D1556053

RELIGION IN NEW SPAIN

Religion in New Spain

Edited by
SUSAN SCHROEDER
and
STAFFORD POOLE

UNIVERSITY OF NEW MEXICO PRESS
ALBUQUERQUE

12   11   10   09   08   07   1   2   3   4   5   6   7

Library of Congress Cataloging-in-Publication Data

Religion in new Spain / edited by Susan Schroeder and Stafford Poole.

p. cm.

Includes bibliographical references and index.

ISBN 978-0-8263-3978-2 (cloth : alk. paper)

1. New Spain—Religion. 2. New Spain—Religious life and customs.

I. Schroeder, Susan. II. Poole, Stafford.

BL2530.N49R45 2007

277.2—dc22

2007002529

Design and composition: Melissa Tandysh

CONTENTS

LIST OF ILLUSTRATIONS

ACKNOWLEDGMENTS

In March 2000 the Stone Center for Latin American Studies and the Dean of Liberal Arts and Sciences of Tulane University sponsored the first France Vinton Scholes Conference on Latin American Colonial History. The title of the conference was "Mexico's Transformative Church: Piety, Pogroms, and Politics." The purpose of the conference was to celebrate the career of Professor Richard Greenleaf and to realize the latest scholarship on religion in New Spain. Above all, we wish to acknowledge the many contributions of Richard Greenleaf, emeritus, Tulane University, to whom the conference was dedicated. In both his scholarly production and his training of graduate students, he has led the field and deserves the gratitude and appreciation of our community of historians.

This volume has been years in the making, and we wish to thank Tom Reese and Sue Inglés of the Stone Center for Latin American Studies for their interest in the project from its inception. We are grateful to Hortensia Calvo, director, David Dressing and Emmett Luty, all of Tulane's Latin American Library, who were most generous with their time and assistance in granting permission for reproduction and photographing the image for the book's cover. We also thank Bill Beezley and Colin MacLachlan for their help along the way, and Nancy Stockton, whose optimism, patience, and excellent editorial skills greatly facilitated our bringing this book to fruition.

Introduction

SUSAN SCHROEDER AND STAFFORD POOLE

Background

"**R**eligion is something you do in a church"—this was the sentiment of the judges in the American West who deliberated native Americans' traditional understanding of spiritual place and ritual.[1] Indeed, sacred space can be anywhere and need not be bound by fictive walls and ceilings. Moreover, religion is immediate, and it is cultural. It can be personal or shared, and it can be based on an attempt to reconcile the mysterious and unmanageable forces of nature, such as storms, droughts, floods, infestations of pests, epidemic diseases, and sicknesses. In this popular form, it is an attempt to control the uncontrollable. Religion can also be an institution that is as all-pervasive as today's media yet, in spite of itself and because of itself, is manifested in a multitude of forms.

These protean qualities of religion are a classic paradigm for the situation in colonial Mexico, where there was a convergence of the institutional church, Spanish popular Catholicism, and indigenous spiritual practices. The unique circumstance of Habsburg royal ecclesiastical authority contributed to the particularity of religious developments in Spain's North American dependency. As an imperial religion, Catholicism was a political-ecclesiastical ideal. Every one of New Spain's inhabitants was expected to conform to the church's precepts. The reality of Mexican Catholicism, however, was a convergence of beliefs and practices and seemed to reflect degrees of actual spirituality, the product, doubtless, of the colony's many cultures; and some peoples were never fully co-opted by Catholic dogma and its ministers.

Of course, the religions of the native populations of the Americas were just as complex and diverse. The beliefs and activities of the indigenes of New Spain were community-based and adhered to what was prescribed by the leaders in the *calpolli* or *tlaxilacalli* (a subdivision of a larger indigenous polity, the *altepetl*, or ethnic state). It is likely that the same leaders and calpolli members supported and participated in the religious activities sponsored by their altepetl.[2] Most groups were subject to an imposed imperial religion that was profound, theologically rich, and spectacular in ritual practice.[3] Moreover, the natives of the Americas, too, were concerned with nature and the uncontrollable and called on a pantheon of deities to order the cosmos. Their rulers were religious figures as well as civil ones. For the Aztecs, by the end of the fifteenth century religion and state were essentially one. This was the same religion that so astounded the invading Spaniards.

The degree of sophistication of beliefs and rituals varied among native groups, but most typically in precontact times participation in religious activities affirmed kinship and family ties, contributed to calpolli identity, and doubtless enhanced altepetl solidarity. More generally for all native Americans, their particular ethnic religious systems served to help make sense of the world, to mark time, and to enrich the course of each of their lives. As a fixture of their cultures, religion was not easily relinquished. Indeed, ongoing research by leading scholars in the field of early Latin American history reveals that native populations in New Spain had great agency in the shaping of colonial religion. These revisionist works nullify the stereotype put forth by some authors who labor to portray the Spanish conquest as

Armageddon and the end of indigenous culture. On the contrary, by any measure religious convergence and continuity were the rule for colonial natives who selectively used the Catholic church and Spanish legal devices to maintain what was theirs.

Much the same can be said for the diverse set of beliefs and practices brought to New Spain by the Spaniards. Too often the difficult, complex theology of the Roman system was neither well understood nor practicable for ordinary Spaniards. According to William A. Christian, fifteenth- and sixteenth-century Spaniards intent on reforming their church saw lay religion as "ignorant, pagan, and lax."[4] Christian focuses on rural Spaniards (a large portion of Spain's population at the time) and finds that religion was local, with devotions to relics and saints largely serving a community's spiritual needs. Families, even entire villages, patronized a given shrine seeking solutions for temporal concerns. For example, propitiation of a favorite saint was believed to help ward off a hailstorm or an infestation of locusts, or cure an ailment. Although contrary to the design of the new, universal post-Tridentine church, across the countryside family and community preferred their local sites and saintly icons. Consider, for example, Medellín in rural Extremadura, the home of conqueror Hernando Cortés, which had at least three churches almost within a stone's throw of one another. Yet Medellín was a long way from either Madrid or Seville, and it is no surprise that the most popular devotional site in sixteenth-century New Castile, the shrine of Our Lady of Guadalupe, was within a day's pilgrimage of Cortés's home.[5]

SUSAN SCHROEDER AND STAFFORD POOLE

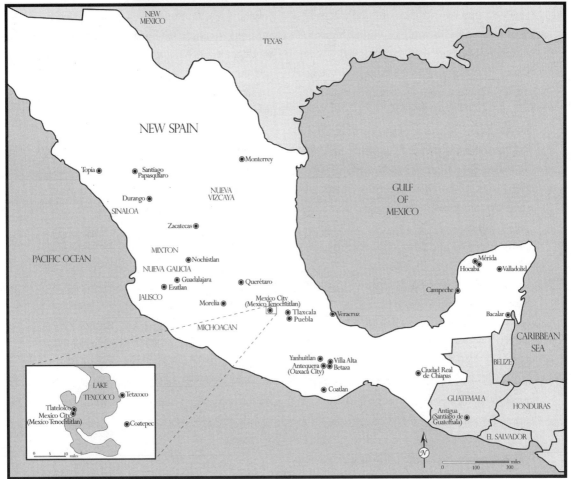

Drafted by Robin H. Gary, 2004

Map: Spain and Mexico. Drafted by Robin H. Gary, 2004.

INTRODUCTION

Politics played a large role in defining the institution of the Catholic church as it was delivered to New Spain. Like the Aztecs, Spain's rulers combined religion and politics in their personae, and it is no coincidence that both the Aztec and the Spanish emperors had a messianic sense of special election. Both societies associated religion with the state and imperialism. King Ferdinand and Queen Isabel were intensely religious themselves, and they used their regal offices to pressure Pope Alexander VI to grant them *patronato real*, the right of ecclesiastical control over newly created colonies. This was a bone of contention between subsequent popes and Habsburg and Bourbon kings for the next three hundred years.[6] Nevertheless, the Catholic kings generally determined who would be appointed ministers in their dominions. Finally overcoming the harangues of fray Bartolomé de las Casas and the legal debates over Spanish jurisdiction in the West Indies, HRE Charles V opted for Saint Augustine's mandate, "compel those outside to come in" as he sent Spanish priests and friars to and across New Spain to evangelize its peoples.[7]

The criteria for who could be Catholic were formulaic and depended not only on one's piety but also one's heredity. *Limpieza de sangre* (purity of blood) was ostensibly a religious concern, and a good Catholic's lineage had to be free of any taint of contamination by intermarriage with Muslims or Jews. Politics inevitably confounded the ideal; exceptions were made for individuals who might be of service to the king.[8] Not all *conversos*, New Christians, or Moriscos were driven from Spain in 1492.[9] They were, however, forbidden to go to the colonies. Here

again, there were ways to get around the law. Jews, for example, are known to have settled in both the newly established capital of Mexico City and regions to the north. Once in the colony, it seems that some Jews took on all the appurtenances of Catholics, and they raised their children as Christians without a hint of their Sephardic beginnings. Others became putative Catholics and overlaid their clandestine beliefs and rituals with a façade of Catholic piety. Yet other Jewish families (especially those living away from the capital) adhered to what could be salvaged of their more orthodox beliefs. Jewish contributions to colonial Mexican religion, while not explicit, were nevertheless a real facet of it, if for no other reason than by their very identity Jews were often suspect and accused of heretical practices.[10]

African and Asian contributions to colonial Mexican religion should not be underestimated either. But they are hard to measure. Since the time of the earliest European invasions, Africans were inhabitants of the colony. They continued to arrive in significant numbers as part of the slave trade. Some had been evangelized in Africa, but the level of indoctrination often was minimal. Most are thought to have become Christians over time, and their enthusiastic organization of and participation in exclusive religious *cofradías* (confraternities) are well known.[11] Nevertheless, African expressions in colonial religion are difficult to document, but doubtless they were manifested in syncretic form through music, dance, song, and other aspects of Christian ceremony.

We know the least about Asian influences. Certainly early on Franciscans and Jesuits made their way to China, Japan,

4

and the Philippines to spread the Gospel, and the Jesuits are known to have taken on many Asian attributes in their ministry.[12] Asian merchant ambassadors and their contingents in Mexico City were a marvel to Spaniards and Indians alike.[13] What of Asian influence or residual in the religious milieu of New Spain? It is a subject awaiting study.

Issues of limpieza de sangre did not initially apply to native Americans when it came to determining who was Catholic. The Indians were categorically excluded since they had never known Christianity. The Franciscans, especially, believed that native peoples were a God-given gift, a means for the church to begin to save itself through their conversion. Conversion of the Indians was also a convenient way for Spain to justify the invasion and occupation of the Americas.

Already, then, we have the politics of the Catholic church, the reform-minded cohorts of pious religious, the cherished spiritualities of native groups, and the beliefs and practices of Spanish settlers. Cortés had dutifully smashed the Indians' temples and idols, replacing them with crosses, the images of saints, and prayers, as he marched toward Mexico Tenochtitlan, the Aztecs' capital. He had his own patron, Saint Peter, whom his parents had invoked because their son had been sickly as an infant and who protected him in his pursuit of gold and glory.[14] However, in times when battles against the Indians were especially difficult and victory was in jeopardy Cortés and his companions called out to Santiago, another saint, for succor.[15] Nevertheless, the various conquest accounts reveal that Cortés, his fellow Extremadurans, and a host of other Spaniards who sailed from Cuba in his company, all with their own brand of religious beliefs, could likely best be described, as William B. Taylor says, as "very good Catholics and very poor Christians."[16] And through this conjunction, for better or for worse, the conquerors and their descendants came to epitomize Mexican Catholicism as living models of Spanish colonial Christian belief and practice.

The utter destruction of Mexico Tenochtitlan also meant the destruction of Aztec political and religious authority. Surviving Nahuas,[17] however, had little intention of giving up a belief system that had served them so well, and they tried to negotiate a compromise of the two theologies. Fray Bernardino de Sahagún's *Coloquios* is a poignant example of a politically devastated people attempting to retain a precious religion that had served them for centuries.[18] They were willing to accept the Spanish kings as sovereigns but not the Spaniards' deity. They wished, instead, to incorporate the Catholic God into their extant belief system.

The Spaniards, though, were adamant and forbade all beliefs and rituals except those sanctioned by the church. The natives made the best of the situation, for not all of Catholicism was repugnant to them. They especially loved the music, song, dance, processions, liturgical calendar, saints, and the spectacle of high church ceremony, for much of it was already familiar through their own practices.[19] Churches were built rapidly and abundantly, and for many natives these sumptuous structures and their ministers were sources of sanctuary and solace as they dealt with horrific cycles of epidemic disease and death and the ongoing adjustments to the needs and wants of their Spanish overlords. The Indians took what suited them best about Christianity, fashioning altars, celebrating favorite saints, becoming accomplished musicians, joining cofradías, and participating in fiestas and processions.[20] Just how much of their enthusiasm was based on orthodox theology is not known, and for all intents and purposes, contrary to the Spaniards, many Indians might be said to be good Christians and not very good Catholics.

Idolatry was a regular concern for the Spanish priests, who doubtless exaggerated its prevalence to serve their own purposes.[21] Not infrequently some indigenous individuals and groups participated in church activities while continuing to worship their old idols. It was not uncommon to find that the natives who conducted the ancient ceremonies were also key figures in town politics and Catholic services. Church authorities rooted out idolaters and when caught most often punished them severely.[22] Idolatry was said to be the work of the devil,[23] and shamans and *curanderos* (healers) were accused of practicing *hechecería*, or witchcraft. It is doubtful that Spanish pogroms and reprisals brought an end to all idolatrous activity. More likely, the worshipers became more discreet, with a practical veneer of Christianity that, when combined, served to ameliorate concerns about natural disasters and other things beyond their control.

The clergy, of course, wore many hats in New Spain. In addition to eliminating witchcraft, they were first and foremost the colony's spiritual leaders. They naturally assumed these roles, filling out a complicated ecclesiastical administrative bureaucracy that spread over the landscape of New Spain. The regular clergy were usually better educated, more stalwart, and more conscientious than secular priests. But generalizations obfuscate the reality. The evidence shows that there were both upstanding and derelict members among both religious and secular clergies. Priests and nuns were also the teachers and the administrators of the colony's charitable institutions. Without their dedication and beneficence there would have been no schools, hospitals, or orphanages. And for more than two hundred years, theirs was an exclusive membership of Spaniards.

Most clergy, it seems, preferred to carry out their duties in large cities, and certainly it was in the urban areas that we find a preponderance of cathedrals, convents, monasteries, and parish churches. Until recently, however, the activities of religious women in these cities have been little studied. Most famous, of course, is Sor Juana Inés de la Cruz, a member of the Hieronymite order, who is celebrated for her intellectual abilities as well as her challenge to misogynist ecclesiastical authorities in Mexico City.[24] Asunción Lavrin has studied nearly every aspect of what can be gleaned from the sources about women religious.[25] With the exception of Sor Juana, the familiar stereotype of a nun was that of a devout, passive, confined person. Lavrin's ongoing research contradicts much of this stereotype, though, and reveals that the women underplayed themselves, for they were literate, active (though still confined), responsible, and highly spiritual.[26] In addition,

SUSAN SCHROEDER AND STAFFORD POOLE

these are the same Spanish-descended women who eventually, although with great reluctance, acceded to the notion of Indian women becoming nuns and having their own convents.[27]

Some priests and friars left the comforts of the cities and went into rural areas.[28] Male religious, especially Franciscans and Jesuits, pioneered the northern frontiers and set up mission-like outposts among the colony's least settled native populations. Their purpose was to bring Christianity, Hispanic culture, and peace to the new territories. Moving into the frontier was always a formidable undertaking, and while some friars and priests enjoyed great success, others suffered martyrdom.

But even among the clergy, colonial business and politics could seldom be kept separate from religion. Money was necessary for the operation of the church. The same money linked the institutional church and its ministers to society. Families garnered substantial prestige when favorite sons (and daughters) became successful clergy, and revenue flowed from the city and countryside to secure these positions.[29] Families could also use their clerical affiliations to influence politics, and business and politics, in some instances, could overshadow, if not overwhelm, spiritual obligations.[30]

Yet Mexican Catholicism flourished through most of the colonial period. Just one glance at the little book *Divine Excess* reveals the exquisite religiosity of New Spain's citizenry.[31] Bourbon reformers did everything they could to curb the extravagance of church activities, and they also deliberately compromised the familiar authority of many of its priests.[32] They restricted

the number of processions and reduced the amount that could be spent from *cabildo* (city council) coffers on religious festivals. Nevertheless, as Linda Curcio-Nagy has shown, official policy rarely dimmed the religious enthusiasms of New Spain's peoples. Surely one of the best means to evaluate popular Catholicism was in its many patterned manifestations at the metropolis's Corpus Christi public processions. Curcio-Nagy offers a fine example of just one event in 1728, when no less than eighty-five confraternities participated in the processions and a canopy extended through the streets for nearly three-fourths of a mile.[33] The viceroy, the judges of the high court, all of the ecclesiastical and city authorities, and the guilds also joined the rank and file to commemorate the holy occasion.

Obviously, everyone who was anyone participated, and likewise everyone else watched. Even cloistered religious must have heard the Indians and their music and the synchronized pealing of the church bells, and perhaps they too draped their balconies with beautiful tapestries to decorate the boulevards below. Gold- and silver-gilded sacred images on *pasos* (portable platforms or litters) decorated with silk, velvet, feathers, and flowers were caravanned through the streets and guilds and cofradías tried to outdo one another to have the most splendid image and grandest paso.[34] Candles, fireworks, and torches lit the festooned passageways, and dancers and musicians set the pace for participants. For the moment, the differences among Indians, blacks, *castas*, and Spaniards were reconciled as all shared the Solomonic purpose of the occasion along with the exuberance of the festivities. Curcio-Nagy quotes Franciscan fray Agustín Vetancurt, who corroborates with his 1698 observation, "The single greatest thing that the city can boast about is the frequency of its religious devotion to the Sacraments, its ostentation of so many festivals, and the generosity of spirit of all of its inhabitants."[35]

The Collection

The chapters in this volume are splendid revisionist samplings of the history of colonial religious culture. They are remarkably diverse and at the same time representative of the rich mosaic of New Spanish society. We learn that the Spanish conquest was not the end-all of indigenous culture; that the Virgin of Guadalupe was a myth-in-the-making by locals as well as foreigners; that nuns and priests had real lives; and that the institutional colonial church, even post-Trent, was increasingly multivalent and seldom if ever above or beyond political or economic influence. Mexican Catholicism is the prevailing leitmotiv of the chapters, yet only a few authors concern themselves with piety or personal spirituality.

Rather, the chapters more broadly encompass aspects of religion in the many regions of New Spain over an extensive period. Striking, too, are the topics that seem tangential to religion altogether—politics and business, for example—but in fact have clear religious dimensions.

The volume has been divided into seven parts that represent general categories that span the colonial era: Encounters, Accommodation, and Outright Idolatry; Native Sexuality and Christian Morality; Believing in Miracles; Taking the Veil and New Realities; Guardian of the Christian Society; The Holy Office of the Inquisition—Racism, Judaizing, and Gambling; Music and Martyrdom on the Northern Frontier; and Tangential Christianity on Other Frontiers: Business and Politics as Usual. The essays, while varying in subject and content, validate the sheer pervasiveness and importance of religion in New Spain while reiterating its many manifestations. How it was particularized by individuals, groups, and institutions is now better known because of the rich, remarkable histories that follow.

NOTES

1. Neil Genzlinger, "If Land is Called Sacred, Bitter Disputes Can Erupt," *New York Times*, August 14, 2001, B5.

2. For information about the calpolli, god carriers, and local deities, see Susan Schroeder, *Chimalpahin and the Kingdoms of Chalco* (Tucson: University of Arizona Press, 1991), 143–49, and the formation of an altepetl with its deity, 122–23.

3. For just two important primary sources, see Diego Durán, *Book of the Gods and Rites and the Ancient Calendar*, ed. and trans. Fernando

Horcasitas and Doris Heyden (Norman: University of Oklahoma Press, 1971), and Bernardino de Sahagún, *Florentine Codex: General History of the Things of New Spain, Book 1: The Gods; Book 2: The Ceremonies; Book 6: Rhetoric and Moral Philosophy*, ed. and trans. Arthur J. O. Anderson and Charles E. Dibble (Santa Fe and Salt Lake City: School of American Research and University of Utah Press, 1970, 1981, and 1969, respectively). Also, see Gary H. Gossen, ed., *South and Meso-American Native Spirituality: From the Cult*

SUSAN SCHROEDER AND STAFFORD POOLE

of the Feathered Serpent to the Theology of Liberation (New York: Crossroad Publishing, 1997).

4. William Christian Jr., *Local Religion in Sixteenth-Century Spain* (Princeton: Princeton University Press, 1989), 4.

5. Christian, *Local Religion*, 121, and for sumptuous visual examples of the Marian cults, see Marie-France Boyer, *The Cult of the Virgin: Offerings, Ornaments, and Festivals* (London: Thames and Hudson, 2000).

6. For background on the principle of royal patronage, see Stafford Poole, "Iberian Catholicism Comes to the Americas," in *Christianity Comes to the Americas*, Charles H. Lippy, Robert Choquette, and Stafford Poole (New York: Paragon House, 1992), 8–10.

7. Quoted in Hans Küng, *The Catholic Church: A Short History* (New York: Modern Library, 2001), 47, and Bartolomé de las Casas, *Historia de las Indias*, 3 vols., ed. Agustín Millares Carlo (Mexico, DF: Fondo de Cultura Económica, 1981); *Tratados*, 2 vols., ed. Agustín Millares Carlo y Rafael Moreau (Mexico, DF: Fondo de Cultura Económica, 1965); and *In Defense of the Indians: The Defense of the Most Reverend Lord, Don Fray Bartolomé de Las Casas, of the Order of Preachers, Late Bishop of Chiapa, Against the Persecutors and Slanderers of the People of the New World Discovered Across the Seas*, trans. Stafford Poole (DeKalb: Northern Illinois University Press, 1974).

8. Stafford Poole, "The Politics of *Limpieza de Sangre*: Juan de Ovando and His Circle in the Reign of Philip II," *The Americas*, 55, no. 3 (1999): 359–89.

9. The terms converso, New Christian, and Morisco describe individuals who have converted to Catholicism.

10. Alfonso Toro, ed., *Los judíos en la Nueva España* (Mexico, DF: Archivo General de la Nación, Fondo de Cultura Económica, 1993); Stanley M. Hordes, "The Inquisition and the Crypto-Jewish Community in Colonial New Spain and New Mexico," in *Cultural Encounters: The Impact of the Inquisition in Spain and the New World*, ed. Mary Elizabeth Perry and Anne J. Cruz, 207–17 (Berkeley: University of California Press, 1991); and Eva Alexandra Uchmany, *La vida entre el judaísmo y el cristianismo en la Nueva España,* 1580–1606 (Mexico, DF: Fondo de Cultura Económica, 1992).

11. For Veracruz, see Patrick J. Carroll, *Blacks in Colonial Veracruz: Race, Ethnicity, and Regional Development* (Austin: University of Texas Press, 2001), and see Matthew Restall and Jane Landers, "The African Experience in Early Spanish America," *The Americas* 57, no. 2 (2000): 167–70, and Matthew Restall, "Black Conquistadors: Armed Africans in Early Spanish America," *The Americas* 57, no. 2 (2000): 171–205.

12. John W. O'Malley, *The First Jesuits* (Cambridge: Harvard University Press, 1993), 60, 76–78, and Charles E. Ronan and Bonnie B. C. Oh, eds., *East Meets West: The Jesuits in China, 1582–1773* (Chicago: Loyola University Press, 1988).

13. For an eyewitness account of delegations of individuals from Asia, see seventeenth-century Nahua historian don Domingo de San Antón Muñón Chimalpahin Quauhtlehuanitzin, *Codex Chimalpahin: Annals of His Time*, James Lockhart, Susan Schroeder, and Doris Namala, eds. and trans. Series Chimalpahin (Stanford: Stanford University Press, 2006), and see Miguel León-Portilla, "La embajada de los japoneses en México, 1614. El testimonio en náhuatl del cronista Chimalpahin," *Estudios de Asia y África* 16, no. 2 (1981): 23–36.

14. Chimalpahin Quauhtlehuanitzin, *Series Chimalpahin: Chimalpahin and the Conquest of Mexico by Francisco López de Gómara*, ed. and trans. Anne Cruz, Cristián de-la-Roa, Susan Schroeder, and David Tavárez (forthcoming).

15. Ibid.

16. Used in another context, but apt, William B. Taylor, *Magistrates of the Sacred: Priests and Parishioners in Eighteenth-Century Mexico* (Stanford: Stanford University Press, 1996), 48.

17. Most of the native peoples who inhabited the central basin of Mexico spoke the Nahuatl language. These speakers are described as Nahuas.

18. Bernardino de Sahagún, *Coloquios y doctrina cristiana: Los diálogos de 1524 según el texto de fray Bernardino de Sahagún y sus colaboradores indígenas*, ed. Miguel León-Portilla

(Mexico, DF: Universidad Nacional Autónoma de México, 1986), and for an example in English, see "The Lords and Holy Men of Tenochtitlan Reply to the Franciscans, 1524 (1564)," in *Colonial Spanish America: A Documentary History*, ed. Kenneth Mills and William B. Taylor, 19–22 (Wilmington, DE: Scholarly Resources, 1998).

19. For just one example, see Robert Stevenson, *Music in Mexico: A Historical Survey* (New York: Thomas Y. Crowell Co., 1952).

20. See "Religious Life" in James Lockhart, *The Nahuas After the Conquest: A Social and Cultural History of the Indians of Central Mexico, Sixteenth through Eighteenth Centuries* (Stanford: Stanford University Press, 1992), 203–60, and Susan Schroeder, "Jesuits, Nahuas, and the Good Death Society in Mexico City, 1710–1767," *Hispanic American Historical Review* 80, no. 1 (2000): 43–76.

21. For one cleric's report, see Hernando Ruiz de Alarcón, *Treatise on the Heathen Superstitions that Today Live Among the Indians Native to This New Spain, 1629*, ed. and trans. J. Richard Andrews and Ross Hassig (Norman: University of Oklahoma Press, 1987).

22. Inga Clendinnen, *Ambivalent Conquests: Maya and Spaniard in Yucatan, 1517–1570* (Cambridge: Cambridge University Press, 1987).

23. See Fernando Cervantes, *The Devil in the New World: The Impact of Diabolism in New Spain* (New Haven: Yale University Press, 1994).

24. There is a wealth of literature about Sor Juana. For a synthetic treatment, see Irving A. Leonard, "A Baroque Poetess," in *Baroque Times in Old Mexico: Seventeenth-Century Persons, Places, and Practices* (Ann Arbor: University of Michigan Press, 1973), 172–92, and for a more comprehensive study, Octavio Paz, *Sor Juana Inés de la Cruz, or The Traps of Faith*, trans. Margaret Sayers Peden (Cambridge: Harvard University Press, 1988).

25. Asunción Lavrin, "In Search of the Colonial Woman in Mexico: The Seventeenth and Eighteenth Centuries," in *Latin American Women: Historical Perspectives*, ed. Asunción Lavrin, 23–59 (Westport, CT: Greenwood Press, 1978), and "Female Religious," in *Cities and Society in Colonial Latin America*, ed. Louisa Schell Hoberman and Susan Migden Socolow, 165–95 (Albuquerque: University of New Mexico Press, 1986).

26. Asunción Lavrin, "La vida feminina como experiencia religiosa: Biografía y hagiografía en Hispanoamérica," *Colonial Latin American Review* 2, no. 1 and no. 2 (1993): 1–26, and see Kathleen A. Myers and Amanda Powell, eds. and trans., *A Wild Country Out in the Garden: The Spiritual Journals of a Colonial Mexican Nun* (Bloomington: Indiana University Press, 1999), and Elisa Sampson Vera Tudela, *Colonial Angels: Narratives of Gender and Spirituality in Mexico* (Austin: University of Texas Press, 2000).

27. Ann Miriam Gallagher, "The Indian Nuns of Mexico City's *Monasterio* of Corpus Christi, 1721–1821," in *Latin American Women*, 150–72, and Asunción Lavrin, "Indian Brides of Christ: Creating New Spaces for Indigenous Women in New Spain," *Mexican Studies/Estudios Mexicanos* 15, no. 2 (1999): 225–60.

28. See William Taylor's exemplary study of rural priests, *Magistrates of the Sacred*.

29. Ida Altman, "A Family and Region in the Northern Fringe Lands: The Marqueses de Aguayo of Nuevo León and Coahuila," in *Provinces of Early Mexico*, ed. Ida Altman and James Lockhart, 253–72, especially 259, 269, and 270 (Los Angeles: UCLA Latin American Center Publications, University of California, Los Angeles, 1976), and see John Kicza, *Colonial Entrepreneurs: Families and Business in Bourbon Mexico City* (Albuquerque: University of New Mexico Press, 1983), 39–40, for a few examples of family and business practices.

30. See D. A. Brading, *Church and State in Bourbon Mexico: The Diocese of Michoacan, 1749–1810* (Cambridge: Cambridge University Press, 1994) and John Frederick Schwaller, *Origins of Church Wealth in Mexico: Ecclesiastical Revenues and Church Finances, 1523–1600* (Albuquerque: University of New Mexico Press, 1985).

31. Ichiro Ono, *Divine Excess: Mexican Ultra Baroque* (San Francisco: Chronicle Books, 1996).

32. Taylor, *Magistrates of the Sacred*.

33. Linda A. Curcio-Nagy, "Giants and Gypsies: Corpus Christi in Colonial Mexico City," in

Rituals of Rule, Rituals of Resistance: Public Celebrations and Popular Culture in Mexico, ed. William H. Beezley, Cheryl English Martin, and William E. French, 1–26 (Wilmington, DE: Scholarly Resources, 1994).

34. For precedents on cofradías and processions in Seville, see Susan Verdi Webster, *Art and Ritual in Golden-Age Spain* (Princeton: Princeton University Press, 1998), and more generally about cofradías in Latin America, see Pilar Martínez López-Cano, Gisela von Wobeser, and Juan Guillermo Muñoz, eds., *Cofradías, capellanías y obras pías en la América colonial* (Mexico , DF: Universidad Nacional Autónoma de México, 1998). Also see Clara García Ayluardo, "Confraternity, Cult, and Crown in Colonial Mexico City, 1700–1800" (PhD diss., Cambridge University, 1990).

35. Curcio-Nagy, "Giants and Gypsies," 1, and see her *The Great Festivals of Colonial Mexico City: Performing Power and Identity in Colonial Mexico City* (Albuquerque: University New Mexico Press, 2004).

PART ONE

ENCOUNTERS, ACCOMMODATION, AND OUTRIGHT IDOLATRY

First humans and then Christians . . .

—José de Acosta, 1580

There were some who had as many as two hundred [wives]; from that number down each man had as many as he liked . . . Neither entreaties, threats, or sermons or anything else sufficed to make them give up all these women and marry one with the sanction of the Church.

—fray Toribio Motolinia, d. 1568

We are not satisfied or convinced by what you have told us, nor do we understand or give credit to what has been said of our gods. It gives us anguish, lords and fathers, to speak in this way . . . As for our gods, we will die before giving up serving and worshiping them . . . We have no more to say, lords.

—fray Bernardino de Sahagún, 1524

[Archbishop doctor don Juan Pérez de la Serna] is now in charge of the altepetl of Tenochtitlan in a good and proper fashion and appears as a good shepherd taking care of the people of Mexico as his sheep, Spaniards and us commoners, all of us his subjects. May our Lord God deign to guard him for me for many years . . .

—Chimalpahin, 1613

Thus, because of their ignorance, they had, and have, such a variety of gods and such different modes of adoration that, having resolved to ascertain the basis of their beliefs and what they all are, we find as little to get hold of as if we tried to squeeze smoke or wind in our fist.

—Hernando Ruiz de Alarcón, 1629

It hardly needs to be said that Native Americans and Spaniards in New Spain were utterly bewildered by one another's appearance and ways of doing things. It was not that they were absolutely unknown to one another, for the Spaniards knew of the Indians that Columbus had put on display when he returned to Spain, and they had also encountered native groups as they passed through the Caribbean Islands. For the natives, word spread rapidly of curious sightings as the Spaniards reconnoitered their way along the Gulf Coast. Even so, the disparity between the two cultures rendered the most well-intentioned diplomatic efforts of little lasting utility.

The Indians, of course, were accustomed to encounters, even warfare, with one another and other polities, and conquest and ethnic miscegenation were processual. But indigenous political protocols, for example, the giving of young women as brides in exchange for peace or subjugation, were not appreciated by the Spaniards, who instead used the women as servants and sexual consorts. The Indians' choreographed and costumed rituals of warfare, while marveled at, were also ignored by the Spaniards.

Many Spaniards, too, came with good intentions. Shortly before her death, Castile's Queen Isabel had declared that the natives of the Americas were her subjects and that they were to be taught to read and write and to be good Christians. The crown's legal instrument of entitlement was the *requerimiento*, or requirement, which, though much maligned now, is a remarkable document. The contract was read to the natives, offering them the option of accepting the Spanish king as their sovereign and the Catholic God as their deity—with the guarantee of perpetual citizenship

and the Faith—or having war declared and suffering death or enslavement. No other European country involved in the Americas came close to providing such a comprehensive (it related to all of Spanish America) and enduring (it lasted until 1917 in Mexico) package of social and legal benefits—schools, hospitals, orphanages, courts, and so on. Some indigenes acquiesced; others waged fierce battles against the invaders. Yet the Spaniards prevailed.

For the natives, it appears, political subjugation to the king of Spain was more tolerable than being forced to abandon their religion and convert to Christianity. They tried to negotiate a compromise with Spanish officials, but to no avail. Only Catholicism was allowed. Reform-minded Franciscans were the first religious to be sent from Spain to evangelize New Spain. For the friars, it was an opportunity to save the church, and they set about establishing *doctrinas* (religious jurisdictions), building churches, preaching, and baptizing countless numbers of Indians. They quickly realized that they needed to learn the natives' languages for the Gospel to be understood, and they began to teach and to learn from the children in their schools. Alphabetic literacy among native peoples greatly helped the friars, but it also allowed the Indians to make the most of Hispanic devices to maintain their own culture. Educated natives were to return to their hometowns as Christian role models in their local governments and churches. Indigenous *fiscales* (church officials) took on many important functions as they assisted their priests. Baptism, monogamous marriage, confession, and penance all became part of their Christian lives. But for many years their conversion to Christianity remained incomplete. One problem was the extremes in theological worldview between the two groups; another was that the natives were largely content with their traditional belief systems.

Kevin Terraciano, in "The People of Two Hearts and the One God from Castile: Ambivalent Responses to Christianity in Early Colonial Oaxaca," has studied Mixtec peoples and their resistance to Christianity. Having been recently subjugated by the Aztecs and then soon thereafter by the Spaniards, the Mixtecs clung tenaciously to their religion and their ethnic autonomy, and we are reminded of the delegation of Nahua elders in Mexico Tenochtitlan who also sought to maintain the integrity of their spiritual beliefs. Lisa Sousa, in "Tying the Knot: Nahua Nuptials in Colonial Central Mexico," discusses Nahua women and Christian marriage. Nahua marriage was already rich in purpose and ceremony, and daughters, mothers, and grandmothers (as community elders as well as relatives) all played key roles in the keeping of marriage tradition in their communities. Sousa brings together both early pictorial and Nahuatl- and Spanish-language texts to demonstrate the importance of local traditions and some of what is gained and lost as Nahuas accommodated to Christianity. David Tavárez, in "Communal Defiance, Divided Allegiances: Zapotec Responses to Idolatry Extirpation Campaigns in Oaxaca," furnishes a moving example of native resistance to Christianity with his account of idolatry. Even as late as the end of the seventeenth century religious authorities were dealing with "Christianized" natives who engaged in the worship of idols. The situation was so distressing that officials were compelled to build a jail just for idolaters. Compounding the situation for the Spaniards was the realization that many of the leaders and practitioners of the ancient rituals were the literate political and church officials who even went so far as to write down the various incantations in the ceremonies. The incantations reveal an awareness of Christianity but are far more telling of the Zapotecs' persisting traditional worldview.

NOTES

Epigraph citations, in order of appearance, are as follows: Claudio M. Burgaleta, *José de Acosta, S.J. (1540—1600), His Life and Thought* (Chicago: Loyola Press, 1999), 48; fray Toribio Motolinia, *History of the Indians of New Spain*, ed. and trans. by Elizabeth Andros Foster (Westport, CT: Greenwood Press, 1977), 149; fray Bernardino de Sahagún, "The Lords and Holy Men of Tenochtitlan Reply to the Franciscans, 1524 (1564)," in *Colonial Spanish America: A Documentary History*, ed. and trans. by Kenneth Mills and William B. Taylor, 22 (Wilmington, DE: Scholarly Resources, 1998); Don Domingo de San Antón Muñón Chimalpahin Quauhtlehuanitzin, *Annals of His Time*, ed. and trans. by James Lockhart, Susan Schroeder, and Doris Namala, Series Chimalpahin (Stanford: Stanford University Press, 2006), 263; Hernando Ruiz de Alarcón, *Treatise on the Heathen Superstitions That Today Live Among the Indians Native To This New Spain, 1629*, ed. and trans. by J. Richard Andrews and Ross Hassig (Norman: University of Oklahoma Press, 1984), 43.

CHAPTER ONE

The People of Two Hearts
and the One God from Castile

Ambivalent Responses to Christianity in Early Colonial Oaxaca

KEVIN TERRACIANO

In 1544, the Inquisition accused three lords from Yanhuitlan of reverting to ancient religious practices and rejecting Christianity.[1] In the same year, three lords from Coatlan were charged with similar crimes against the church.[2] The two cases are related in that the lords of Coatlan referred to meetings with nobles from Yanhuitlan and other communities in the Mixteca Alta. This essay uses testimony from the two trials as evidence of indigenous responses to Christianity in the early colonial period, focusing on the confused and ambivalent words and actions of native nobles in Oaxaca who experienced the first wave of assaults against their beliefs and practices. In the first few decades after the conquest, native lords were confronted with a choice: to accept the new religion in place of traditional beliefs or to maintain those beliefs while converting nominally

to Christian practices. As one historian has noted, most indigenous people never made the choice.[3] In the trials from Yanhuitlan and Coatlan, however, it is clear that some people were forced to choose between their sacred ancestors and the "one god from Castile," as they referred to the Christian God. The testimony of native priests, lords, and slaves allows us to consider the psychological impact of the spiritual conquest on a generation of Mixtecs, Zapotecs, and Nahuas in early colonial Oaxaca.

The historical record tells us little about how the introduction of Christianity affected indigenous nobles of the first post-conquest generation who came into direct contact with Christianity. The silence is not surprising. Most writings from the early period come from the friars, who inform us mainly about what they did, or what they thought they had done. Native-language writing, which has revealed so many aspects of indigenous culture, was not practiced until one or two generations after the conquest. In general, native-language writings do not address responses to Christianity in the immediate postconquest period, except how select nobles understood or did not understand Christian concepts. Early colonial native commentaries on religion tend to come from the converted few who participated in church-sponsored projects. One outstanding exception to this general rule is the famous trial testimony of don Carlos Mendoza Ometochtzin, the *cacique* (local ruler) of Tetzcoco, who was executed for speaking openly about his beliefs. Aside from ecclesiastical chronicles, records of inquisitorial investigations are some of the only sources that document native responses to the introduction of Christianity in the early sixteenth century.

Inquisition records are valuable sources for the study of native beliefs and practices. The trials in Yanhuitlan and Coatlan, for example, elicited testimony from dozens of Spanish and indigenous witnesses, including unbaptized native priests who described their ritual practices in detail. Of course, it is important to keep in mind the limitations of these records. First of all, the questions asked of witnesses in the trials were based on European categories of thought about pagan religion. The inquisitors' questions, prepared in response to accusations made by Spaniards, dictated the types of information that were recorded in the trials. Native witnesses were asked to elaborate on "idols," sacrifices, and any signs of opposition to Christianity. Reconstructions of native beliefs and practices based solely on

these trials are likely to be superficial and biased. Second, not all of the testimonies are entirely credible, especially considering how both Spaniards and native peoples used the inquisitorial process to defame their enemies. Many factors motivated witnesses to testify against the accused. Third, it is important to remember that observable practices in the 1530s and 1540s represent responses to a state of crisis and change provoked by the conquest and recurring diseases. The trials in Yanhuitlan and Coatlan coincided with an epidemic (1545–1548) and drought. Fourth, in these Spanish-language documents, native witnesses spoke through at least one translator, so that the transmission of concepts was subject to distortion and reinterpretation.

Despite these biases and distortions, many historians have used inquisition records to shed light on cultural beliefs and practices.[4] Let us reconsider some of the limitations. First, it is true that the questions were usually limited to a narrow focus on certain notorious practices, but observant Christians recognized many of these practices as fundamental elements of Mesoamerican religious systems, even if they did not understand them entirely. In this early period, it is relatively easy to distinguish indigenous practices from European introductions. Native witnesses who responded to the questions did not necessarily conceal the truth. Sometimes, witnesses raised additional issues in their testimonies, which the inquisitor pursued in subsequent questioning. Discrepancies between the inquisitor's questions and the native respondent's answers represent how each side viewed the same matter. Second, if native witnesses fabricated stories to implicate their enemies in idolatries, they nonetheless articulated specific rituals and acts that were imbedded in their own cultural imagination and experience. Multiple native descriptions of ceremonies, taken as a whole, represent a collective commentary on ritual practices. Some of these descriptions correspond with representations of ritual acts in the preconquest codices, or are corroborated by colonial Nahuatl-language sources or records based on the oral tradition. Native priests and lords who described their own participation in sacrificial rituals had little to gain by such confessions.[5] While many accused simply denied everything, others spoke freely, and a few recanted their statements when they realized the full implications of earlier testimony. Finally, it is true that we should not place too much emphasis on specific terminology elicited in the course of the trial, unless the original native language was retained; in general, the names of people, places, and deities are the only native-language items preserved in the documentation. But in terms of bridging language gaps, most native nobles knew Nahuatl as a second language, and the translation process that relied on Nahuatl as a lingua franca was well developed in Oaxaca by the 1540s. Thus, despite their limitations, inquisitorial records are valuable sources of information for the early period.[6]

The first part of this essay interprets the inquisitorial investigations in Yanhuitlan and Coatlan as struggles for local power that involved many players, including the native nobility, local rivals from other communities, the Dominicans, and the Spanish encomenderos. The second part examines how the lords responded to Christian beliefs and practices. The third and final part considers the impact of the trials on these lords and their communities.

Conflicts of Interest

In 1544, Licenciado don Francisco Tello de Sandoval assumed the position of apostolic inquisitor of New Spain. He relieved fray Juan de Zumárraga, the first bishop of Mexico City, who had been criticized in Spain for his handling of native idolatries.[7] In particular, Zumárraga had condemned the cacique of Tetzcoco to a sentence of death in 1539. Even though the accusations against don Carlos Mendoza Ometochtzin did not involve allegations of human sacrifice, he was hanged and burned at the stake for his open defiance of church and crown. In December of 1544, Tello de Sandoval ordered the arrest of the governor and cacique of Yanhuitlan, don Francisco and don Domingo, while Bachiller Pedro Gómez de Maraver, visitor of the bishopric of Oaxaca and dean of its cathedral, continued gathering evidence against the lords.[8] The investigation in Yanhuitlan involved many Spaniards and Mixtec nobles from the area, as well as native slaves and priests who had served in the houses of the lords.

A Spaniard named Martín de la Mesquitta, the *corregidor* (magistrate) of Texupa and a resident of Antequera (Oaxaca City), provided the first testimony against don Francisco. Mesquitta went to Yanhuitlan to arrest the son of don Francisco for his alleged participation in a violent confrontation with officials from Etlatongo. When he arrived at don Francisco's house, he encountered a ceremony in progress.

KEVIN TERRACIANO

Mesquitta entered the house as a man ran out carrying a cloak filled with bloody feathers, straws, and reeds. He looked around the house and saw some small images in a dark chamber, several bundles, and stacks of *cajetillas* or small bowls for food and offerings.[9] This was the first of many statements recorded against don Francisco and the nobles of Yanhuitlan.

The first round of testimony seemed to confirm the Dominicans' fears that pagan beliefs continued to thrive in the most populous and prosperous area of the Mixteca, at the very center of their regional operations and nearly two decades after their arrival. In fact, they had been forced to abandon their convento twice before 1544. The friars acknowledged this sad state of affairs. Fray Martín de Santo Domingo, a resident of Coixtlahuaca, confessed that the faith had made no impact whatsoever in communities around Yanhuitlan. In Molcaxtepec, he lamented, the church was a straw shed that could accommodate no more than ten people. When saying mass in the shed, fray Martín could barely elevate the host without scraping it on the ceiling.[10] Ironically, the richest community in the Mixteca had the least impressive church building, images, and adornments, and the worst reputation for continued idolatries and drunken feasts. The friars' exaggerated claims that other communities in the Mixteca had embraced the Christian faith wholeheartedly only heightened the tragedy of Yanhuitlan.

In reality, the church suffered from a lack of resources in this densely populated, mountainous region of multiple, dispersed settlements. The Spanish presence consisted of a small group of friars and a handful of administrators who were scattered in less than a dozen *cabeceras* (plural of cabecera, the head-town of a given colonial jurisdiction). In the many *ñuu* (local Mixtec states) surrounding Yanhuitlan, there were no churches or resident priests. Language barriers had forced the friars to rely on a few bilingual boys to translate their sermons into Mixtec. Many native priests confessed that they had never seen a friar before the trial.[11] Despite acknowledging these limitations, the friars blamed their failures on the native lords and the Spanish encomendero of Yanhuitlan.

The Mixtec governor of Yanhuitlan was the first defendant to testify before the grand inquisitor of the Holy Office in Mexico City. Don Francisco sidestepped or denied every accusation made against him: he had nothing to do with drunken feasts; if he sometimes appeared inattentive during mass, it was because he was a sick, old man; he made the same types of offerings that Christians made to the dead; if boys had been sacrificed, let their parents come forth and complain, and let their relatives identify them with paintings. Finally, when asked if he knew anybody who was opposed to Christianity, he replied, "I don't know anything about anybody."[12] He knew that the friars were very disappointed with the situation in Yanhuitlan, but he attributed their frustration to a longstanding conflict with the Spanish encomendero, Francisco de las Casas.[13]

In his defense, don Francisco deflected attention to a bitter feud between the local encomendero and the Dominican order. Indeed, many friars openly accused Francisco de las Casas of obstructing their

PEOPLE OF TWO HEARTS AND THE ONE GOD FROM CASTILE

mission. Fray Francisco de Mayoraga blamed the idolatries on the encomendero's unwillingness to cooperate with the friars. One friar testified that the encomendero continually impeded evangelization because he wanted "the natives to go through him first" and, in fact, "he wanted everything to go through his hands."[14] Fray Bernardo de Santa María claimed that the encomendero's lack of support had forced them to abandon Yanhuitlan. The encomendero intervened when friars punished Indians for their sins, he interfered with plans for the building of a church, and he even encouraged native nobles to ignore the friars.[15] The Dominicans clearly resented Francisco de las Casas' influence and used the trial to discredit his position.[16]

The feud represented a typical confrontation between friars and encomenderos over the control of native resources. The encomienda of Yanhuitlan was disputed from the beginning, when Hernando Cortés assigned the grant to his cousin, Francisco de las Casas.[17] To the encomendero, the foundation of a large convent in Yanhuitlan competed with his own plans for native labor and tribute. They would want to build a large church, and they would expect many things to go through their hands, so to speak. Even the business of confiscating images was subject to competition. Native witnesses testified that Francisco de las Casas had instructed them to bring their images to his house, and not to the friars. One cacique reported that they brought some very good stones to him, and he took them in secrecy.[18] Since some of the pieces were inlaid with gold and precious stones, it is easy to imagine the encomendero's

motivation for making a secret pact. In Coatlan, the lords accused secular priests of confiscating idols for this same purpose.[19] Friars were not above this practice, either. When fray Benito Hernández discovered a cave full of images and offerings in the Mixteca Alta, he used the jewels and gold from the images to purchase silver and vestments for the sacristy of the church in Achiutla.[20] Tombs and images provided start-up capital for the Christian enterprise; similarly, temples supplied building materials for new churches.

Indigenous nobles found themselves caught in the middle of this worldly conflict, but they were not passive victims. Just as native groups in central Mexico used ecclesiastical conflicts to advance their own interests, including competition among the orders and between the secular and regular clergy, the lords of Yanhuitlan defended themselves by exploiting a conflict between the encomendero and the friars.[21] Apparently, the lords of Yanhuitlan and the encomendero had reached a working agreement that did not include the friars. The agreement was simple: the encomendero would not interfere too much with local affairs if he received a specified amount of tribute. The encomendero did not pose an immediate threat because he did not live in Yanhuitlan. Here was an arrangement that Mixtecs could accept, based on their own conventions of paying tribute to a distant lord. In contrast, resident priests who sought to destroy temples, images, writings, and rival priests were quite unprecedented and unacceptable.

At the same time, deep-seated conflicts and rivalries divided the Mixtec

KEVIN TERRACIANO

participants of the trial.[22] Don Francisco was fully aware of this fact. He acknowledged Yanhuitlan's previous legal disputes with Etlatongo, Jaltepec, and Suchitepec. All these disputes had gone before the Royal Audiencia in Mexico City. The Spanish political reorganization that made Yanhuitlan a cabecera over many other ñuu had made matters worse. In this colonial arrangement, *sujetos* (subject towns) were subordinated to cabeceras in matters of local administration, government, and tribute payment. Nobles and caciques from these subject communities seized the opportunity to denounce Yanhuitlan and its rulers. Etlatongo led the attack. Apparently, don Francisco's son had provoked a skirmish with officials from Etlatongo over some native slaves. This incident led to the initial confrontation between Mesquitta, the corregidor, and don Francisco, when the Spanish official barged into the governor's house. The fact that lords from Yanhuitlan possessed slaves from Etlatongo indicates that the two communities had engaged in warfare at some point in the recent past. In 1544, Etlatongo filed a legal suit against Yanhuitlan and its encomendero. The nobles of Nochixtlan supported Etlatongo by filing a similar suit against Yanhuitlan. In fact, the two communities were allied through dynastic intermarriage. Don Francisco and don Domingo singled out the rulers of Suchitepec, an ally of Etlatongo, as embittered rivals who resented their status as a sujeto of the cabecera of Yanhuitlan. Rather than serving the cabecera, they sought to establish their own autonomy.[23] Political conflicts encouraged many witnesses to testify against Yanhuitlan. Local allegiances were so strong that the only witnesses from Yanhuitlan who denounced the lords were boys in the service of the friars. The slaves who condemned the lords for their idolatrous words and actions were from elsewhere; even the native priests came from outlying communities. Rival lords offered the most enthusiastic denunciations. Pre-existing conflicts among autonomous ñuu were complicated by colonial changes.

Spaniards offered damaging testimony against the lords of Yanhuitlan for their own reasons. Some of the Spanish witnesses had quarreled in the past with people from Yanhuitlan. One of the most vocal accusers, Bachiller Gómez de Maraver, had insulted the lords of Yanhuitlan more than once, calling them "no more Christian than a horse."[24] Luis Delgado, a lieutenant of the Spanish *alcalde mayor* who thought of himself as a Christian vigilante, could hardly conceal his contempt for the lords of Yanhuitlan.

At the same time, four Spaniards testified on behalf of don Francisco, confirming the bitterness of inter-community rivalries and acknowledging the conflict between Francisco de las Casas and the friars. Whereas no Dominican defended the lords of Yanhuitlan, a secular priest named Juan de Ruanes openly contradicted the friars.[25] He called don Francisco a good Christian who had done his best to attend church regularly, and he dismissed many of the accusations as petty gossip. Ruanes said that he had witnessed don Francisco preaching to groups of native people in the church patio. The Spanish witnesses defended don Francisco and the other lords of Yanhuitlan on several counts. Don Francisco ingested tobacco before mass, they said, but many Indians, Africans, and Spaniards used tobacco to stave off hunger, to alleviate the pain of headaches and toothaches, and to provide energy. Rather than encouraging drunkenness, one witness thought that the native officials of Yanhuitlan tended to punish drunkenness too harshly. Another witness observed that the lords positioned men at the back of the church to ensure that nobody would sneak out during the mass. The fact that at least four Spanish witnesses spoke on behalf of the native nobles and testified that Yanhuitlan was being victimized by native and Spanish factionalism complicates our general impression of the trial as a Spanish assault on Mixtecs. Although the relationship between these witnesses and the encomendero is unclear, I suspect that they favored the encomendero's position for their own personal reasons. The spiritual conquest invited multiple struggles for power and influence.

The same observations may be made for Coatlan, a complex cabecera with multiple "estancias" in a border area shared by Nahuas, Mixtecs, and Zapotecs.[26] Coatlan was the site of a violent two-year rebellion against the Spanish invasion, beginning in 1525, in which many people were killed. Repression and disease followed in the 1530s. A dispute over the encomienda was settled in favor of Andrés de Monjarráz, whose son, Gregorio, inherited half after it was divided by the crown. Meanwhile, the Dominicans were forced to relinquish Coatlan to the secular clergy in 1538, probably due to a lack of resources.[27] In December of 1544, a secular priest of Oaxaca, Pedro de Olmos, submitted a report concerning idolatries and sacrifices in Coatlan. Tello de Sandoval ordered an investigation based on the report. Whereas the encomendero of Yanhuitlan did not appear to testify in the record of the trial, Gregorio Monjarráz testified against the lords of Coatlan. He charged them with multiple crimes and sins: organizing sacrificial slaughters; burning a Christian cross in the marketplace; and raping his female Indian slave.[28] He recommended harsh punishment for the lords. After the trial, Monjarráz was charged with excessive violence and cruelty, and he lost his encomienda. Although less is known about the specific circumstances of the case of Coatlan, it is clear that native rivalries fanned the flames of the Inquisition. Many of the witnesses came from Tututepec, a traditional rival of Coatlan.[29]

Ambivalence and Resistance

When the native governor of Chachuapa testified in 1545 that the people of Yanhuitlan sacrificed things both to their ancestors' images and to the "one god from Castile," he used the phrase the "people of Yanhuitlan were of two hearts."[30] This expression, translated from Mixtec, makes the common association of *yni*, "heart," with volition and spirit.[31] This ambivalent, two-hearted allegiance was understandable. To the Mixtecs, the introduction of a new ethnic deity after the conquest was to be expected.[32] Apparently, many people had accepted the god from Castile. But accepting a new deity did not entail rejecting all others, nor did the continuation of ancient practices and beliefs signify a rejection of Christianity. Don Francisco had acknowledged the god from Castile by attending mass and

KEVIN TERRACIANO

observing many Christian customs, but he had not embraced Christianity wholeheartedly. When asked if he knew any Christian prayers in Latin, Castilian, or Mixtec, he replied that he knew two or three words; when asked to say those two or three words, he admitted that he could not remember them.[33]

Several witnesses claimed that the people of Yanhuitlan were "lukewarm" in matters of the faith.[34] They accused the lords of "going through the motions" without truly knowing or caring about God. When the lords attended mass, they went reluctantly and did not pay attention. Don Francisco was accused of chewing tobacco, refusing to kneel, looking away from the altar, putting his head down, and falling asleep during mass. After mass, the nobles sat around and drank pulque, joking that they had not understood a word of the sermon. They ate meat on Fridays and they made their servants work on the Sabbath. Spaniards saw these transgressions as signs of blatant indifference or latent resistance.

Spaniards sought out and persecuted signs of ambivalence and resistance. In response, the lords of Yanhuitlan tried to appease zealous Spaniards by reassuring them that they had accepted Christianity. Luis Delgado recalled the time when nobles from Yanhuitlan offered him gifts of clothing and gold in exchange for his acceptance of them as good Christians.[35] The nobles tried to convince him that they had given up their images when they were baptized, and that there was no longer any need to look for signs of idolatry. Apparently, the strategy did not work. Armed with a musket and sword, Delgado confiscated several images

from a *cacica* (female lord) in Tacosaguala who confessed that she was guarding the images on behalf of Yanhuitlan. When several nobles of Yanhuitlan tried to rescue the images from Delgado's house by attempting to bribe him, he smashed and burned the images in their presence. Delgado reminisced how a noble named Domingo Estumeca fell to his knees and cried at the sight of the destruction.[36]

The investigation in Coatlan reveals intimate glimpses of how the lords were forced to placate Christians by relinquishing their precious images. In 1546 the lords confessed that a priest had come to Coatlan to destroy their images about eight years earlier. The three lords and four *tequitlatos* (tribute collectors) secretly assembled the images and separated the most esteemed and noble ones ("los mayores y principales") from the lesser ones ("los menores"). They gave the least favored images to the Christian priest while keeping the most precious ones for themselves. Then they made a speech before the remaining "principales" or important ones. One of the lords of Coatlan, don Alonso, recalled what they had said to the images on that sad day in 1538:

> We reasoned with them, telling them how the priest had come for them and that in order to meet his demands, we gave him the lesser ones, which were separated from the rest. The remaining ones will be hidden and guarded where nobody can find them. And we promised that we would keep them as gods, like before, and that they should not be angry, and that they should remain calm.[37]

The cacique, don Hernando, remembered the speech in similar terms. He said to the images: "You already know how the Christians have come around asking for you and looking to burn you, and that we would be mistreated and killed if we did not give them anything. So it is better that we gave the priest those lesser ones."[38] He pleaded with them not to be angry. Once the priest had gone from Coatlan, they honored the remaining images by sacrificing a male and female slave before them, offering the victims' hearts to them as a propitiatory gesture. In don Hernando's words, a priest performed the sacrifices "so that they [the images] would not be angry." The third brother, don Juan, recalled how they had confessed to the images their fear of the Christians, and how they had reaffirmed their resolve to worship and take care of them as before. The three lords of Coatlan conversed with their deities in very respectful terms. Some of the deities were ranked higher than others, reflecting the society in which they were adored. The least noble of the images were sacrificed to the Christian priest for the greater good of the most esteemed.

Eventually, the lords of Yanhuitlan began to wonder whether their half-hearted acceptance of the Castilian god had angered their own deities, who were punishing them with sickness and drought. Disease was widespread in the 1530s and 1540s, especially in 1538 and from 1545 to 1548.[39] According to one indigenous witness, when the lords of Yanhuitlan gathered in the palace of don Francisco to devise a strategy for dealing with drought, hunger, and disease, they concluded that the recent baptisms and masses had angered Dzahui, the rain deity. Don Francisco allegedly concluded that "If Jesus Christ were a god, he would not give the commoners such hunger." He reasoned that "our gods are angry because some of us follow the god of the Christians."[40] They assembled the necessary items for sacrifice, drank pulque, and invoked Dzahui.[41] When don Francisco painted himself with charcoal and made sacrifices to Dzahui, he supposedly cried out "now I'm no longer Christian, I'm what I used to be."[42]

The trials in Yanhuitlan and Coatlan featured much evidence of resistance to Christianity. The nobles of Yanhuitlan were notorious for mocking the new faith and denouncing the friars and native converts. According to witnesses, don Francisco bragged about not being Christian and reminded people that their ancestors had not come from Castile, nor did they understand the ways of the Christian god.[43] People from Yanhuitlan mocked native Christians from other communities with gestural and verbal insults. The cacique of Nochixtlan testified that the nobles and commoners of Yanhuitlan insulted his people when they passed along the borders or on the road, shouting "there go the Christians of Castile, the chickens."[44] The governor of Chachuapa remembered the time when, in the market of Suchitepec, they were accosted by officials from Yanhuitlan and accused of abandoning the traditional practices. He claimed that they wanted to bar native Christians from going to the Suchitepec marketplace because it was a major source of their sacrificial items. The governor recalled how people from Yanhuitlan had scorned them

KEVIN TERRACIANO

with derisive gestures, exposing their genitals to them and saying "well, since you are Christians."[45]

Christianity forced nobles to participate in the destruction of the old system or to stand aside and witness its demise. One Spaniard recalled don Francisco's reaction on the day they demolished the ancient temple. When fray Dionisio de la Anunciación ordered commoners to tear down the temple remains that were left standing next to the church, don Francisco tried to obstruct their work. According to Luis Delgado, when the men began to raze the structure, don Francisco warned them that the gods would get their revenge.[46] Don Francisco allegedly prohibited people from surrendering their images to the friars. When the cacique of Molcaxtepec was about to hand over his images to a friar, don Francisco berated him and cried out "Why are you bringing your gods to the friars? These are your ancestors whom you should guard and adore."[47]

The friars appropriated ancient sacred spaces for their new churches and Christian images, but the old temples and deities were not forgotten. According to a slave of Molcaxtepec who had served in the palace of Yanhuitlan, don Francisco instructed people to worship the deities of their ancestors in the church patio, where the temple used to stand. Another native witness was more explicit about the church's location on sacred ground: don Francisco told people to invoke the sacred ancestors, to burn copal, and "to worship in the place where the houses and temples of the deities used to be, on the southern side of the church patio."[48] This was the place where many

Mixtecs, including don Francisco, had been accused of letting blood from their ears on the ground. As he admitted in his own confession, don Francisco had been punished with lashes by fray Bernardo de Santa María for his performance of this ritual act.[49]

Clandestine practices were a predictable response to Spanish repression in the early colonial period. Certain ritual acts were confined to concealed spaces and remote places, involving fewer people. Small, bundled images were worshipped in houses or carried to remote mountains and caves. Fray Diego de Santa María, who claimed to have burned piles of images, admitted to the existence of many concealed continuities.[50] For example, native priests hid themselves or changed their appearance by dressing differently and washing when the friars came around.[51] One priest named Cuizo (2-Ocelot) was *alguacil* (native constable) of Yanhuitlan until a Spanish official removed him from office in 1544.[52]

Christians had time and power on their side. Secret rites divided communities into factions, pitting converted natives against their unconverted neighbors. The proselytizing, disruptive, and divisive nature of Christianity invited communities, factions, and individuals to police each other's activities. Diego Hernández, a native church attendant of Yanhuitlan who translated sermons into Mixtec, testified that the lords had tried to kill him because he preached Christianity and denounced the ancient deities.[53] Most people in Yanhuitlan would not speak to him. Often, friars trained boys for these specialized church skills, encouraging them to identify elders who had not converted. Outsiders with prying eyes were most threatening because they were not subject to local authorities or peer pressure. Thus, when many people from Yanhuitlan and surrounding communities gathered in Topiltepec for a sacrificial feast to Dzahui, the rain deity, nobles warned the commoners in their speeches not to say a word about the ceremony to anyone, especially to native Christians from Teposcolula, Nochixtlan, and Etlatongo.[54] When this type of large-scale, corporate activity was no longer possible or expedient, when the collective nature of ritual practices was reduced to a few people who risked their lives to perform secret rites in remote places, clandestine cults ceased to pose a serious threat to Christianity in Yanhuitlan.[55]

The case of Coatlan abounds with evidence of crisis, confusion, indecision, and conscious resistance. Agustín de San Francisco, a native church official in Tututepec, was informed by merchants from his community that the people of Coatlan continued to perform many traditional practices, including human sacrifice.[56] According to Diego de Albino, a noble from Tututepec, emissaries from the communities of Yanhuitlan, Xaltepec, Tilantongo, Elotepec, Teozapotlan, Tiltepec, and many other Mixtec and Nahua communities gathered in Coatlan in 1543 to discuss strategies for responding to the Christian threat. They celebrated a feast in which they ate and drank, painted, sacrificed blood from their ears and tongues, and performed many other rites and ceremonies. When the feast was over, Albino recalled the following speech that the lord don Hernando made to the assembled group:

Brothers, I beg you to tell your caciques and nobles what you have seen here, and I beg them that they should do the same there. They should sacrifice and call upon their gods as they have done before, and they should not listen to the doctrine of the [Christian] priests. Here are the gods of our ancestors; they should resuscitate their gods . . . I am the valiant and great lord don Hernando, I have many bows and arrows and many people, and if I were to kill the priests or the Christians, then the *tatuan* (*tlatoani*, or ruler) of Mexico will pardon me.[57]

He warned against giving images to Christian priests, who sought them for the gold and precious stones from which they were made. When don Alonso, the cacique of Mistepec, suggested that it might be best to give up the images in order to retain power in the region, don Hernando insulted him before all the other nobles in the patio of his palace.[58] He challenged don Alonso to explain why he had not buried his father in the traditional manner, and he berated and insulted the other nobles who had accepted Christian practices and who had spoken with priests. He was proud to have guarded the ways of his ancestors, and to remain "lord in his own land." Apparently, even by 1543, don Hernando clung to the notion that the tlatoani of Mexico Tenochtitlan was the ultimate political authority in the land.

According to several native witnesses, don Hernando had made some provocative statements about Christian priests, whom he called *gallinas* (hens).[59] Pedro de Olmos attributed the following speech to don Hernando:

If the Christians have their god, then we have our own gods, and if they have their laws and commandments, then we have ours, too. We should not associate ourselves with the Christians, nor should we accept the sticks (staffs of office) that the viceroy sends because they are not our friends. We have listened to the priests and dealt with Christians for more than twelve years, but we have not accepted their words, nor do we want to accept what they say because it is all lies.[60]

He admonished people to stay away from the friars. One day, when Bartolomé Sánchez, the vicar of Coatlan, was preaching the Gospel to nobles and commoners, don Hernando stood up and shouted at him that the Gospels were nothing but lies written down on paper. Another time, when Sánchez began to reprehend the nobles in his sermon for not attending mass regularly, they walked out of the church and went to the market, leaving him to say mass to himself. When the priest later confronted them for ignoring him, they threatened to beat him.[61] Sánchez also recounted how he had entered don Hernando's house one day to investigate alleged idolatries. He found don Hernando and other nobles with their warclubs, bows, and arrows, getting drunk. When the priest tried to enter, don Hernando grabbed him by the beard and sexually insulted him.[62]

The lords of Yanhuitlan and Coatlan struggled to accept Christianity while resisting the destruction of their sacred relations. They were persecuted for their ambivalence and resistance.

Epilogue

The lords of Yanhuitlan were imprisoned for two years, and more than forty witnesses came forth to denounce or support them. Meanwhile, the community of Yanhuitlan was forced to pay for the proceedings. In 1546, they paid 500 pesos for the legal expenses of the Holy Office.[63] Likewise, Coatlan was ordered to pay 1,000 pesos in 1547 for the cost of the trial.[64]

In 1546, the inquisitors began to search Yanhuitlan for buried corpses and other evidence of human sacrifice. In the house of don Juan's neighbor, where don Juan allegedly had buried a sacrificed girl, they exhumed the body of a boy or girl whose skull was broken into fragments; the chamber contained several pieces of "blue stone" (turquoise). Nearby, the corpse of an adult was bundled in a reed mat, surrounded by jade stones, pieces of silver, and eight jars.[65] The owner of the house testified that the bones belonged to a mother and her child. The investigation proved inconclusive. The accounts of witnesses who claimed to have seen sacrifices and burials led the inquisitors on a wild search for bodies. In Molcaxtepec, officials dug around in a canyon called Yuchaco, where boys were allegedly sacrificed and buried. They found nothing.[66]

While officials searched for bodies, seven native priests were arrested and placed in chains. Two of the priests were too sick to walk, and another was an elderly, feeble man, so only four of the priests were interrogated. Two of them had testified earlier. One of the most talkative priests, Caco of Coscatepec, admitted that he had performed numerous sacrifices.[67] When the cacique of Coscatepec had died, for instance, he sacrificed several boys. When the cacique of Yanhuitlan died around 1539, don Francisco and don Juan had ordered him to make sacrifices. One time, he confessed, they sacrificed five boys on a hill near Coscatepec. But the second time Caco was called upon to clarify his testimony, he retracted part of his statement. Specifically, he denied that the lords of Yanhuitlan had ordered him to make any sacrifices. Meanwhile, the other three priests were evasive in their replies. Cuyuizo denied performing human sacrifice and concluded that "he did not know anything" about the lords of Yanhuitlan.[68] When the judge admonished him to tell the truth, he replied that he did not know anything more. Cocoane and Xixa, both about twenty years old, denied letting blood from their ears or tongues and, in the end, denied that they had ever been priests.[69] When asked about the severe scars on his tongue, Cocoane said that it was from eating maize stalks; in response to questions about the scars on his ears, Xixa said that his mother had pierced them when he was a boy. By this time, most of the accused priests had realized that it was better to deny everything than to admit anything.

As testimony against the lords of Yanhuitlan continued, and the lords continued to deny the charges made against them, the documentation comes to a dead end. The case is incomplete. The last page ends in the middle of don Domingo's denials. We can only guess how long the trial continued beyond the last page of the document, and whether the inquisitors tortured the accused, as they had done elsewhere in New Spain. We do not know the verdict. It is likely that

the trial was suspended indefinitely when the inquisitor Tello de Sandoval returned to Spain in 1547. Richard Greenleaf suspected that the encomendero of Yanhuitlan, who bailed don Domingo out of jail in 1546 for the sum of 2,000 pesos, may have exerted pressure on the inquisitorial proceedings by vouching for the lords of Yanhuitlan.[70] It is likely that the entire case was dropped.

The record of the trial in Coatlan continued into 1547 but also ended without a verdict. Whereas the lords of Yanhuitlan denied every serious charge, in spite of explicit confessions by native priests with whom they allegedly were associated, the three lords of Coatlan confessed to guarding images and performing sacrifices, even after baptism. Don Hernando defended himself with the disclaimer that he had been deceived by the devil and that he was not opposed to Christianity. By his own admission, he did not know a thing about the faith. He remembered that he had been baptized by a tall priest from Castile, whose name he did not know. He admitted that the baptism had meant nothing to him. At the end of his confession, he begged the court for mercy and promised to live as a Christian. The three lords were imprisoned in Mexico City when the documentation ends in 1547.

The Dominicans used the inquisitorial process to challenge an encomendero, to confront ambivalent and resistant nobles, and to establish their presence in Oaxaca. The trial in Yanhuitlan strengthened church and crown in the Mixteca Alta. The most prominent indigenous nobles of Yanhuitlan and Coatlan were forced to declare their allegiance to Christianity, and the Dominicans reasserted control over the indoctrination of the area by 1548. In that year, the encomienda of Yanhuitlan was limited to half its original grant; the other half fell under crown control as an *alcaldía mayor*. Francisco de las Casas bequeathed his half to his son, Gonzalo de las Casas, who helped finance the construction of the great church of Yanhuitlan.[71]

The trial exposed a generation of indigenous nobles who could scarcely comprehend the radical changes that had taken place in the course of two decades. Driven by local enmities and struggles for power, indigenous people and Spaniards alike used the inquisitorial proceedings to bring down their opponents. When the alleged words and deeds of the accused came under scrutiny, the defendants concealed their lingering doubts about the new religion and its leaders. There was no room for dialogue or discourse here. Perhaps the lords of Coatlan and Yanhuitlan had heard about the cacique of Tetzcoco who was publicly executed only a few years earlier. After two years of imprisonment and interrogation, they were not prepared to burn for their own ambivalent beliefs. As the trial records from Oaxaca come to a sudden end, leaving us with nothing more on the matter, we can only imagine what these people thought about the one god from Castile and the consequences of his conquest.

NOTES

I would like to thank Stafford Poole, Susan Schroeder, and Lisa Sousa for reading and commenting on this essay. I am especially grateful to Lisa for her assistance in reading parts of the original, lengthy trial records used in this study, which are stored in the Inquisición section of the Archivo General de la Nación (AGN) in Mexico City. For a full discussion of these two cases from Oaxaca and Mixtec religion, in general, see the chapter titled "Sacred Relations" in Kevin Terraciano, *The Mixtecs of Colonial Oaxaca: Ñudzahui History, Sixteenth through Eighteenth Centuries* (Stanford: Stanford University Press, 2001), 252–317.

1. Archival General de la Nación (AGN), Inquisición, 37: 5, ff. 7–11. In New Spain, the episcopal or apostolic Inquisition, under the direction of the bishop and then the archbishop, had jurisdiction over native idolatries until 1571. For an introduction to this case, see Richard Greenleaf, *The Mexican Inquisition of the Sixteenth Century* (Albuquerque, New Mexico: University of New Mexico Press, 1969), 76–79, and Ronald Spores, *Mixtec Kings and Their People* (Norman: University of Oklahoma Press, 1967), 25–27. See also María Teresa Sepúlveda y Herrera, *Procesos por idolatría al cacique, gobernadores, y sacerdotes de Yanhuitlan, 1544–1546* (Mexico City: Instituto Nacional de Antropología e Historia, 1999) for an analysis and transcription of sections of the trial involving the lords of Yanhuitlan. Jiménez Moreno and Mateos Higuera transcribed brief excerpts from the case in their study of the Codex of Yanhuitlan, in Wigberto Jiménez Moreno and Salvador Mateos Higuera, eds., *Códice de Yanhuitlan* (Mexico City: Instituto Nacional de Antropología e Historia, Museo Nacional, 1940), 37–49. The surviving record of this investigation, dated from 1544 to 1546, is one of the lengthiest inquisitorial records involving native peoples of New Spain.

2. AGN, Inquisición, 37: 6. Berlin provided a partial transcription of the 55-page document, with no accompanying analysis, in Heinrich Berlin, *Fragmentos desconocidos del Códice de Yanhuitlán y otras investigaciones mixtecas* (Mexico City: Antigua Librería Robredo de José Porrúa e Hijos, 1947), 35–38.

3. Nancy Farriss, *Maya Society Under Colonial Rule: The Collective Enterprise of Survival* (Princeton: Princeton University Press, 1984), 298–99.

4. On the use of Inquisition sources, see Carlo Ginzburg, *The Cheese and the Worms: The Cosmos of a Sixteenth-Century Miller*, trans. by John and Anne Tedeschi (New York: Penguin Books, 1982), xvii–xxvi; and Carlo Ginzburg, *Clues, Myths, and the Historical Method*, trans. by John Tedeschi and Anne Tedeschi (Baltimore: The Johns Hopkins University Press, 1986), 156–64. For colonial Mexico, see Greenleaf, *The Mexican Inquisition* and Richard Greenleaf, "Historiography of the Mexican Inquisition: Evolution of Interpretations and Methodologies," in *Cultural Encounters: The Impact of the Inquisition in Spain and the New World*, ed. Elizabeth Perry and Anne J. Cruz, 248–76 (Berkeley and Los Angeles: University of California Press, 1991), 248–76, and Serge Gruzinski, *Man-Gods in the Mexican Highlands: Indian Power and Colonial Society, 1520–1800* (Stanford: Stanford University Press, 1989), 3–5. For colonial Peru, see Kenneth Mills, *Idolatry and Its Enemies: Colonial Andean Religion and Extirpation, 1640–1750* (Princeton: Princeton University Press, 1997), 5–7. See also Sabine MacCormack, *Religion in the Andes: Vision and Imagination in Early Colonial Peru* (Stanford: Stanford University Press, 1991), 3–14, on the relevance of colonial sources in general for the study of Andean religion.

5. Even these statements must be read with caution and tested against other statements and sources. See Greenleaf, "Historiography of the Mexican Inquisition," 264–65, and Mills, *Idolatry and Its Enemies*, 45, on using the testimony of native witnesses as historical evidence.

6. See Ginzburg, *Clues, Myths, and the Historical Method*, 156–64. In an essay titled "The Inquisitor as Anthropologist," Ginzburg reminds us that no source is neutral and that, ironically, the inquisitor and the scholar often seek the same types of information.

7. Greenleaf, *The Mexican Inquisition*, 75–77.

8. Ibid., 77; Jiménez Moreno and Mateos Higuera, *Códice de Yanhuitlan*, 26. Gómez de Maraver had presented Tello de Sandoval with evidence of idolatries in Yanhuitlan, including human sacrifice.

9. AGN, Inquisición, 37: 5, f. 104.

10. Ibid., 7, f. 191.

11. Ibid., 7, ff. 203–4.

12. Ibid., 8, f. 212.

13. Ibid., 8, f. 215v.

14. Ibid., 7, f. 205v.

15. Ibid., 7, f. 206. This claim was made by fray Francisco de Villegas.

16. On the general Dominican conflict with encomenderos in the 1540s, see Lewis Hanke, *The Spanish Struggle for Justice in the Conquest of America* (Philadelphia: University of Pennsylvania Press, 1949), 81.

17. Yanhuitlan was converted to a corregimiento from 1531 to 1536 before being reassigned to Francisco de las Casas as an encomienda in 1537. After his death and the trial, half of the encomienda reverted back to crown control in 1548. See Jiménez Moreno and Mateos Higuera, *Códice de Yanhuitlan*, 13–14, and María de los Ángeles Romero Frizzi, *Economía y vida de los españoles en la Mixteca Alta: 1519–1720* (Mexico City: Instituto Nacional de Antropología e Historia, 1990), 47–61.

18. AGN, Inquisición, 37: 7, f. 200v.

19. Ibid., 6, f. 144.

20. Francisco de Burgoa, *Geográfica descripción*, Vol. 1 (Mexico City: Editorial Porrúa, 1989), 341.

21. On ecclesiastical "dissensions" see Robert Ricard, *The Spiritual Conquest of Mexico; An Essay on the Apostolate and the Evangelizing Methods of the Mendicant Orders in New Spain: 1523–1572*, trans. by Lesley Byrd Simpson (Berkeley and Los Angeles: University of California Press, 1966), 239–63; on native responses to ecclesiastical conflicts in the Valley of Mexico, see Charles Gibson, *The Aztecs Under Spanish Rule: A History of the Indians of the Valley of Mexico, 1519–1810* (Stanford: Stanford University Press, 1964), 110.

22. On native collaboration in the "spiritual conquest," see Ricard, *The Spiritual Conquest*, 273, and Serge Gruzinski, *The Conquest of Mexico: The Incorporation of Indian Societies into the Western World, 16th–18th Centuries*, trans. by Eileen Corrigan (Cambridge: Polity Press, 1993), 59–60.

23. AGN, Inquisición, 37: 8, f. 231. On Yanhuitlan's conflicts with its neighbors, see Ronald Spores, *The Mixtecs in Ancient and Colonial Times*

(Norman: University of Oklahoma Press, 1984), 209–10.

24. AGN, Inquisición, 37: 9, f. 287.

25. Ibid., 8, f. 252.

26. Coatlan is located in a multilingual area, between Zapotec Miahuatlan and Mixtec Tututepec. It was also closely connected to the Mexica empire, so that many of its nobles had Nahuatl names and spoke Nahuatl. The case of 1544–1547 indicates that Coatlan maintained close relations with several Mixtec communities, including Yanhuitlan, Tlaxiaco, Teposcolula, Tilantongo, Achiutla, Xaltepec, and Tututepec. Interpreters in this case spoke Nahuatl, Mixtec, and Zapotec. Witnesses in the case made frequent references to the Mexican (Nahua) and Mixtec pueblos around Coatlan.

27. Peter Gerhard, *A Guide to the Historical Geography of New Spain* (Cambridge: Cambridge University Press, 1972), 188–89.

28. Some Spaniards owned native slaves who were captured in "just wars." The document does not indicate the origin of this slave. Slaves may have been taken in the fierce military campaigns of the 1530s.

29. According to the *Relación geográfica* of 1580, Coatlan had been engaged in a state of intermittent warfare with Tututepec. René Acuña, *Relaciónes geográficas del siglo XVI: Antequera*, vol. 1 (Mexico City: Universidad Nacional Autónoma de México, 1984), 84.

30. AGN, Inquisición, 37: exp. 7, f. 195, and exp. 9, f. 266.

31. This phrase, "be of two hearts" (*cuhui uhui yni*) is probably a Mixtec metaphor; it appears in the *Doctrina en lengua mixteca*, which was first published in 1567 (I consulted a copy of the *Doctrina*, by Benito Hernández, in the Huntington Library). Goody defines ambivalence as "being in two minds" about something; see Jack Goody, *Representations and Contradictions: Ambivalence Toward Images, Theatre, Fiction, Relics, and Sexuality* (Oxford: Blackwell Publishers, 1997), 22–31. On the topic of ambivalence in colonial discourse, see Homi Bhabha, *The Location of Culture* (Routledge: London and New York, 1994), 85–92.

32. On this aspect of conversion, see Ricard, *The Spiritual Conquest*, 274; Farriss, *Maya Society Under Colonial Rule*, 293; and James Lockhart, *The Nahuas After the Conquest: A Social and Cultural History of the Indians of Central Mexico, Sixteenth through Eighteenth Centuries* (Stanford: Stanford University Press, 1992), 203.

33. AGN, Inquisición, 37: 8, f. 212.

34. Ibid., 7, f. 206. This was Francisco de Villegas, a resident of Antequera, who claimed that the people of Yanhuitlan would not attend mass if they were not forced to do so. Ricard also commented on the indifference of native peoples to the faith and, in fact, emphasized native "indifference" over "organized hostility"; see Ricard, *The Spiritual Conquest*, 269.

35. AGN, Inquisición, 37: 7, f. 184v.

36. Ibid., 7, ff. 185–185v. The name "estumeca" was derived from the Nahuatl *oztomecatl*, a type of long-distance merchant.

37. Ibid., 6, f. 152.

38. Ibid., 6, f. 149v.

39. Gerhard, *A Guide to the Historical Geography of New Spain*, 23.

40. AGN, Inquisición, 37: 7, f. 198v. The witness was Domingo from Etlatongo, a former slave of don Francisco, the cacique of Yanhuitlan.

41. Ibid., 7, ff. 202–3. The witness was Diego of Etlatongo, a slave of don Juan, the governor of Yanhuitlan.

42. Ibid., 7, f. 197.

43. Ibid., 7, ff. 201v–202.

44. Ibid., 7, f. 193v.

45. Ibid., 7, f. 196.

46. Ibid., 7, f. 186. This testimony indicates that the church was built beside the old structures, not on top of them. A provisional church was built before the old temple had been completely destroyed. This earlier structure was not the grand building that stands in Yanhuitlan today.

47. Ibid., 5, f. 118v.

48. Ibid., 5, f. 118.

49. Ibid., 8, f. 229v.

50. Ibid., 7, f. 186v.

51. Ibid., 5, f. 118.

52. Ibid., 7, ff. 198–99.

53. Ibid., 7, f. 189.

54. Ibid., 5, f. 116v.

55. See Farriss, *Maya Society Under Colonial Rule*, 292, 309, on clandestine practices in Yucatan.

56. AGN, Inquisición, 37: 6, f. 142. Agustín testified in Nahuatl.

57. Ibid., 6, f. 144.

58. Ibid., 6, ff. 144–144v.

59. Ibid., 6, f. 140. This was the same term employed by nobles of Yanhuitlan for Christians.

60. Ibid., 6, f. 128v.

61. Ibid., 6, ff. 129, 137, 140v–141.

62. Ibid., 6, ff. 136–136v. He called him a "cuylono ciguata." The term "cuylono" includes the Nahuatl verb *cui*, "take," which also referred to the act of sex. "Cuilono" could be a Spanish version of the passive, agentive form of the verb, *cuiloni*, "one who is taken." Or perhaps it is based on the noun *cuilonyotl*, which refers to sex between men, or the verb *cuilontia*, "commit sodomy." For this sixteenth-century Nahuatl-language terminology, see Alonso de Molina, *Vocabulario en lengua castellana y mexicana y mexicana y castellana* (Mexico City: Editorial Porrúa, 1992), 26v

(2nd numeration). "Ciguata," derived from the Nahuatl *cihuatl* (woman), may refer to his role as the taken one, or it is simply an insult to his masculinity. Elsewhere in this case, Sánchez was called a "ciguata" when he tried to reprimand a native person who was hiding an image along the road. Also, don Hernando was alleged to have called native Christians "ciguatas" and other insulting names, including "gallinas." The Nahuatl-language terms were probably altered in their translation to Spanish.

63. AGN, Inquisición, 10, ff. 330–330v.

64. Ibid., 6, f. 148.

65. Ibid., 10, f. 335v.

66. Ibid., 10, f. 337.

67. Ibid., 10, f. 337v.

68. Ibid., 11, f. 345v.

69. Ibid., 11, ff. 346–47.

70. Ibid., 10, f. 341; Greenleaf, *The Mexican Inquisition*, 79.

71. Romero Frizzi, *Economía y vida de los españoles en la Mixteca Alta*, 58.

CHAPTER TWO

Tying the Knot

Nahua Nuptials in Colonial Central Mexico

LISA SOUSA

Writing in the mid-sixteenth century, fray Diego Durán complained of some of his indigenous parishioners, "After I married some young men and young women, with all the solemnity and ceremonies that the sacrament demands, after leaving the church, they went to a house of some elder men and elder women and they married them again, with the ancient ceremonies and rites."[1] Durán's comment reveals the contested nature of marriage concepts and practices in sixteenth-century New Spain. In the first generations after the conquest, ecclesiastics dedicated their energies to promoting Christian marriage. In doing so, they incorporated some aspects of the Nahua marriage ceremony into the Christian ritual, and significantly altered others. Yet, even with the development of a hybrid ceremony, Christian rites could not replace the symbolic acts performed

during native nuptial rituals that served to reinforce fundamental social relations based on age, gender, and status. Rather, Nahuas developed parallel rituals to legitimate marriage.

Several recent studies of marriage in New Spain have used Spanish literature and records from bigamy, divorce, and marriage opposition cases to examine marital relations and expectations, intergenerational conflicts over choice of spouses, and the influence of concepts of honor and virtue on nuptial practices.[2] These works have made important contributions to the social history of marriage. However, they focus primarily on the Spanish population of the viceroyalty, leaving native perspectives and practices little understood. This article begins to address this gap in the literature by analyzing Nahua nuptial concepts and rituals and their adaptation under colonial rule.

This essay uses ecclesiastical writings, Nahuatl-language sources, and pictorials to examine how differing rituals reflected the values of New Spain's multiethnic society. The language, gesture, and behavior of participants and the use of multivocal symbols articulate social and sacred ideologies. The ritual process is shaped by and shapes a society's conceptualization of ideal social and sacred relations. Ritual also marks the differing stages of life and recognizes the transition from one state to another. In the colonial context of New Spain, where language barriers often hindered communication between friars and the native population, ritual acts took on further significance.

Let us begin by describing and interpreting the type of Nahua nuptials that Durán would have witnessed in the mid-sixteenth century.

Nahua Marriage Ceremonies

In Mesoamerica marriage was celebrated with elaborate rituals and festivities. There were several stages to the Nahua wedding ceremony, including a bridal procession, a series of speeches, cloth exchange, and feasting and drinking. An image from the Codex Mendoza, a pictorial manuscript with Spanish glosses drawn by Nahua artists around 1540, depicts the procession and the speechmaking portions of the ritual (see fig. 2.1). Marriage signified the passage from childhood to adulthood, a formidable step in a young person's life. Various aspects of the Nahua ceremony highlighted the transition that the bride and groom underwent in marriage. The festivities began with a proces-

sion of the bride's party from her home to the groom's home. Women carrying pine torches escorted a woman who carried the bride, as if she were a child. According to Mesoamerican pictorial conventions, the bride bearer's larger size in the Codex Mendoza suggests that she was older and/or of higher status. The procession represented the liminal state of the bride, who was removed from her household as a child and by the end of the ceremony would join the groom's household as a woman.[3] The bride's arrival at the groom's house at dawn, bathed in the light of the pine torches, symbolized the renewal and regeneration that the marriage would bring to the couple and their households. Celebration of the marriage in the early morning also harmonized with the Nahua belief that the sun provides moral order.[4] In contrast, night, which eclipses day, is associated with immorality and danger. Just as the sun provides order to the world, the institution of marriage regulates sexual, social, and economic relations within the community.

The Nahua bride wore the sign of her liminality with her face paint, which associated her with the Nahua goddess of sexuality, Tlazolteotl. Tlazolteotl's name is a compound derived from *tlaçolli* (trash) and *teotl* (god[dess]). She was said to have ruled over *in teuhtli, in tlaçulli* (the dust and the trash).[5] The deity was associated with fertility, sexuality, and sexual excess, including adultery. Read as a multivocal symbol, the face paint both expressed Nahua concerns for reproduction in marriage and associated the bride with the realm of the deities and with pollution.

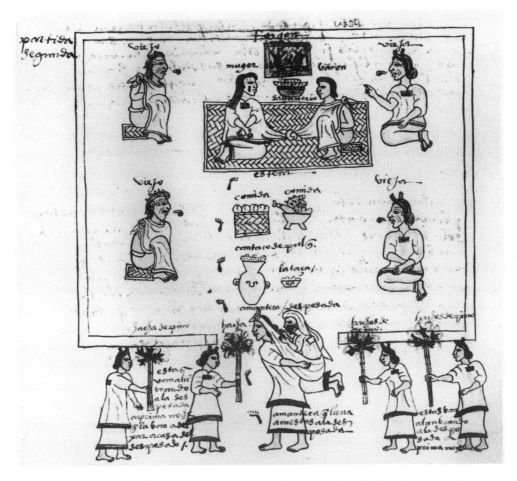

Figure 2.1: Nahua marriage ceremony from the *Codex Mendoza* (Arch. Selden. A1, 61r). Courtesy of The Bodleian Library, Oxford University.

Speeches made during the marriage ceremony also underscored the transition from childhood to adulthood. The mother of the bride expressed concern about the suitability of the young man as her daughter's husband, but also spoke of how the ritual would transform him:

Macaçamo xommauilmati, ca ie motlalticpac, ca ie mixcotian, ca ie centetl in monemiliz, ca aiocmo aviliez in moiollo,

ca ie oticcauh in telpuchtlavelilocaiutl inneivintiliztli, in vetzquiztli, in camanalli, ca ie titlapaltzintli.[6]

Do not take the marriage lightly, because it is now your world and your special realm; your life is now different. Your attitude is no longer to be frivolous, because you have already left behind the misbehavior of youth—drunkenness, laughter, and joking. Now you are a married man.

Similarly, the young bride was advised:

In axcan, ca ic intech tompachivi in ilamatque: ie toconpeoaltia in ilamane-miliztli: axcan xiccencacoa in pipillotl, in coconeiutl: aiocmo tiuhquin tipil-tontli tiez, aiocmo iuhquin.[7]

Now you have with this approached the old women; you are already beginning the life of an old woman. Now leave childishness entirely behind; you are no longer to be like a little child.

The speaking roles of the mothers, in which the bride's mother addressed the groom and the groom's mother addressed the bride, represented a symbolic exchange of children. As part of the wedding ceremony, speeches served to extend the authority of parents and elders over the young couple.

Nahua marriage rituals also formalized cooperative labor relations and the management of resources between husband and wife and their respective households. While the bride and groom were seated on a reed mat, which was both a bed and a symbol of authority in Mesoamerica, elders and respected guests counseled the bride and groom on their duties in marriage.[8] The Codex Mendoza image shows two older men and two older women flanking the couple; the artist depicted their advanced age by drawing wrinkles on their faces, and he indicated their roles as orators by placing speech scrolls in front of their mouths. Several examples of the types of speeches that were made at Nahua wedding ceremonies were written down in the sixteenth and seventeenth centuries.

The conservative nature of the language and content suggests that these speeches bear little Christian influence and that they reflect Nahua attitudes toward idealized marital relations and the gendered division of labor. Elders and honored guests discussed marriage as a partnership in which husband and wife performed distinct, but complementary duties. In one Nahuatl-language example an orator advises the groom to provide for people in his household and counsels the bride to dedicate herself to cleaning, cooking, weaving, and managing the household.[9] Similarly, in the Florentine Codex mothers of the bride and groom spoke in complementary terms, telling the couple that a wife was to trade in local markets and that a husband was to travel to distant markets to sell their goods.[10] The late sixteenth-century *Relación geográfica* of one central Mexican community corroborates evidence in the Codex Mendoza and Nahuatl-language speeches, reporting that two elders instructed the groom to "take care in working and providing food for your wife," and admonished the bride to "take care in serving and making food for your husband."[11]

Rituals involving cloth constituted another important part of the marriage ceremony. Cloth exchange was used throughout Mesoamerica to establish and maintain social and sacred relations. For example, nobles presented gifts of cloth to one another during feasts to strengthen alliances, and people made cloth offerings to temples and deities. Throughout the Nahua region, the bride's mother presented her son-in-law with a new loincloth and cape, and the groom's mother gave her daughter-in-law a new skirt and blouse. The exchange of cloth represented the reciprocal relations of the bride's and groom's households, and the new garments symbolized their new lives as adults. During the marriage ceremony the groom's cape and the bride's blouse were tied together while they were seated on the mat, as depicted in the Codex Mendoza image. Some accounts specify that a midwife performed this highly symbolic act.[12] In Nahuatl-language sexual metaphors, gender-specific clothing represented the male and female bodies, and the term *nemecatiliztli* (tying oneself) was used to mean "to have sexual relations with someone."[13] Thus the couple's place on the mat/bed, the tying together of clothing, and the participation of midwives in this aspect of the ritual symbolized the fertile sexual union of the bride and groom.

Like cloth, food and drink were central to Nahua ritual expression. During the nuptials the bride and groom shared tortillas, turkey, and pulque, expressing their mutual obligations to sustain one another. As husband and wife, they would feed, clothe, and provide each other with life's necessities. The Codex Mendoza highlights the significance of these acts by displaying food and drink at the center of the composition. According to the Florentine Codex, the groom's mother also fed her son and her daughter-in-law tamales from the same bowl, representing the groom's mother's responsibility to nurture the daughter-in-law who joined their household.[14] The act highlighted the mother-in-law's special duty to protect her daughter-in-law and to treat her as her own child. After the

wedding, feasting and drinking went on for as long as four days.[15] The couple withdrew to a room where they consummated the marriage, as "old women" sat outside holding vigil and drinking.[16] When the couple emerged four days later, they concluded the festivities with one last round of speeches, feasting, and drinking in a ceremony called the *huexiuhtlahuana* (parents-in-law get drunk).[17]

The Codex Mendoza illustration and sixteenth-century accounts of the marriage ritual reflect underlying concepts of gender parallelism and complementarity. The spatial relationship between the couple in the Mendoza image suggests equality of age and status between the bride and groom, and the alignment of male and female elders and their equivalent speeches allow men and women an equal role in the ritual. The speeches and ceremonial acts reinforced a gendered division of labor and formalized cooperative work and resource arrangements between households. These accounts of the marriage ceremony portray idealized social relations between husband and wife, elders and youth, and the families of the bride and groom.

What did the friars think of these "ancient rites and ceremonies," as Durán called them? During the sixteenth century, ecclesiastics contemplated the validity of native marriage.[18] While some in the church may have been sympathetic to the validity of the indigenous institution in preconquest times, they agreed that Christian marriage, as dictated by canon law, must be encouraged under colonial rule. Thus the friars upheld the Christian sacrament of marriage as a model of virtue and civilization. How then did ecclesiastics promote Christian marriage among the indigenous population of New Spain?

Christian Marriage Practices

Christian marriage united husband and wife in a monogamous, indissoluble union. Over the course of the sixteenth century, a good number of Nahuas must have willingly celebrated marriage in the church. According to fray Toribio de Benavente Motolinia, the Franciscans were overwhelmed by the natives' requests for the marriage sacrament by the 1530s. Writing in 1537, he boasted,

> There are days when they [the Franciscans] marry a hundred couples, and other days two, three, or even five hundred, and as the priests are so few it gives them a great deal of work, for it happens that one priest may have many to confess, baptize, betroth and marry, and besides he has to preach and say mass and do other things that cannot be neglected.[19]

To emphasize his point, Motolinia refers to the phenomenon in different *altepetl* (Nahua ethnic state) of central Mexico where the friars betrothed and married anywhere from 200 to 1,000 couples a day. Like the exaggerated reports of mass baptisms, Motolinia's ecstatic account is surely intended to aggrandize the Franciscans' accomplishments as the first order in New Spain, and cannot be accepted at face value. The scarcity of priests trained in indigenous languages relative to the native population alone suggests that a good number of native people never celebrated the holy

sacrament of marriage. The first priorities among the friars were baptism and instruction in the fundamental tenets of the faith. Ecclesiastics were also hesitant to extend the sacrament to neophytes whose understanding of the faith was limited. Census records indicate that, at least in some areas of central Mexico, marriage remained limited even a generation after the conquest. In her study of a circa 1540 census from the Morelos region, which provides data on 315 joint family and nuclear households, Sarah Cline found evidence of only one couple who had married in the church.[20]

Although the precise numbers of Nahuas who married in the church can never be known, it is clear that the friars advocated the institution in sermons and ceremonies. In preaching to native audiences, religious emphasized that marriage was necessary for regulating sexual relations. In their Nahuatl-language sermons, fray Juan de la Anunciación preached that marriage allowed individuals to live in a "sacred way," and fray Bernardino de Sahagún asserted that marriage was necessary in order to avoid "liv[ing] wickedly."[21] Fray Alonso de Molina also advised the couple who came to the church seeking the sacrament that those who married for the love of God would be redeemed.[22] In New Spain, as in Western Europe, the church promoted the marriage of Saint Joseph and the Virgin Mary as the model of the ideal union of man and woman.[23]

The friars recognized and utilized the power of ritual in the colonizing process. They believed that if they could attract nobles to Christianity by offering participation in church sacraments and festivities as a privilege, then the commoners would follow. Motolinia revealed the friars' strategy, writing,

> In order to uproot the old feasts, they [the friars] celebrate the Christian festivals with great pomp, not only in the services and administration of the sacrament, but also with dances and entertainment; all of this is necessary to wean them away from the evil customs into which they were born.[24]

Motolinia's account of what he purports to be the first Nahua-Christian wedding, held in Tetzcoco in 1526, shows how friars carefully choreographed the ceremony as a display of power and prestige in the new colonial order to encourage holy matrimony among native neophytes.[25] He tells how don Hernando, brother of the cacique of Tetzcoco, and seven other nobles "who had been brought up in the house of God" and their brides were the first to receive the sacrament of marriage. The elaborate festivities included a mass, followed by feasting and dancing in the cacique's home. Both Spaniards and indigenous nobles attended the ceremony and brought gifts for the couples.[26] Motolinia admits the friars' tactics for promoting Christian marriage, writing, "Because this wedding was to be an example for the whole of New Spain, the full and solemn nuptial mass was used, with benedictions and pledges and a ring, as the Holy Mother Church commands."[27] Initially, the sacrament was administered selectively to young indigenous men who had been educated by the friars to accept monogamy as the norm.[28] Marriage was a privilege that

the church bestowed upon its faithful allies in its effort to convert indigenous nobles and commoners alike.

Canon law outlined a series of impediments that established the terms of acceptable unions and sexual relations.[29] *Impedimentos dirimentes* (insurmountable obstacles) provided grounds for denying marriage or for invalidating an existing marriage, regardless of whether the marriage had been consummated or the couple had children. Prior marriage (when the spouse was still living), previous public engagement, being underage (younger than fourteen for boys and twelve for girls), being a pagan or having joined the clergy (which was not an option for indigenous men) were among the impedimentos dirimentes. Consanguineal, affinal, or ritual kinship also constituted an insurmountable obstacle.

Christianized indigenous officials were to play a significant role in the enforcement of canon law in their own communities. This was a practical solution to the shortage of ecclesiastics, especially those trained in indigenous languages, a problem that persisted throughout the colonial period. Motolinia discusses the duties of local officials as early as the 1530s, reporting that in every community the friars trained native assistants, called *licenciados* (licentiates) because of their expertise in impediments and canon law regarding marriage. The licenciados investigated kinship and other matters that might provide grounds for denying the sacrament to a couple.[30] While there is little evidence to support Motolinia's claim that licenciados were functioning in "every community" by this early date, his comments reveal the church's ambitious, although not always successful, plans to reform native marriage practices.

Molina's *Confesionario mayor en la lengua mexicana y castellana* (1569) illustrates the church's attempts to impose Christian marriage as stipulated by canon law on the Nahuas of central Mexico.[31] The bilingual Nahuatl and Spanish confessional manual contains instructions on preparing a Nahua couple for the Christian sacrament of marriage and a brief description and illustration of the wedding ceremony. Molina directed the book to both native *fiscales* (native officials with responsibility for many church functions) and notaries, like those described by Motolinia, who initially interviewed the couple, and the priest, who examined the betrothed and their witnesses before performing the marriage ceremony. If the bride and/or groom were not from the altepetl, the notary was to notify the priest in the candidate's home community so that he could investigate whether impediments existed and announce the banns, making public the couple's intention to marry. Thus the *Confesionario* includes instructions and model dialogues between the priest, local officials, the couple, and their witnesses.

Molina opens the section on marriage with a warning that the existence of an impediment would invalidate a marriage. Seeking to discover impedimentos dirimentes, the fiscal and notary asked the bride and groom their ages, status, whether they had been baptized, and whether they had exchanged the marriage promise with anyone else.[32] Investigation of status (Molina includes slave, widow, and virgin on his list) prevented the possibility that a person might marry based on false information

about his or her spouse; such a discovery would invalidate the required consent and thereby annul the marriage.[33] The couple was also asked if their union was consensual, since, as a sacrament, marriage could only be entered into freely and voluntarily.

By far, the greatest concern expressed in Molina's *Confesionario* was over any potential relationship of consanguinity, affinity, or spiritual kinship between the couple. According to Molina's model, the fiscal and priest were to ask the betrothed and their witnesses five separate times whether the bride and groom were related. The priest warned them against lying, which would warrant strong punishment, including excommunication. Impediments based on kinship were to be emphasized again when the banns were read on three consecutive Sundays and holy days of obligation. The great emphasis placed on kinship as an impediment may have resulted from the ability of closely related kin to marry in Nahua society, which the friars observed during the first decades after the conquest. The importance placed on this matter explains the friars' frustration with those who knowingly violated impediments when they married; these cases reveal not only deception on the part of the couple, but also broader collusion between family and community members who did not make the impediment known.

Several aspects of the Christian marriage rite described by Spanish ecclesiastics would have seemed familiar to native audiences, providing a common ground for its acceptance by Nahuas. As in preconquest times, native spiritual authorities prepared couples for marriage. Whereas calendar readers and prognosticators traditionally counseled the bride and groom before marriage and determined their compatibility, the colonial native fiscal who initially interviewed the couple helped determine who could and could not marry. One's family and friends might also participate as witnesses to the Christian ceremony, although the broader roles that they would have performed in indigenous weddings would have been circumscribed. The priest's repeated use of the terms *nopilhuane* (my children) and *notlaçopilhuane* (my beloved children) to address the couple and their witnesses invoked kinship in order to legitimize the friar's role in the creation of alliances between families.[34] Gift exchange, feasting, and dancing, as described in Motolinia's account of the wedding in Tetzcoco, provided an element of continuity in native spiritual practices and forms of legitimating agreements and transactions. Emphasizing the sacred nature of the ritual, Molina instructed the bride and groom to come to the church on the day of their marriage with their hands and faces washed, and their clothing clean and neatly arranged. These directions clearly expressed the church's prohibition against the use of body paint and adornment in the ceremony. On the other hand, Molina's order would have appealed to the Nahua ritual of bathing before any ceremony, and the exchange of new garments was a standard feature of the Nahua wedding ceremony.

In addition to the similarities in the performance of wedding rituals, Nahuas would have found parallels in the content of Christian and native nuptials. Nahuas would have related to the church's emphasis on the importance of procreation in marriage. Molina reminds his parishioners:

"And another thing, one is to be married for having children, not for earthly pleasure, which would just be in vain" (*Oc cenca ye yeuatl ypampa yn nepilhuatiliztli nenamictilo: amo yehuatl ypampa yn çan nenquizqui tlayelpaquiliztli*).[35] This admonition resonates with Nahua expectations that a couple would have children, who would bring new life to a household and, among the nobility, who would serve as heirs to the rulership. According to early seventeenth-century models of Nahuatl-language speeches that were made during marriage negotiations and wedding ceremonies, the bride's parents and other guests spoke of the hope that the union would bear children.[36] In one example, an honored guest ponders the possibility that the bride may produce an heir to the throne; speaking to her in elegant, metaphorical Nahuatl, he says: "I wonder if we will also be so fortunate that a jewel and plume of ours will split and break off from you, will bloom and blossom out from your womb and throat, the sprout and blossom of the lord ruler, the Tlacateuctli" (*aço ça nen no tocnopiltiz inic motechzinco tzicuehuaz tlapaniz in tocozqui in toquetzal, aço xotlaz aço cueponiz in moxillantzinco in motozcatlantzinco in itzmolinca in icelica in ixotlaca in tlacatl in tlatoani in tlacateuctli*).[37] Other model speeches show guests making similar remarks to the groom and parents of the married couple.[38]

Molina's *Confesionario* demonstrates that the friars appropriated some Nahua traditions and included them in the Christian ceremony.[39] Usurping the role of the Nahua elders, the priest reminded the bride and groom of their duties in marriage: "Through reciprocity you are to help one another with [things] on earth, you are not to be idle" (*ynic nepanotl ammopalehuizque yn itechpa tlalticpac, amo nenca*).[40] He advised the groom, "it is a man's duty to work very hard to acquire what is needed to eat and drink for himself, his wife and his children" (*ca ytequiuh yn oquichtli ynic cenca tlatequipanoz, ynic quimixnextiliz yn itech monequiz yn quiquaz yn quiz yn yeuatl yuan yn iciuauh no yeuantin yn ipilhuan*).[41] A wife's duties were also made clear: "And likewise the woman is to greatly help her husband: her duties are to guard the belongings, to be in the house, to live in the house, to sweep, to wash, to spin, to weave, to grind [corn], to make food, [and] to raise children" (*Auh çano yuhqui yn cihuatl, ynic* *cenca quipaleuiz yn inamic: ca ynauatil ynic uelquipiez yn tlatquitl: cali yez cali nemiz, tlachpanaz, tlapacaz, tzauaz, hiquitiz, teçiz, tlaqualchiuaz, tlacauapauaz*).[42] Although Molina's Nahua assistants clearly influenced the ideology and terminology, the inclusion of indigenous customs in the ceremony followed a Christian tradition of absorbing local practices as a way of asserting church authority over marriage. In fact, the ceremony brought to the Americas had evolved over the course of centuries and had incorporated local customs, including the presentation of the ring to the bride, which derives from Roman practices of alliance building, and the joining of hands, which was part of the ancient Jewish ceremony.[43]

Figure 2.2: Nahua-Christian marriage ceremony in Alonso de Molina, *Confesionario en la lengua mexicana y castellana* (1569), f. 57. Courtesy of the John Carter Brown Library at Brown University.

LISA SOUSA

A comparison of the iconography of the Codex Mendoza image and of a woodcut showing the Christian marriage of a native couple from Molina's *Confesionario* underscores the differences between Christian and Mesoamerican concepts of gender relations and marriage (see fig. 2.2). The image in Molina's book represents the church's vision of the proper social order in the mid-sixteenth century. All native participants are subordinated to the Spanish friar, who represents authority within the colonial ethnic hierarchy. In contrast, the elders, the keepers of wisdom and knowledge in indigenous tradition, are silenced. Colonial authority was to be vested in Spanish Christian males, rather than community elder men and women and parents who guarded the practice of ancient rites. Symbols of reciprocity, including the food and drink that signified the binding of social and economic relations between husband and wife and their respective households, are absent. The bride's face paint, the procession at dawn, and references to the participation of elders and the midwife are gone. The illustration reveals the church's attempt to transform Nahua ritual and to restructure social relations in colonial times. The image also speaks powerfully to the importance of ritual as a colonizing tool in sixteenth-century New Spain.

Concluding Remarks

As in other areas of cultural contact, Spaniards sought to change indigenous practices that they considered objectionable. In terms of marriage, friars worked to replace traditional practices of serial monogamy and polygyny with monogamous, indissoluble Christian marriage. However, when grounds for convergence and mutual understanding existed, Nahua customs, beliefs, and institutions survived and, in some cases, flourished. Thus Nahua practices that did not violate Christian principles, such as the universality of marriage in native communities, did not trouble ecclesiastics. Areas of commonality, including the regulation of sexuality and alliance building, gave the friars a foundation to build upon as they introduced Christian marriage.

During the sixteenth century, hybrid Nahua-Christian marriage rituals developed, which combined European and indigenous traditions. While these ceremonies may have attracted Nahuas to the sacrament, they did not entirely replace native rites. As Durán noted, the church enjoyed only limited success in its attempt to transform indigenous marital concepts and practices, for the Nahuas continued to find meaning in their traditional ceremonies.

NOTES

1. Fray Diego Durán, *Historia de las indias de Nueva España e islas de tierra firme* (Mexico City: Editorial Porrúa, 1967, 2 vols.), I: 5, 56.
2. Recent studies of marriage in New Spain include: Patricia Seed, *To Love, Honor, and Obey in Colonial Mexico: Conflicts Over Marriage Choice, 1574–1821* (Stanford: Stanford University Press, 1988); Silvia Marina Arrom, *The Women of Mexico City, 1790–1857* (Stanford: Stanford University Press, 1985); Richard Boyer, "Women, *La Mala Vida*, and the Politics of Marriage," in *Sexuality and Marriage in Colonial Latin America*, ed. Asunción Lavrin, 252–86 (Lincoln: University

of Nebraska Press, 1989), and Boyer, *Lives of the Bigamists: Marriage, Family, and Community in Colonial Mexico* (Albuquerque: University of New Mexico Press, 1995); Ramón A. Gutiérrez, *When Jesus Came, the Corn Mothers Went Away: Marriage, Sexuality, and Power in New Mexico, 1500–1846* (Stanford: Stanford University Press, 1991); and Thomas Calvo, "The Warmth of the Hearth: Seventeenth-Century Guadalajara Families," in *Sexuality and Marriage in Colonial Latin America*, ed. Asunción Lavrin, 252–86 (Lincoln: University of Nebraska Press, 1989). For marriage in other parts of colonial Latin America, see Susan M. Socolow, "Acceptable Partners: Marriage Choice in Colonial Argentina," in *Sexuality and Marriage in Colonial Latin America*, ed. Asunción Lavrin, 209–46 (Lincoln: University of Nebraska Press, 1989), and María Beatriz Nizza da Silva, "Divorce in Colonial Brazil: The Case of São Paulo," in *Sexuality and Marriage in Colonial Latin America*, ed. Asunción Lavrin, 313–40 (Lincoln: University of Nebraska Press, 1989). Brief discussions of native marriage practices can be found in: Louise Burkhart, *The Slippery Earth: Nahua-Christian Moral Dialogue in Sixteenth-Century Mexico* (Tucson: University of Arizona Press, 1989); Susan Kellogg, *Law and the Transformation of Aztec Culture, 1500–1700* (Norman: University of Oklahoma Press, 1995); S. L. Cline, ed. and trans., *The Book of Tributes: Early Sixteenth-Century Nahuatl Censuses from Morelos* (Los Angeles: UCLA Latin American Studies Center Publications, Nahuatl Studies Series, Number 4, 1993); and Robert Ricard, *The Spiritual Conquest of Mexico: An Essay on the Apostolate and the Evangelizing Methods of the Mendicant Orders in New Spain: 1523–1572*, trans. Lesley Byrd Simpson (Berkeley and Los Angeles: University of California Press, 1966).

3. *Codex Mendoza*, facsimile with commentary by Frances F. Berdan and Patricia Anawalt (Berkeley and Los Angeles: University of California Press, 1992, 4 vols.), Vol. III: f. 61; fray Bernardino de Sahagún, *Historia universal de las cosas de Nueva España: Codice Laurenziano Mediceo Palatino 218, 219, 220*, 12 books (Florence: Giunti, 1996), Book II: f. 14v and Book VI: f. 109v; and René Acuña, ed., *Relaciones geográficas del siglo XVI*, 10 vols. (México City: Universidad Nacional Autónoma de México, 1981–1988), 7: 264.

4. James M. Taggart, *Nahuat Myth and Social Structure* (Austin: University of Texas Press, 1983), 63.

5. Sahagún, *Historia universal*, Book I: f. 7r–v.

6. Ibid., Book VI: f. 113v.

7. Ibid., Book VI: f. 110r–v.

8. Acuña, *Relaciones geográficas*, 8: 70–71. For an example of the Nahuatl-language speeches made by nobles at wedding ceremonies, see Frances Karttunen and James Lockhart, eds. *The Art of Nahuatl Speech: The Bancroft Dialogues* (Los Angeles: UCLA Latin American Center Publications, 1987), 122–27.

9. Karttunen and Lockhart, *The Art of Nahuatl Speech*, 108–11.

10. Sahagún, *Historia universal*, Book VI: f. 113r–v.

11. In reference to the pueblo of Ayutla, in the Relación de Xalapa, Cintla y Acatlan, in Acuña, *Relaciones geográficas*, 3: 289.

12. Relación de Tezcoco (Acuña, *Relaciones geográficas* 8:70–71); and Sahagún, *Historia universal*, Book II: f. 14v. The Nahuatl term *titici* (sing. *ticitl*, physician, prognosticator, healer) is used in the Spanish text of the Florentine Codex. See also Sahagún, *Historia universal*, Book VI: f. 112.

13. For a discussion of gender-specific clothing as a metaphor for the male and female body, see Lisa Sousa, "Women in Native Societies and Cultures of Colonial Mexico" (PhD diss., University of California, Los Angeles, 1998), 159–62. Burkhart notes the use of the term *nemecatiliztli* in sermons (*The Slippery Earth*, 154–56).

14. Sahagún, *Historia universal*, Book VI: f. 132.

15. Ibid., f. 112v. The couple remained on the mat for three days according to the Relación de Cempoala (Acuña, *Relaciones geográficas*, 7: 77) and Relación de Epazoyuca (Acuña, *Relaciones geográficas*, 7: 86). They were left on a mat for an unspecified number of days according to the Relación de Tlacotepeque (Acuña, *Relaciones geográficas*, 7: 301).

16. Ibid.

17. Ibid.

18. According to Stafford Poole, "the religious

favored the validity of native marriage, the diocesans did not." Charles H. Lippy, Robert Choquette, and Stafford Poole, *Christianity Comes to the Americas, 1492–1776* (New York: Paragon House, 1992), 40.

19. Fray Toribio de Benavente Motolinia, *History of the Indians of New Spain*, trans. and ed. Elizabeth Andras Foster, 150 (Berkeley: Cortés Society, 1950).

20. Cline, *The Book of Tributes*, 52.

21. Burkhart, *The Slippery Earth*, 156–57.

22. Fray Alonso de Molina, *Confesionario en la lengua mexicana y castellana* (Mexico City: Universidad Nacional Autónoma de México, 1984 [1569]), 51v.

23. For a discussion of the evolution of marriage practices in Tuscany and the importance of the marriage of the Virgin as a theme in Italian painting, see Christiane Klapisch-Zuber, *Women, Family, and Ritual in Renaissance Italy*, trans. Lydia Cochrane, with a forward by David Herlihy, 178–212 (Chicago: University of Chicago Press, 1985). On the promotion of Joseph and Mary as the model couple in New Spain, see Burkhart, *The Slippery Earth*, and Charlene Villaseñor-Black, "Love and Marriage in the Spanish Empire: Depictions of Holy Matrimony and Gender Discourses in the Seventeenth Century," *The Sixteenth Century Journal* 32, no. 3 (fall 2001): 637–68.

24. Motolinia, *History of the Indians of New Spain*, 150.

25. Ibid., 148–49.

26. Motolinia mentions an elaborately decorated marriage bed, which had been set up at the cacique's house, where the bride and groom greeted guests. This may have followed the indigenous custom of the married couple being seated on a mat during the marriage ceremony and the festivities that followed.

27. Motolinia, *History of the Indians of New Spain*, 148.

28. Ibid., 149.

29. For discussions of the impediments to marriage, see Seed, *To Love, Honor, and Obey in Colonial Mexico*, and Socolow, "Acceptable Partners," 209–46.

30. Motolinia, *History of the Indians of New Spain*, 151.

31. Molina, *Confesionario en la lengua mexicana y castellana*, 45–58.

32. Seed notes that the impediment of public honesty concerned a prior public engagement with a close relative of the intended spouse; however, Molina is much more general, asking only whether either the bride or groom had exchanged the promise of marriage with anyone else first. See Seed, *To Love, Honor, and Obey in Colonial Mexico*, 85.

33. On this point see Seed, *To Love, Honor, and Obey in Colonial Mexico*.

34. Molina, *Confesionario en la lengua mexicana y castellana*, 49, 50v, 51v, 56, and 57.

35. Ibid., 53v–54.

36. Karttunen and Lockhart, *The Art of Nahuatl Speech*, 122–23.

37. Ibid., 124–25.

38. Ibid., 127 and 110–13.

39. Arthur J. O. Anderson notes the use of Nahuatl rhetoric in his comparison of Nahuatl huehuetlatolli and a sermon and the *Manual del christiano* by fray Bernardino de Sahagún, but he comes to somewhat different conclusions about the significance of this practice. Arthur J. O. Anderson, "Aztec Wives," in *Indian Women of Early Mexico*, ed. Susan Schroeder, Stephanie Wood, and Robert Haskett, 55–85 (Norman and London: University of Oklahoma Press, 1997).

40. Molina, *Confesionario en la lengua mexicana y castellana*, 55v.

41. Ibid.

42. Ibid., 55v–56.

43. Klapisch-Zuber, *Women, Family, and Ritual in Renaissance Italy*, 178–212.

CHAPTER THREE

Communal Defiance, Divided Allegiances

Zapotec Responses to Idolatry Extirpation Campaigns in Oaxaca

DAVID TAVÁREZ

On September 14, 1700, a confrontation that presaged the end of local attempts to maintain dual spheres of worship in colonial Zapotec communities took place in San Francisco Cajonos, a town in the southern reaches of the *alcaldía mayor* of Villa Alta. Sometime between eight and eleven o'clock at night, following a confidential report from San Francisco residents don Juan Bautista and Jacinto de los Ángeles,[1] the town vicar fray Alonso de Vargas and the minister fray Gaspar de los Reyes caught many of the inhabitants of San Francisco Cajonos engaging in a communal ritual act in the house of Joseph Flores, the chief officer (*mayordomo*) of the local confraternity of Saint Joseph. Flores's guests—who included many of San Francisco's inhabitants—had plucked and beheaded some turkeys, and were in the process of bleeding a doe to death in order to fill some

containers with its blood, as they repeated some prayers in Zapotec before images of Christian saints with their faces turned toward the walls. One detail held the mendicants' attention: several male and female children who were praying on their knees imparted a jarring touch of innocence to what seemed to be a despicable act. The celebrants fled the house, leaving the friars to confiscate the remains of the sacrificed animals and other implements.

On the evening of the next day, an enraged native crowd surrounded the church of San Francisco, where the Dominicans, the two informants, and about a dozen non-Indians had sought refuge. Vicar Vargas took out an image of the Virgin Mary and asked the crowd to disperse, but only received mocking responses and hostile remarks. The mob shouted threats and threw stones at the church, while its

46

defenders used arquebuses to shoot first into the air and then into the crowd, killing at least one native rebel. However, when the defenders ran out of ammunition, they decided to surrender the two native informants. After don Juan Bautista and Jacinto de los Ángeles were handed over, they were taunted, whipped at the pillory, and taken away to a nearby mountain where they were executed. Juan Antonio de Mier y Tojo, *alcalde mayor* (chief magistrate) of Villa Alta, immediately began an investigation into the fate of the two Zapotec informants. The townspeople initially claimed that the informants had fled the Cajonos area, but after the imprisonment and interrogation of about thirty-four revolt participants, the alcalde mayor obtained a full confession. After a protracted trial for rioting, murder, idolatry, and insubordination that lasted from November 1700 until January 1702—requiring several consultations with the viceroy and the Audiencia—Mier y Tojo handed down an especially unforgiving form of exemplary punishment. On January 11, 1702, fifteen of the Cajonos rebels were hanged and quartered after being sentenced to death without appeal, and their remains were exhibited in San Francisco Cajonos and along the main road to Oaxaca. The following day, two more defendants were paraded in an *auto de fe*.[2]

The structural features of this rebellion—the apparent lack of a guiding ideology or premeditation, the collective nature of the response against the ministers, the swift punishment of the informants— suggest that a key triggering factor was the interference of the Dominicans and their informants, which may have broken the collective expectation that some of these communal realms could be maintained beyond the reach of the church and its agents in the local sphere. Such an approach echoes E. P. Thompson's well-known model of a peasant "moral economy," which argues that peasant populations may rebel against the ruling class once the traditionally accepted boundaries of economic and political subjugation are trespassed by government officials. However, unlike James Scott's precise formulation of an economic model that depicts boundary conditions for the moral balance between rulers and subjects, the task of defining what demands or contingencies may trigger the collective defense of a moral economy in a colonial situation may call for a more complex—and subjective—assessment of the meaning of boundaries and expectations.[3]

Before we can produce a full account of implicit expectations in a situation of colonial hegemony, we should provide an adequate account of local strategies in the context of colonial evangelization, and we should relate these strategies to the production of specific arrangements for local forms of worship that coexisted with more orthodox practices. Therefore, in order to attain a full understanding of the drive and motivations of this particular native revolt, we must address the series of confrontations among native ritual specialists, native officials, and colonial authorities that took place in the last quarter of the seventeenth century in southern Villa Alta, both before and after the 1700 revolt at Cajonos. It is only through a lengthy examination of evidence regarding ecclesiastical attempts to investigate and suppress certain ritual practices, native strategies for maintaining local spheres of worship beyond the reach of these attempts, local factionalism as it assessed the wisdom of engaging in a rebellion, and the relative political weight of various colonial authorities that we may arrive at a full account that may be tied to a thesis of a higher order—either the moral economy argument, or another argument describing the emergence of peasant and native consciousness in a colonial context.[4] This essay should be read as a first step in this direction.

This essay begins with a brief appraisal of the ecclesiastical policies against idolatry suspects in Villa Alta that were implemented between the late 1660s and the early 1700s. This appraisal will introduce a specific local response to extirpation efforts in Villa Alta between 1700 and 1706: the defense of local control over dual spheres of worship in the Zapotec towns of Betaza and Lachitaa. Rather than reducing these events to an inventory of economic or political fulcra that pushed moral consensus in one direction or another, this essay will depict the collective objectives of Zapotec office holders in action as they strove to defend a local notion of autonomy supported by their public engagement in collective ritual practices. It should be stressed here that a full discussion of local factionalism is beyond the scope of this essay, which focuses instead on a description of the social and economic organization that maintained a separation between two parallel realms of ritual practice: one Christian and official, and the other local and collective. Finally, this essay will present a hypothesis regarding the contrasting local responses to ecclesiastical

measures against idolatry in Cajonos in 1700, and in Betaza and Lachitaa in 1704.

Civil and Ecclesiastical Idolatry Extirpation Policies in Oaxaca, 1665–1696

A consideration of the "spiritual conquest" of Villa Alta from the mid-sixteenth century onward goes well beyond the scope of this chapter. Therefore, this essay will discuss ecclesiastical policies toward idolatry suspects—which have been incorporated into John K. Chance's extensive discussion of colonial Villa Alta[5]—beginning with the indigenous rebellion of Tehuantepec in 1660, which may be seen as the initial fulcrum behind a period of confrontations and tense impasses between native communities and ecclesiastical and civil authorities in both Villa Alta and the Isthmus area in Oaxaca. On March 22, 1660, a large group of Zapotecs who had congregated in the Isthmus town of Tehuantepec for Holy Week celebrations rioted against and killed their alcalde mayor Juan de Avellán, along with two of his associates. The rebels then appointed new local authorities, sought the support of neighboring native communities via letters and meetings, and maintained control over the surrounding region for the following year. Exactly two months later, on Corpus Christi, the Zapotecs of Nexapa also rose up in arms, forcing a military standoff which was resolved only through the mediation of bishop Cueva y Dávalos. During 1660 and 1661, the rebellion spread like wildfire—to use its chroniclers' simile of choice—through several Chontal, Huave, Mixe, Zapotec, and Zoque communities.

This sequence of events occupies a

unique place in the historiography of New Spain due to its multiethnic character and its sudden expansion over a large swath of Oaxaca. One may ask what could have motivated native peoples from linguistically and culturally diverse communities to form an unprecedented (and short-lived) alliance against Spanish rule. There exist two complementary analyses that have attempted a response to this question. One analytical view—espoused by Hector Díaz-Polanco et al.[6]—rehearses a cumulative theory that resembles the moral economy argument: taxation abuses related to the *repartimientos*,[7] followed by the punishment and humiliation of recalcitrant native elites, may have provided a spark for the Tehuantepec rebellion. On the other hand, Marcelo Carmagnani stresses the symbolic use of social space by native rebels and colonial officials, and emphasizes the differential participation by native actors at various stages in the rebellion.[8] In his view, rather than a rebellion, this movement was a confrontation against the expanding political role of the alcalde mayor, which collided with the reformulation of communal identity in seventeenth-century Oaxaca.

In a development that seems to confirm Carmagnani's observations about the expanding powers of alcaldes mayores in seventeenth-century Oaxaca, between 1665 and 1736 Villa Alta's alcaldes mayores and deputy governors (*tenientes de alcalde*) presided over at least a dozen trials against Indians accused of engaging in idolatry or sorcery, according to surviving records.[9] Under other circumstances, the attempt to take native defendants of crimes against the faith before a civil judge would

have been regarded as a violation of the ecclesiastical jurisdiction over such crimes. Nevertheless, the extant trials housed in the judicial archives of two alcaldías mayores in Oaxaca—Villa Alta and Teposcolula—provide evidence to support the argument that, besides marking a transition in episcopal policies toward idolatry, the decade of the 1660s was also characterized by more frequent judicial interventions by civil authorities in cases of native idolatry and superstition.[10]

Both bishops Monterroso (1665–1678) and Del Puerto (1679–1681) held in high esteem the cooperation of civil authorities in inaccessible regions regarded as prone to rebellion, as was the case in Villa Alta. In fact, it was during Del Puerto's brief tenure as bishop that the six towns in the Cajonos region—San Francisco, San Mateo, San Pedro, Santo Domingo, San Pablo, and San Miguel—regained their saliency as strongholds of idolatry in the consciousness of the extirpators.[11] In a 1679 letter to the crown, Del Puerto reports the discovery of a "high priest" who, along with four others, exercised a parallel ministry in some of these six towns. These specialists received the same deferential treatment accorded to Christian priests, heard confessions, and admonished their followers not to confess with the Christian priests. Del Puerto had these specialists imprisoned in the royal jail of Oaxaca City, intending to exile them permanently from their native communities.[12]

Isidro Sariñana (1683–1696), Del Puerto's successor, was the first bishop of Oaxaca to support extirpation efforts with the establishment of a novel punitive institution in Oaxaca City: a prison devoted to the permanent seclusion of "teachers of idolatries" and recidivist idolaters that would be known as the "perpetual prison of idolaters."[13] After arguing that such a prison was required to curb native idolatry, Sariñana obtained a grant of 3,000 *pesos de oro* from the crown for the project and began building this prison only a few streets west of the cathedral, and announced its completion in a 1692 letter to the crown. However, Sariñana's prison lasted only a few years: First, an earthquake devastated many buildings in Oaxaca City, including this prison; then, in November 1696, Sariñana died, leaving the prison's finances in a state of uncertainty. Sariñana's prison building had been so devastated by the earthquake and the subsequent lack of funds that bishop fray Ángel Maldonado (1702–1728) abandoned it in order to establish a new prison in a different area of Oaxaca City. Bishop Maldonado inherited Sariñana's punitive project, and turned it into one of the supporting pillars of the exacting extirpation campaigns he carried out in Villa Alta in the first decade of the eighteenth century.

Although the September 1700 Cajonos rebellion was unusual in its defiance of ecclesiastical authority, the Dominicans resident in southern Villa Alta could not have been surprised by the acts of collective defiance, and by the unyielding persistence of suspicious practices in southern Villa Alta. Two documents drafted to counter Maldonado's contention that idolatry had prospered in Villa Alta due to Dominican leniency—a December 1704 letter from fray Joseph Castilla to his provincial, and a July 1706 Dominican testimony drawn up before an *escribano* (notary)—indicate

that at least fifteen Dominicans had worked as extirpators of idolatry in the last decades of the seventeenth century in the Villa Alta towns of Yatee, Yaa, San Francisco Cajonos, Zoogocho, and Yatzachi.[14] Unfortunately, few details about the trials organized by these extirpators have survived. On the other hand, an April 1691 riot in the town of Zoochila—which was triggered by a Dominican friar's attempt to arrest some of the town's officials and its choirmaster—bears some structural resemblance to the Cajonos revolt of 1700, except for its resolution. After a short-lived confrontation, the Zoogocho rebels, the Dominican minister, and colonial officials reached an uncertain point of equilibrium when the town officials were freed, motivating the rebels to put down their weapons, return to their daily lives, and beg the forgiveness of the Dominican minister—which was granted immediately—only days after the rebellion.[15]

Maldonado's Amnesty: A Novel Approach to Extirpation Policies

Between 1702 and 1728, Oaxaca Bishop fray Ángel Maldonado would assume a particularly activist position on the issue of native ritual practices, which would lead to the loss of parish control by the Dominicans and would join the growing influence of the alcaldes mayores of Villa Alta as external factors that impinged on the internal affairs of native communities. Upon his arrival in Oaxaca on July 20, 1702, Bishop Maldonado learned about the 1700 Cajonos revolt and the current state of the legal procedures, and decided to carry out a personal inspection (*visita*).[16] On November 1702,

DAVID TAVÁREZ

Maldonado departed on an exhaustive visita of Villa Alta, during which he inspected seventeen endowed curates (*beneficios*), confirmed more than 4,000 natives, undertook a number of abridged idolatry proceedings, and sent several idolatry convicts to be incarcerated in the new prison for idolaters he had erected near the orchards of Santo Domingo el Grande in Oaxaca City as a substitute for Sariñana's prison.[17]

During his first visit to Villa Alta in late 1702 and early 1703, Maldonado discovered that the idolaters of this region were not only rebellious, but also highly accomplished authors of clandestine ritual texts. In order to extract information about local maestros, ritual practices, and ritual texts, Maldonado appointed the parish priest of Ejutla, Joseph de Aragón y Alcántara—Sariñana's leading secular extirpator during the 1680s—as his Visitor General, and took him along on his first visit.[18] However, as Maldonado later indicated in a Latin epistle to Clement XI in April 1708, his first scrutiny of the inhabitants of Villa Alta only led him to suspect that they concealed "even greater abominations."[19] In order to motivate the natives of Villa Alta to confess their idolatrous activities, turn in their ritual texts, and denounce their local maestros in exchange for an absolution, Maldonado tried an innovative approach to the announcement of his amnesty measures. According to later testimony presented to the crown by Dominican Procurator General Antonio de Torres, Maldonado selected one of the eleven defendants from San Francisco that were surrendered to him by the alcalde mayor, placed his pectoral around his neck, and ordered him to travel throughout the region of

Villa Alta announcing his offer of absolution.[20] Maldonado's offer was simple and non-negotiable: in exchange for denouncing their ritual specialists, turning in the clandestine ritual texts that several generations of extirpators had called "books of the devil," and making a full confession about communal and private ritual practices, each native community would benefit from both a general absolution and an amnesty from any formal trial.

When Maldonado returned to Villa Alta for a second visita in 1704, he organized an exhaustive investigation into native ritual practices. He was assisted in this task by several extirpators: the indispensable Visitor General Aragón y Alcántara, the Dominican minister of San Ildefonso fray Joseph de Contreras, and the secular priests Miguel Martínez de Salamanca, Domingo Zenlí y Cerdán, and Juan Manuel de Urbina.[21] Following cooperation guidelines that had been established through earlier extirpation attempts between the bishopric and Villa Alta, the alcalde mayor Diego de Rivera y Cotes assisted Maldonado and Aragón y Alcántara during their visit, and turned over the testimonies of about forty-five "teachers of idolatry" who had been imprisoned in the royal jail of Villa Alta.[22] Maldonado's offer of mercy, coupled with the fresh memory of the exemplary punishment that had been visited upon the Cajonos rebels, convinced many residents of Villa Alta communities to yield at least some of their specialists and ritual implements. At the request of Maldonado, between November 1704 and February 1705, the elected authorities of most of the 104 native communities in Villa Alta—representing a

COMMUNAL DEFIANCE, DIVIDED ALLEGIANCES

native population of about 60,000 according to Maldonado's count—journeyed to San Ildefonso to register a communal confession before Aragón y Alcántara in order to benefit from Maldonado's amnesty. Through this innovative extirpation strategy, Maldonado harvested 103 separate manuscript versions of the 260-day Zapotec ritual calendar, or *piyè*, and about thirty-seven Zapotec ritual songs, which had been composed to be performed during communal ritual practices to the beat of a cylindrical drum called *nicachi* in Zapotec and *teponaztli* in Nahuatl.[23]

Maldonado vs. the Dominicans: Ecclesiastical and Political Reforms, 1704–1712

Maldonado's growing disillusionment with the state of doctrinal education in native communities in Villa Alta and elsewhere lead him to take a reformist position that clashed with the interest of the Dominicans in preserving the status quo. Shortly after his 1704 Villa Alta visit, Maldonado proposed to the crown the creation of six new curates. In an intermediate chapter celebrated in May 1705, the Dominicans agreed to this petition, but requested that these curates be filled by Dominicans. Maldonado agreed, and these regulars were given their appointments through the bishop—a novel form of episcopal intervention in doctrinal matters that the Dominicans had long regarded as internal. In August 1706, Maldonado upped the ante by asking the crown to confirm the creation of eleven new curates—Zoochila, Tabaa, Yalálag, Betaza, Lachixila, Comaltepec, Latani, Santa María, Puxmetacán, Ayutla, and Atalacatepec.[24]

The Dominicans attempted to counter-act Maldonado's proposals at every step, both in Oaxaca and at the Council of Indies. Although the details of this controversy exceed the scope of this essay, the arguments for and against the division of curates that were based on the proliferation of idolatry may be summarized into two broad categories: the effectiveness of Dominican doctrinal administration and the number of ministers that Villa Alta and other geographically isolated regions required for the administration of sacraments. These pitched confrontations were interrupted in June 1712 when pro-Dominican forces in Madrid convinced King Philip V to remove Maldonado from Oaxaca by appointing him to the diocese of Orihuela—a small but comfortable bishopric in Murcia (Spain). However, since Maldonado had already reached an agreement with the Dominican provincial, he was able to reject this offer in December 1712, arguing that the common agreement would solve the impasse over the partitioning of curates.[25]

From Omens to Confrontation: Communal Resistance to Extirpation in Betaza

Between November 1702 and November 1704, Maldonado and his emissaries spread a clear and succinct message: each of the 104 communities in Villa Alta had to surrender specialists and implements linked to local communal practices, or face severe punitive measures. The newly expanded range of these punishments had been richly illustrated by the spectacle of the decaying body parts of the Cajonos rebels along the road to Oaxaca. Toward the end of 1702, Maldonado himself brought his message to the towns

DAVID TAVÁREZ

of San Melchor Betaza and Santo Tomás Lachitaa in Villa Alta. Betaza was a relatively large town, with an estimated population of 935 residents in 1703; the neighboring community of Lachitaa shared numerous political and kinship links with Betaza and had an estimated population of only 178 individuals in 1704. It should be noted that, prior to 1704, the people of Betaza celebrated only eight Christian holidays per year under the supervision of a visiting priest.[26]

In spite of Maldonado's visit, the townspeople of Betaza and Lachitaa were not ready to renounce their communal ritual practices. According to Agustín Gonzalo Zárate, a former town official of Betaza in 1702—and the specialist whose arrest would trigger a revolt in this town—hardly a month had passed after the bishop's visit before the town engaged in another communal ritual celebration. Sometime during the next year, it was decided that the town would consult a realm that exceeded that of the powerful alcalde mayor in Villa Alta, as well as that of their enterprising but remote bishop. Through the mediation of ritual specialists who were experienced interpreters of the visions produced by *cuana betao*,[27] the town of Betaza would ask its own tutelary deities what would befall them. Two ritual specialists—Simón de Santiago and Nicolás de Espina Aracena—ingested cuana betao before the entire town, who awaited the response of the local deities assembled outside the *Yoo Yagtao*—a house that provided these specialists with the darkness and quiet required to communicate with the cuana betao entities. Both Santiago and Aracena reported having received the same premonition. Santiago, the eldest of the two,

would later declare before the alcalde mayor that the deities of Betaza had revealed

that they had fallen into the hands of God the Father [*que ya habían dado en manos de Dios Padre*] that the Christian doctrine would come into town, and that the Spaniards would come in and take away their parents and grandparents—meaning their idols. The first would be *Goque Yagchila*, and in fact, he was brought out and burned in the town square of [Villa Alta] later.[28]

Santiago's elegiac tone was echoed by Espina Aracena, who confessed that the town deities had told them that "the law of their ancestors would be lost; the Spaniards will come and take away the things we have from our ancestors."[29]

Due to public concern about the bishop's visit, communal celebrations in Betaza were carried out only three times in 1703, as opposed to eight to ten times in the previous year. Although the trial records provide only fragmentary information about the rationale for these practices, it could be argued that these collective observances were linked to particular ritual observances in the 260-day Zapotec ritual calendar, and had as their main objective the propitiation of local deities in order to obtain good harvests and well being for the community. Later that year, visiting priest fray Francisco de Orozco came to ask the people of Betaza to surrender their ritual implements, but the townspeople denied having any.[30] After this visit, Betaza's officials called a communal meeting, and discussed whether they would surrender their implements, specialists, and calendrical texts. According to Agustín Gonzalo Zárate, in spite of the fateful omens and mounting ecclesiastical pressure, the entire town decided not to yield to Maldonado's order, and asserted that, rather than turn in their ritual implements, "they would first surrender and give up their own blood."[31]

Following a pattern of intercommunity communication—a local diplomacy of sorts that was also pursued by rebel communities during the Tehuantepec (1660) and Cancuc (1712) rebellions, Betaza's town council sent letters to neighboring towns informing them of their decision to resist Maldonado's proclamation, and asking them for support. According to Juan Martín de Cabueñas, Betaza's governor, the council sent a letter asking the neighboring communities of Yaa, Yatee, and Lachirioag not to break ranks with Betaza and not to turn in their idols or fruit stocks—which were used for the illegal production of alcoholic beverages—even if events led to a "great legal proceeding."[32]

Idolaters Against the Alcalde Mayor: The Failure of Native Resistance in Betaza

The communal resolve of the inhabitants of Betaza and Lachitaa was tested by several incidents that occurred on December 17, 1703, during a local fair that took place in Yalálag, a town located a few kilometers to the south.[33] In spite of their decision to resist Maldonado's proclamation, Betaza's town officials were apparently not concerned about any immediate consequences, for several of them went down to Yalálag's fair. Among the crowds of outsiders who thronged in the town square, Bernardo

García, a Spaniard from Villa Alta, recognized Agustín Gonzalo Zárate, a ritual specialist from Betaza whose detention had been requested a short time earlier by Bishop Maldonado. Another visitor from Betaza was don Pedro de Paz, a former alcalde and gobernador who possessed such confidence about Betaza's communal decisions that he approached one of the *regidores* (councilmen) of Yalálag and scolded him by saying:

Perhaps the people of Yalálag are women, for they do not deserve to wear pants, and it would be better if they wore their women's petticoats, or else why should they have turned in their idols without resistance? They should not have turned them in without fighting to the last drop of their blood.[34]

After this exchange, Yalálag governor don Juan de la Cruz conferred with García, and arrested Zárate, Paz, and four other Betaza and Lachitaa officials who were at the fair.

Initially, the people of Betaza seem to have interpreted these arrests as a direct attack on them from the community of Yalálag. In fact, upon learning of the detention of their husbands, some of the prisoners' wives left Betaza with one of their alcaldes in order to complain to the alcalde mayor that the officials of Yalálag had seized their husbands without justification.[35] Shortly after his detention, Zárate was able to send a nephew back to Betaza with news about the arrests. Therefore, one of Yalálag's couriers was detained in Betaza by an angry crowd, who placed him under detention. However, an anonymous

DAVID TAVÁREZ

informant from Betaza sent word to Diego Rivera y Cotes, alcalde mayor of Villa Alta, that a courier bearing a letter for him had been detained in his town. Since the courier bore a letter for the alcalde mayor, the people of Betaza had gone beyond mere local conflict, and were now engaged in an act of disobedience against the provincial representative of the crown. Cotes immediately ordered his alguacil mayor to lead a force of sixteen men into Betaza in order to make inquiries. This small army retrieved both courier and letter, and escorted a group of Yalálag residents to the town of Villa Alta along with the five remaining prisoners from Betaza and Lachitaa, who were placed in the town's jail along with Zárate, who arrived separately.

The decisive intervention of Cotes in Betaza seems to have defused Betaza's planned resistance to idolatry extirpation campaigns. After the Christmas holidays, Cotes issued a formal order of arrest against eleven residents of Betaza and three men from Lachitaa, which included the people seized earlier in Yalálag. This order had the effect of discouraging any would-be revolt leaders, since it included all of the former elected office holders in Betaza and Lachitaa who, as ritual specialists, had orchestrated communal ritual practices in both towns during the previous decade. The arrested leaders from Betaza included Fabián de Vargas (a *fiscal* [church official] in 1703), don Pedro de Paz (former regidor, alcalde, and gobernador), Simón de Santiago El Tuerto (Betaza's eldest specialist), Agustín Gonzalo Zárate (a regidor in 1702), Joseph Bolaños (a former alcalde), Agustín Gutiérrez de Benito (the town's escribano since circa

1686), Agustín Gonzalo (an alcalde in 1693), Nicolás Martín (an alcalde in 1703), and Nicolás de Espina Aracena and Simón de Santiago (Betaza's foremost cuana betao drinkers). For Lachitaa, this list included Pedro Cano (a cuana betao drinker), Nicolás de Celis (a renowned specialist and a former fiscal, escribano, and *maestro de doctrina* [teacher of doctrine]), and Joseph de Celis (a *belao*, or ritual singer and musician, who had also been fiscal three times). On January 14, 1704, after a defense attorney was appointed to represent these thirteen defendants, a parade of witnesses began wending its way before Cotes. The defendants provided Cotes with detailed accounts about various subjects: communal decisions regarding Maldonado's proclamation, the activities of past and present local "teachers of idolatry," and, most importantly for Cotes, the financial measures that were taken by the community to fund clandestine ritual practices. The defendants' declarations reflect a solid consensus on the identity of the most respected ritual specialists in Betaza: Simón de Santiago El Tuerto, Nicolás de Espina Aracena, Fabián de Vargas, and Nicolás Martín.

The Social and Financial Management of Communal Ritual Practices in Betaza

Communal ritual practices in native communities were a collective undertaking that was financed by both individual contributions and collective sources of revenue. Betaza was not an exception to this pattern, and it seems to have developed a parallel system in which various methods were used to collect funds for two distinct budgets, one for Christian devotional practices, and the other for clandestine communal ritual practices. In Betaza, town officials took collections to satisfy the yearly demand for tribute to the crown. A group of twenty-four mayordomos—replaced on a rotating basis—raised three pesos each in order to cover expenditures for the visiting priest and for the seven public Christian holidays that he led yearly. Additional funds for Christian celebrations were raised by the only religious confraternity in town, the Cofradía del Rosario.[36] Then, whatever communal funds remained every year after satisfying the demands of the crown and the church were devoted to communal ritual expenses. The escribano Gutiérrez estimated that, every year, about 170 pesos of uncollected tribute to the crown remained in the town, along with about 27 pesos that remained from the collections taken to fund the visits of their priest.[37] At least once, 25 pesos were appropriated from the budget of the Cofradía del Rosario for a non-Christian purpose: they were given as payment to Nicolás de Celis, Lachitaa's foremost specialist, so that he would impart his knowledge of ritual practices to two Betaza men—Nicolás Martín and Nicolás de Espina Aracena. Joseph de Celis, Nicolás's brother, was a belao, and taught his ritual specialization to four Betaza residents: Gaspar Bautista, Fabián Luis, Joseph Luis, and Juan Gerónimo.[38]

Gutiérrez, Vargas (who was a fiscal in 1703), and former alcalde Bolaños indicated two other methods for raising funds for communal ritual practices. The first one was an outright collection of between one or one and a half *reales* per household head, which was used to fund immediate expenditures.

The second one involved a set of communal obligations and money lending practices that mirrored the financial practices of indigenous sodalities in other native communities.[39] Three mayordomos—Juan de Paz, Juan de Celis, and Agustín García—supervised the plowing of three land plots that corresponded to Betaza's three subdivisions, and kept three dwellings in which celebrants ate and drank after the communal celebrations. After the maize obtained from these plots was sold, profits were lent to people in the community at a high interest rate of 37.5 percent—or three reales for each peso that was borrowed.[40] Through the accumulation of communal funds earmarked for communal ritual practices, the town had bought ten teams of oxen that were used primarily to plough the three land plots mentioned above. Moreover, in order to raise additional funds, these teams of oxen were also rented out for a daily rate of three reales.[41]

The following deposition by Fabián de Vargas—son of a famous "teacher of idolatry" who owned transcriptions of ritual songs and was a respected ritual specialist himself—deserves to be quoted *in extenso*, as it depicts both the range of activities comprised in communal ritual practices and the various expenditures that were involved:

During the communal idolatries [the specialists] sacrifice two or three deer, and many turkeys and puppies, and they make the men fast and avoid their wives for thirteen days, and during this time, rather than going to the steam baths, they bathe in the river at the cock's first or second crow. They confess with the priests before the sacrifices, bringing each a real or a real and a half. In order to receive these reales, the regidores are present there, and the amount they should bring is determined beforehand by the town council, the escribano, and the other priests. They also bring four young boys to these communal sacrifices; . . . these boys behead the turkeys and the dogs, and open the deer chests while the priests hold these animals. . . . In a piece of paper made from tree bark, they pour [the animals'] blood; then, everyone comes in, gets on their knees, and over the bloodied paper, they toss a bit of ground tobacco called *pisiete,* which each Indian carries in a little gourd. . . .

After making those sacrifices, the alcaldes purchase some thin candles from the money that remains, and place them on the altars at the church, and then they order people to sing a litany. A large feather that adorns the images of Our Lady is taken to the sacrifices, and the person who plays the teponaztli and sings diabolic songs wears it on his head. . . . During the sacrifices, they post guards in various places, so they may give a warning if they see a Spaniard or any suspicious person.[42]

Although the vocabulary of the court interpreter has reduced the original Zapotec terms to routine Christian designations—such as "priests" or "diabolic songs"—this description depicts the entire town council at work, orchestrating collective ritual action, receiving individual

contributions, and participating in these ritual practices. While an outside observer might fall into the temptation of designating these practices as a hybrid mixture of Christian and native practices, the attitude of the celebrants is rather clear: they were conceived by the town as collective ritual practices that were essential to the communal identity and well being of Betaza. Therefore, they were practiced clandestinely and under the potential risk of discovery by outsiders. From a local perspective, these practices belonged in a communal realm that was kept relatively separate in spatial, budgetary, and social terms from local public Christian celebrations.

Conclusions

How may one explain the fact that native resistance in Betaza did not lead to a violent confrontation with colonial authorities, as had occurred in Cajonos three years earlier? Other than assuming that mere fright convinced the Betazans to yield, one could propose that Betaza's town council misread the arrest of their specialists at the Yalálag fair: based on previous experience, they did not expect a neighboring native community to take the side of idolatry extirpators, and they believed that the arrests were a collective act of aggression on the part of Yalálag. When a small army arrived from Villa Alta making inquiries, it was too late to organize armed resistance, and the town officials and leading ritual specialists had little choice but to surrender to the powerful alguacil mayor Joseph de la Sierra. At this point, Betaza's fight against extirpation was a losing proposition in both ideological and political terms: Betaza's neighbors had

COMMUNAL DEFIANCE, DIVIDED ALLEGIANCES

not pursued the path of resistance that they had vowed to support through their clandestine correspondence, and Betaza's neighbors seemed ready to accept Maldonado's offer of amnesty rather than risk another rebellion. Betaza's former elected officials had concluded that rebellion was not in the cards, and thus yielded easily to Cotes's questions about their communal ritual practices, allowing an exceptionally detailed description of the social organization of clandestine ritual practices in a native community in New Spain to be inscribed in the legal record.

The 1703–1704 Betaza idolatry trial provides us with a richly detailed perspective into the local reformulation of a prescriptive political system that was imposed by the colonial regime. Betaza's councilmen refashioned the obligations and faculties of their posts as alcaldes, escribanos, and regidores in order to reproduce a separate social and economic realm for collective ritual practices. It would be rather misleading to simply label these practices as clandestine; from the perspective of Betaza's residents, they were both public and collective exercises, but they were clandestine and illegitimate from the extirpators' perspective. In the manner of other native officials—most notably, the church officials of San Miguel Sola who circulated copies of the 260-day Zapotec ritual calendar among a network of at least thirty-five text users and specialists[43]—Betaza's town officials led a dual existence as leading members of their town council and as ritual specialists who participated in collective and private ritual practices. As in Sola, this attempt to reproduce a position of authority in both a legitimate political sphere and in a clandestine realm for local ritual practices was eventually suppressed by the colonial authorities.

We should not assume, in spite of the town officials' claim about local consensus, that the people of Betaza uniformly embraced this dual system and offered unconditional support for an agenda of defiance. It is more appropriate to interpret the local arrangements on behalf of traditional ritual practices as a project that was embraced by a particular faction of town officials. In fact, there exists evidence of local resistance to the policies set forth by town officials. On February 4, 1704, a few weeks after the interrogation of Betaza's officials began in Villa Alta, the vicar of Betaza, fray Joseph Cardona, celebrated mass and pronounced a communal absolution from idolatry over the entire town. However, the town authorities—which seem to have had a clear picture of who had supported them and who had collaborated with the priests—punished some of the inhabitants whom they regarded as traitors the day after Cardona's absolution. Betaza resident Juan Mateo would report that he was intercepted as he walked down the street by a man called Juan Luis, who assaulted him, accusing him of betrayal to the people of Betaza. At that point, Betaza's alcalde incarcerated him and accused him of having gone to Villa Alta to give accounts about their customs, and had him tied to the pillory and whipped several times. Before being released, he was ordered to pay a five-peso fine.[44]

In their attempts to refashion local political offices, the people of Betaza, Lachitaa, and Yalálag attempted to profit from a de jure separation between indigenous and nonindigenous subjects: as native subjects, they endeavored to maintain a dual system of public religious practices that would only be viable in a relatively isolated indigenous community. The social reproduction of a dual system in these communities was facilitated by their geographic isolation and by the laxity of the evangelization policies that were pursued by Dominicans and secular priests in the area during the first half of the seventeenth century. However, during the second half of the seventeenth century, two policy changes began to have substantial effects in Villa Alta. On the one hand, two activist bishops—Sariñana and Maldonado—embraced a more severe set of legal measures and punitive efforts against alleged idolaters; on the other, the office of the alcalde mayor in Villa Alta expanded its reaches into idolatry extirpation measures, and increased its economic and political impact among natives through a greater control of policies that appropriated goods and labor in native communities. In the most terrible of ways, local Zapotec deities had the last word. When Betaza's ritual specialists consulted their local deities through the mediation of hallucinogens, they understood that the time of the Spaniards and God the Father—a second civil and ecclesiastical conquest in the slowly unfolding cycle of colonial evangelization projects—had finally arrived in the isolated mountain ranges of Villa Alta.

NOTES

The abbreviations used in this essay are as follows:

AGI: Archivo General de Indias, Seville, Spain

AGN: Archivo General de la Nación, Mexico

AGOP: Archivio Generale dell'Ordine dei Predicatori, Rome, Italy

AHAO: Archivo Histórico del Arzobispado de Oaxaca, Mexico

ALC: Archivo del Lic. Luis Castañeda, Oaxaca, Mexico

ANSM: Archivo de Nuestra Señora de la Merced, Oaxaca, Mexico

ANO: Archivo de Notarías de Oaxaca, Mexico

ATEP: Archivo Judicial de Teposcolula, Oaxaca, Mexico

AVA: Archivo Judicial de Villa Alta, Oaxaca, Mexico

1. Although a strong local historical tradition—which Archbishop Gillow embraced during his 1889 inquiry into the Cajonos revolt—identified don Juan Bautista and Jacinto de los Ángeles as native *fiscales*, neither of them was designated with this title in the 1700–1702 Cajonos trial documents. While they both acted in the stead of conscientious fiscales, they did not seem to hold such title in September 1700. It should be noted that the Catholic church proclaimed them as Blessed in the summer of 2002.

2. ANSM, Mártires de Cajonos; ALC 1270, 161v–169v; AHAO Mártires de Cajonos, S-4, 615–31; Eulogio Gillow, *Apuntes históricos sobre la idolatría e introducción del cristianismo en Oaxaca* (México: Ediciones Toledo, [1889] 1990), 174–81.

3. See E. P. Thompson, "The Moral Economy of the English Crowd in the Eighteenth Century," *Past and Present* 50 (1971): 76–136, and James C. Scott, *The Moral Economy of the Peasant* (New Haven: Yale University Press, 1976). The moral economy argument has been presented as a suggestive analytical framework for a colonial Maya rebellion in Kevin Gosner, *Soldiers of the Virgin: The Moral Economy of a Colonial Maya Rebellion.* (Tucson: University of Arizona Press, 1992).

4. See Steve J. Stern, "New Approaches to the

Study of Peasant Rebellion and Consciousness: Implications of the Andean Experience," in *Resistance, Rebellion and Consciousness in the Andean Peasant World*, ed. S. Stern, 3–25 (Madison: University of Wisconsin Press, 1987). For an example of contending analyses of colonial native rebellions tied to religious practices, see the characterizations of the complexity of the various forms of native cultural consciousness that informed the 1712 Tzeltal rebellion at Cancuc in Kevin Gosner, "Religion and Rebellion in Colonial Chiapas," in *Native Resistance and the Pax Colonial in New Spain*, ed. S. Schroeder, 47–66 (Lincoln: University of Nebraska Press, 1998), and Juan Pedro Viqueira, *Indios rebeldes e idólatras: dos ensayos históricos sobre la rebelión india de Cancuc, Chiapas, acaecida en el año de 1712* (Tlalpan, DF: CIESAS, 1997).

5. See John K. Chance, *The Conquest of the Sierra* (Norman: University of Oklahoma Press, 1989).

6. The most extensive analysis of the 1660 Tehuantepec rebellion to date is Héctor Díaz-Polanco et al., *El fuego de la inobediencia. Autonomía y rebelión india en el obispado de Oaxaca* (México: CIESAS, 1996).

7. *Repartimientos* were the appropriation of local raw and manufactured goods by colonial authorities through a mandatory exchange for goods manufactured elsewhere that natives did not need, and at unfavorable exchange ratios. Alcaldes mayores manipulated these ratios for their own advantage. See Chance, *The Conquest of the Sierra*.

8. See Marcelo Carmagnani, "Un movimiento politico indio: La 'rebelión' de Tehuantepec, 1660–1661," in Días-Polanco et al., *El fuego*, 81–102.

9. See Díaz-Polanco et al., *El fuego*, and Marcelo Carmagnani, *El regreso de los dioses: El proceso de reconstitución de la identidad étnica en Oaxaca, siglos XVII y XVIII* (México City: Fondo de Cultura Económica, 1988).

10. During the 1660s, we find at least one idolatry trial initiated by Juan de Baena, the notary public, or *escribano*, and teniente de alcalde mayor in Teposcolula: a case against Catalina Mendoza and Melchor Hernández of Tamasulapa, accused of performing "idolatrous" practices in order to murder town mayor Domingo de Ayala in 1662 (ATEP 502). On the other hand, Diego de Villegas y Sandoval Castro, alcalde mayor of Villa Alta in 1653–1655, and again from late 1665 until late 1667, appeared to be an especially active civil extirpator of idolatries under the aegis of bishop Monterroso (1665–1678), for he presided over at least three idolatry trials in 1665 and 1666: the trial of Luis de Vargas of Yojovi (AVA Criminal 19) and the related trial of Vargas's murderer, Lucas de los Reyes in 1665 (AVA Criminal 20); the trial of Juan Gonzalo and Pedro de Viloria of Lachirioag in 1666 (AVA Criminal 22); and finally, the multitudinous trial of eleven residents of Lachirioag accused of engaging in suspicious acts that could have been idolatrous in 1666 (AVA Criminal 23). Moreover, at least three of Sandoval Castro's successors are known to have presided over idolatry trials in Villa Alta—don Fernando de Velasco y Castilla, Captain Cristóbal del Castillo Mondragón (AGI Mexico 357, AGOP XIII.12760), and Captain don Alonso Muñoz de Castilblanque, who began an idolatry trial against six defendants from San Francisco Cajonos in 1684 (AVA Criminal 49), but surrendered both the procedure and its defendants to ecclesiastical jurisdiction at the request of Bishop Sariñana (1683–1696). A detailed discussion of the failed prosecution of a group of idolatry defendants from the Villa Alta town of Lachirioag in 1666 appears in David Tavárez, "Idolatry as an Ontological Question: Native Consciousness and Juridical Proof in Colonial Mexico," *Journal of Early Modern History* 6, no. 2 (2002): 114–39.

11. The association between Villa Alta and suspicions of idolatry was not a novel one at this point. The Dominican fray Pedro Guerrero began the first systematic extirpation campaign in the region in 1560, when he convinced scores of natives to turn in their idols. Guerrero apparently achieved this objective through indiscriminate use of the whip, which motivated the suicide of a ritual specialist in Tabaa (AGI Mexico 358, exp. 3 bis). A summary of early extirpation attempts in Villa Alta appears in Chance, *The Conquest.*

12. AGI Mexico 357.

13. Sariñana was inspired not only by the

DAVID TAVÁREZ

previous experiences of his predecessors, but also by other inquisitorial precedents. In Mexico City, in the early seventeenth century the Holy Office erected a *prisión perpetua* for proselytizing Jews (*judaizantes*) and heretics—see Solange Alberro, *Inquisición y sociedad en Mexico, 1571–1700* (México: Fondo de Cultura Económica, 1988). In the archbishopric of Lima, a prison for idolaters called *Casa de Santa Cruz* was finished in 1618, and ceased to exist as such before 1639; its inmates were to remain imprisoned for unspecified periods of time, earning a living by weaving textiles. See Iris Gareis, "Repression and Cultural Change: The 'Extirpation of Idolatry' in Colonial Peru," in *Spiritual Encounters: Interactions Between Christianity and Native Religions in Colonial America*, ed. N. Griffiths, and F. Cervantes, 234 (Lincoln: University of Nebraska Press, 1999). Sariñana's prison project is described in several letters to the crown found in AGI Mexico 357.

14. AGI Mexico 881, 882.

15. AHAO Mártires de Cajonos S—1.2; Gillow, *Apuntes*, 93–99.

16. Maldonado brought to the bishopric of Oaxaca his abilities as an experienced theologian. He obtained a doctorate in theology at the University of Alcalá, and taught there for several years before taking the title of *magister* in his order of Saint Bernard. Although he was named to the bishopric of Comayagua (Honduras) in August 1699, he received a second appointment as bishop of Oaxaca by Innocentius XII only several months later. See José Antonio Gay, *Historia de Oaxaca* (México: Editorial Porrúa 1998), 387.

17. AGI Mexico 877.

18. Ibid.

19. AGI Mexico 880.

20. This vivid detail was provided in a report to the crown written circa 1710 against Maldonado by Antonio de Torres, procurator general of the Dominican Order in Oaxaca, found in AGI Mexico 880. Although Maldonado wrote a point-by-point rebuttal of this report, he remained suspiciously silent on the subject of this most peculiar emissary.

21. AGI Mexico 879, 882.

22. AGI Mexico 882, 296r–391v.

23. A survey of the pocket calendars and the communal ritual practices of Villa Alta appeared in the first monograph devoted to the topic— José Alcina Franch, *Calendario y religión entre los zapotecos* (México: UNAM, 1993). The first contemporary translation of one of the Zapotec songs of Villa Alta appeared in David Tavárez, "The Passion According to the Wooden Drum: The Christian Appropriation of a Zapotec Ritual Genre in New Spain," *The Americas* 62, no. 3 (2006): 413–44.

24. AGI Mexico 880 and 881.

25. AGI Mexico 880. Maldonado's institutional proposals for addressing widespread idolatry went beyond ecclesiastical reforms. Both Maldonado and the alcalde mayor Rivera y Cotes presented the crown with the ambitious suggestion of congregating all the towns in Villa Alta into groups of four hundred married couples; they also recommended appointing Spanish language teachers in each town, as well as allowing the alcalde mayor to name local representatives as he saw fit; see AGI Mexico 882. As Chance (*The Conquest*) has noted, many natives opposed these proposals, and there is no extant evidence that these *congregaciones* were carried through. Native resistance to this measure was so great that some towns offered large bribes to the alcalde mayor if he desisted from carrying out congregaciones.

26. See Chance, *The Conquest*. Betaza and Lachitaa's abridged liturgical year featured the observance of Epiphany (which also celebrated Saint Melchor, Betaza's patron saint), Christ's purification at the Temple, Easter, the feast of the Holy Spirit, Corpus Christi, Our Lady of the Rosary, All Saints, and Christmas. Before 1704, visiting priests did not perform such celebrations in Betaza itself, but in an isolated location in between the towns of Betaza and Lachitaa. See AVA Criminal 117, 28v, 27v.

27. According to multiple testimonies, certain Zapotec ritual specialists took the seeds of a plant called cuana betao in Sierra Zapotec, ground them, and drank them with water. This plant is probably *Turbina* (or *Rivea*) *corymbosa*, a vine of the morning glory family with hallucinogenic properties, which was known as *ololiuhqui* in Nahua communities.

28. AVA Criminal 117, 39v–40r, my emphasis. An

ongoing translation project led by the author that focuses on the Zapotec ritual song corpus seized during Maldonado's campaign (AGI 882, Calendarios 100–102) has confirmed that a subset of these songs celebrated Coque Yagchila and other local deities.

29. AVA Criminal 117, 37v.

30. Ibid., 60r.

31. Ibid., 24 r–v.

32. Ibid., 60r.

33. Yalálag held an important place among the Zapotec communities of southern Villa Alta due to three factors: its role as a regional market hub, its location on the road between Oaxaca and the cabecera of Villa Alta, and its position as the largest town in southern Villa Alta, with an estimated population of 1,577 residents in 1703. See Chance, *The Conquest*, 48.

34. AVA Criminal 117, 9r.

35. Although the extant records do not indicate the existence of conflicting claims over outlying lands and forests between Yalálag and Betaza during this period, Betaza and Lachitaa seem to have had land conflicts with their northern neighbors of San Andrés Yaa; see AVA Criminal 207.

36. AVA Criminal 117, 17v.

37. Ibid., 28v.

38. Ibid., 47v, 49v.

39. Central Mexican indigenous sodalities routinely constituted themselves as productive and money-lending enterprises. A particularly well-documented operation during the 1760s in the Nahua community of Tlapa in what is now central Guerrero is described in Danièle Dehouve, "The 'Money of the Saint': Ceremonial Organization and Monetary Capital in Tlapa, Guerrero, Mexico," in *Manipulating the Saints*, ed. A. Meyers and D. E. Hopkins, 149–74 (Hamburg: WAYASBAH, 1988). In Tlapa, the "money of the saint"—a collective fund raised by pooling monetary contributions from cofradía members—was used as a source of revenue for the cult of the saint. Both members and nonmembers of the cofradía borrowed amounts from this fund at usurious rates of interest that ranged from 25 to 50, and even to 100 percent, provided that both principal and interest were returned by the year's end.

40. AVA Criminal 117, 17 r–v.

41. Ibid., 28v.

42. Ibid., 16r–18r.

43. See Gonzalo Balsalobre, "Relación auténtica de las idolatrías, supersticiones, vanas observancias de los indios del obispado de Oaxaca," *Anales del Museo Nacional de México* (1ª Época) 6, [1656] 1892, 229–60, and Tavárez, "La idolatría letrada: Un análisis comparativo de textos clandestinos rituales y devocionales en comunidades nahuas y zapotecas, 1613–1654," *Historia Mexicana* 194, 49, no. 2 (1999): 197–252.

44. AVA Criminal 117, 51r.

PART TWO

NATIVE SEXUALITY AND CHRISTIAN MORALITY

The carnal woman is an evil woman who finds pleasure in her body. . . . She consumes her inner substance—a brazen, a proud, a dissolute woman of debauched life. . . . She parades; she moves lasciviously; she is pompous.

—fray Bernardino de Sahagún, c. 1577

The worst thing that he did was that he came into my house four times, trying to take my wife by force in order to sow sin [fornicate] with her. He desired this, but he did not fulfill his desire.

—Diego Pox, notary, Tabí, Yucatan, late sixteenth century

Tuesday, 6 November [1658], at eleven in the morning they took fifteen men from the Royal Court jail, in order to burn fourteen of them, and one, because he was a boy, they gave him two hundred lashes and sold him to a *mortero* for six years, all for having committed the sin of sodomy among themselves for many years.

—Gregorio Martín de Guijo, 1658

In that time there will be lies and madness, and also lust and fornication . . .

—Chilam Balam of Chumayel

I deny all of this, and I believe that no good Christian person, much less a priest, could do such a thing . . .

—Padre Cristóbal de Valencia, 1609

Once Pope Alexander VI granted the Patronato Real to Catholic Kings Ferdinand and Isabel in 1494, all of Spain's dominions were destined to be Christian and subject to their patronage. The crown's ministers to the colonies were reform minded but steeped in medieval theological beliefs and practices. Thus, social norms and morals in the colonies derived from these archaic prescriptive policies. The sacraments afforded spiritual protection from birth to death, and the faithful knew the promise of Heaven when they adhered to them.

The natives had their own codes of behavior, and for the Nahuas they are commonly referred to as sumptuary laws. These laws regulated everything from the consumption of alcoholic beverages and thievery to adultery. Most all were regarded as criminal acts, and the perpetrators suffered the harshest of penalties, even capital punishment.

Their rigidly controlled society was a boon to the Spaniards, who expected to supplant the natives' social controls with their own strict civil and religious laws. But the natives were not eager to change their ways to suit the Spaniards. For example, to partake of the holy sacrament of marriage meant that a man married just one woman. But native rulers were accustomed to having many wives, and did not easily give up this practice. There was also considerable hypocrisy, for Spanish men did indeed marry in the church but were known to have multiple other sexual partners. Even some priests who had taken vows of celibacy were known to cohabit with women and were not infrequently reported to authorities for soliciting sexual favors in the confessional. The "most nefarious sin," sodomy, was loudly abhorrent to the invading Spaniards and the clergy who followed them. But indigenous

homosexual activity was probably not as prevalent as was first reported. Moreover, among native peoples it was not necessarily considered a deviant practice. Rather, moderation in all things was the ideal for Mesoamericans.

Some of the indigenes' traditional beliefs about proper social behavior meshed with Spanish ways of thinking and doing things. But, ultimately, colonial morals and social norms conformed to what best served to maintain the integrity of the community. Sonya Lipsett-Rivera, in "Language of Body and Body as Language: Religious Thought and Cultural Syncretism," studies the sexual and social comportment of native women based on Nahuatl-language sources. Her interest is in the Nahuas' notion of self and body and the culture of the body. Here, then, religion is implicit, but issues of honor, class, and gender can be made explicit in one's body language. John Chuchiak adds greatly to the panorama of indigenous studies as he takes us to the Yucatan Peninsula. In "*Solicitantes* in the Colonial Diocese of Yucatan and the Yucateca Maya, 1570–1785," Chuchiak examines a rich assortment of Yucatec Maya and Spanish documents to bring to light issues relating to sexuality— both that of Mayas and Spaniards—and how sexuality was used to the advantage of each group against the other. Most surprising, perhaps, are the graphic descriptions of sexual abuse by clergy against both native men and women as well as the astonishing number of accusations.

Epigraph citations, in order of appearance, are as follows: fray Bernardino de Sahagún, *Florentine Codex: General History of the Things of New Spain, Book 10—The People*, ed. and trans. by Arthur J. O. Anderson and Charles E. Dibble (Santa Fe and Salt Lake City: School of American Research and University of Utah Press, 1961), 55; Documentos de Tabí, Yucatan, 33; Pete Sigal, *From Moon Goddess to Virgins: The Colonization of Yucatecan Maya Sexual Desire* (Austin: University of Texas Press, 2000), 90; Gregorio Martín de Guijo, *Diario, 1648–1664*, vol. 2, ed. Manuel Romero de Terreros, 105–6 (México: Editorial Porrúa, 1953) (The definition of mortero is uncertain, and could mean "stone cutter" or "one who dealt with cadavers."); Munro Edmunson, *The Ancient Future of the Itza: The Book of Chilam Balam of Tizimin* (Austin: University of Texas Press, 1982), 23; Peticion y respuesta por parte del acusado, Padre Cristobal de Valencia, en contra de los indios de su partido, Archivo de la Nacion, Ramo de Inquisicion, vol. 472, exp. 5, ff. 6v–7v.

CHAPTER FOUR

Language of Body and Body as Language

Religious Thought and Cultural Syncretism

SONYA LIPSETT-RIVERA

Walking, strolling, or sauntering down the street a woman's body spoke to the eyes of those around her. Both spectator and the object of his or her attention understood the messages conveyed by corporeal movement, clothes, gaze, and body alterations. In middle-period New Spain, the language of the body derived from the cauldron of cultural contact of early Mexico was an idiom shared by two traditions: Nahua and Spanish. The common understandings existed because of a process of cultural syncretism. Religious syncretism has most often been examined in terms of rituals and practices. But Spanish religious also imported moral beliefs that affected daily life. Many of these moral teachings referred to the body in ways that would not have been entirely foreign to the Nahuas. Because of superficial similarities, a common bodily language developed in the early

contact period and was still very much in place in the early nineteenth century. This language of morality and body affected the day-to-day dealings of women and men of all classes and ethnicities (see Javier Villa-Flores's Chapter 12 for more on gesture and body language).

The moral teachings of the Catholic church combined with concepts of hierarchy and precedence joined to form a culturally syncretic sense of body and honor. Because on the surface, Spanish and Nahua ideas about the body and about honor could easily converge, the body served as a means to communicate or impose a multitude of messages. In this chapter, I intend to propose that the body and corporeal language could be used as a medium for cultural transference in early Mexico and that, by the end of the colonial period, the body served as a canvas for social messages. Bodies and their coverings or alterations conveyed very clear indications as to morality, class, and gender. Bodies symbolized the inner person of which clothes were an indicative extension. Bodies were also a canvas for acting out personal interactions. Tensions were executed on another person's body within a code that allocated different values to a particular body part and different actions depending on the relationship between aggressor and victim.

Cultural Syncretism

In his latest book, Hugo Nutini proposes that there are two forms of cultural syncretism—guided and spontaneous.[1] The two types share many elements but differ in the level of intervention that colonial authorities could exert upon the process. Nutini suggests five elements for the process of cultural syncretism. In both guided and spontaneous cultural syncretism, similarities between the two traditions in terms of administrative elements or institutions have to exist. One of the cultures dominates the other. The third factor is the element that determines whether the process is guided or spontaneous. With forced conversion, if the Spanish religious (in this case) could guide and manipulate the two cultures then the process was guided. Nutini argues that where colonial authorities did not have the capacity to guide this process, then the fourth factor was altered, and it happened much more quickly and without the guidance of the dominant culture. In a guided process, the cultural changes would happen very slowly. The result was a culture in which the origins of elements within a cultural tradition can no longer be recognized as coming from one or the other tradition because they form part of a syncretic culture. Nutini, of course, derived this model from an exhaustive study of the Day of the Dead. He follows the Nahua rituals for the dead and shows how in the second stage of cultural syncretism, the pre-Hispanic structures were all but eliminated but that Catholic structures were influenced by Nahua beliefs. In the next stage, the reasons for certain practices were forgotten but these structural elements persisted.[2] Clearly Nutini developed his ideas by examining a particular religious ritual with substantiated roots in the Nahua ideology. I argue, however, that his model can be applied to slightly more diffuse cultural traditions such as beliefs about body and honor. The interactions of such beliefs are harder to pinpoint because they did not function within a structure such as the Day of the Dead. They were applied in the course of day-to-day activities. Nevertheless, I believe that this construct is applicable because there are so many ideological similarities between Nahua and Spanish cultural traditions regarding the interrelated categories of body and honor. These similarities formed a bridge between the two cultures. In the process of cultural syncretism, then, the very different rationales—the ideology—was forgotten and the structure, that is the practices, became a shared tradition. According to Nutini, the colonial process of cultural syncretism was formalized by the early nineteenth century and then stabilized but, of course, it was never static.[3] It is for this reason that I look to pre-Hispanic ideas and the moral teachings of sixteenth-century Spaniards

LANGUAGE OF BODY AND BODY AS LANGUAGE

to establish the culture of body and honor that I apply to middle-period New Spain. I contend that the language of the body cannot be understood without previously examining it at its source: early colonial cultural contact.

In order to develop a framework to classify the kinds of messages communicated by bodies, I use both Nahua and Spanish sources. Missionaries recorded invaluable information including the *huehuetlatolli*, or talks of the elders, and the Florentine Codex, to name two. I also rely heavily on the excellent analyses by Alfredo López Austin and Louise Burkhart.[4] Spanish ideas about the body are amply documented in the abundant morality literature. These sources reveal striking similarities in the way that the Nahuas and the Spanish perceived the various parts of the body. Their rationales were frequently very different but superficially their beliefs provided a cultural bridge for syncretism. The ideological framework of the body is relatively easy to document but, unlike Nutini's example of the Day of the Dead, for concepts of the body there is no obvious structure or ritual that supported corporeal concepts. Rather, ideas of the body were played out formally and informally on a daily basis but were subject to both official and informal controls. Therefore, although ideas can be documented, their enforcement—although present in the documents—is more elusive. Using criminal cases and acts of violence, I show how people acted upon their beliefs about the body and honor. The body provided a medium for messages but also a structure to act upon beliefs and enforce them.

Body and Honor

Codes of honor derived from the Mediterranean have been amply explored and applied to colonial Mexico.[5] Ideas of honor affected many aspects of daily life. They were also intimately connected to ideas about the body because honor was expressed in a bodily fashion. Honor also assigned values to different parts of the body. The body provided a two-way system of communication for honor. It expressed a person's honor, for example, by the way an individual held him or herself in the presence of others. But, it was also a canvas for other people to express their beliefs about the honor of an individual. When a crowd of people cut off a woman's or a man's hair, it expressed in a concrete and palpable manner its opinion of that person's honor. Yet the physical act was also a symbolic one—one that conveyed messages about the person's loss of honor. The head was the central receptacle of honor; its position conveyed social status as well as dishonor. It also became the most important metaphor to express relationships of honor. Thus, in the church, Christ was the head and the faithful the rest of the body; in politics, the king took that position over his subjects; and in marriage, the husband was expressed as the head and his wife the limbs.[6] The body was a symbol for the inner person; the way a woman or man dressed expressed their connection to moral norms and prevailing ideas about honorable conduct. The body therefore served as a symbol and a canvas in the daily negotiation of honor. This language was derived from the cultural syncretism of the early colonial period.

Although the transfer of honor codes

SONYA LIPSETT-RIVERA

from Spain to the colonial world is very well documented, scholars do not generally apply this construct to the Nahuas. Alfredo López Austin, however, does refer to "the concept of honor" when he explains the way that Mexica nobles instilled in their children a belief in their inherent moral cleanliness due to their lineage. López Austin believes that the emphasis on moral purity was linked to an effort to preserve noble families' power but also to maintain the strength of their collective *tonalli*—an animistic force located in the skull.[7] Such ideas about the intrinsic superiority of moral conduct of those born within noble families were not very different superficially from the Mediterranean idea of honor. The derivation of honor from ancestors and the way that it imparted a supposed superior morality was something that the Mexica and the Spanish shared. The ideology of the Nahuas regarding the tonalli in particular was different but the structural elements were very similar. From a young age, Mexica children were socialized to accept their position in what López Austin terms a "hierarchical environment." The child learned to respect birth-order rankings as well as the "vital forces" of their elders. Respect for this distinction was reinforced with the threat of bodily harm, in a manner that the Spanish would not have recognized or believed.[8] But the ultimate product—a society in which rank and status was linked to lineage and nebulous concepts such as honor—was familiar to Iberians. The ideology was different but the resulting structure—a hierarchical society—was familiar to both cultures.

If the Mexica had concepts of lineage and morality that could easily be merged into the structural elements of the Spanish code of honor, how did this relate to the interrelated concepts of body and honor? The Nahuas had very complex beliefs about their bodies and the animistic forces that inhabited them. They also recognized social position by signs such as clothes, hair, allowed food—all rights acquired from either birth or accomplishments.[9] These concepts as well as ideas about the importance of moderation in all bodily activities had some resonance in the Spanish ideas about the head, clothes, bodily alterations, and appetites. The basis for Nahua ideas about the body was far removed from that of the Spanish but the superficial similarity allowed the creation of a culturally syncretic ideology of the body.

Head

Because of its relationship with the tonalli, López Austin assigns the head a special place in Nahua beliefs. It was central to human relations. Mexica society recognized men or women of noble birth, who were therefore honorable, by their heads and faces. According to López Austin, the "hierarchy of superiority was correlated to the most noble part of the human body, and by their faces the highest-ranking men were patently recognized."[10] A person's breath was imbued with both emotions and moral value, and the face reflected that person's particular character. The head expressed emotions through signs but also could produce symbols, for example, a nod of the head.[11] Mexica rulers and nobles adorned their heads with jewelry such as lip and earplugs and headdresses of rare and valuable feathers.[12] The ruler's head was so imbued with honor and so respected that none could look him in the face. The eyes could also convey a sexual message. In fact the Florentine Codex specifies that "whoever fixes his gaze, whomever stares at a woman unknown to him, commits fornication with his staring." Although it was the man who committed a sin with his eyes, a woman faithful to her husband held the responsibility of avoiding this gaze.[13] As such, a good woman eschewed attracting attention to her head by her bodily practices. In the Florentine Codex, the Nahua mother told her daughter: "never long for, never desire the color, the cosmetics, the darkening of teeth, the coloring of the teeth, the coloring of the mouth; for they denote perverseness, they mean drunkenness." These physical marks were associated with "the restless ones, the dissolute ones, the evil women," "the ones called harlots."[14] Prostitutes as well as Otomí and Huastec women (peoples considered socially and morally inferior by the Nahuas) reddened their teeth with cochineal.[15] The mouth was a highly eroticized organ.[16] The description of "Bad Women and their Various Ways of Being" elaborates on this picture. She has a "vain face, excessively made-up," "she makes herself shine with unguents," "she puts cochineal on her teeth, her hair hangs loose—half-combed—she forms horns with her hair."[17] The use of improper personal ornamentation seems to have concentrated upon the head. Because the head held so much symbolic importance in conceptions of honor, it also attracted attention. Those who had honor, such as the ruler or nobles, could emphasize this attribute by decorating their heads. But those without it, or with a dubious claim to honor, had to refrain from such ornamentation. The connection between honor and sexuality is also very explicit. Because the head and the mouth in particular were erotic zones, the honor of a woman consisted in de-emphasizing this aspect.

Within European notions of the body, honor was also centered in the head.[18] As stated previously, the relationship between the head and the rest of the body provided the central metaphor of Spanish society for authority over subjects and therefore honor. Men and women conveyed their respect for others by bowing their heads in the presence of persons of higher stature and their superiority by holding their heads high.[19] In the middle period, a young man of the upper classes was either advised to keep his head straight, neither bending it forward nor leaning it to one side, or to keep it slightly bent although with a straight back.[20] In middle-period New Spain the symbolism of the head is seen mostly in its inverse—the pulling down of the head as a humiliation.[21] There was also a relationship between the head and morality. Women who claimed to be pure covered their heads while out of the house as this practice indicated their honesty.[22] According to the moralist Francisco de Osuna, proper women used a plain veil "for the angels."[23]

The head's lowered position meant an avoidance of direct eye contact or staring. Women especially were to avert their eyes. At the same time, just like in Nahua society, women took responsibility to prevent the male gaze because, as the moralist Gaspar de Astete stated, it was "like killing with a poisoned knife."[24] An eighteenth-century author went further. Don Joaquín Moles, with words that seem to echo the Florentine Codex, states that "when a man looks at a woman with lust he has already committed adultery in his soul." He believed that the eyes were the soul's doors.[25] The virginal woman's appearance was not meant to please men's eyes but rather to delight the pure eyes of her "husband" Jesus Christ.[26] Women sinned when their appearance attracted men's lascivious looks.[27] In middle-period New Spain, an anonymous author advised that young men should learn to discipline their eyes neither moving them around nor looking fixedly and arrogantly at others. This author stated, "when you talk to someone do not fix your gaze on their face but keep it a bit lower especially if the other person is of superior rank or a different sex."[28] The eyes and the two-way communication that they could engage in with a woman's body therefore were fraught with danger.

For both the Nahuas and the Spaniards the head was a repository for much symbolism, in the way it was adorned, held, and moved. Belief in the tonalli may have faded but because of structural similarities in conceptions of the head, the syncretic culture of the era privileged the head as symbolic of a person's honor. Thus attacks upon rivals or miscreants often entailed a pulling down of the head. This action was a direct attack upon a person's honor, forcing him or her into a submissive position. Pulling a person's head down was often considered a justification for attacks but certainly it was always insulting.[29] For example, an official in Mexico City pulled Juan Velásquez's braid when the latter was rude. The official retaliated to Velásquez's

slight to his position and honor by bringing him into line and attacking Velásquez's honor.[30] Officials often used this humiliating act to bring plebeians into line.[31] Many Mexicans of the middle period accepted the officials' right to pull hair and thus bring the head into a submissive dishonorable position, but they did not accept that others might do so. When Salvador de Ayala pulled Juana de Dios's hair in Coatepec in 1771, the witnesses were emphatic that Ayala had not been reelected as a town official and therefore no longer held any rights to pull down her head.[32] Such actions humiliated by attacking the central part of bodily honor but also by bringing down the natural position of the body, wrenching the head involuntarily into a lower and less honorable position.

The way that people looked at one another was also potentially dangerous. In daily practices, a direct stare could easily provoke an attack. Moreover, women who looked intently at each other in early nineteenth-century Mexico often fought.[33] Although in these cases, the offending gaze does not seem to have had a sexual connotation, the symbolic danger of a focused stare seems to have been considerable. The direct gaze was related to perceptions of honor because such staring was not possible to someone of higher stature. Among many other messages imparted by this action, it conveyed an insulting opinion of the recipient's stature and honor. Attracting men's lustful looks was another type of danger. When not reciprocated certain men and some women attacked, scratching women's faces or even, at times, killing women who rebuffed their advances.[34] In Nahua culture, the face was symbolic of the person and revealed social status. It should not be surprising, therefore, that the face could act as a type of canvas to mark people socially. People not only pulled down the head but also tried to scar the face as revenge for sexual transgressions. Usually men scratched women's faces because they refused their advances or wanted to end a relationship. Women marked other women's faces if they believed that the victim was flirting or involved with their husband or lover. Many men who committed such acts stated that they did so to scar the women's faces and make them unattractive.[35] On a deeper level they were expressing an old belief that people were known by their faces. The culture of middle-period New Spain promoted a sexualized communication between the eyes of men watching and those of women who broke the bonds of modesty. But, for a woman permanently marked by a former lover, this visual flirting must have been more difficult. Did she then keep her head lowered in order to hide her scars? Her face and her head could no longer be held in the same way, and she was forced into the kind of modesty advocated by both Nahua and Spanish moral authorities. The kind of communication between eyes and bodies that was highly sexualized in the syncretic colonial culture was no longer possible for these victims.

Hair

Although clearly associated with the symbolism of the head, hair also had its own particular messages. In Nahua culture hair, like the head, was associated with the tonalli. It protected the tonalli and so

cutting and washing hair was risky. Persons performing demanding or dangerous work—such as priests or long distance merchants—avoided such actions.[36] It was both humiliating and hazardous to have all one's hair shorn. At the same time hairstyles conveyed messages of masculinity and femininity. Warriors were distinguished from other men by particular haircuts, but those who failed in battle were shaved.[37] Hair also conveyed messages in particular contexts. For example, upon their return from the battlefront, messengers sported unkempt hair if the Mexica had been defeated but tidy and covered in a white cloth if victorious.[38] Nahua women also communicated their sexuality according to their hairstyle. Prostitutes wore their hair loose.[39] Among many other customs frowned upon by the Nahuas, Otomí women decorated their hair with feathers.[40] Female adulterers are depicted as having unruly hair. In fact, unruly, disheveled hair seems to have been a metaphor for misbehavior.[41] Clearly the Nahuas understood hair to be intimately associated with the symbolic importance of the head but also believed it to be representative of masculinity and femininity. Cutting hair was symbolically important and potentially degrading.

Although the Spanish did not believe that hair had magical qualities, it did impart messages of gender and sexuality. Long hair was associated with the feminine and when men wore their hair longer than the norm, they upset gender ideas. Spanish moralists condemned this practice. Trujillo decried male aspiration for beauty in long hair saying that it showed that these men did not appreciate their luck to be men. He asked, in a rhetorical fashion, "How many women would like to be a man like you and have your liberty?" He noted that men's shorter hair was a sign of their superiority over women.[42] Of course, as noted above, women were supposed to cover their hair. Clearly they did not because their hairstyles were the source of much moralist indignation. Women attracted attention to their hair by adorning it with pearls, gold bangles, and by curling it. Such embellishments, like those Otomí feathers derided by the Nahuas, demonstrated a loose character—one that was not sufficiently engaged in interior spirituality. As such they caused others to sin and sinned themselves.[43] Cutting a woman's hair communicated very precisely that she had engaged in illicit sexuality. It denied her the capacity to continue such conduct because without hair, the woman lost part of her femininity.

In colonial culture, hair cutting as a humiliation crossed gender lines for the indigenous population. It retained its associations with illicit sexuality for women. Those who chose to punish a sexually transgressive woman did so to mark her and castigate her.[44] But indigenous men also suffered this fate when they challenged colonial authority.[45] Hair remained an important identifier for indigenous peoples—they continued to wear it in ways that were related, if not identical, to pre-Hispanic hairstyles.[46] Because hair continued to be an important symbol, attacks on hair were highly symbolic. Inevitably attacks in middle-period Mexico entailed some pulling of hair. Such acts may simply have been practical—hair was easily grabbed in a fight. Also, by pulling hair,

the opponent was more easily controlled. But testimony makes clear that the act of hair pulling was considered humiliating in itself. Clearly, colonial authorities understood this relation, as they seem to have always used hair as a means to humiliate and control. Hair cutting was traditionally the punishment for female adulterers. But two middle-period New Spanish husbands inverted this language. When their wives discovered their illicit affairs and denounced them to the local authorities, these men cut off their wives' braids.[47] An incident with similar overtones occurred in 1850 between José María Ramíres and his wife. When she accused him of adultery, he in turn accused her of illicit relations (invented according to her) and pulled her around by the hair, wounding her quite badly. In this case, it almost seems that he was trying to pull her hair out by the roots.[48] Some hair cutting does not seem to arise from sexual tensions. In 1850 María Cornelia Ortiz attacked her employer and tried to cut off her hair for what she considered an unjustified scolding.[49]

Women also cut the hair of those whom they believed violated norms of chastity, but in particular those who seemed to threaten a sexual relationship with their husbands or lovers. In Xochimilco, Rita Trinidad suffered this fate at the hands of a group of women ostensibly for only talking to one of the group's husbands.[50] Clearly hair cutting had evolved from its origins as a punishment for sexually promiscuous women. It served an inverted punishment for men whose adultery was challenged by their wives but also as an act of rebellion for a resentful servant. Because both men and

LANGUAGE OF BODY AND BODY AS LANGUAGE

women were the recipients and the actors in hair cutting, hair and the head served as a way to symbolically act out the language of dishonor and humiliation. It was probably a language borrowed from colonial authorities but one that also had its roots in older notions of the symbolism of hair.

Clothes

Because clothes were placed next to the body they imparted messages about the body. What people wore communicated not only their wealth, class, and ethnicity, but could also reveal their morality. Indeed, according to the Spanish moralists, clothes reflected the inner being. The ancient Nahuas also believed in the importance of the messages conveyed by clothes. Sumptuary law, in Mexica society, reserved cotton for the elite and cactus or palm fibers for others but also the wearing of sandals, the decoration (embroidery, color, feather work), and the length of cloaks were all regulated.[51] For example, for commoner men, the length of cape was limited unless their legs were injured at war.[52] Among Aztec women, there were limitations on the type of adornment of clothes and those who wore excessively adorned clothes were tarred with the brush of immorality. The clothes of a proper woman were to be "honest and suitable," without excess of luxury or detailing, but they should reflect rank.[53] In the mother's speech to her daughter, she states: "In order that thou wilt live prudently, thou art not to clothe thyself [excessively]. Thou are not to place on thyself finely worked clothing, replete with design, for it achieveth gaudiness." But she adds: "Nor art thou to take rags; thou art not to place on thyself

the goods, the property of the vassals for it achieveth ridicule. In moderation art thou to clothe thyself, not in gaudiness, in vanity."[54] The association between flashy clothes and poor conduct is drawn when the "bad mature woman" is called a whore and gives one of her attributes as "she decks herself out presumptuously." The evil young woman also "is shameless, she dresses presumptuously."[55] The Mexica also made a connection between the quantity of clothing and sexual desires. Fewer clothes allowed the body to harden with the cold and allowed dangerous sexual energies to be dissipated.[56] On the other hand, the absence of certain clothes denoted immorality. For example, the Mexica considered that Huastec men who customarily did not wear loincloths to be dissolute.[57]

For the Spanish moralists, the connection between clothes and sin originated in the story of Adam and Eve. As a result of their fall from grace, the first couple had to begin to cover themselves and thus clothes should be coarse and hard.[58] Talavera explains that Adam chose a fig leaf over flowers or delicate leaves to cover himself because they "are hard and harsh." "Because I sinned," said Adam, "I lost the mantle of innocence and sanctity, so I know that I am worthy of this clothing that causes no delight, but rather bites at my flesh and tames the rebellion of my body."[59] Like the Aztecs, some moralists believed that excessive clothing was sinful, but the ways that clothes could represent a damaged soul were numerous.[60] Clothes of a certain type were "dishonest" and thus signaled the bad qualities of the person wearing them. For example, they might demonstrate an adulterous heart, a bad conscience, a lack of chastity, or luxuriousness. Such clothes were comparable to an advertisement, and moralists likened women who wore them to taverns as advertising the sale of wine or prostitution.[61] When dressing women made a choice whether to be on the side of the devil or Christ. The devil could work through women and their sinful clothes to take souls.[62] Women also signaled their choice for Christ by their clothing's color and fabric. Silk, velvets, and other luxurious materials as well as purple dresses demonstrated a false and vain soul that rejected Christ. The body's coverings were indicative of the inner being.[63] Clothes that attracted attention could cause men to sin by their lustful gaze, but the women who dressed this way also sinned by their actions.[64] The only women who had a dispensation from this rule were those who were married. Wives could dress in a way to keep their husband's attention and sexual interest in order to prevent the man from sinning by committing adultery.[65] Despite this exception, some moralists warned wives to please their husbands by their modesty and by staying home rather than dressing provocatively.[66] Dress was one of the principal ways that people defined their bodies and gave themselves an identity either as sinner or saved. By color, cloth, and quantity, women defined their inner being and entered into a relationship with those who looked at them.

Clothes were a necessary evil inherited from the first sin. By their regulation, clothes could, however, prevent further transgressions. But there were other ways that external adornments interacted with the body. Such outerwear could actually alter the body in many fashions and thus interfere with God's work. Women particularly tried to make their bodies more curvaceous or attempted to appear taller. They changed their hair color, whitened their complexion, and pierced their ears. By doing so they were fooling with God's work.[67] Those who committed this sin fell into the hands of the devil and were considered dishonest because they were trying to trick men.[68] It was akin to adultery.[69] Anything that changed God's disposition in creating the individual bodies was sinful and inherently disturbing morally. It attracted sinful attention but it also mocked God's will.

The moralists expected that individuals would dress to reflect the status that God gave them, including clothes gendered according to their sex. Their major worry was that men would wear women's clothing. Doing so flew in the face of God's beneficence in making them men. And yet, there were men who grew their hair too long (a sign of female inferiority) and who wore luxurious fashions that denoted a certain femininity.[70] But it was also sinful for women to pass themselves off as men. Osuna and Vives were concerned that many female fashions were too masculine.[71] In middle-period New Spain I found few references to cross-dressing although the feminization of men through dress and fashion continued to cause anxiety. But, in 1844, María de los Santos was apprehended dressed as a man. When questioned, she stated that she put on men's clothing in order to catch up with a man who impregnated and then abandoned her. When she tried to approach him dressed in the normal manner as a woman,

LANGUAGE OF BODY AND BODY AS LANGUAGE

he escaped. It was only in her masculine disguise that she was able to approach him.[72] So, rather than rebelling against God's order, her reasons were very practical.

Body Movement

People could also communicate with others in the way they moved their bodies. In both Spanish and Nahua traditions, corporeal movement either attracted attention or was neutral within the environment of the streets. Women particularly had to moderate the way they walked through crowds in order to avoid unnecessary motion or action. The Florentine Codex described the proper way to walk for women. It had to be orderly and measured: "And when thou art to travel [do it] also prudently. Thou art not to travel in great haste, nor art thou to amble; for [to amble] achieveth pompousness; [haste] meaneth restlessness. Thou art to go deliberately; thou art only to move thy feet along the road."[73] According to Burkhart, the regular pace recommended by Nahua mothers was designed to avoid stirring up dust or *tlazolli*.[74] In fact, in the Florentine Codex, the father's definition of maturity in his daughter emphasizes just this aspect: "because now you do not walk lifting up the earth."[75] The bad woman was "full of movement, a walker," "a strutting woman," "she moves lewdly," "she moves voluptuously."[76] The improper Nahua woman indicated her state by her movement; she did not show the bodily restraint expected of her and she did not limit the spatial range of her deambulations. She walked in the markets; on roads and streets she followed the "path of the rabbit, of the deer," that is, of vagrancy.[77]

It was not enough to simply walk with the proper cadence, eye contact and suitable posture were also significant. As stated previously in this chapter, the movement of the eyes and the act of visibly looking or staring were offensive. But I raise the issue here once more because it was related to the whole picture of a woman as she walked through the streets. It was part of her bodily movement. Did she stare and move her head around to look at others and see if she had attracted attention? If so, her bodily movement would not be stable. She would invite the stares of passersby. Wicked women went "around calling with [their] eyes . . . smiling at people" and also drew attention to themselves by whistling, clapping, and making noises.[78] The elders instructed proper Nahua women that on the street they should be "neither laughing, nor looking out of the corner of your eye, do not look at those coming toward you nor in their faces, but rather you must walk straight on."[79] A respectable woman was not supposed to answer strangers on the streets but also not to appear hostile.[80] Husbands expected their wives to remain impassive to strangers on the street, since it was a mark of their marital loyalty that they did not allow these lascivious inspections to break their concentration.[81] Yet, the bearing of the good woman was not supposed to be subservient, in fact, the young woman was also told to keep a straight back and neither cover her mouth or face with shame.[82] Her bodily stance clearly had to reflect her own sense of honor. In fact, it seems that a simple walk was a bit of a balancing act for most women; they should not look around or in someone's eyes but they should not bend over to prevent this; they were supposed

SONYA LIPSETT-RIVERA

to remain aloof from those surrounding them but not appear antagonistic.[83] Proper feminine behavior was a slender path that narrowly defined a woman's precise movements, attitude, and deportment.

The Spanish moralists were no less adamant that women display a proper corporeal conduct walking in the streets. According to these authorities, respectable women walked with a steady rhythm, neither hurrying nor dawdling. This measured pace and modesty of movement conveyed the seriousness of the individual. Martín de Córdoba defined the ideal pace in this manner as "to be ordered in one's movements in such a way as to not walk too fast nor dawdle: nor should one break one's pace." Such an unequal pace was, according to this author, "a type of luxuriance" that demonstrated lewdness. Women were supposed to "show modesty and measure in all acts and external movements."[84] Young men were also instructed on the proper manner of walking. It was important to maintain a moderate pace, without jumping or running and without either stamping feet or dragging them along the ground. In addition authors warned young men not to push or shove or wave their arms about, but rather to keep an adequate distance from those around them avoiding all bodily contact.[85]

Apart from the telltale walk of the loiterer, another indicator of depravity was found in the way women looked around themselves. Modest women indicated this quality by "not having roving eyes, not looking because she is looked at."[86] Astete also stressed the proper pace for women's walk. In addition he noted that whenever a woman came to a spot where other people had congregated, she had to show shame in her face—that is, she had to keep it averted and lowered—and her body should reflect a proper upbringing.[87] In middle-period New Spain Licenciado don Juan Francisco Domínguez reiterated this feminine model. He stated that it was extremely "agreeable [to see] a woman who is moderate in her movements . . . who shows in her eyes the humility of her soul."[88] Domínguez extended the earlier teachings about body movement and its connection to the eyes. In fact his statement reveals remarkable similarities with those other moral teachings that connect clothes to the inner being. Here the way a woman averted her eyes as a result of her proper body language showed that her soul was pure. In the proposal for the establishment of a school for girls in Mexico, the rules emphasized that young girls would learn this type of reserve: "They will not run lightly from one place to another, but will walk slowly as they come and go from their house."[89] In her nineteenth-century travel account, Fanny Calderón de la Barca noted that very few women (by this, she was no doubt referring only to women of high social standing) walked in the streets or even parks. She saw only "a few ladies in black gowns and mantillas [who] do occasionally venture forth on foot very early to shop or attend mass."[90] Her explanation for this reluctance was a combination of fashion and indolence but it does seem to conform to the ideal of the moralists.

Fanny Calderón de la Barca depicted elite ladies on the *paseos* (promenades), which they partook from the vantage point of their carriages. They did so "in full dress and silence for a given space of time, acknowledging by a gentle movement of their fan, the salutations of their fair friends from the recesses of their coaches, and seeming to dread lest the air of heaven should visit them too roughly."[91] Again, this author is perplexed by this conduct but it makes perfect sense if one has been trained to refrain from brusque movements and direct eye contact in public. The emphasis of these commentators was that women should not see or be seen; they were to be passive objects of the male gaze and thus accept their role as subordinate.

Conclusions

In middle-period New Spain the body provided a canvas for insults and attacks upon honor. Because the body was a symbol, all its symbolic extensions such as clothes, colors, makeup, ornaments, and even padding reflected both the outer being and the inner being. Attacks on the body were the result of a reciprocal communication using this symbolism and body language. But the language was derived from older traditions. It was the result of a process of spontaneous cultural syncretism that occurred in the early colonial period. On a deeper level, Nahua ideas regarding the body were very different from those of the Spanish. The animistic entities that the Nahuas believed inhabited the body certainly had little correspondence with the Spanish soul. But their emphasis on moderation in all bodily attributes—dress, sexuality, walking, and looking—is strikingly similar to contemporary Spanish ideas on these topics. These superficial similarities provide a bridge for cultural communication and for the formation of a syncretic culture of the body.

The fusion of Spanish and Nahua morality concerning the body was not entirely harmonious. For example, Spanish religious authorities objected to the typical male attire of a loincloth and insisted that indigenous men wear trousers.[92] Here Nahua ideas about the appropriateness of such clothes clashed with the Spanish desire to cover the body more completely. Yet on many other levels the language assigned to the body and interpreted from corporeal position and movement were not so far apart. As the Nahua ideology that was the foundation for this bodily language faded away, colonial Mexicans were left with a structure for bodily communication. This corporeal language was concentrated on the head as the central receptacle of bodily honor. The head's position, covering, and its movement all imparted messages to spectators. The eyes were particularly important because through their movements they could attract attention. Also their motion served to change the head's position. Hair also held an important symbolic importance and in fact seems to have preserved some connection to Nahua ideology at least in terms of the hairstyling. But the actions taken upon the head and the hair derived from a shared culture. The act of pulling the head down by the hair as well as hair cutting were clearly humiliating acts that transcended cultural boundaries. Proper body position as well as movement stressed moderation as well as the knowledge of when to bow and when to be erect. Such movements were very much related to the hierarchy of power in early colonial and later middle-period New Spain. Bodies had to reflect the rankings of honor within these societies;

SONYA LIPSETT-RIVERA

otherwise they would suffer humiliating reprisals. The body thus was a commonly shared language but also a mutually understood canvas for acts of forced deference.

People used a bodily language derived from the cultural syncretism of the early colonial period without reference to its antecedents. But clearly acts such as fixed staring as a challenge to the object of such a gaze were part of an earlier preoccupation with the eye's movements. The continued use of hair pulling as a ritual humiliation was related to an understanding of bodily concepts of honor. The marking of women's faces provides one of the most interesting aspects of this bodily language. I have not found any indication that this was based upon an earlier practice of either Spaniards or Nahuas. Yet it clearly seems to derive from the notion that the face represents the person and that the head is the central place in the body to attack because of its association with honor. Of course there was a practical side to such attacks that was stated by some of the perpetrators. They wished to mark their victim in such a way as to limit his/her sexual/social life because they would no longer be attractive. But many other methods exist that can disfigure a person. The choice of the face seems to point back to older ideologies that had faded with time. By the middle-period a structure of bodily language was all that remained of Spanish and Nahua bodily ideologies.

NOTES

1. Hugo Nutini, *Todos Santos in Rural Tlaxcala: A Syncretic, Expressive, and Symbolic Analysis of the Cult of the Dead* (Princeton: Princeton University Press, 1988), 17–18.

2. Ibid., 79.

3. Ibid., 81.

4. Alfredo López Austin, *The Human Body and Ideology. Concepts of the Ancient Nahuas*, vol. II. (Salt Lake City: University of Utah Press, 1988); Louise Burkhart, *The Slippery Earth: Nahua-Christian Moral Dialogues in Sixteenth-Century Mexico* (Tucson: University of Arizona Press, 1989).

5. For a discussion of the literature and concepts of honor see Lyman Johnson and Sonya Lipsett-Rivera, eds., *The Faces of Honor: Sex, Violence and Illegitimacy in Colonial Latin America* (Albuquerque: University of New Mexico Press, 1998), 1–17.

6. Juan de Cerda, *Libro intitulado vida política de todos los estados de mugeres: en el qual dan muy provechosos y Christianos documentos y avisos, para criarse y conservarse debidamente las mugeres en sus estados* (Alcalá de Henares: Casa de Juan Gracian, 1599), 323v; Francisco de Osuna, *Norte de los estados en que se da regla de bivir a los mancebos: y a los casados; y a los viudos; y a todos los continentes; y se tratan muy por estenso los remedios del desastrado casamiento; enseñando que tal a de ser la vida del cristiano casado* (Sevilla: no publisher, 1531), 90v–91v; Colin M. MacLachlan *Spain's Empire in the New World; The Role of Ideas in Institutional and Social Change* (Los Angeles: University of California Press, 1988), 9.

7. López Austin, *The Human Body*, vol. I, 393.

8. Ibid., 395–96.

9. Ibid., 172.

10. Ibid.

11. Ibid., 171.

12. Frances Berdan, *The Aztecs of Central Mexico, An Imperial Society* (New York: Holt, 1982), 47.

13. López Austin, *The Human Body*, vol. I, 305.

14. Bernardino de Sahagún, *Florentine Codex: General History of the Things of New Spain*, ed. and trans. Charles E. Dibble and Arthur J. O. Anderson, 101 (Salt Lake City and Santa

Fe: University of Utah Press and the School of American Research, 1953).

15. Inga Clendinnen, *Aztecs, An Interpretation.* (Cambridge: Cambridge University Press, 1991), 193; Chloe Sayer, *Mexican Costume* (London: Colomale Books, 1985), 68.

16. Clendinnen, *Aztecs*, 193.

17. As cited in López Austin, *The Human Body*, vol. II, 278.

18. Mijail Bajtin, *La cultura popular en la Edad Media y en el Renacimiento. El contexto de François Rabelais* (Madrid: Alianza Editorial, 1988), 132, 150.

19. William B. Taylor, *Magistrates of the Sacred; Priests and Parishioners in Eighteenth-Century Mexico* (Stanford: Stanford University Press, 1996), 230–31; Cheryl E. Martin, *Governance and Society in Colonial Mexico; Chihuahua in the Eighteenth Century* (Stanford: Stanford University Press, 1996), 98; Ramón Gutiérrez, *When Jesus Came, the Corn Mothers Went Away: Marriage, Sexuality, and Power in New Mexico, 1500–1846* (Stanford: Stanford University Press, 1991), 183; Juan de Escoiquiz, *Tratado de las obligaciones del hombre,* (Madrid: Imprenta Real, 1803), 114–16; Anonymous, *Reglas de la buena crianza civil y christiana Utílisimas para todos, y singularmente para los que cuiden de la educación de los Niños, a quienes las deberían explicar, inspirándoles insensiblemente su practica en todas ocurrencias* (Puebla: Oficina de Don Pedro de la Rosa, 1802), 14.

20. Joaquín Moles, *Doctrina para niños y adultos a la mente de San Carlos Boromeo, y del catolicismo romano* (Madrid: Imprenta de Pantaleon Aznar, 1803), 112–14; Anonymous, Reglas, 8–9.

21. Martin, *Governance and Society*, 99; Sonya Lipsett-Rivera, "De Obra y Palabra: Patterns of Insults in Mexico, 1750–1856," *The Americas* 54, no. 4: 515–18.

22. Pedro Galindo, *Verdades morales en que se reprehendan y condenan los trages vanos, superfluos, y profanos; con otros vicios, y abusos que oy se usan: mayormente los escotados deshonestos de las mugeres* (Madrid: Francisco Saenz, 1678), 49.

23. Osuna, *Norte de los estados*, 143v.

24. Gaspar de Astete, *Tratado del buen govierno de la familia y estado de las viudas y doncellas* (Burgos: Juan Baptista Varedio, 1603), 211, 217–18.

25. Moles, *Doctrina para niños*, 132.

26. Astete, *Tratado del buen govierno*, 263–64.

27. Thomas de Trujillo, *Libro Llamado Reprobación de Trajes, Con un Tratado de Lymosnas* (Navarra: no publisher, 1563), 80; Galindo, *Verdades morales*, 334–35.

28. Anonymous, *Reglas*, 8–9.

29. Archivo Judicial del Tribunal Superior del Districto Federal, Ramo Penales, vol. 4, exp. 3, 1788 (hereafter AJTS, Penales, vol. 4, exp. 3, 1788); Archivo General de la Nación, Criminal, vol. 222, exp. 15, ff. 283–313v, 1771 (hereafter AGN, Criminal, vol. 222, exp. 15, ff. 283–313v, 1771); AGN, Criminal, vol. 38, exp. 16, ff. 305–36, 1809; AGN, Criminal, vol. 118, exp. 13, ff. 473–81, 1807; AGN, Bienes Nacionales, leg. 663, exp. 9, 1812; Yale Library-Puebla Collection, box 5, series 2, folder 72, 1745 (hereafter YL-PC, box 5, series 2, folder 72, 1745); Archivo Judicial de Puebla, 1836, paquete 3, exp. 689 (hereafter AJP 1836, paquete 3 exp. 689); AJP 1850, exp. 3325; AJP 1776, no. 4345, f. 31; AJP 1836 #179, f. 16; AJP 1856, paquete 4 (Proceso contra Joaquina Rojas); AGN, Criminal, vol. 570, exp. 7, ff. 75–81, 1795; AJP, 1846, no exp. number (Proceso contra María Justa Palacios); AJP, 1846, exp. 616; AJP 1856, paquete 4, no exp. number (Proceso contra Juana María Bautista y Josefa Bárbara); AJP 1850, exp. 3390; AJP 1850, exp. 1287; AJTS, Penales, vol. 4, exp. 14, 1785; AJTS, Penales, vol. 4, exp. 26, 1785; AJTS, Penales, vol. 6, exp. 71, 1791; AJTS, Penales, vol. 9, exp. 2, 1797; AJTS, Penales, vol. 11, exp. 16, 1750; AJTS, Penales, vol. 11, exp. 68, 1752; AJTS, Penales, vol. 10, exp. 57, 1772; AJTS, Penales, vol. 3, exp. 2, 1777; AJTS, Civil, vol. 141, no exp. number, 1779; AJTS, Civil, vol. 113, no exp. number, 1756; AJTS, Civil, vol. 110, no exp. number, 1754; AJP, 1850, exp. 1287.

30. AJTS, Penales, vol. 4, exp. 3, 1788.

31. Taylor, *Magistrates of the Sacred*, 234–35.

32. AGN, Criminal, vol. 222, exp. 15, ff. 283–313v, 1771.

33. AJP 1846, no. exp. number (Proceso contra María Luisa Torres); AJP 1834, paquete 1, Puebla, no exp. number (Proceso contra Maria de la Luz Ruiz); AJP 1856, paquete 5, no exp. number (Proceso contra Rafaela Pérez).

34. Scratching women's faces was common. See AGN, Criminal, vol. 459, exp. 5, ff. 237–83, 1817; AGN, Criminal, vol. 131, exp. 27, 1727; AGN, Criminal, vol. 131, exp. 27, ff. 425–80, 1802; AGN, Bienes Nacionales, leg. 717, exp. 100, 1853; AGN, Criminal, vol. 2, exp. 19, ff. 326–65, 1776; AGN, Criminal, vol. 12, exp. 9, ff. 276–89v, 1744; AGN, Criminal, vol. 275, exp. 1, ff. 1–101, 1766; YL-PC, box 5, series 2, folder 75, 1823; AJP 1850, no. 3324 and 1343 (Proceso contra Micaela Armenta); AGN, Civil, leg. 39, parte 5a, no exp. number, 1854 (Proceso contra Refugia Ramírez); AGN, Civil, leg. 133, parte 2, exp. 7, 1838; AJP 1846, no exp. number (Proceso contra Mariano Gómez); AJP 1836, paquete 1, no exp. number (Proceso contra María Lugarda Ignacio); AJP 1850, exp. 3319; AJP 1846, exp. 616; AJP 1856, paquete 2, no exp. number (Proceso contra Gertrudis); AJP, 1856, paquete 2, no exp. number (Proceso contra María de Jesús Arroyo); AJP 1856, paquete 1, no exp. number (Proceso contra Petra Briseño); AJP 1856, paquete 4, no exp. number (Proceso contra Catarina Mendiola); AJP 1856, paquete 2, no exp. number (Proceso contra José Trinidad Sánchez); AJP 1850, exp. 3180; AJP 1856, paquete 6, exp. 38; AJP 1856, paquete 5, no exp. number (Proceso contra Juana Martinez); AJP 1850, exp. 3329; AJTS, Penales, vol. 3, exp. 62, 1776.

35. Lipsett-Rivera, "De Obra y Palabra," 518–19.

36. López Austin, *The Human Body*, vol. II, 170, 221.

37. Inga Clendinnen, "The Cost of Courage in Aztec Society," *Past and Present* 107 (1985): 56.

38. Burkhart, *The Slippery Earth*, 90.

39. Clendinnen, *Aztecs*, 193.

40. Sayer, *Mexican Costume*, 68.

41. Burkhart, *The Slippery Earth*, 90.

42. Trujillo, *Libro Llamado*, 19, 92–94v.

43. Astete, *Tratado del buen govierno*, 210.

44. Gutiérrez, *When Jesus Came*, 203–6; Susan Socolow, "Women and Crime: Buenos Aires 1757–97," *Journal of Latin American Studies* 12 (1980): 49.

45. Taylor, *Magistrates of the Sacred*, 233; David Frye, *Indians into Mexicans; History and Identity in a Mexican Town* (Austin: University of Texas Press, 1996), 77–78.

46. Gutiérrez, *When Jesus Came*, 205; Charles Gibson, *The Aztecs Under Spanish Rule; A History of the Indians of the Valley of Mexico, 1529–1810* (Stanford: Stanford University Press, 1964), 144.

47. AGN, Criminal, vol. 278, exp. 7, ff. 239–62, 1796; AGN, Civil, vol. 2045, exp. 11, 1794.

48. AJP 1850, no. 3325, 4 folios.

49. AJP, 1850, no. 1287.

50. AGN, Criminal, vol. 41, exp. 25, ff. 389–89v.

51. Patricia Anawalt, "Costume and Control. Aztec Sumptuary Laws," *Archaeology* 33 (1980): 1, 35–37.

52. Berdan, *The Aztecs of Central Mexico*, 47.

53. Sahagún, *Historia general de las cosas de Nueva España*, vol. I (Madrid, Alianza Editores, 1988), 370.

54. Sahagún, *Florentine Codex Book*, 10, 100.

55. As cited in López Austin, *The Human Body*, vol. II, 271.

56. López Austin, *The Human Body*, vol. II, 381.

57. Burkhart, *The Slippery Earth*, 60.

58. Trujillo, *Libro Llamado*, Aj, 4; Astete, *Tratado del buen govierno*, 61.

59. Hernando de Talavera, *Reforma de trages ilustrada por el maestro Bartolome Ximenez, regente del estudio de letras umanas a Villanueba de los Infantes* (Baeça: Juan de la Cuesta, 1638), 12.

60. Trujillo, *Libro Llamado*, 36v.

61. Galindo, *Verdades morales*, 5, 33.

62. Ibid., 18–19; Moles, *Doctrina para niños*, 127.

63. Osuna, *Norte de los estados*, 124, 126v; Astete, *Tratado del bien govierno*, 61, 207.

64. Astete, 219–20; Trujillo, *Libro Llamado*, 80; Galindo, *Verdades morales*, 134–35.

65. Trujillo, *Libro Llamado*, 79v–80; Osuna, *Norte de los estados*, 125; Astete, *Tratado del bien govierno*, 223.

66. Trujillo, *Libro Llamado*, 84v; Galindo, *Verdades morales*, 45.

67. Trujillo, *Libro Llamado*, 86; Astete, *Tratado del bien gobierno*, 214; Talavera, *Reforma de trages*, 53; Juan Luis Vives *Instrucción de la mujer cristiana* (Buenos Aires: Espasa-Calpe, 1948), 58.

68. Trujillo, *Libro Llamado*, 87; Vives, *Instrucción*, 57.

69. Astete, *Tratado del bien govierno*, 214.

70. Trujillo, *Libro Llamado*, 19, 92–94v; Galindo, *Verdades morales*, 14–5; Osuna, *Norte de los estados*, 132.

71. Osuna, *Norte de los estados*, 132; Vives, *Instrucción*, 68.

72. AJTS, *Penales*, vol. 12, exp. 57, Mexico City, 1844.

73. Sahagún, *Florentine Codex Book* 10, 100; Gerónimo de Mendieta, *Historia eclesiástica indiana* (Mexico City: Editorial Porrúa, 1971), 118; Alonso de Zorita, *Life and Times in Ancient Mexico: The Brief and Summary Relation of the Lords of New Spain*, trans. Benjamin Keen (New Brunswick: Rutgers University Press, 1963), 148.

74. Burkhart, *The Slippery Earth*, 137.

75. Sahagún, *Historia general*, vol. I, 366.

76. As cited by López Austin, *The Human Body*, vol. II, 273, 276–78.

77. López Austin, *The Human Body*, vol. II, 279; Louise Burkhart, "Moral Deviance in Sixteenth-Century Nahua and Christian Thought: The Rabbit and the Deer," *Journal of Latin American Lore* 12, no. 2 (1986): 107–39.

78. López Austin, *The Human Body*, vol. II, 277–79.

79. Mendieta, *Historia eclesiástica*, 118.

80. Sahagún, *Historia general*, vol. I, 371.

81. López Austin, *The Human Body*, vol. I, 305.

82. Sahagún, *Historia general*, vol. I, 371.

83. Ibid.

84. Martín de Cordóba, *Jardín de las nobles donzellas*. (No place: no publisher, 1542) Part II, Chapter 9, no page numbers; see also Cerda, *Libro intitulado vida política*, 17v; Vives, *Instrucción*, 95.

85. Escoiquiz, *Tratado de las obligaciones*, 112–14; Anonymous, *Reglas*, 11–12.

86. Cerda, *Libro intitulado vida política*, 9v–10, 17v; Vives, *Instrucción*, 71, 94.

87. Astete, *Tratado del bien govierno*, 228.

88. Juan Francisco Domínguez, *Vida y virtudes de la Reyna del cielo María Santíssima, Madre de Dios*, (Mexico City: Imprenta Madrileña, 1803), 52.

89. AGI, Audiencia de México, leg. 724, exp. 16, 68, 1686.

90. Fanny Calderón de la Barca, *Life in Mexico* (London: Dent, 1970, first ed. 1843), 105.

91. Ibid., 112.

92. Berdan, *The Aztecs of Central Mexico*, 177.

SONYA LIPSETT-RIVERA

CHAPTER FIVE

Secrets Behind the Screen

Solicitantes in the Colonial Diocese of Yucatan and the Yucatec Maya, 1570–1785

JOHN CHUCHIAK

Introduction

On July 6, 1609, Francisco Ek and his son Clemente traveled from the Maya town of Hocaba to the city of Mérida to appear before fray Hernando de Nava, the commissary of the Holy Office of the Inquisition in the province of Yucatan. Francisco Ek presented a petition that the interpreter, fray Rodrigo Tinoco, translated from Maya. Francisco Ek pleaded, "We come before your Excellency . . . in order to tell you and let you know how it is that Padre Cristóbal de Valencia perverts the good Christian doctrine in the town of Hocaba."[1]

Ek told a terrible tale, one filled with sexual violence and clerical misconduct. According to the Mayas, Father Cristóbal de Valencia called Clemente Ek to a confession in his sacristy. The priest suddenly appeared naked, telling Ek:

Come and take my private parts in your hands and play with them because this is the service of God and it is the office of the saints who are in heaven . . . and if you do not comply with this and play with my private parts go and bring me your wife because she has a large vagina and has slept with the entire village.[2]

Ek responded in shock, "Why do you say this Father, this is a very shameful thing . . . look here is the sacred chalice and you say this in front of it." The priest angrily retorted, "Don't you come here and preach to me . . . I will have my way with you without anyone ever knowing it and if not I will kill you tonight!"[3] According to Ek, the priest cursed and attacked him. He then pulled down Ek's breeches and grabbed his penis, squeezing it until blood ran. He then mockingly challenged Ek, "Go and complain about this to the bishop or the inquisitor . . . I have the power to burn you alive, and I am not afraid . . . even if four hundred bishops come here I will not dirty my pants out of fear . . . I am the bishop here."[4]

Following this sexual violation, Clemente Ek and his father went to denounce the priest before the Inquisition. The horrified commissary of the Inquisition, outraged at the accusation, ordered the priest's arrest and an immediate investigation.[5] Following the graphic accusations of these two Maya men, the clerical career of a parish priest came to an abrupt end. Padre Valencia lost his post as the parish priest of Hocaba to face a trial that eventually lasted for several years. Francisco Ek and his son Clemente had forced their oppressive parish priest from office.

Trial testimony revealed that Cristóbal de Valencia, parish priest and *vicario* (vicar) of the Maya town of Hocaba, was a well-known pervert and a pederast. By all accounts, he had taken sexual advantage of virtually all members of his parish, either in private or in the sanctity of the confessional. Testimony and accusations poured into the investigator's office as Mayas from the towns of Hocaba, Sanlahcat, Yaxcaba, and Hoctun came forward to denounce the priest for sexual abuse.[6] The ecclesiastical authorities considered Father Valencia's abuse of the sacrament of confession to be the most abhorrent and damning accusation. A parish priest who sexually molested his parishioners or lived in open concubinage with Indian women seldom proved an important enough accusation to merit serious sanctions.[7] Accusations of impropriety in the confessional or solicitation of sex

during confession, in contrast, ended a clergyman's career.[8]

Things, however, were not always as they seemed. Valencia argued that the accusations should not be taken at face value. He stated that the Mayas falsely testified against him because he had punished them for crimes of drunkenness and idolatry. As stated in the report of the priest's confession:

Both this native and other natives testify falsely against him out of the hatred that they have for his having punished them for their crimes against God and their other vices and sins which he preached against publicly. He refers the inquisitor to the testimony and opinions of the other parish priests who have served in the province of Hocaba who know and can tell him how it is public knowledge that the Maya from the town of Hocaba have a common practice of raising false testimony against their priests in order to get rid of them.[9]

This leaves the historian with the question of whom to believe, the Mayas or the priest. The overwhelming number of Mayas who testified against the priest suggests either a high level of sexual depravity on the part of the clergyman or an impressive ability of the Mayas to join together in a conspiracy to remove their priest. Whatever the answer, the trial against Padre Valencia reveals the intricate nature of sexual relations and morality in colonial Yucatan.

The Mayas, following the conquest, found themselves threatened by an alien culture that sought to impose an entirely new code of sexuality and morality upon

JOHN CHUCHIAK

longstanding traditions and beliefs. The Mayas quickly learned that Spain's cultural codes could be manipulated and turned against those seeking to impose their religion and morality on them. Historian Guido Ruggerio has argued that in the fourteenth and fifteenth centuries in Europe two very different worlds of sexuality emerged: the world of marriage and procreation, and the libertine world in which women were raped, prostitutes pursued, nuns seduced, and boys sodomized.[10] When the Spaniards conquered the province of Yucatan, they encountered a third world of traditional Maya sexual customs. The Maya, in turn, got caught in a confusing sexual universe, where Spanish libertines raped and abused them while simultaneously preaching the values of marriage and chastity. The Yucatec Mayas, however, quickly learned how to use the European's contradictory attitude toward sexuality and morality for their own purposes. Accusations of sexual misconduct, especially against priests and friars, became powerful weapons for colonial Mayas who proved otherwise powerless to defend themselves against the economic and/or sexual abuses of their priests and friars. The use of Europe's sexual morality to defend Maya culture is a metaphor for how the Mayas proved able, despite oppressive adversity, to protect themselves during the centuries of colonial rule.

This case against Cristóbal de Valencia is but one of many formal accusations of sexual misconduct and solicitations of sex in the confessional in colonial Yucatan (see Appendix). Maya accusations of fornication and sexual misconduct are widespread in colonial documents. These denunciations and petitions against their Catholic clergymen reveal the intricate layers of sexual morality and sexuality that existed in New Spain. These testimonies illustrate how Maya and Spanish Christian concepts of sexuality and sexual perversion diverged, intermingled, and collided. The clash between these different cultural concepts is most evident in the accusations against clergymen found guilty of solicitation, or *solicitación*. The conflicting views of sexual normalcy and perversity indicate that in the early colonial period there had been an attempt at a "sexual conquest." This conquest proved incomplete and must be seen as a metaphor for how the Mayas used Spain's culture as a political weapon to defend their own civilization. The Spanish tried to "conquer" the sexuality and morals of the Yucatec Mayas by imposing their values forcibly on the region. At the same time, as they attempted to impose their moral first world of sexuality on the Mayas, they also brought the Mayas into the second world of libertine sexuality and abuse. The Mayas exploited these contradictions, creating a universe where they defended their traditional third world of sex and sexuality from the Spaniards by pitting the colonizer's first world of morality against the second world of libertine sexuality. The astute Mayas shrewdly used accusations of sexual misconduct to defend their unique culture, including their sexual mores, against their Spanish overlords, administrators, and priests. This Maya struggle to maintain their traditions against the Spaniards, however, also transformed their own views of sexuality as these three worlds collided.

Although a majority of Yucatec Mayas undoubtedly suffered real sexual abuse, a significant number of them cleverly manipulated European sexual morality in order to subvert the colonial system. The many worlds of sexual exploitation, abuse, and accusation illustrate how the politics of culture, morality, and sexuality helped to shape colonial Yucatan as the Mayas skillfully maneuvered the two worlds of Spanish sexuality against each other, all the while struggling to maintain their own view of sex and sexuality that had little to do with either the strict chastity of Spanish Catholicism or the passionate sexuality of the Renaissance libertine.

Precontact Maya Attitudes and Sexual Morality

Sex and concepts of sexuality have played a major role in determining how people respond to their environment. When two different cultures come into contact, their concepts of sex and sexuality also clash and conflict. Maya concepts of sexuality differed markedly from those of the Spanish. The earliest conquerors commented on aspects of Maya sexuality that they considered strange or different from their own concepts. For instance, fray Diego de Landa observed that sodomy, or the nefarious act against nature, appeared oddly absent. He wrote that "I have not learned of their doing this in this country, nor do I believe they did so."[11]

Other early observers and later Franciscan historians such as fray Diego López de Cogolludo also noted the precontact Mayas' rigorous punishments for sexual crimes such as adultery and rape.[12] According to these observers, precontact Yucatec Maya women lived chaste and virtuous lives.[13] Their modesty was such that they avoided looking men in the eyes for fear of provoking their desires. If a young girl did look at a man, her mother punished her for her indiscretion. This idyllic view of Maya chastity and sexual purity, whether exaggerated or not, quickly changed after initial contact with the Europeans.

Colonial Maya Sexuality and Sexual Morality: A Clash with Spanish Catholicism

The image of a chaste and sexually pure Maya world came under assault during the early colonial period. Many clergymen believed that morality changed when the Mayas came into contact with the Europeans. Landa had stated that Maya women were so chaste before the arrival of the Spaniards that it was a marvel to behold.[14] In order to explain the virtue of Maya women, Landa gave an example of the violence of the sexual conquest. He noted one instance of sexual violence:

> Captain Alonso López de Avila, father-in-law of the Adelantado Montejo, captured a handsome and graceful Indian girl during the war at Bacalar. She, in fear of death for her husband, had promised him never to yield herself to another, and for this nothing could persuade her, even fear of death, to consent to violation; so that they threw her to the dogs.[15]

With the advent of forced sexual relations between the Europeans and Maya women, Maya conceptions of sex and sexuality began to change. The so-called sexual conquest violently assaulted traditional Maya views of morality and sexuality.

Tellingly, the Maya books of *Chilam Balam* also connected the arrival of the Europeans with the advent of their suffering:

When misery came, when Christianity came from these many Christians who arrived with the true divinity, the True God. For this indeed was the beginning of misery for us, the beginning of tribute, the beginning of tithes, the beginning of strife over purse snatching, the beginning of strife with blowguns, the beginning of strife over promotions, the beginning of the creation of many factions.[16]

The *Chilam Balam* of Chumayel lamented that the arrival of the Spaniards coincided with the advent of shameful lust and a loss of virtue:

Many village girls became prostitutes before them and behind them too. They did not understand the expectations of the foreigners: neither their Christianity, nor their payment of tribute . . .[17] The foreigners who have come here, they brought shame when they came . . . Lust and sex are their priests that are coming to administer things here because of the foreigners.[18]

Landa's image of the virtue of Maya women before the conquest conflicts with the later seventeenth-century view of Maya sexual promiscuity that fray Diego López de Cogolludo describes as the standard of his day. López de Cogolludo lamented the loss of this chastity and decency and an increase in adultery and rape: "Today when they should be better Christians, it is a sad thing to observe the lasciviousness that exists among them today, and this is no doubt caused because they do not punish these sins with the rigor that they did before."[19]

The violence and rape caused by the Spanish conquest and the introduction of a new system of morality and government no doubt changed the Mayas' own concepts of sexuality and sexual morality. No longer could the Mayas' caciques and *batabob* (governors) punish their commoners with the death penalty for adultery, rape, or sexual promiscuity. Instead they had to rely on the secular Spanish officials and judges who were notoriously lax in their persecution of sexual offenses. Even the Holy Office of the Inquisition had no power to enforce sexual morality among the Mayas.[20] Instead this job was left up to the bishops, their ecclesiastical courts of the *Provisorato de Indios*, and their officials in the local Maya towns called *vicarios*. The earliest bishops gave explicit instructions to the local ecclesiastical judges or vicarios concerning the sexual crimes and sexual morality of the Mayas. Fray Francisco de Toral, the first bishop, ordered that the local vicarios be especially vigilant in teaching the Mayas about the sacraments of confession and matrimony and with the aid of interpreters have them confess their sins and lusts of the flesh.[21] Subsequent bishops would continue to issue explicit orders to their vicarios to be vigilant and control the sexual morality of their Maya parishioners. As late as 1765, church authorities in the province revealed their continued preoccupation over the Mayas' sexual offenses when they ordered their parish priests to be especially careful about these vices and preach against them at the pulpit.[22]

One of the first actions of the early friars was to stop all pre-Hispanic practices that were considered "deviant or sexually promiscuous," such as Maya concubinage and promiscuous sexual relations, especially those of the Maya nobility. The early friars viewed this task as their attempt to "civilize" the Maya. Fray Bernardo de Lizana wrote in 1633 that the early Franciscans had the job of "domesticating [the Mayas] and placing them in good order and civility, procuring that they wear clothes because before they went around naked, and making them form orderly republics and towns."[23]

The later missionary friars' views differed greatly from the initial positive observations of precontact Maya sexual morality. The later friars viewed the Mayas and their religion and culture as savage and inhuman. They remarked that their religion and culture broke all "divine and natural laws."[24] Especially in their observations of Maya sexual practices and marital relations, the Franciscans and Spanish authorities found traditions that they wished to change.

As early as 1553 Spanish officials in the province issued ordenanzas that attempted to regulate Yucatec Maya sexual morality and marital relations. The Royal Visitador from the Audiencia of Guatemala issued a series of ordenanzas at the request of the Franciscans that attempted to reform and restrict Maya sexual practices. From that point onward, the Catholic church and the Spanish authorities regulated and controlled Yucatec Maya sexuality, desire, and sexual relations. The ordenanzas of Tomás López Medel included several decrees concerning fornication and Maya marital relations. The royal official noted, "even

though the sacrament of matrimony was used among the natives of this province, they commit grave errors and abuses."[25] The decree ordered that:

All those who after having been baptized had and lived with many women . . . are to manifest all of the women that they have to the bishop or the friars who will examine them to determine which one should be the legitimate wife so that they should leave behind all of the others.[26]

Anyone who continued to fornicate with many women or who refused to leave his other wives would be punished with "one hundred lashes." The decrees also mandated a similar penalty for those Maya men and women who committed adultery. According to the decree, anyone surprised in the act of committing adultery would receive "one hundred lashes and have their hair shorn off."[27] Similarly, anyone who continued to practice polygamy or adultery faced harsher penalties. The ordenanzas also prohibited Maya caciques and principals from keeping Maya women as slaves because the Spaniards believed that these female slaves were kept as "lovers and concubines in great offense of their legitimate wives and the sacrament of matrimony." Fray Diego de Landa mentioned that the caciques often engaged in sexual relations with their female slaves, because they believed that it was "a man's right to do with his own property as he wished."[28]

Regardless of these prohibitions and even the stiff penalties attached to them, more than twenty years after the conquest the Spaniards and the clergy

JOHN CHUCHIAK

began to observe an increase in the sexual promiscuity of the Yucatec Mayas. For example, as testified to by the Spaniard Juan Hernández in a trial about the sexual promiscuity of several Maya:

I have seen that the natives here in this province commonly get married while they are still boys of a young age . . . many marry at the age of ten or twelve and they live a married life with their wives, and it is common among them that they have carnal access with women at a very early age, unlike the Spaniards.[29]

The Church's Message on Sexuality and Abuse: The Clergy and Sexuality

After the clergy learned the Maya language, the job of instructing the Mayas in Spanish Christian concepts of sexual morality became the task of both the Franciscan order and the secular clergy of the newly established bishopric. Christian morality, as Louise Burkhart also noted for the Franciscans' work among the Nahuas, was defined according to the Ten Commandments and the Seven Mortal Sins, "which were part of the basic doctrine that everyone was expected to memorize."[30] The official view of the Catholic clergy enforced by the Council of Trent in 1563 was that "virginity or celibacy is better and more conductive to happiness than marriage."[31]

Within this concept of sexuality, vaginal intercourse conducted by a married couple remained the only sexual expression permitted. However, even this was viewed as shameful and only served the purposes of procreation. The clergy taught that the "less pleasure sustained during sex the better, and if it was possible one ought to experience no pleasure at all."[32] The friars also preached often on the virtue of virginity and the sinfulness of sexual activity outside of marriage.[33]

Thus, the most important message taught to the Mayas was that celibacy remained the most desirable state. The early friars also taught the Mayas that the Catholic clergy were celibate and had to remain celibate, not only during the conducting of religious services, but throughout their lives. This concept of clerical celibacy conflicted with traditional Maya concepts of ritual celibacy, which though required for the conducting of certain religious ceremonies and feasts, was not a permanent characteristic of the Maya priesthood.[34]

The clerical preoccupation with sexual morality and sexual practices is evident in the earliest doctrines and Christian confession manuals published in the Maya language.[35] For instance, the surviving seventeenth-century confession manual translated into Yucatec Maya, called *Confessionario breve para confesar a los Indios*, placed a great deal of emphasis on discovering and making the Mayas confess their sexual sins and other perversions.[36] One of the longest sections of this confession manual deals with the sin of fornication. The priest or confessor is instructed to ask questions that followed a supposedly normal exchange between confessor and Maya confessant. For example:

Yanxin açipil ti hunpay chuplal
    Have you fornicated with some woman?

Haytulx tubaob
> With how many?

Hay tenhi ti hun tulicunx tihuntuli
> How many times with one and
> with the other?

Yan uxiblil cuchi
> Did she have a husband?

A uenelob xin
> Are they your relatives?

Bicx auonelil ti
> How are they related to you?

Yonelob xin a chuplil
> Are they relatives of your wife?

Yanxin a dziboltic huupay chuplal
> Have you desired any woman?

Haytulx tubaob
> How many?

Haytenhi a dzibolticob
> How many times have you desired
> them?

Yanhi ua auoltiçipil tiob cuchi
> Did you have the will to fornicate
> with them?

Yanxin abaxtic aba
> Have you touched yourself
> dishonestly?[37]

The Spanish clergy's preoccupation with sexual deviance and sexual morality is evident not only in this confession manual, but it can be seen in many of the words that they elicited from their Maya informants for their earliest dictionaries. For instance, in many of the Franciscan dictionary entries that dealt with sex and sexuality, the clergy attached the Maya word *keban* to words for sexual practices and sexual positions. The clergy used the word keban which meant "a sad or miserable thing"[38] to roughly translate for the Spanish term

"sin," or *pecado*. The Catholic Christian relationship between sex and sin was thereby perpetuated by the later friars' teachings. Just as Louise Burkhart noted for the Franciscan's missionary efforts among the Nahuatl-speaking natives of central New Spain, the missionary's "aim was translation, not linguistic investigation."[39]

As many other examples of Maya terms for sexual positions and sexual acts illustrate, the Franciscan friars associated Maya sexuality and sexual practices with sinfulness and dirtiness. The friars began to record common Maya sayings that also gave evidence of their view of the increase in sexual promiscuity among the Mayas. One such common phrase was *Baxalech choo u baxalech kuch*, which meant "You are the plaything of mice and buzzards." The friars glossed the meaning of this phrase as "You are an evil woman who gives herself to everyone and everyone comes to you like rodents go to bread and buzzards to putrid flesh."[40] In this way, they attempted to inculcate a negative view of sexual promiscuity and lasciviousness. Their conceptions came from the Christian Catholic view of sexuality dictated by the Council of Trent in 1563.

The Mayas, however, had a sexual morality that did not view sex as inherently evil. Maya conceptions of sex and sexuality defined and placed sexual pleasure and sexual relations within certain constructs and relationships that depended on one's social class and one's status in society. Whereas Maya commoners were only allowed to enjoy sexual relations within the confines of a monogamous marriage, the Maya nobility and caciques were allowed during the precontact period to engage in and enjoy sexual relations with many wives and with many of their female slaves and servants. Even during the colonial period, the Maya nobility attempted to continue to assert their sexual prerogatives over many women, even including some of the wives of their own commoners. For instance, in 1569 the Maya nobleman and governor from the region of the town of Tabi tried to force a commoner's wife to have sexual relations with him. According to the commoner, "The worst thing he did was that he came into my house four times, trying to take my wife by force in order to sow sin [fornicate] with her. He desired this, but he did not fulfill his desire."[41]

As this case against a Maya nobleman illustrates, with the full force of Spanish colonial society and the church on their side, Maya commoners could thwart the continued prerogatives and sexual advances of the Maya nobility. During the later colonial period, Maya women too were able to use the Spanish system to protect themselves from lascivious Maya noblemen and even unwanted sexual advances from Spaniards.[42]

The Priests/Confessors and the Mayas: The Secrets Behind the Screen

For the Spanish Catholic church during the colonial period, the single most abhorrent crime that a clergyman could commit was the crime of *solicitación ad turbia intra confessionem*.[43] According to medieval Spanish law, the clerical crime of soliciting sex in the confessional was tantamount to heresy, and a grievous sin considered one of the worst committed against the majesty of God. The old Castilian law of the *Siete Partidas*, on which many of the laws of the Indies were

based, declared that "ecclesiastics are always bound to live in a chaste manner, especially after they have taken holy orders."[44] Any clergymen who solicited sex in the confessional or who engaged in open fornication would be removed from his parish.[45] The Holy Office of the Inquisition also issued several edicts specifically denouncing the sin of solicitation and requiring all Christians to denounce any cases of solicitation to their local commissary of the Inquisition.[46]

Technically in canon law, the crime of solicitation was the use of the sacrament of penance, either directly or indirectly, for the purpose of drawing others into sins of lust.[47] In the province of Yucatan and in New Spain in general, the term solicitación came to adopt a wider meaning and a broader definition. It came to be associated with any attempt to initiate sexual contact between a priest or confessor and anyone else before, during, or after a confession. The actual solicitation of sex in the confessional was not absolutely necessary to try a priest for solicitation. The actual act of soliciting sex or engaging in sexual relations could take place before or after a confession either in the church, the priest's private dwelling, or any other place close to or attached to the church or convent.[48] The mere fact that the soliciting priest was also a licensed confessor made any sexual overture or act of the priest a sin against the sacrament of penance and an abuse of office.[49]

The seriousness of an accusation of solicitation of sex in the confessional made them a powerful weapon for the Mayas in their battles against their parish priests.[50] In many instances, the Mayas used accusations and their knowledge of their priests' and friars' illicit sexual relations as a weapon against them.[51] They had learned well the lessons that the priests and friars had taught them about sexuality and sexual perversion, and they used these lessons as weapons to attack their clergymen when they had no other recourse as a matter of resistance. For example, in one instance in 1774 an anonymous Maya wrote a long petition denouncing the hypocrisy of his or her local parish priests.[52] The Maya denounced them for sexual depravity:

> I, the informer of the truth, tell you what you should know about Father Torres, Father Díaz, squad corporal, Father Granado, sergeant, and Father Maldonado. They say false baptism, false confession, false last rites, and false mass. Nor does the True God descend in the host when they say mass, because they have stiff penises. Every day all they think of is intercourse with their mistresses. In the morning their hands smell bad from playing with their mistresses. Father Torres only plays with the vagina of that ugly black devil Rita. He whose hand is disabled does not have a disabled penis. It is said that he has up to four children by this black devil. Likewise, Father Díaz, squad corporal, has a woman from Bolonchen called Antonia Alvarado, whose vagina he repeatedly penetrates before the whole community, and Father Granado bruises Manuela Pacheco's vagina all night. Father Maldonado has just finished fornicating with everyone in his jurisdiction and has now come here to carry out his fornication. The whole community knows this. When Father Maldonado makes his weekly visit, a woman from Pencuyut named Fabiana Gómez provides him with her vagina. Only the priests are allowed to fornicate without so much as a word about it. If a good commoner does that, the priest always punishes him immediately. But look at the priests' excessive fornication, putting their hands on these whores' vaginas, even saying mass like this. God willing, when the English come may they not be fornicators equal to these priests, who only lack carnal acts with man's arses. God willing that smallpox be rubbed into their penis heads. Amen. I, the Informer of the truth.[53]

The use of this petition is illustrative of the Mayas' abilities to take the Catholic Christian teachings on the immorality of sexual behavior and turn them against their own priests and friars. In this petition, the author, no doubt a Maya nobleman, subtly challenged the clergy's teachings concerning fornication and polygamy. His use of the phrase "If a good commoner does that," shows that he is trying to relate and identify himself as a common Maya, but his education and erudition betray him as a member of the noble class that remained the most affected by Franciscan and clerical prohibitions of polygamy and fornication. As Pete Sigal noted in reference to this petition, the petitioner reveals quite a bit about Spanish colonialism and the impact of the sexual conquest.[54] This petition is also a brilliant act of Maya resistance against their clergy. The author achieved his desired effect of shocking the ecclesiastical authorities. The official of the Inquisition who translated the document was so offended that he added his own opinion to the translation, saying that the accusations were "scathing, audacious, and grossly excessive," since he argued that it was well known that the clergy treated the Mayas with "respect and veneration."[55] The anonymous Maya petitioner attempted to use his knowledge of Spanish sexual morality to attack his parish priests. Apparently, the tactic worked because during the pastoral visitation of the region several of the friars and priests mentioned in this petition were removed and tried for solicitation.[56]

Thus, Maya petitions and denunciations against the sexual deviance of the clergy served as powerful weapons. In one of the earliest cases against a clergyman for soliciting sex in the confessional, a similar Maya petition complained about the parish priest and vicario Andrés Mexía:

> While he gives confession to women, he says, "If you do not give yourself to me, I will not give you confession." This is how he abuses the women. He will not give them confession unless the women go to him. Unless the woman fornicates with him. This is the whole truth about why the women are so upset.[57]

Initially, Mexía was removed, but after a long trial he was eventually reinstated in the Peto region from 1582–1589.[58] Andrés Mexía returned with his own countercharges, claiming that the Mayas were quick to lie under oath and often committed perjury. He stated before the Inquisitors that the Mayas were, in his opinion,

> People who very easily commit perjury and who ordinarily get drunk and are easy to convince and persuade to give testimony against someone in contradiction to the truth . . . They are out to see who they can take advantage of and for any small occasion or interest they contradict themselves [declare false statements].[59]

Apparently, the Inquisition officials eventually believed Mexía's arguments because they exonerated and reinstated him. The Maya officials from the local town of Tetzal quickly realized that the reinstated Mexía might harbor a grudge against them for their initial complaints against his solicitation. In a bold move, the members of the Maya town government of Tetzal showed their cunning and understanding of the reality of colonialism by writing a letter of apology and forgiveness to the Inquisition on Mexía's behalf, no doubt trying to assuage the priest's anger upon his return. They cunningly used Spanish ideas of Christian forgiveness and blamed the whole thing on the gossip of Maya women:

> Because of Christianity we gave up our anger with the padre and that which we previously said about him. Nor do we ask anything of him. Nor do we have anything else to say about it, because it is all over. We tell the truth. We'll remember none of it a second time, because we know nothing about it except for taletelling and women's gossip.[60]

It was not long, however, before the Mayas used another accusation of solicitation of sex in the confessional against Padre

Mexía. In late March 1589, a group of Maya women from the Peto region denounced Padre Mexía again for sexually abusing them in the confessional.[61] Once more, Mexía argued that they held animosity against him, but he was not as successful this second time.[62] Eventually condemned, the Inquisitors sentenced Mexía to the perpetual privation of confessing women as well as a sentence of banishment from the province for two years and a fine of 100 pesos.[63]

In another case against a Franciscan friar in 1599, the Mayas utilized their denunciations of sexual impropriety in the confessional as a powerful weapon against their abusive friar. A group of Maya women from the towns of Motul and Cacalchen denounced their friar for soliciting sex in the confessional and for molesting them while they confessed. Through the interpretation of fray Julián de Quartas, four young Maya women denounced their friar to the Franciscan Provincial fray Alonso de Rio Frio.[64] They accused fray Pedro de Vergara of soliciting sexual relations from them and ultimately raping them during their confessions. According to Ana Kuk, a Maya woman from Motul, fray Pedro had said "lascivious words to her and shown her his penis after which she grew saddened and left without confessing."[65] Beatriz Dzib, also from the town of Motul, denounced that Vergara had solicited her as well during the act of confession. She claimed that fray Pedro "placed his hands on her breasts and tried to make her touch his penis."[66] In the town of Cacalchen, however, María Cocom made the worst allegations, alleging that fray Pedro de Vergara made her sit between his legs before him while he "touched her breasts and forced her to touch his penis."[67] When the young girl began to cry, the friar reportedly forced her to her knees and then raped her, telling her when he finished that "she should not tell anyone about what had happened there."[68]

According to other information gathered later, fray Pedro de Vergara had also raped Maya women in other towns.[69] More petitions from Maya women and men arrived and the provincial of the Franciscan order, scandalized by the friar, wrote that after having been warned the friar still "had not changed his ways, but rather continued these vile actions and did other things worthy of punishment."[70] Based on the Mayas' petitions and testimony, the provincial removed the friar. However, by October of 1600 fray Miguel López, a Franciscan official who visited the province, heard of the case and reviewed it. He discovered that many of the husbands of the same Maya women who denounced Vergara had been previously punished by him for the crime of idolatry.[71] Fray Miguel wrote that the Inquisition should reconsider the case:

These Maya [who testified against him] are less than firmly planted in the faith and they have proceeded to denounce fray Pedro de Vergara out of desires for revenge since they had ample cause to hold hatred for him because, as the *guardián* (Franciscan official) of their convent and as a translator of their language, he had persecuted them for their idolatries with all of the care and diligence necessary of his office and, in punishing them, he used harsh measures and cruelty. Due to his extirpation of idolatry, there has not been a single convent in which the Indians have not raised severe complaints against him for his excessive cruelty and, even now, during the present chapter meeting of our order, I have received verbal petitions from the Indians of several villages where he has never yet served as guardian, not because he has done anything, but rather because out of their fear, and knowing the fame of his cruelty, they hoped that he would not be assigned to their guardianía . . . For these reasons I am sure that the Indians referred to in this case have the same hatred for him since he was the translator in various cases against idolatry in their town . . . Thus I am of the opinion that we delay any punishment for some time until we can be sure that should any of the witnesses in this case wish for revenge they will not be able to gain it in this manner.[72]

Again, the 1609 case against the parish priest Cristóbal de Valencia discussed in the introduction is another typical case in which the Mayas used denunciations of sexual impropriety against a clergyman who had punished them for their own excesses. Clemente Ek was not the only one who denounced Padre Valencia. More than one hundred other Mayas gave depositions against the priest. One of the many witnesses who testified against Valencia was Pablo Chan, a resident of the town of Hoctun. According to Pablo Chan, Padre Valencia,

with a diabolical soul and indignant in the ministry and office of a priest, called the said Indian one day and ordered him to put his virile member into his mouth and that the said Indian placed his virile member into the mouth of the accused and he took his own member into his hands and he played with it until he spilled his own natural seed.[73]

Valencia, in his own defense, argued similarly that Pablo Chan, Clemente Ek, and many of the other Maya witnesses used their denunciations to gain revenge against him. The record states that "the natives give this false testimony against him because he had punished them for their own crimes against the faith and their idolatries and drunkenness that they engage in frequently, and for this reason they declare these falsehoods against him."[74]

Again, as in the case against fray Pedro de Vergara, the Mayas apparently used accusations of sexual impropriety to rid themselves of a repressive clergyman. During the same period, the bishop of Yucatan stated that the Mayas often lied and testified falsely against their clergymen. He wrote to the crown concerning these denunciations of clergyman: "I, inquiring about the matter, discover that the Indians come with lies because they are obligated to go and hear mass or the doctrine, or that proceedings for some crime or sin against the faith are brought against them."[75]

Whether the Mayas told lies or the truth, the important thing to note is that their accusations proved effective in removing their clergymen, at least temporarily during the duration of the trial.

As these and other cases show (see Table 5.1), many Mayas may have used denunciations of solicitation as weapons to remove priests and friars that punished them or abused them for what they viewed as the Mayas' own sins. Accusations of solicitation served as a weapon that empowered Maya men and enabled them to gain revenge against the repressive measures of clergy who engaged in the extirpation of idolatry. Maya women also took the initiative in denouncing their parish priests or friars for sexual advances in the confessional or in the church.

Maya women became empowered by the use of these accusations, using them to protect themselves from the abuse of a jealous husband who suspected them of marital infidelity. For example, two Maya women from the Peto region denounced their interim parish priest, Bachiller Antonio Ramón de la Cueva, in 1730 for the crime of solicitation *ad turpia intra confessionem*. Fearful that their husbands might discover that they were not virgins when they married, they decided to blame their loss of virginity on an abusive parish priest who was well known to exploit his parishioners.[76] Whether or not they were actually raped in the confessional, the Maya women used the accusation of being raped by their priest as a shield to protect themselves from their jealous husbands' abuse. In order to minimize their own public shame, the two women intelligently asked a second Spanish confessor to denounce the priest for them.[77] Another Maya woman named María Uxul brought a similar case against the assistant parish priest of the town of Mama, Bachiller Félix de Malavar, in the same year.[78] Apparently, her husband also had abused her for suspicions of infidelity.

In many other cases, Maya men made use of claims that the local clergyman either raped or solicited sex from Maya women in the confessional in order to gain revenge for abuses committed against them. For example, in 1780 Félix Cocom, the Maya *maestro de capilla* (choirmaster) of the town of Uman, denounced his own parish priest, Bachiller Luis Antonio de Echazarreta, for sexual misconduct and solicitation.[79] According to later testimony, the priest not only solicited sex during confession, but he also mistreated young pregnant Maya women. Apparently, he frequently attacked unwed mothers or pregnant Maya women by yelling at them, "Come here you whores, you little pigs, mules of the devil that is what you are, slaves of the devil's fornication, come and tell me who are the fathers of the bastard children that you have in your womb."[80]

Padre Echazarreta's offenses did not stop with insults. Many of the younger Maya women who attempted to marry, such as Francisca Cauiche, testified that the priest had raped them during their marriage talks and confessions while they resided in the church.[81] Apparently, while they stayed in the church at night the priest called them to his room. Francisca Cauiche later testified that after dinner one night she was summoned to his room by the priest's sister doña Ignacia, who dragged her by her arms and locked her in the priest's room.[82] Father Echazarreta then pulled her forcibly to the bed and threatened her, "If you do not have carnal relations with me, I will not marry you." Francisca kicked and resisted and told him, "My Lord, I cannot have relations with you because you are Christ on earth!" The priest replied,

> My daughter, I have permission and a license to have relations with anyone

even a young virgin like you ... I should be the first to taste of the fruits that will soon belong to those *cabrones*, besides if you have any trouble in the future with your husband because of this just come to me and tell me so I can punish him.[83]

According to other witnesses, the parish priest apparently molested all of the young girls who came to him for marriage instruction and confession.[84] In his initial denunciation, Félix Cocom argued that Father Echazarreta's public sexual scandals were so horrendous that they set a bad example for the entire town. Cocom appealed to the Catholic fears of public scandal when he wrote sarcastically in his petition: "All of this My Lord appears upon seeing it to cause me many sins, because if a spiritual Padre can do and consent to these things in his Holy Convent, what will I not do with this bad example."[85]

However, Cocom's denunciation was less motivated out of altruistic interest in protecting the Maya women of his town and more motivated by individual plots of revenge. Cocom attempted to use the denunciation of solicitation and sexual misconduct to gain revenge against Padre Echazarreta for having had him mercilessly whipped and then ordering the Maya *fiscales* (church officials) to smear human excrement in his mouth.[86] Apparently, the parish priest had him punished for appearing drunk in public and swearing and insulting him with foul words.[87] The Maya women who were involved in this case were at first reluctant to press the issue, but Cocom's denunciation forced them

to testify against the priest. Although the priest's sexual abuse of the women was a fact, it was not the motivating factor in his denunciation. In fact, two of the women who were molested by the priest actually received much grief from their husbands due to their participation in the case.[88] The Maya women and one Spanish woman, who the priest also molested, would have preferred to keep their sexual molestation a secret. However, the value of using the denunciation of sexual impropriety as a weapon proved irresistible for Félix Cocom and the other members of the town council of Uman. The Maya officials had become angered at Echazarreta's failure to pay them or even feed their town's workers for labors they conducted on the town church.[89] In the end, the authorities removed the priest from his parish, not for the host of abuses and extortions he committed, but rather for his few sexual indiscretions.

A similarly large corpus of trials for clerical solicitation exists. The few examples given here serve to illustrate the ways the Mayas used denunciations of sexual abuse to rid themselves of clergymen who abused and punished them for their own supposed crimes against the Catholic faith.[90] Although sexual abuse almost certainly did occur in most of these cases, it was not until the Mayas found themselves abused in other ways that they used the accusations of sexual impropriety against their clergymen. In most cases, the Mayas accepted and even covered up the sexual indiscretions of their clergymen.[91] As long as the clergy did not engage in open violation of traditional Maya concepts of celibacy during the conducting of religious rituals, such as mass, confession, or baptism, then the Mayas would ignore their sexual impropriety. Thus, in many cases of sexual misconduct both Maya men and women willingly kept the secrets behind the screen as long as the clergyman did not abuse them in other ways. But, if a local clergyman attempted to punish the Mayas of his parish too rigorously for their traditional religious practices or for what he viewed as their sexual immorality, then the Mayas would complain about his hypocrisy. When the local priest enforced the Spanish Catholic code of sexual morality, the Mayas complained about the "priest's excessive fornication" as they did in that 1774 petition. In many instances, the accusation of sexual immorality was the last of many attempts to remove abusive clerics and friars. In the cases against Andrés Mexía and Luis Antonio de Echazarreta, a long series of complaints against economic and labor abuses preceded denunciations for solicitation. However, the Spanish authorities, themselves complicit in Mexía and Echazarreta's corruption and extortion of the Mayas of their parishes, turned deaf ears to their complaints. Only after the Holy Office of the Inquisition got involved in solicitation cases did the Mayas manage to remove their abusive priests.

Conclusion

The Mayas' response to the "sexual conquest" illustrates the ability of a militarily conquered people to exploit every weakness in the colonial system to preserve their traditional culture. In the case of the Mayas who denounced their priests, they skillfully used the contradictory worlds of Spanish sexual morality against them. If we are to believe the testimonies of the Mayas who denounced their parish priests as pedophiles or sexual abusers, the picture we gain is one of rampant sexual promiscuity among the clergy. Although many of the Mayas' testimonies may have been exaggerated, there is evidence of the clergy's lax morality in the frontier province of Yucatan. To argue that the Mayas used accusations of sexual abuse as a weapon of political and cultural self-defense is not to deny that actual abuses took place with all too alarming frequency throughout the colonial era.

Among the higher clergy, sexual immorality appears to have been commonplace. For example, in 1700 a priest of the cathedral, Doctor Gaspar Joseph Rodríguez, complained that the entire ecclesiastical membership of the Cathedral chapter had engaged in sexually immoral behavior. He wrote to the crown:

> Many of the priests and even the *prebendados* (prebends) have illicit relationships with women, and they even have children by them . . . The dean of the chapter does not go to the meetings, instead he screws around with four girls and gives them his pensions as "dowries" . . . the archdean also has a lover with whom he fornicates . . . The *maestraescuela* (officer in a cathedral chapter) also has a lover with whom he fornicated, a mestiza woman named Josepha Montalvo, whom he offered as a whore informally to a member of the secular *cabildo* (council). They all fornicate with mestizas and indias . . . but I should tell no more so as not to offend Your Majesty's chaste ears.[92]

JOHN CHUCHIAK

If this is an accurate image of the higher better-educated clergy in Mérida, what could one expect from the undereducated and often illiterate clergy who served in the Maya parishes and guardianías? Maya testimony suggests a pattern of widespread sexual abuse, which appears to continue past independence from Spain in the nineteenth century.[93] This leads to the question of whether Maya accusations of the clergy's sexual misconduct is evidence of sexual deviance, or were they part of a brilliant use of Catholic sexual preoccupations and conceptions against their own clergy? This question, however, ignores the most important arena of sexual conflict, where traditional Maya sexuality collided with the contradictory Spanish worlds of morality and lasciviousness. In these encounters, the sexually abused Mayas found themselves used as political weapons against the colonial system by Maya lords who resented their loss of sexual prerogatives.

In the end, one is left with the lingering and unanswerable question of who actually won the "sexual conquest." Perhaps the best way to explore this question is with Guido Ruggiero's metaphor of two European sexual worlds. The first world of Spanish Catholic morality, with its virtues of chastity and virginity, clearly failed to conquer the Spanish, much less the Mayas. The second world of Spanish lasciviousness found itself checked by the first world and also failed to "conquer" the Mayas. At the same time, the Maya world of pre-Columbian sexuality found itself under assault by both worlds of Spanish sexual mores. In this culturally complex universe of sexual worlds there were neither winners nor losers, only an intermingling, colliding, and chaotic brew of clashing cultures that defined the evolution of the province of Yucatan during the colonial period. It is the wreckage of worlds colliding, reforming, and colliding again that serves as the best metaphor for the creation of a unique postconquest Maya culture that successfully protected their civilization from both the sexual aggression of the Spaniards and their alien concepts of Catholic sexual morality even as the conflict itself transformed their traditional culture.

Table 5.1 Sample Cases of Clerical Solicitation in the Diocese of Yucatan, 1578–1808

Date	Accused Clergyman	Crime	Accuser	Incident	Outcome
1578	Andrés Mexía, cleric [Yalcon, Ekpedz, Tetzal, others]	Solicitación ad turpia intra confessionem	Maya cabildo and numerous Maya women from towns of Ekpedz and Tetzal	Solicitation of sex and sexual relations in confessional	Temporary removal
1580	Various clergymen	Solicitación ad turpia intra confessionem	Maya women and men	Solicitation of sex in confessional	Permanent removal

continued on next page

Date	Accused Clergyman	Crime	Accuser	Incident	Outcome
1580	Fray Juan de Santanella, Franciscan	Solicitación ad turpia intra confessionem	Maya women, town government	Solicitation of sex in confessional, sexual molestation	Permanent removal
1582	Fray. Pedro Núñez, Franciscan	Solicitación ad turpia intra confessionem	Various Maya women	Solicitation of sex in confessional, sexual molestation	Permanent removal
1589	Andrés Mexía, cleric (Calotmul, Peto)	Solicitación ad turpia intra confessionem	Maya women and cabildos of towns of Peto and Calotmul	Solicitation of sex and rape in the confessional	Permanent removal
1599	Fray Pedro de Vergara, Franciscan (Motul)	Solicitación ad turpia intra confessionem	Maya women from the towns of Motul and Cacalchen	Solicitation of sex in the confessional, rape, molestation	Temporary removal, reinstatement
1600	Br. Andrés Fernández de Castro, cleric	Solicitación ad turpia intra confessionem	Several Spanish and Maya women	Solicitation of sex during confession	Temporary removal
1605	Diego de la Camara, cleric	Solicitación ad turpia intra confessionem	Maya women	Solicitation of sex during confession	Temporary Removal
1610	Cristóbal de Valencia, cleric	Solicitación ad turpia intra confessionem, pecados contra natura, actos nefandos	Maya men and boys from Hocaba, Sanlahcat, Hoctun	Solicitation of sex during confession, homosexual acts, forced oral sex	Permanent removal
1613	Fray Cristóbal de Moreno, Franciscan [Campeche]	Solicitación ad turpia intra confessionem	Maya women	Solicitation of sex in the confessional	Permanent removal
1621	Fray Francisco Gutiérrez, Franciscan	Solicitación ad turpia intra confessionem	Maya women	Solicitation of sex in the confessional	Permanent removal
1624	Fray Julián Orbita, Franciscan	Solicitación ad turpia intra confessionem	Maya and Spanish women	Solicitation of sex in the confessional	Permanent removal
1730	Br. Antonio Ramón de la Cueva, cleric	Solicitación ad turpia intra confessionem	Bernardina Chan, Thomasa Huchim	Solicitation of Sex in the confessional	Permanent removal
1730	Br. don Felix de Malaver, cleric	Solicitación ad turpia intra confessionem	Cecilia Uxul (Mama)	Solicitation of sex in the confessional	Permanent removal

Date	Accused Clergyman	Crime	Accuser	Incident	Outcome
1750	Br. Alfonso Pérez, cleric	Solicitación ad turpia intra confessionem	Maya women	Solicitation of sex in the confessional	Permanent removal
1751	Fray Francisco Guzmán, Franciscan	Solicitación ad turpia intra confessionem	Maya women	Solicitation of sex in the confessional	Permanent removal
1757	Br. Mateo González, cleric	Solicitación ad turpia intra confessionem	Maya, mulatto, and Spanish women	Solicitation of sex in the confessional	Permanent removal
1777	Fray Francisco Guzmán, Franciscan (repeat offender)	Solicitación ad turpia intra confessionem	Marcela de Campos, other women	Solicitation of sex in the confessional, assault	Died during trial
1780	Luis Antonio de Echazarreta, cleric	Solicitación ad turpia intra confessionem, fornication, other crimes	Francisca Cauice, Manuela Pacheco, Felix Cocom	Solicitation of sex in the confessional, sexual misconduct	Permanent removal
1780	Fray Pedro Ortega, Franciscan	Solicitación ad turpia intra confessionem	Spanish, mestiza women	Solicitation of sex in the confessional	Permanent removal
1781	José Manzanilla, cleric	Solicitación ad turpia intra confessionem	Maya, mulatto, and Spanish women	Solicitation of sex in the confessional	Died during trial
1785	Pablo Raymondi, cleric Italian	Solicitación ad turpia intra confessionem	Various Maya and mestiza women	Solicitation of sex in the confessional	Permanent removal
1794	Br. Julián Quijano, cleric (Bacalar)	Solicitación ad turpia intra confessionem, sodomía, acto nefando	Francisco Uicab	Solicitation of sex in the confessional, sodomy, homosexual acts	Permanent removal
1795	Antonio Pacheco, Cleric	Solicitación ad turpia intra confessionem	Micaela Dzib	Solicitation of sex in the confessional	Died during trial
1797	Juan Dionisio Frasqui, Cleric	Solicitación ad turpia intra confessionem	Maya women	Solicitation of sex in the confessional	Permanent removal
1798	Br. José Rafael Jiménez, cleric (Tixkokob)	Solicitación ad turpia intra confessionem	María Isabel Torralbo, Mestiza	Solicitation of sex in the confessional	Permanent removal
1808	Fray Lorenzo de Avila, Franciscan	Solicitación ad turpia intra confessionem	María Encarnación	Solicitation of sex in the confessional	False accusation

Source: Archivo General de la Nación (Mexico City), Ramo de Inquisición, vols. 35, 69, 85, 90, 122, 123, 249, 281, 288, 295, 303, 337, 472, 926, 935, 954, 988, 1046, 1187, 1250, 1284, 1369, 1373, 1380, 1468; Archivo General de las Indias (Seville), Audiencia de México, 248, 369, 1030–36, 3053, 3063, 3068. 3168; AGI, Escribania de Camara, 313 B, 317; Archivo Histórico Nacional (Madrid), Inquisición, 1735; Archivo Historico del Arzobispado de Yucatán (Mérida), Asuntos Terminados, 5; AHAY, Visitas Pastorales, vol. 1.

NOTES

1. *Petición en lengua Maya de Clemente Ek y Francisco Ek su padre contra el cura beneficiado del pueblo de Hocaba, Cristobal de Valencia por varios cosas indecentes*, 6 de julio, 1609, Archivo General de la Nación (AGN), Ramo de Inquisición, vol. 472, exp. 5, f. 1v–3r.

2. Ibid., f. 2v.

3. *Testimonio y declaración de Clemente Ek en contra de su cura Cristobal de Valencia*, 6 de Julio, 1609, AGN, Ramo de Inquisición, vol. 472, exp. 5, f. 10r.

4. Ibid., f. 10r–10v.

5. *Mandamiento de prision contra Padre Cristobal de Valencia hecha por su paternidad Fr. Fernando de Nava, comisario del Santo Oficio*, 6 de Julio, 1609, AGN, Ramo de Inquisición, vol. 472, exp. 5, f. 4r–4v. As the commissary's reaction illustrates, the ecclesiastical authorities remained especially adamant in rooting out what they viewed as "sodomy," the "nefarious act," or any type of homosexual relations between clergymen and parishioners. For a complete study of Christian intolerance and historical views on homosexuality see David F. Greenberg and Marcia H. Bystryn, "Christian Intolerance of Homosexuality," *American Journal of Sociology* 88, no. 3 (November 1982): 515–48. Also for the case of colonial Latin America see Federico Garza Carvajal, "An Emasculation of the 'Perfect Sodomy' or Perceptions of 'Manliness in the Harbours of Andalucía and Colonial Mexico City, 1560–1699.'" Paper presented at the 1998 Latin American Studies Association Meeting in Chicago, September 24–26, 1998. For an earlier discussion of the connection between the Christian concept of "crimes against nature" and homosexual behavior, see F. E. Frenkel, "Sex-Crime and its Socio-Historical Background," *Journal of the History of Ideas* 25, no. 3 (July–September 1964): 333–52.

6. For only a few of the one hundred or more denunciations see *Testimonio y declaración de Juan May, vecino de Tixpehual, contra Padre Cristobal de Valencia*, AGN, Ramo de Inquisición, vol. 472, exp. 5, f. 11v–13r; *Presentación de capitulos y cargas en contra del padre Cristobal de Valencia hecha por los indios del pueblo de Hocaba*, AGN, Ramo de Inquisición, vol. 472, exp. 5, f. 13v–17r; and *Petición del cacique y oficiales del pueblo de Xochel en contra de su cura Padre Cristobal de Valencia*, AGN, Ramo de Inquisición, vol. 472, exp. 5, f. 17r–32r.

7. According to canon law and tradition, the local bishop had to warn and admonish parish priests who had concubines or engaged in illicit sex three times before they removed them from office. For specific examples of Spanish custom and law concerning the sexual immorality of clergymen, see the statutes in the *Siete Partidas*. See *Las Siete Partidas: Vol. 1, The Medieval Church: The World of Clerics and Laymen*, trans. Samiel Parsons Scott and ed. Robert I. Burns, S.J., 100–103 (University of Pennsylvania Press, 2001). Also see the decrees concerning sexual offenses, clerical celibacy and misconduct in the Council of Trent's proceedings in D. Ignacio López de Ayala, *El dacrosanto y ecuménico Concilio de Trento traducida al idioma castellano* (Librería de Garnier Hermanos, Méjico, 1855). For the case of New Spain (Mexico), see Mariano Galván Rivera, *Concilio III provincial mexicano celebrado en México el año de 1585*, Eugenio Mallefert y Compañia, Editores (México, 1859). For specific Yucatecan examples of these ecclesiastical regulations, see *Synodo diocesano celebrado por su señoria ilustrisima el Dr. Juan Gomez de Parada*, 1721, AGI, Audiencia de México, 1030. Also see *Synodo diocesano celebrado en el año de 1737 en el obispado de Yucatán*, 1737, AGI, Audiencia de México, 3168. This laxity in dealing with the sexual offenses of the clergy was not an aberration in the New World; even in Europe before the reforms of the Council of Trent, the church turned a blind eye to all but the most open and scandalous violations of the vows of celibacy. For the best and most complete study of the concepts of sex and sexuality and the dilemma between sexual practices and church doctrine, see Asunción Lavrin, "Sexuality in Colonial Mexico: a Church Dilemma," in *Sexuality and Marriage in Colonial Latin America*, ed. Asunción Lavrin, 47–95 (Lincoln: University of Nebraska Press, 1989). For a good description of the European reality, see Merry E. Weisner-Hanks, *Christianity and Sexuality*

in the Early Modern World: Regulating Desire, Reforming Practice (Oxford: Routledge Press, 2000), 118–21. For other discussions of the historical trajectory of Christian intolerance and laxity, see Christie Davies, "Sexual Taboos and Social Boundaries," *American Journal of Sociology* 87, no. 5 (March 1982): 1032–63.

8. To date the most complete discussion of the phenomenon of the solicitation of sex in the confessional is found in Stephen Haliczer, *Sexuality in the Confessional: A Sacrament Profaned* (New York: Oxford University Press, 1996). Also see Jorge René González M., "Clérigos solicitantes, perversos de la confesión," in *De la santidad a la perversión: o de porqué no se cumplía la ley de Dios en la sociedad novohispana*, Edición de Sergio Ortega (México: Grijalbo, 1986), 239–52. For a study of the types of punishments and censures given to solicitantes, see Solange Alberro, "El discurso inquisitorial sobre los delitos de bigamia, poligamia y de solicitación," in Solange Alberro et al., *Seis ensayos sobre el discurso colonial relativo a la comunidad doméstica: matrimonio, familia y sexualidad a través de los cronistas del siglo XVI, el Nuevo Testamento y el Santo Oficio de la Inquisición* (México: Departamento de Investigaciones Históricas, INAH, Cuadernos de trabajo, 35, 1980), 215–26.

9. *Repuesta y Confession del Padre Cristobal de Valencia a las cargas hechas contra el por los Mayas del pueblo de Hocaba y su partido*, 1 de octubre, 1609, AGN, Ramo de Inquisición, vol. 472, exp. 5, f. 117r–34r.

10. For an excellent analysis of Renaissance sex and sexuality see, Guido Ruggerio, *The Boundaries of Eros: Sex Crime and Sexuality in Renaissance Venice* (Oxford: Oxford University Press, 1985). Also see Ruggerio, *Binding Passions: Tales of Magic, Marriage, and Power at the end of the Renaissance* (Oxford: Oxford University Press, 1993).

11. See Matthew Restall and John Chuchiak, "The Friar and the Mayas: Fr. Diego de Landa's *Relación de las Cosas de Yucatán*," unpublished translation and manuscript, 35, or see Fr. Diego de Landa, *Yucatan Before and After the Conquest*, ed. and trans. William Gates (Dover Publications), 52.

12. Cogolludo remarks that the Mayas had harsh punishments of death for adulterers and rapists. He stated, "They punish vices with rigor . . . The man or woman who commits adultery received the death penalty by shooting them with arrows . . . thus they abhorred this sin and they punished even noble and principal persons." Fr. Diego López Cogolludo, *Los tres siglos de la dominación española en yucatan o historia de esta provincia*, tomo I and II, Akademische Druck-u. Verlagsanstalt, Graz, Austria, 1971, tomo I, 331.

13. Landa, *Yucatan Before and After the Conquest*, 54–55.

14. Ibid.

15. Ibid.

16. See Munro Edmonson, *Heaven Born Mérida And Its Destiny: The Book of Chilam Balam of Chumayel* (Austin: University of Texas Press, 1986), 109–10.

17. Ibid., 146.

18. Ibid., 148.

19. Cogolludo, *Historia de Yucatán*, Tomo 1, 331.

20. The crown and church early on excluded the Indians from the jurisdiction of the Holy Office of the Inquisition and placed them under the jurisdiction of the episcopal courts of the *Provisorato de Indios*. See Richard E. Greenleaf, "The Inquisition and the Indians of New Spain: A Study in Jurisdictional Confusion," *The Americas* 22 (1965): 138–66. For a complete study of the *Provisorato de Indios* in the diocese of Yucatan, see John F. Chuchiak, "The Indian Inquisition and the Extirpation of Idolatry: The Process of Punishment in the Provisorato de Indios of the Diocese of Yucatan, 1563–1821" (PhD diss., Tulane University, 2000).

21. See *Avisos del muy illustre y reverendisimo señor Don Fray Francisco de Toral, obispo de Yucatán, para los padres curas y vicarios de este obispado*, sf, AGI, Audiencia de México, 369, 12 folios.

22. *Instrucción que dio el Juez Provisor y Vicario General de la Provincia de Yucatán para los curas de almas y sus tenientes*, 19 de julio, 1765, Archivo Histórico del Arzobispado de Yucatán (AHAY), Asuntos Terminados, 5 folios. Earlier episcopal synods also focused on specific clerical preoccupations over Maya fornication, bestiality and other "crimes against nature" such as sodomy (*el pecado nefando*). See the

documents of the Synod of 1722, especially, *Formula del edicto de pecados publicos que todos los domingos primeros de Quaresma se ha de publicar por los Curas y Vicarios de este obispado*, 1722, AGI, Audiencia de México, 1040, f. 230r–232v.

23. Fr. Bernardo de Lizana, *Devocionario de nuestra señora de Izamal y conquista espiritual de Yucatán*, ed. René Acuña (Mexico, UNAM, 1995), 67.

24. Ibid., 68.

25. Cogolludo, *Historia de Yucatán*, tomo I, 93. Here Cogolludo gives us the complete set of ordenanzas of Tómas López.

26. Ibid., 93.

27. Ibid.

28. Landa, *Yucatan Before and After the Conquest*, 46.

29. *Testimonio de Juan Hernandez, vecino de Mérida en el proceso contra pecados nefandos*, 15 de enero, 1563, AGI, Justicia, 248, 3 folios.

30. Louise Burkhart, *The Slippery Earth: Nahua-Christian Moral Dialogue in Sixteenth-Century Mexico* (Tucson: University of Arizona Press, 1989), 25.

31. W. C. Brownlee, *The Doctrinal Decrees and Canons of the Council of Trent*, trans. from the first edition printed in Rome in 1564 (New York: Charles K. Moore, 1842), 89, and cited in Burkhart, *The Slippery Earth*, 152.

32. Burkhart, *The Slippery Earth*, 153.

33. See Pete Sigal, *From Moon Goddesses to Virgins: The Colonization of Yucatecan Maya Sexual Desire* (Austin: University of Texas Press, 2000), 94–128. Also see Burkhart, *The Slippery Earth*, 154.

34. For a complete discussion of Maya priesthood and the colonial survival of traditional Maya religious practices, see John F. Chuchiak, "Pre-Conquest *Ah Kinob* in a Colonial World: The Extirpation of Idolatry and the Survival of the Maya Priesthood in Colonial Yucatán, 1563–1697," in *Maya Survivalism: Acta Mesoamericana*, vol. 12, ed. Ueli Hostettler and Matthew Restall, 135–60 (Germany: Markt Schwaben, Verlag A. Saurwein, 2001). For specific information on the ritual celibacy of the Maya priesthood, see Sigal, *From Moon Goddesses to Virgins*, 18–21.

35. Catholic attempts at controlling and reshaping Maya sexual practices have recently been dealt with in a new book by Pete Sigal, *From Moon Goddesses to Virgins*. Moreover, in this task, Catholic confession manuals were useful tools for the evangelization of the indigenous people of Mesoamerica. In the pages and translations of these confession manuals, the clergy attempted to "conquer," "reform," and reshape indigenous conceptions of sex, sexuality, eroticism, and acceptable moral behavior. Several recent studies have analyzed these confession manuals in order to understand more about both colonial Catholic and indigenous sexual practices and sexual morality. For a few examples, see Luis Arias González and Agustín Vivas Moreno, "Los manuales de confesión para indígenas del siglo XVI: hacia un nuevo modelo de formación de la conciencia," *Estudios de Historia Moderna* 10 and 11 (1992/1993): 245–59. Their analysis offers a close examination of these confession manuals, which they argue reveal much about the nature of the interaction of priests and indigenous peoples and the mind sets of both groups. For another example of the use of confession and confession manuals to dominate and change indigenous conceptions of eroticism and sexuality, see Sylvia Marcos, "Missionary Activity in Latin America: Confession Manuals and Indigenous Eroticism," in *Religious Transformations and Socio-political Change: Eastern Europe and Latin America*, ed. Luther Martin, 237–53 (New York: Mouton de Gruyter, 1993). Similarly, for the now classical study of the use of the sacrament of confession as a form of domination and social control, see Serge Gruzinski, "Individualization and Acculturation: Confession among the Nahuas of Mexico from the Sixteenth to the Eighteenth Century," in Lavrin, *Sexuality and Marriage in Colonial Latin America*, 96–117. Gruzinski describes the sacrament of Christian confession of sin as a form of ideological control and subjugation. Another similar interpretation of the use of the confessional as a tool of colonial domination is found in Jorge Klor de Alva, "Sin and Confession among the Colonial Nahuas: The Confessional as a Tool for Domination," in *Memorias de la reunión de historiadores mexicanos y norteamericanos*, 7th. ed., Oaxaca, Mexico, 1985 (México:

Universidad Nacional Autónoma de México, 1992), vol. 1, 91–101. Klor de Alva also portrays the act of Christian confession as a means of social control. He was one of the first to suggest that questions posed in Nahuatl-language confessionals hold vital information about indigenous sexuality and worldviews.

36. The complete title of the *Confessionario* is illustrative of the early clergy's goals in controlling and dominating Yucatec Maya sexual practices: *Confessionario breve, para confesar a los indios, ponense las preguntas ordinarias en la lengua y la de Castilla, segun las culpas que acostumbran cometer y en que ordinariamente pecan y se les pregunta*, printed seventeenth-century confession manual in the Yucatec Maya language, Private Collection, Mérida, Yucatan, Mexico.

37. These questions and others related to confessing sexual sins are found in *Confessionario Breve para confesar a los indios*, 17th Century, f. 234v–35v.

38. For various colonial definitions of the word keban see *Calepino de Motul: Diccionario Maya-Español*, vol. 1 (Mexico: UNAM), 417–18.

39. See Louise Burkhart, *The Slippery Earth*, 23.

40. *Calepino de Motul*, vol. 1, 80.

41. Quoted from Pete Sigal, *Moon Goddesses to Virgins*, 90. The same document and incident was also discussed by Matthew Restall, *The Maya World: Yucatec Culture and Society, 1550–1850*, (Stanford: Stanford University Press, 1997), 144. Restall also discussed the same document in "He Wished it in Vain: Subordination and Resistance Among Maya Women in Post-Conquest Yucatan," in *Ethnohistory* 42, no. 4: 577–94. The original can be found in the *Documentos de Tabí*, held in the LAL of Tulane University.

42. Several instances of Maya women using the Spanish system to protect themselves from Maya noblemen and Spaniards are found in various documents submitted by the bishop of Yucatan against the sexual misconduct of parish priests and Franciscan friars. See especially *Informaciones del Obispo de Yucatán contra los abusos de algunos frailes y clerigos del obispado*, 1702, AGI, Audiencia de Mexico, 1035.

43. Stephen Haliczer's book, *Sexuality in the Confessional*, remains one of the best treatments on the crime of solicitation.

44. *Las Siete Partidas*, vol 1.

45. Ibid.

46. For several of the more important edicts of the Holy Office in Mexico against the crime of solicitation, see *Edicto de fe de los Inquisidores de Mexico contra el crimen de la solicitación*, 30 de Abril, 1620, AGN, Edictos, vol. 1; *Edicto de fe de los Inquisidores de Mexico contra los solicitantes*, 13 de Mayo, 1624, AGN, Edictos, vol. III, f. 45–46; *Edicto de fe de los Inquisidores de Mexico contra los solicitantes*, 13 de Mayo, 1651, AGN, Indiferente General. For a study of these edicts and the crime of solicitation, see Jorge René González Marmolejo, "El delito de solicitación en los edictos del tribunal del Santo Oficio, 1576–1819," in Solange Alberro et al., *Seis ensayos sobre el discursos*, 169–211.

47. Definition of solicitation in *The Catholic Encyclopedia*, 1911. However, the definition and scope of the crime of solicitation was often confused by the bishops and inquisitors who investigated these crimes. For several instances where commissaries of the Inquisition and bishops inquired and sought information concerning the definition and methods to define the actual crime of solicitation, see *Carta de Fr. Diego de Landa, Obispo de Yucatán. Consultando sobre casos de solicitacion y averiguando sobre su jurisdicción*, 1578, AGN, Ramo de Inquisición, vol. 90, exp. 8, 3 folios. Also see *Carta con dudas del Maestro Alonso Martin Bermejo, Comisario del Santo Oficio en Yucatán sobre confesores solicitantes*, 1580, vol. 85, cxp. 8, 2 folios.

48. In terms of the surviving documents concerning the crime of solicitation committed by Yucatecan clergy, it appears that the term solicitation was used most often in references to soliciting sex from a parishioner within the priest's private chambers or the sacristy. Many of the cases involved the solicitation of sex while engaged in confessing the women and men in these places. See the chart in Table 5.1 for descriptions of specific cases under study. Many of the major cases against priests and friars who solicited sex in the confessional can be found in the following archives: AGN, Ramo de Inquisición, vols. 35, 69, 85, 90, 122,

123, 249, 281, 288, 295, 303, 337, 926, 935, 954, 988, 1046, 1250, 1284, 1369, 1373, 1380, 1468; also many documents relating to solicitantes in Yucatan are found in AGI, Audiencia de México, 1030–36, 3063, 3068; similar documents relating to Inquisition trials and proceedings are found in AHN, Inquisición, 1735; AHN, Competencias.

49. All parish priests and confessors had to have an explicit license from their bishop in order to conduct and hear confessions. In the diocese of Yucatan, it took a special license to be able to confess both women and men. Each cleric or priest was examined and periodically they were inspected during pastoral visitations in order to ensure that they did not abuse the sacrament of penance and solicit sex in the confessional. During the pastoral visitations to the province, the Yucatecan bishops issued a series of questions to the Maya town officials and principal residents of each town. The most important questions focused on the lifestyle and abuses of the clergy. The bishops wanted to know if "the Indians know of or have heard that the priests and their assistants have women or have engaged in illicit relations with them publicly or secretly." See *Interrogatorio por el cual deben ser examinados los sugetos mas dignos de cada pueblo sobre las conductas y operaciones de sus cura de alma*, in AHAY, Visitas Pastorales, vol. 1, exp. 4, Visita Pastoral al pueblo de Oxkutzcab, 1782, f. 13r–15v. The answers to all of these thirty questions are then recorded. Most often the Maya hid the sexual crimes of their clergy, but in a few instances they revealed their priest's sexual indiscretions.

50. For other excellent studies that examine the relationship between indigenous people and their parish priests and the inherent conflicts that arose between them, see William B. Taylor, *Magistrates of the Sacred: Priests and Parishioners in Eighteenth-Century Mexico* (Stanford: Stanford University Press, 1996). Also see Robert Haskett, "Not a Pastor, but a Wolf: Indigenous-Clergy Relations in Early Cuernavaca and Taxco," *The Americas* 50, no. 3 (Jan. 1994): 293–36.

51. *Expediente de las quejas de los indios del pueblo de Becal contra su cura Br. Bernardo Echiverria*, 1768, AGI, Mexico, 3053, 63 folios.

52. Matthew Restall was one of the first to note that this petition served as a form of revenge against what the Mayas perceived as the hypocritically punitive reaction of Spanish priests to Maya sexual activity. (Restall, *Maya World*, 161). Restall argues that the issue was a matter of control, for the "Maya view priests as outsiders without the authority or status to pass judgment and demand punishment over this aspect of Maya life." However, I believe at the heart of this is the fact that the Mayas in this petition did not challenge the priests' authority, but instead they used these accusations to get back at the entire Spanish system of sexual morality that had attempted to "conquer" Maya sexuality and encompass it within the bounds of the more restrictive sexual morality of Spanish Catholicism. Restall did note that the "public sexual behavior" alleged was a potent weapon. Thus, based on Spanish Catholic fears of "public scandal" these were the types of charges that would warrant the removal of a priest. For more detailed discussions of the removal of priests for solicitation, see Jorge René González, "Clérigos solicitantes, perversos de la confesión," in *De la santidad a la perversión*, 239–52.

53. The original document can be found in AGN, Ramo de Inquisición, 1046. This fascinating document has been examined and analyzed previously by Matthew Restall (1997), and Peter Sigal (2001). Although exceptionally vivid in its detail and the quality of its sarcastic prose, this Maya petition is not alone. Other similar petitions also exist in the archives (See AGI, Escribanía de Camara, 313B, 317; also see AGN, Ramo de Inquisición, vol. 69, f. 472, and others).

54. Sigal, *Moon Goddesses to Virgins*, 65.

55. Restall notes the Inquisition official's horror and his notations in reaction against the petition. Restall, *Maya World*, 141–42. The original is found in AGN, Ramo de Inquisición, 1187, exp.2, f. 59–61.

56. See AHAY, Visitas Pastorales, vol. 1.

57. See Sigal, *Moon Goddesses to Virgins*, 75–76. The original Maya petition is found in AGN, Ramo de Inquisición, vol. 69.

58. Andrés Mexía was partially exonerated when he proved to the Inquisitors that many of the Mayas who declared against him were the

same ones he had punished for idolatry and other "*faltas de doctrina.*" Also, he stated that the Mayas denounced him under the inducement and sinister plot of their local Spanish encomendero who Mexía had punished for his own sexual indiscretions with two local Maya women. Mexía declared in his self defense, "All that they said against me was done out of the sinister inducement of their encomendero who wishes me ill because I conducted a trial against him for living in concubinage in the said town with two married Indian women and for this reason he has had animosity and he has openly stated that he would do anything in his power to harm me." See Response to charge number 46 in *Respuestas del clerigo Andrés Mexía contra los cargos que le hicieron los indios de su partido*, 1578, AGN, Ramo de Inquisición, vol. 69, exp. 5, f. 191v.

59. *Respuestas del clerigo Andres Mexía*, 1578, AGN, Ramo de Inquisición, vol. 69, exp. 5, f. 192r.

60. Taken from Restall, *Maya World*, 164. The original Maya document can be found in the Inquisition trial against Andrés Mexía. See AGN, Inquisition, vol. 69, exp. 5.

61. See *Testimonio y declaración de Maria Tun, india del pueblo de Peto contra su cura Andrés Mexía*, 1589, AGN, Ramo de Inquisición, vol. 69, exp. 5, f. 318r–19r; also see *Testimonio y declaración de Maria Col, india del pueblo de Peto contra su cura Andrés Mexía*, 1589, AGN, Ramo de Inquisición, vol. 69, exp. 5, f. 319r–20r; also *Testimonio y declaración de Mencia Puc, india del pueblo de Peto contra su cura Andrés Mexía*, 1589, AGN, Ramo de Inquisición, vol. 69, exp. 5, f. 320r–21r. Other testimonies and denunciations are found in the same volume, AGN, Inquisition, vol. 69, exp. 5, f. 268–78.

62. See *Peticion de Andrés Mexía beneficiado de Calamud y Peto en que oppone de enemistad contra los indios que le han informado contra el delicto de solicitud y presenta recaudos como ya son amigos*, 1589, AGN, Ramo de Inquisición, vol. 69, exp. 5, f. 273r–274v.

63. *Sentencia y votos hecho por los inquisidores de Mexico contra el clerigo presbitero Andres Mexia por el crimen de solicitacion a sus hijas de confession*, 13 de julio, 1590, AGN, Ramo de Inquisición, vol. 69, exp. 5, f. 325r.

64. *Carta del Provincial del orden de San Francisco,*

Fr. Alonso de Rio Frio dando cuenta de unas peticiones de algunas indios en contra de Fr. Pedro de Vergara por el delito de solicitación, AGN, Ramo de Inquisición, vol. 249, exp. 1, 3 folios.

65. *Declaracion de Ana Kuk, en contra de Fr. Pedro Vergara por el crimen de Solicitacion*, 16 de noviembre, 1598, AGN, Ramo de Inquisición, vol. 249, exp. 1, f. 12.

66. *Declaracion de Beatriz Dzib, en contra de Fr. Pedro Vergara por el crimen de Solicitacion*, 16 de noviembre, 1598, AGN, Ramo de Inquisición, vol. 249, exp. 1.

67. *Declaracion de Maria Cocom, en contra de Fr. Pedro Vergara por el crimen de Solicitacion*, 16 de noviembre, 1598, AGN, Ramo de Inquisición, vol. 249, exp. 1.

68. *Carta del provincial del orden de San Francisco en Yucatán sobre el caso de solicitación en contra de Fr. Pedro de Vergara*, 1598, AGN, Ramo de Inquisición, vol. 249, exp. 1.

69. *Carta de Fr. Juan de Santa Maria, guardian del convento de Campeche en contra Fr. Pedro de Vergara y sus abusos de los indios*, 14 de marzo, 1599, AGN, Ramo de Inquisición, vol. 249, exp. 1.

70. *Carta de Fr. Alonso de Rio Frio contra Fr. Pedro de Vergara escrita a los Señores Inquisidores de Mexico*, 16 de noviembre, 1599, AGN, Ramo de Inquisición, vol. 249, exp. 1, f. 26.

71. *Carta del visitador Fr. Miguel López acerca del caso de Fr. Pedro de Vergara con informacion sobre el odio que le tienen los indios que han declarado contra el en el caso de solicitación*, 20 de octubre, 1600, AGN, Ramo de Inquisición, vol. 249, exp. 1.

72. *Carta de Fr. Miguel López*, 20 de octubre, 1600, AGN, Ramo de Inquisición, vol. 249, exp. 1. Interestingly, this is the last document in the Inquisition trial against him. There is no record of any punishment administered. No doubt the Inquisitors believed that the Mayas had used falsified testimonies to remove their priest. Moreover, Fr. Pedro de Vergara would go on to serve in the Franciscan missions of the Sierra where he appeared around 1603.

73. *Declaración y testimonio hecho por Pablo Chan, indio natural del pueblo de Hoctun en contra de su cura Cristobal de Valencia*, Julio

1609, AGN, Ramo de Inquisición, vol. 472, exp. 5, 4 folios.

74. *Confesión del clerigo Cristóbal de Valencia con sus respuestas a los cargos impuestos contra el por los indios de su partido,* AGN, Ramo de Inquisición, vol. 472, exp. 5, 14 folios.

75. *Carta del obispo de Yucatan sobre sus relaciones con el gobernador,* 10 de Octubre, 1606, AGI, Audiencia de México, vol. 369, 4 folios.

76. See *Proceso del Santo Oficio contra el Br. Don Antonio Ramon de la Cueva, cura interino que fue del partido de Peto, por solicitante,* 1730, AGN, Ramo de Inquisición, vol. 1046, exp. 4, f. 107–26.

77. *Carta del comisario del Santo Oficio, Br. Nicolas Leyton, con informacion sobre la solicitacion ad turpia de unas indias en la confession por Padre Don Antonio Ramon de la Cueva, cura interino de Peto,* 21 de marzo, 1730, AGN, Ramo de Inquisición, vol. 1046, exp. 4, f. 108r–09r.

78. *Carta del comisario del Santo Oficio, Br. Nicolas Leyton, con informacion sobre otra delito de solicitación,* 29 de Marzo, 1730, AGN, Ramo de Inquisición, vol. 1046, exp. 4, f. 112r–13r.

79. *Peticion en Lengua Yucateca contra el cura Don Antonio hecho por el Maestro de Capilla del pueblo de San Francisco de Uman,* 1781, AGI, Audiencia de México, vol. 3064, 10 folios.

80. *Peticion en lengua Yucateca contra el Cura Don Luis Antonio de Echazarreta,* 1781, AGI, Audiencia de México, vol. 3064, 10 folios.

81. See various denunciations against Padre Echazarreta in AGI, Audiencia de México, 3064.

82. *Declaracion y testimonio de Francisca Cauiche en contra el cura de Uman,* 26 de abril, 1781, AGI, Audiencia de México, vol. 3064, 4 folios.

83. *Petición y denuncia hecha por Felix Cocom, maestro de capilla del pueblo de Uman contra su cura por abuses que le habia hecho,* 1781, AGI, Audiencia de México, vol. 3064, 4 folios.

84. *Declaración de Don Andres Tinal, Cacique del pueblo de Tahuman contra su cura,* 1781, AGI, Audiencia de México, vol. 3064, 4 folios; also see *Carta y petición del cacique y oficiales indios del pueblo de Uman con unas quejas contra su cura,* 1781, AGI, Audiencia de México, vol. 3064, 6 folios.

85. *Peticion en Lengua Yucateca contra el cura Don Antonio hecho por el Maestro de Capilla del pueblo de San Francisco de Uman, Felix Cocom,* 1781, AGI, Audiencia de México, vol. 3064, 10 folios.

86. *Petición y denuncia hecha por Felix Cocom, maestro de capilla del pueblo de Uman contra su cura por abuses que le habia hecho,* 1781, AGI, Audiencia de México, vol. 3064, 4 folios.

87. *Declaración de Don Ignacio Quintal, español, sobre los abusos del cura de Uman,* 1781, AGI, Audiencia de México, vol. 3064, 4 folios.

88. Both Francisca Cauich and Manuela Pacheco, a Spanish woman, complained that the root causes of their troubles with their husbands came from their having been raped and violated by the priest. See *Carta y petición del cacique y oficiales indios del pueblo de Uman con unas quejas contra su cura,* 1781, AGI, Audiencia de México, vol. 3064, 6 folios.

89. See the official complaints of the cacique don Andres Tinal and the other town officials of Uman, *Petición en lengua Yucateca con traducción de las quejas del cacique y cabildo del pueblo de Uman contra los abusos de su cura interino,* 1780, AGI, Audiencia de México, vol. 3064, 4 folios. Specific instructions and official ecclesiastical quotas were set to regulate the clergy's use of Maya labor. A table of fees, called the *arancel,* existed to regulate these economic interchanges. For an example of these regulations and other laws prohibiting clerical exactions in the province of Yucatan, see *Arancel de lo que cada indio debe contribuir para el sustento de su cura en el discurso del año,* 1737, AGI, Audiencia de México, vol. 3168; also see *Arancel para los derechos que se deben llevar en este curato y vicaria de Campeche,* 1763, Archivo Histórico del Arzobispado de Yucatán, (AHAY), Asuntos Terminados, box #1, exp. 14. For a detailed examination of the abuses and exploitation of the Mayas both by legal and illegal means, see John F. Chuchiak, "Ca numiae, lay u cal caxtlan patan lae: El tributo colonial y la nutrición de los Mayas, 1542–1812: Un estudio sobre los efectos de la conquista y el colonialismo en los Mayas de Yucatán," in *Iglesia y sociedad en América Latina colonia* (Centro Coordinador y Difusor de Estudios Latinoamericanos, Universidad Nacional Autónoma de México, 1995), 117–225.

90. It is interesting to note that a large number

of priests and friars denounced for solicitation had previously punished their accusers for serious infractions of Catholic law such as witchcraft, idolatry, and public drunkenness. See Chuchiak, "The Indian Inquisition and the Extirpation of Idolatry," 512, n. 119.

91. The complicity of many Maya parishioners in the sexual misconduct of the clergy is evident during many of the Inquisition and episcopal courts' trials of sexual misconduct. For one example, see *Informacion del Obispo de Yucatan sobre los excesos de religiosos saliendose de noche vestidos de seglares y los escandalos públicos y concubinatos que tienen*, AGI, Audiencia de México, vol. 1035, 42 folios.

92. *Carta del Dr. Don Gaspar Joseph Rodriguez Vizario, Clerigo Presbitero del Obispado de Yucatán sobre los beneficios de la Provincia y su mala conducta*, 1700, AGI, Audiencia de México, Legajo 312, 7 folios.

93. Accusations of sexual abuse by the clergy continued long into the early national period. The section of the National Archives of Mexico that contains material confiscated from the church archives (*Bienes Nacionales, Bienes Nacionalizadas*) shows that as late as the middle of the nineteenth century parish priests were accused of abuse and sexual misconduct by the Mayas.

PART THREE

BELIEVING IN MIRACLES

But, whoever it was, it was considered a miracle, as it truly turned out to be. And not only did the Spaniards see him [Santiago], but the Indians felt the weight of his attack upon their squadrons, which he seemed to dazzle and render stupid.

—Francisco López de Gómara, 1552

There is also another thing from which I took heart and was encouraged to write your miracles in the Nahuatl language; it is what your beloved servant Saint Bonaventure says: that the great, marvelous, exalted miracles of our Lord God are to be written in a variety of languages so that all different peoples on earth will see and marvel at them, . . .

—Luis Laso de la Vega, 1649

Once the consummate Virgin, the heavenly Lady of Guadalupe, was in her precious home, she worked many and innumerable miracles, with which she befriended the local people and the Spaniards, . . .

—Luis Laso de la Vega, 1649

The redeemer of the world no longer wants miracles to be worked because they are not necessary, because our holy faith is so well established by so many thousands of miracles as we have in the Old and New Testaments.

—fray Juan de Zumárraga, d. 1548

For the greater part of the colonial era, Mexico City was the largest, most populous, and wealthiest urban capital in North America. The city center, or *traza*, was *the* place to be, with the grandest houses, churches, and political and judicial edifices clustered around the square. Stores, markets, and vendors of all sorts set up shop in their midst to capitalize on the traffic as people went about their business.

Ideally, only Spaniards lived in or near the traza; native peoples and other ethnic and racial groups were consigned to its outer margins. But Spaniards needed domestic help and laborers for personal and official projects. As a result, the heart of the metropolis was inhabited by a composite of all of New Spain's societies.

The city's churches were also a major attraction for the citizenry, and they served as their own centers within the hub, with fountains supplying locals with fresh water and bells tolling the time of day and warning of important news. The churches were sanctuaries as well as the source of the city's social services. Parish communities were racially eclectic, and one church might have several *cofradías* (confraternities) made up of blacks, natives, and Spaniards, respectively.

Parishioners knew one another, attended mass together, and celebrated the major festival days as best they could. Complete understanding of the complexities of Catholic theology may not have been universal in the parish, or the city, for that matter. But most of Mexico City's residents cared deeply about the church as they knew it and found spiritual comfort in the patronage of favorite saints or religious icons.

Life in the capital was not easy, for it was often inundated by floods and its citizens suffered the inexorable seasons of epidemic disease. Poverty was endemic for many of the capital's ordinary citizens. Yet in the course of the most mundane circumstance, marvelous things occurred, and miracles were among the most wondrous. Miracles were the work of God, and they served to enhance or renew one's faith in the Almighty. They also attenuated profound despair or grief in the face of one's powerlessness or sense of inevitable loss.

Martha Few's "'Our Lord Entered His Body': Miraculous Healing and Children's Bodies," tells of the faith of Mexico City's ordinary citizens and their belief in the powerful attributes of their holy images. We also learn of dreaded childhood conditions, the deaths of children, and then blessed recoveries. Priests, too, witnessed these miraculous events, which most often were cause for the ringing of church bells across the city and generalized celebration. Jeanette Peterson turns our attention to the cult of the Virgin of Guadalupe and early seventeenth-century graphic representations exulting her extraordinary abilities. In "Canonizing a Cult: A Wonder-Working Guadalupe in the Seventeenth Century," Peterson examines both a painting and an engraving dating to the early 1700s that became visual expressions of a legend long (apparently) in the making. She notes too that more than likely these manifestations went hand-in-hand with specific counterreformation campaigns to promote interest in the saints and supernatural happenings.

NOTES

Epigraph citations, in order of appearance, are as follows: Francisco López de Gómara, *Cortés: The Life of the Conqueror by His Secretary*, ed. and trans. Lesley Byrd Simpson, 47 (Berkeley: University of California Press, 1964); Luis Laso de la Vega, *The Story of Guadalupe: Luis Laso de la Vega's Huei tlamahuiçoltica of 1649*, ed. and trans. Lisa Sousa, Stafford Poole, and James Lockhart, 57 (Stanford and Los Angeles: Stanford University Press and UCLA Latin American Center Publications, 1998); Fray Juan de Zumárraga, *Regla cristiana breve*, edición crítica y estudio preliminario por Ildefonso Adeva, Prólogo Josep-Ignasi Saranyana (Pamplona: Ediciones Eunate, 1994), 36.

CHAPTER SIX

"Our Lord Entered His Body"

Miraculous Healing and Children's Bodies in New Spain

MARTHA FEW

In the aftermath of Columbus's first voyage to the Americas, disease played a central role in shaping colonial encounters between indigenous and European peoples. While much recent research has addressed the role of epidemic disease and its devastating effects on native peoples, more work needs to be done on analyzing the role of illness and the illnesses experienced in the daily lives of European, African, indigenous, and mixed-race peoples in colonial society.[1] This work begins to address this gap by looking at an especially poignant aspect of illness in daily life—sick and dying children. Though no concrete numbers exist for children's mortality rates in New Spain, child sickness and death most likely formed an integral part of family and community life in Latin America throughout the colonial period.[2]

This essay analyzes family and community responses to sick children through miraculous healing accounts, where children on the brink of death became healed through what those involved described as divine intervention. Such accounts contain detailed descriptions of children's illnesses, along with family and community healing strategies taken over the course of the sickness. Parents, relatives, neighbors, priests, and colonial officials witnessed the miraculous healing events, highlighting the public nature of both illness and healing in colonial society. The miraculous healing of a sick child and even, in some cases, the child's resurrection from death, became occasions for community celebrations, setting off fireworks, and the pealing of church bells.

Images of children's bodies and their transformation formed a central focus of miraculous healing accounts, and they provide evidence for multiple meanings of embodiment in New Spain.[3] Children who returned from the brink of death had flexible and open bodies, capable of being entered by divine beings, and in cases of miraculous resurrection, the ability to transform from the cold rigidity of a corpse back into a living body. After recovering, the children often described crossing the boundary between the earthly and heavenly worlds to communicate with divine beings such as the Virgin Mary, God, Jesus, and various saints. Miraculous healing accounts not only highlight bodily transformations, but also the children's changed status in the aftermath of the illness, reshaped and reconstructed through divine power, in a sense reborn as a wonder or marvel in community life. Don Domingo de San Antón Muñón Chimalpahin Quauhtlehuanitzin, a Nahua historian writing in Mexico City in the seventeenth century, captured the essence of this process when he wrote: "And on the fourteenth of December of the year 1600, Thursday, San Diego brought a child back to life again. The child who was revived was also greatly marveled over as well."[4]

Descriptions of the miraculous healing of children can be found across New Spain in the colonial period, in the capital cities of Santiago de Guatemala and Mexico City, in regional towns such as Ciudad Real de Chiapas, as well as in smaller rural settlements such as Esquipulas and Ciudad Vieja. The historical sources I use in this essay come from a range of colonial era sources, including contemporary histories, a confiscated devotional book dedicated to the healing shrine of the Black Christ of Esquipulas, Inquisition testimonies, and indigenous language annals. The range of colonial documents that contain miraculous healing

accounts focused on children suggests that not only did the Catholic church control such accounts through formal, institutional channels, but that stories of seemingly incurable children miraculously returned to health occupied an important part of local discourses and activities in daily life.

Miraculous healing accounts offer descriptions of illness experiences and provide evidence about the strategies that family members, neighbors, and religious officials used in seeking cures. These strategies provide glimpses of popular ideas about children, illness, and their bodies and how their families and religious officials viewed the children after they healed. And while men and women in the local community considered the healed children exceptional and even miraculous, the accounts also offer evidence of broader understandings, expectations, and fears of childhood illness and hopes for survival in colonial society.

Familial and Community Responses to Child Sickness and Death

Miraculous healing events involving children took place in many kinds of social spaces in colonial society. These included distant healing shrines, such as the shrine of Nuestro Señor de Esquipulas, located east of Guatemala's capital city of Santiago (now Antigua). Local healing shrines, such as the Franciscan convent in Santiago de Guatemala, also provided images and items associated with healing, including the oil from the lamp of the image of Nuestra Señora de Alcántara.[5] Other less formal spaces in colonial society, however, also became sites for the miraculous healing of children, including homes, where parents and family members cared for the sick and elderly, and water wells, where children sometimes fell and lay injured or dying while onlookers tried to rescue them. All of these were public spaces, where parents, family members, and relatives kept watch over sick and dying children, medical doctors and curanderos visited in attempts to heal the sick child, priests came to administer the last rites, and families prayed for divine intervention.

When children became sick, parents did not immediately search for a miraculous cure and ask for divine intervention. Instead, family members waited until the illness continued for a period of months or years, caused particularly painful or "monstrous" symptoms or bodily changes, or reached the point where the child was on the verge of death. Many of the miraculous healing accounts highlight the central role of the mother in searching for a cure, especially her enduring devotion to caring for the sick or injured child, and her decision to elicit the help of a priest, or to ask for a saint, the Virgin, or Christ to intervene on behalf of her child.

The following undated miraculous healing account highlights the role of the mother in the search for a miraculous cure. It describes a two-year-old boy, the only child of Estefanía Vásquez de Jaén and Andrés de Espinoza Moreira, who lay dying "by slowly wasting away."[6] The parents consulted both licensed physicians and popular healers, but no one could cure the boy. The boy would not breast feed, nor could he open his eyes, and "everyone began to think he would die." At the point where the child "was almost dead and without a pulse," the

mother decided to act. The mother, at the side of the sick child's bed, made a promise that if the child lived through the night, at dawn she would take him to the chapel of Our Lady of Alcántara in the church of Nuestro Señor de San Francisco, located in the barrio of San Francisco on the near southeast side of Santiago de Guatemala.

In Santiago, Our Lady of Alcántara first became associated with miraculous healing during a 1601–1602 epidemic.[7] The epidemic of *dolor del costado* (chest or side pain; can also refer to a respiratory disorder) and *tabardillo* (typhus) began with an inflammation of the tonsils accompanied by the formation of pus and, by the second or third day, one developed a burning fever, which quickly killed the afflicted.[8] As the epidemic spread outward from the capital, Franciscan friars invoked the intercession of the Virgin Mary through the image of Our Lady of Alcántara. The friars began to experiment with the oil from her lamp as an antidote against the contagion, and they also carried the image in a general religious procession. In the aftermath of the rituals, the contagion began to subside: many avoided the plague, others became healed, and still others "returned as from death to life." From that point on in Santiago de Guatemala, the image of Our Lady of Alcántara, and in particular the oil from her lamp, became associated with miraculous healing properties.

When the dawn arrived and her child had survived the night, Estefanía Vásquez de Jaén took her son to the chapel at the Franciscan church. When she arrived, she found fray Juan de Alcover in a corner praying before the image of Our Lady of Alcántara. "With tears the grieving mother told of her pain" and she asked the friar to say mass for the child. Fray Juan agreed, warning her that the successful effect of the mass on her son's illness depended on the "purity" of the mother's faith. He then anointed the child above the heart with the healing oil from the lamp and said mass.

The healing event itself centered on feeding the baby's body. The baby boy had a wasting sickness, and one aspect of that sickness was that he could not breast feed. The baby began to heal, however, at the moment the friar raised the host while saying mass: at that point the boy opened his eyes and began to smile. The boy continued to heal after the completion of the mass, when he began to breast feed. In the process, the child not only healed but somehow became transformed. The friars on hand during the miraculous cure commented "that the boy had become something other than what he was."

Miraculous Healing and Children's Bodies

Eating and healing events were linked, in particular, at shrines known for their miraculous healing earth. The shrine of Nuestro Señor de Esquipulas, a black Christ image located in eastern Guatemala, became associated with miraculous healing when the sick and afflicted ate the earth from the site. Believers sought the earth from the Esquipulas shrine to cure "fevers, sores, and *males de corazón*," described enigmatically as "a steam or gas, that because of its quantity and quality pains the heart, and [the pain] lasts until the vapor or gas resolves itself."[9] In 1715, three girls went to the shrine in search of a cure for mal de corazón, and

became miraculously healed after eating "the holy earth." The Esquipulas earth became known as the "medicine of the poor, and the healing potion of all the destitute."

Eating imagery also pervades a 1603 account from the city of Santiago de Guatemala, where Antonia, the one-year-old only child of doña María de Porras y Alvarado, and Capitán Luis Aceytuno de Guzmán, *alcalde ordinario* (local magistrate), also lay dying from an illness that caused her to "waste away."[10] She too became miraculously healed after ingesting milk. Sick for two months, the baby girl suffered from weakness, fainting spells, an upset stomach, and fever. In May of 1603, the girl's condition worsened, and she appeared "in the throes of death, with deadly nausea." Kinsfolk gathered at the girl's sickbed, including her mother, her grandmother, doña Magdalena de Monzón, and her aunt, doña Juana Chinchilla. At nine in the morning on May 31, the grandmother took the dying baby in her arms. "The girl began to shake and shudder, stretching out her arms and legs," and her mouth twisted "as a person who tried to force out the soul [from their body]." The baby then gave "three gasps of death" and died. Her eyes then became white and ruptured.

The baby died in her home in the presence of relatives, all of whom agreed that the girl had indeed died and left "this present life." Death watches in the sick room were primarily female activities: the baby's mother, grandmother, aunt, and other relatives were present at the time of her death. The father, however, was "outside of the house," and the women sent word to him only after his daughter had died. He then returned home, and everyone dressed for the funeral, planned for that afternoon. The dead baby's body became "as stiff as a cadaver," and relatives placed the little girl's body in her cradle, dressed her for burial, and ordered a coffin built.

News of the baby girl's death soon spread to the surrounding community, probably fueled by her extreme symptoms, and the fact that she came from an elite family. Many relatives and neighbors came to the house to pay their respects. As the mother cried at her daughter's death "with [all] the sorrow of her heart," she made one last effort for her daughter. She appealed to the image of San Diego that had been placed in the baby's crib, asking him to intercede and bring her daughter back to life.

A few moments later, the mother reportedly heard a "little moan" and she went over to the cradle, uncovered the baby's face, and felt for a pulse. She then cried out "the girl has a pulse," and everyone present cheered and ran to the cradle to see the child. The mother then fed the baby a drop of milk with a spoon, and the baby opened her eyes and began to move "as if alive." Forty days later the girl became completely healed. Word of the miraculous resurrection quickly spread throughout the capital. The process of the baby's recovery also included feeding her body; the breast milk played a central role in bringing the child back to life. In addition, the baby's body proved remarkably flexible according to witnesses, transforming effortlessly from a stiff cadaver back into a living body.

In the aftermath of her resurrection from death, the baby girl also became transformed. The one-year-old began to speak, and asked "in her badly formed words . . . why they had cried so much for her when she was with her *tata Dios* (daddy God), and that as soon as her parents gave birth to another daughter, she would go to heaven, and she would not return no matter how much they prayed to San Diego." The baby girl described crossing the boundary between the world of the living and the world of the dead to communicate with divine beings, in this case to talk with her "daddy God," and prophesied that as soon as her parents gave birth to another daughter, she would die again.

In 1604 in Ciudad Real de Chiapas, Antonio, the son of Francisca del Castillo and Juan Domínguez, had a "monstrous hernia or rupture" that healed when he communicated with San Diego and San Jacinto.[11] From the time the boy was very young, his hernia had grown to the size of "an ordinary bottle of [olive] oil," which caused him to feel continuously exhausted. The boy could sit up but could not walk, and "his little body was gaunt and weak as an infant's." The parents, desperate for a cure, brought their son to the altar of San Diego in the Franciscan church in Ciudad Real. They asked a friar, fray Juan de Orduña, to "entrust" the boy to God. The friar told Antonio to spend the day praying the rosary before the image of San Diego, lit two beeswax candles, and accompanied Antonio in prayer. At noon, fray Juan fed the boy, and then the two continued to "pray fervently."

Twice during their afternoon prayers the sick boy heard a voice coming from the image of San Diego, but he could not understand what the image said. Fray Juan called to the other Franciscans and asked them to stop praying so they could listen, and then the voice was heard again.[12] Still the boy could not understand the words. At this point the friar intervened and interpreted the words for the boy: "Do you know what San Diego is telling you? . . . he is telling you to go and speak to his brother San Jacinto who will cure you." He then picked up Antonio, carried him to the church of Santo Domingo, and placed him before the image of San Jacinto. Fray Juan then spoke to the image of San Jacinto, "as if he spoke to a person whom he could hear." The friar told Antonio to wait for an answer and returned to his own church to pray with the other Franciscans.

A short while later, the Dominicans entered the church and went to pray in the choir loft. From there, the friars witnessed the "*maravilla*" (marvel or miracle): the image of San Jacinto extended his hand and gestured to the boy to come forward. By the time the Dominican friars had descended from the choir loft to the altar, they found that the image of San Jacinto had the boy's hernia truss in his hand. The boy told the friars that San Jacinto had ordered him to remove the truss, and then San Jacinto healed him. In this example, the boy began to hear the voices of San Diego and San Jacinto after the friar fed him lunch. He then communicated with San Jacinto, removed his hernia truss, and became healed. There is no further information about whether the monstrous hernia remained, or if it shrank and disappeared.

Children's deaths in the midst of the various epidemics that swept through New Spain throughout the colonial period probably caused a great deal of family and community stress and distress. In 1680 in the indigenous town of Zamayac, the seven-year-old niece of Antonia Pech, a member of the local indigenous elite, fell gravely ill during a smallpox epidemic that killed many of the local children.[13] The girl became so gravely ill that "she arrived at the point of death without hope of living." At this point, the sick girl's aunt, who "loved her as a daughter," made a promise to San Nicolás that if the girl lived, she would serve in the local *cofradía* (religious sodality) dedicated to him for a period of one year.

One night, after Antonia had served the cofradía for six months, the sick girl cried out to her aunt from her sick bed, telling her "to look at San Nicolás, and that he stood over there." The girl repeated the words to her aunt "with much happiness," and said that San Nicolás had watched over her during her illness, and that he said he would cure her. The sick girl then asked for something to eat, and "from then on it was as if she had been rid of the sickness." Even though the girl did not heal instantaneously, she did heal quickly to the astonishment of everyone, "because no one believed that she would live."

The images of transformation also pervade the following account of a miraculously healed *mulato* boy thought to be a saint. In June of 1694, Santiago's Inquisition received a letter from fray José Delgado, parish priest from the nearby town of San Juan Amatitlan, charging Sebastiana de la Cruz "for giving her son adoration and worshiping him as a son of God."[14] De la Cruz, a widowed *mulata*, had lived for many years in the town of Amatitlan, but two years before moved to the capital of Santiago de

"OUR LORD ENTERED HIS BODY"

Guatemala, where she lived with her thirteen-year-old mulatto son Bartolomé Catalán.

A neighbor, Juana Ximénez, a fifty-year-old Spanish widow, testified that Bartolomé had become gravely ill with some type of illness (*achaque*). Bartolomé's mother asserted that as the boy lay on his sickbed, "Our Lord entered his body" and healed him. Bartolomé confirmed that "his father, Our Lord" healed him in that way. During his illness, the archangel Gabriel took Bartolomé to heaven, baptized him, and then brought him back to earth.

The neighbor Juana Ximénez's testimony focused on Bartolomé's transformation after being miraculously healed. She reported that de la Cruz told her that her son transformed into "Father Our Lord." De la Cruz then saw her son transform and wave his hand as if giving a blessing, and she fell to her knees. Ximénez commented that "[de la Cruz] appears certain that Our Lord had placed himself in his [Bartolomé's body] in the form of an angel."[15] One night while carrying Bartolomé to bathe, Ximénez also saw the boy transform and give a blessing. In addition, she described Bartolomé's continuing ability to speak with divine beings, including "his mother Nuestra Señora de la Soledad," who visited him and spoke to him.

The embodiment of a chosen child, miraculously healed or revived, proved flexible, open to the entrance of divine beings, and capable of physical and/or spiritual transformation. Descriptions of the miraculous healing process in children frequently contained images of eating and feeding, whether symbolically by raising of the host during mass, or physically, through breast feeding. Many of the healed children described leaving their bodies to travel to heaven. In the aftermath of the miraculous healing, the family and community viewed the children as somehow changed, chosen, and special. Bartolomé, the thirteen-year-old mulatto boy, also became transformed in the aftermath of his miraculous healing—his mother, family, and the local community came to worship him as a saint, and he began to perform miracles in their home, becoming a public "marvel" of sorts, a status that rested on community knowledge of his miraculous healing and acknowledgement of his changed status.

Representations of Healed Children as "Marvels" in Colonial Society

Bartolomé Catalán became "reborn" in the aftermath of his illness, occupying a special status in the local community, transformed from a boy into a saint. Sebastiana de la Cruz also told her *comadre* María Mendoza that she kissed Bartolomé's feet and hands "because God has protected him [from the illness] to be a bishop." After Bartolomé's illness, when he felt well enough to travel, de la Cruz brought her son from the capital to convalesce in her home in Amatitlan, among her grown children and their families and the neighbors and friends she had known for twenty years or more. From his home in Amatitlan, Bartolomé began to "perform miracles" in front of family members and neighbors, who gathered at his home.[16]

After their return, gossip and rumor soon spread through the town about Bartolomé's special status. One neighbor remarked that he heard that Bartolomé "could do things that appeared to be more like things done with the light of God than things from this life or other natural things." When another neighbor talked one day with three other men, he heard that his mother, de la Cruz, "venerates Bartolomé . . . as a son of God," and that he "performs miracles" and says mass every night in her home. Community members asserted that Bartolomé had direct communication with Jesus Christ through the altar in his mother's home and through the image of the crucified Christ in the parish church. One day Bartolomé ordered his older brother Lorenzo to go pray and give thanks to the Christ image in the church. When Lorenzo entered the church, the statue of Christ, whose altar stood next to the entrance, nodded his head to him. Bartolomé also gave the impression that he spoke to the image of the *Limpia Concepción* (Immaculate Conception), located on their home altar. Their neighbor, Juana Ximénez, often saw Bartolomé pray at the altar before the image. She said that "many times" he would return horrified after looking at the image, and tell everyone to kneel "because Our Lady was coming," and so they all knelt. Bartolomé's brother Lorenzo asserted that Bartolomé spoke to Jesus Christ and the Virgin Mary, and that one time he saw him kneel down before the home altar, and it appeared that the image spoke to him. Lorenzo asked Bartolomé what the Virgin Mary said, and he said that she asked him "if the people in the house were being cared for, and if they had enough to eat."

Each night Bartolomé went into a trance and said mass in "ecstatic rapture" in front of those gathered. Bartolomé reportedly levitated in the air while he said mass and called on Saints Rafael, Miguel, and Gabriel, while Juana Ximénez, the widowed mestiza,

and María Candelaria, a black woman, walked around him carrying crosses. Martín García, a free mulatto, added that it was "public knowledge" that Bartolomé "se ponía en cruz" (put himself up on the cross). Word of Bartolomé's special status and his activities spread throughout Amatitlan, and crowds of people flocked to de la Cruz's house to watch him perform miracles.

Miraculously healed children such as Bartolomé became objects of wonder in colonial society—men and women from different ethnic and social groups discussed the stories of their illness and remarkable recoveries, their ability to communicate with divine beings, and celebrated the roles of their parents, especially the mother, in the request for divine intercession. The healed children became objects of curiosity and sometimes even worship in a historical context of the prevalence of epidemic disease and illness and their devastating effects on both adults and children.

Word of a miraculously healed child could spread quickly and result in spontaneous city-wide celebrations, such as those described by the Nahua historian Chimalpahin.[17] Chimalpahin wrote a history of Mexico City (1579–1615) in annals form in Nahuatl at some point in the first quarter of the seventeenth century. In it, as mentioned above, he referred to a miraculous healing that occurred in December of 1600, describing a community-wide acknowledgment and celebration of the marvelous child:

> The aforementioned Monday . . . was when San Diego revived a small child; it was a great miracle that was performed.

"OUR LORD ENTERED HIS BODY"

When [the child] passed away, its mother brought it to the church and laid it before San Diego. With heavy weeping she prayed to the beloved of God, San Diego. And when he had approved her prayer, the child came back to life. After it had revived, the bells began to ring everywhere because of it. All the friars and Spaniards saw [the miracle].[18]

Public knowledge and celebration of miraculous healing crossed racial and status boundaries of colonial society. In Mexico City in September of 1615, a one-and-a-half-year-old boy, the son of a Nahua woman commoner, fell into a small well and died from his injuries. He then became miraculously revived through the divine intervention of San Nicolás de Tolentino. According to Chimalpahin, the event cause city-wide celebrations:

Bells began to ring at the church of San Agustín, and at the Colegio of San Pablo, at Santa Cruz Contzinco, at San Sebastián, at our precious mother Nuestra Señora de las Mercedes, and at the Casa Profesa, announcing that the child . . . had fallen into a small well, and by a miracle San Nicolás de Tolentino helped and revived him on the eve of his feast day. The said child had really died, for he lay dead for two and a half hours until the said saint revived him. And when it was dark, as night was coming, the bells rang everywhere in all the churches all over Mexico [City], at the cathedral and the monasteries, especially at San Agustín, and the Spaniards everywhere burned wood on their roofs, and some burned it

in the street outside their houses, and in the monasteries they shot off rockets, and many Mexica commoners did the same, burning wood on their roofs.[19]

Conclusion

What makes childhood illness and healing particularly meaningful and revealing in this context is how residents of Mexico City and other towns and cities across New Spain noticed and celebrated wonders in their daily lives such as the resurrection of the small child who fell in a well, and the power of a saint to bring him back to life. In this sense the wonder of a miraculous healing contradicted and destabilized expectations, providing tangible evidence of hope and a counterpoint to the prevalence of illness and epidemic disease in daily life in New Spain.[20] On the surface, accounts of the miraculous healing of children may seem similar to the same sorts of events in Europe, yet they reflected broader concerns with and discourse about the meaning of illness and death in the Americas.

That context for believing in miracles in colonial Guatemala and the rest of New Spain included the church's ongoing campaigns of religious conversion of native peoples. Descriptions of miraculously healed children, set within a Catholic framework, provide evidence of how colonial institutions such as the church formally mediated supernatural signs and sought to put its own ideological spin on miraculous healing. In addition, the accounts reveal how popular understanding of Catholicism mixed with local concerns for sick children and celebrations of their return to health in this multicultural setting.

The research support of a Rockefeller Foundation Postdoctoral Fellowship at the Newberry Library (1999–2000) is gratefully acknowledged. In developing this article, I benefited from conversations with Susan Schroeder, Janine Lanza, Christopher H. Lutz, Peter Hulme, and from audience comments at the Scholes conference on "Mexico's Transformative Church," at Tulane University in March 2001. Susan Schroeder graciously shared with me accounts of the miraculous revival of children from don Domingo de San Antón Muñón Chimalpahin Quauhtlehuanitzin in *Annals of His Time*, ed. and trans. James Lockhart, Susan Schroeder, and Doris Namala (Stanford: Stanford University Press, 2006). This essay forms part of my current book project, *Colonial Medicine and Healing Cultures in Guatemala, 1680–1830*.

1. See, for example, Alfred W. Crosby, *The Columbian Exchange: Biological and Cultural Consequences of 1492* (Westport, CT: Greenwood Press, 1972). Noble David Cook analyzes the effects of epidemic disease on all sectors of society in the colonial Americas, outlining how its effects varied regionally and temporally in his important work *Born to Die: Disease and New World Conquest, 1492–1650* (Cambridge: Cambridge University Press, 1998).

2. While my analysis differs, Nancy Scheper-Hughes's work, *Death Without Weeping: The Violence of Everyday Life in Brazil* (Berkeley and Los Angeles: University of California Press, 1992), which addresses child death and its impact on motherhood, family, and community life in poor communities in northeastern Brazil in the 1970s and 1980s, helped me think about children and illness in a larger cultural and historical context.

3. Here, I build on the work of Carolyn Walker Bynum's analysis of resurrection belief and the meaning of embodiment in *The Resurrection of the Body in Western Christianity, 200–1336* (New York: Columbia University Press, 1995), especially xv, xviii, and 2.

4. Chimalpahin, *Annals of His Time*. For more on Chimalpahin, see Susan Schroeder, *Chimalpahin and the Kingdoms of Chalco* (Tucson: University of Arizona Press, 1991).

5. For a comparative analysis of images used for curing in urban centers in sixteenth-century Spain, see William A. Christian Jr., *Local Religion in Sixteenth-Century Spain* (Princeton: Princeton University Press, 1981).

6. Francisco Vázquez, *Crónica de la Provincia del Santísimo Nombre de Jesús de Guatemala*, 4 vols. [1714–1716] (Guatemala: Tipografía Nacional, 1937), vol. 4, 219–20, 227.

7. Also known in Santiago as Nuestra Señora de Loreto.

8. Hans J. Prem has classified *dolor de costado* as an upper respiratory illness. See his chapter "Disease Outbreaks in Central Mexico During the Sixteenth Century," in *Secret Judgments of God: Old World Disease in Colonial Spanish America*, ed. Noble David Cook and W. George Lovell, 44 (Norman: University of Oklahoma Press, 1991).

9. Br. D. Nicolás de Paz, *Novena y bosquejo de los milagros y maravillas que ha obrado La Santisima Imagen de Christo Crucificado de Esquipulas, con la que se pueden preparar a celebrar fiesta el dia de quince de enero* (Reprint, Mexico 1791), not paginated. The definition of *mal de corazón* was found in *Diccionario de Autoridades* (Madrid: Real Academia Española, 1726–1739), 459.

10. Vázquez, *Crónica de la Provincia*, vol. 4, 235–37.

11. Ibid., 237–38.

12. It is unclear from the text if just the boy heard the words, or if the friar heard them as well.

13. Vázquez, *Crónica de la Provincia*, vol. 4, 313.

14. Archivo General de la Nación (Mexico City), Ramo de Inquisición, vol. 609, exp. 4, f. 335–69 (1694). I have published an earlier analysis of this case in a section of "Women, Religion, and Power: Gender and Resistance in Daily Life in Late Seventeenth-Century Santiago de Guatemala," *Ethnohistory* 42, no. 4 (fall 1995): 627–37, and in my book *Women Who Live Evil Lives: Gender, Religion, and the Politics of Power in Colonial Guatemala* (Austin: University of Texas Press, 2002). Mario

Humberto Ruz has also written about this case in the context of multiethnic social relations in colonial Guatemala in his essay "Sebastiana de la Cruz, alias 'La Polilla': Mulata de Petapa y Madre del Hijo de Dios," *Mesoamérica* 23 (1992): 55–66.

15. "y que vió esta declarante que el dicho muchacho se transpuso, y con la mano echó una venedicción y entonces se hincó de rodillas a dicha Sebastiana y esta declarante tambien pareciendo seria cierto que nuestro Señor se le metia en el cuerpo por angelito." The meaning of what went on regarding Bartolomé here is ambiguous and difficult to translate. I chose to translate se transpone and transponerse as "transform," though it might also be translated as "to become possessed," as if by a spirit or being. While I have been unable to locate a definition for the verb *transponer* as a reflexive verb as it is used in this context, transponer (not reflexive) can mean to hide, to make disappear, or to switch over. Christopher H. Lutz, March 2001, personal communication.

16. It is unclear from the documentation whether or not Bartolomé practiced miracles in Santiago, though apparently his religious activities lasted for a few years before the local priest intervened. In any case, colonial authorities did not investigate until he and his mother traveled back to Amatitlan.

17. Chimalpahin, *Annals of His Time.*

18. Ibid.

19. Ibid.

20. Here I build on the work of Lorraine Daston and Katharine Park, *Wonders and the Order of Nature: 1150–1750* (New York: Zone Books, 1998), esp. 10–11.

CHAPTER SEVEN

Canonizing a Cult

A Wonder-Working Guadalupe in the Seventeenth Century

JEANETTE FAVROT PETERSON

The turning point in the evolution of the cult of the Mexican Virgin of Guadalupe is attributed to the role of two mid-seventeenth-century creole chroniclers, Miguel Sánchez and the vicar of the Guadalupe shrine, Luis Laso de la Vega. With their compelling accounts of the 1531 apparition of Guadalupe to the native Juan Diego, Sánchez and Laso de la Vega elevated a devotional image to that of an *acheiropoietic* image, one "not made by human hands," but divinely imprinted on Juan Diego's cloak (fig. 7.1). Based on a meticulous compilation of the textual sources, historians have concluded that these foundational narratives in Spanish and Nahuatl officially launched the cult of Guadalupe

Figure 7.1: Virgin of Guadalupe, anonymous, 16th century. Oil and tempera on cloth; 175 x 105 cm. Basilica of Guadalupe, Mexico City.

and converted her into a "proto-national" saint. To phrase it another way, the period in New Spain's religious history prior to 1648 and 1649 is one that is characterized as "Before Guadalupe."[1]

The earliest known visual representation of the climax of the Guadalupe legend is found in the first published account of the apparition story in Miguel Sánchez's 1648 chronicle (fig. 7.2). In this engraving of her fourth apparition, before a reverential audience that includes a kneeling bishop Zumárraga and his ecclesiastical entourage, Juan Diego reveals the likeness of the Virgin Mary imprinted on his outstretched mantle or *tilma* (*tilmatli* in Nahuatl). While the Virgin of Guadalupe had made her presence known only to the neophyte Juan Diego on three previous occasions at Tepeyac, north of Mexico City, in this last, more public apparition the Virgin of Guadalupe materializes as a permanent sign of her reality. The vaporous apparition is remapped on a cloth said to be the same titular icon venerated today in the Guadalupe basilica in Mexico City. Referred to as the "tilma image" in this paper, the icon

Figure 7.2: Fourth Apparition of the Virgin of Guadalupe, anonymous engraving. 16.4 x 11.6 cm. In: *Imagen de la Virgen María . . . de Guadalupe*, Miguel Sánchez, 1648.

JEANETTE FAVROT PETERSON

Figure 7.3:
Virgin of Guadalupe, Baltasar
de Echave Orio, 1606.
Oil on cloth. 170 x 111 cm.
Private collection, Mexico.

depicts the Virgin Mary standing on a crescent moon within a mandorla of solar rays,
her iconography closely following the bibli
cal description of the woman in Revelation
(12:1) who is "clothed with the sun, and the
moon under her feet." This streamlined version of the apocalyptic woman is the Marian
image referred to as *Maria in sole* or the
mulier amicta sole that became the basis for
the rendering of the Immaculate Conception
as it was slowly standardized during the
course of the sixteenth century. The tilma
image of the Mexican Virgin of Guadalupe
also relies on representations of the Virgin
Tota Pulchra (Perfectly Beautiful) that extol
symbolically the purity of Mary, as well as on

fifteenth-century images of the Assumption
of the Virgin.[2]

As an art historian less skeptical of the
evidentiary role of images, I will examine two of the earliest artworks that occupy
the putative vacuum of textual documentation between 1531 and 1648 to suggest that the
church was canonizing a cult already firmly
established around a new wonder-working
Virgin by the first decade of the seventeenth
century. Of the few surviving depictions of
the Virgin of Guadalupe securely dated to
this time frame, two artworks include a 1606
painting by Baltasar de Echave Orio and a
1613 engraving by Samuel Stradanus (figs.
7.3 and 7.4).[3] It is an image that gives birth

Figure 7.4: Indulgence for alms toward the erection of a church dedicated to the Virgin of Guadalupe, Samuel Stradanus, ca. 1613–1615. Copper engraving. 32.7 x 20.9 cm. The Metropolitan Museum of Art, Gift of H. H. Behrens, 1948 (48.70).

JEANETTE FAVROT PETERSON

to the Guadalupe cult and subsequent pictorial referents to the originary tilma image serve to substantiate and corroborate its supernatural efficacy for a heterogeneous and growing colonial constituency. The ability of images to tell a more inclusive or alternative story makes them indispensable for understanding the subtexts that are often unarticulated in written documentation; they can also reveal the discrepancy between ideological positions and social realities. I will argue that these earliest Guadalupe images did not invent but recorded stories already circulating at the time of their production, including a conviction in Guadalupe's thaumaturgic powers and, as a corollary, a growing belief in her supernatural origins. In this interpretation, the official creole authors of the mid-seventeenth century, such as Sánchez and Laso de la Vega, capitalized on narratives long embedded in popular belief. Moreover, the Guadalupe representations we will examine also signal a shift in the mature colonial church's acceptance of the authenticating role of the miraculous. Fearing idolatry during the early stages of evangelization, the mendicant orders in particular disputed portentous claims made for new cult images, including those of the Mexican Virgin of Guadalupe.[4] By the late sixteenth and early seventeenth centuries the cult of saints was reinvigorated by the militancy of the Counter Reformation; newly canonized saints and advocations of the Virgin Mary went hand-in-hand with an increase in the official recognition of supernatural happenings.

Representing the Sacred Cloth

The 1606 painting signed by the Spanish artist Baltasar de Echave Orio is a unique and remarkably faithful copy of the sixteenth-century tilma icon (fig. 7.3). In addition to approximating its model's proportions, Echave Orio went so far as to fabricate his work out of two similarly joined vertical canvas strips to simulate the sewn panels of the tilma Guadalupe.[5] The painting is also unusual for the attention Echave Orio pays to the fabric of the cape or tilma itself, creating a twofold reality. The cloth drapes in ample folds on either side of the Virgin's depiction. The illusion of its solid physicality is reinforced by representing the cloth as hanging, the upper edges tacked at the corners and the hem billowing softly at the lower frame. The luminous image of Guadalupe, although imprinted on the textile surface, appears to be impervious to its sway, hovering apart from the laws of gravity. Thus Echave Orio creates on his canvas a cloth that appears to be tangibly real and a permanent relic. The sign that it bears, however, is rendered as a transcendent image in an aureole of solar rays.

The Basque artist Echave Orio immigrated to Mexico between 1573 and 1580, an accomplished writer and painter who soon thereafter began executing commissions for members of the church. By the time he produced his Guadalupe painting, Echave Orio had worked on all or portions of five major *retablos* or altarpieces, including that of the main altar in the old cathedral in Puebla, and he had received commissions from the Holy Office of the Inquisition.[6] While the patron of the 1606 Guadalupe painting remains unknown, it is telling that sixteen of Echave Orio's paintings were slated for the retablo of Santiago Tlatelolco, the Franciscan monastery church most closely associated with the Guadalupe apparition legend as the site of Juan Diego's religious instruction. We can thus hypothesize that Echave Orio executed this earliest extant reproduction of the Virgin of Guadalupe in response to the requirements of an ecclesiastical patron, perhaps one associated with the Franciscan order at Tlatelolco.

Echave Orio scrupulously follows Tridentine dictates to create his decorous and didactic themes. In a transitional late Renaissance style, his compositions are straightforward and convincing in spite of some disregard for adequate pictorial space, sudden theatrical shifts of light and dark, and an occasional use of acrid colors.[7] It is the restraint of his full-bodied figures and his three-dimensional treatment of draperies that are fully evident in Echave Orio's rendering of Guadalupe. While there is painstaking effort to duplicate the outlines, proportions and ornamental details of the original cult image, the artist puts his unique interpretative stamp on the representation by demarcating the facial features and flowing mantle of the Virgin with sharply sculpted edges and strongly contrasting highlights and shadows.

This work makes a claim for the inherent mediating power of the sacred cloth itself, much as paintings of the head of Christ on Veronica's veil, or the sudarium, are "images within an image."[8] As Western Christendom's answer to the Byzantine mandylion of Edessa, the traces left by the sweat and blood of Christ after Veronica wiped his face on the road to Golgotha were said to have created a *vera icon* (true image), hence the names given the myriad recreations of this cloth as Veronica's veil or the sudarium.[9] By the thirteenth century the Veil of Veronica venerated in Rome initiated a tradition of the indulgenced image, promising indulgences of ten days to those who recited a special prayer in front of the image.[10] Cloth images of the Holy Face multiplied throughout Europe in the fourteenth and fifteenth centuries, each copy tracking its genealogy to one of the putative original cloths taken from Christ himself. Once the icon's miraculous powers were locally established, pilgrimages and alms were sure to follow, as was true of the well-known relic of the Holy Face (*Santo Rostro*) in the cathedral of Jaén, Spain.

The importance given textiles as carriers of holy signs and the multivalence that inheres in cloth as relic, gendered garment, and skin are traceable to both prehispanic and European Christian traditions.[11] It cannot be coincidental, therefore, that Baltasar Echave Orio's painting evokes both the acheiropoetic imprint of the Virgin of Guadalupe and the very substance of its textile support. The artist is signaling the iconic status of Guadalupe as a singular and physical devotional image and, at the same time, clearly suggesting that the image of the Virgin is unpainted or "not painted by human hands," in the manner of the sudarium. While unconvinced by assertions that this work offers proof of the existence of the apparition legend at this time,[12] oral versions of such a myth may well have been circulating. Once the preternatural origins of the image are established, the need for an appropriate recipient of the vision is the logical next step. The creation of the humble seer whose faith is stronger than the skeptical ecclesiastical hierarchy as articulated in the Juan Diego narrative, is an adaptation of familiar European Marian apparition

JEANETTE FAVROT PETERSON

stories.[13] However, the growing belief in Guadalupe's divine authorship is already detectable in Echave Orio's painting and will be linked to an ever expanding corpus of miracle stories in the Samuel Stradanus engraving executed seven years later.

The Stradanus Engraving

The obvious care exercised by Echave Orio to duplicate the titular icon is not apparent in the unconventional Virgin of Guadalupe featured in the 1613 Stradanus print (fig. 7.4). In the Stradanus, our eye is first fixed on the central upper panel featuring a recognizable but loosely quoted Virgin of Guadalupe hovering above an altar in a cloud bank. Below her image, a textual panel details the fundraising purposes of the print and the benefits that will accrue to the generous donor, namely a grant of forty days of indulgence or relief from purgatory, in exchange for a donation to the building effort.[14] The inscription in the central column terminates with the heraldic insignia of the patron, Archbishop Juan Pérez de la Serna.

By the turn of the seventeenth century the cult of Guadalupe was sufficiently well established to merit embarking on an ambitious building program to replace the shrine at the foot of Tepeyac hill. As the cult set down more substantial architectural roots with the inauguration of a new sanctuary in 1601, there arose a critical need. The Mexican church had both to raise needed funds and to justify the expenditures such an ambitious project entailed. Soon after taking office as archbishop in 1613, Pérez de la Serna reinvigorated the lagging campaign to finish the building and by 1614 construction was well underway.[15] Although

the broadsheet is customarily dated to sometime between 1615 and 1622 when the church was consecrated, I place it closer to 1613, not only because it is dedicated to Juan Pérez de la Serna, but because in the engraving's request for alms the text indicates that the construction work is ongoing (la obra que se va haziendo). Clearly an extra infusion of subsidies was necessary at the outset of the building effort and the Stradanus broadsheet became a valuable commodity in this renewed campaign. To do so required that the devotion be planted firmly in American soil within a matrix of miraculous testimonials that would verify the efficacy of the cult image. For just such a purpose, the church commissioned Samuel Stradanus, a Flemish artist recently working in New Spain, to design an appropriate fundraising tool with accessible visual appeal. Stradanus designed a copper plate for the production of multiple broadsheets, each 8.3 inches by 12.8 inches. That this engraving enjoyed widespread circulation can be inferred by the current condition of the plate, from which the illustration is a twentieth-century restrike. The surface of the plate is so worn as to render almost unintelligible certain details of the design, an index of its use and reuse to produce large quantities of prints.

The artist, Samuel Stradanus (Latinized from the Flemish, van der Straet) identifies himself twice on the plate: on the altar at the feet of the Virgin (as Samuel Stradanus Excudit) and, again, at the base of the print in the Latin dedication as Samuel Stradanus Antwerpiensis Sculptor. About this Stradanus we have little concrete data either personally or professionally.[16] The copper engraver is recorded as being active in Mexico at least by 1604 when a signed and dated engraved portrait embellishes the publication *Obediencia* by Arias de Villalobos. Thereafter, only a scattered handful of extant engravings (four frontispieces, a map, and another portrait) remain to testify to what must have been a sizable output in the notoriously ephemeral medium of paper prints. His frontispiece for the *Proceedings of the Third Mexican Church Council* (1585) confirms the artist's status as well as his privileged working relationship

with Archbishop Juan Pérez de la Serna, who was responsible for its belated publication in 1622.

Stradanus appears to have been an educated humanist, having undergone his training in Flanders, presumably in Antwerp, consistently and proudly cited as his native city after his signature on almost every one of his prints. The style used by Samuel Stradanus reflects a well trained artist, familiar with the conventions of pictorial space, figural composition, and the heraldic flourishes of the decorative

#1 #2 #3 #4 #5 #6 #7 #8

Figure 7.5:
Reading order of the engraving by Samuel Stradanus.

JEANETTE FAVROT PETERSON

frontispieces for which he is best known. The artist is clearly more fluent in Latin than in his newly adopted Spanish, judging by the number of misspellings in the captions under the miracle vignettes. The Latin text adjacent to Pérez de la Serna's coat of arms is an honorific, almost obsequious, dedication by Stradanus to his patron.

The general composition and iconography of the Stradanus broadsheet can be categorized as a type of "graphic sermon," common in Spain and elsewhere. The engraving is divided into tidy, bounded sections, in a retablo or altarpiece format used to commemorate discrete events in the lives of Christ, the Virgin Mary, and Christian saints. Typically this composition foregrounds the honored holy figure or saint; rotating around and/or flanking the central figure are the hagiographic stories that advertise the ability to heal and safeguard adherents from life's perils. As portable sermons, these widely disseminated prints taught doctrinal, biblical, and moral lessons by illustrating the model of a virtuous, often sacrificial, life.[17] The Stradanus print is a busy image, functioning on many levels. It is a devotional as well as an instructive image through the miracle narratives that are inscribed in the eight small vignettes that flank the central icon. The conventional reading order of this cycle of miraculous episodes moves from the upper to the lower images on the left margin then vertically down the scenes on the right, numbered correspondingly as images #1–#8 in this text (see fig. 7.5). The broadsheet is also an indulgenced image, promoting, through the central column of text, the reciprocal relationship between the liturgical novenas and the generous alms of the devotee, with the fruits of that devotion eventuating in the remission of the pains of purgatory.

The Devotional Guadalupe Image

The most prominent panel in the Stradanus engraving is occupied by the Virgin of Guadalupe herself as she hovers midair in a cloudburst, filled with fifteen almost imperceptible angel heads, as if she had just descended from her heavenly abode (fig. 7.6).[18] Most essential ingredients make the image of Guadalupe instantly recognizable and some scholars have described the Stradanus rendering as "classic."[19] Samuel Stradanus portrays the Virgin of Guadalupe in her characteristic prayerful attitude with one bent knee standing on a crescent moon, wearing a star-studded robe whose lower corners are sustained by a single angel-caryatid. She wears a delicate spiked crown, a feature that appears throughout the colonial period, finally painted out of the tilma image in the nineteenth century in preparation for Guadalupe's official coronation.[20] Yet, in contrast to the 1606 Echave Orio painting, the Stradanus interpretation of the Virgin is by no means a close copy of the titular image. Moreover, she is treated as a free floating vision, not as an icon framed by a cloth support. In the multiple renderings of Guadalupe found in the Stradanus engraving, the tilma disappears altogether. Here the miraculous powers attributed to Guadalupe are channeled through the Virgin's presence in the lives of New Spain's inhabitants and through the implicit sacrality of her shrine-home and its environs. It is the proper liturgical setting that is emphasized for this otherwise

Figure 7.6:
Virgin of Guadalupe:
Central panel,
copper engraving
by Samuel Stradanus
(detail of Figure 7.4).

levitating Virgin Mary as she is surrounded
by all of the traditional paraphernalia of a
recognized cult image: the altar top, candlesticks, four hanging lamps, and the ana-
tomical replicas or *milagros* (miracles) that
dangle above her to verify her prodigious
power, as discussed below.

Stradanus deviates from the prototype in
representing his Guadalupe with the ampli-
tude of a robust Flemish matron. Rather than
the more erect posture and reserved, down-
cast facial expression of the tilma image, the
engraved Virgin is animated by a beatific

smile and the dynamic sway of her pose. The
creases and folds of her dress and mantle
only generically follow the patterns displayed
in the painted original, with the corners of
her robe given a pronounced, breezy flip.
Lace trimming at both the collar and sleeve
cuffs provides an elegant ornamental touch
in contrast to the otherwise plain bindings
of the tilma image. In short, while it is clear
that Stradanus was very conversant with the
sacred model, it is also apparent that reproductions of the Virgin were not yet codified
nor dependent on the painstaking tracings

JEANETTE FAVROT PETERSON

derived from a template so commonplace in the mass production of "true" Guadalupanas after the mid-seventeenth century.[21] Rather, the artist may have worked from his own sketches of the tilma painting or alternatively, from secondhand renderings. His meticulous attention to anecdotal details of dress, interior decor, and domestic objects in the miracle scenes and the more fulsome proportions he gives the Virgin betray the artist's Flemish origins. A predilection for

homely realism can be appreciated in image #1 of the canopied bed (see fig. 7.7), with its elaborate spindle headboard, and in such genre incidentals as the inkwell and crucifix on the table in image #4 (see figure 7.8).

Although the solar rays of Guadalupe's radiant nimbus are all but effaced in the illustrated print, a result of damage suffered by the worn copper plate, a few emanating rays are visible at the lower edge of the clouds (fig. 7.6). Additionally, the Virgin of

Figure 7.7:
Miracle #1, Bartolomé Granado and his silver head *milagro*. Copper engraving by Samuel Stradanus (detail of Figure 7.4).

CANONIZING A CULT

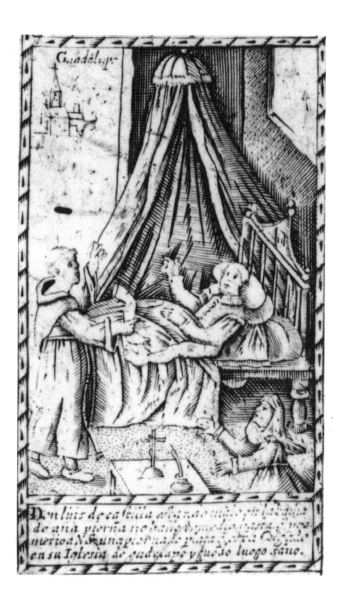

Figure 7.8:
Miracle #4, don Luis de Castilla
and his silver leg *milagro*.
Copper engraving
by Samuel Stradanus
(detail of Figure 7.4).

Guadalupe is surrounded by external light sources from two tall candles on the altar as well as four large hanging lamps. Given the installation of Guadalupe over an altar and the presence of candlesticks and lamps, it is likely that the artist based his rendering of Guadalupe on a common European type of devotional image sometimes known as an *andachtsbild*. Broadly defined,

andachtsbilder can be thought of as aids to prayer and meditation that focused on such themes as the Holy Face or Veronica, a half-length figure of Christ as the Man of Sorrows, or the Madonna and Child. After 1450, single figure devotional images were combined with narrative scenes and, exploiting the new print medium, engravings quickly replaced painted panels. These

JEANETTE FAVROT PETERSON

paper andachtsbilder were cheap and fast to produce in all sizes, often by the very monasteries or pilgrimage churches that featured the object of veneration; purchased or given in exchange for a donation, the prints served to protect their owners as well as to embellish and sanctify domestic shrines.[22]

The panel featuring Guadalupe within the larger Stradanus broadsheet displays the same compositional format and modest size (11 cm in width) as a popular small-scale printed andachtsbild. Moreover, the duplication of the artist's name both at the base of the altar, as well as below within the lowest inscription in the engraving, suggests that Stradanus may have already recycled this design, or intended to do so, as an independent print. It is also telling that the loop in the upper cord "frame," to indicate where to secure or hang the print, is centered over Guadalupe's head. If indeed this section of the Stradanus graphic was designed and produced independent of the larger broadsheet, it may have acted as the prototype for the almost identical engraving in Miguel Sánchez's 1648 account (compare figs. 7.6 and 7.9).

The surfeit of artificial light sources from

Figure 7.9:
Virgin of Guadalupe, anonymous engraving. 15 x 11.7 cm. In: *Imagen de la Virgen María . . . de Guadalupe*, Miguel Sánchez, 1648.

Figure 7.10:
Miracle #6, Anonymous
victim of falling lamp.
Copper engraving
by Samuel Stradanus
(detail of Figure 7.4).

candles and hanging lamps that frame the Virgin of Guadalupe reflects a time-honored tradition in Christian shrines, where devotional images are bathed in luminosity to underscore their celestial origins and preternatural powers. From the fourteenth century on, the Extremaduran monastery of Guadalupe boasted splendid lamps made of silver and gilded silver that were given as trophies and votive gifts by persons of note, including Philip II and Hernán Cortés.[23] Stradanus himself could have personally observed these oil-burning lamps within the primitive Mexican Guadalupe shrine. Miles Philips, in his 1568 visit to the Guadalupe shrine at Tepeyac, was dazzled by the number of lamps, inspiring the inflated remark that "there are as many lamps of silver as there be days in the year, which, upon high days, are all lighted."[24]

JEANETTE FAVROT PETERSON

That oil lamps such as these could be hazardous to the health is noted in the sixth Stradanus miracle scene where, to quote the caption text, "A man was praying on his knees when a very heavy lamp fell on his head and he was not hurt nor was the lamp dented, nor did the oil spill out nor was the glass even broken" (fig. 7.10).[25] The extravagance of such lamps was measured not only by their manufacture in precious metals, but also in the very costly nature of the oil needed to fill them, underscoring the wealth of the sixteenth-century Guadalupe shrine. Moreover, both wax and oil had a talismanic and curative function. The seventh Stradanus miracle recounts the healing nature of lamp oil. Juan Pavón, who was the sacristan of "Our Lady," cured his son of a throat abscess (*apostema*) by rubbing lamp oil on the afflicted region.[26] In the image (fig. 7.11), the sacristan is shown holding his son and dipping his hand into the nearby lamp, conveniently lowered. A woman, perhaps the mother, kneels in front of Guadalupe's altar, displaying the piety appropriate to bring about the cure. And this sanctified interior is firmly localized in the capital city shown through the open door as an assemblage of turrets, domes, and a prominent cross, which Stradanus glosses as "La Gran Cuidad [*sic*] de Mexico" (The Great City of Mexico).

A Book of Miracles

The miraculous powers of the Virgin of Guadalupe are advertised through the presence of the tiny, disarticulated body parts that hang above her head (fig. 7.6). Modeled either from wax or, more likely, of silver, six replicas (three heads, two legs, and one hand) have been given in thanksgiving for the Virgin's curative powers of those same limbs. Three of the Stradanus miracle scenes involve the supplicant's exchange of silver ex-votos, sometimes called milagros, as concrete evidence that the holy figure effectively intervened in the destinies of her constituency. In miracle image #1, Bartolomé Granado suffered "terrible head and earaches" which were cured by the nine-day services (*novenas*) he attended at the shrine of Guadalupe and his gift of the silver head which he hung in the church.[27] In the caption to miracle image #4 (fig. 7.8), don Luis de Castilla is said to be "ill in bed with a bad leg that would not heal until he promised Our Lady a silver leg that was hung in the church of Guadalupe and then he was healed." The cure was effected when the silver leg was hung, probably near the image of the Virgin herself as shown in figure 7.6. The commentary correlates healing with the vow fulfilled; however, in the image, Stradanus has captured the dangerous hiatus between the promise of the ex-voto and the resolution of the malady. Into a single scene, the artist has compressed Castilla's awkward display of his leg as it is thrust out of the bedcovers as well as his gift of the silver milagro in the shape of a leg, held aloft by a tonsured friar like some prosthetic trophy.[28] Although this is only one of two miracles in which the image of Guadalupe does not appear, note the gloss of the name "Guadalupe" over her shrine in the background.

Miraculous events that involved the Virgin Mary as a celestial advocate proliferated soon after Christianity was introduced to the Americas. Not only did the Virgin actively abet the conquest, but she was also an ally in the Spaniards' continuing battle against diabolical forces; in addition, the Virgin rewarded Christian piety through her powers to heal and safeguard.[29] The great majority of miracles were modeled on medieval European precedents and, although in many cases highly idiosyncratic, all carried communal ramifications. Then, as now, once miracles were recorded in word or picture, personal interventions entered the public domain and enacted what Pilar Gonzalbo Aizpuru has called a "spiritual complicity" between the shrine and the local populace.[30] In the mainstreaming of extraordinary events the sacred entered the realm of the possible for all believers; holy favors were thus shared with the world beyond the shrine.

While an oral tradition accumulates almost immediately after a devotion is

JEANETTE FAVROT PETERSON

successfully initiated, a permanent "book of miracles" may be produced much later to certify the holy favors. By 1598, for example, the official history of the Spanish Guadalupe in Extremadura included an inventory of 150 miracles, 50 cited in each of the three previous centuries.[31] It is likely that a Spanish precedent for the Stradanus engraving existed, given the countless prints of the older Black Virgin that were sent from the mother house in Spain to the Americas. A later manifestation of this "altarpiece" genre in the Andean colonies may be seen in an eighteenth-century Cuzco style painting dedicated to the Extremaduran black Madonna (fig. 7.12). Although the small panels revolving around the central image of the Spanish Guadalupe represent the discovery of this Romanesque sculpture and her authenticating miracles, the painting is so strikingly similar to the Stradanus engraving in its layout of the narrative cycles as to suggest that it was based on an early and analogous print.[32]

The Stradanus broadsheet enumerates eight supernatural events and thus acts as the first "book of miracles" for the Tepeyac cult. Moreover, Lisa Sousa, Stafford Poole, and James Lockhart suggest that the Stradanus graphic may have acted as the prototype for the stories recorded in the Miguel Sánchez account (1648) and in Luis Laso de la Vega's *Nican Motecpana* (1649). They note that the eight Stradanus miracles are duplicates of the later published miracle episodes, in places repeated verbatim.[33] There are three miracles on the Stradanus engraving (images #5, #6, and #8, as numbered on fig. 7.5) that are also later recorded in Miguel Sánchez and Laso de la Vega. In addition,

five stories on the Stradanus print are comparable to healing episodes in Laso de la Vega (images #1, #2, #3, #4, and #7 on fig. 7.5). However, slight discrepancies between the Stradanus image and the Laso de la Vega written account argue for independent and perhaps multiple sources available to the Flemish artist and creole authors. Some of the differences can be explained by the need to compress the storylines in the condensed text of the Stradanus print; in particular, Luis Laso de la Vega's tales elaborate on those found in the engraving. However, where specific names are later changed or omitted, only the use of varied sources for the same basic miracle stories would account for these discrepancies. To give one example, in miracle image #2 Stradanus specifically cites "Catharina de niehta," but Laso de la Vega, in two relevant miracles involving the healing waters of the spring, more generally calls the petitioner "a humble woman named Catalina" or "a Spanish woman," but never by her full name nor revealing the fact that she was a nun. Laso de la Vega would not have intentionally elided this kind of specificity as names and places (and, rarely, dates) anchored miracles in historical reality. We can only conclude that Laso de la Vega did not have the Stradanus to refer to but may well have used a source also known to the Flemish engraver.[34] Moreover, Samuel Stradanus did not himself fabricate the miraculous incidents, but I would argue derived them from miracle narratives well established by 1613. He may have been given one or several written compilations, possibly from narratives collected by Archbishop Juan Pérez de la Serna himself. In addition, Stradanus may have sought inspiration

CANONIZING A CULT

Figure 7.12: Virgin of Guadalupe, Spain, anonymous, Cuzco School, Peru. Oil on cloth, 18th century. 82.5 x 62.2 cm. New Orleans Museum of Art, Museum Purchase 74.270.

JEANETTE FAVROT PETERSON

from painted ex-votos already being displayed in the Mexican shrine as his figural style suggests.

Without exception, all Spanish books of miracles credit the cult image with saving the life of one or more hapless horseback victims; the Stradanus print is no exception. Miracle image #5 tells the story of the son of a wealthy hacendado, don Antonio de Carvajal, whose horse bolted on his trip from the Guadalupe shrine to Tulancingo (fig. 7.13). Although according to the caption the "horse dragged him through some canyons" with the boy's foot caught in the stirrup, "Our Lady" appeared to him and "kept him from all harm." As we can see in figure 7.13, the doll-like figure of the young boy dangles precariously from the stirrup.

Figure 7.13:
Miracle #5, don Antonio
de Carvajal and his son's
horseback riding accident.
Copper engraving
by Samuel Stradanus
(detail of Figure 7.4).

CANONIZING A CULT

This is one of two miracles documented in the Stradanus in which the Virgin is said to have appeared (*habia aparesido*) and through her very presence prevented harm or reversed the ill effects of disease. And indeed a faint and tiny Virgin of Guadalupe hovers in the upper left hand corner. It may be that Stradanus had also included the horse genuflecting in obeisance to this vision, although the background is now too damaged to read. The actual event, said to have taken place in 1555, was commemorated with two lost sixteenth-century paintings, one given to the Guadalupe shrine and the other intended for the Carvajal hacienda in Tulancingo; this story continued to be a popular subject for Guadalupanas well into the eighteenth century.[35]

The remaining two miracle scenes are important for the supernatural status they seem to confer on the Virgin of Guadalupe. In the eighth miracle image, the vicar, Father Juan Vázquez de Acuña, was at the altar to say mass and waiting for the candles to be lit (fig. 7.14). Suddenly the candles were "alit miraculously by N. S. [*Nuestra Señora*]."[36] The text rather dryly records this most innocuous of wonders performed by the Virgin of Guadalupe, an underwhelming event in which no one is snatched from the jaws of disaster or prevented from bodily harm. Although the text is terse, the image describing the Stradanus miracle #8 is rich in details analogous to the more ample storytelling of Sánchez and Laso de la Vega. Having been extinguished by strong winds, the candles in the shrine are relit, in one version, by the very brightness of the Queen of Heaven "like tassels of flame" and, in another, by brilliant flashes of lightning.[37]

However miniaturized, the artist's staging cleverly invites us to enter through the pointing spectators and to move from the lower to the highest registers, from the profane to the sacralized spheres. The kneeling sacristan at the altar rail marks the entry into sanctified space where the vicar, as mediator of dogma, is saying mass at the altar. At the apex of the hierarchical composition, the Virgin of Guadalupe participates in yet another level of transubstantial reality. The ambiguity of the Stradanus image may be intentional, for the diagonal rays can be read either as streaming toward her through the open side windows or as emanating from the Virgin herself. Guadalupe competes with the candles, lamps, and even rays of lightning as a generative source of radiant light. Like the "Mass of St. Gregory" by Israhel van Meckenem, a Flemish print well known in sixteenth-century New Spain, the distinction between ordinary and extraordinary vision is blurred (fig. 7.15). In the legend, Pope Gregory's mass is interrupted by his visceral experience of Christ's torso or full-length body rising up behind the altar. Gregory's vision created an authorized portrait of Christ, the *imago pietatis*, but also put the stamp of papal approval on countless images of indulgence, of which Meckenem's were the first in the print medium.[38] In Stradanus' miracle image #8 the Virgin of Guadalupe also vacillates between a weightless, diaphanous apparition and a tangible iconic representation that occludes a view of the apse wall with her three-dimensional mass. In this sense the Virgin of Guadalupe participates simultaneously in two realms, the immaterial and the palpably real, both necessary states

JEANETTE FAVROT PETERSON

of being for any cultic image to command faith and funds.

The second Stradanus story (miracle image #2) focuses on the miraculous spring and may be the most crucial for its proven antiquity, bicultural significance, and direct reference to the Virgin's apparition (fig. 7.16). The engraving conflates portions of several miracles later recorded individually by Laso de la Vega on the healing of two different women by the curative waters of the fountain.[39] In Laso de la Vega's account, however, neither of the petitioners is named Catharina de Niehta, nor is she described as the nun that Stradanus so explicitly represents with unmistakable robe and wimple. The text accompanying miracle image #2 records that "Catharina

Figure 7.14:
Miracle #8, Father Juan Vázquez
Acuña and the relit candles.
Copper engraving by
Samuel Stradanus
(detail of Figure 7.4).

CANONIZING A CULT

de niehta had had dropsy for 11 years without any hope of recovery. She came to novenas and drank the water from the fountain where Guadalupe appeared, and she was promptly cured."

The medicinal powers of a natural spring with "brackish" waters were noted at Tepeyac on the northwest edge of the salty portion of Lake Texcoco and connected with the nearby sixteenth-century shrine of Guadalupe. According to Miles Philips, writing in 1568,

At this place there are certain cold baths, which arise, springing up as though the water did seethe: the water whereof is somewhat brackish in taste, but very good for any that have any sore or wound, to wash themselves therewith, for as they say, it healeth many: and every year once upon Our Lady day, the people use to repair thither to offer, and to pray in that church before the image, and they say that Our Lady of Guadalupe doth work a number of miracles.[40]

JEANETTE FAVROT PETERSON

Figure 7.16:
Miracle #2, Sister Catharina
de Niehta and the fountain.
Copper engraving by
Samuel Stradanus
(detail of Figure 7.4).

In the sacred landscape, water sources were associated with life-giving powers, fertility, and healing. As just one example of a popular Marian cult in Spain during this period, the Virgen de la Salud near Valencia was said to have emerged from a bubbling spring.[41] In New Spain, as in Europe, these sites were often pre-Christian in origin; the friar Diego Durán warned of the lingering Precolumbian superstitions associated with springs which "aroused false divinity and mystery."[42] Later in the seventeenth century, the Guadalupe apologists, Luis Becerra Tanco and Francisco Florencia, emphasized the special draw of the medicinal waters of the Guadalupe spring for native Americans, especially women and children, alluding to the persistence of its preconquest importance. Moreover, both authors also associate the location of the spring with the fourth apparition of the Virgin of Guadalupe when she commands Juan Diego to pick roses from Tepeyac hill as "signs" of her unique powers. In 1675 Becerra Tanco even hypothesizes that it is at the very site of the spring that the miraculous painting was imprinted on Juan Diego's cloak.[43]

In this regard, the wording of the Stradanus text under the second miracle image may be significant, pointing to either partial or prototypical apparition stories already being disseminated. Stradanus specifically states that Catharina drinks water from the fountain "where Guadalupe appeared" (*adonde se aparessió N. S. de Guadalupe*) and then she was cured. The text is ambiguous, however, about whether the appearance of Guadalupe was a historical event, as part of a nascent apparition legend, or occurred to effect Catharina's cure. Unfortunately, the print does not now reveal a tiny hovering Virgin of Guadalupe, as it does in miracle image #4, where Carvajal's son claimed her image appeared to him during his riding accident.

Conclusion: The Canonizing Image

With adroit economy, Stradanus has communicated the essential ingredients of each story, highlighting the protagonists, particularly the primary recipient of the Virgin's grace, as well as the supporting cast. In the box-like interiors of each ex-voto, narrative is served by the sharply diagonal walls that create convincing stages for each of the scenes and generally converge on the principal figures, making the story line intelligible at a glance. Walls are eliminated where unimportant;

perspective is "bent" or ignored. In several of the ex-votos, Stradanus has compressed not only space but time, simultaneously representing (or implying) two or more episodes of the same narrative. In the Catharina miracle, for example, the nun is depicted sequentially at three stages of the story (fig. 7.16). First, through the open right wall of the sanctuary, the nun is seen drinking the healing water at the distant well. As the story progresses, the nun becomes increasingly larger, awakening from her sleep induced by drinking the curative fluid just outside of the shrine, and finally, center front, kneeling before the Guadalupe altar.

Life-altering events unfold in bounded spaces that are charged with dynamic motion and heightened emotion. Within the compact scenes, as in the third miracle where friar Pedro de Valderrama's toe is healed, figures fall, leap, gesticulate, and register astonishment at what is unfolding before their eyes (fig. 7.17).[44] Stradanus frames the scenes so as to slice figures who are entering from below or from the sides to enhance their immediacy and the drama of the moment. By and large the figures are handled competently but with economy of line and some puppet-like stiffness, perhaps an intended duplication of the naïve or "folk" quality of known ex-votos.

Although landscape details have suffered from the worn condition of the plate, sketchy urbanscapes do ground the events in real places and are crucial for localizing the cult in New Spain. Silhouettes of distant cities are marked as Christian communities with pointed spires surmounted by visible crosses. Although the capital city is invoked twice, as Mexico Tenochtitlan (fig. 7.16) and

JEANETTE FAVROT PETERSON

as "La Gran Ciudad de Mexico" (fig. 7.11), firmly situating the cult and shrine in the capital, the more distant cities of Tulancingo and Pachuca also appear with names glossed, suggesting a growing dissemination of the cult. The Virgin of Guadalupe is omnipresent in six of the eight miracle scenes—even when the text contradicts the need, citing other elements, such as the lamp oil, that are responsible for effecting the cures. The iconic figure is always pivoted frontally in spite of an angled point of view. Thus, the viewer is repeatedly reminded of the beneficial presence of the visionary Guadalupe and her "home," the shrine, as the consecrated space where such miraculous events take place, clearly justifying the erection of an even grander setting for the wonder-working icon.

The fundraising function of the Stradanus engraving is patently evident in that many of the beneficiaries of its miracles are

Figure 7.17:
Miracle #3, Father Pedro
de Valderrama and his toe.
Copper engraving
by Samuel Stradanus
(detail of Figure 7.4).

Spaniards or creoles and, with the exception of the churchmen, from a social and economic stratum that could afford to be generous. On the whole the Stradanus vignettes are populated with an upperclass clientele, such as the fashionable Bartolomé who emerges from his bed in figure 7.7 and his equally well-heeled companion in breeches, collared ruff, and feathered hat who holds the silver votive head. Yet it is important to recognize the intent to demonstrate that Guadalupe's blessings could benefit all her people, children and adults, men and women, European and native, the latter embodied in the sole (and token?) representative of the indigenous population in the sacristan, Juan Pavón of miracle image #7.[45]

Prints such as that by Stradanus were the foot soldiers in the Catholic church's militant challenge to Reformist criticism.[46] A flood of graphics was produced by the Counter Reformation church following the canonization of new saints, such as the Spanish St. Isidore Labrador in 1622. Strikingly similar to the Stradanus engraving, the commemorative print of St. Isidore includes four lateral panels each detailing in picture and word the authenticating hagiography of this farmer-saint who became so immensely popular among the agrarian populace of the Americas. The inclusion of text made images more acceptable to meet Reformist criticism: not only did words carry out the Tridentine mandate to instruct, but they assisted in sidestepping the danger of confusing representation with divine prototype.[47] In this spirit, the Stradanus engraving complies with the need for eyewitness testimony to provide

an acceptable foundation of "truthful" data that are grounded in specificity of protagonist and place and expressed in vernacular and Latin texts. Yet pictures continued to be the primary mode of communication in semiliterate societies, given the language barriers that were even more acute in the polyglot New World.[48] It is the images in the Stradanus that carry the burden of proof to authenticate Guadalupe as a genuine, not counterfeit, sign with potent agency. They verify the untranslatable, the mysterious workings of the supernatural. And as Lorraine Daston notes, miracles in the seventeenth century were in themselves evidence of divine revelation, characterized as God's "signature" or indexical signs of the Godhead.[49] Together, the play between text and image create a powerful tool for verifying Guadalupe's portentous forces.

The Echave Orio painting and the Stradanus engraving were clearly church sponsored and sanctioned efforts to promulgate the cult, but I argue they officially endorsed beliefs and customs already entrenched at the popular level. We have no evidence to indicate the intended viewer(s) for the 1606 painting, but the artist's treatment of the sacred cloth suggests that the icon of the Virgin of Guadalupe was being interpreted as acheiropoetic. The Stradanus broadsheet more explicitly speaks to a promotional campaign intended to secure and expand the cult to a broader, more inclusive, audience, using not only a belief in Guadalupe's heavenly origins but amassing an incontrovertible phalanx of miraculous events. I would argue that neither of these artworks is entirely a top-down manifestation nor were they invented from whole cloth. They represent official recognition of popular beliefs thus ensuring a positive reception.

An indigenous peasant was the recipient of Guadalupe's grace in the first miracle recorded at the shrine. In a letter to Philip II dated 1575, Viceroy don Martín Enríquez de Almanza specifically mentions the story of a "shepherd" (*ganadero*) who had his health restored by going to the Guadalupe shrine at Tepeyac and, with this event, propelled the worship of Guadalupe across ethnic lines.[50] As James Lockhart notes, both Spaniard and native reinforced the growth of cults, venerating the same holy objects and readily endorsing miraculous events that occurred even in the "other's" world.[51] However, at this early time, the specific intercessor, whether the Spanish or Mexican Virgin of Guadalupe, both of which may have been venerated at the shrine, is left ambiguous.[52]

At Tepeyac, as at other early colonial shrines, native participation was enthusiastic on Christian feast days through the staging of elaborate performances in dance, song, and theater that were given a distinctly indigenous cast. Ritualized hunts, sea battles, and choreographed chants characterized as "war songs" are documented as honoring the Virgin of Guadalupe in 1566,

1585, and 1595.[53] Becerra Tanco recollects the great dances (*mitotes*) and sung narratives that marked the native celebration of the Virgin of Guadalupe's feast day before the devastating inundation of Mexico City in 1629. To the rhythmic beat of the preconquest upright drum, or *teponaztli*, native songs commemorated in verse the apparition legend and various miracle stories associated with Guadalupe. Becerra Tanco emphasizes the strength of sung histories passed down from one generation to another among the indigenes and cites the vocal medium as one of the primary methods of preserving and transmitting the Guadalupe legends.[54] If we are to believe Becerra Tanco, a strong tradition of orality kept these beliefs intact among the indigenous worshippers. By performing the Guadalupe miracles they were recording and perpetuating memory. Thus the Stradanus narratives can be interpreted as a response to these extant oral and performative stories. The 1613 engraving only articulated in concrete form what was already in the collective memory and harnessed Guadalupe's perceived powers securely under the jurisdiction of the church, canonizing a cult long before the middle of the seventeenth century.

NOTES

1. "Before Guadalupe" is the title of Louise M. Burkhart's (2001) study of the Virgin Mary in early colonial (pre-1648) Nahuatl literature. See Louise M. Burkhart, *Before Guadalupe: The Virgin Mary in Early Colonial Nahautl Literature* (Albany, NY: Institute for Mesoamerican Studies, 2001). On the campaign to legitimize Guadalupe as the primary Virgin Mary in New Spain by creole authors referred to as the "four evangelists" for their

fervor in establishing the historicity of the Virgin of Guadalupe, see Francisco de la Maza, *El guadalupanismo* [1953] (Mexico City: Fondo de la Cultura Económica, 1981); Jacques Lafaye, *Quetzalcoatl and Guadalupe: The Formation of Mexican National Consciousness, 1532–1815*, trans. Benjamin Keen (Chicago: University of Chicago Press, 1976); James Lockhart, *The Nahuas After Conquest* (Stanford: Stanford University Press, 1992), 248; Stafford Poole, *Our*

Lady of Guadalupe: The Origins and Sources of a Mexican National Symbol: 1531–1797 (Tucson and London: The University of Arizona Press, 1995), 100–171; and D. A. Brading, *Mexican Phoenix: Our Lady of Guadalupe* (Cambridge: Cambridge University Press, 2001), 54–145. In addition to Miguel Sánchez, *Imagen de la Virgen María Madre de Dios de Guadalupe* (Mexico City: Bernardo Calderón, 1648) and Luis Laso de la Vega, *Huei tlamahuicoltica*, ed. and trans. Primo Feliciano Velázquez (Mexico City: Carreño e hijos, 1649), the other creole pro-apparitionist authors among the "four evangelists" are Luis Becerra Tanco, *Felicidad de México* (Mexico City: Viuda de Bernardo Calderón, 1675) and Francisco de Florencia, S.J., *La Estrella de el norte de México* [1688] (Barcelona: Antonio Velázquez, 1741).

2. See Jeanette Favrot Peterson, "Creating the Virgin of Guadalupe: The Cloth, Artist and Sources in Sixteenth Century New Spain," *The Americas* 61, no. 4 (April 2005): 571–610. The Marian typology of Tota Pulchra is derived from Song of Solomon 4:7, "*Tota pulchra es, amica mea, et macula non est in te*" (You are all fair, my love; there is no flaw in you). The visual hybridity of the Mexican Virgin of Guadalupe as the Immaculate Conception forms part of my broader study on the iconographic changes that occurred in transporting the Guadalupe cult from Spain to New Spain. See Suzanne L. Stratton, *The Immaculate Conception in Spanish Art* (Cambridge: Cambridge University Press, 1994), 39–66, for the evolution of Immaculate Conception imagery in early modern Spain.

3. Although curiously few extant pre-1648 copies of the Virgin of Guadalupe have been located, her putative role in quelling the floodwaters that inundated Mexico City between 1629–1634 stimulated the manufacture of "mountains" of copies, many of them "false" and scandalously painted, according to Cayetano de Cabrera y Quintero, *Escudo de armas de México: Ma. Santissima en su portentosa imagen del mexicano Guadalupe* (Mexico City: Vda. de D. Joseph Bernardo de Hogal, 1743), bk. 3, #715–17. Such was the poor quality of most of these reproductions that in 1637 the Ecclesiastical Council of Mexico City issued an edict intended to control their production and to confiscate those of inferior make. Elisa Vargas Lugo,

"Iconología guadalupana," in *Imagenes guadalupanas: Cuatro siglos* (Mexico City: Centro Cultural Arte Contemporaneo, 1988), 76–80, plates 48, 49, 52; Elisa Vargas Lugo, "Algunas notas más sobre iconografía Guadalupana," in *Anales del Instituto de Investigaciones Estéticas* (Mexico City: Universidad Nacional Autonóma de México, 1989), 59, has suggested three other reproductions of the tilma image from this pre-1648 period. A mural in the Augustinian monastery of Yuririapúndaro, Gto., assigned to friar Pedro Salguero and thus dated to 1621–1627, is problematic in my view, and more likely an eighteenth-century work. More certain are signed and dated canvases by Rodrigo Delapyedra (1625) at the church of Santo Desierto, San Luis Potosí, and by Luis de Tejeda (1632) in the Convento del Desierto, Tenancingo, Mexico.

4. Both the image and its putative miraculous powers were contested by the Franciscan provincial, Francisco de Bustamante, in 1556. His iconoclastic sermon was reconstructed through testimonials by several eyewitnesses referred to collectively as the "Información de 1556," in Ernesto de la Torre Villa and Ramiro Navarro de Anda, *Testimonios históricos guadalupanos* (Mexico City: Fondo de Cultura Económica, 1982), 36–141.

5. The dimensions of the Echave Orio painting are 170 by 111 cm (67" x 44") as compared with the tilma painting of Guadalupe in the Basilica in Mexico City of 175 by 105 cm (69" x 41¼"). Apparently, 51 cm. were cut from the top of the tilma canvas in 1766 to accommodate the painting to a new frame. Manuel Ortiz Vaquero, "Tres ejemplos de pintura guadalupana," *Imagenes guadalupanas: Cuatro siglos* (Mexico City: Centro Cultural Arte Contemporaneo, 1988), 29, notes that two panels were used by Echave Orio almost certainly to replicate the model. Vargas Lugo, "Algunas notas más sobre iconografía Guadalupana," 60–61, concludes that Baltasar de Echave Orio's emphasis on the sacred cloth of Juan Diego's tilma is unique and only reappears in eighteenth-century paintings reflecting the resurrection of an interest in Juan Diego himself.

6. Baltasar de Echave Orio (b. 1547/48–1619/23) was promptly given commissions for altarpiece paintings that are ennumerated in

Guillermo Tovar de Teresa, *Pintura y escultura del renacimiento* (Mexico City: Instituto Nacional de Arte e Historia, 1979), 180–84; see also Marcus Burke, *Pintura y escultura en Nueva España: El barroco* (Mexico City: Grupo Azabache, 1992), 28–29, 33.

7. For an example, see Echave Orio's painting "Vision of St. Francis in Porciuncula" of 1609, in Burke, *Pintura*, 28.

8. Hans Belting, *Likeness and Presence*, trans. E. Jephcott, 428 (Chicago and London: University of Chicago Press, 1994), speaks of the "twofold reality" of the head of Christ on "Veil of Veronica," and also refers to it as an "image within an image." On the separation of the cloth ground from the immaterial Holy Face of Christ on the sudarium, also see Joseph Leo Koerner, *The Moment of Self-Portraiture in German Renaissance Art* (Chicago and London, 1993), 86, 89.

9. On the history of Veronica's Veil as an acheiropoetic image see Belting, *Likeness*, 208–24, and Koerner, *The Moment*, 80–126. The Western adaptation of the Veronica myth and its first sudarium was displayed at St. Peter's in the thirteenth century, but disappeared during the sack of Rome in 1527.

10. See Sixten Ringbom, *Icon to Narrative: The Rise of the Dramatic Close-up in Fifteenth-Century Devotional Painting* (Åbo: Åbo Akademi, 1965), 23–24.

11. On the metaphorical interplay of skin-cloth traced through biblical and theological history, see Ewa Kuryluk, *Veronica and Her Cloth* (Cambridge and Oxford: Basil Blackwell, 1991).

12. As asserted by Jaime Cuadriello, *Maravilla americana: Variantes de la iconografía guadalupana*, s. XVII–XIX, (Mexico City: Patrimonio cultural del occidente, 1989), 33.

13. Similarities in the structural patterns of European Marian legends are discussed by William A. Christian, *Apparitions in Late Medieval and Renaissance Spain* (Princeton: Princeton University Press, 1981) and William A. Christian, *Local Religion in Sixteenth-Century Spain* (Princeton: Princeton University Press, 1981), 3–26. An explanation of the "shepherd's cycle" and its relevance to both Spanish and Mexican Guadalupe cults

can be found in Victor Turner and Edith L. B. Turner, *Image and Pilgrimage in Christian Culture* (New York: Columbia University Press, 1978), 41–57.

14. The central inscription on the Stradanus print reads as follows: "The renowned don Juan de la Serna, by the grace of God and the Holy Apostolic See, Archbishop of Mexico of the Royal Council of the King, Our Lord, etc., remits forty days of indulgences that have been conceded by the Holy Apostolic See, granted to whomever possesses a copy of this image of Our Lady the Virgin of Guadalupe and gives a donation to the ongoing construction of the new church, her Holy house and shrine, to which all faithful should contribute as there are not enough [funds] to finish, and this is very pious work on behalf of the Virgin" (author's translation).

15. While the Metropolitan Ecclesiastical Council approved construction in 1600, it is unclear whether the new church dedicated to the Virgin of Guadalupe was begun in 1601, suspended and then recommenced in 1609, or only initiated in 1609. In 1612 the architect, Juan Pérez de Soto, had to stop for lack of funds but it was at this point that the election of the archbishop, Juan Pérez de la Serna, breathed new life into the enterprise. This sanctuary is known as the "old" basilica which was demolished in 1694 when the "new" basilica was begun and ultimately consecrated in 1709. On this history consult Fidel de Jesus Chauvet, "Historia del culto guadalupano," in *Album conmemorativo del 450 aniversario de las apariciones de Nra. Sra. de Guadalupe* (Mexico City: Ed. Buena Nueva, 1981), 42–43; Efraín Castro Morales, "El santuario de Guadalupe de México en el siglo XVII," in *Retablo barroco a la memoria de Francisco de la Maza* (Mexico City: Universidad Nacional Autonóma de México, IIE, 1974), 70.

16. Samuel Stradanus is not to be confused with the better known Joannes or Jan Stradanus (1523–1605), also known as Jan van der Straet. Of the scant biographical data that have been found on Samuel Stradanus (sometimes written Estradanus), we know he was working in Mexico at least by 1604 and married there in 1626. Within his active engraving period, Stradanus produced an engraving

for a 1602 publication from Córdova, Spain (signed Samuel Hoochstradanus) and subsequently his graphics were commissioned for Mexican publications: a portrait and frontispiece from 1604, the frontispiece from the *Sucesos de las Islas Philipinas* by Doctor Antonio de Morga (1609), a frontispiece, map, and portrait from 1618, and finally, the frontispiece for the *Sanctum Porvinciale Concilium Mexici* of 1622. On these, see Manuel Romero de Terreros, *Samuel Stradano: Imagen de la Virgen Nuestra Señora de Guadalupe* (Mexico City: Ediciones Arte Mexicano, 1948), and Manuel Romero de Terreros, *Grabados y grabadores en la Nueva España* (Mexico City: Ediciones Arte Mexicano, 1948), 343–45, plate 539. The 1602 engraving can be found in the Biblioteca Nacional in Madrid, Spain (photograph #3.33149).

17. On the sermonizing use of prints in this compositional format, with the saint or holy figure surrounded by biographical and hagiographic narratives, see Juan Carrette et al., *Grabado en España, s. XV–XVIII. Summa Artis, v. XXXI* (Madrid: Espasa Calpe, 1996), 155. Belting, *Likeness*, 249, refers to this genre as "vita" or reading icons. A variant of this format is the Virgin of the Rosary by Doménech, one of the earliest fifteenth-century prints in Spain (Carrette et al., *Grabado en España*, fig. 6); for later examples of this genre, see Carrette et al., *Grabado en España*, figs. 276 and 416.

18. In his 1688 account of the Guadalupe cult, Florencia, *La estrella*, 33, claimed that certain sixteenth-century caretakers of the shrine doctored the image by adding "cherubims" or angel heads around the solar mandorla. These angel heads were later erased, although the cloud bank continued to be visible in the scalloped edge of the mandorla throughout Guadalupe's iconographic history. At the time Stradanus worked on his engraving, these cherubims may still have been visible, or, he simply added them based on conventional depictions of the Virgin Mary, given that Echave Orio does not include them in his 1606 painting.

19. See Chauvet, "Historia del culto guadalupano," 44.

20. Although controversial to this day, it appears that the crown was absent, probably painted out

by 1893, when the official coronation ceremony was held for the Virgin of Guadalupe; see Jeanette Favrot Peterson, "The Virgin of Guadalupe: Symbol of Conquest or Liberation," *Art Journal* 51, no. 4 (winter 1992): 45.

21. Juan Correa was among the first artists to devise a paper template of the original icon in the 1660s, from which hundreds of copies were subsequently made. See Elisa Vargas Lugo and J. G. Victoria y Curiel, eds., *Juan Correa: Su vida e su obra* (Mexico City: UNAM, 1994), 273; Jeanette Favrot Peterson, "Juan Correa y la Virgen de Guadalupe," in *Los siglos de oro en los virreinatos de América 1550–1700* (Madrid: Sociedad Estatal para la Conmemoración de Los Centenarios de Felipe II y Carlos V, 1999). However, I propose an earlier use of templates in a 1656 Guadalupe painting by José Juárez; "The Virgin Guadalupe with Apparitions by José Juárez [1656]," in *Painting the New World* (Denver: Denver Art Museum, 2004), 158–59. By replicating the colors and symbolic details, but especially the precise measurements and proportions, something of the power of the originary image was thought to be transferred to the copies.

22. On andachtsbilder, see Ringbom, *Icon*, 52–58; Belting, *Likeness*, 425–26. Christian, *Local*, 100, discusses the sale of *estampas* (prints) at Spanish shrines and their use for curing. Specific miracles attributed to prints of the Spanish Virgin of Guadalupe (worn in hats or inside a devotee's jacket) are cited by Gabriel de Talavera, *Historia de Nuestra Señora de Guadalupe* (Toledo: Thomás de Guzmán, 1597), in his history of the Extremaduran sanctuary, f. 248v, 322–23.

23. On sixteenth-century votive gifts donated by Christopher Columbus and Hernán Cortés, see Talavera, *Historia*, f. 153–57. Hanging lamps festooned the main altar in the Spanish Guadalupe church, such as Philip II's gift of a votive lamp of gilded copper to mark the 1571 victory at Lepanto, in Sebastián García Rodríguez, ed., *Guadalupe: Siete siglos de fe y de cultura* (Guadalupe: Ediciones Guadalupe, 1993), 71, 419.

24. Miles Philips, "The Voyage of Miles Philips, 1568," in *The Principal Navigations, Voyages and Discoveries of the English Nation*

[1589] (Glasgow: James MacLehose & Sons, 1904), 419.

25. The Spanish texts under each miracle scene are challenging to decipher because of the effaced condition of the copper plate. My own transcriptions of the captions have benefited from, but do not always follow, previous publications of the texts, including that of Romero de Terreros, *Grabados*; Chauvet, "Historia del culto guadalupano," 44–45; and Pilar Gonzalbo Aizpuru, "Lo prodigioso cotidiano en los exvotos novohispanos," in *Dones y promesas: 500 años de arte oferenda* (Mexico City: Fundación Cultural Televisa, 1996), 67.

26. The full caption under miracle image #7 reads: "The Great City of Mexico; Juan Pavón, sacristan of Our Lady, had a son ill with an abscess of his throat which he rubbed with the oil of a lamp of Our Lady, and . . . And thus he was cured without requiring other treatment."

27. The full caption under miracle #1 reads: "Bartolomé Granado had terrible head and earaches; there was no remedy; he went to novena. He took a silver head which is hanging in the church and he was miraculously cured."

28. The anonymous friar who displays the silver leg in the Stradanus print is indirectly identified as the Franciscan Pedro de Valderrama by Luis Laso de la Vega. See Lisa Sousa et al., *The Story of Guadalupe: Luis Laso de la Vega's Huei tlamahuiçoltica of 1649* (Stanford: Stanford University Press, 1998), 109. Valderrama is also the protagonist of miracle image #4 in the Stradanus print.

29. On the prodigies of the Virgin Mary in the early colonial period, see Luis Weckmann, *The Medieval Heritage of Mexico*, trans. Frances M. López-Morillas (New York: Fordham University Press, 1992), 163, 260–74, 276–86; Lockhart, *The Nahuas*, 244–46; Burkhart, *Before Guadalupe*, 131–46. And on the growth of confirmed miracles in the seventeenth century, see Antonio Rubial García, "Tierra de prodigios: Lo maravilloso cristiano en la Nueva España de los siglos XVI y XVII," in *La iglesia católica en México*, ed. Nelly Siguat, 357–64 (Michoacán: El Colegio de Michoacán, 1997) and Luisa Elena Alcalá, "Imagen e historia: La representación del milagro en la pintura colonial," in *Los siglos de oro en los virreinatos de América 1550–1700* (Madrid: Sociedad Estatal, 1999), 107–25.

30. On the relationship between miraculous cult image and shrine, see Gonzalbo Aizpuru, "Lo prodigioso cotidiano," 52; Thomas Calvo, "El exvoto: Antecedentes y permanencies," in *Dones y promesas: 500 años de arte ofrenda* (Mexico City: Fundación Cultural Televisa, 1996), 35–36, and Christian, *Local*, 102–5 for Spain.

31. Gabriel de Talavera, prior of Jeronymite monastery of Guadalupe, in 1597 wrote one of the first histories of the cult of the Spanish Guadalupe and Book V in his history is devoted to the 150 miracles, some of which have parallels in the Stradanus engraving.

32. On this Cuzco school painting of the Spanish Virgin of Guadalupe, see Pál Kelemen, *Peruvian Colonial Painting* (New York: The Brooklyn Museum, 1971), Plate 34. Arturo Alvarez Alvarez, "Guadalupe: Dos imagines bajo una advocación," in *Guadalupe: Siete siglos de fe y de cultura*, ed. Sebastián García, 523–33 (Madrid: Ediciones Guadalupe, 1993), reviews possible iconographic connections between the Extremaduran Virgin of Guadalupe and the Guadalupe cults that took root in the Americas.

33. Sousa et al., *The Story*, 13–17. The miracle stories are in Sánchez, *Imagen*, f. 82v–87v. Transcriptions of Luis Laso de la Vega's fourteen miracle texts (*Nican Motecpana*) are found in Laso de la Vega, *Huei*, 57–83, and in Sousa et al., *The Story*, 92–113. Descriptive analyses of the Stradanus miracles have been undertaken by Romero de Terreros, *Grabados*; Chauvet, "Historia del culto guadalupano, 44–45 and figs. 11, 12; and Poole, *Our Lady*, 118–24.

34. The references to a woman benefiting from the curative springs at Tepeyac are found in Laso de la Vega's miracles 8 and 10, as translated by Sousa et al., *The Story*, 105–9. Other minor discrepancies include the spelling of Antonio Carbelar in the Stradanus miracle image #5 as opposed to don Antonio Carvajal in Sanchez and Laso de la Vega (miracle #4) and the substitution of "a Spaniard" as the protagonist in the falling lamp miracle for Stradanus' "anonymous man" (*un hombre*) in miracle #6.

35. These now lost paintings may have been

commissioned either by don Antonio de Carvajal himself, a wealthy landowner and an *alcalde* (magistrate) in Mexico City, or by his son, Andrés de Carvajal y Tapia, according to Gonzalbo Aizpuru, "Lo prodigioso cotidiano," 79, who does not give the source of these data. An illustration of an eighteenth-century painting on this theme can be found in Vargas Lugo, "Iconología guadalupana," plate 111.

36. The full caption under miracle image #8 reads: "Father Juan Vázquez Acuña, vicar of the Virgin, was waiting at the altar to say mass, saw that the candles to be lit were alit miraculously by Our Lady."

37. Both Miguel Sánchez and Luis Laso de la Vega trace the extinction of the candles to windy conditions, but they differ in their interpretation of how they were subsequently relit. Sánchez cites two solar rays as the cause whereas Laso de la Vega attributes their relighting to the effects of the emanating "rays of the heavenly Lady" (Torre Villar and Navarro de Anda, *Testimonios*, 250–51; Sousa et al., *The Story*, 103).

38. See David Landau and Peter Parshall, *The Renaissance Print 1470–1550* (New York and London: Yale University Press, 1994), 58.

39. Luis Laso de la Vega refers to the curative spring waters in three of his fourteen miracles (his 7th, 8th, and 10th miracle stories), with two episodes close to, but not exact duplicates of, miracle image #2 in the Stradanus print (Sousa et al., *The Story*, 105–9).

40. Philips, *Voyage*, 419.

41. On the association of Spanish shrines with the healing properties of springs, see Christian, *Local*, 83–85.

42. Diego de Durán, *Historia de las Indias de Nueva España e Islas de la Tierra Firme*, ed., Angel Ma. Garibay K, 2 vols. (Mexico City: Ed. Porrúa, 1967), I:173.

43. Becerra Tanco, *Felicidad*, f. 7 and 7v.; Francisco de Florencia in Torre Villar and Navarro de Anda, *Testimonios*, 363–64.

44. The legible caption under miracle image #3 reads: "Father Pedro de Valderrama, a discalced Franciscan, had a toe . . . then it was healed and he went on foot from Guadalupe to Pachuca."

45. The Nahua term for the staff of the church is *teopantlaca* or "church people," of whom the sacristan was one of the lesser officials in charge of maintaining the Eucharist and sacristy; Lockhart, *The Nahuas*, 215–18.

46. On the extensive use of prints by a militant church, see Carrette et al., *Grabado en España*, 158–63.

47. See Belting, *Likeness*, 465–70.

48. Michael Camille, "The Book of Signs: Writing and Visual Difference in Gothic Manuscript Illumination," in *Word and Image* 1, no. 2 (1985): 133–48, offers instructive parallels on the ongoing, powerful role of images in late medieval pictorial manuscripts.

49. Lorraine Daston, "Marvelous Facts and Miraculous Evidence in Early Modern Europe," in *Questions of Evidence: Proof, Practice and Persuasion across the Disciplines*, ed. James Chandler et al., 265–66 (Chicago: University of Chicago Press, 1994).

50. Viceroy Enríquez's visit is recorded in Torre Villar and Navarro de Anda, *Testimonios*, 148–49.

51. Lockhart, *The Nahuas*, 244–46.

52. The exact nature of the cult image in the early shrine of Guadalupe has been embroiled in polemic from the very outset. I argue that when the painted Mexican tilma image of the Mexican Virgin of Guadalupe was installed in the Tepeyac shrine around 1555, it began to compete with another Marian image, perhaps a copy of the Spanish sculptural image that was already being venerated in the shrine. Thus at the viceroy's visit in 1575, when a church had replaced the earlier *ermita* or shrine of 1555–1556, it is unclear which of the two images was being given credit for the shepherd's miraculous cure.

54. On the celebration of Guadalupe's feast day, see Luis Reyes García, *Anales de Juan Bautista* (Mexico City: Biblioteca Lorenzo Boturini, Insigne, Nacional Basílica de Guadalupe, 2001), f. 6v, 151; Max Harris, *Aztecs, Moors and Christians: Festivals of Reconquest in Mexico and Spain* (Austin: University of Texas Press, 2000), 151–52.

55. Becerra Tanco, *Felicidad*, f. 12v., 14–14v.

JEANETTE FAVROT PETERSON

PART FOUR

TAKING THE VEIL AND NEW REALITIES

One day, when I was at a meal, and was in no way interiorly recollected, my soul began to experience a suspension and recollection of such a kind that I thought some rapture was coming upon me, and I saw this vision, which lasted but the usual brief space of time—that of a lightning flash. I thought Our Lord Jesus Christ was near me, in the form of which his Majesty is wont to reveal Himself to me.

—Teresa of Avila, 1515–1582

And so whenever I receive some favor from Our Lord, I already know it is a warning that I shall suffer more and more, because I am enjoying and suffering at one and the same time . . .

—Madre María de José, 1656–1719

From the moment I was first illuminated by the light of reason, my inclination toward letters has been so vehement that not even the admonitions of others. . . . nor my own meditations. . . . have been sufficient to cause me to forswear this natural impulse that God placed in me; the Lord God knows why, and for what purpose.

—Sor Juana Inés de la Cruz, 1648–1695

The traditional view of colonial women of high social standing was that they had only two options regarding the course of their lives—to marry or to enter a convent—and that they had little to say about their choice of spouse or religious house. Moreover, if they were second or third daughters in the household, they inevitably were fated for life in the convent since families tended to channel their financial assets into a generous dowry for a first, or preferred, daughter, in order to attract the best possible suitor and ensure a profitable match. Women entering nunneries also received dowries to sustain themselves, but typically the monetary investment was less. Daughters in prestigious marriages and convents brought great esteem to families for both built on New Spain's social and economic corporate institutions and also helped to maintain the elaborate structure of the church.

Until very recently, there was little information about the lives of women once they took the veil. A few nuns had magnificent portraits painted of themselves wearing elaborate crowns of jewels and flowers that reflected the sumptuousness and splendor of their spiritual undertaking. The portraits have legends furnishing brief sketches about the women, their families, and the order. Other paintings reveal information about the religious orders themselves and the requisite habits. Convents fulfilled some of the many social obligations of the Catholic church: nuns served as teachers, nurses, and providers of safe haven for orphans and other people in need. Most women, upon taking their vows, were cloistered for the rest of their lives.

But what of their lives once confined? For their own edification, some became accomplished musicians and performed in concert or participated in and enjoyed their own theater productions. Others became specialty cooks or producers of fine handicrafts. Sor Juana Inés de la Cruz is legendary for her intelligence—some of which was realized in her poetry, plays, and songs—and her struggle to continue her literary interests in the face of discrimination and reprimand from misogynist clerical authorities. Sor Juana had become a nun by choice and believed that piety and intelligence were not necessarily contradictory attributes for women.

Nunneries were typically in the cities and subject to the authority of a local bishop, but otherwise the nuns had their own rules and managed their own affairs. They were brides of Christ, and their vows obliged them, first and foremost, to lead truly pious lives. Yet the measure of their spirituality was always subjective at best, except for those who kept records of their experiences. More than personal career biographies or hagiographies of favorite saints, new research reveals that many nuns kept diaries detailing their struggles for spiritual perfection. Several of the nuns were mystics, and all experienced rapturous divine visions of one sort or another. The journals are intimate and profound, and we are only now beginning to appreciate these holy women's exquisite anguish.

Asunción Lavrin, in "Female Visionaries and Spirituality," introduces the topic of female religious to this collection. Too often what is known of the lives of nuns was penned by their spiritual confessors. Lavrin wishes to let the women speak for themselves and thus discovers the "purest vision of their spirituality." In "The Indigenous Nuns of Corpus Christi: Race and Spirituality," Mónica Díaz continues the discussion of female religious spirituality while focusing on the issue of racism in New Spain. Using a rich collection of sources, she also delves into questions of class, intellectual capability, literacy, and the public versus private voice of religious. For more than two hundred years, convents had been the exclusive province of Spanish women. But native women were interested in spiritual vocations, too. Díaz tells of their struggle, and eventual success, to have a convent for themselves alone.

NOTES

Epigraph citations, in order of appearance, are as follows: Teresa of Avila, *The Complete Works of Saint Teresa of Jesus*, vol. 1, ed. and trans. E. Allison Peers, 354 (London and New York: Sheed and Ward, 1957); Madre María de José, *A Wild Country Out in the Garden: The Spiritual Journals of a Colonial Mexican Nun*, ed. and trans. Kathleen A. Myers and Amanda Powell, 80 (Bloomington: Indiana University Press, 1999); Octavio Paz, *Sor Juana or, The Traps of Faith*, trans. Margaret Sayers Peden, 416 (Cambridge: Harvard University Press, 1988).

CHAPTER EIGHT

Female Visionaries and Spirituality

ASUNCIÓN LAVRIN

Female visionaries and mystics have emerged as one of the most inspiring themes of recent European medieval historiography. They have injected new life into the study of Christian spirituality as well as the history of women, and their writings are now considered a new literary genre worthy of translation and interpretation. The names of Hildegarde of Bingen, Clare of Assisi, Catherine of Siena, Margery Kempe, and Julian of Norwich are perhaps the best known among medieval visionaries, but they are only a few of a group that is constantly broadening in scope. Elizabeth Petrof's anthology of visionary writers, published in 1986, contains twenty-eight selections.[1] None of the authors resided in the Iberian Peninsula. According to Jodi Bilinkoff, there were no writings of medieval visionaries or mystics in the Iberian Peninsula, until the fifteenth century.[2] In the sixteenth century

Teresa of Avila and her "brother in religion," John of the Cross, represented the finest flowering of Spanish mysticism.

Students of Spanish female literature in the fifteenth and sixteenth centuries have already rediscovered a significant number of writings by visionaries and mystics that will place the peninsula in a special place as a latecomer of distinction in the halls of early modern literature.[3] Given the development of mysticism in sixteenth- and seventeenth-century Spain, it is not surprising to find visionaries in the New World. Of all the cultural transfers that took place in the sixteenth century between Spain and its newly founded colonies, the canonic foundation of religion was possibly the least liable to be altered. Orthodoxy had to be rigidly maintained against the threat of Protestantism and deviant forms of spirituality within Roman Catholicism.

In Spain itself observance was reformed, whenever possible, to adjust Roman Catholic spirituality to the new rules guiding the church after the Council of Trent (1545–1563). Threats to the authority of the church such as *alumbradismo*, a form of direct communication with God, became a great concern for the ecclesiastical authorities and the Inquisition. By the end of the sixteenth century the Spanish church was under much tighter internal controls and in a position to exercise them in its American possessions.[4] Religion was one of the strongest vehicles of Spanish cultural diffusion in the New World. This does not mean that observance was rigidly copied from Spanish models without any local challenge. In the Americas Christianity was a recent transplant to a soil that had nurtured hundreds of non-Christian beliefs before the Spanish arrival, and "idolatry" was still not just suspected, but confirmed among the newly converted indigenous population. Observance, the specific manner of following Catholic beliefs in rituals and daily life, was closely monitored in New Spain as well as in the rest of the colonies, precisely because they began to take certain local forms that looked intolerable to the authorities.

In his study of the *alumbrados* of Mexico, Alvaro Huerga states that the inquisitorial investigations of these and other forms of unorthodoxy points to *criollización* or adaptation to the physical and psychological challenges of the new society. The Inquisition was keenly aware of subtle reinterpretations and sought to uproot them.[5] Late sixteenth- and early seventeenth-century bishops and archbishops arriving in New Spain, fresh from the peninsula, scrutinized observance

in all branches of the church. They enacted new regulations to correct any transgressions and used their episcopal authority to survey the behavior of the clergy and regular orders.

The models of observance and spiritual perfection that we find in biographies and conventual chronicles written in the seventeenth and early eighteenth centuries suggest that there was a desire to create unchallengeable guides of correctness for religious as well as for the laity. The orthodoxy dictated by the Council of Trent had to rely on strengthening the spiritual linkage between Spain and New Spain and the most solid supporters of Roman Catholicism: the members of the church and the Spanish social elite. In theory, they served as models for the recently converted. Should they offer diluted or wrong examples to the indigenes and the populace, the church and Christianity could lose their authority. The church had great trouble maintaining its control over the personal behavior of the laity, and it also strove to keep its ascendancy over its own members.

The desire to maintain orthodoxy helps to explain the tight control over nuns. Some novohispanic nunneries were given new rules, their habits were inspected to achieve proper modesty, and their conventual observance subjected to stricter regulations.[6] Nuns' writings and, more importantly, the type of spirituality that flowered in women's convents was held under tight scrutiny. The possibility of distortion of faith and observance was not totally unfounded. In the years between the foundation of the first nunnery ca. 1550 and the first quarter of the seventeenth century there were some internal reverberations about observance in some convents, while the first cases of transgressions by nuns, beatas, male clergy, and friars were examined by the Inquisition.[7] Peninsular nuns led by Marina de la Cruz, inspired by the writings of Teresa de Jesús and the reformed observance practiced by her Carmelite nuns, began to plan the foundation of a more observant nunnery because Jesús María was, in their opinion, "relaxed" and did not fill their bill of religious observance. In mid-seventeenth century, Franciscan provincial fray Francisco de la Rúa demanded from Franciscan nunneries a return to a more austere observance of the rules of poverty. The few cases of alumbrada nuns that reached the Mexican Inquisition confirmed the suspicion of religious authorities that heterodoxy among the closed walls of the brides of Christ could take place.[8]

Spanish, as well as other European theologians examined all manifestations of female spiritual visions. A unique religious vocation such as that of Teresa of Avila was subjected to praise as well as to criticism for unorthodoxy. So were those of several other Spanish women whose writings or visionary experiences were not totally acceptable to a traditional male hierarchy for whom the greatest virtue in women was silence and obedience. While approving the autobiography of Sor Isabel de Jesús, one of the readers declared that he began reading it "with the greatest repugnance . . . because I did not think it was right that a woman should write on doctrine for the public when there are so many books by very learned men."[9] Isabel Ortiz, a sixteenth-century beata, gained a deserved reputation as a spiritual advisor and wrote a small book on

meditation and prayer. When she attempted to have it published, the Inquisition's examiner disapproved it, stating that "a woman's book should not be approved or printed," following Paul's prohibition of women docents in the church.[10] This was the spirit that led prelates to exercise strict vigilance over women's writings, confining them to manuscript form in conventual archives or, worse, destroying them. On the other hand, men took advantage of their authorial role to write women's lives. Chroniclers and biographers, by virtue of their sex and training, used histories of convents and biographies written by women as the raw materials from which they wrote funeral sermons, conventual chronicles, and lives of exemplary nuns.[11]

Women's writings in New Spain were under similar strictures. Most Mexican nuns wrote at the command of their confessors for their own spiritual development, and not for publication, but in the pages of their letters and diaries, they lay bare their emotions and religious beliefs. There is no certainty as to how many of them were written and destroyed throughout the colonial period, but conventual chronicles suggest that there were more than those so far recovered. With the possible exception of Sor María Anna Agueda de San Ignacio in eighteenth-century Puebla, whose works were published in 1758 with the support of her bishop, Domingo Pantaleón Alvarez de Abreu, novohispanic nuns never assumed that their writings would go beyond the hands of their confessors.

In 1993, Josefina Muriel dedicated one chapter of her book on feminine culture to the mystics of New Spain. She identified eleven nuns who were known to have written, even though their work remains to be published or studied.[12] At this point, we can add several more, such as Sor María Marcela, a capuchin nun in Querétaro, Sor María de Jesús Felipa, of San Juan de la Penitencia, and beata Francisca de los Angeles, from Querétaro. Recent works are bringing their writings out of archival seclusion.[13] These women, identified as "visionaries" and/or "mystics," are the counterpart to those who flourished in Spain between the fifteenth and the eighteenth century.

Visionaries and Mystics

Perhaps the first issue to be clarified is whether there is any difference between a mystic and a visionary. For all intents and purposes, most authorities seem to conflate them, assuming that a mystic was also a visionary. For example, Elizabeth Petroff assumes that visions are part of the mystic experience, as she writes, "There was a self-fulfilling element in the common medieval assumption that the natural bent of women's religious impulses was contemplative and visionary." Kathryn J. McKnight's study of Sor Francisca Josefa de la Concepción, better known as "la monja de Tunja" (New Granada) calls her a "mystic." Fernando Iturburu also uses the word "mysticism" in his study of the Peruvian nun Sor Josefa de la Providencia, and Manuel Ramos Medina entitles his study of Mexican Carmelite nuns, Místicas y descalzas.[14] Given that Teresa of Avila was the preferred model followed by all colonial nuns, it is relevant to state that her experiences mix both states of mystic union and visions.[15] Gillian Ahlgren, who has thoroughly analyzed

Saint Teresa's writings, states that "Teresa's contemporaries saw evidence of her spiritual powers through such concrete signs as levitation, ecstasy, and prophecy."[16] Ahlgren concludes that Teresa made "clear the interdependence of the visionary and mystical traditions."[17] On the other hand, Rowan Williams, noting our contemporary interest in mystic experiences, argues that while Teresa invented mysticism by charting her own spiritual progress, she would not have assumed that "visionary and paranormal" experiences could be used as "evidence for the way the universe is."[18] Visionaries are, in most cases, mystics, and all mystics experienced visions. Therefore, when I use the word visionary I imply somebody who is also following the path of mysticism and seeking union with God. The experience of that union is what mattered to mystics, but doctrine made it clear that the soul and God were not identical; they remained of a different essence or nature. This union had no ultimate objective except that ineffable experience, but it could also be a venue whereby an important truth was communicated as a revelation for the benefit of the receiver and that of her community.[19] The most complex narrative of the mystic experience in sixteenth-century Spain was that of John of the Cross, whose poetry and detailed explanation of the process of mystic union remain unsurpassed. His explication of the mystic process does not fit neatly into "stages," but as a follower of Teresa of Avila, he refined the understanding of the latter. Doubtless, along with Teresa, he left a profound influence on novohispanic spirituality.[20]

Visionaries and mystics raised contradictory views. While one school of religious reform extolled the knowledge that could be received from direct communication with God, another upheld intense suspicion of visions, especially those held by women who were prone to be deceived by the devil. Nonetheless, the abundant literature on saintly lives of the period, whether lived by members of the church or simply pious lay people, brims with miracles, ecstasy, revelations, and similar forms of direct communication with God. Julio Caro Baroja, commenting on this fact, underlines, not without some irony, that what was written and admitted by theologians (about visions and ecstasy) could not but become acceptable and accepted as religiously valid.[21] But by the beginning of the seventeenth century, the Roman Catholic church had already built its own walls of protection against false visionaries. In 1607, Fr. Leandro de Granada published a treatise on the nature of visions and a doctrinal analysis of such revelations in order to help the faithful, and even more so, their confessors, to differentiate between the genuine orthodox vision and the deceit of the devil.[22] In New Spain, Miguel Godínez (Michael Wadding), S.J., teacher of Theology at the Colegio de San Pedro y San Pablo in Mexico City, wrote a classic treatise on mystical theology in which he defined canonical mystical behavior, its failures and rewards. Having worked in New Spain and taken under his direction some Mexican nuns, his analysis of visions, raptures, and ecstasy is indispensable to judge the nature of visionaries.[23]

An important element in the understanding of vision and mysticism and the intertwined nature of both is the fact that theologians and mystics have explained the perception of spiritual experiences using metaphorical language. They wrote as if the spirit, in perceiving the divine, had interior acts corresponding to the senses.[24] They could write of a movement upwards, or outwards, a sense of enwrapment, a sense of burning in love, or a sense of "holy liquefaction" in which the person loses himself or herself as though he or she did not exist or have a clear understanding of the self. Fragrances can be smelled, burning feelings felt or soft touches experienced, the rivers of graces are tasted, and even God is also tasted as a sweet experience. He could also be the whisper of a breeze or silent music. That such sensations are not physical, but provide knowledge and certainty, was undeniable to those who experienced and wrote about them. To avoid confusion with the false experiences of charlatans and feigned beatas, they have to declare that such visions were not seen with the physical eyes but with the eyes of the soul.

Evelyn Underhill, whose work on mysticism seems to stand the test of time, is a useful tool to analyze the several stages of mystical union, although I am aware of variations in terminology and the description of the process in other authors.[25] Underhill posits several stages for the development of the soul, of which the most important are: awakening of the self, illumination, contemplation, and final union with God. Her scheme is an expansion of the basic stages described in the seventeenth century by Godínez, who simply identified three classic states of purgative, illuminative, and unitive ways (*vías*). The awakening of the self is a state in which the individual apprehends God, and becomes aware of a destiny that involves the pursuit of the highest contact with Him.[26] This awakening can be carried out through a vision or can be simply a perception within. This is followed by the purgative stage or purification of the self, in which, according to her, "The self must be purged of all that stands between it and goodness." The sense of imperfection or unworthiness moves the individual to seek mortification and privation to rid herself of worldly attachments. As Underhill puts it, "purification is a perpetual process" for the soul moves from moments of happiness to moments of depression. Acts of physical mortification are seen as exercises in gaining control over the body and all personal passions. Further, they are ways of identifying with the suffering of Christ in his passion, especially since the latter is an example of how the path to perfection demands sacrifice and how personal sacrifice is an offering to God, an inescapable imitation of Christ.[27] Practices to fulfill this form of *imitatio Christi* were very popular in post-Tridentine Catholicism.

The following stage is the illumination of the self whereby the individual gains consciousness of being in touch with God.[28] This is a door that opens to a new world of understanding. It is at this stage that Underhill sees the need to use an extensive imagery to convey the joyous feeling of discovery. This stage is passive; it provides peace and exultation, but the individual and God remain two and separate. It is after the enlightenment that Underhill places the "voices and visions" that describe the most commonly held experience of the visionaries. Visions left the soul infused with humility and holy fear, promoting charity, peace, piety, and devotion.[29] Voices and visions have been most intensely subjected to scrutiny to prove or disprove their existence and the balance of mind of those who experienced them. Women who claimed visionary experiences raised doubts among many post-Tridentine theologians, although they never denied the feasibility of visions. Godínez devoted the last section of his treatise to identifying true from false visions and the states of rapture, ecstasy, and suspension. As a good Jesuit, he stated that visions were not necessary for the exercise of virtues in the spiritual life. He defined two types of visions: "intellectual," the highest caliber, which is more abstract and detached from the world, and "sensitive," in which the senses are involved. The latter were liable to be pasture for the devil's tricks, and women seemed, in his opinion, inclined to "bad" or deceitful visions.

Underhill and modern followers are not interested in verifying visions as facts. Rather, they are seen as "symbolic expression, ways in which the subconscious activity of the spiritual self reaches the surface-mind." Put this way, as a metaphor for an inner reality and a venue for conveying a spiritual reality, the veracity of any vision ceases to be relevant. But, in the seventeenth and eighteen centuries, the greatest concern of all who experienced "visions," as well as that of the church authorities, was to verify they were not the product of deceit induced by the devil and that they were "real" contacts with God or the saint. Indeed, the rigid censorship that the church imposed on its members—writers or not—is reflected in the carefully worded expressions of orthodox visionaries, who were educated in the restrictions applicable to visions. Such restrictions did not deter vividly recounted experiences, which became part and parcel of the baroque expression of spirituality. In Spanish culture the process of visualizing the scenes of meditation, the events in the life of Christ or the saints, and similar religious themes was encouraged since the late sixteenth century, especially by Saint Ignatius of Loyola, and this method became essential to the expression of spirituality in the seventeenth century.[30]

Ecstasy and rapture are the two deeper stages and part of the process of union with God. In ecstasy—or trance—the consciousness of the world is lost. The value of the ecstasy resides in its aftermath, when the individual understands that he or she has received the grace of union with God. Rapture is understood as having a violent and passionate nature. As Saint Teresa put it, in a trance the soul gradually dies to outward things; in rapture there is a swift transport and the soul is carried away as if leaving the body.[31] Unfortunately, the mystics also experienced drawbacks in their search for God. Ecstasies burned emotions and created stress and eventual withdrawal from that state into one of dryness (*sequedad*), solitude, depression, even despair, which Godínez calls *desamparo*, and John of the Cross identified as the *noche oscura*.[32] Godínez also spoke of a "dark union" in which the soul fears what it loves and suffers because it is unsure of God's love. Such states of doubt and dryness are temporary. They were regarded as forms of purification that could bring renewed spiritual strength. When such roadblocks were removed, the process toward union would proceed.

Finally, the unitive state was reached. It is the most fascinating and the most impregnable because it was assumed to be transcendental and beyond description. Images of fire and burning were used, but unutterable happiness, the nullification of all cares, the enrichment of the soul beyond description, were the norm to convey the ultimate meeting of the soul with its creator.

We no longer believe that there was a clear progress from awakening to the final union of the soul with God. Underhill's scheme is helpful but it should not be taken as a pattern for all visionary experiences, or understood as a model of linear development to be found in all visionaries. There are no clear cut divisions among the spiritual "stages." They seemed to have been experienced at different times throughout life. It is more accurate to talk about states rather than stages, and this is the nomenclature I shall use. Other analysts use a different approach. For example, W. W. Meissner, in analyzing the mystic experience in Saint Ignatius de Loyola, travels backward from the mystic experience to the practice of asceticism and penances as the venue to achieve the union with God, and he ends his study with a detailed analysis of the psychological and even pathological features of the spiritual life.[33]

The Spiritual Features of the Writings of Mexican Nuns

Novohispanic nuns followed Iberian and Roman Catholic canons very closely, and they were quite aware of the writings of Saint Teresa. They also read lives of saints as part of their conventual training and heard canonically orthodox messages in the sermons delivered in their churches. However, few of the writers cite the sources of their literary or religious inspiration.[34] The writings available to us vary in character: some are letters; others are monthly accounts, and others are of a mixed nature combining narratives of the convent, autobiography, and accounts of a spiritual nature. For this work I have reviewed the writings of Sor María de San José, Augustinian of the convents of Santa Mónica in Puebla and San José in Oaxaca; Sor María Marcela, capuchin in Querétaro; and Sor Sebastiana María Josefa de la Santísima Trinidad and Sor María de Jesús Felipa, both of the convent of San Juan de la Penitencia. Sor María de San José wrote the most complex of all these texts, combining autobiography, accounts of her spiritual life, the history of her own writings, and the story of the founding of the convent of Santa Mónica in Oaxaca, in over one thousand folios. She also composed a book of spiritual exercises in honor of the Virgin Mary. Sor María Marcela wrote an autobiography, which included her life before her entrance into the convent and an account of her spiritual life after her profession; Sor Sebastiana left an extensive account of her spiritual life in the form of letters addressed to her confessor. From Sor María de Jesús Felipa, we have eleven monthly accounts of her spiritual life, also addressed to her confessor.

Following Underhill, the awakening of the self as the opening of the soul to God is not necessarily described in all diaries or autobiographies. Fortunately, Sor María de San José remembered her own awakening. It occurred through several visions and voices that began to explain to her the meaning of Christ's passion and that of her own life very early on.[35] For Sor María Marcela, the understanding of having achieved communion with God came without any visions. It was an illumination or understanding after many years of religious life that strengthened her faith and confidence in having elected the right path in life:

The aforementioned state followed such an intimate union of God and the soul that it felt like in the tightest and most indissoluble of embraces, so firm and permanent that I am persuaded that no amount of will can separate the soul from God or untie this knot. Thus, the soul began to shed all doubts or suspicions; the security of this state is hard to compare to any.[36]

Purgative states or desamparo were constant in all of these nuns' spiritual lives. They typically passed from states of happiness and serenity to states of despondency and self-abatement. Perhaps Sor Sebastiana María Josefa de la Santísima Trinidad is the one who most consistently suffered periods of depression:

My lack of consolation is such that I give myself as lost, not knowing what to do, or how I should go to another [confessor], or how to continue doing the little that I do; everything is a confusion of thoughts that I strive to lay aside; it is in vain that I attempt stopping this struggle. I lack for words, and without them I lay embarrassed before the sweetness of my most patient Husband, life of my soul. My anguish suffocates

FEMALE VISIONARIES AND SPIRITUALITY

me and makes my heart burst. I suffer much within.[37]

The alternation of joy and despair were also known to Sor María Marcela:

The vespers of great favors were days of great want, and after the celebrations I returned to my state of vigilance; I suffered from grave darkness and dense dimness in my understanding. It seems that all the roads of prayer were closed, and I only found an exit once in a while, which seemed lightning shedding a new light, and this convinced me that God was there; and then I began to confess and adore, and love Him and to be in Him. This lasted a short time, and then the light returned. I stayed in this condition for over one year, in this interplay of manifestations. Some other times I found myself abandoned as in a field, alone, and lacking all manner of shelter, or anywhere to turn my eyes to, sad, dry and without God, but always in conformity with His will.[38]

The illuminative state is well represented in all writings and is the one that seems to generate the most visions. Each vision bears the imprint of the nun who experienced it, since it was a product of her education, life experience, emotional state, and spiritual development. When visions are narrated by biographers or hagiographers, they become grist for their mills. The result is that such visions expand and intensify, often becoming bizarre and truculent, teasing the imagination of readers rather than reflecting the experience of the visionary.[39] The nuns' own descriptions are less prone to exaggeration. Writing in the second half of the eighteenth century, there is no baroque exaggeration in Sor María Marcela's writings. On one of those few occasions when she saw the Virgin Mary, Saint Joseph, and Saint Michael, the sight produced a sense of joy and enhanced her faith:

One year, on the day of the betrothal [of Mary and Joseph] she showed herself to the eyes of the intellect, most beautifully and richly adorned, with a crown of stars, the moon at her feet, and dressed with the sun. This sun that dressed her up and made her most luminous was given to me to understand that it was her most sainted son. Saint Joseph showed himself to me one year on his saint's day, when I had made him a tunic of acts of humility, a cape of charitable deeds, a staff of firm hope, and a diadem of conformity. Saint Michael has showed himself to me three times. One was during prayer, and I was very worried because I thought I did not have purity. He placed himself in front of the eyes of my soul, very handsome and beautiful, in a posture that gave me an understanding of what was purity in intention and inspired me to believe that I have it, and he left me most consoled and in peace. The posture was as follows: standing in the air, with feet not touching the ground, and the arms lifted towards heaven, one behind the other, as that of one who is walking towards heaven.[40]

In the illuminative state the nun finds the fulfillment of peace and certainty about having found God. Although Sor Sebastiana María Josefa de la Santísima Trinidad found few moments of happiness in her spiritual life, when she did her experience was very similar to that of other nuns:

> I received inner consolation and solace from seeing the beauty and happiness of the Divine Countenance, who made me understand that my soul pleased Him. It was like a most beautiful lighted sky (I cannot tell well because I am confused and I am unable to express it). The light was better than that of the sky, and the Divine Majesty was there as a resplendent cloud of stunning beauty, and his most pure mother and my Lady and the source of all my good, my mother Mary . . . It is not up to my lowliness to tell; my ignorance cannot understand it because it is all so different from what we experience here. It was a white thing and better than all the clarity around it. I felt my heart loose inside my body, as if in the air.[41]

It is difficult to define the border between illuminative and unitive in these statements, but there is no doubt that novohispanic nuns experienced both. Sor María de San José underlined the ineffable feeling of union by saying "his Majesty draws nearer to do me some favor, which is so far within the interior of my soul that I can find no terms to make myself understood."[42]

Sor María de Jesús Felipa

Because I have been reading Sor María de Jesús Felipa very closely, I would like to offer a vignette of her spirituality as an example of how novohispanic visionaries and mystics could flourish in silence and humility, without leaving a ripple in history or raising any theological suspicion. Sor María de Jesús Felipa eludes us to the present. Pending further research, I know next to nothing about her family or her profession. She lived in the convent of San Juan de la Penitencia and was writing a spiritual diary in 1758, one year after the death of Sor Sebastiana María Josefa de la Santísima Trinidad.[43] The diary covers the months between February and December, at which point it is truncated.[44] As many other nuns, she wrote at the insistence of her confessor, whose name remains unknown. The diary has been meticulously reviewed by a person who took the trouble of crossing out and making unreadable almost all the names of the persons Sor María mentioned. This desire to cover the identity of her sisters suggests the concern of the unknown "censor-reader" to preserve the anonymity of those engaged in affective relationships with the nun and to protect the privacy of the cloister.

In the 228 pages of Sor María's diary we find the key features of the inner life of a typical visionary. It is largely an introspection of spiritual states, with relatively few instances of information about the daily life of the convent. Throughout eleven months the nun analyzes the progress, or lack thereof, of her spiritual life and engages in a dialogue with her confessor in which the main topics are her acts of penitence, her relationship with God and her efforts to enhance it, her concern for the souls of purgatory, and for her own salvation and that of her sisters in religion.

In her writing we can find all the expected features of the spiritual journey except that of the awakening of the self, which she may have experienced already and may have recorded elsewhere. The conflictive waning and waxing between purgative and unitive states is strongest between February and June. Throughout this period she sought her main source of consolation in the Virgin Mary, but she also called on Santa María Egipciaca and Santa Margarita de Cortona. It is the absence of her Beloved (God-Christ) that sinks her into deep despair:

> It is true that it seems that he has thrown me in a sea of many and undescribable tribulations because it is all darkness inside. . . . The soul experiences the absence of her beloved, and in this absence she lacks all consolation, human or divine, because there is nobody to offer a respite.[45]

The darkness of abandon is accentuated by the knowledge of all the sins committed against God and is reminiscent of Godínez's "desamparo" and John of the Cross's la noche oscura:

> I am tormented for the sins of the world. In the midst of this dark night, I see and I feel and I would like to die rather than learn about the offenses that keep me in that hideous night . . . Oh, what intimate pain pierces me; to look for my absent beloved and instead of finding him among His brides, among His ministers, among Christians, all I see are their sins in their malice. And I see myself the worst of all, seeking Him who, on other occasions, has striven to lift me to His grace with different gifts and diverse benefices. And now, in this darkness I

do not know whether in everything I see I will offend Him.[46]

Despite all, Sor María de Jesús Felipa experienced unions with God. Thus, in April she beautifully expressed that concept of understanding the presence of God within and without her, as follows:

> I know that God is everywhere in essence, presence, and will, and that His kingdom is within me, and that I received Him in the sacrament, God and true man, with all His virtues, and that I am His child and this Lord, my creator, having redeemed me with so much travail is my redeemer; his treasures are mine; his virtues and the gifts he bears are mine.[47]

Sor María de Jesús Felipa experienced a transformation in her life when, in June, she began to have visions of heaven, conversations with Christ and the Virgin Mary, and also long conversations with her guardian angels, who took her for a visit of heaven, where she sees Saint Augustin, Saint Francis, Saint Dominick, and Saint Catherine of Siena. Her contact with God allowed her the experience of "deification," "*me endiosó mi esposo*," and the understanding of the dual nature of his divinity and his humanity. Christ showed himself to her as a good-looking youth of thirty who assured her that He had signaled her with His esteem and that this would be made public through her writings. This experience is like a dream and very much like a form of ecstasy:

> And I lay in a sweet enchantment as if sleeping, but in this dream I enjoyed

the harmony of the music of the angels. And my custodian [angels] in the said manner, instilled in me the fire of love. I was in the church and the *coro*, but not as it is, but as if it were all of diamonds, and broader and longer . . . and the religious and all present, were very white, as if they were covered with snow.[48]

The most important result of this vision is the validation of her sufferings as a means to reach God, and the reaffirmation of the state of grace. This, in her words, made her drunk with love and she compared herself to a lover who could not express his love for a lady.[49] The universal theme of love with God, part of the affective states of ecstasy, is a fixed element in all mystic writing, reaffirmed in Spain by John of the Cross. Throughout this process of increasing contact with the divine, Sor María de Jesús Felipa engages in a series of physical disciplines to experience the humanity of Christ's sufferings in the cross. This was also a favorite theme of the medieval Italian visionary, Angela de Foligno. Spanish and Spanish American nuns were very much within the mainstream of early modern spirituality in considering their bodies the locus of God. To find a similar trait in Mexican nuns' writings is thus not surprising.

Sor María de Jesús Felipa also witnessed the Holy Trinity (a true feat for Catholic visionaries of that period) after beginning spiritual exercises in which she set up several chambers in her soul and was guided by her guardian angels to see the divinity of God.[50] This passage has the strong imprint of Saint Teresa. In her own words:

And other [occasions] I am taken to another place full of delightful and beautiful rooms richly and exquisitely decorated, in which it seems that I am within God himself, partaking of His attributes and perfections . . . and find myself lacking everything when I am left in the view of this divine sun that consumes and annihilates me until as a soft tide He lifts me giving me all his love and telling me: my dove, you have nothing and because of this, I give you, because I mark the most despised with the sign of my cross.[51]

In a long speech Christ explains to the nun not only her mission but the nature and meaning of His sacrifice and the certainty of His punishment to those who abandon or ignore Him. This was a true mystic union, because through this conversation she experienced the knowledge of the mysteries of the Trinity.

Do not fear, my soul; I am your shelter. He said all that to me while He explained the light through which he worked on me, and I felt a strength never experienced before, a burning love that breathed arrows into me. And I found in this conversation the many ways of learning the mysteries, while I paid homage to God in the union of the mystery of the Trinity and the essence of His being, and I understood with a special light how the three divine persons were in my soul, embracing it tightly and making it splendent.[52]

Sor María de Jesús Felipa also had visions, conversations, and explanations from the

Virgin Mary, and long explanations from the guardian angels on the nature of God's love and actions.[53] The result of these visions was a growing confidence in herself, in her role of helper of the souls in purgatory, as well as in her role as a venue for God's will and protector of her convent.

Mexican Spirituality: A Final Overview

The influence of Saint Teresa's life, and later her canonization in the seventeenth century, kindled the imagination of many cloistered women and encouraged them to write their experiences, which very much resemble those described by the saint. Teresa was not the only inspiration, however. Late medieval saints such as Saint Catherine of Siena offered models of spirituality and observance that lent form and substance to the counter-reformation church. In the writings briefly reviewed here we see elements of sixteenth-century and baroque or mid-colonial spirituality, such as the affective ties with God and the saints, and the need to suffer in imitation of Christ in order to achieve personal redemption. It is a spirituality that feeds itself on an intensive and continuous introspection born from the obligatory enclosure and the concept of *recogimiento*, or gathering into oneself. Recogimiento, formulated in the sixteenth century by Francisco de Osuna, was the foundation of that interior world in which the most wondrous and the most painful could be experienced, and the only locus for an encounter with God.[54] It was the venue used by the most important Spanish mystics.

Seventeenth- and eighteenth-century baroque spirituality used recogimiento as a foundation, but added new elements inspired by the post-Tridentine ecclesiastical authorities such as spiritual and physical regulation and discipline, the mediation of the confessor in his pedagogical, supervisory, and paternalistic role, the cult of the Virgin and the saints, and the regular use of the sacraments of communion, contrition, and penance. Monastic rules carefully prescribed hours of prayer and hours of nonreligious activities, supervised readings, and trained their minds in the exercise of virtue and good works to ensure orthodoxy. The written expression of this mid-colonial spirituality was also highly emotional and heavily laced with metaphors that lent it sensuality and immediacy. Within these confines, the flights to God were observed and judged by the male hierarchy, but they were not forbidden. Because they were possible, they flourished as a desirable outlet for spiritual fulfillment.

It is important to understand how the approved forms of visions and mystic proclivities differed from those experienced by "false mystics" who came under the purview and indictment of the Inquisition.[55] To begin, nuns were not wanderers in the outside world, but cloistered women firmly under the control of ecclesiastic authorities. They belonged to a select group of women considered the choicest among the female sex: the brides of Christ who had given up freedom, free will, and attachment to material pursuits and human love to earn their privileged status. They had tested their mettle through a novitiate that trained their minds and bodies to meet the demands of orthodoxy. Their readings and apprenticeship led them to the appropriate channels of belief and observance.

Their visions followed canonical form and concepts. They rarely challenged the established patterns of mystic experience delineated by Saint Teresa and John of the Cross and other earlier sources of canonical correctness that all confessors and higher authorities knew well and could test in their spiritual daughters.

Nuns who experienced visions and mystic states were recipients of God's love and never actors on their own volition. They were humble and approached divinity with awe, respect, and humility. They surrendered their will to God, above all, and to their religious superiors. Their writings were private and meant to help them seek the right path for salvation. Thus, even though their orthodox writings contained material that bore similarities to those of false beatas, the contextualization of their experience made them different for those in charge of judging them.

Spanish and Mexican religious culture between 1600 and 1750 had some variations, but, nonetheless, they had a core of features that conferred a certain homogeneity to the experiences of female visionaries. José Luis Sánchez Lora, an authority on Spanish Baroque culture, makes a distinction between abstract mysticism and the counter-reformation obsession with visions, assuming that the latter was part of the religious expression after the last quarter of the sixteenth century.[56] He believes that true mysticism died in the sixteenth century and that baroque spirituality was a literary construction, artificial and annihilating.[57] While, indeed, there is some truth in his interpretation, we would be much the poorer if we discarded the visionaries'

writings and experiences as mere exaggerations of a religious culture obsessed with theatricality and hyperbole but lacking a true mystical value. We cannot ignore the substance because of the wrapping. The theatricality and hyperbole he criticizes is mostly the creation of the biographers, not the nuns themselves. The substance was a world imagined and lived by women and carefully described in its most intimate spaces as an expression of expansive female protagonism, despite the inevitable presence of the confessor. The written dialogue with this male authority figure satisfied the church's requirement for supervision and the need to share one's experience with a minister of the faith. In the confessor these women found an interlocutor who in their world was a necessary element for their spiritual development. Without him they may not have written at all; with him, they could sustain, verify, and ratify the validity of their experiences and, in some cases, establish a vibrant exchange of ideas based on testing each other's mettle. As I have observed in previous work, and as also observed by Kathleen Myers and Amanda Powell, lines of authority frequently became blurred and male authorities sought a source of faith and enlightenment in these women.[58]

In the final analysis, while forms of observance may have irritated peninsular male authorities, female Mexican spirituality followed the best tradition of sixteenth-century recogimiento, even if sometimes dressed up in baroque garb. As visionaries the novohispanic nuns surveyed in this article searched for God with love, a sixteenth century element, by detaching themselves from the enjoyment of worldly cares and human appetites, and pursuing the achievement of moral virtue.[59] They were painfully aware of what they considered the imperfections of their souls and lives and tried, as hard as they could, to become more perfect in the eyes of God through suffering and purgation. All of the aforementioned are key features of "the ascent of Mount Carmel," as explained by Saint John of the Cross.[60] It is true that most Mexican nuns did not possess his extraordinary gifts, but that cannot be expected in women who only had a limited education and who remained defined and constrained by their own chosen cloistered world. Indeed, under these circumstances, their writings are the most remarkable evidence of the female endeavor for self-expression. The knowledge of who they were and why they wrote remains a challenge and much remains to be done, but as we get deeper into their world I am convinced that we will discover that women's spirituality was more than a mere female caprice or an accident in the history of New Spain.

NOTES

1. Elizabeth Alvilda Petroff, *Medieval Women's Visionary Literature* (New York: Oxford University Press, 1986). Elizabeth A. Lehfeldt, *Religious Women in Golden Age Spain. The Permeable Cloister* (London: Ashgate, 2005). See also, as examples, Sabina Flanagan, *Hildegard of Bingen: A Visionary Life* (London: Routledge, 1998); Clarissa Atkinson, *Mystic and Pilgrim: The Book and the World of Margery Kempe* (Ithaca: Cornell University Press, 1983); Susan Mosher Stuard, ed., *Women in Medieval History and Historiography* (Philadelphia: University of Pennsylvania Press, 1987); and Jo Ann Kay McNamara, *Sisters in Arms: Catholic Nuns Through Two Millennia* (Cambridge: Harvard University Press, 1996).

2. Jody Bilinkoff, *The Avila of Saint Teresa: Religious Reform in a Sixteenth-Century City* (Ithaca: Cornell University Press, 1989), 96, and, by the same author, "Navigating the Waves (of Devotion): Toward a Gendered Analysis of Early Modern Catholicism," in *Crossing Boundaries Attending to Early Modern Women*, ed. Jane Donawerth and Adele Seef, 161–72 (Newark: University of Delaware Press, 2000); Geraldine McKendrik and Angus MacKay, "Visionaries and Affective Spirituality during the First Half of the Sixteenth Century," in *Cultural Encounters: The Impact of the Inquisition in Spain and the New World*, ed. Mary Elizabeth Perry and Anne J. Cruz, 93–104 (Berkeley: University of California Press, 1992).

3. See, for example, Ronald E. Surtz, *Writing Women in Late Medieval and Early Modern Spain: The Mothers of Saint Teresa of Avila* (Philadelphia: University of Pennsylvania Press, 1995); Julio Caro Baroja, *Las formas complejas de la vida religiosa: Religión, sociedad y carácter en la España de los siglos XVI y XVII* (Madrid: Akal Editor, 1978), 33. See also, Amy Katz Kaminsky, ed., *Water Lilies: An Anthology of Spanish Women Writers from the Fifteenth Through the Nineteenth Century* (Minneapolis: University of Minnesota Press, 1996); Sherry M. Velasco, *Demons, Nausea, and Resistance in the Autobiography of Isabel de Jesús, 1611–1682* (Albuquerque: University of New Mexico Press, 1996); Cristina Segura Graíño, ed., *La voz del silencio: Fuentes directas para la historia de las mujeres (Siglos VIII–XVIII)* (Madrid: Asociación Cultural Al-Mudayna, 1992); Jesús Gómez López e Inocente García de Andrés, *Sor Juana de la Cruz: mística e iluminista toledana* (Toledo: Diputación Provincial, 1982); María Pilar Manero Sorolla, "Visionarias reales en la España aúrea," in *Images de la Femme en Espagne aux XVIe et XVIIe siècles*, coord. Agustín Redondo, 305–18 (Paris: Presses de la Sorbonne Nouvelle, 1994); Mario Hernández

Sánchez-Ibarra, *Monjas ilustres en la historia de España* (Madrid: Ediciones Temas de Hoy, S.A., 1996); Isaías Rodríguez, O. C. D., *Santa Teresa de Jesús y la espiritualidad española* (Madrid: Consejo Superior de Investigaciones Científicas, 1972); Manuel Serrano y Sanz, *Apuntes para una biblioteca de escritoras españolas* (Madrid, 1903); Elizabeth Teresa Howe, *The Visionary Life of Madre Ana de San Agustín* (Woodbridge: Tamesis, 2004).

4. Julio Caro Baroja, *Las formas complejas de la vida religiosa*; Angela Muñoz Fernández, *Acciones e intenciones de mujeres: Vida religiosa de las madrileñas (ss. XV–XVI)* (Madrid: hora y HORAS, Editorial, 1995); Jesús Imirizaldu, *Monjas y beatas embaucadoras*, Biblioteca de Visionarios Heterodoxos y Marginados (Madrid: Editora Nacional, 1977); Isabelle Poutrin, *Le Voile et la Plume: Autobiographie et sainteté féminine dans l'Espagne moderne* (Madrid: Casa de Velázquez, 1995).

5. Alvaro Huerga, *Historia de los alumbrados*, vol. III, *Los alumbrados de Hispanoamérica (1570–1605)* (Madrid: Fundación Universitaria Española, 1986), 16, 784–85.

6. Asunción Lavrin, "Vida conventual: Rasgos históricos," in *Sor Juana y su mundo: Una mirada actual*, ed. Sara Poot Herrera, 35–91 (México: Universidad del Claustro de Sor Juana, 1995) and "De su puño y letra: Epístolas desde el claustro," *Actas del Segundo Congreso Internacional Sobre el Monacato Femenino en el Imperio Español* (México: Centro de Estudios de Historia de México CONDUMEX, 1995), 43–62; Antonio Rubial García, "Un caso raro: La vida y desgracias de Sor Antonia de San Joseph, monja profesa en Jesús María," in *El monacato femenino en el imperio español*, coord. Manuel Ramos Medina, (México: CONDUMEX, 1995); Jorge Traslosheros, *La reforma de la iglesia del Antiguo Michoacán: La gestión episcopal de Fray Marcos Ramírez de Prado, 1640–1666* (Morelia: Universidad Michoacana de San Nicolás Hidalgo, 1995); Elisa Sampson Vera Tudela, *Colonial Angels: Narratives of Gender and Spirituality in Mexico, 1580–1750* (Austin: University of Texas Press, 2000); Jacqueline Holler, *"Escogidas Plantas": Nuns and Beatas in Mexico City, 1531–1601* (New York: Columbia University Press, 2005).

7. Richard Greenleaf, *The Mexican Inquisition of the Sixteenth Century* (Albuquerque: University of New Mexico Press, 1969), and Isabelle Poutrin, *Le Voile et la Plume*, 51–69; Jacqueline Holler, "The Spiritual and Physical Ecstasies of a Sixteenth-Century Beata: Marina de San Miguel Confesses Before the Inquisition (Mexico 1598)," in *Colonial Lives: Documents on Latin American History, 1550–1850*, ed. Richard Boyer and Geoffrey Spurling, 77–100 (New York: Oxford University Press, 2000).

8. AGN, Inquisición, vol. 5, exp. 4 (1564); vol. 8, exp. 1 (1568); vol. 166, exp. 5 (1598); vol. 186, exp. 1 (1598–1601); vol. 718, exp. 10 (1701); Manuel Ramos Medina, "Isabel de la Encarnación, monja posesa del siglo XVII," in *Manifestaciones religiosas en el mundo colonial americano*, vol. 1, coord. Clara García Ayluardo y Manuel Ramos Medina, 41–51 (Mexico: CONDUMEX, INAH, Universidad Iberoamericana, 1993); Alvaro Huerga, *Historia de los alumbrados*, 609–714; Richard E. Greenleaf, *The Mexican Inquisition*, 133–37.

9. See Sherry Velasco, *Demons*, 97.

10. Angela Muñoz Fernández, *Acciones e intenciones*, 203.

11. Francisco Pardo, *Vida y virtudes heroycas de la Madre María de Jesús, religiosa . . . en el convento de la Limpia Concepción . . . de la ciudad de los Angeles . . .* (México: Viuda de Bernardo Calderón, 1676); Carlos de Sigüenza y Góngora, *Parayso occidental* (1684) (México: UNAM/CONDUMEX, 1995); Asunción Lavrin, "La vida femenina como experiencia religiosa: Biografía y hagiografía en hispanoamérica colonial," *Colonial Latin American Review* 3–4 (1993): 27–52; Rosalva Loreto López, "Oir, ver y escribir: Los textos hagio-biográficos y espirituales del padre Miguel Godínez, ca. 1630," in *Diálogos espirituales: Manuscritos femeninos hispanoamericanos, siglos XVI–XIX*, ed. Asunción Lavrin and Rosalva Loreto L., 156–200 (Puebla: BUAP/UDLA, 2006).

12. Josefina Muriel, *Cultura femenina novohispana* (México: UNAM,1993), 313–471.

13. Kathleen A. Myers, and Amanda Powell, eds., *A Wild Country Out in the Garden: The Spiritual Journals of a Colonial Mexican Nun* (Bloomington: Indiana University Press, 1999); Kristine Ibsen, *Women's Spiritual Autobiography in Colonial Spanish America* (Gainesville: University Press of Florida, 1999); Asunción Lavrin, "La escritura desde un

mundo oculto: espiritualidad y anonimidad en el convento de San Juan de la Penitencia," *Estudios de Historia Novohispana* 22 (2000): 49–75; Ellen Gunnarsdóttir, *Mexican Karismata: The Baroque Vocation of Francisca de los Angeles, 1676–1774* (Lincoln: University of Nebraska Press, 2004).

14. Elizabeth A. Petroff, *Medieval Women's Visionary Literature*, 6; Kathryn Joy McKnight, *The Mystic of Tunja: The Writings of Madre Castillo 1671–1742* (Amherst: University of Massachusetts Press, 1997); Fernando Iturburu, *(Auto)biografía y misticismos femeninos en la colonia* (New Orleans: University Press of the South, 2000); Manuel Ramos Medina, *Místicas y descalzas* (México: CONDUMEX, 1997); Elia J. Armacanqui-Tipacti, *Sor María Manuela de Santa Ana: Una teresiana peruana* (Cusco: Centro de Estudios Regionales Andinos Bartolomé de Las Casas, 1999); Isabelle Poutrin, *Le Voile et la Plume*, 89–100.

15. Santa Teresa de Jesús, *Libro de su vida* (Garden City, NY: Doubleday and Company, 1991), see Chapter XX and Chapter XXVIII.

16. Gillian T. W. Ahlgren, *Teresa of Avila: And the Politics of Sanctity* (Ithaca: Cornell University Press, 1996), 83.

17. Ibid., 112. See also Alison Weber, *Teresa of Avila and the Rhetoric of Femininity* (Princeton: Princeton University Press, 1990).

18. Rowan Williams, *Teresa of Avila* (Wilson, CT: Morehouse Publishing, 1991), 148–49.

19. Nelson Pike, *Mystic Union: An Essay in the Phenomenology of Mysticism* (Ithaca: Cornell University Press, 1992), 28, 33, 35, 37.

20. San Juan de la Cruz, *Subida del Monte Carmelo: Noche oscura, Cántico espiritual, Llama de amor viva* (México: Editorial Porrúa, S.A. 1984).

21. Caro Baroja, *Las formas complejas*, 82, 89–90, 94. For a discussion of the place of mysticism in the doctrinal body of the church, see Jaroslav Pelikan, *The Christian Tradition: A History of the Development of Doctrine*, vol. 4, *Reformation of Church and Dogma (1300–1700)* (Chicago: University of Chicago Press, 1984), 63–68.

22. Cited in Caro Baroja, *Las formas complejas*, 36 (on treatises on prophecies, see 37–38).

23. Michael Wadding, an Irish Jesuit, changed his original name to Miguel Godínez. Miguel Godínez, *Práctica de la teología mística* (Quito: Imprenta de V. Valencia, 1856).

24. Pike, *Mystic Union*, 42.

25. Evelyn Underhill, *Mysticism* (New York: Doubleday, 1990); Melquíades Andrés Martín, *Los recogidos: Nueva visión de la mística española (1500–1700)* (Madrid: Fundación Universitaria Española, 1975).

26. Ibid., 176–97.

27. Ibid., 198–231.

28. Ibid., 232–65.

29. Godínez, *Práctica*, 220–38. His careful advice to confessors on how to distinguish good from bad visions suggests how concerned he and others were about fraudulent pseudo-mystics. For beatas before the Mexican Inquisition, see Dolores Bravo, *Ana Rodríguez de Castro y Aramburu, ilusa, afectadora de santos, falsos milagros, y revelaciones divinas: Proceso inquisitorial en la Nueva España (siglos XVIII y XIX)* (México: UNAM, 1984); Jacqueline Holler, "I, Elena de la Cruz: Heresy and Gender in Mexico City, 1568," *Journal of the Canadian Historical Association* 4 (1993): 143–60; "The Spiritual and Physical Ecstasies of a Sixteenth-Century Beata: Marina de San Miguel Confesses Before the Mexican Inquisition," in *Colonial Lives: Documents on Latin American History, 1550–1850*, ed. Richard Boyer and Geoffrey Spurling, 77–100 (New York: Oxford University Press, 2000); Nora Jaffary, *False Mystics and Deviant Orthodoxy in Colonial Mexico* (Lincoln: University of Nebraska Press, 2004).

30. *Ejercicios espirituales de San Ignacio de Loyola* (Santander: Sal Terrae, 1986). Also see Nora Jaffary, *False Mystics*, and Antonio Rubial García, *Profetisas y solitarios: Espacios y mensajes de una religión dirigida por ermitaños y beatas laicos en las ciudades de Nueva España* (Mexico: UNAM/Fondo de Cultura de Económica, 2006).

31. Santa Teresa de Jesús, *Libro de su vida*, chapters XXV, XXVIII, and XXXVIII. See also Godínez, *Práctica*, 230–38. For him, raptures helped to strengthen virtue, charity, and humility. A true state of rapture was luminous and heated, soft and strong, and it came from God. Ecstasy was an excess of love in the heart, its source being divine love.

32. Underhill, *Mysticism*, 380–412; Godínez, *Práctica*, 66–72, 55; San Juan de la Cruz, *Subida del Monte Carmelo*, 209–56.

33. W. W. Meissner, S.J., M.D., *Ignatius of Loyola: The Psychology of a Saint* (New Haven: Yale University Press, 1992), 279–345. As features of the mystic experience, he identifies ineffability, noetic quality (cognitive state); transiency, which signifies that the experiences are very short; passivity, ecstasy and rapture, and *loquelae* or auditions in addition to visions.

34. One exception is María de San José, who cited Augustine, Bernard of Clairvaux, John of the Cross, and Teresa of Avila. See Myers and Powell, *A Wild Country*, 278.

35. Myers and Powell, *A Wild Country*, 81, 84, 85, as examples of the messages from God to her.

36. Vida de la Madre María Marcela, f. 125.

37. Cartas en las cuales manifiesta a su confesor las cosas interiores y exteriores de su vida la V. M. Sor Sebastiana Josefa de la Santísima Trinidad, Mexico, Biblioteca Nacional, f. 30.

38. Vida de la Madre María Marcela, f. 156.

39. Agustín de la Madre de Dios, *Tesoro escondido en el santo Carmelo mexicano, mina rica de ejemplos y virtudes en la historia de los carmelitas descalzos de la provincia de Nueva España* (México: Probursa-Universidad Iberoamericana, 1985), 318–35.

40. Vida de la Madre María Marcela, f. 162.

41. Cartas (de) la V. M. Sor Sebastiana Josefa de la Santísima Trinidad, f. 164.

42. Myers and Powell, *A Wild Country*, 155. See also 134, 135, 136, and 158. The lack of words to describe such states suggests a unitive state.

43. Sor Sebastiana was one of the white novices who had been placed in the Indian convent of Corpus Christi, and whose presence was so hotly contested that she was forced to transfer to a convent for white nuns. For further reference, see Asunción Lavrin, "Indian Brides of Christ: Creating New Spaces for Indigenous Women in New Spain, *Mexican Studies/Estudios Mexicanos* 15, no. 2 (summer 1989): 225–60.

44. Sor María de Jesús Felipa, Diary of a Religious Mexican, Feb.–Dec. 1758, Library of Congress, Washington DC, Manuscript Division MM59;

Asunción Lavrin, "Sor María de Jesús Felipa: Un diario espiritual de mediados del siglo XVIII (1758)," in *Monjas y beatas: La escritura femenina en la espiritualidad barroca novohispana, siglos XVII y XVIII*, ed. Asunción Lavrin and Rosalva Loreto, 111–60 (Mexico: Archivo General de la Nación/Puebla: Universidad de las Américas, 2002) and "La escritura desde un mundo oculto: espiritualidad y anonimidad en el convento de San Juan de la Penitencia," *Estudios de Historia Novohispana* 22 (2000): 49–75.

45. Sor María de Jesús Felipa, Diary, f. 1, 20.

46. Ibid., f. 40.

47. Ibid., f. 43–44.

48. Ibid., f. 89–90.

49. Ibid., f. 92.

50. Ibid., f. 98.

51. Ibid., f. 103–4.

52. Ibid., f. 107. The mystic union through the understanding of the Trinity was a Teresian imprint.

53. Ibid., f. 120.

54. Francisco de Osuna, *Tercer abecedario espiritual* (Madrid: B. A. E., 1911). See also Antonio Márquez, *Los alumbrados: Orígenes y filosofía (1525–1559)* (Madrid: Taurus, 1980).

55. For a study of false mystics under Inquisitorial purview in Peru, see René Millar Carvacho, "Falsa santidad e Inquisición: Los procesos a las visionarias limeñas," *Boletín de la Academia Chilena de la Historia*, nos. 108–9 (2000): 277–305; Antonio Rubial, "Josefa de San Luis Beltrán, la cordera de Dios: Escritura, oralidad y gestualidad de una visionaria del siglo XVII Novohispano" (1654), in *Monjas y beatas*, 161–204.

56. José L. Sánchez Lora, *Mujeres, conventos, y formas de la religiosidad barroca* (Madrid: Fundación Universitaria Española, 1988). Frances Beer does not discuss this topic, and the assumption is that all mystics had visions. See Frances Beer, *Women and Mystical Experience in the Middle Ages* (Woodbridge, England: Bydell Press, 1993).

57. Sánchez Lora, *Mujeres, conventos*, 238–66.

58. Asunción Lavrin, "La vida femenina como experiencia religiosa"; Myers and Powell, *Wild Country*, 316–23; Kathleen Ann Myers, "La influencia mediativa del clero en las vidas de religiosos y monjas," in *Sor Juana y su mundo: Una mirada actual. Memorias del Congreso Internacional*, coord. Carmen Beatriz López-Portillo, 341–53 (Mexico: Universidad del Claustro de sor Juana/ UNESCO/Fondo de Cultura Económica, 1998); Jodi Bilikoff, *Related Lives: Confessors and Their Female Penitents, 1450–1750* (Ithaca: Cornell University Press, 2005).

59. Teresa de Jesús, *Libro de las fundaciones* (Madrid: Espasa Calpe, 1991), 76. "All souls are for loving . . . the profit of the soul does not consist in thinking much but in loving much."

60. Antonio de Nicolás, *St. John of the Cross: Alchemist of the Soul* (York Beach, ME: Samuel Weiser 1996), 157–93.

CHAPTER NINE

The Indigenous Nuns of Corpus Christi

Race and Spirituality

MÓNICA DÍAZ

One of the rare available writings by an indigenous nun is a biographical account of the founding abbess of Corpus Christi, the first convent in colonial Mexico for indigenous women. The account, which is addressed to the author's confessor, ends with a vague report of a mysterious occurrence. The writer recounts that the father of a Spanish novice who had been accepted into Corpus Christi had made preparations to kill the indigenous nuns who were living there. He had set up a ladder to climb the wall of the convent, yet the night he planned to enter and kill the nuns, someone murdered him in the winery. The writer concludes and glosses the anecdote by stating that she and her fellow indigenous nuns suffered very much while Spanish nuns and novices lived among them.[1]

The episode recounted by the nun of Corpus Christi—which in 1724 became the first convent to allow indigenous women of colonial-era Mexico to enter as nuns— illustrates the racial conflicts that existed within and surrounded the convent. The existence of Corpus Christi incurred strong opposition from various people who doubted the spiritual and intellectual capacity of Indians. Some religious authorities, with the support of powerful lay people in colonial society, demonstrated their opposition by allowing Spanish nuns and novices into the convent. The Spanish nuns clashed with the indigenous nuns, generating more vigorous animosity on all sides.

The animosity, however, had roots in a longstanding debate about race in New Spain and began to emerge even before Corpus Christi first opened its doors, when the convent for indigenous women was merely a possibility for public consideration. At that time, different factions of the religious authorities formulated and expressed conflicting positions on the question of indigenous women's capacity to become nuns. The debate that took place reveals the importance that race had for the Spanish population. Spaniards propagated their ideology of racial hierarchy "that placed the Spaniards on top, *castas* (individuals with mixed racial backgrounds) in the middle, and Indians and Africans at the bottom," and organized society accordingly.[2] The exercise of Spanish superiority was at stake in the opinions of the individuals who fervently opposed convents for Indians.

Racial ideologies in the colonial period were fused with gender ideologies. The opening of the first convent for indigenous women in Mexico City focused controversy on indigenous women and exposed the gendered dimensions of racial beliefs. According to Kristine Ibsen, during the colonial period in Spanish America, "man was associated with the soul, spirit, and reason, and woman with the body, carnality, and sinfulness."[3] Because, in addition, the "qualities" and the "nature" of the indigenous people remained the subject of debate, Indian women experienced a double alienation by virtue of their sex and their race "from any place in the spiritual hierarchy, and particularly from such an exalted one as religious profession."[4]

In what follows, I analyze three documents that allow us to glimpse the complexities of the racial debate and conflicts that took place in colonial Mexico as a consequence of the opening of Corpus Christi. First, I examine the hagiographical account of Catharina Tegakovita, an indigenous woman from New France. The

account appeared in Spanish translation in Mexico as part of the defense of indigenous women's spirituality. Second, I analyze two chapters of the *vida* of Sebastiana Josefa de la Santísima Trinidad, a nun who once lived among the indigenous nuns in Corpus Christi. The priest who wrote the biography intended to document an exemplary life, yet he indirectly mentions the racial conflict that was provoked by the presence of Spanish nuns and novices in the convent. Last, I consider one part of a document recently found in the archives of Corpus Christi. The manuscript is a group of biographical accounts entitled *Apuntes de algunas vidas de nuestras hermanas difuntas* (Notes about the Lives of Some of our Deceased Sisters). The accounts are the products of at least three different handwritings, all by anonymous authors. Surface linguistic clues indicate that all of the writings came from a feminine hand, and at least one of them from an indigenous hand.

For each of the three documents, my analysis is intended to draw out the racial, gendered, and spiritual concerns that guide the authors. Ultimately, I show that the interplay of gender and genre takes a principal role in the construction of the authors' arguments. The identity and position of the author relate closely to the sorts of rhetorical framework that are employed in addressing questions of spirituality and race.

Historiography

The last decades have seen the creation of a new subfield within colonial studies, which is at times referred to as "conventual writing," according to Kathleen Myers.[5] The first important works written in the 1960s and 1970s about religious women coincided with the feminist politics and the interests of scholars in writing a history of women.[6] In the 1980s, the discoveries of key documents written by women allowed a new space for research and analysis, where the boundaries between history and literature blurred. Colonial studies have since aimed for interdisciplinary scholarship. Important works published in the 1990s, such as Jean Franco's *Plotting Women* and Schlau, Arenal, and Powell's *Untold Sisters*, compiled previous research on conventual writings in the canon of literary studies and enriched textual analysis with historical contextualization. Myers states, "One of the driving forces behind these broadening trends was the push to discover and analyze new sources that told the stories of previously voiceless people in traditional literary and historical studies."[7]

Scholars have pursued attempts to recover the voices of indigenous women from the colonial period—previously voiceless people in traditional studies—but they have not yet uncovered the documents that would provide direct access to indigenous women's perspectives. Individuals working in the field of conventual writings have used numerous documents about indigenous nuns in order to understand and develop a history of these women, without the need of autobiographical accounts, as scholars have done for many *criolla* nuns.[8] By identifying the several filters of gender and racial domination in documents written about indigenous women by others rather than the women themselves, scholars have endeavored to draw out the voice of the voiceless. These efforts, however, have had limited

success, and we continue our quest for clear proof of the intellectual life of indigenous women in the colonial period.

The indigenous nuns of Corpus Christi were literate and expressed themselves in writing, as did many other women in colonial Mexico, inside and outside of the walls of the convent. In the introduction to *Indian Women of Early Mexico*, Susan Schroeder argues that the indigenous nuns "did know Latin, and some definitely knew how to write, as is apparent in their petitions, licenses, and other record books."[9] Ann Miriam Gallagher states that indigenous nuns "were instructed in Christian doctrine, all could read Latin for the Divine Office, and all had attained some proficiency in the domestic arts."[10] Their writings, however, are not easy to find since they were neglected because of gender and racial biases.

Until now we have only one known manuscript from the convent of Corpus Christi, a series of anonymous biographies about some indigenous nuns in the convent and others about the criolla founders. The manuscript was published by Josefina Muriel in 1963, entitled *Las indias caciques de Corpus Christi* (The Noble Indian Women of Corpus Christi). The manuscript was written in the third person, and most likely it was composed by a priest basing his writings on biographies, or *vidas*, written by the nuns in the convent.[11] Although Muriel believes that indigenous nuns wrote the manuscript she found, scholars in the field have begun to suggest the contrary by describing the different kinds of rhetoric usually used by priests in their writings and by the nuns in their written confessions or vidas.[12] Moreover, scholars have shown that priests would adapt the writings of the nuns without giving them any credit for their work. Asunción Lavrin mentions that the interest in making of them exemplary and didactic compositions was used to justify the intellectual appropriation and the dis-closure of the confidences exchanged in a relationship that was supposed to be direct, personal, and secret.[13] Jean Franco also studies the process by which the nuns' writing goes from private to public. She states that the language of the writer nun had to be polished by the lettered priest, since the language of the women was considered rustic. Consequently, the priests usually edited the nuns' compositions.[14] Immediate proof that the manuscript published in 1963 was not written by the nuns is the recent finding of the original texts in the archives of the convent. This important finding changes and contributes to the body of work that has been done on the subject.

A number of important studies followed Muriel's initial research on the founding of Corpus Christi. Asunción Lavrin has analyzed the conflicts in the convent during its first years as well as the racial divergences within the convent.[15] Ann Miriam Gallagher wrote her doctoral dissertation in 1972 about the family background of the indigenous nuns of Corpus Christi and another convent in Querétaro, and has an article on the same subject.[16] Elisa Sampson published a book in which she studies the debate that surrounded the founding of the convent for Indian women and the different kinds of images that were constructed for these women.[17] Mariselle Meléndez wrote an article about the racial identity constructed in the manuscript about the indigenous

nuns of Corpus Christi, and María Justina Sarabia Viejo treats a similar subject using materials from the General Archive of Indies in Seville.[18] All of these works have greatly contributed to the knowledge of one of the most important occurrences in New Spain, the acceptance of indigenous nuns into a convent.

Convents began appearing in Spanish America thirty years after the conquest. Fray Juan de Zumárraga, the first bishop of New Spain, asked the crown to send Spanish nuns to establish centers of Christian life among the female indigenous population, but Charles V opposed the idea since according to him it was too early in the process of the conquest.[19] Although some of the first missionaries instructed indigenous girls in the Catholic faith, the nunneries founded in the sixteenth and seventeenth centuries were for Spanish and criolla women. Church authorities believed that indigenous people could not comprehend the meaning of monastic life. For much of the early colonial period, they restricted indigenous women to the role of servants or *donadas*[20] within convents. Finally, in 1724 Viceroy don Baltasar de Zúñiga, marquis of Valero, and clerical authorities established the convent of Corpus Christi in Mexico City, a convent for indigenous noble women. Clerical authorities believed that the nobility would be better educated and more prepared for monastic life than other Indians. Moreover, the authorities believed that there was a large group of Indians who wanted to profess, and they wanted to limit the number of candidates. In 1737, the convent of Cosamaloapan, the second for indigenous women, appeared in Morelia; and

MÓNICA DÍAZ

in 1782, the convent of Nuestra Señora de los Angeles was opened in Oaxaca. Early in the nineteenth century, the marquis of Castañiza, director of Mexico City's former Jesuit school for indigenous girls of Nuestra Señora de Guadalupe in Mexico City, transformed it into a convent. This convent was the first to open to indigenous women regardless of social class in 1811.

Gendered Racial Beliefs

A convent for indigenous women had not been allowed before 1724, and the opening of the convent signified a change in racial and gender politics in the religious arena. Previous research has shown that the transition was not easy and not immediate, and even despite the change of politics, groups continued to fight to restrict indigenous women to servile roles. The entry of indigenous women into the convent was in reality part of a continuous negotiation between the indigenous nobility, priests, and colonial authorities. The negotiation did not end when the convent opened its doors; rather, it continued and involved the indigenous nuns as active participants. The first convent was intended only for members of the indigenous nobility, who maintained a special position of power, particularly during the first years of the colony. They allowed the Spaniards to interact with the rest of the indigenous population, the *macehuales* (commoners), by filling the roles of intermediaries between the colonizers and colonized. In their positions as intermediaries, they had privileges that distinguished them from the rest of the Indians, yet they did not have the same social and economic status as the Spaniards. Indigenous nobility remained racially inferior to Spaniards in colonial society and in the religious hierarchy.

Indigenous noble men were able to participate in religious life earlier than indigenous noble women. Although not in a monastery per se, the indigenous nobility was able to learn Christian devotional practices as well as to read and write in Latin, Nahuatl, and Spanish. Louise Burkhart writes that the Colegio de Santa Cruz at Santiago Tlatelolco, founded in 1536 by the Franciscans, had as its primary goal an "educational program to train assistants who would help the friars attain the language skills they needed to preach to the rest of the native population."[21] In reality, as Burkhart explains, the training of the Colegio de Santa Cruz became empowering to members of the indigenous nobility; they not only learned to speak Latin and Spanish in addition to Nahuatl, but also "had been taught to reason according to Western as well as Nahua logical principles and to construct arguments according to Western as well as Nahua rhetorical arts."[22] Initially, Franciscan friars thought about training the Indians for the priesthood, but they backed away from that idea, "not because they lacked intellectual ability but because they were overendowed with sensuality."[23]

By the time the convent of Corpus Christi was open, indigenous men were allowed to become priests, but indigenous women had few opportunities in the colonial church. There were convents that allowed indigenous girls to enter in order to receive an education and to learn about Christianity, yet they could not become nuns. When church authorities had to give a reason for their opposition to indigenous women becoming nuns, they mentioned the problem of sensuality, which had previously been assigned to indigenous men. Asunción Lavrin summarizes, "The ugly double-headed monster of intellectual ineptitude and sexual incontinence which had stalled the process of acceptance on indigenous men in the clergy revisited the scene to taint the process for women."[24] Allan Greer argues that "according to their detractors, the *indias* lacked one other, indispensable virtue: constancy. Presumably the vows of poverty and obedience posed no difficulty to humble native women; rather it was the vow of chastity that was at issue."[25] When the debate was opened to several priests' opinions about the ability of indigenous women to become nuns, the Franciscans, Augustinians, and Dominicans responded that the convent for Indian women was necessary and that many of these women had already shown the capacity to live a religious life in the convents for Spaniards and criollas.[26] The Jesuits, although not all of them, were against the indigenous convents.

In the midst of the debate about the ability of native women to become nuns appeared a document that would argue in favor of indigenous nuns. In 1724, to counterbalance the negative campaign against the new convent, Juan de Urtassum published a hagiographical account about an indigenous woman from New France, entitled *La gracia triunfante en la vida de Catharina Tegakovita*.[27] The original account was authored by Francisco Colonec and translated from the French by Juan de Urtassum, a Jesuit. The translation appeared in a three-part volume in New Spain. In the first part of the work, Juan Ignacio de Castorena, who

was vicar-general of the Indians, wrote a *Parecer* in which he defended the capacity of indigenous women to become nuns. The second part is the biography of Catharina in the form of a hagiographical account, and the last part consists of several short accounts of indigenous women who had been known to lead exemplary lives. With regard to the racial debate of Corpus Christi, the first and last parts of the Spanish version of *La gracia triunfante* are the most important ones. The hagiographical account of Catharina appears merely as an exemplary life of an Indian in support of the agenda that Urtassum and Castorena shared. The translated account of Catharina was the result of the two men's efforts to present convincing evidence that indigenous women could be chaste and pure. They defined the spirituality that indigenous women needed to enter the convent in terms of chastity, purity, and continence.

Because the main point of contention was the lack of chastity among indigenous women, Castorena attempts to defuse the debate in the first part of the book: "The reason seems convincing, as it is noticeable, founded on the Scriptures and Fathers in what the Holy Spirit dictated to the pen of the wise man: Nobody can be pure if God does not make him chaste. We owe the gift of continence to your mercy."[28] In this paragraph, Castorena argues that the favor of God is required in order to be chaste. According to him, if God grants that favor to religious men and women in all parts of the world, then he would not deny that favor to indigenous women. He contends that chastity or continence does not come from human will but from divine favor and that one racial or gender group cannot be excluded from God's will.

In the third point of the apology, Castorena goes on to contest the criticisms and reasons that were given to oppose the foundation of Corpus Christi. Against the idea that indigenous people could not comprehend the meaning of religious monastic life, Castorena argues, "I ask, didn't they have the ability to go from the ignorance of our holy mysteries to the knowledge of them? Then why wouldn't they have the ability to go from the knowledge of the mysteries and obligations of being a Christian to the knowledge of the Evangelical advises?"[29] Castorena argues that the indigenous people were capable of understanding the mysteries of Christianity and becoming Christians, and that same capacity would allow them to understand the duties of monastic life. During the time of the debate, the indigenous women to whom they were referring had been Christians for generations. There was not much chance of a false Catholic among them, according to Castorena.

The second part of *La gracia triunfante* presents the life of Catharina Tegakovita, an Iroquois Indian.[30] Catharina's main virtue is her purity. Her parents attempted to persuade her to marry, but she resisted because her love of purity was stronger. The hagiography states that her people persecuted her until she left her village. After her departure, she took her first vow: the vow of chastity. The narration, in the style of a hagiographical account, touches on particular topoi such as the sufferings and pains that Catharina endured with happiness and patience. The life of Catharina Tegakovita was a pretext for writing extensively and with precise examples about the virtues of indigenous women. The third part, which starts in chapter six, begins with the following explanation: "Herein a brief notice of the exemplary life of some of the Indians of this New Spain is given; and in particular of the continence, which they professed, and which they maintained until their blessed death."[31]

Urtassum includes in the last part of the volume short narratives about the lives of several indigenous women who had lived a life of chastity. The cases of exemplary indigenous lives that Urtassum offered in *La gracia triunfante* were taken from other texts; maybe the most recognized ones are of Petronila de la Concepción and Francisca de San Miguel, which are included in *Paraíso occidental*, written by don Carlos de Sigüenza y Góngora. None of the indigenous women featured were nuns because they were not yet allowed that privilege. Like Catharina, they were women who lived according to the model of perfection found in hagiographies and who adhered to a secret vow of perpetual virginity. Magdalena de Pátzcuaro, for example, had experiences similar to those of Catharina. She was sick and offered her vow of chastity in return for healing. Later her parents tried to have her marry, but she refused because of her vow. "She concluded her prayer by making a vow of perpetual virginity to her [Mary's] Holy Son, proposing in virtue and imitation of Him, to preserve her body whole and without stain for the rest of her life."[32]

The book, then, not only demonstrates that there were indigenous women who were worthy of being nuns because they could remain chaste during their entire

THE INDIGENOUS NUNS OF CORPUS CHRISTI

lives, but also became part of the central racial debate in which the proponents of the convent endeavored to change the images of indigenous women and portray them as chaste as other religious women. *La gracia triunfante* was a piece of religious literature that challenged the gendered racial beliefs that religious men had about indigenous women. Through the work, the two Jesuit authors were able to present new images of these women and influenced the founding of the first convent for indigenous women.

Suffering as Spirituality

Another example of religious literature that is part of the racial debate is the *Vida de la venerable Madre Sor Sebastiana Josepha de la SS. Trinidad.*[33] The argument of this work is more subtle than that of *La gracia triunfante*, and the purpose of the author was different from that of Urtassum and Castorena. In reality, this vida was not intended to make a direct contribution to the debate, but it has a chapter that comments on the racial tensions caused by the presence of a Spanish nun in the convent for indigenous nuns. The vida demonstrated that predominant perceptions of indigenous women had not changed completely in the colonial setting and that conflicts between races continued even after the founding of the convent. The vida of Sor Sebastiana Josepha is particularly important because she was one of the criollas accepted into the convent of Corpus Christi. The vida written by one of her confessors is based on letters and spiritual accounts that she wrote. For this reason, the content of the vida is important not only for what was taken from Sebastiana's writings but also for the position that the priest takes

in the conflict, since he rewrote the nun's experiences leaving the reader with a modified version of what Sebastiana in fact wrote. Chapter fourteen of the vida describes the entry of Sebastiana into Corpus Christi, and chapter fifteen explains briefly her time at the convent and her eviction from it.

Fray Joseph Valdés expresses his sadness over Sebastiana's departure from the convent, presenting Corpus Christi and the nuns as a place of perfection and virtue. He is sympathetic to the indigenous nuns, and does not express opposition to the expulsion of Sebastiana from the convent. The combination of loyalties to both the indigenous nuns and the Spanish nun is surprising. Fray Joseph narrates the unfortunate chapter of Sebastiana's life in Corpus Christi without negatively portraying the indigenous nuns.

Fray Joseph starts the chapter by praising the convent: "The convent, I say, religious, penitent, austere, and exemplary of noble religious ladies of Corpus Christi in where they live to heaven and die to the world; the caciques that come from all over this kingdom as candid doves flying to their nest and royal dovecote."[34] Beginning in the first paragraph, fray Joseph enumerates the several virtues of the convent and stresses the noble character of the inhabitants. He suggests that the indigenous nuns attained perfection because of the extremely austere and regulated life that they pursued, and he recounts that Sebastiana tried to conform to their austere way of life. Fray Joseph goes on to assert that it is more admirable to be the "weak sex" (*el sexo débil*) and practice such penances and mortifications on their bodies, while living happily and walking with ease. The question of chastity does not figure into his description of the indigenous women's spirituality. Instead, suffering and mortification are the key elements of his narrative.

Sebastiana took the veil in the convent of Corpus Christi. She did not have money to pay the dowry to get into any convent but she had a sponsor who paid for her to be a Bridgettine nun. But in that convent they would only give her the white veil and her inclination was to be able to participate as a black-veiled nun. Through another intercessor, the Marquise of Salvatierra, Sebastiana got into Corpus Christi. "The Commissary General having given license, although with resistance and with the nuns' disgust because they did not want to accept Spaniards. But in the end, with the intercession of several people and the persuasion of the prelates, they accepted three back then, and among them our venerable Sebastiana, about whose virtue they have heard much news."[35]

There were more than a couple of people who were opposed to maintaining the indigenous character of the convent of Corpus Christi, even though it had been decided by a royal *cédula* (mandate). The admission of Spaniards into Corpus Christi created great turmoil,[36] but little is known about the reaction of the indigenous nuns when the Spaniards entered the convent. One of the biographical accounts included in the *Apuntes* gives voice to one of the nuns who saw her convent in danger of being lost to the Spanish government, as had happened with the convent of Santa Clara in Querétaro, which accepted the daughter of the cacique Diego de Tapia as a nun. He was the main benefactor of the convent

and his only request was to see his daughter as a black-veiled nun. His intention was to make that convent one that would accept indigenous women; but no other indigenous woman was ever accepted, and it remained a convent for criollas.[37] In the *vida* fray Joseph mentions this occurrence: "And going back to what happened for her eviction, it is good to remember that having founded this convent as it was founded with the finality of receiving in it only noble Indians and not wanting to receive Spaniards because they [the Indians] were fearful to end up without this convent, as they had lost another one."[38]

In the biographical account of the *Apuntes*, the writer takes as her mission the narration of some episodes from the life of Sor Petra de San Francisco, one of the founding nuns and first abbess of Corpus Christi. Sor Petra was a criolla nun who came from the convent of San Juan de la Penitencia and who was, according to this biographer, very kind to the indigenous novices and nuns. The anonymous writer does not limit herself to the account of Sor Petra's life and virtue, rather she takes advantage of the opportunity to write and be read by an ecclesiastical authority in order to relate the truthful version of the conflicts in Corpus Christi. The writer uses a candid and colloquial style. She writes as if she was speaking to the reader, who in this case is *Vuestra Paternidad*, surely the confessor of the nuns at the moment. In that style, she offers the following portrayal of Sor Petra: "She would give us our good lashes and then if we were crying she would caress us and she would tell us: This is over my children. They gave more lashes to our husband and did worse

THE INDIGENOUS NUNS OF CORPUS CHRISTI

things to his majesty."[39] In this anecdote, the narrator recounts that Sor Petra would severely punish the nuns of the convent when they made a mistake and then talk to them lovingly. She would give them another opportunity to behave properly, but the narrator suggests that they usually would err again and receive reprimands from Sor Petra. The lesson that Sor Petra wanted to teach them was that their sufferings could not be surpassed by Jesus's suffering. The idea of suffering as an essential element of spirituality, which was implied in the vida, is mentioned as the teachings of Sor Petra.

When the biographer finishes recounting the life of Sor Petra, she continues writing about the racial conflicts in the convent. The writer clarifies that the founding nuns—all of them criollas—were not the ones who caused trouble for the indigenous nuns, but were the nuns that Father Navarrete admitted into the convent once Sor Petra died. The biographer directly addresses the racial conflict, unlike fray Joseph in the vida. Fray Joseph refers only to the need for Sebastiana to leave the convent because Corpus Christi was never intended for criolla nuns and that the indigenous nuns were afraid of losing the indigenous character of their convent; he never explores the problems between the two racial groups. The narrator of Sor Petra's life in the Apuntes, by contrast, more closely relates racial concerns and spirituality.

In colonial documents, the relation between gender and genre is a clear one. By comparing the style of fray Joseph and that of the anonymous female biographer of the Apuntes, we can find obvious distinctions that were related to the gender of the writer. Several critics have studied the stylistic differences of vidas written by men and those by women. For example, Kathryn McKnight argues that the men who wrote vidas usually do not indicate a confessional relationship as the basis for their context, reveal little internal conflict, and contain quite a bit of self-affirmation. In addition, the writings were clearly intended for publication, which marked a great divergence between male and female writing production.[40] The last characteristic can be considered symbolic of the different public and private spaces that women and men occupied. The vida written by a nun as a request from her confessor, belonged to the private arena, and even when it circulated among the priests in order to be published, it had to go through the editorial revisions of the confessor. The texts written by men could be composed with the purpose of being published, and men could choose from a different variety of genres, most of which were forbidden for women.

The style of the vidas found in the Apuntes differs in important ways from that of Las indias caciques de Corpus Christi by Josefina Muriel. As I mentioned before, the biographer of the Apuntes is able to combine spiritual commentary or a hagiographical style with the racial discussion—with issues that would not be part of a hagiographical account. The vidas in the manuscript published by Muriel are clearly hagiographical; their style is rigid and formulaic, and their language is polished and sophisticated. Clearly, the texts were written with the purpose of being published, and most likely a priest wrote them. All the accounts are composed to portray exemplary lives, models for readers to follow. With the Apuntes in hand,

MÓNICA DÍAZ

we are able to compare the two sets of texts and discover differences in style and content that lead us to believe that the *Apuntes* were the basis for the manuscript published by Muriel. Moreover, we find clear linguistic clues that let us know that the writer or writers were indigenous nuns.

It is difficult to assert that all of the biographers were indigenous, but we can be sure of the one writing about Sor Petra because of the content of her account. As she writes in describing the true conflict between the Spanish nuns and the indigenous nuns: "And, our father, even when they say that our founding mothers created a war, no it was not like that, it was not until our mother closed her eyes when Father Navarrete sent us another four nuns from the Convent of San Juan and other three novices, but these two ladies from San Juan were the ones who made the war."[41] The author explains that these two criollas would constantly accuse the indigenous nuns of wrongdoing before Father Navarrete. Because of the accusations that the two nuns made, Navarrete would punish the indigenous nuns and take away their veils. The author claims that he also wanted to force the indigenous nuns to vote for the Spanish novices to become nuns in the convent. Navarrete, from what we know from this account and that of fray Joseph, was not convinced that the indigenous nuns should live in a convent without criolla nuns. Asunción Lavrin has analyzed a letter by the Commissary General Navarrete in which he admits that he has the lowest opinion of the capacity of the Indians to rule in any way or to direct themselves.[42]

The nuns, however, did not accept what Navarrete requested because, according to the author, "the mind-set of the sponsor of the convent was that it was only for Indians." The author states that the indigenous women had to endure the difficult situation created by the presence of Spanish nuns and novices until God allowed the arrival of a royal *cédula* and the papal brief that expelled the nuns and novices from the convent. Her comments suggest that the indigenous nuns were not only well aware that the conflict within the convent was a result of racial difference, but they also knew that people were supporting their cause outside the convent walls. The biographer finished her narration by telling the story recounted at the beginning of this work, ending with: "At last, our Father Navarrete stopped. And it was a lot, a lot that we suffered."[43]

Her report about the suffering caused by the Spanish nuns and novices in the convent is brief, yet it is substantial enough to provide more information about the life of the indigenous nuns in the convent. Most of the information provided in this account was either erased or modified when the priest edited the text and rewrote it as the hagiography that was included in the group of texts published by Josefina Muriel. What we now know is that the indigenous nuns were in fact participating in the racial debates and conflicts that were part of Corpus Christi, in this case, by letting other priests know about their sufferings and problems—to assert the cause of their race in one of the few forums accessible to them.

Final Considerations

The materials examined in this work argued that indigenous women required two main virtues, chastity and suffering, in order to be nuns. The authorship of the texts influenced the arguments stated in them. The two Jesuits, Juan de Urtassum and Juan Ignacio de Castorena, focused their attention on the virtue of chastity, which was a requisite of monastic life. The vida, although also composed by a man, was based on the writings of Sebastiana. That text and the biographical account of the indigenous nun stressed the virtue of suffering. For men, the most important issue was the control of the Indians' sexuality. For women in the convent, the main concern was to appreciate their suffering and to recognize a resemblance with their ultimate spiritual authority, Jesus, as Sor Petra had taught the indigenous women.

These three texts are windows through which we can appreciate the racial and gender negotiations that allowed the founding of Corpus Christi. Racial and gender ideologies were important overlapping elements in the arguments of the texts, but each of the authors takes different approaches. For Sebastiana and fray Joseph, the question of race was not as important as it was for the indigenous nun, who was affected directly by it. The indigenous nun wrote her account with a specific reader in mind—a man, most probably a confessor. Consequently, a power relationship guided the production of this particular text, yet from the text emerges an example of a fearless nun who denounces the injustices committed by Father Navarrete and commends the great sufferings of herself and her sisters. In the first part of her account, in which she writes about Sor Petra, the nun most likely responds to the petition of the confessor or the abbess to write about her sisters who had passed away. In the last part of her account, in which she touches on the racial conflict in the convent, we can recognize an autonomous voice, the voice of one who wants to be heard. The biographer wanted to let her readers know about the conflict in Corpus Christi and the individuals involved in it. She wanted to make known that the Spanish nuns had caused the indigenous nuns to suffer. Ultimately, the indigenous women received their reward for their sufferings. The Spanish nuns and novices left the convent, and the indigenous women were left with a convent of their own.

NOTES

My thanks go to Peter Guardino, Kathleen Myers, and Ethan Sharp for their valuable suggestions.

1. *Apuntes de algunas vidas de nuestras hermanas difuntas*, México, Convento de Corpus Christi.

2. R. Douglas Cope, *The Limits of Racial Domination, Plebeian Society in Colonial Mexico City, 1660–1720* (Madison: University of Wisconsin Press, 1994), 4.

3. Kristine Ibsen, *Women's Spiritual Autobiography in Colonial Spanish America* (Gainesville: University Press of Florida, 1999), 1.

4. Elisa Sampson Vera Tudela, "Fashioning a Cacique Nun: From Saint's Lives to Indian Lives in the Spanish America," in *Gender & History* 9 (1997): 181.

5. Kathleen Ann Myers, "Crossing Boundaries: Defining the Field of Female Religious Writing in Colonial Latin America," *Colonial Latin American Review* 9 (2000): 151.

6. Josefina Muriel, *Las indias caciques de Corpus*

Christi (México: UNAM, 1963); Asunción Lavrin, "Religious Life of Mexican Women in the XVIII Century" (PhD diss., Harvard University, 1963); Ann Miriam Gallagher, "The Family Background of the Nuns of Two 'Monasterios' in Colonial Mexico: Santa Clara, Querétaro; and Corpus Christi, Mexico City, 1724–1822" (PhD diss., The Catholic University of America, 1972).

7. Myers, "Crossing Boundaries," 153.

8. *Criollo* refers to a person of Spanish descent, born in Mexico. See, for example, Kathleen A. Myers and Amanda Powell, *A Wild Country Out in the Garden, The Spiritual Journals of a Colonial Mexican Nun* (Bloomington and Indianapolis: Indiana University Press, 1999); Kathryn Joy McKnight, *The Mystic of Tunja, The Writings of Madre Castillo 1671–1742* (Amherst: University of Massachusetts Press, 1997).

9. Susan Schroeder, Stephanie Wood, and Robert Haskett, eds., *Indian Women of Early Mexico* (Norman and London: University of Oklahoma Press, 1997), 9.

10. Ann Miriam Gallagher, "The Indian Nuns of Mexico City's Monasterio of Corpus Christi, 1724–1821," in *Latin American Women, Historical Perspectives*, ed. Asunción Lavrin, 163 (Westport and London: Greenwood Press, 1978).

11. The genre of the *vida* or "spiritual life" appeared in two different styles. It could be a confessional autobiography or a hagiographic biography; the first was usually written by the nun to her confessor, and the second could have been written by a nun about one or more nuns in the convent or by a priest about a nun or nuns.

12. See, for example, Kathleen A. Myers, "The Mystic Triad in Colonial Mexican Nuns' Discourse: Divine Author, Visionary Scribe, and Clerical Mediator," *Colonial Latin American Historical Review* 6 (1997): 479–524; Asunción Lavrin, "La vida femenina como experiencia: biografía y hagiografía en Hispanoamérica colonial," in *Colonial Latin American Review* 2 (1993): 27–51.

13. Lavrin, "La vida femenina," 31.

14. Jean Franco, *Las conspiradoras: La representación de la mujer en México*, trans. Mercedes Córdoba (México: El Colegio de México/FCE, 1994), 37.

15. Josefina Muriel, *Conventos de monjas en la Nueva España* (México: Editorial Jus, 1995); Lavrin, "Religious Life." Lavrin's dissertation deals with the conflicts that took place in Corpus Christi between some of the Spanish founder nuns and the Indian ones. Later, fray Pedro de Navarrete, Commissary General of the Franciscan order, allowed more Spanish novices into the convent. She mentions a letter in which Sor María Teresa de San José, while abbess, wrote to the Council of Indies asking for the expulsion of three Spanish novices. Lavrin, "Indian Brides of Christ: Creating New Spaces for Indigenous Women in New Spain," *Mexican Studies/Estudios Mexicanos* 15, no. 2 (1999): 225–60.

16. Gallagher, "The Indian Nuns," 150–66; Gallagher, "The Family Background." In a phone interview that I had with Ann Miriam Gallagher she shared with me what a great experience she had when living with the nuns in Corpus Christi while doing her research. She had the opportunity to have complete access to that archive (they have moved to another convent) and used the records and books of entries that would give her the information she needed.

17. Elisa Sampson Vera Tudela, *Colonial Angels: Narratives of Gender and Spirituality in Mexico 1580–1750* (Austin: University of Texas Press, 2000).

18. Mariselle Meléndez, "El perfil económico de la identidad racial en los Apuntes de las indias caciques del convento de Corpus Christi," *Revista de Crítica Literaria Latinoamericana* 46 (1997): 115–33; María Justina Sarabia Viejo, "La Concepción y Corpus Christi. Raza y vida conventual femenina en México, siglo XVIII," in *Manifestaciones religiosas en el mundo colonial americano*, ed. Clara García Ayluardo y Manuel Ramos Medina, 179–92 (México: INAH, UIA, CONDUMEX, 1997).

19. Lavrin, "Religious Life," 29.

20. *Donadas* were laywomen who lived in the convent, primarily for educational reasons.

21. Louise M. Burkhart, *Holy Wednesday: A Nahua Drama from Early Colonial Mexico*

THE INDIGENOUS NUNS OF CORPUS CHRISTI

(Philadelphia: University of Pennsylvania Press, 1996), 57.

22. Ibid., 59.

23. Ibid., 60.

24. Asunción Lavrin, "Indian Brides of Christ," 244.

25. Allan Greer, "Iroquois Virgin: The Story of Catherine Tekakwitha in New France and New Spain," in *Colonial Saints: Discovering the Holy in the Americas*, ed. Allan Greer and Jodi Bilinkoff, 235–50 (New York and London: Routledge, 2003). Even though the indigenous women described here were noble, they occupied a lower position than Spaniards in the social hierarchy and could therefore be considered "humble." Moreover, indigenous nobles were not necessarily rich; their nobility was due to their purity of blood and their heritage.

26. Antonio Rubial, "La exaltación de los humillados. Indios y santidad en las ciudades novohispanas del siglo XVIII," *Actas del III Congreso Internacional de Mediadores Culturales. Ciudades mestizas, intercambios y continuidades en la expansión continental, siglos XVI–XIX* (México: CONDUMEX/INAH, 2000).

27. *La gracia triunfante en la vida de Catharina Tegakovita, india Iroquesa, y en las de otras, así de su Nación, como de esta Nueva-España*, (Henceforth *La gracia triunfante*), México año de 1724, Biblioteca Nacional, Sala Mexicana.

28. *La gracia triunfante*, Parecer.

29. Ibid.

30. Urtassum locates the province of the Iroquois to be on the border of New Mexico, he also argues that they were never conquered by the French.

31. *La gracia triunfante*, 211.

32. Ibid., 217.

33. *Vida de la venerable madre Sor Sebastiana Josepha de la SS. Trinidad, Religiosa de Coro, y Velo negro en el Sagrado Convento de San Juan de la Penitencia de Religiosas Clarisas de esta Ciudad de México*, [Henceforth *Vida*] México año de 1765, Biblioteca Nacional, Sala Mexicana.

34. *Vida*, 100.

35. Ibid., 102.

36. Lavrin, "Religious Life"; Muriel, *Conventos de monjas*; Sarabia Viejo, "La Concepción y Corpus Christi."

37. See Gallagher, "The Family Background."

38. *Vida*, 108.

39. *Apuntes*, 7–8.

40. McKnight, *The Mystic of Tunja*, 56–57.

41. *Apuntes*, 9.

42. Lavrin, *Religious Life*, 30.

43. *Apuntes*, 10.

PART FIVE

GUARDIAN OF THE CHRISTIAN SOCIETY

The Holy Office of the Inquisition—Racism, Judaizing, and Gambling

---

It is a pity that Agustín Alvarez is not considered to be pure of blood because. . . . I consider him the best of all possible candidates.

—Mateo Vázquez de Lecca, 1590

[The Inquisition] would be one of the most important things in the service of God for use against the Spaniards, mulattoes, and mestizos who offend our Lord [but] for now it should be suspended in what concerns the natives because they are so new to the faith, weak [*gente flaca*], and of little substance.

—don Sancho Sánchez de Muñón,
d. 1600

In this book, he will be able to see all what God did to David and to those who kept the Law God gave to Moses. Through guarding this Law and its ceremonies he will attain the merits King David and the others attained. By fulfilling the commandments he will receive God's blessing; not keeping them he will be cursed by God.

—Antonio Correa Núñez, n.d.

I enter this house [i.e., church], I will worship neither wood nor stone, but only God who governs the universe.

—Converso's silent act of faith, n.d.

The lot is cast into the lap; but the whole disposing thereof is of the Lord.

—Proverbs 16:33

Piensan que Dios anda favoreciendo a bellacos.
(They think God is on the rogues' side [as in "luck is on my side"].)

—Pedro de Covarrubias, 1543

Catholic Kings Ferdinand and Isabel and their successors expended great effort to realize Christian orthodoxy throughout their dominions. It was an enormous, expensive undertaking, and much to their dismay they were not entirely successful. It is true that many individuals in the colonies were exemplary Christians; others, though, eschewed Catholicism altogether. Native peoples and Africans, for example, were often selective in their accommodation of the Gospel, for they preferred their own religious traditions. Spaniards, too, most nominally Catholics, were selectively observant and many tended to use the church for personal advantage. Moreover, the familiar Spanish trope, "I obey but do not comply" (*obedezco pero no cumplo*), conveniently explained away any deviation from the requisite norms. Thus, the church's clergy labored to bring heterodoxy under control.

The Holy Office of the Inquisition, established in Castile in 1478, was the perfect institution to implement the crown's policy of religious conformity. The tribunal had an elaborate bureaucracy that fanned out across the countryside to root out heresy. The court had its own jail, and it was not uncommon for the accused to languish in their cells for years, waiting for their cases to be resolved. Pogroms and autos de fe served as horrific periodic public reminders of the crown's rigid position regarding untoward religious activity.

In 1571, the Holy Office was established in Mexico City, and in its early years the court adjudicated cases concerning everything from witchcraft and judaizing to bigamy and blasphemy. Over the course of the colonial period, however, its priorities shifted somewhat, and the persecution of Jews and persons accused of practicing witchcraft lessened, at least as far as we can tell from extant court records. This is not to say that the Holy Office lost its authority; on the contrary, its reach was wide and relentless throughout the viceroyalty, and it continued as a formidable means to both monitor and punish anyone whose behavior was thought to be problematic.

Issues of *limpieza de sangre* (purity of blood) had been fundamental to the court's purview in Spain, and these concerns were just as great in New Spain. Individuals wishing to enter the priesthood or take the veil, seeking political or legal office, or wanting to marry into a family of high social standing were required to furnish proof of their legitimacy and freedom from tainted lineage. Ancestors and relatives suspected of African, Jewish, or Moorish heredities, or individuals engaged in certain undesirable lines of employment, were all suspect and thus ineligible as candidates. Investigations to prove legitimacy or to counter accusations of tainted blood could be lengthy and expensive, and it was not uncommon for family fortunes to be lost during the process. María Elena Martínez, in "Interrogating Blood Lines: 'Purity of Blood,' the Inquisition, and *Casta* Categories," treats the issue of limpieza de sangre—its insidious development and purpose in Spain and then its characteristically imperfect form in the colony. Although the importance of the idea of pure lineages probably never really diminished in either place, it was more difficult to keep things straight in New Spain.

Religious noncompliance was of course

thought to be heretical, and eliminating it was the exclusive prerogative of the Inquisition. Stanley Hordes, in "Between Toleration and Persecution: The Relationship of the Inquisition and Crypto-Jews on the Northern Frontier," emphasizes the importance of distance from Mexico City for the survival of Crypto-Jewish religious beliefs and practices. Hordes contextualizes his study of Jews in New Spain with information about the cycles of persecution by the Holy Tribunal and the way in which Portuguese immigrants and their descendants, in particular, seemed to be the most active and successful in perpetuating Jewish culture.

Then, Javier Villa-Flores, in "On Divine Persecution: Blasphemy and Gambling," brings to light another side of religious activity altogether. Not only do we know more about the prevalence of gambling in the colony, but we learn that perennial losers inevitably blamed their God for their failing. Moreover, their blasphemous curses were a public insult, which was costlier, ultimately, than their monetary losses at the gaming tables. Yet Villa-Flores's study of gambling and blasphemy is especially revealing of the pervasiveness of Catholic belief, for the Christian God was always faulted, not fortune or bad luck.

NOTES

Epigraph citations, in order of appearance, are as follows: Stafford Poole, "The Politics of *Limpieza de Sangre*: Juan de Ovando and His Circle in the Reign of Philip II," *The Americas* 55, no. 3 (1999): 359; J. Jorge Klor de Alva, "Colonizing Souls: The Failure of the Indian Inquisition and the Rise of Penitential Discipline," in *Cultural Encounters: The Impact of the Inquisition in Spain and the New World*, ed. Mary Elizabeth Perry and Anne J. Cruz, 14 (Berkeley: University of California Press, 1991); Moshe Lazar, "Scorched Parchments and Tortured Memories: The 'Jewishness' of the Anussim (Crypto-Jews)," in *Cultural Encounters: The Impact of the Inquisition in Spain and the New World*, ed. Mary Elizabeth Perry and Anne J. Cruz, 180, 176 (Berkeley: University of California Press, 1991); Pedro de Covarrubias, *Remedio de jugadores* (Salamanca: Juan de Junta, 1543), xxxvi.

CHAPTER TEN

Interrogating Blood Lines

"Purity of Blood," the Inquisition, and *Casta* Categories

MARÍA ELENA MARTÍNEZ

Most students of early modern Iberia are familiar with the statutes of *limpieza de sangre* (purity of blood) that certain Spanish institutions began to adopt in the second half of the fifteenth century and that continued to spread during the next one hundred years. Initially inspired by suspicions that recent Jewish converts to Catholicism, known as *conversos*, were not sincerely committed to their new faith, the statutes made "pure" Christian ancestry a requirement for certain ecclesiastical and public posts, among other things. Institutions that established such requirements included cathedral chapters, university colleges, military orders, and the Inquisition, each of which had its own procedures for the certification of limpieza. The spread of the statutes, the factors that led to their implementation, and the ways in which the issue of purity of blood came

to be manipulated by individuals or rival political factions have been studied by various historians of early modern Spain.[1] Far less attention has been paid, however, to the actual process of "proving" limpieza and its transplantation to the New World. This chapter focuses on these issues. In particular, it is concerned with the way that the Holy Office of the Inquisition first investigated and defined purity of blood, and with some of the legal steps, mechanisms, and problems associated with its certification in both Spain and Mexico. These issues are important for what they reveal not only about power and honor in different contexts, but also about the relationship between law, religion, and the birth of colonial *casta* (mixed ancestry) categories. Thus, after sketching the spread of the purity of blood statutes and development of procedures to certify limpieza by the

Inquisition in Spain, the chapter discusses the emergence and operation of similar requirements in Mexico and some of the ways the Holy Office's genealogical inquiries promoted the construction of classifications of mixed ancestry.

The Spanish Statutes of Purity of Blood and the *Probanza de Limpieza de Sangre*

Although they did not emerge until the second half of the fifteenth century, the history of the Spanish statutes of limpieza de sangre really begins in 1391. In that year a wave of anti-Semitic violence swept through Seville and other cities that resulted in the death of hundreds, perhaps thousands, of Jews.[2] According to Domínguez Ortíz, the suddenness and number of Jewish conversions to Christianity that followed the massacres created the impression that they had been insincere.[3] The issue of identifying "authentic" versus "false" Christians produced a great deal of commotion within several institutions, especially some of the religious orders, and by the mid-fifteenth century it was feeding suspicions that the new converts were threatening to undermine the faith. In subsequent decades these suspicions only grew as reports of alleged "judaizers" (crypto-Jews) multiplied, prompting Ferdinand and Isabel, "the Catholic Kings," to establish the Inquisition in Castile.[4] By the end of the 1480s, the Holy Office had been extended to León and Aragón (a papal Inquisition had existed in the latter kingdom since 1232 but by the fifteenth century it was largely inactive), and its seat had been transferred from Seville to Toledo, where the Supreme Council of the Holy and General Inquisition (the "Suprema") was from then on to be based.[5] The Suprema was in charge of coordinating activities between tribunals in Castile, León, and Aragón and later would also be responsible for overseeing all matters handled by the Holy Office in the Americas.

It is important to emphasize that the Spanish Inquisition was a tribunal set up to investigate charges of heresy among Christians, and in particular among conversos. It had no jurisdiction over Jews and dealt not with Judaism per se but with the problem of crypto-Judaism. It is also worth stressing that although the statutes of purity and the Holy Office are usually paired in the historiography, their emergence followed somewhat different trajectories. When the Inquisition was founded, some institutions had already adopted limpieza de sangre requirements. In fact, the Holy Office did not officially demand proof of "purity of blood" from its officials until after the mid-sixteenth century. By then, statutes were in place in certain cathedral chapters, religious orders, university colleges, brotherhoods, guilds, and in the three main military orders (Santiago, Alcántara and Calatrava).[6] But if the Inquisition was relatively slow in adopting the requirement for its officials, once it did, it played a prominent role in promoting the preoccupation with "purity of blood."

Although there is no consensus on the precise origins of the purity statutes, historians do tend to agree that their emergence was linked to the conversions that followed the 1391 pogroms and that a key moment in their history was Toledo's 1449 *Sentencia-Estatuto*. Issued by members of the town council at a moment when converso tax collectors were being made the scapegoats of Juan II's repressive fiscal policies, this local decree made converted Jews and their descendants ineligible for public offices and all municipal appointments.[7] Supporters of the statute claimed that the conversos could not be trusted because their conversions were questionable and because of their deep hatred of "Old Christians." The city, they argued, had to protect itself and the Catholic faith by ensuring that only people who derived from unsullied Christian lineages were in positions of power. From that moment on, claims about the treachery and heretical tendencies of Jewish converts to Catholicism were repeated again and again as different secular and religious establishments took similar exclusionary measures.

The purity statutes were initially modeled after canon law's treatment of heretics, according to which those that deviated from the faith and their descendants were to be deprived of access to public and religious offices and various honors. The statutes, however, identified two categories of "impurity": descent from condemned heretics and descent from Jews or Muslims.[8] The converted descendants of Jews and Muslims were considered "stained" because they supposedly had not yet fully embraced Catholicism and were therefore potential heretics. But, also following heresy laws, most institutions at first limited the transmission of the status of impurity to two generations, that is, to the convert's grandchildren. That Toledo's Sentencia-Estatuto did not was certainly a bad omen, but in general early purity requirements applied the two-generation rule. This started to

change, however, in the 1530s. The church of Córdoba, for example, did not place a limit and neither did the cathedral of Toledo. By the mid-sixteenth century, most leading religious and secular bodies did not restrict how far back the search for Jewish, Muslim, and even heretical ancestors could go.[9]

Thus, what had officially begun as a temporary tool to ensure the purity and integrity of the faith had in the course of a century developed into a mechanism for creating a hierarchical sociopolitical order based almost exclusively on blood and on the categories of Old and New Christians. The importance of this shift cannot be emphasized enough, for it made the concept of limpieza take on a much more essentializing quality than it had had at the beginning, a process that was signaled by the increasing deployment of the word *raza* (race) against the converts and their descendants. Because the term had profoundly negative connotations, Old Christians seldom applied it to themselves.[10] For them, to have raza essentially meant to have Jewish, Muslim, and, in some cases, even Protestant antecedents. Religion, "blood," and race hence became inextricably intertwined as the notion of limpieza transformed into a discourse, that is, as it was systematically deployed by a number of key institutions, as it became strongly implicated in all sorts of practices and power relations, and as it helped to constitute social subjects.[11]

It was also around the mid-sixteenth century that official support for the doctrine of purity of blood became more explicit. After much maneuvering by the infamous Archbishop Juan Martínez Silíceo, both the papacy and the crown approved the

MARÍA ELENA MARTÍNEZ

decision of the cathedral chapter of Toledo to demand proof of limpieza from its members—the pope in 1555 and Philip II in 1556. Royal support of the statutes was accompanied by the rise of genealogical investigations intended to certify whether a person's ancestors were "stained" or not. Several key institutions, among them the Inquisition and the Consejo de Órdenes, began to systematize the procedures for how to conduct the investigations. In the case of the Holy Office, the shift was prompted by a series of royal decrees that made proof of limpieza mandatory for all of its members, except the inquisitor general. The most important of these decrees came at the end of 1572, when the Supreme Council was issued instructions on how to verify purity and Old Christian ancestry.[12] Significantly, the instructions did not establish a limit on a how far back "stains" could be traced. As of the 1570s, the Suprema thus began sending detailed orders to all Inquisition tribunals, including those that were just being established in the New World, for how to go about producing a "probanza de limpieza de sangre." How, then, was a person's purity of blood certified?

Within the Inquisition itself, the process normally began when the individual who wished to be considered for an office or the title of *familiar* (a lay informant for the Inquisition) presented his genealogical information, called an *información de genealogía y limpieza de sangre* at the given tribunal. If the petitioner was married, he also gave the genealogy of his wife. The Holy Office's preoccupation with verifying that the spouses of its personnel had "clean" ancestry was linked to its concern with preserving its institutional honor as well as the purity of lineages. Since the status of limpieza was established by biological parenthood and through both bloodlines, a male's marriage to an "impure" woman "contaminated" his descendants. The Inquisition tried, with mixed success, not to associate itself with "stained" families and therefore insisted that its married officers submit proof of purity for their wives, even if they wed after receiving their titles. Each genealogical history had to include the names and places of origin (*naturaleza*) and residence (*vecindad*) of the person's parents and four grandparents or *cuatro costados* (four corners). These data were supposed to enable officials to examine local registers and people that might provide details about the petitioner's ancestors and reputation.

Once the genealogical information was recorded, the inquisitors selected the commissioner (*comisario*) who was to conduct the secret investigation, usually a parish priest, and he in turn chose the secretary that was to accompany him. The actual inquiry consisted of various steps, the first of which involved going to the petitioner's birthplace and examining all available public, private, and ecclesiastical records—such as parish registers when they existed, Inquisition archives, and censuses—that might contain information regarding the person's birth status, lineage, and general family history. Illegitimacy tended to disqualify the candidate not only because it was considered "infamous" by law (a public dishonor), but also because it called into question his biological parenthood, thus making it impossible to ascertain his purity of blood. If no stain of illegitimacy or any other irregularities were found, the comisario proceeded to conduct the oral part of the investigation. With the help of the local or district familiars he identified eight to twelve people who could serve as unbiased "witnesses" in the case. In keeping with the Spanish tradition of privileging the viejos (elders) of each town as sources of information and authority, these individuals were to be selected from among the oldest Old Christian males of the community.

There were thus two main types of "proofs" involved in a normal probanza. The first came from written records, namely registers and archives, and attested mainly to the legitimate birth of the candidate and his immediate ancestors. The second was oral and relied on the memory of a select group of men. It was this latter source of information or evidence that usually established the purity or impurity status of the individual, not necessarily because it was preferred, but because the Spanish documentary revolution that greatly multiplied and systematized public and ecclesiastical records was just beginning. Once the witnesses were chosen, the most important and solemn part of the entire process took place: the actual interrogations. The people who testified were told to guard the "secret" of the Holy Office and had to swear to tell only the truth. Penalties for lying were severe: by the early seventeenth century they included the threat of excommunication. During the questioning, the secretary recorded the testimonies verbatim and one or several public notaries were present to attest to the legality of procedures.

Since several people were interrogated, the whole process could take several days, sometimes months, and even years. The length of an investigation largely depended on the number of places in which it had to be conducted and on whether doubts about the limpieza of the petitioner or any one of his ancestors were raised. If the latter occurred, the commissioner had to try to determine on which bloodline the stain supposedly ran and if there was any "hard evidence" to substantiate the claim, such as the existence of sanbenitos. These were penitential garments that persons convicted for heresy by the Inquisition had to wear and which, after they died, were left hanging, indefinitely, in local churches with a sign identifying the individual to whom they had belonged. The idea was to continue to publicly shame the heretic and his or her descendants, among other things so that "pure" families would try to avoid being "contaminated" by them. In essence, the sanbenitos served as a visual type of proof of impurity that helped to maintain a community's memory of its stained lineages and surnames.

After all the witnesses were interrogated and the comisario wrote down his impressions of the proceedings and any other pertinent information, the case was sent back to the inquisitors. They verified that all aspects of the investigation had been conducted according to proper legal form, evaluated the evidence, and issued a decision. The case in its original form was stored in the Holy Office's archives, which thereby created and preserved genealogical histories. Those who were declared to have the quality of purity of blood were generally given three or four official copies of the probanza, which could serve as proofs

MARÍA ELENA MARTÍNEZ

of eligibility for a post, title, or institution that had limpieza requirements. Though not necessarily accepted by other establishments, the Inquisition's purity certifications were generally recognized as among the most important because of the relative rigor of its investigations. In short, these were the steps involved in producing a probanza at the end of the sixteenth century. Except for the increasing attention paid to the social status of candidates for posts or titles in the Holy Office,[13] thereafter the process remained pretty fixed.

Several aspects of the Holy Office's process of certifying purity are worth noting. First, no lawyers were involved and decisions, which normally could not be appealed, were mainly based on the information gathered by the commissioner. Second, the purity status of an individual was established primarily through negative proof. Detecting impure ancestry—through records of people tried by the Holy Office, sanbenitos, hearsay, and so forth—was much easier than finding positive or conclusive proof of limpieza de sangre. The latter was in fact impossible because genealogies could only be traced to a certain point and there were obvious limits to communal memory. Thus, the best that the Inquisition and other establishments could do to establish someone's purity of blood was to show that there appeared to be no evidence to the contrary. Third, the "proof" of purity came primarily in the form of oral testimonies. What ultimately determined a person's eligibility to access the privileged sectors was the "public voice and fame" (*pública voz y fama*). As various scholars have observed, this aspect of the process was the most

radical as well as the most problematic because it essentially meant that the whole case relied on the presumed impartiality of witnesses.[14] But there was, of course, no real way to ensure that people were telling the truth. For the petitioner of a probanza, the best scenario was that the witnesses selected held him in high regard and would not try to profit from the case; the worst was that someone involved in the investigation had a vendetta against him or his family.

A fourth feature of the probanzas was that they were quite expensive, even when no bribes were involved.[15] When the petitioner initiated the process, he had to make a deposit, the sum of which was based on the estimated costs of sending commissioners to one or various places and of compensating all other local officials participating in the certification procedures. To this payment might be added others, depending on how long and labyrinthine the investigation turned out to be. Fifth, the interrogations were closely scripted. By the seventeenth century, the comisarios tended to be equipped with a questionnaire, which sometimes included blank spaces for the answers.[16] The questions seldom varied, and those that pertained to limpieza basically told the witness how to respond (see appendix). Thus, most answers recorded in the probanzas are almost as formulaic as the questions themselves, which only serves to underscore the role that institutional practices played in the production of knowledge. Indeed, the rigidity of the interrogation method meant that there was little room for witnesses to define purity of blood in any other way than the Inquisition dictated, at least while they were giving testimonies.

INTERROGATING BLOOD LINES

And finally, the questionnaires used by Inquisition officials throughout the seventeenth century reveal that, in addition to determining if there were any "stains" whatsoever in the petitioner's genealogy, the purity interrogations were also meant to assess the general standing of the person in the community, especially with regard to lifestyle, moral conduct, character, and values.[17] Thus, when asked to comment about these issues, witnesses sometimes referred, in general terms, to the marital status, sexuality, and family life of the candidate, as well as to whether he was tranquil (*pacífico*), loyal to his Majesty, and had rendered services either for the republic or the church. The issue of female chastity also sometimes surfaced, for if any woman in the genealogical tree was thought to be unchaste then the paternity (and hence also purity) of her children was put into question. Thus, as Hernández Franco has observed, the legal discourse of limpieza—embodied in the questionnaires used by comisarios— helped to construct and reproduce a particular cultural model, one that was not only premised on the imagined Christian genesis of Spanish society but also promoted certain religious, social, and sexual practices, notions of honor, and most of all loyalty to crown and faith.[18] In other words, the mechanisms established to certify limpieza were ultimately intended to ensure that only persons of a certain status and whose beliefs and behavior were in consonance (or seemed to be) with the cultural-political projects of the church and state could have access to the power, wealth, and honor that being officially recognized as "pure" implied. These mechanisms and

the cultural model that they promoted were transferred to the Americas, where they would be adapted to colonial conditions and social relations.

"Purity of Blood" in Early Colonial Mexico

In the Americas, the concept of limpieza was important even before any statutes of purity were implemented because Spaniards who lacked it were prohibited from migrating to there. In New Spain the first edict banning the arrival of those lacking purity credentials was passed in 1523. Various other decrees excluding Jews, Muslims, conversos, *moriscos* (Muslim converts to Christianity), Gypsies, heretics, and the descendants of those categories from the Indies were to follow.[19] Together these laws amounted to a limpieza requirement for going to the New World.[20] Thus, the role of Spanish monarchs in promoting purity of blood concerns was, from the start, more marked in the Americas than in the metropole. According to Henry Kamen, in Spain the statutes were limited to a small number of predominantly private Castilian institutions and were never part of the public laws.[21] Although these claims are debatable, it is fair to say that the crown's support of purity policies were generally more overt in Spanish America. This difference can in part be attributed to the importance that the project to convert the native population acquired in the aftermath of the military defeat of the Aztecs. The Catholic Kings had at one point considered the possibility of allowing converted Jews to migrate to the Americas, for a price, but fears that they would become a source of "contamination" quickly led them to change their minds. As the Mexican Inquisitor Alonso de Peralta was later to explain, his Majesty prohibited the presence of New Christians in the Indies because of concerns that the indigenous people would unite with them or follow their ways.[22]

The concern with allowing only Old Christian Spaniards to travel to the Indies intensified as official support for the metropolitan limpieza requirements increased, particularly with the cathedral of Toledo's adoption of a purity statute.[23] Excepting a few categories, emigrants were required to present certificates of purity of blood, along with royal licenses to travel, at Seville's Casa de Contratación (Royal House of Trade). Then again, these were not always submitted or were falsified and the bureaucratic mechanisms set up in Seville, especially during the early period, were not efficient enough to prevent some New Christians from traversing the Atlantic. News of their growing presence in New Spain prompted the crown and vice-regal officials to begin making purity of blood a requirement for various colonial institutions and professions.[24] Limpieza status also gradually became necessary for certain religious orders, confraternities, convents, and guilds, among other establishments.[25] It was in the area of government and ecclesiastical offices, however, that the issue of purity of blood first figured prominently. The status was necessary for a number of imperial posts, including royal councilors, judges, and secretaries, and in certain instances (depending on the region and period) for alcaldes (mayor, judge), corregidores (magistrates), and regidores (councilmen).[26]

By contrast, in Spain limpieza appears not to have been necessary for the last three offices.[27]

In charge of determining the purity of blood credentials of individuals seeking public posts and royal grants were audiencias (high courts) and sometimes town councils. In 1601, for instance, Antonio Rueda presented his información de limpieza to Mexico City's audiencia in order to be considered for the job of royal secretary.[28] The corregidor accepted the petition and ordered the probanza made. It consisted of an interrogation of several witnesses, who attested to the purity of blood of Rueda's parents, grandparents, and all other ancestors. The probanza was approved by an audiencia judge and sent to the Council of the Indies. Also sent was a copy of a limpieza certification that in 1548 Rueda had obtained from the corregidor of Alba de Tormes (near the Spanish city of Salamanca) and which he presented at the Casa de Contratación before embarking for the New World. Another aspirant to the post of royal secretary in New Spain was Pedro de Salmerón, who had been born in Castile. In 1601 he expressed his desire to do an información de limpieza before Mexico City's audiencia.[29] Six witnesses, most from Serrano's native town, declared that he descended from the "caste of Old Christians, and not from the castes of confesos, Jews, or Moors, nor from the newly converted." When finished, the información was sent to Spain, where a second probanza was made in the town of Villanueva de la Fuente. There the alcalde ordinario took testimonies of four people who had known Serrano and his family and who said they knew that they were all of pure blood and Old Christian ancestry.

In cities without audiencias, candidates for religious or secular offices usually submitted proof of their services and qualifications as well as their genealogies to the town council. Thus, in 1569 Pedro García Martínez requested a canonry in the Puebla cathedral and presented the cabildo with an información attesting to the fact that he was an experienced priest and of "clean lineage and caste."[30] The alcalde interrogated seven witnesses and when he was finished approved the probanza and wrote down his endorsement of the candidate. The case was then sent to Philip II and his Royal Council of the Indies, and García Martínez was given three legal copies of his purity certification. García Rodríguez Pardo, undertook the same process in Michoacan's town council in the 1560s. He too solicited a canonry. To that effect, Rodríguez Pardo presented a probanza made in the town of Guayangareo (Michoacan) attesting to his qualifications as a priest. He also submitted a certificate of purity of blood that he had made in Spain before an alcalde in 1548, just before migrating to America.[31]

Some town councils also required purity of blood of their own members. Although the extent to which these bodies examined genealogical qualifications varied according to context, the most important ones in New Spain, those of Mexico City and Puebla, emphasized the issue of limpieza throughout most of the colonial period. Civil government was thus to be primarily in the hands of Old Christians and the same can be said of ecclesiastical posts. While it is true that certain

institutions had the right to establish their own membership rules and that there was no formal statute of purity for bishops and priests, generally speaking the members of the secular and regular clergies were expected to be Old Christians and pure of blood.[32] Limpieza requirements for priests became more regularized with the 1574 passage of the Ordenanza del Patronazgo, which consolidated the crown's control of all ecclesiastical benefices, including cathedral chapter appointments.[33]

During the last third of the sixteenth century, the number of probanzas requested in New Spain increased, a trend that was related to at least three developments. One was the union of the crown of Portugal with Castile (1580–1640), which accentuated fears among colonial officials about Portuguese conversos making their way to the Americas.[34] Another factor was the religious-political climate of the Counter Reformation. In the second half of the sixteenth century, Catholicism was clearly on the defense and nowhere was this truer than in Spain, which envisioned itself as the divinely chosen guardian of the faith. Efforts to enforce a post-Tridentine Catholic orthodoxy within Hispanic society at large were accompanied by more aggressive policies to prevent both the spread of heresy and the revival of idolatry in the Americas. These concerns with ensuring that the Indies remained "uninfected" and that the Indians did not relapse into their pagan practices helped justify entrusting colonial governance, both civil and spiritual, only to Old Christian Spaniards. Finally, the third development that helped to make the probanzas more commonplace in New Spain

MARÍA ELENA MARTÍNEZ

was the 1571 establishment of the tribunal of the Holy Office of the Inquisition.[35]

Perhaps it was just a coincidence, but Philip II issued the aforementioned decree outlining the rules and procedures for investigating the purity of blood of inquisitorial staff shortly after the Mexican and Peruvian Inquisitions were founded. These two American tribunals were therefore immediately informed that their officials had to supply proof of limpieza for themselves and their wives.[36] This meant that persons concerned with adding "luster" to their lineages through titles and posts had to carefully consider whom to marry. But who exactly applied for certification of blood purity with the Holy Office? First, as in Spain, the Inquisition in Mexico investigated the limpieza status of its officials and familiares. Though unsalaried, the title of familiar was coveted because it implied that the holder had passed the "purity test" and because it gave him automatic local influence by transforming him into an official informant of the Inquisition. Thus, applicants for the post often consisted of recent immigrants who hoped to infiltrate established circles of power. By the early seventeenth century, however, many familiares were members of New Spain's most established families, and their titles were frequently passed down in patrimonial fashion.[37] The Inquisition also sometimes conducted probanzas for candidates for public offices. As noted earlier, these usually had their purity of blood certified by audiencias or town councils, but sometimes they requested certificates of purity from the Inquisition because, at least in New Spain, they were considered the most prestigious.

As to the actual process of certifying purity of blood, the Inquisition soon discovered that in the colonial context it was no easy task. First there was the problem of distance between the Americas and Spain. As opposed to the genealogical investigations made by the ordinary justices (alcaldes and corregidores) and the audiencia, those done by the Holy Office required detective work in all the places of origin and long-term residence of the petitioner's parents and grandparents.[38] A single probanza could therefore entail inquiries in various towns, oftentimes by different Mexican and Spanish tribunals. In this sense, the Inquisition was truly a transatlantic institution, at least initially. Consider the case of Juan Esteban, whose ancestors were born and lived in several different places. When he applied to be a familiar in the late 1630s, his genealogy had to be certified in Logroño, Valladolid, Jerez de la Frontera, and Mexico City itself.[39] If the petitioner was married, the investigations could easily multiply, making the process of certification even longer and more expensive than in Spain.

Another problem was that the towns founded by the colonists did not yet have genealogy books and barely had any parish and census records. The American Inquisitions were ordered to keep registers of all the people they processed and lineages they investigated,[40] but until a solid infrastructure for tracing ancestries was created the genealogical evidence gathered in the colonies mainly had to consist of oral testimonies. However, as the Peruvian inquisitors pointed out, in the Indies everyone was a newcomer except the Indians, which meant that finding an adequate number of witnesses was sometimes a formidable challenge.[41] Commissioners could not always identify enough people who were from the same place of birth as the candidate and who could thus attest to his ancestry. In New Spain the certification process was also complicated by the fact that, by the time that the Inquisition tribunal was founded, the viceroyalty had a small but important population of Spaniards who had been there for about a half a century. Because it was not until the cathedral of Toledo's adoption of a statute that probanzas de limpieza began to be done on a regular basis, many first colonists and settlers had not made proofs of purity. How were their descendants' peninsular origins and family histories going to be reconstructed? This problem became more serious in the early seventeenth century, when the number of creoles who solicited offices and titles started to increase.

Initial difficulties with verifying ancestries sometimes forced the inquisitors to be flexible with some of the requirements for purity certification. This did not mean, however, that the probanzas were mere formalities. A great number, for example, involved investigations in different towns and more than one phase of interrogations. Furthermore, the process occasionally resulted in the discovery of Jewish, heretic, and, to a lesser extent, Muslim ancestors and therefore in the disqualification of the petitioner. Two examples will suffice. The first is provided by the case of Doctor Santiago de Vera, who applied to be an advisor for the Mexican Holy Office. He was an alcalde in Mexico City's chancellery and when his probanza was being made

was named president, governor, and general captain of the audiencia that was just being established in the Philippines. It is not clear whether Vera had already submitted his genealogical information in order to be appointed as alcalde or whether he had to show proof of purity to assume the presidency of the new tribunal. In any event, he did have to establish his limpieza to be a member of the Holy Office and that process did not turn out to be easy.

Vera's probanza involved inquiries in several Spanish towns, including Seville (for his paternal bloodline) and Madrid (for the maternal one). Because his paternal grandfather had married twice, the Seville commissioner had first to determine who his biological grandmother was and then her purity status.[42] As it was, he quickly concluded that most, if not all, of the petitioner's bloodlines were "unclean." According to some of the witnesses and the Holy Office's local archives, Vera's paternal grandfather (at one point a royal secretary) was the son of Juan de Sevilla and Violante Ruiz, who had both been tried for heresy, declared guilty, and "reconciled" with the church. The family's history with the Inquisition did not end there. Juan de Sevilla's parents had purportedly also been reconciled and those of Violante Ruiz had been condemned for heresy. The witnesses made similar claims about the parents of Vera's paternal grandmother, Isabel de Cazalla. The Seville inquisitors saw no reason to proceed with the investigation in Madrid. Vera was a "*confeso descendiente de condenados y reconciliados por la ley de Moysen*" (a convert [or converso], a descendant of people condemned [by the Inquisition] for

MARÍA ELENA MARTÍNEZ

practicing the Law of Moses and reconciled [with the church]) and therefore clearly not eligible for purity of blood status). It mattered not that his "infamy" derived from his paternal great grandparents and great-great grandparents.[43]

The second example is provided by the genealogical investigation of Lucas de Madrigal, a resident of Puebla de los Ángeles. In the early seventeenth century his genealogy was investigated in Madrid, where he claimed that he and his ancestors had been born. However, the commissioner assigned to the case, don Diego de Guzmán, had difficulty finding people who knew of Lucas or his ancestors, and who could attest to their naturalezas. He first interrogated six people and then six more. None of the witnesses gave any indication that Lucas or his ancestors were known to be impure. But they could not establish Madrid as the Madrigals' place of origin and were reluctant to speak about their limpieza, although one did mention that the petitioner's brothers had had their purity certified before entering Alcalá's university college. Guzmán continued to investigate Lucas's genealogy and discovered that he had done a purity probanza before he left for New Spain and, furthermore, that when his family had returned to Spain from Vienna (the father was serving the empress as a shoemaker) it had had its nobility certified by virtue of a privilege granted by the emperor. The commissioner also confirmed that some of the family members had in fact lived in Madrid and had been buried in its cemeteries. Lucas's sister, furthermore, was a nun in the convent of San Ildefonso de Talavera and had

had to submit a probanza de limpieza there. Still, Guzmán was not satisfied because doubts about the family's geographical origins remained, and if he could not be sure of the Madrigals' naturalezas, then the testimonies in favor of their purity status in Madrid were for the most part irrelevant. Because determining place of birth was extremely important to the certification of purity, the investigation continued.

Meanwhile, the Seville tribunal was studying the genealogy of Madrigal's wife, María Dávila. Inquiries were conducted in Cádiz for her maternal ancestors and in Medina Sidonia for her paternal ones. In the first town the commissioner was informed that María Dávila's maternal grandparents, Pedro de Sierra (a priest) and María de Paredes, had arrived from elsewhere and had not been married. Furthermore, of the twelve potential witnesses that the commissioner identified, only two were willing to testify. The other ten said that because María de Paredes had a reputation for being "*no de las mas recogidas*" (loose) they could not be certain that the father of her child was really the priest Pedro de Sierra. At least from her maternal bloodline, María Dávila's limpieza could thus not be established, but neither had it been directly challenged. In Medina Sidonia, the story was different. Twelve witnesses were interrogated, all of whom declared that María's father, Alonso Jiménez Dávila, and his ancestors were known to be neither pure nor Old Christians. The first witness (who like three others was a familiar) said that he had been told by many community elders that both of Alonso's parents derived from conversos and that, indeed, for as long as he could remember he had been

INTERROGATING BLOOD LINES

hearing just that. Thus he held the family to be New Christians. The same witness added that he had no knowledge of anyone being penanced or condemned by the Holy Office or having any other infamy. He did recall, however, that the town's elders and others used to say that Catalina Rodríguez (Alonso's mother) descended from a "*fulano*" Mantillo who had been forced to wear a sanbenito that the inquisitors later hung on the wall of the church. Other witnesses gave similar testimonies and mentioned hearing about the ancestor that had been "sanbenitado" (forced to wear a San Benito). When the interrogations in Medina Sidonia were over, the comisario wrote in his report that María Dávila was not pure of blood because her father's community considered him to be a descendant of New Christians. The case was sent to Seville and from there to Mexico, where presumably Lucas de Madrigal was not given a certificate of limpieza.

Although the Mexican Holy Office denied purity of blood status to various other candidates for familiaturas or posts, it is important to stress that the genealogical investigations that it commissioned were not always as rigorous as the two above examples would suggest.[44] Its initial flexibility—due in large part to the problems associated with doing probanzas in the colonies that were discussed earlier—proved to be beneficial for New Spain's most established creole families, which in the first half of the seventeenth century consolidated their control over local religious and public posts. In the early seventeenth century, for instance, the Suprema gave American tribunals permission to accept probanzas that followed the

guidelines for only three of the "four quarters" because of "the difficulties that those of the Indies have in knowing the origins of all their grandparents."[45] Consequently, a number of probanzas were approved even though the origins of one grandparent remained obscure. This relative flexibility probably helped some families with New Christian ancestors establish their purity of blood. It also had implications for some individuals of Spanish and native descent.

Neither the crown nor the Suprema ever declared native people to be impure, but their status as recent converts was not exactly conducive to their being accepted into places that required proof of Old Christian ancestry. Furthermore, the discovery of the persistence of idolatry in Yucatan and other parts of New Spain not only eroded Franciscan enthusiasm with the evangelization project but made religious authorities increasingly suspicious about the sincerity of native conversions. Already by the 1530s some native people were tried for idolatry and heresy and some were even forced to wear sanbenitos. For example, don Carlos, the cacique of Tetzcoco, was tried by Inquisitor fray Juan de Zumárraga for being a "heretical dogmatizer," convicted, and executed. His sanbenito was displayed in Mexico City's main church until 1570, when indigenous people were removed from the Inquisition's jurisdiction because of their status as "neophytes." Subsequently, they could not be tried for heresy, but questions about their ability to remain or become fully Catholic continued to shape Spanish perceptions and policies. Indeed, as of the mid-sixteenth century, religious and secular institutions started to deploy the

MARÍA ELENA MARTÍNEZ

argument that the Indians' commitment to Christianity was unstable in order to postpone admitting them as full members and ordaining them as priests.[46]

The question of what to do with the descendants of Spanish-Indian unions who applied for posts that required proof of limpieza, however, was more complicated. In Mexico, the Holy Office raised it in 1576. In that year Ruiz de Ayala was denied a *familiatura* (title of familiar) because his wife had an Indian grandmother (the rest of her grandparents were Spanish). Among the reasons that were offered for the denial was that the religious origins of Indians were uncertain, possibly Hebrew, and that this cast suspicions on the trustworthiness and qualifications of both *mestizos* and *castizos*. Native ancestry was thus not explicitly treated as a source of impurity, but the religious status of indigenous people was nonetheless starting to function as an excuse to exclude them and other colonial categories from certain offices and posts. As to the purity classification of individuals of African ancestry, the Inquisition did not discuss the issue at this time, perhaps because the possibility that they would serve in any religious or public post was already understood to be out of the question. That discussion would take place, but not until about a century later.[47] Nevertheless, it is clear that by the late sixteenth century the discourse of limpieza de sangre was being extended to blacks. Not only were some Spaniards linking "blackness" and "impurity,"[48] but some probanzas de limpieza began to list black and mulatto ancestors as sources of impure blood.

For instance, when in 1600 Pedro Serrano (a native of Seville), applied to be a royal secretary in the Philippines, he submitted his genealogical information in order to prove that his ancestors were "clean from the races of moriscos, Jews, blacks, and mulattoes and had not been punished by the Holy Office" but instead had always been pure and Old Christians.[49] Serrano might have been surprised to discover that a few years later, Catalina Reyes requested a probanza before Seville's alcalde in order to establish that she was the daughter of a white Old Christian male and an "Old Christian woman of dark skin" (*morena ateçada y cristiana vieja*) who had been a slave. Reyes wanted to accompany her employer Isabel Cervantes to New Spain, but first needed to obtain proof that she was both free and pure of blood. She claimed that her mother had been freed before giving birth to her, which thanks to the principle of the "free womb" meant that she too was free. And as to her purity status, Reyes declared, "I and my son and my parents are and were Old Christians of clean caste and generation, without any stains or races from Moors or Jews nor from the newly converted to our holy Catholic faith," and presented two witnesses to support her statement.[50] Thus, even though it appeared in some of the probanzas done by Spaniards in the late sixteenth century, the association between "blackness" and "impurity" was only just emerging (it would become more common as the system of transatlantic slavery was consolidated) and was certainly being challenged by people of African ancestry such as Catalina Reyes, who argued that her Catholic antecedents entitled her to the status of purity of blood.

The discourse of limpieza would be even

INTERROGATING BLOOD LINES

more ambiguous when it came to individuals of Spanish-Indian ancestry because of the native people's official status as pure. As the purity investigation done for Ruiz de Ayala suggests, as early as the 1570s the Holy Office was beginning to use its genealogical inquiries to produce some of the casta categories. By the end of the century, commissioners in charge of doing probanzas were making distinctions between mestizos and castizos in order to determine whether or not to certify a person's limpieza status. This is illustrated quite clearly in the genealogical inquiries that were done in 1590 for Juan de Reina and his wife. The canon Santiago, who served as the Holy Office's commissioner in Puebla, informed the inquisitors in Mexico City that he had investigated whether Reina's wife was a mestiza or castiza. After conducting interrogations and determining that her father was a Spaniard and her mother an Indian, Santiago stopped the información and asked for further instructions from the Inquisition.[51] Significantly, the commissioner indicated in his report that he would have proceeded with the investigation if the woman had been a "castiza," implying that by that point the category was not incompatible with the concept of purity of blood, at least not as much as "mestiza."

By 1624, the frequency of petitions for certification by individuals who had some native ancestry led the Suprema to declare that having one-quarter native ancestry (quarto de Indio) was not an impediment to becoming a familiar if the candidate was deemed to be otherwise qualified.[52] The decree was one of the first indications of the institutionalization of the "passing"

phenomenon that characterized Latin American colonial race relations, whereby people of mixed ancestry were, under certain circumstances, in this case with the right religious history and percentage of Spanish (Old Christian) blood, able to claim limpieza de sangre. The ideological basis of the sistema de castas—the colonial system of classification based on different proportions of Spanish, indigenous, and African blood—was thus starting to emerge, and as suggested by some of the Inquisition's early probanzas, its logic initially was linked to the religious status of different colonial groups.[53] The genealogical investigations also indicate that the Holy Office's emphasis on establishing biological parenthood and purity from all four grandparents encouraged the creation of categories of mixed ancestry. These categories had antecedents in Spain, where the Inquisition had occasionally been classifying people according to their proportions of "old" and "new" Christian blood.[54] Only in the New World, however, did classifications of "mixture" become central to the organization and reproduction of the hierarchical social order.

The 1624 ruling essentially enabled creole (Spaniards born in the Americas) families with some native ancestry to access Inquisition posts and titles and in general to prove their limpieza de sangre. The process of certification continued to be favorable to them until the mid-seventeenth-century visit of Inquisitor Medina Rico to New Spain. This official had just spent years investigating complaints of abuses by inquisitors in Cartagena de Indias (which also had a tribunal), and had accused many of corruption and of accepting bribes from

MARÍA ELENA MARTÍNEZ

Portuguese merchants. When the scrupulous *visitador* inspected the Mexican Holy Office's archives, he was shocked to discover that of about one hundred and fifty limpieza files that he had had a chance to review, only about seven or eight were technically complete. As a consequence, he spearheaded efforts to make the investigations conform to the original guidelines, especially the one that called for verifying the purity of the parents and grandparents in their Spanish towns of origin.[55] For starters, the visitador asked familiars and Inquisition officers to return their titles and to refrain from using them until their probanzas were in fact complete. Because many of those who were singled out by Medina Rico were members of important Mexican families, the orders erupted into a public scandal. Even the reputations of familiars whose probanzas were complete ended up tarnished, and they did not hesitate to express their outrage.[56]

Medina Rico's interventions were also not well received by the Mexican inquisitors. In a letter to the Suprema they warned that the majority of those whose "grandparents and great grandparents had shed their blood conquering the lands in the service of God, the spread of the Catholic faith, and of the Royal Crown" were now unable to account for their Spanish origins. They would thus not be able to prove their purity of blood, the inquisitors added, which meant that they would not be able to qualify for anything:

> All we have to report to Your Highness is that there are families in these Kingdoms of New Spain that are so ancient that they almost arrived with

the conquest . . . The sons of those that first populated these Kingdoms cannot give their grandparents' exact origins [naturaleza] in Spain because they came more than one hundred years ago to these parts, where their purity status has been maintained in the highest opinion. And as usually happens that the grandparents are very rich, the children have something, and the grandchildren beg, if they [the descendants of the conquerors and first settlers] are not helped in this regard their purity status and reputation will suffer. [They] cannot afford to pay to have their proofs done in all the probable places of origins of their Elders, who perhaps having their privileges and good fortune assured did not try to prove their qualities when they had the chance.[57]

The inquisitors continued discussing the detrimental effects that having to prove the purity of their bloodlines in Spain would have on the descendants of the conquerors and first settlers. In the process, they described a system of religious and public posts in central Mexico that had been controlled, namely through the probanzas, by a few leading creole families.

Conclusion

In New Spain, the requirements of purity of blood were first put into place in order to exclude Spanish New Christians and potential heretics from domains of power and privilege as well as to ensure that the project to establish the Catholic faith would not be undermined. The colonial discourse of limpieza thus differed from the metropolitan one in that it was inextricably linked to the Christianizing mission, which in Mexico centered on the idea that Old Christian Spaniards were to guide the native people in spiritual and secular matters until they had been fully converted. To this end, Spanish kings not only made the condition of limpieza a precondition for going to the Indies, but ordered colonial officials to make sure that it was made a requirement for certain professions, offices, and honors. Thus, if the notion of purity of blood never became part of the general laws of Spain, it did play a prominent role in colonial policies, especially during the reign of King Philip II. By the end of the sixteenth century, the concepts of purity of blood and Old Christian ancestry had become critical ideological components of the creation and reproduction of the secular and religious hierarchies of the viceroyalty of New Spain.

These concepts were accompanied by an elaborate system of certifying pure Catholic ancestry that helped transfer the metropolitan obsession with lineage and with detecting Jewish, Muslim, and heretical blood, to New Spain. But its significance was much broader than that. First, the hundreds, perhaps thousands, of probanzas that were ordered from the colonies and that involved an even greater number of testimonies by people from towns all over Spain must have reinforced the ideology of purity of blood in the metropole itself, which might help to explain why it continued to have salience long after the New Christians were considered a serious threat to the Catholic faith. Second, while in Spain the statutes of limpieza arguably ended up helping the traditional nobility to remain in power,[58] in

Mexico the requirements in essence created a privileged group out of the descendants of the conquerors and first colonists, who were favored for public and religious posts, albeit not the top ones, in exchange for their loyalty to both Catholicism and the king. This aristocracy, which consisted of a few interrelated families from Mexico City, Puebla, and Morelia, transmitted certificates of purity, familiaturas, and offices as if they were titles of nobility.

And third, the legal and generational formulas for proving purity of blood, which emphasized legitimate birth, biological parenthood, and ancestry from both bloodlines, helped to produce colonial categories of mixed ancestry. Crucial in this process was the Inquisition, whose genealogical investigations had by the late sixteenth century helped to make the distinction between mestizos and castizos important for determining the status of limpieza de sangre. Native ancestry was never declared impure, but the Indian's recent conversion disqualified them from claiming Old Christian ancestry, at least for a few generations. The genealogical rules developed by the Inquisition thus amounted to a discourse of limpieza de sangre in which purity and Indian lineage were not necessarily opposed, but in which conversion to Christianity and Spanish blood were the favored means to full redemption. A similar logic would be applied to the descendants of Spanish-black unions, but in their case the status of limpieza de sangre would always be more difficult to achieve, in part because of the different legal-theological status that Africans occupied within Hispanic society vis à vis the Indians, but

MARÍA ELENA MARTÍNEZ

also because of their eventual association with slavery.

Various bodies, including audiencias, town councils, and religious orders, would gradually adopt formulas similar to those of the Inquisition for establishing purity of blood status. Together these institutions helped to produce the sistema de castas, the system of classification that in theory determined a person's access to privileges and institutions mainly on the basis of descent. In New Spain this system did not crystallize until around the mid-seventeenth century but, as this chapter has shown, its origins can be traced to the last third of the sixteenth century, when that uniquely Hispanic cultural model that privileged Old Christian ancestry started to be adapted, along with the Inquisition, to the colonial context.

APPENDIX

Questionnaire Used by the Mexican Inquisition During the First Half of the Seventeenth Century

How to interrogate the witnesses in investigations of purity:

1. First, [ask] if they know the said person for whom the investigation is being done. [Ask also] how do they know him, for how long, and what his age is.
2. [Ask] if they know the father and mother of the said person. And if they do, [ask] where they are native to and where they have lived, and where they have been *vecinos* (residents, citizens) and for how long, and how they know.
3. [Ask] if they know [the paternal grandparents] of the said person. And if they have any information whatsoever about any other ancestors on the paternal line, they should declare how it is that they know them and for how long, and where they are originally from, and where they have been vecinos and had residence.
4. [Ask] if they know [the maternal grandparents] of the said person, and where they are originally from, and where they have been vecinos, and resided, and how they know them and for how long.
5. [Ask] the witnesses whether any of the general questions apply. [These basically tried to ascertain whether the witness was an enemy or close relative of the person whose genealogy was being investigated.]
6. [Ask] if they know whether the person for which this investigation is being made is the son of the said [parents] and is thought, considered, and commonly reputed to be their legitimate son. Ask them to declare the affiliation and how they know.
7. [Ask] if they know whether the said person's father and paternal grandparents, and all other ancestors by the paternal line, all and each and every one of them were and are old Christians, of clean blood, without the race, stain, or descent from Jews, Moors, or Conversos, or from any other recently converted sect, and

as such have been thought of, and considered and commonly reputed to be. And that there is no fame or rumor to the contrary and if there was, the witnesses would know, or would have heard, because of the knowledge and information that they had and have about each and every one of the said persons.

8. [Ask] whether they know if the said person or his father or paternal grandparents which are named in the previous question, or any other ancestors, have been punished or condemned by the Holy Office of the Inquisition, and if they have incurred any other infamies that would prevent them from having a public office and honor. They should say what they know about this, and what they have heard, and what they know about the good habits, character, and judgment of the said person.

9. [Ask] if they know that the said mother of the said person and the named maternal grandparents and all other ancestors by his mother's side each and every one of them have been and are old Christians, clean and of clean blood, without the race, stain, or descent from Jews, Moors, or Conversos, or from any other recently converted sect, and as such have been thought of, and considered and commonly reputed to be. And that as such

they are held by public voice and fame and by common opinion, and that there is no fame or rumor to the contrary and if there was, the witnesses would know, or would have heard, and that there is no possibility that they wouldn't, given the information that they had and have of each and every one of the said persons.

10. [Ask] if they know whether the mother of the said person or any of the other ancestors which were specified in the previous question have been condemned or punished by the Holy Office of the Inquisition, and whether any of them have been associated with any other infamies that would prevent them from having a public office and honor.

11. [Ask] if they know that everything that they have declared is public voice and fame.

The person who conducts the interrogation should make sure that the witnesses respond promptly to each point in each question, without accepting general responses to the question. And as for any other questions not in the interrogatory, he should only make those that from the depositions are deemed necessary to investigate the truth, without making any irrelevant questions.[59]

1. The literature on the statutes is too extensive to cite here. For the classic study see Albert A. Sicroff, *Los estatutos de limpieza de sangre: controversias entre los siglos XV y XVII*, trans. Mauro Armiño (Madrid: Tauros Ediciones, S.A., 1985).

2. See Cecil Roth, *The Spanish Inquisition* (New York: W. W. Norton, 1964), 20–22, and Philippe Wolff, "The 1391 Pogrom in Spain: Social Crisis or Not?" *Past and Present* 50 (1971): 4–18.

3. Domínguez Ortiz, *La clase de los conversos en Castilla en la edad moderna* (Granada: Universidad de Granada, 1991), 10.

4. See Henry Kamen, *The Spanish Inquisition: A Historical Revision* (New Haven and London: Yale University Press, 1998), 43–44.

5. Jaime Contreras and Jean Pierre Dedieu, "Estructuras geográficas del Santo Oficio en España," in *Historia de la Inquisición en España y América: las estructuras del Santo Oficio*, vol. II, ed. Joaquín Pérez Villanueva and Bartolomé Escandell Bonet, 5–47 (Madrid: Biblioteca de Autores Cristianos, Centro de Estudios Inquisitoriales, 1993).

6. Henry Charles Lea, *A History of the Inquisition in Spain*, vol. II (New York: Macmillan, 1906), 285–90; Juan Hernández Franco, *Cultura y limpieza de sangre en la España moderna: puritate sanguinis* (Murcia: Universidad de Murcia, 1996), 38–39; and Domínguez Ortiz, *La clase de los conversos en Castilla*, 54–68.

7. Domínguez Ortiz, *Los judeoconversos en la España moderna* (Madrid: Editorial MAPFRE, S.A., 1992), 15.

8. Note, however, that the connection between Islamic descent and "impurity" was not made on a consistent basis until about the mid-sixteenth century. Julio Caro Baroja, *Razas, pueblos y linajes* (Madrid: Revista de Occidente, 1957), 108.

9. Lea, *A History of the Inquisition*, vol. II, 297–98.

10. On the linkage of the term *raza* with the notion of impurity, see Joan Corominas, *Diccionario crítico etimológico de la lengua castellana*, vol. III (Berne, Switzerland: Editorial Francke, 1954), 1019–21.

11. On the concept of discourse as a system of meaning production, as "practices that systematically form the objects of which they speak," see Michel Foucault, *The Archaeology of Knowledge*, translated from the French by A. M. Sheridan Smith (New York: Pantheon Books, 1972), esp. 44–49.

12. See Archivo Histórico Nacional (hereafter AHN), Inquisición, Libro 1243.

13. See, for example, Jean Pierre Dedieu, "Limpieza, Pouvoir et Richesse: Conditions d´entrée dans le corps des ministres de 1´inquisition. Tribunal de Tolède, XIVᵉ–XVIIᵉ siècles," *Les sociétés fermées dans le monde Ibérique (XVIᵉ–XVIIIᵉ siècle)* (Paris: Editions du Centre National de la Recherche Scientifique, 1986), 168–87.

14. See, for instance, Domínguez Ortiz, *La clase de los conversos*, 75.

15. For Spain, see Lea, *A History of the Inquisition*, vol. II, 302–6. In Mexico, according to one report sent to the Suprema in the mid-seventeenth century, a normal probanza cost the petitioner between 1,500 and 2,000 pesos, sometimes even as much as 4,000. AHN, Inquisición, Libro 1057.

16. For a questionnaire that was used in Toledo, Spain, in the early seventeenth century, see Archival General de la Nación (AGN), Judicial, v. 5, exp. 5; and for an almost identical one that was used in Mexico during the same time, see AHN, Inquisición, Libro 1056. The latter is included and translated in the appendix.

17. See the final part of question eight in the appendix.

18. Hernández Franco, *Cultura y limpieza de sangre*, 15–17.

19. See, for example, Archivo General de Indias (Seville) (AGI), México 1064, L. 2.

20. Luis Lira Montt, "El estatuto de limpieza de sangre en el derecho Indiano," *XI Congreso del Instituto Internacional del Derecho Indiano* (Buenos Aires: Instituto de Investigación de Historia del Derecho, 1997), 39.

21. Kamen, *The Spanish Inquisition: a Historical Revision*, 235–39.

22. AHN, Inquisición de México, Libro 1050: Letter from Inquisitor Peralta, 1604.

23. J. I. Israel, *Race, Class and Politics in Colonial Mexico, 1610–1670* (London: Oxford University Press, 1975), 93.

24. In 1535, for instance, Viceroy don Antonio de Mendoza was ordered through a *real cédula* (royal law) to make sure that those people barred from practicing medicine and obtaining university degrees in Spain were also not allowed to do so in Mexico. See John Tate Lanning, "Legitimacy and *Limpieza de Sangre* in the Practice of Medicine in the Spanish Empire," *Jahrbuch Für Geschichte* 4 (1967): 43.

25. On purity requirements in colonial Mexican guilds see Manuel Carrera Stampa, *Los gremios mexicanos: la organización gremial en Nueva España 1521–1861* (Mexico City: Edición y Distribución Ibero Americana de Publicaciones, S.A., 1954), esp. 51–52 and 226–44.

26. Ann Twinam, "The Negotiation of Honor: Elites, Sexuality, and Illegitimacy in Eighteenth-Century Spanish America," in *The Faces of Honor: Sex, Shame, and Violence in Colonial Latin America*, ed. Lyman L. Johnson and Sonya Lipsett-Rivera, (Albuquerque: University of New Mexico Press, 1998).

27. See, for example, fray Agustín Salucio, *Discurso sobre los estatutos de limpieza de sangre* (Valencia: Artes Gráficas Soler, 1975 [1599]), 2v. However, it is important to point out that in the American context, the practice also varied. In Mexico, for example, proof of purity of blood seems to have been required only by certain town councils, and corregidores and judges also did not always submit probanzas.

28. AGI, México 121, Ramo 1.

29. Ibid.

30. AGI, México 282.

31. AGI, México 281.

32. Thus, in the early seventeenth century, a scandal broke out in Mexico because the archbishop was rumored to lack the quality of limpieza de sangre. He was not removed from his post, but the Holy Office reported that his religious order had tried to expel him when it received news of his "tainted" ancestry and that one of his nephews had not been admitted into the Order of Santiago for the same reason. AHN, Inquisición de México, Libro 1050: Letter from the Mexican Inquisition to the Suprema, 1604.

33. See John Frederick Schwaller, *The Church and Clergy in Sixteenth-Century Mexico* (Albuquerque: University of New Mexico Press, 1997), 81–109, esp. p. 87.

34. Domínguez Ortiz, *Los judeoconversos en España y América* (Madrid: Ediciones Istmo, 1971), 134.

35. On inquisitorial activities in Mexico before the Holy Office was officially established, see Richard E. Greenleaf, *The Mexican Inquisition of the Sixteenth Century* (Albuquerque: University of New Mexico Press, 1969), 7–157.

36. There was even a time when genealogical investigations were conducted for deceased spouses, but the practice apparently ended in 1612. See AHN, Inquisición de México, Libro 1051.

37. See Javier Eusebio Sanchiz Ruiz, "La limpieza de sangre en Nueva España: el funcionariado del tribunal del santo oficio de la inquisición, siglo XVI" (Master's thesis, Facultad de Filosofía y Letras, Universidad Nacional Autónoma de México, 1988).

38. AHN, Inquisición de México, Libro 1050.

39. AHN, Inquisición de México, Libro 1054.

40. AHN, Inquisición de México, Libro 1050: correspondence from the Mexican Inquisition, 1574–75.

41. AHN, Inquisición de México, Libro 1049: letter to the Suprema, April 14, 1603.

42. AGN, Inquisición, vol. 77, exp. 34: Correspondence of the Mexican Inquisition, 1582.

43. AHN, Inquisición de México, Libro 1048, f. 139–140v: Letter from the Mexican Inquisition to the Suprema, October 22, 1583.

44. For a few more examples, see AHN, Inquisición de México, Libro 1048, and AHN, Inquisición de México, Libro 1049.

45. AHN, Inquisición, Libro 1058.

46. For more on the subject of ordination see Stafford Poole, "Church Law on the Ordination of Indians and *Castas* in New Spain," *Hispanic American Historical Review* 61, no. 4 (1981): 637–50.

MARÍA ELENA MARTÍNEZ

47. See María Elena Martínez, "Religion, Purity and 'Race': The Spanish Concept of *Limpieza de Sangre* in 17th Century Mexico and the Broader Atlantic World," paper presented at the International Seminar on the History of the Atlantic World, Harvard University, August 8, 2000.

48. See, for instance, fray Prudencio de Sandoval, "Historia de la vida y hechos del Emperador Carlos V," in *Biblioteca de Autores Españoles*, vol. 82 (Madrid: Ediciones Atlas, 1955 [1606]), 319.

49. AGI, México 121, Ramo 1. My translation.

50. AGI, Indiferente, 2072, N. 44. My translation.

51. Archivo General de la Nación (AGN) (Mexico City), Inquisición, vol. 82: Letter from the canon Santiago regarding the genealogical investigations of Juan Reina and his wife, 1590.

52. AHN, Inquisición de México, Libro 1057.

53. Claudio Lomnitz has also proposed that colonial Mexico's sistema de castas was partly based on a religious logic in his *Exits from the Labyrinth: Culture and Ideology in the Mexican National Space* (Berkeley and Los Angeles: University of California Press, 1992), 261–81.

54. Elaine C. Wertheimer, *Jewish Sources of Spanish Blood Purity Concerns* (Brooklyn, NY: Adelantre, The Judezmo Society, 1977), 15.

55. AHN, Inquisición, Libro 1056: Report from Visitador Pedro Medina Rico on the proofs of limpieza for the Mexican Holy Office's ministers and familiars, 1657.

56. See, for example, AHN, Inquisición, Libro 1057: Letter from Juan de Aguirre to the Suprema, 1659.

57. AHN, Inquisición de México, Libro 1055: Letters from the Mexican inquisitors to the Suprema, July 20, 1650 and August 8, 1651.

58. See, for instance, Juan Antonio Maravall, *Poder, honor, y élites en el siglo XVII* (Madrid: Siglo Veintiuno editores, 1984), 173–250.

59. AHN, Inquisición, Libro 1056.

CHAPTER ELEVEN

Between Toleration and Persecution

The Relationship of the Inquisition and Crypto-Jews on the Northern Frontier

STANLEY M. HORDES

Introduction

To the popular mind, the Mexican Inquisition conjures up images of torture chambers, prisoners strapped to the rack, their screams echoing throughout the Palacio de la Inquisición, or perhaps *autos de fe*, with countless numbers of Jews burning at the stake, the stench of their flesh permeating the streets of Mexico City. Did these ghastly events really take place? Certainly, but rarely with the frequency or intensity that many authors would have us believe.

The perception that the Holy Office of the Inquisition had engaged in the relentless and continuous persecution of crypto-Jews[1] in New Spain (and throughout the Indies) is largely the function of the Black Legend, anti-Spanish historiography that developed from the early nineteenth to the mid-twentieth century,

represented principally by Protestant, Northern European scholars, and later by authors analyzing the Mexican Inquisition from the perspective of Jewish history.[2] The works produced by this school of historiography placed a heavy emphasis on the role that the Holy Office played in the persecution of crypto-Jews, despite the fact that the Mexican inquisitors concerned themselves far more with mundane breaches of faith and morality, such as blasphemy, bigamy, witchcraft, impersonation of priests, and solicitation of women in the confessional. Moreover, these authors often engaged in the inappropriate imposition of moral value judgments backward in time, ranting against the "moral depravity" of the Inquisition, and its "corrupt," "unjust" procedures, such as holding "unfair trials," where "flimsy evidence" was admitted.[3] If this outrage were directed at modern contemporary institutions, few would dispute these harsh words of condemnation. The imposition of such twentieth-century judgments backward to the sixteenth and seventeenth centuries, a decidedly less enlightened and less ecumenical age, however, runs counter to standards of responsible historical scholarship.[4]

It is my thesis that, in contrast to the interpretation outlined above, the policy of the Holy Office of the Inquisition in New Spain toward crypto-Jews was one more of toleration than persecution, relative to the experience between the two entities in Spain. Furthermore, the more distant from the metropolis, the less intense and less frequent the attention paid by the inquisitors to the *conversos* (converts from Judaism to Catholicism), even within the context of this policy of relative toleration.

Iberian Backgrounds

The roots of New Spain's crypto-Jewish settlement penetrate deeply into the history of Spain and Mexico. While legend placed Jews in the Iberian Peninsula as early as the sixth century BC, more solid accounts trace the origins of the community to the diaspora that occurred in the Late Roman Empire, when Jews expelled from their ancestral homeland found themselves scattered all across the Mediterranean region. Under the rule of the Visigoths, patterns of economic life began to emerge among Spanish Jews that would change little for centuries. Concentrated for the most part in towns in Cataluña and Andalucía, and in Toledo, they engaged in commerce, both internal and overseas, and administered estates of Christian nobility. Some

Jews owned their own land and farmed it themselves, or utilized slave labor. Relations between Jews and the ruling Visigoths were by no means peaceful. Codes were enacted that severely restricted the opportunity for Jews to hold office, intermarry, and build synagogues. Increasingly through the sixth and seventh centuries, zealous Visigoth kings sought the conversion of Spanish Jews, achieving moderate success. Those who retained their faith, such as their descendants in New Mexico who were also forced to pursue their religious beliefs in a hostile environment, tended to observe such basic rituals as sanctification of the Sabbath and festivals, dietary laws, and circumcision.[5]

With the Muslim invasion of the Iberian Peninsula in 711, Spanish Jews received a reprieve from persecution and attempts at forced conversions. While the Muslims by no means pursued a policy of total religious freedom, the general atmosphere was one of toleration of non-Muslim religious practices.[6] Barriers to social and economic mobility, imposed earlier by the Visigoths, were by and large removed. Jewish communities in areas under Muslim rule, and eventually in Christian areas as well, were allowed a large degree of autonomy in the administration of their affairs. Geographically, Jewish settlement expanded throughout the peninsula, initially to the major cities in Andalucía, such as Córdoba, Seville, Granada, and eventually through the twelfth and thirteenth centuries, into the more heavily Christian regions of Castile, León, and Aragón. During this period Jews tended to pursue urban trades as artisans, craftspeople, and shopkeepers, in addition

BETWEEN TOLERATION AND PERSECUTION

to serving as tax farmers for Christian nobles. In so doing, they often found themselves the object of scorn and hostility at the hands of their poorer and relatively more rural Christian neighbors.[7]

The hostility toward the Jews of Spain that had been growing among Christian commoners, nurtured by generations of civil wars, taxes, and religious crusades against the "infidel," began to manifest itself more clearly through the fourteenth and fifteenth centuries. The church mounted a concentrated campaign to convert the Spanish Jews to Christianity through a combination of both peaceful and violent means. This conversion effort achieved a high degree of success, especially among those wealthier and better educated elements of the Jewish communities. For many of them the transition from Judaism to Christianity was made without a great deal of inner spiritual conflict, for it represented a change of religion in name only. But many conversos and their offspring did not take their new faith seriously. They continued to participate in the social, political, and religious affairs of their old synagogues. The pain of conversion was further eased by the new and unprecedented opportunities now available to these "New Christians." Barriers that hitherto prevented them as Jews from rising to economic, social, or political prominence now disappeared, and there came upon the scene instantaneously a new class of nobles, courtiers, municipal office holders, and literary figures, obviously distinguishable from their Old Christian counterparts by their origin, manner, and appearance.[8]

The presence of a large and prosperous group of apparently insincere converts became increasingly disturbing to the Old Christian community through the fifteenth century. Anti-converso sentiment, which spread throughout Spain, soon found itself manifested in the official policies of ruling monarchs. The two emerging rulers, Ferdinand of Aragón and Isabel of Castile, capitalized upon this hostility in order to unite their subjects and thus solidify control in their dominions. The establishment of the Holy Office of the Inquisition in Spain by the Catholic Monarchs in concert with Pope Sixtus IV in 1483 may be seen as a logical institutional manifestation of the deeply rooted religious feeling against the conversos and also of the royal desire to implement their sovereignty over their newly consolidated realms. Moreover, the Catholic Monarchs, through the Inquisition, sought to break down the economic power of the increasingly influential middle class, largely composed of Jews and conversos.[9]

The ranks of the Spanish conversos were further swelled as a result of Ferdinand and Isabel's edict, issued on March 31, 1492, expelling the Jews from Castile and Aragón. Estimates vary on the number of Jews who opted to leave the Spanish realms, but it seems safe to conclude that of the estimated two hundred thousand Jews living in Castile and Aragón in 1492, well over half of them fled to safer havens. Of these exiles, most sought refuge across the frontier in Portugal, the others fleeing to France, Italy, and Turkish-controlled regions of the eastern Mediterranean. Those who remained in the Spanish kingdoms submitted to the conversion process and became, at least nominally, *cristianos católicos* (Catholic Christians). From this time

STANLEY M. HORDES

forward, Catholicism was to be the only legally practiced religion in Spain and in the vast empire of the Indies that was about to be uncovered by Christopher Columbus in the very same year of the expulsion.[10]

The observance of Jewish rites and customs, now outlawed, was forced underground, to be practiced only in the secrecy of one's home. No longer Jews, those New Christians who chose to continue these observances did so as Christians, in violation of ecclesiastical law, and were often prosecuted for these relapses by the Holy Office of the Inquisition, the institution charged with the enforcement of Catholic orthodoxy among Spanish Christians, Old and New alike. The situation was markedly different for the estimated sixty thousand to one hundred and twenty thousand Spanish Jews who migrated westward across the Iberian Peninsula to join the smaller native Jewish population of Portugal. Although they too were forced to either convert or leave the country by edict of Manoel I in 1497, conversion was for the most part nominal and enforcement of orthodoxy lax. In sharp contrast to the pressure on Spanish conversos to abandon all vestiges of their old faith, the attitude in Portugal was far more tolerant, and Portuguese New Christians tended to continue to observe Judaic laws and rituals discreetly, yet in an atmosphere of relative security. Thus, through the sixteenth century in Portugal there arose a new and distinct group of crypto-Jews, differing from the Spanish conversos by the retention of their old faith and religious practices.[11]

The Portuguese conversos distinguished themselves by their vigorous activity in the economic sphere, not only in the peninsula, but also in Portugal's overseas colonies in America, Asia, and Africa, where they played a crucial role in organizing and financing the initial commercial enterprises. For a variety of reasons, the last half of the sixteenth century witnessed an intensity of royal and ecclesiastical activity against crypto-Jews in Portugal. As in Spain, New Christians represented a threat as a rising middle class, bourgeois elements against the older ruling aristocracy. Furthermore, the Protestant Reformation sparked a new spirit of vigilance among religious elements within the country, and a consequent strengthening of the powers of the Inquisition. Sealing the fate of the Portuguese crypto-Jews was the union of Spain and Portugal under the rule of Philip II, which came about as a result of a crisis of succession in 1581. The resulting increase in the activity of the Portuguese Inquisition against the crypto-Jewish community stimulated a veritable invasion of Portuguese New Christians into the Spanish realms from the 1580s through the early decades of the seventeenth century.[12]

Crypto-Jewish Settlement in New Spain

Within a few years, Portuguese crypto-Jews were also finding their way to distant parts of the Spanish Indies, including the viceroyalty of New Spain. The heaviest period of immigration occurred in the 1620s. This was owing to a variety of factors. Undoubtedly many crypto-Jews sought to take advantage of the relaxation in the immigration laws.[13] However, it is also clear that an equally strong motive for emigrating was the improvement of their material condition. In addition, New Spain served as a potential haven for crypto-Jews who wished to practice their secret religious rites in an atmosphere of relative security. In contrast to the Iberian Peninsula, where the Holy Office posed a constant threat to New Christians, the Mexican Inquisition was not particularly concerned with the persecution of *judaizantes* (judaizers). With two exceptional periods of activity against crypto-Jews, one in the 1580s and 1590s, and the other in the 1640s, the Holy Office focused its attention upon less spectacular breaches of Catholic orthodoxy, such as witchcraft, bigamy, blasphemy, and the solicitation of women by priests. Thus, once the troubled Iberian crypto-Jews left their homeland for New Spain, they were able to begin new lives, relatively free from the persecution of the past, and pregnant with the expectation of a comfortable material existence.

Those conversos who arrived from Spain and Portugal in the late sixteenth and early seventeenth century did not find themselves in a completely alien environment. Viable crypto-Jewish communities had flourished in Mexico City and other towns in New Spain since the early 1500s. Mexican crypto-Jews tended to pursue mercantile trades in greater numbers compared with other endeavors. Their careers encompassed a wide variety of trading activities. Some crypto-Jews, stationed for the most part either in Mexico City or Veracruz, engaged in trade across the Atlantic, importing goods from Spain, as well as slaves from Angola, while exporting silver, dyestuffs, and other New Spanish products. Others worked out of Acapulco, and concerned themselves with the Philippines trade. Still others sought to take advantage of the profitable cacao trade with Maracaibo

and Caracas, while certain other conversos maintained commercial ties with Peru. Exploiting the sources and markets within the viceroyalty of New Spain itself offered opportunities to many more crypto-Jewish merchants, including those who carried goods to remote areas of the far northern frontier of New Spain.[14]

As indicated above, Mexican crypto-Jews were able to practice their secret faith in an atmosphere of relative toleration, with the exception of the late 1580s and 1590s, and the 1640s. During these two periods, due to a series of complex factors, the Holy Office of the Inquisition embarked on vigorous campaigns against the conversos. The first of these, which lasted from 1589 to 1604, was initiated in response to the activities of one Luis de Carvajal, *el mozo* (the Younger), Portuguese New Christian and nephew of Luis de Carvajal y de la Cueva, the governor of Nuevo León.

The elder Luis de Carvajal was born around 1539 in the small Portuguese mountain town of Mogadouro to a converso family. He made his first journey to New Spain in 1567, as a merchant carrying a cargo of wine to sell in Veracruz, Mexico City, and Zacatecas.[15] Recognizing the opportunities for exploiting the agricultural and mineral resources in the far northeastern frontier of New Spain, Carvajal sailed back to Spain in 1578 to submit a proposal to King Philip II. In return for opening up the Nuevo Reino de León for Spanish colonization, Carvajal asked the king for two major concessions: (1) that he be appointed governor; and (2) that no investigations be conducted into the ethnic background of the colonists he recruited to populate the new settlement.

STANLEY M. HORDES

Under the terms of the royal *cédula* (mandate) issued by King Ferdinand in 1501, it was illegal for anyone of Jewish or Moorish descent to emigrate to the Indies. To be sure, many conversos and their offspring did come over legally, but they came under assumed names or doctored documents of *limpieza de sangre* (purity of blood). Philip II agreed to these terms, and by means of a formal *capitulación* (agreement) signed on May 31, 1579, Luis de Carvajal received his mandate to initiate his colonization effort.[16] He immediately began to recruit approximately one hundred people from Spain and Portugal, most of converso origin, and brought them to New Spain, establishing his capital at Cerralvo in Nuevo León.

The young colony survived the material challenges presented by a hostile environment. In religious matters, as well, it appears that the settlers were left alone to worship as they pleased, as long as they did so quietly. However, this atmosphere of calm was soon to be shattered, when one of the colonists betrayed the standard of discretion. Shortly after his arrival in New Spain, the governor's fourteen-year-old nephew was told of his Jewishness by older relatives. In contrast to the response of his contemporaries, young Luis de Carvajal decided that if he was a Jew, he was going to live openly as a Jew. Not only did he begin to practice his religion in full view, but he also initiated efforts to reconnect other New Christians back to Judaism.[17] Even in an atmosphere of relative toleration demonstrated by New Spanish society, this behavior could not be endured. The Holy Office of the Inquisition, recently elevated to the status of tribunal, had been watching the growth of the Portuguese converso community in New Spain over the course of the previous few years and expressed concern over the potential for the spread of the practice of *la ley muerta de Moisén*—the Dead Law of Moses.[18]

The reaction on the part of the inquisitors in Mexico City was strong and swift. Between 1589 and 1596, almost two hundred persons were arrested for the crime of judaizante, focusing on the Carvajal family, and extending to crypto-Jewish activity all over the viceroyalty. Young Luis de Carvajal was arrested in 1589, and was "reconciled" in the auto de fe of 1590. Undeterred by this castigation, young Carvajal resumed his proselytizing efforts, was rearrested by the Inquisition, and convicted for relapsing into Judaism. He was burned at the stake in the auto de fe of 1596, along with several members of his family.[19] After 1604, the policy on the part of the Holy Office returned to one of relative toleration towards the crypto-Jews of New Spain, with only sporadic arrests in the 1620s and 1630s. During the first four decades of the seventeenth century, the converso community grew substantially both in numbers and in commercial influence.[20]

The second intense campaign began in 1642, motivated in large measure by events across the ocean. In 1640, a successful revolutionary movement for Portuguese independence from the king of Spain stimulated in New Spain a fierce xenophobic reaction against all those of Portuguese background. It was feared that the Portuguese in Mexico City, Veracruz, and the northern mining areas would rise up in revolt against Spanish authorities and attempt to deliver the viceroyalty to the new Portuguese king. A newly appointed anti-Portuguese viceroy initiated a comprehensive crack-down against this perceived foreign threat. Included among this target group were the estimated two thousand crypto-Jews in the viceroyalty, most of whom possessed Portuguese roots. By 1649, hundreds of crypto-Jews were arrested, tried, and con-victed of the crime of "Observing the Law of Moses." As in the previous campaign, a few were executed, but most were reconciled and returned to resume their lives and careers.[21]

After the mid-seventeenth century, the policy on the part of the Holy Office toward the crypto-Jews of New Spain returned to one of relative toleration. From this point until the demise of the Mexican Inquisition with the independence of Mexico from Spain in 1821, the inquisitors had very lit-tle interest in prosecuting judaizante cases, concentrating instead on more mundane breaches of heresy. Many of the descendants of New Spain's crypto-Jews, generation by generation, assimilated and acculturated into mainstream Catholic society, losing all vestiges of Judaism. But others appear to have held on to elements of their ancestral faith, either retaining residual Jewish prac-tices, or even passing along a consciousness of a Jewish heritage.

The Frontier as Refuge

Before, during, and after the two aber-rant periods of inquisitorial persecution against the crypto-Jews in New Spain, it appears that the far northern frontier served as a haven for conversos attempting to avoid arrest by the Holy Office. Solange Alberro, in her ground-breaking 1988 work, *Inquisición y sociedad en México, 1571–1700,* emphasized this fact in her analysis of seventeenth-century Zacatecas. The second-most important city in the viceroyalty of New Spain, Zacatecas served as an impor-tant mining center and mercantile distribu-tion point for the region.[22]

Alberro argued that the great distance of Zacatecas from the center of authority in Mexico City and its geographical isolation from other major communities "facilitated laxity and backsliding, practically assuring exemption from punishment" by the Holy Office.[23] The permissive atmosphere of this northern mining community fostered an environment where heretical acts lost their character as social transgressions, and, as a consequence, behavior that would not have been tolerated in the capital passed virtu-ally unnoticed in *tierra adentro* (the inte-rior region of New Spain). The frontier offered two major advantages for crypto-Jews seeking anonymity: remoteness from inquisitorial officials and an ample market for the goods and services provided by con-verso merchants. Alberro observed that, although several members of this commu-nity were denounced before the Mexican tribunal, only a minority of these cases was ever prosecuted.[24] The testimony provided by inquisition records, however fragmen-tary, represents a unique window through which the role that these crypto-Jews played in the economy and society of the northern frontier can be viewed better.

On the basis of this documentation, a clear picture emerges of converso participa-tion in commerce from a variety of perspec-tives. The trade with the northern mining area was largely controlled by merchants based in Mexico City, who received on

STANLEY M. HORDES

consignment such diverse items as wine from Spain, silk from the Philippines, cacao from Venezuela, cloth from *obrajes* (factories) in Tlaxcala, and wax from Campeche, and then sold this merchandise on credit to traveling merchants bound for Zacatecas and other mining towns. These individuals comprised a mobile, adventuresome group, seldom remaining in one place for more than a few years at a time. For many, their trading experience in the mining areas was but one of several spheres of mercantile activity in which they had engaged during their lifetime. With few exceptions, these crypto-Jews were immigrants from Portugal and Spain who had come over at a young age to seek their fortunes. Their experiences reflected the needs and the hardships of the environment in which they lived. Some of them participated in the defense of the mining frontier against Indian attacks. Others suffered the loss of their wares along the highway at the hands of thieves. The danger and risk of their enterprises necessitated the development of interdependence and cooperation among the travelers, both crypto-Jews and Old Christians alike. Often, groups of traders undertook journeys together or joined in *compañías* (partnerships) for mutual aid and protection.[25]

Most of the traveling crypto-Jewish merchants tended to transact their business with certain other conversos who stationed themselves in the various communities of the northern mining areas. Most prominent among these individuals was Simón López de Aguarda. López received shipments from his contacts in Mexico City, transported to Zacatecas by mule train, and exchanged them for silver, which he sent southward.

Several crypto-Jewish merchants, based in other towns, also brought their goods to López, depositing them in his store on the *plaza pública* (public plaza).

López performed other important functions in the northern mining community, most significantly in his role as a source of credit. At the time of his arrest in 1642, debts owed to him by residents of the mining region totaled almost 10,000 pesos.[26] In addition he served as *fiador* (bondsman) for several miners, thus enabling them to purchase mercury, a crucial commodity in the processing of silver. Residents of Mexico City also entrusted López to transact business for them in Zacatecas by means of powers of attorney. In the noncommercial area, López served the Spanish mining community with distinction as captain of the presidio of Atotonilco.[27]

Religious observance on the part of crypto-Jews of Zacatecas and the surrounding areas tended to follow the same pattern demonstrated in other parts of New Spain. Customs included abstaining from eating pork, porging of animals prior to slaughter, and fasting on Yom Kippur.[28] Inquisition records even cite the existence of a synagogue in the city from the early seventeenth century.[29] Moreover, like their coreligionists living elsewhere in the viceroyalty, Zacatecan conversos followed similar patterns of endogamy, taking care to marry within the community.[30] Despite the formal prohibition of judaizing activity in New Spain, the practice of the Law of Moses in Zacatecas was, according to Alberro, "conscious, coherent, and deliberate," thus indicating that the northern mining region functioned effectively as a zone of refuge.[31]

Crypto-Jewish Settlement in New Mexico

"If Zacatecas constitutes a zone of refuge in comparison with the central region of the viceroyalty," according to Alberro, "New Mexico is, as [France V.] Scholes states, 'a heaven for social outcasts from the mining camps of Zacatecas, Santa Bárbara and Parral.' . . . That is to say, the zone of refuge from the zone of refuge."[32] Indeed, it appears that New Mexico, like the mining areas of Zacatecas, also served as a focus of settlement of crypto-Jews seeking to escape persecution from the Mexican Tribunal of the Holy Office of the Inquisition.

The origins of European exploration of New Mexico date to 1540, when Francisco Vázquez de Coronado led an expedition of over one thousand men and women west and north from Mexico City into what is today the U.S. Southwest.[33] The Spanish explorers, in search of the mythical, wealthy "Seven Cities of Cíbola," found little in the way of precious metals. But, perhaps more important, they encountered groups of sedentary Indians, whom they labeled "pueblos," due to the concentration of the native population in towns. A combination of severe winters, failure to discover the treasures of "Cíbola," and a debilitating injury to Vázquez, compelled the Spaniards to return home to Mexico City, thus leaving the colonization of New Mexico for another, more permanent enterprise five decades later.[34]

The campaign of the Mexican Holy Office against the crypto-Jews of Nuevo León of the 1580s and 1590s, discussed above, was to have a direct impact on the later exploration and settlement of New Mexico at the end of the sixteenth century. Upon the arrest of Governor Luis de Carvajal by the Inquisition for tolerating the presence of judaizantes under his administration, he left behind in Nuevo León as lieutenant governor of the province a seasoned military leader, Gaspar Castaño de Sosa. Like Carvajal, Castaño was born in Portugal, and was possibly of crypto-Jewish origin.[35] Soon after receiving word of Governor Carvajal's conviction and appearance in the auto de fe of February 24, 1589,[36] Castaño rounded up the some 170 colonists (comprising men, women, and children) in Cerralvo and left on an uncharted, unlicensed expedition to the north. This "Colony on the Move," as Matson and Schroeder[37] referred to it, reached the Río Grande,[38] traveled upriver to its confluence with the Río Pecos, trekked up the Pecos, crossing Glorieta Pass into the Río Grande Valley, and finally stopped near the pueblo of Santo Domingo in an attempt to establish the first permanent Spanish colony in New Mexico.

Under the terms of the Spanish colonial system in the late sixteenth century, however, the Castaño de Sosa *entrada* (expedition) of 1590 comprised an illegal expedition. Not only had Castaño failed to secure permission from the viceroy to leave Nuevo León (although his emissaries had made attempts to do so), but he had neglected to inform anyone in authority that he was embarking on such a venture. Moreover, Castaño's was the only expedition into the northern frontier of its day not to include a priest or any member of a religious order.[39] The close ties maintained by Castaño to Governor Carvajal, the coincidence of the timing of his hasty (and illegal)

STANLEY M. HORDES

departure for the north upon hearing of Carvajal's problems with the Inquisition, the absence of a priest on the expedition, and the allegations of his own familial ties to the crypto-Jewish community, all suggest strongly that Castaño might have initiated the dangerous entrada for the purpose of leading other crypto-Jews to a secure haven on the far northern frontier.

Unfortunately, little is known about the background of the members of the Castaño de Sosa expedition. No muster roll has ever been found, that would provide clues as to the Iberian, or possibly crypto-Jewish, origins of its participants. While certainly not conclusive, possible links may be established by comparing the names of colonists tried for judaizante with those found in contemporary trial records of the Mexican Inquisition, names such as Rodríguez, Nieto, Díaz, Hernández, and Pérez.[40] The participation of Juan de Vitoria Carvajal also raises some interesting questions. Certainly the coincidence of his tenure in Nuevo León suggests a familial connection to Governor Luis de Carvajal.[41] Could Vitoria Carvajal have represented a hitherto unidentified branch of the family attempting to escape to the north?

Not all of the participants in the Castaño enterprise remain lost to history, however. One of the members of the Castaño expedition who can definitely be linked to converso origins was Alonso Jaimes. Born in the Canary Islands, Jaimes tried to pass himself off as an Old Christian before immigration officials in an attempt to emigrate to New Spain in 1574. He had convinced Francisco Rodríguez to perjure himself by alleging that Jaimes was "free from all Muslim or Jewish blood." Recognizing the attempt to circumvent the prohibition of descendants of Jews to emigrate to the Americas, Inquisition officials in the Canaries arrested Jaimes and accused him of being "a descendant of a line of conversos, reconciled by the Inquisition." Unbeknownst to either Jaimes or Rodríguez, the inquisitors had maintained a dossier on Jaimes's family, tracing them back five generations to Jews from various parts of Spain and Portugal who, after converting to Catholicism in 1492, had sought refuge in the Canaries. Rodríguez was fined eight *ducados* (Spanish currency) for his perjury. And, despite all the attention from the Las Palmas tribunal of the Holy Office, Jaimes apparently was able to emigrate to New Spain within a few years after his unpleasant encounter with Inquisition officials.[42]

When the viceroy of New Spain was informed of Castaño's departure from Nuevo León, he sent Juan Morlete, a former associate of Castaño's, to arrest him and his entire party, not for practicing Judaism, but for having conducted an illegal expedition. Castaño was convicted of treason and exiled to the Philippine Islands, where he died shortly thereafter.[43] Many of the survivors of the entrada returned to Nuevo León and participated in the founding of the town of Monterrey in 1596.[44] Others remained in central Mexico, fearful, perhaps, of attracting the attention of the Inquisition, now in the throes of its vigorous campaign against the converso community of New Spain.

By the late 1590s the king had realized the efficacy of establishing a defensive outpost in the far northern frontier of New Mexico. Several candidates put forth their names for consideration to lead such an expedition. One in particular enjoyed the support of the Mexican Inquisition, Francisco de Urdiñola. Urdiñola was a *comisario* (commissary) of the Holy Office, who, in the eyes of the inquisitors, would be in a position to ensure the purity of blood and orthodoxy of the colonists heading north.[45] Viceroy don Luis de Velasco, however, had no intention of allowing a competing jurisdiction to interfere in such a secular venture. Charges were brought against Urdiñola for the murder of his wife and several servants, and in the face of such serious allegations, Velasco simply could not permit the comisario to remain under consideration to lead the entrada to the north. The viceroy declared the mission suspended indefinitely.[46]

The next year, Velasco chose don Juan de Oñate, the son of a wealthy and powerful northern miner, and himself a descendant of converted Jews,[47] to serve as *adelantado* (he who advances the frontier), and charged him with the task of establishing a new colony in the distant frontier of New Mexico. Among the people whom Oñate approached to join him in this effort were some of the survivors of the Castaño de Sosa expedition. After all, they had returned from New Mexico just a few years earlier and consequently knew well the route northward, the terrain, and had firsthand knowledge of the Pueblo Indians who inhabited the lands to be conquered and occupied. In short, Oñate must have realized the potential for these survivors of the Castaño expedition to help him establish his new colony on a strong footing.

For their part, those survivors who did not return to Nuevo León might well have felt themselves somewhat vulnerable to arrest by the Inquisition, which, as has been demonstrated, was in the midst of its heaviest phase of activity against New Spanish crypto-Jews. Whether for push or pull factors, at least two members of the Castaño entrada decided to return with Oñate in 1598, Juan de Victoria Carvajal and Juan Rodríguez Nieto. The latter appears to be the same Juan Rodríguez, identified by the Mexican Inquisition as a fugitive the previous year, and who was burned in effigy in the auto de fe of 1601 for practicing Judaism.[48] Another member of the 1590 expedition, Alonso Jaimes, whose Jewish origins are discussed above, could be found in Oñate's military encampment at Casco in 1596.[49] Another of Oñate's soldiers, Cristóbal de Herrera, was arrested several years later in Zacatecas and denounced before the Inquisition on suspicion of practicing Judaism.[50] Alberro, in her discussion on the history of the Inquisition in Zacatecas, referred to Herrera as "un verdadero judaizante" (a true judaizer).[51] The supplier of the Oñate expedition was a merchant by the name of Baltasar Rodríguez, possibly the same Baltasar Rodríguez, merchant of Nuevo León and brother of Luis de Carvajal, who had eluded attempts by Inquisition agents to arrest him several years earlier.[52]

Bartolomé Romero, a soldier accompanying Oñate to New Mexico in 1598, was listed on the muster roll as born in Corral de Almaguer, in the region of Toledo, the son of Bartolomé Romero.[53] His mother was María de Adeva, possibly a relation of the Benadevas, a prominent Jewish, and later converso, family of Sevilla at the turn of the sixteenth century.[54] Baptismal records from Corral de Almaguer note that

STANLEY M. HORDES

other Romeros from the town either served as godparents of New Christians, or were, themselves, descendants of conversos.[55] Yet another Romero from Quintanar de la Orden, located about fourteen miles from Corral de Almaguer, was convicted of judaizante by the Inquisition of Cuenca in 1589.[56]

Despite the presence of New Christians in New Mexico from the earliest years of Spanish settlement, the Inquisition, represented in the colony by the Franciscan friars, appeared unconcerned about the possibility of the practice of Jewish heresy in its midst. This was due to a variety of factors, including the general disinterest by the Mexican Holy Office in judaizante cases in the early seventeenth century, and the remoteness of New Mexico from the capital. Perhaps most significantly, the Franciscans were preoccupied with the struggle for power with the civil authorities in this far northern frontier outpost.[57]

During this period of inattention it appears that several more descendants of conversos emigrated northward along the Camino Real into New Mexico, including Simón de Abendaño, from Ciudad Rodrigo,[58] along the Spanish-Portuguese border; Diego de Vera, from the Canary Islands;[59] and the Portuguese Manuel Jorge. Suspicion of Judaic background extended even to the ranks of the Franciscan order. The investigation into the limpieza de sangre of fray Esteban de Perea, born in Villanueva del Fresno, on the Spanish-Portuguese border, nominated to the position of *custos* (custodian) in 1629, contained testimony alleging that the nominee's ancestors had been Jewish.[60] The Franciscan authorities chose to overlook this potentially damaging evidence, however, and confirmed Perea to the post.

It was not until 1662 that Inquisition agents in New Mexico began to focus on crypto-Judaism. At four o'clock on the morning of August 27, comisarios of the Holy Office burst into the home of Governor Bernardo López de Mendizábal, arresting his wife, Teresa de Aguilera y Roche. Also taken that year were the governor himself and Sargento Mayor Francisco Gómez Robledo. All three were charged with secretly practicing Judaism. Arrested on unspecified charges of heresy were Capitán Cristóbal de Anaya Almazán, Sargento Mayor Diego Romero, and Capitán Nicolás de Aguilar.[61] The documentation generated by the politically motivated trials of these individuals offers a glimpse into crypto-Jewish activity in New Mexico during the period preceding these arrests, when neither the inquisitors nor anyone else in the colony appeared to be bothered by such heretical practices.

Testimony emanating from these trials revealed customs clearly identified as Jewish being practiced by early New Mexican settlers. Several witnesses testifying against Francisco Gómez Robledo insisted that it was common knowledge in the colony that his father, Francisco Gómez, was a Jew.[62] The elder Gómez, born in Coina, Portugal, came to New Spain in 1604 in the retinue of Juan de Oñate's brother, Alonso, heading north to New Mexico shortly thereafter. During his nearly half century in the colony, Gómez held several civil and military positions.[63] Not only was Francisco Gómez Robledo found to have been circumcised,[64] considered by inquisitors as a certain indication of judaizing,[65] but his younger brothers, Juan and Andrés, were as well. It is worthy to note that in 1662 testimony against the latter two, the witness, Domingo López de Ocanto, conveyed the impression that knowledge of the circumcisions was widespread among the community:

They were asked if they knew, or if they had heard of any person or persons who were circumcised. He replied that he only knows that Juan Gómez and Andrés Gómez, sons of Francisco Gómez, deceased, citizens of the Villa of Santa Fe, who are of the age of this witness, when they were young boys used to bathe together, and that it appeared to him that they had their parts circumcised, *and that all of the young men of that age know this.* (emphasis added)[66]

As a result of this revelation, Inquisition prosecutor Rodrigo Ruíz suggested that:

Juan and Andrés Gómez, brothers, sons of Francisco Gómez and doña Ana Romero [read Robledo] with regard to the aforesaid sign of circumcision or cutting, which demonstrates that they are observers of Judaism, as a consequence should be severely castigated by the Holy Office with the penalties established by law.[67]

Despite the clear indications of Judaic identity and practice, and the stern admonition by prosecutor Ruíz, Francisco Gómez Robledo was acquitted of all charges, and neither Juan nor Andrés was ever prosecuted by the Inquisition.

So, too, did the record generated by the trials of Governor Bernardo López de Mendizábal and his wife, Teresa de Aguilera y Roche, suggest a connection to a Jewish background. López, arrested for judaizante in 1662, swore that he was of pure Old Christian noble origin, and that none of his ancestors had ever been castigated by the Inquisition.[68] He rather conveniently neglected to mention that one of his maternal great-grandfathers, Juan Núñez de León, had been penanced by the Mexican Inquisition for judaizante in 1603.[69] Testimony against Aguilera included Sabbath observance, such as changing linens and bathing on Fridays, and reciting prayers in secret on Friday evenings.[70]

Cristóbal de Anaya Almazán, as cited above, had been arrested on an unspecified charge of heresy. His testimony, however, appears to have suggested a fear of charges against him for practicing Judaism:

Item—he also says and declares that in August of the previous year, in the pueblo of Sandía, having complied with the order brought by the Holy Tribunal, don Fernando de Durán y Cháves said to the witness that he had taken back that which the Holy Tribunal had ordered, to which the witness responded to him, "I, too, take back what I said so that the people should not be saying what is being said, that perhaps they arrested me for practicing Judaism, which was said before don Agustín de Cháves, Padre fray Raphael, and doña Catalina Vásques, from whom I also ask for mercy as a Catholic Christian."[71]

During the course of the 1660s persecutions in New Mexico, testimony emerged from the trial of Governor López that shed light on the Jewish practices of another early colonist. Padre fray Nicolás de Villar related that during Lent of 1657, one of his Franciscan brethren had told him that a young girl, the eldest daughter of Portuguese blacksmith Manuel Jorge, confessed to him that "she observed the Law of Moses with exquisite rites and ceremonies." The priest did not report her heresy to anyone, since the Mexican Tribunal was 500 leagues distant, and he was not aware of the presence of any Inquisition official in the colony.[72]

Conclusion

The examples cited above suggest that the crypto-Jewish identity and practices of early New Mexico colonists were quite well known both to the general populace and to religious officials. But, absent extraneous factors, in this case the effort in the 1660s on the part of the Franciscans to break down the political power of Governor López de Mendizábal, the authorities, both civil and religious, appeared to be unconcerned about this heresy in their midst. In this sense, the New Mexico experience supports the thesis that the frontier served as a haven for those fleeing from the authority of the Inquisition. The farther one found oneself from the metropolis, the greater the sense of toleration. In the case of the crypto-Jews, those who fled from their homes in Spain and Portugal found a relatively safe haven in central Mexico. During the two aberrant periods of persecution by the Mexican Holy Office in the sixteenth and seventeenth centuries, New Christians were able to escape to an even more secure environment on the far northern frontier of New Spain. Indeed, it appears that the distant outpost of New Mexico represented, in Solange Alberro's words, "the zone of refuge from the zone of refuge" with regard to its policy of toleration of a crypto-Jewish presence.

NOTES

The author would like to acknowledge the Estate of Eva Feld for its support of the research that formed the basis of this article. His book, *To the End of the Earth: A History of the Crypto-Jews of New Mexico*, was published by Columbia University Press in 2005.

1. The term "crypto-Jews" refers to individuals baptized as Catholic Christians and living outwardly as such, but secretly practicing Judaic rites and customs. While the terms converso and New Christian strictly should pertain to those Jews who actually converted to Catholicism, it will be extended in this article to the descendants of the original conversos who lived as crypto-Jews.

2. See Stanley M. Hordes, "Historiographical Problems in the Study of the Inquisition and Crypto-Jews in Mexico," *American Jewish Archives* 34, no. 2 (November 1982): 138–52.

3. Seymour B. Liebman, *The Jews in New Spain: Faith, Flame and the Inquisition* (Coral Gables: University of Miami Press, 1970), 88, 101, 105; Cecil Roth, *A History of the Marranos* (Philadelphia and New York: The Jewish Publication Society of America, 1932; Meridian Books, 1959), 102–5.

4. The twentieth century was not without more objective, analytical treatments of the history of the Mexican Inquisition, which placed inquisitorial activity within proper social and political contexts, for example, France V. Scholes, *Church and State in New Mexico,*

1610–1650 (Albuquerque: Historical Society of New Mexico, 1937), *Troublous Times in New Mexico, 1659–1670* (Albuquerque: Historical Society of New Mexico, 1942), and "The First Decade of the Inquisition in New Mexico," *New Mexico Historical Review* 10 (1935): 195–241; Richard E. Greenleaf, *The Mexican Inquisition of the Sixteenth Century* (Albuquerque: University of New Mexico Press, 1969), *Zumárraga and the Mexican Inquisition: 1536–1543* (Washington, DC: Academy of American Franciscan History, 1962), "The Inquisition in Eighteenth-Century New Mexico," *New Mexico Historical Review* 60, no. 1 (1985): 29–60; Eva Alexandra Uchmany, *La vida entre el judaísmo y el cristianismo en la Nueva España, 1580–1606* (Mexico, DF: Archivo General de la Nación and Fondo de Cultura Económica, 1992); and Solange Alberro, *Inquisición y sociedad en México, 1571–1700* (Mexico, DF: Fondo de Cultura Económica, 1988).

5. Yitzhak Baer, *A History of the Jews of Christian Spain*, 2 vols. (Philadelphia: The Jewish Publication Society of America, 1971), vol. 1, 15–22; Stanley G. Payne, *A History of Spain and Portugal*, 2 vols. (Madison: University of Wisconsin Press, 1973), vol. 1, 12.

6. For a more elaborate discussion of the nature of religious toleration in Muslim Spain, see Philip K. Hiti, *History of the Arabs* (London: Macmillan and Company, 1937); Gabriel Jackson, *The Making of Medieval Spain* (Norwich: Harcourt Brace Jovanovich, 1972); and Américo Castro, *The Structure of Spanish History* (Princeton: Princeton University Press, 1954).

7. Jackson, "The Making of Modern Spain," in Jackson, *The Making of Medieval Spain*, 100–107; Payne, *A History of Spain and Portugal*, vol. 1, 18; Baer, *A History of the Jews in Christian Spain*, vol. 1, 22–24.

8. Detailed accounts of upward mobility of Spanish conversos may be found in Baer, *A History of the Jews in Christian Spain*, vol. 2, 270–77; Manuel Serrano y Sanz, *Orígenes de la dominación española en América* (Madrid: Bailly-Ballière, 1918); Francisco Márquez Villanueva, *Investigaciones sobre Juan Álvarez Gato* (Madrid, 1960); Márquez Villanueva, "Conversos y cargas concejiles en el siglo XV," in *Revista de Archivos, Bibliotecas y Museos*

63 (1957): 503–40; Márquez Villanueva, "The Converso Problem: An Assessment," in *Collected Studies in Honour of Américo Castro's Eightieth Year* (Oxford: Lincombe Lodge Research Library, 1965), 317–33; Benzion Netanyahu, *The Origins of the Inquisition in Fifteenth Century Spain* (New York: Random House, 1995); Henry Kamen, *The Spanish Inquisition : A Historical Revision* (New Haven and London: Yale University Press, 1998).

9. Payne, *A History of Spain and Portugal*, vol. 1, 209.

10. Several specialists of Jewish history theorize that Columbus's departure from Spain in 1492 was no mere coincidence, but that he and other crypto-Jews sought to avoid the new restrictions imposed by Fernando and Isabel by sailing westward in search of the Indies. See, for example, Roth, *A History of the Marranos*, 271; Jacob Beller, *Jews in Latin America* (New York: Jonathan David, 1969); Simon Wiesenthal, *Sails of Hope: The Secret Mission of Christopher Columbus* (New York: Macmillan, 1973); Jonathan Sarna, "The Mythical Jewish Columbus and the History of America's Jews," in *Religion in the Age of Exploration*, ed. Bryan F. Le Beau and Menahem Mor, 81–95 (Omaha, NE: Center for the Study of Religion and Society, The Klutznik Chair in Jewish Civilization, Creighton University Press, 1996).

11. Payne, *A History of Spain and Portugal*, vol. 1, 229–30; Julio Caro Baroja, *La sociedad criptojudía en la corte de Felipe IV* (Madrid: Imprenta y Editorial Maestre, 1963), 23.

12. Payne, *A History of Spain and Portugal*, vol. 1, 230; Caro Baroja, *La sociedad criptojudía*, 36.

13. Liebman, *The Jews in New Spain*, 188–89.

14. See Hordes, "The Crypto-Jewish Community of New Spain, 1620–1649: A Collective Biography," (PhD diss., Tulane University, 1980).

15. Alfonso Toro, *La familia Carvajal* (México, DF: Editorial Patria, 1944), vol. 1, 25–26.

16. Ibid., 39–40; Archivo General de Indias, (hereafter cited as AGI), Indiferente, Legajo 416, L. 7, "Asiento y capitulación con el Capitan Luys de Carvajal sobre el descubrimiento y población del Nuevo Reyno de León" (Aranjuéz, May 31, 1579), f. 1v.

STANLEY M. HORDES

17. For details on the activities of Luis de Carvajal, el Mozo, see: Liebman, *The Jews in New Spain*, chapters 7 and 8; Martin Cohen, *The Martyr* (Philadelphia: The Jewish Publication Society of America, 1973); Liebman, *The Enlightened: The Writings of Luis de Carvajal, el Mozo* (Coral Gables: University of Miami Press, 1967); Greenleaf, *The Mexican Inquisition of the Sixteenth Century*, 169–71; Toro, *La familia Carvajal*.

18. Archivo Histórico Nacional (Spain) (hereafter cited as AHN), Inquisición, Legajo 1047, f. 168r and v, Correspondence from the Supreme Council of the Inquisition to the Mexican Tribunal, Madrid, August 20, 1588.

19. See Liebman, *The Jews in New Spain*, chapters 7 and 8; Cohen, *The Martyr*; Toro, *La familia Carvajal*; Liebman, *The Enlightened*; Greenleaf, *The Mexican Inquisition of the Sixteenth Century*, 169–71.

20. See Hordes, "The Crypto-Jewish Community of New Spain," chapter 3.

21. Hordes, "The Inquisition as Economic and Political Agent: The Campaign of the Mexican Holy Office Against the Crypto-Jews in the Mid-Seventeenth Century," *The Americas* 39, no. 1 (July 1982): 31–38.

22. See Peter J. Bakewell, *Silver Mining and Society in Colonial Mexico: Zacatecas, 1546–1700* (London: Cambridge University Press, 1971).

23. Alberro, *Inquisición y Sociedad en México*, 390.

24. Ibid., 390–402.

25. Archivo General de la Nación (México) (hereafter cited as AGN), Ramo de Inquisición, tomo 414, exp. 2, Testificaciones de Manuel Rodríguez Núñez contra diversas personas (1644), f. 170. See also, Hordes, "The Crypto-Jewish Community of New Spain," 88–94.

26. AHN, Inquisición, Legajo 1737, exp. 20, Libro de la razón de la visita, f. 415–48, computed from the *relación de los pleitos* pertaining to López.

27. AHN, Inquisición, Legajo 1736, exp. 4, Diferentes autos y papeles tocantes a la visita, f. 289v, 293, 296–97, 302, 304. López also received praise from both the capitan general of Nueva Vizcaya and the alcalde mayor of Guanacevi for his actions in the defense of Spanish settlements against Indian attacks in 1626 and 1627.

28. AGN, Inquisición, tomo 510, f. 334, Denuncia contra Gabriel, mozo, Cuencamé (1625); AGN, Inquisición, tomo 435, f. 445, Denuncia contra Thomas de Sosa, Zacatecas (1650), as cited in Alberro, *Inquisición y Sociedad en México*, 403; Hordes, "The Crypto-Jewish Community of New Spain," 120.

29. Alberro, *Inquisición y Sociedad en México*, 401, 403–4.

30. Ibid.; Hordes, "The Crypto-Jewish Community of New Spain," 119.

31. Alberro, *Inquisición y Sociedad*, 408.

32. Ibid., 391–92. The quote from Scholes derives from France V. Scholes, "The First Decade of the Inquisition in New Mexico," *New Mexico Historical Review* 10, no. 3 (1935): 216.

33. No studies have yet been undertaken to ascertain the participation of crypto-Jews on the Vázquez de Coronado expedition, but recent genealogical research has established that Vázquez's wife, Beatríz de Estrada, was the granddaughter of Men Gutiérrez, relaxed in effigy by the Inquisition of Toledo, for practicing Judaism. See José Antonio Esquibel, "The Jewish-Converso Ancestry of Doña Beatriz de Estrada, Wife of Don Francisco Vásquez de Coronado," *Nuestras Raíces* 9, no. 4 (Winter 1997): 134–43.

34. See Herbert Eugene Bolton, *Coronado: Knight of Pueblos and Plains* (New York, London and Toronto: Whittlesey House; Albuquerque: University of New Mexico Press, 1949); Richard Flint and Shirley Cushing Flint, eds., *The Coronado Expedition to Tierra Nueva: The 1540–1542 Route Across the Southwest* (Boulder: University of Colorado Press, 1997).

35. Martin Cohen in *The Martyr*, 103–4, suggested a familial link between Castaño de Sosa and the crypto-Jewish community of Nuevo León. Richard Santos, in *Silent Heritage: The Sephardim and the Colonization of the Spanish North American Frontier* (San Antonio: New Sepharad Press, 2000), 297–98, referred to Castaño as a "suspected Crypto-Jew." Unfortunately, neither author provided references, archival or otherwise, for these assertions. Investigations are currently underway to ascertain the family history of Gaspar Castaño de Sosa; while no specific tie has yet been established, several other Portuguese

"Castaños" and "Sosas" were identified as crypto-Jews in New Spain in the sixteenth and seventeenth centuries.

36. AGN, Inquisición, Lote Riva Palacio, tomo 11, exp. 3, "Proceso contra Luis de Carvajal, Governador del Nuevo Reino de León," f. 69; José Toribio Medina, *Historia de la inquisición en México* (Mexico, DF: Ediciones Fuente Cultural, 1905), 128; Eva A. Uchmany, *La vida entre judaísmo y el cristianismo*, 55.

37. Albert Schroeder and Dan Matson, *A Colony on the Move: Gaspar Castaño de Sosa's Journal, 1590–1591* (Santa Fe: School of American Research, 1965).

38. The precise location of Castaño's crossing of the Río Grande is a subject of scholarly debate. Schroeder and Matson, as well as George P. Hammond and Agapito Rey, placed the site near Del Rio, Texas. On the other hand Santos claimed that the expedition made the crossing farther downriver, near Piedras Negras. He identified the name of the crossing as *el paso grande de los judíos*, but offered no primary citation for this, beyond his reference to its use by the U.S.-Mexico Border Commission in 1850. See: Schroeder and Matson, *A Colony on the Move*, 32–33; George P. Hammond and Agapito Rey, *The Rediscovery of New Mexico, 1580–1594: The Explorations of Chamuscado, Espejo, Castaño de Sosa, Morlete, Leyva de Bonilla and Humaña* (Albuquerque: University of New Mexico Press, 1966), 249; Santos, *Silent Heritage*, 286–87.

39. Hammond and Rey, *The Rediscovery of New Mexico, 1580–1594*, 28–39.

40. Liebman, *The Inquisitors and the Jews in the New World* (Coral Gables: University of Miami Press, 1974), 1–164.

41. AGI, Sección de Audiencia de México, Legajo 25, pt. 1, 244–45 (pagination from University of New Mexico, Center for Southwest Research photostats).

42. Museo Canario (Las Palmas), Fondo Antiguo, CXXXIII-20-Proceso seguido en el S. O. contra Francisco Rodríguez, vecino de Garachico, porque en cierta información de limpieza de sangre que para pasar Indias con cierta cantidad de vino hizo Juan Núñez Jaimez, declaro ser este cristiano viejo, siendo notorio descendiente de los Almonte, naturales de Lepe,

reconciliados por el Tribunal, f. 941r–943v; CLII-2-Libro Segundo de Genealogías, f. 1r, 36v.

43. Hammond and Rey, *The Rediscovery of New Mexico*, 39–48.

44. Alonso de León, *Relación y discursos del descubrimiento, población y pacificación de este Nuevo Reino de León* (México, 1649), republished in *Historia de Nuevo León* (Monterrey: Centro de Estudios Humanísticos de la Universidad de Nuevo León, 1961), 60.

45. AHN, Inquisición, Correspondence from Mexican Tribunal to the Supreme Council of the Inquisition, México, March 31, 1595. Microfilm, Reel 3, f. 7r and v.

46. Hammond and Rey, *Oñate, Colonizer of New Mexico, 1595–1628*, 5; Marc Simmons, *The Last Conquistador: Juan de Oñate and the Settling of the Far Southwest* (Norman: University of Oklahoma Press), 58.

47. José Antonio Esquibel, "New Light on the Jewish-converso Ancestry of Don Juan de Oñate: A Research Note," *Colonial Latin American Historical Review* 7, no. 2 (Spring 1998): 174–90; Esquibel, "Four Additional Lines of Descent from the Ha-Levi Family of Burgos, Spain, to the Present," *Beyond Origins of New Mexico Families*, Special Feature, January 2001, available at http://pages.prodigy.net/bluemountain1/halevi.htm.

48. Liebman, *The Inquisitors and the Jews in the New World: Summaries of Procesos, 1500–1810 and Bibliographical Guide* (Coral Gables: University of Miami Press, 1974), 130; Alfonso Toro, *Los judíos en la Nueva España: Documentos del siglo XVI correspondientes al ramo de inquisición* (Mexico, DF: Archivo General de la Nación y Fondo de Cultura Económica, 1932, 1993), 12, 62. The latter source lists the trial of Ruy Díaz Nieto and Juan Rodríguez in succession as expedientes 1 and 2 of AGN, Inquisición, tomo 157.

49. Hammond and Rey, *Oñate*, 130, 148, 158–60; Hammond and Rey, *The Rediscovery of New Mexico*, 245–95.

50. Hammond and Rey, *Oñate*, 297; Tulane University, Latin American Library, Liebman Collection, box 2, vol. 5, f. 194–97, AGN, Inquisición, tomo 309, f. 171–200 (typescript), "Causa contra Cristóbal de Herrera, mercader,

vecino de la ciudad de Zacatecas" (1614). Both the Inquisition trial and the Oñate muster roll indicate that Herrera was born in Jeréz de la Frontera, the son of Juan de Herrera.

51. Alberro, *Inquisición y sociedad en México*, 405–6.

52. Hammond and Rey, *Oñate*, 102–8; AGN, Inquisición, Lote Riva Palacio, tomo 12, exp. 3, "Proceso contra Baltasar Rodríguez de Andrada, o de Carvajal" (1589).

53. Hammond and Rey, *Oñate*, 293.

54. AHN, Libro de Bautismos, Corral de Almaguer, Libro 1, April 5/7, 1557, Baptism of Bartolomé Romero, f. 359v; Juan Gil, *Los conversos y la inquisición sevillana* (Seville, Universidad de Sevilla, 2000), vol. II, 37, 80, 330. Following the persecution of the Benadevas in the late fifteenth and early six-teenth centuries, several members of the family fled from Sevilla; The Benadevas of Sevilla were also cited as the maternal line of Diego de Ocaña, one of the earliest crypto-Jews penanced by the Mexican Inquisition in 1528. See AGN, Inquisición, tomo 77, exp. 35, Autos y diligencias hechas por los sambenitos antiguos y recientes y postura de los que sean de relajados por este Santo Oficio (México, 1574–1632), f. 221r, Testimony of Bernardo de Albornoz (México, July 9, 1574); AGN, Inquisición, tomo 223, exp. 43, Abecedario de relaxados, reconciliados y penetenciados en la Nueva España con nombre y tto. del Sto. Officio assi por los ordinarios del distrito como por la Inquisición Apostólica despues que en la tierra se fundó a los 4 de Noviembre del año de 1571 (1576), f. 718r.

55. AHN, Libro de Bautismos, Libro 3, March 26, 1581, July 8, 1589, and May 27, 1590.

56. Archivo Diocesano de Cuenca, Archivo de la Inquisición, Legajo 323, exp. 4642, Isabel Romero, muger de Alonso del Campo, Quintinar de la Orden, 1589, judaísmo, reconciliada.

57. See France V. Scholes, "The First Decade of the Inquisition in New Mexico"; Scholes, *Church and State in New Mexico, 1610–1650* (Albuquerque: Historical Society of New Mexico, 1937); Scholes, *Troublous Times in New Mexico, 1659–1670*; Joseph P. Sánchez, *The Rio Abajo Frontier, 1540 to 1692: A History of Early Colonial New Mexico*, 2nd ed. (Albuquerque: The Albuquerque Museum, 1996).

58. Secondary sources on the history of Ciudad Rodrigo indicate that the Abendaños were a prominent fifteenth-century Jewish family. Moreover, baptismal and marriage records from the town's diocesan archives document several Abendaños living in the old *judería*, on the same street where the synagogue had stood.

59. Research through the inquisition records of the Museo Canario (Las Palmas), suggests a common ancestry of Diego de Vera and Pedro de Vera, convicted of practicing secret Judaism in the Canaries in 1609. Museo Canario (Las Palmas), Fondo Antiguo XLIV-10-Proceso seguido en el S. O. contra Esteban de Jerez, por declarar en cierta información que Francisco de Vera Muxica era cristiano viejo siendo como era, descendente de judíos, conversos, etc. (1609).

60. AGN, Inquisición, tomo 268, exp. 5, "Carta de la inquisición de Llerena acompañando datos acerca de la genealogía de fray Estéban de Perea, franciscano" (1630), f. 1–3v.

61. AGN, Concurso de Peñalosa, Legajo 1, no. 3, "Prisión y embargo de bienes de doña Teresa de Aguilera y Roche en 27 de agosto de 1662 años," f. 396r–97r; Legajo 1, no. 5, "Auto de prisión, embargo y remate de bienes del Capitan Nicolás de Aguilar, año de 1662," f. 475r; Legajo 1, no. 6, "Autos de prisión embargo y remate de bienes del Sargento Mayor Francisco Gómez Robledo, fecho el año de 1662," f. 245r; Legajo 1, no. 7, "Autos de prisión embargo y remate de bienes del Sargento Mayor Diego Romero—Año de 1662," f. 294r; AGN, Inquisición, tomo 594, exp. 1, "Primera audiencia de don Bernardo López de Mendizábal, por proposiciones irreligiosas y escandalosas. Mexico, April 28, 1663," f. 2r.

62. AGN, Inquisición, tomo 583, exp. 3, "Proceso y causa criminal contra el Sargento Mayor Francisco Gómez Robledo . . . por sospechoso de delitos de judaísmo" (1663), f. 270v, 275r, 278v, 293r, 295r–v; 308v.

63. Fray Angelico Chávez, *Origins of New Mexico Families in the Spanish Colonial Period* (Santa Fe: William Gannon, 1954, 1975), 35–36.

64. AGN, Inquisición, tomo 583, f. 353r–v;

BETWEEN TOLERATION AND PERSECUTION

373v–374r; 379v–80v. On September 5, 1663, three surgeons appointed by the inquisitors found that Francisco Gómez Robledo had three scars on his penis that appeared to have been made with a sharp instrument. The defendant protested that he was not circumcised, but rather that the scars were caused by small ulcers that he had suffered. He asked for, and received a second examination, conducted on June 23, 1664. This time the three surgeons were accompanied by an Inquisition doctor. The second inspection not only confirmed the findings of the first, but revealed two other scars. They concluded that the scars were created "by a sharp instrument . . . [and] could *not* have originated from any another cause" (emphasis added) (f. 380v). Scholes appears to have misread the original document when he indicated that the inspection revealed, "'it *was* possible that they had resulted from another cause'" (emphasis added). See Scholes, "Troublous Times in New Mexico," 193. Unfortunately, in her effort to discredit the historical basis for crypto-Judaism in New Mexico, folklorist Judith S. Neulander failed to consult the original record, relying instead on Scholes. See Neulander, "The Crypto-Jewish Canon: Choosing to be 'Chosen' in Millenial Tradition," *Jewish Folklore and Ethnology Review* 18, no. 1–2 (1996): 49.

65. See Hordes, "The Crypto-Jewish Community of New Spain," 120–21; and David Gitlitz, *Secrecy and Deceit: The Religion of the Crypto-Jews* (Philadelphia: Jewish Publication Society of America, 1996), 202–7. In the case of Gómez Robledo, it appears that the foreskin was not entirely removed as part of his ritual circumcision. This is consistent with the observation by David Gitlitz: "By the seventeenth century in Mexico, some Judaizing conversos did not remove the foreskin at all, but rather scarred it with a longitudinal cut in an attempt to comply with the requirement of the law and deceive the Inquisitors. When Inquisition doctors examined Gabriel de Granada in Mexico in 1645 they 'found a mark . . . running longitudinally and with a scar, made apparently with a cutting instrument'" (*Secrecy and Deceit*, 206).

66. AGN, Inquisición, tomo 598, exp. 7, "Testificaciones que se an sacado a pedimiento del dr. fiscal de uno de los quadernos que se remitieron por el comisario del Nuevo

México contra Juan Gómez, vezino de dicho Nuevo México" (1662–1663), Testimony of Domingo López de Ocanto Convento del Sr. San Francisco del Pueblo de Sandía, April 4, 1662, f. 119v.

67. AGN, Inquisición, tomo 598, exp. 7, "Testificaciones que se an sacado a pedimiento del dr. fiscal de uno de los quadernos que se remitieron por el comisario del Nuevo México contra Juan Gómez, vezino de dicho Nuevo México" (1662–1663), Petition by Dr. Rodrigo Ruiz (México, July 23, 1663), f. 116r.

68. AGN, Inquisicion, tomo 594, exp. 1, "Primera audiencia de don Bernardo López de Mendizábal, por proposiciones irreligiosas y escandalosas" (1663), f. 5v–6r.

69. AGN, Inquisición, tomo 210, exp. 2, "Proceso contra Juan Núñez, balanzario de la Real Caja, por alumbrado y sospechoso de judaizante" (1598–1609).

70. AGN, Inquisición, tomo 596, exp. 1, "El Señor Fiscal del Santo Oficio contra doña Teresa de Aguilera y Roche, mujer de don Bernardo López de Mendizábal, por sospechosa de delitos de judaísmo" (1663), f. 1or–40r. Scholes, in "Troublous Times in New Mexico," dismissed the value of the testimony presented against the governor and his wife, as well as against Francisco Gómez Robledo, arguing that "Actual eyewitness accounts . . . were given by only four or five persons who were members of the López household" (160), and that such testimony represented nothing more than "petty gossip and spiteful rumor-mongering" (196–97). Furthermore, he pointed out, both López and Aguilera either denied the charges, or explained that the timing of their practices was purely coincidental. It is this author's opinion that testimony by a number of eyewitnesses should not be summarily disregarded simply because they were servants. Nor should the obviously self-serving explanations of the defendants be given particularly heavy weight either. Many scholars of the Mexican Inquisition, including this author, have suggested that the Holy Office was often motivated by political concerns extraneous to the issues of heresy. But the mere fact that the inquisitors, or even the witnesses, themselves, may have maintained other agendas does not

STANLEY M. HORDES

necessarily discredit the validity of the charges of crypto-Judaism. See, for example, Hordes, "The Inquisition as Economic and Political Agent: The Campaign of the Mexican Holy Office Against the Crypto-Jews in the Mid-Seventeenth Century," *The Americas* 39, no. 1 (July 1982).

71. AGN, Inquisición, tomo 610, exp. 7, "Denunciaciones contra Juan Domínguez de Mendoza. Nuevo México" (1667), Denuncia de Christóbal de Anaia Almazan (Santo Domingo, May 3, 1666), f. 66v–67r.

72. AGN, Inquisición, tomo 593, exp. 1, "El Santo Oficio contra Bernardo López de Mendizábal por proposiciones hereticas y sospechosos en el delicto de judaísmo" (1662), f. 162r.

CHAPTER TWELVE

On Divine Persecution

Blasphemy and Gambling

JAVIER VILLA-FLORES

Introduction

On August 27, 1596, Diego Flores, an inhabitant of Jalapa, lost a good amount of money at cards. Since this was the second day of a losing streak, Flores was manifestly frustrated: "God's not tired of punishing me (*hacerme mal*)!" he uttered in despair. To the dismay of his denouncer, Colonel Luis Pérez, Flores's frustration was soon transformed into defiance, for he also exclaimed angrily while looking at the sky, "He should be tired of punishing me by now (*era razón de que estuviese cansado*)! God be damned (*voto a Dios*)! You'll have to be tired (*pues de cansaros tenéis*)!" That day the defiant gambler was taken to prison on orders of *Comisario* (Commissary) Francisco Carranco. However, the Holy Office only decided to initiate an investigation after eight months had elapsed. When prosecutor Martos de Bohórquez finally reported on

this case on March 13, 1597, he asserted that Flores had blasphemously depicted God as a whimsical creature who acted without a reason and was subject to human passions. Grounding his demand for a thorough investigation of this crime upon Flores's misattribution of human characteristics to God, Bohórquez never contested the gambler's conviction that God's hand actively intervened in the games. On the contrary, his main concern and motive of outrage was Flores's suggestion that even at the seemingly trivial scale of gambling games God could conduct Himself without a purpose. The Holy Office issued an order of arrest accordingly, but the man had managed in the meantime to escape from his prison in Jalapa and could not be found. Some neighbors heard the rumor he had been hanged on a ship coming from Havana, where Diego apparently had been sentenced as a slave-galley. In any event, he had disappeared not to be seen again.[1]

The case of Diego Flores constitutes an early example of the tendency among losing gamblers in New Spain to engage in blasphemy as an exercise of negative retribution, reproach, and even self-defense against the supreme divinity who had ruled against them in the games. Indeed, like Flores, several gamesters broke into insults and blasphemous utterances against God, the Virgin, and the saints in an angry reaction manifesting their conviction that their repeated losses were not random, but divinely ordained. Paradoxically, the same providential premises that led gamblers to blaspheme in New Spain—that is, the belief that God enjoyed not only supreme clairvoyance, but actively intervened in the affairs of this world—also comprised the basis on which moralists and theologians condemned gambling. Medieval Christians such as Boethius, Dante, and even Aquinas had emphasized that the existence of a divine providence did not rule out the action of chance or luck, but many post-Reformation theologians asserted that nothing could take place in the world without God's will. Although this extreme version of providentialism was not universally shared, it was believed widely enough to override ancient notions of a capricious Fortune, Fate, or chance.[2] In New Spain, both Inquisitors and blaspheming gamblers were convinced that even at the gaming table the workings of divine providence were constantly manifested. However, while losing gamesters protested God's unchangeable decrees, officers of the Mexican Inquisition stressed conformity and expected players to be content with their lot, for human beings only have a feeble insight into the mysterious purposes of the Almighty. It was only with the expansion of the notion of chance at the beginning of the eighteenth century that the tie between gambling results and providentialist intervention was finally broken. Since gaming losses were now attributed to bad luck or misfortune and not to the works of a punishing and persecuting god, blasphemous reproaches became less frequent at the gaming table.

This chapter explores the complex relationship between gambling and blasphemy as social practices associated with social disarray, moral decay, and danger in New Spain. Early in colonial times, authorities banned gambling games for constituting a motive for fights, quarrels, and social discord, and established fines for the transgressors. The frequency of blasphemous utterances at the games, however, represented a motive of even bigger concern for both the colonial church and the state. Colonial authorities assumed that blasphemy almost always had devastating consequences. In a sense, it was the very opposite of a "crime with no victim." Blasphemy was deemed a natural cause of famine, pestilence, earthquake, and shipwrecks. Since it was not only the sinful who were chastised, the pressure for religious conformity was necessarily great. Secular and ecclesiastical authorities severely punished this crime for endangering the colonial enterprise, offering a bad example of Christian behavior to the Indians and other subjects, and attacking God's honor. Although the Audiencia of Mexico also had jurisdiction to punish this crime, the vast majority of blasphemers were tried by the Mexican Holy Office. Accordingly, inquisitors regularly sentenced the blaspheming gamesters to pay a fine, receive a public flogging, serve a term slaving in the king's galleys, exile, and, in rare cases, the cutting off of part of the tongue. In spite of risking a severe punishment, many gamblers resorted to blasphemous utterances and deprecatory gestures not only to express their anger and frustration but also to offer their audiences an image of strong belligerence after they had experienced a humiliating defeat resulting from the intervention of the Christian God.

Blasphemy and Gambling

Blasphemy and gambling had long been associated in Christian thought. When medieval writers chose to refer to gambling, they usually pointed out the concomitant quarrels and blasphemies as a reason to condemn games in which betting was involved. Because of the moral dangers it represented for the participants, canon law prohibited gambling from early Christian times. In 306 CE the Council of Elvira threatened those guilty of gambling with excommunication, although they could be restored to communion after a year of amendment. The Fourth Lateran Council (1215) also prevented clerics from playing or even being present at games of chance. No less severe was the Council of Trent (1545–1563) in its denunciation of gambling, but it left to the bishops' discretion the decision as to what games were to be deemed illicit according to circumstances of person, place, and time. Further church councils drew up lists of games in which dice and some forms of cards were banned. Although taking part in games was not utterly prohibited—moralists frequently exalted the virtues of "honest recreation" or *eutrapelia*, which provided rest and relaxation to the participants—gambling was always censured.[3] If indulging in gaming to excess, Christian writers thought, gamesters could lose not only considerable amounts of money, but also precious life time. Furthermore, gaming easily led participants into fraud, theft, cheating, an idle life spent in bad company, and blasphemy.[4] Sixteenth- and seventeenth-century moralists were convinced that there were "no other human dealings or interactions (*trato o conversación*) [in which] the admirable Name of God and His saints [was] so regularly blasphemed as in the games."[5] As Puebla's bishop Juan de Palafox put it in his posthumous *Luz a los vivos* (1661), "*jurar* and *jugar* [to blaspheme and to play] are twin brothers, and legitimate offspring of vice."[6] Following John Chrysostom and Bernardin of Siena, spiritual writers commonly depicted gamesters as faithful attendants to a satanic mass in which oaths and blasphemies played the part of litanies and exclamations of hallelujah, while the recited creed expressed their firm conviction that they were not going to die and pay for their sins.[7] John Chrysostom believed that "it is not God who gives us the chance to play, but the devil," and Bernardin of Siena was convinced that Lucifer had invented the gambling games themselves as a parody of transubstantiation; indeed, since the goods (*substantiae*) of a player were transferred to the hands of another one, gambling could be considered as a wicked imitation of the utmost sacred mystery of Christianity.[8] In

JAVIER VILLA-FLORES

Francisco Luque Fajardo's *Fiel desengaño contra la ociosidad y los juegos* (1603), the repentant cardsharp Florino even goes to the extreme of declaring that for gamesters the biggest incentive in playing was to have an opportunity to blaspheme.[9] Although some moralists such as Nicolás de Avila (1610) believed that the devil himself instigated gamesters to blaspheme or even spoke through their mouths against God, most rejected this idea as a way of diminishing the transgressors' responsibility for their own utterances.[10] Indeed, like Francisco de Alcocer in his *Tratado del juego* (1559), most writers believed that gamblers intentionally transgressed all commandments and incurred all mortal sins. They thus described the gamblers' gatherings as infernal reunions in which threats were common, lies and perjury regularly took place, and promises were rarely kept.[11]

Given the diabolic nature of gaming, it was inevitable that moralists and writers at the time would refer to the deck of cards as an anti-bible of forty-eight sheets, *el descuadernado* (an unbound book), read by idle people of all classes who scandalously intermixed with the purpose of playing. Indeed, as Luque Fajardo reminded his readers, *baraja* (deck of cards) originally meant fight and confusion, and it was because of this confusion (created by the baraja) that nobles mingled with plebeians in the same way that *oros* (coins) and *bastos* (batons) intermixed when cards were shuffled.[12] According to moralists, the nefarious character of the games was revealed by the cards themselves: the coins represented the sin of greed and the skin color (yellow) of those who spent the whole day and night at the gaming table; the cups, both the excess of drunkenness and gluttony that occurred in conjunction with the games; the batons, the bestiality and brutality among the players; and, finally, the swords manifested the often mortal hatred and disputes triggered in the games. Clearly, cards were nothing but instruments put in the hands of human beings by the devil to create social disarray and offend the supreme divinity.[13] Since that sin was based on human intention, moralists urged Christians to avoid places and occasions where they could willingly put their own salvation at risk, such as those in which gambling or "forbidden games" were taking place and in which blasphemy allegedly constituted a diabolical form of "prayer."[14]

Forbidden Games in New Spain

The condemnation of gambling in New Spain was not only expressed in religious terms but also in secular terms, particularly in the form of legal banishment of those ludic practices known as *juegos prohibidos* (forbidden games). This concept was widely used by moralists to describe those games that paved the way to blasphemy, mockery, anger, fights, pain, despair, lies, curses, and perjury, but these same moralists made no attempt to offer a clear definition of such games.[15] Spanish legislation designated as forbidden, however, those games in which *suerte* (betting), *envite* (chance), or *azar* (hazard) were involved. Although under this broad classification most table games were to be banned, *ordenanzas* (royal decrees) frequently used the expression "dice and cards" as a synonym for forbidden games. Yet while dice were always proscribed, some

ON DIVINE PERSECUTION

games of cards were allowed on condition that the amount of money gambled was not superior to 10 gold pesos in a twenty-four-hour period. In truth, however, even the "forbidden games"—of which a 1771 royal decree offered a list—were allowed if the bets placed did not exceed two reales and the amount collected was used to buy food for those attending the games. These conditions were, of course, rarely observed.[16]

Beginning in 1511 Governor Diego Colón was instructed to forbid gambling games on the island of Cuba, and in 1518 the crown tried to eradicate the gambling games in the Antilles, or at least to tune down the passions involved by limiting the bets that could be placed to ten ducats. In 1525 the cabildo of Mexico City banned the card and dice games that were played even in the viceregal palace. For its part, Viceroy don Antonio de Mendoza ordered in 1538 the closure of the gambling houses or *tablajerías*, as they were known at the time.[17] Despite these prohibitions, gambling went on everywhere because those in charge of enforcing the regulations were frequently involved in the games. A good case in point was Hernando Cortés. Before his departure to New Spain, the conquistador was clearly instructed by Diego de Velázquez to prevent his men from playing cards or dice because of the resulting scandals and blasphemies against God and His saints, and the detrimental effects of the games on military discipline.[18] Shortly before the *Noche Triste* (the sad night), however, Pedro Valenciano, one of his company, made "playing cards as good and well painted as those of Castile, using the hides from the drums."[19] Cortés not only allowed gambling games while he

was captain-general and governor of New Spain, but also organized card games at his own house. The conquistador charged a house's commission, and even prohibited playing cards in any other place of Mexico City but his house.[20]

Corregidores (royal district governors) and governors also exploited with success the passion for gambling that was shared by every class. Hosting frequent *tertulias* (gatherings), these high magistrates transformed their mansions into gambling houses for well-to-do people where they charged the players a fixed fee per round, and even obtained monetary gratuities from the guests upon departure.[21] In contrast to people in the lower echelons of society—blacks, mulattoes, and mestizos—whose attachment to gambling was seen as one more expression of their "evil ways of life," elite Spaniards allegedly attended the magistrates' soirées for the sole purpose of entertainment.[22] Since these leading citizens did not engage in the games for money but only to socialize and find some relaxation, Jerónimo Castillo de Bobadilla stated in his *Política para corregidores* (1597) that the rigorous measures recommended against gambling dens should not apply to them.[23] However, the Council of Indies frequently found the entertaining social life that these magistrates carried on at their homes offensive because the card games often went on for days and the hosts left their duties as *oidores* (judges of the Audiencia or high court), corregidores, and governors unattended. More strikingly, although licensed gambling houses had been again outlawed in 1609 and 1618, some corregidores were so bold as to establish their own tablajerías and to prohibit the existence of any other gambling establishments, thus assuring themselves a source of revenue. Such a blatant abuse of authority was not without its critics. Moralists such as fray Antonio de Ezcaray, a *doctrinero* (priest serving in a doctrina, or parish, for neophytes) of Santiago de Querétaro who spent fifteen years in the Indies, asserted that governors and corregidores who made profit out of gambling games incurred mortal sin and could only be forgiven upon complete restitution of their gains to the players.[24] For all the severity of their criticism, however, the clerics themselves were sharply divided on the issue of gambling, with some decrying playing for money as a diabolical activity and many others heavily addicted to the games. Thus, in the same way those salaried and high magistrates were admonished in royal legislation not to organize or play cards for money at any place or time, clerics were flatly warned by every church provincial council (1555, 1565, and 1585) not to gamble lest they risk excommunication.[25]

Despite all its efforts to eradicate games of chance, even the Spanish crown benefited from the widespread practice of gambling. In frank contradiction to its avowed high moral standards, the crown decided to obtain an economic gain from the taste for cards by monopolizing their production and diffusion in the Iberian world through the creation of the *estanco de naipes* (monopoly of gambling cards), one of the oldest monopolies of the Spanish state. For many years Spain had been importing cards from France, but in 1528 the Spanish crown decreed that all cards should be manufactured in the home country and then exported to the colonies. Ten years later, the *Casa de Contratación* (House of Trade) in Seville prohibited the taking of cards and dice to the Indies.[26] Thus, for several decades the sole gaming cards allowed in the colonies were those produced by the royal factories at Madrid and Málaga, as certified by the royal seal normally printed in the *as de oros* (ace of coins) of each pack. In 1576 a royal decree established that all gambling cards used in New Spain had to be printed in the colony, but the price of a pack was still far superior to that of a card set clandestinely produced in Mexico or brought from some place else. Although royal decrees banning tablajerías and gambling games clearly affected the demand for cards in New Spain, the estanco yielded good profits for many years until its fusion with the monopoly of tobacco in 1768.[27] It is clear in this context that although royal and colonial authorities frequently voiced concerns about the practice of gambling in New Spain, they also profited from the diffusion of card games at all levels and even participated in the organization of the games. Only women were explicitly banned from participating in games of cards, dice, board games, and others. As stated in an ordinance issued by the cabildo of Mexico City in 1583, however, female players were not unusual, a fact that moralists and colonial authorities found utterly scandalous and most damaging for the colony.[28] In this way, from the elegant soirées of corregidores and *gente principal* (high society), to the "infernal" gatherings conducted in inns, taverns, *obrajes* (textile workshops), prisons, and tablajerías, gambling went on everywhere, thus becoming one of the first and

ON DIVINE PERSECUTION

most extended forms of the circulation of money in New Spain. As will be seen, however, the thrill and attractiveness of gambling in colonial Mexico frequently resided in much more than the possible transfer of wealth between the participants.

Chance and Providentialism

Indeed, aside from the money involved, throwing dice or playing cards were also attractive activities because they were deemed to depend not on the whim of chance, but on God's immediate will. At a time in which God's omnipotence was so strongly emphasized, it was simply impossible to attribute to chance the results of one's own game. "The lot is cast into the lap," said the Proverbs (16:33), "but the whole disposing thereof is of the Lord." Although it is difficult to establish to what extent the official eschatological thinking of the church coincided with the perspective of common Christians, it is a fact that this kind of providentialist belief was widespread among people of all classes. Throughout Medieval and Early Modern Europe, society as a whole had long been accustomed to referring potentially contentious decisions to lot as a way of knowing God's will in cases of urgent necessity.

According to William Christian, casting lots was a widely used procedure in Castile to find helper saints in times of need.[29] This practice was accepted by Augustine and Aquinas if there was urgent necessity, provided due reverence was observed. The method had long been sanctioned by Judeo-Christian tradition, as is clear from the numerous examples offered in the Bible.[30] Moralists and theologians regularly classified all these instances of divine intervention in three broad categories: *sors divinatoria*, when God's aid was invoked to know what was going to happen; *sors consultoria*, to know what ought to be done; and *sors divisoria*, to find out what was to be given to whom. As procedures involving the distribution of wealth, games of chance were subsumed under the latter category. Beyond the blasphemous utterances produced as a result of participating in the games, this implied that the games of chance themselves—lusory lots, as they were known by the casuists—were often seen as a mockery of the sors divisoria, for they constituted an illegitimate and sinful way of resorting to divine providence to decide which gamester should receive the wagered property or money.[31]

Given this extended conviction that divine order operated in the midst of the apparent randomness of the games, it is understandable that losing gamesters engaged in blasphemy as a desperate exercise of negative reciprocity against the Divinity who "loaded the dice." Indeed, although moralists frequently defined blasphemy as nothing less than a naked act of vengeance against a guiltless God, gamesters in New Spain often broke into insults against the divinity because they attributed to His hand the results of the games. As is shown in several trials for blasphemy in the early days of colonial society, divine providence was understood as God's active intervention in this world, not only as His supreme clairvoyance and foreknowledge. In this sense, players witnessed more than God's unchangeable decrees at every turn of cards; they also experienced his power.

JAVIER VILLA-FLORES

Take for instance the case of Pedro de Sosa, a man who in 1536 found himself losing at cards in such a way that he cried in despair, "I renounce him who does it (*reniego de quien lo hace*)!" meaning by "it" his repeated losses. Then, in a further gesture of defiance he gave himself to the devil.[32] Similarly, in 1526, Alonso de Carrión ascribed his continuous losses to God and also uttered "may it spite God who does so much harm to me (*pese a dios que tanto mal me hace*)!" while looking at the sky.[33] Ten years later, Carrión was again denounced for voicing a similar utterance, although this time, as if trying to protect himself, he added rhetorically, "I neither believe in you, nor can you hurt me any more (*ni me puedes hacer más mal*)!"[34] That same year, in 1536, Archbishop and Inquisitor fray Juan de Zumárraga also tried and sentenced Juan de Porras for expressing in despair that God could scarcely punish him any harder (*no puede hacerme más mal*) after he badly lost at cards.[35] Although it is possible that some gamesters felt indeed the victims of God's whims, those who experienced repeated losses at the games like Porras, Carrión, Sosa, and others, were certainly convinced that they had long been singled out. In these circumstances, blasphemy seems to have represented a way of protecting themselves against a divinity that persistently "punished" them with defeat at cards.

In recognizing the work of a transpersonal power, however, the players were not necessarily surrendering all kinds of agency and falling into a state of complete subjection to the being who had control over the outcome of the games. On the contrary, gamblers often attempted to influence the supreme divinity by means of a vast array of activities and artifacts, among which blasphemy was probably the most radical one. For example, while Joseph de Messa (alias *El Semita*) used to play in 1670 with a rosary about his neck,[36] others carried gold medals and crucifixes that in case of extreme necessity could also be used to place a bet, as Juan Baeza did in Mexico City in 1545 and Diego Moreno in Huachinango in 1569.[37] Gamblers also gave monetary gifts, *baratos*, to bystanders, and alms to occasional beggars when they won, thus using money both as an amulet and a way of attracting God's favor through a token of Christian charity.[38] Prayers and spells were invoked at the time, although not always successfully. In 1695, while playing *albur*,[39] Joseph de Saucedo prayed before turning the card face up, "may the Holy Virgin be there!" Yet when he saw his opponent's card emerge instead of the expected epiphany, he shouted, "what a shitty Faith (*qué fe de mierda*)! What's the purpose of believing if it's of no use at all!"[40] For his part, Gonzalo Hernández de Figueroa went to the chapel of his prison before a game started and threatened a Christ on a crucifix, "there you are hunchback (*encorvado*)! You better favor me now in the games or I'll do it!" without specifying what he intended to do in retaliation. The use of all these different strategies hardly gave the players the power of forcing a favorable outcome in the games, but they certainly knew they were already coercing God into taking decisions on "what was to be given to whom." In this sense, even those who lost at the games had some degree of mastery, for they were at least in control of the conditions of their own losing. Obviously, as Catherine Bates has emphasized, this is not enough to make the player himself *the* God, "able to give and take away. But, it does perhaps make him *a* god, able to create the conditions in which giving and taking will occur." Gamblers were certainly deprived of the power of decision, but even the downtrodden knew that in gambling they could have the power of decidability, that is, "the ability to arrange the circumstances which will decide who the winner is."[41]

A Persecuting God

But what about those who repeatedly lost at gaming? How could they avoid feeling persecuted when, in game after game, the powers-that-be seemed to rule against them while they bankrupted themselves and beggared their families in the process? In such conditions, certainly, the results of the game merely confirmed that the players were impotent before a God perceived as rarely giving but almost always taking away. As might be expected in such cases, blasphemy constituted a particularly dramatic and confrontational act of verbal defiance that went far beyond its occasional production as an outburst of anger and frustration.

Take, for example, the case of Gonzalo Hernández de Figueroa, the proud son of conquistador Gonzalo Hernández de Mosqueda, who was condemned on an April morning in 1571 to the unusually harsh sentence consisting of public infamy and abjuration, four hundred lashes, and perpetual service as a galley slave. For Hernández, an inveterate gambler reduced to absolute misery, the sentence constituted the final episode in a long affair with the Holy Office, for he had already faced the tribunal on

five occasions on recurrent charges of blaspheming God upon losing at cards. The first time Hernández was tried by the Mexican Inquisition he was only seventeen years old. He had been accused in 1559 of bragging after losing a game that he wanted to fight with God "in the open" (*a campo raso*). Because of his young age and the political influence of his father, however, he was released after spending some time in the stocks. Three years later he was tried again for renouncing God and uttering some other blasphemies after losing the huge amount of 300 gold pesos at cards. In his defense he stated that, as a Christian and son of a conquistador who had done so much with arms and horses for the expansion of the Catholic faith, he could not have possibly blasphemed. Although he also alleged to be a *hijodalgo* (nobleman) and *deudor cercano* (close relative) of Viceroy don Antonio de Mendoza, Inquisitor Luis Fernández de Anguis condemned Hernández to pay 5 gold pesos plus the costs of the trial, and to hear mass in the cathedral with a candle in his hands, a sentence his defensor considered "unjust and ignominious."

This punishment notwithstanding, Hernández faced the Inquisition three more times between 1565 and 1569. A frequent attendant at gambling houses, taverns, and private homes where "forbidden games" took place, the conquistador's son recurrently engaged in heated disputes over gambling debts, which occasionally ended up in insults, fist fighting, and sworn animosities. As might be expected, several of his denouncers and witnesses for the prosecution in the ensuing trials were former participants in those violent encounters.

JAVIER VILLA-FLORES

To mitigate the harshness of the sentences resulting from these often lengthy and costly trials, the *encomendero* (individual who enjoys the right to tribute and labor from natives) Gonzalo Hernández de Mosqueda made use of all his political influence in his son's favor. Yet to the father's almost certain dismay, each time the Inquisitors were increasingly hard on Hernández. On August 27, 1565, Inquisitor Barbosa condemned the blaspheming gamester to spend two years in exile and pay 6 gold pesos because he had hurled "I don't believe in the Catholic faith!" and other sinful expressions at the cards. One year later, Hernández was denounced for saying that God had no power to do him any good and was therefore sentenced by Inquisitor Barbosa to pay 18 gold pesos and contribute two jugs of oil for the *Santísimo Sacramento* (Holy Eucharist); in addition, he was to be banished from Mexico City for three more years. Leaving his wife and children in his father's house, he went to live in exile in Acatzingo. One year before concluding his sentence, however, in 1569, he was seen and arrested at a tavern in Mexico City. When the *alguaciles* (bailiffs) came to get him, Hernández escaped to the house of his father, which was close to the drinking establishment. Then, while his mother and sisters despairingly obstructed the constables' work, he ran to the church nearby seeking sanctuary, where despite his efforts, he was finally apprehended and disarmed. Looking at the cross on the altar, he uttered in anger, "may it spite you (*pese a tí*), because I know who is doing this!" a phrase he had also used at the gaming tables. On July 26, 1569, after a four-month trial, Inquisitor Esteban de Portillo condemned Hernández to pay 50 gold pesos and to receive 100 lashes. Although he was to be whipped in a secret chamber, the sentence clearly represented a debasement of the culprit's social standing, for corporal punishment was usually reserved for individuals at the bottom of society.

When Hernández faced the Holy Office still one more time, in September 1570, the prosecutor alleged that he was now eligible to be burned at the stake as a heretic. The Inquisition sentenced him, however, to pay 30 gold pesos and to serve five years as a galley slave. Since Hernández alleged complete destitution and incapability of providing for his wife and family, the Inquisitor cancelled the fine but ordered the culprit to be imprisoned until he could be transferred to San Juan de Ulúa, the island-fortress of Veracruz, and serve his time on one of the king's ships. When the Inquisitor found two months later that Hernández had pledged himself to the devil while playing cards in jail, he increased the sentence of galley service by one year. This only added to the already strong resentment and despair the gamester experienced as a result of his miserable situation. In the months preceding his final sentence, Hernández repeatedly expressed, among other things, that he would prefer to have money over achieving canonization as a saint and that he would not accept the glory [of Heaven] even if God gave it to him. Given his profound conviction that God's hand intervened in every turn of cards, his anger and frustration at the gaming table were understandably supreme. As the outraged Inquisitor later learned, Hernández frequently uttered while looking at the sky, "may it spite You,

ON DIVINE PERSECUTION

Jewish rascal, (*pese a tí bellaco judío*) for you . . . persecute me so much, one day you'll regret this!" Almost a year later, having entered and frequently lost countless battles against superior forces in the games, a destitute and orphaned Hernández heard from the lips of Inquisitor Esteban Portillo the unusually harsh sentence against him.[42]

It is interesting to note that, like Hernández, many other losing gamblers claimed to be persecuted by Christ or God. Indeed, although other divinities of the Catholic pantheon such as the Virgin Mary, Saint Peter, and Saint Stephen were either praised, invoked, or vilified during games, Christ was the favorite target of frequent losers. In a reversal of the teachings of Catholic theology, Christ, the persecuted and sacrificed scapegoat for humanity's sins, was thus transformed by angered gamesters into a relentless cruel persecutor. Consider the case of Domingo de Yrregui who was denounced on November 13, 1612, for saying during the card games organized for a celebration in honor of the viceroy in Acapulco "that he knew God for His works better than his own hands, and that God did not help him but only persecuted him." Conflating the Son with the Father, Yrregui manifested that God did not get along with people of good birth, but only with Jews because He also was a Jew. "What was then the use of whipping him?" Yrregui asked, "He deserved even more lashes!" Besides, God had badly reciprocated his devotion, because ever since he had confessed after a decade of not approaching the sacraments, he had lost in the games. That same day Isabel María de Gonzalo Rodríguez attested before Comisario Pedro García de Herencia

that Yrregui had also called Christ a sodomite (*bujarrón*) and sworn that he would not confess, hear mass, or fast anymore because God did not do anything for him. Nine years later, Yrregui was still scandalizing his neighbors in the harbor of Acapulco. According to a letter of Comisario Agustín de Mexía, dated August 18, 1621, while looking at the sky Yrregui had uttered, "Oh Nazarene, neither you nor anyone of your race has ever done me any good!"[43] In addressing Christ as a Jew, both Yrregui and Hernández distanced themselves from the "Crucified" while also denying the Passion as a source of their perpetual indebtedness to God. In fact, as Yrregui saw it, it was Christ himself who did not reciprocate with those who were faithful to him. Indeed, partaking in the sacraments, a key ritual to remembering and acknowledging the irredeemable debt contracted by the believers to God through His son's death, was seen by Yrregui as a way of indebting God himself. The gamester probably reasoned if he continuously lost in the games it was because God did not pay up, or repaid "in a bad way" the debt he had contracted with those who were faithful to him.[44] The cases of Gonzalo Hernández and Domingo Yrregui were obviously outside the norm, but as will be seen in the following section their expressions of outrage, impotence, and indignation were only the extreme manifestation of feelings shared by many other gamesters for what they deemed an undeserved punishment from an all-powerful supreme deity.

Gesticulating Gamesters

The impossibility of exerting any kind of control over the outcome of the games was usually mirrored, moralists pointed out, by the lack of self-control exhibited by the players at the gaming table. In the dangerous theater of disguises that constituted the real world, gambling games were deemed an occasion in which the participants' "true self" was revealed and their secret vices were exposed, not only through imprecative speech but also through derogatory gestures.[45] As perceivable movements of the body, gestures had been considered since antiquity expressions of the inner movements of the soul and, consequently, used to judge the moral inclinations of the person performing them. If duly disciplined, however, body gestures could not only reveal the human soul but also contribute to its improvement. Accordingly, a strong emphasis on self-restraint and control formed part of the moral discipline of the Counter-Reformation following the dignified ideal of Spanish "gravity." Obviously, nothing could be farther from the disciplined decorum of the Iberian model than the unruly and impious spontaneity of a gathering of "desperate and furious men" (*hombres rabiosos y desesperados*), as gamblers were called by moralists such as Pedro de Covarrubias.[46]

Insofar as they constituted a language of the soul, gestures were a focus of new interest starting in the twelfth century; but they received revived attention again during the early modern period. Following a monastic tradition stretching back to the Middle Ages, Christian writers paid especial attention to those parts of the human body considered more "expressive," such as the hands, the face, and the eyes.[47] This tradition is still alive in contemporary efforts by scholars from diverse disciplines to compile "dictionaries of gestures."[48] Yet, given the fact that gestures have a meaning only through interaction, when they occur in a spatialized situation where communication is carried on, it seems a mistake to reduce gesture analysis to a description of body part movements as decontextualized signifying units. As Jean-Claude Schmitt and Jacques Le Goff have convincingly argued, gestures only acquire a social significance when performed before an audience, in compliance or defiance of moral and social norms, and in relation to hierarchical spatial orientations such as right and left, front and back, or, more significantly, high and low—undoubtedly, the most important of the spatial orientations for the Judeo-Christian tradition.[49]

Since the source of cosmic power was situated in the sky while satan inhabited the underground, it was only natural that the high/low aspect would play a crucially important role in the performance and appraisement of gestures related to reverence and/or misdemeanor during gambling games. For instance, turning the eyes up to heaven, a bodily movement normally associated with prayer, was often considered a corporal means of identifying God as a referent of one's words or actions. Thus, even euphemical expressions such as "*pese a tal*" (literally, "may so-and-so regret it") could be considered blasphemous if uttered while looking at the sky.[50] Similarly, bodily gestures that normally belonged to the recurrent repertoire of ridicule and offense, such as giving a "fig" (thumb protruded between clenched index and middle or middle and ring fingers),[51] or biting one's thumb, acquired blasphemous connotations if performed while raising the eyes to heaven.[52]

Spitting, a gesture associated with profound contempt and disdain, was especially significant as constituting a metaphor of contumelious speech, as noted in the second of *Las Siete Partidas* (1256–1263), the Castilian law code of Alfonso X: "Those who revile (*denuestan*) [God and the saints] are similar to those who spit to heaven and receive their spit back in their face."[53] Surely more than the force of gravity was at play here: since the Christian celestial beings could hardly be harmed by the invectives of human aggressors, this bodily excrescence (like all blasphemous speech) came back to haunt its producers. This depiction notwithstanding, spitting seems to have been in reality a "low" gesture, usually accompanied by derogatory speech. In 1565, for instance, Hernando de Rivera was denounced in Mérida for giving his parents' souls and his own to the devil while throwing the cards away and spitting on the ground after looking at the sky with contempt (*airadamente*).[54]

Trivial as it might seem, spitting could have grave consequences if performed on sacred objects. In what constitutes one of the rare cases in which a blasphemer was condemned to lose part of his tongue, Francisco Tijera (or possibly Teixeira) was tried in 1564 for spitting on a painting of a crucifix and uttering "many blasphemies and offenses against God our Lord and His saints." According to his denouncer, Francisco de Ventanilla, Tijera had spent a whole night playing cards with him in Toluca. Having gone to the extreme of wagering and losing his own shirt, a doublet, and a cloak, Tijera

spat with anger at the painting, which hung on one of the walls, also adding "may he who painted you regret it (*pese a quien te pintó*)!" Writing from his prison in March of the same year, Tijera begged for mercy alleging his ignorance of the presence of a crucifix in the room and asserting that he had acted only out of anger and was the son of Christians. The tribunal remained unconvinced. A sailor in the fleet of the king of Portugal, Tijera had spent three years imprisoned in Algiers after his capture by the Turks. Knowing this, the *provisor* (chief ecclesiastical judge of a diocese) of Toluca suspected he had renounced the Christian faith while imprisoned, and even asked Tijera what were the words he said in "Muslim language" (*lengua mora*) the day he spat on the crucifix. Some time later, on March 18, 1564, Tijera was paraded in the streets of Toluca mounted on a donkey with a rope around his neck and naked to the waist while a crier announced his crime. Upon arrival at the public gallows, an executioner administered three hundred lashes to him and cut off part of his tongue.[55]

Casting objects to the ground was another recurrent gesture among gamblers. Although rosaries and medals with the *Agnus Dei* (Lamb of God) were occasionally thrown to the floor, gaming cards were among the first objects to touch the earth in an angry outburst.[56] Denouncers and witnesses usually reported this action to illustrate the anger, frustration, or despair of the blaspheming gamesters. When in 1555 Constable Antonio Márquez cast gaming cards that had a printed cross on one side to the floor, however, he provoked enough indignation among his fellow gamblers to be denounced to the provisor of Oaxaca. In his formal accusation the prosecutor stated that after the game was over Márquez had also cast to the ground other objects which had cruciform shapes such as his staff of office (*vara de justicia*) and his own sword. While he broke his staff in several pieces and later gave it to the devil, he threw his sword to the floor and uttered "let the devil take this sword with its cross included!"[57] Like other gamesters, Márquez performed all these bodily acts in anger, jousting against the supernatural in such a way as to make it difficult for the others to miss them. In the same way that participants of rituals and social dramas created personae by performing before an audience, losing gamblers like Márquez offered an image of strong belligerence by means of irreverent gesticulations and utterances against the supreme divinity. In a sense, it was as though players thought it necessary to assert their personal independence and autonomy precisely when a superior force had just shown that it was an impossible claim to make.

Not all gestures were directed against the Godhead, however; there were also extreme manifestations of despair, frustration, and intense grief over the loss of money. Besides pulling their beards, biting their hands, and crying, gamesters could even undergo fits, contortions, and tantrums that would give them a sinister resemblance to those possessed by the devil. Or at least that is what Matheo Pardo de Soto, priest of the cathedral of Mexico, and fellow minister thought. On a cold November night of 1694, Pardo and his colleague were summoned to a gambling house in Mexico City to see an *endemoniado*, a

person diabolically possessed. When they arrived, they found a furious man lying on the ground making strange faces, writhing, and making violent contortions while he hurled "many blasphemies and *reniegos* (blasphemies)" and called up the demons. The person in question, a destitute individual called Baltasar de los Reyes, had fallen into a trance upon losing everything he had at cards. After the arrival of the priests, he continued in this lamentable state for three solid hours until he was so tired that he fell asleep on the floor. Seeing him sleeping, Pardo and his colleague decided to go to dinner at around 11:00 p.m. and return later. When they came back to the gambling den, they brought with them the book of exorcisms by Remigio (*Remigius*), a container of holy water, a cross, and a stole. They then asked Baltasar to kneel before the Virgin of Dolores to start his act of contrition. He performed the ritual in a proper manner, although he also mixed some unidentified *impertinencias* (offensive words) into his prayers. Reporting on these events five days later, Pardo told the inquisitor that Baltasar had a reputation for going into this kind of trance every time he lost. In his own deposition, however, Baltasar asserted that he had never experienced such a thing before, and only lost his senses because he felt an enormous grief in his heart upon losing. He also stated he had no recollection of what happened, and accepted no responsibility for the words and disorderly gesticulations that took place in the gambling house. Like other individuals possessed by demons, the gambler had experienced corporal automatism manifested by a multiplicity of tantrums and contortions, and had articulated

ON DIVINE PERSECUTION

a blasphemous language of which "other" was seemingly the author.[58]

By the end of the seventeenth century, however, the Holy Office looked with great suspicion on such cases of diabolism. Only two years before Baltasar was heard before the Holy Tribunal, the Mexican Inquisition had dismissed a spectacular case of massive possession in a Querétaro convent by stating that the pretended demoniacs feigned to be possessed "as a mere pretext to blaspheme and to utter heretical remarks, thus causing great and unnecessary scandals."[59] Luckily for Baltasar, the inquisitor merely decided to dismiss his case and forget about the whole matter. His decision was probably somewhat influenced by the fact that Baltasar was very young (twenty-four years old), and declared himself to be profoundly depressed because he had recently lost a child and lived in absolute misery.[60]

Private Homes and Gambling Houses

It is clear that gamesters hardly exhibited the cultivated stoicism of the members of European Renaissance courts, who impassively lost huge amounts so as to not reveal an immoderate and base attachment to money. On the contrary, gambling was a social event in which passions and violence were often triggered and in which quarrels, fighting words, and blasphemies could lead to the intervention of both secular and ecclesiastical authorities. Knowing this, Renaissance writers as disparate as gambling scholar Gerolamo Cardano and philosopher and moralist Juan Luis Vives recommended some guidelines in terms of social intercourse at the moment of gambling. Stressing the importance of carefully choosing place, time, and playing mates, Vives warned his readers against playing in gambling houses and choosing troublemakers as opponents, that is, irascible individuals or scandal-mongers whose presence could easily lead to dreadful tragedies. For his part, Cardano emphasized the relevance of playing with opponents "of suitable station in life," for short periods, for low stakes, in respectable places (such as the house of a friend), and on suitable occasions (as at a holiday banquet).[61]

Although it is not unlikely that some players in New Spain took into consideration several of the caveats expressed by Vives and Cardano before joining others in the games, their recommendations were all seen as ideal conditions, which might not often be met in reality. Surely the best way of preventing quarrels and avoiding drawing the attention of the colonial authorities consisted in playing with people the players knew and trusted and, if possible, at the house of one of the participants. Besides, since gambling for high stakes was illegal in New Spain, only in this way could the necessary secrecy for the unfolding of the games be guaranteed. Playing in private homes also yielded other advantages, such as evading the fees charged by the owners of the gambling houses, the fines for high-stakes gambling, and the bribes to the authorities who occasionally raided the gambling houses. Finally, by gambling at the houses of friends players were not forced to use the more expensive "royal" cards, but could employ decks of cards clandestinely printed or imported from another country. Since it was in their interest to avoid drawing the attention of the authorities, it is unlikely that gamesters were particularly eager to denounce their opponents for blaspheming. In fact, there is evidence that gamesters tried different strategies to avoid blasphemous utterances, for example, exerting some control over possibly risky conversation gambits, reprimanding cursing gamesters, or even establishing a fine for an individual who blasphemed.[62]

Were all these strategies to fail, however, an immediate denunciation did not necessarily ensue, for on many occasions players waited a long time before taking the case to the Inquisition. In the 1536 trial against Angel de Villasaña for blasphemy, for instance, Juan de Alvarado stated in 1536 that Villasaña had renounced God a year before, and that seven or eight years earlier the same defendant said either "*pese a dios*" (God be damned!) or "*no creo en dios*" (I don't believe in God).[63] Similarly, two of the witnesses against Juan de Porras declared in 1536 that the defendant was a "consummate blasphemer," for they had seen him blaspheme every time he played and lost, a candid statement that suggests that they previously heard such statements from the accused, or even shared a gaming table with him, and had decided not to denounce him.[64] Of course, the only reason we know about these cases is that important conflicts took place among the players. Both Villasaña and Porras were tried by bishop fray Juan de Zumárraga as part of a group of gamesters who knew each other for some time and not infrequently sat at the same gaming table. For some unknown reason, however, social disharmony entered the group and triggered multiple denunciations before the tribunal. On a single day—

July 7, 1536—Diego Palma denounced Angel de Villasaña, Juan de Villagómez, and Alonso de Carrión, all of whom, he assured the inquisitor, had the "habit" of blaspheming (*costumbre de blasfemar*). That same day Juan de Alvarado bore witness not only against Angel de Villasaña, but also against Francisco de Maldonado. Hernán Pérez de Carrión also presented himself voluntarily on that date to declare against Angel Villasaña, Juan de Villagómez, and Alonso de Carrión. Finally, Alonso de Carrión was also said to have witnessed Villasaña blaspheme, and Juan de Villagómez was mentioned as a possible witness against Pedro de Sosa.[65]

We do not know what triggered the denunciations of July 7, 1536, but it is possible that many of the accusations had their roots in bitter disputes over money and gambling debts. Given the fact that high-stakes gambling was not legal, gaming debts were not recognized by the state. The economic obligations acquired by the participants at the games, therefore, were predicated only upon the value of their own word. The importance of honoring gaming debts was even emphasized by Christian theologians and critics of gambling, for although gambling was utterly condemned, welshing would only compound, not cancel, the sin.[66] There was always the possibility of avoiding paying up, however, or more strikingly, trying to get one's money back or pawned property returned through the intervention of the Holy Office. For example, in 1557 Juan Mexía was denounced by Bernardo Ortiz for uttering "many words of blasphemy" such as "by God's life." Having gathered what he judged sufficient evidence, the prosecutor drew up an order for Mexía's arrest. While the defendant waited in prison for his trial, his denouncer, Bernardo Ortiz, visited him. According to some prison witnesses, Ortiz asked Mexía to give him back some clothes he had left in pawn. Since Mexía refused to do so unless his denouncer cleared his debt, Ortiz said he would do as much harm as possible to him, in a clear allusion to the accusation he had made before the Inquisition.[67] Similarly, Gonzalo Hernández asserted in one of his trials, that of 1567, that Gonzalo de Arciniega had testified against him because Hernández refused to give him back some things he left in pawn without paying his gambling debt. He also added, however, that several of the other witnesses presented by the prosecutor were his enemies because Hernández himself refused to pay up his own debts when he realized that his opponents were true card sharps. Two years later, Hernández was denounced by a man whom he had slapped in the face and called "thief" for not playing well but *cautelosamente* (cautiously). According to Gonzalo Hernández, the man in question, Rodrigo Calderón, swore he would do his best to provoke the arrest of Gonzalo by the Holy Office, an endeavor in which he clearly succeeded.[68]

Things were much more complicated, of course, if in addition to the quarrels and conflicts between the players the testimony was added to by bystanders or witnesses of all classes, as was usually the case when the games took place at popular gambling houses. In these areas, money circulated not only in the form of bets, but also as *baratos* (gratuities), gambling fees, and bribes. Failure to meet their economic obligations in any of these different forms could provoke important conflicts for the players, but even refusing to give alms to the occasional beggars could represent a source of problems.

On February 8, 1662, for example, Ana Muñoz Vera, a poor woman of thirty-eight years of age, went to beg at a gambling house situated in the street of El Portal de la Acequia in Mexico City. There she found an individual called Jaime Viadel playing cards with other men. Joining a group of female beggars who were already there, Ana asked Viadel for money. The gamester threw half a *real* (one-eighth of a silver peso) to them, but one of the women grabbed the coin claiming that she had been waiting longer than the rest. While Ana waited for another act of generosity, a woman begged Viadel to give her a coin "for the love of the Virgin," but received as alms an irritated response from the player: "Go whore fuck yourself with the Virgin's prick!" Looking perhaps for some revenge but also profoundly scandalized, both Ana and María de la Rua, the other beggar, denounced Viadel to the Inquisition.

The owner of the gambling house, Pedro Fernández de Quiróz, denied that blasphemous utterances were expressed in his establishment although he later admitted that Viadel addressed the beggars, using the word "*puta*" (whore). The prosecutor charged that the gamester was a "vicious man contaminated with heresy" and an order of arrest was issued. After a trial that lasted for several months, Viadel was finally sentenced to hear mass at a public *auto de fe* marked by the usual signs of the blasphemer: gagged, with a rope about his neck, and, most strikingly, with a *green* candle in his hand (a sign that his remarks were found heretical). In addition, being under suspicion of heresy, he was to make the abjuration *de vehementi*.[69] Then he was to be paraded on a beast of burden naked to the waist, while a crier proclaimed his offense and he was scourged by two hundred lashes. Lastly, he was ordered to serve as a galley slave for ten years and be carefully instructed by the priests of the prison in the basics of Christian doctrine.[70]

The case of Viadel was, of course, not isolated. Throughout the colonial period, frequent fights, quarrels, and blasphemies drew the attention of colonial authorities to gambling houses as plebeian places of social disorder and moral corruption, a concern also often voiced by preachers in their homiletic sermons. As late as 1691, the popular Jesuit Juan Martínez de la Parra decried from his pulpit at La Profesa church those "infernal caverns," "caves of dragons," and "homes of demons" that contaminated the inhabitants of New Spain and were "the reason of all sorrows." He severely criticized the owners of gambling houses (*coymes*), for making a living out of the condemnation of their blaspheming clientele.[71]

This moral preoccupation with the decline of customs apparently represented by the practice of gambling acquired more dramatic overtones after a crucial event took place in the public life of colonial Mexico City. On June 8, 1692, a roaring mob formed by Indians, mestizos, and mulattoes rioted against the Spanish government due to a shortage of wheat and corn. The mob set the viceregal palace aflame, burned the *ayuntamiento* (city council) buildings, and sacked

the merchants' shops of the central city while crying, among other things, "Down with the Spaniards and the *gachupines* (Spanish peninsulars), who are eating up our corn!" "Death to the viceroy and his wife!" "Death to the corregidor."[72] As a result of the riot, the disturbed colonial authorities executed nine individuals, ordered nearly thirty public floggings in the space of two and a half weeks, and orchestrated a policy of racial and social segregation that excluded Indians from the center of the city and other areas. "From then on," writes Juan Pedro Viqueira, "the authorities and the elites perceived the dissipated customs of the people as potential seeds of social subversion that needed to be weeded out."[73]

As might be expected, colonial authorities regarded with particular suspicion those places of plebeian subculture such as taverns, markets, *cofradías* (confraternities), and gambling houses that could serve as a breeding ground for rebellious behavior and nests for future threats against the colonial authorities. Thus, after an Indian was robbed and killed in a tablajería, Viceroy Alburquerque ordered the suppression of all gambling houses on June 21, 1707, and canceled all licenses previously given for organizing games of chance. As the angered administrator of the playing card monopoly, Juan Unzueta, pointed out to the king, the decree did not apply to the most important gambling houses, where wealthy people and leading citizens constituted the main clientele. The viceroy had clearly targeted a locus of popular socializing in an effort to enforce order and control over what were deemed to be centers of vice, disorder, and crimes. His successor, the Marqués de Casafuerte, was no less severe and his repressive policy reduced the number of gambling houses in Mexico City from thirty-six to only fourteen.[74]

Although still clearly a criticized activity from the point of view of Christian religion, popular gambling came more and more to be considered a secular danger as well, a ludic practice that led both to the financial ruin of the participants and their families, and to the corrosion of social order and hierarchy. The increasing revenues derived from the sale of cards, however, and the participation of the authorities in the games canceled out in practice the desire to combat the disorders as expressed in the renewed decrees issued against gambling games in 1745, 1768, and 1771. By the end of the eighteenth century, the monopoly of cards was one of the more lucrative fiscal measures of the Spanish crown and gambling, clandestine or not, went on everywhere.

Conclusions

For all their harshness and obsessive preoccupation with order, the social concerns of Bourbon authorities are undoubtedly closer to the modern rhetoric of games as a self-destructive madness and source of social disorder than the religious convictions that informed both the condemnation of gambling games and the production of blasphemous utterances around a gaming table in the Habsburgs' New Spain. Once closely related, games of chance and religion had become in modern times rivals for the promotion of what the scholar of play Brian Sutton-Smith calls "altered states of consciousness," that is, states of mind that make it possible to transcend everyday

cares and concerns and to be "lost" in play.[75] Inveterate gamblers are no longer seen as sinners but as pathological addicts to an activity that allows them little to no control over their winnings, losses, or psyches.[76] In fact, trying to exert some influence upon the outcome of games by means of amulets, prayers, or threats has been now considered by scholars such as Roger Caillois as a "corruption" of the games, for the results should be ruled by an "impersonal neutral power, without heart or memory, a purely mechanical effect. With superstition, the corruption of *alea* (game of hazard) is born."[77]

Yet in the eyes of sixteenth- and seventeenth-century moralists and inquisitors, the real corruption of games started when the legitimate need for relaxation before going back to work was transformed into a way of tempting God in games of "chance," of robbing him of precious time in church by playing on Sundays, of participating in thefts, quarrels, and other crimes to continue gambling and, most importantly, of transmuting the human voice into a diabolical source of contempt, reproach, and blasphemy against God. In his famous essay on Balinese cockfights, Clifford Geertz contrasted money gambling, which he labeled "shallow play," to status gambling, or "deep play." While most gamblers participated in the first kind of play "just for the money," a select group wagered their esteem, honor, dignity, and respect in the cockfights.[78] In New Spain, however, the denial of the possibility of luck or accident frequently transformed playing for money into "deep play," for the believers in Providence could hardly account for a bad outcome in the games without jeopardizing their self-esteem. Since

God's hand was behind each turn of the cards, a bad result could mean either punishment for past offenses or an unjust disregard of the gambler by the supreme divinity. In these conditions, blasphemy constituted not only a cultural tool to express anger and frustration, but also a way of "fighting," if only symbolically, the supreme divinity and His celestial court and momentarily rescuing the self-esteem of the losing players. As the notion of chance registered a renewed and increased expansion as an operative force unrelated to divine power at the beginning of the eighteenth century, however, the relationship between gambling games and providentialism was fatally damaged.[79] It is likely that this shift made the utterance of blasphemous reproaches at the gaming tables less frequent over time. Gambling losses were increasingly attributed to bad luck or even misfortune in the form of the "unknown designs of God," not to cause-and-effect punishments from an angry, whimsical, and persecuting God.

NOTES

This article is based on materials consulted in the following archives: Archivo General de la Nación, México City; Archivo del Arzobispado de México, México City; Archivo General de Indias, Seville; the Bancroft Library; and the Huntington Library. I would like to thank Eric Van Young for commenting on a previous version of this chapter and Connie Dickinson and Stafford Poole for helpful suggestions to improve its quality. I am also grateful to the Huntington Library for a Francis J. Weber Research Fellowship in Roman Catholic History, the University of California Institute for Mexico and the United States (UC MEXUS) for a dissertation grant, CONACYT México, and support from the John Carter Brown Library, the Newberry Library, and the Department of History of the University of California, San Diego.

1. Archivo General de la Nación, México City, Ramo Inquisición (hereafter AGN Inq.), t. 146, exp.4, f. 263–80v.

2. For a discussion of the conflictual relationship between Fortuna and Providencia in fifteenth-century Spain and its theological implications for understanding thorny issues such as predestination and the existence of evil on earth, see Juan de Dios Mendoza Negrillo, *Fortuna y providencia en la literatura castellana del siglo XV* (Madrid: Anejos del boletín de la Real Academia Española, 1973), esp. chaps. 1, 2, and 7. On the idea of Fortune as a concept in conflict with the idea of God's absolute sovereignty, see the classical work of H. R. Patch, *The Goddess Fortuna in Medieval Literature* (Cambridge, MA: Cambridge University Press, 1927).

3. Antonio de Ezcaray, *Vozes del dolor* (Sevilla: Thomas López de Haro, 1691), 348; Jean-Pierre Étienvre, *Márgenes literarios del juego. Una poética del naipe siglos XVI–XVIII* (London: Tamesis Books Limited, 1990), 43. Literally defined as the "well-turning," *eutrapelia* was the Aristotelian virtue of he who "turns" to play or relaxing activities without losing himself in them and with the sole purpose of resting before returning to serious matters. Following Aristotle, Aquinas stressed the importance of relaxation and exercising eutrapelia as "virtue in play." See Aquinas, *Summa* II–II q. 168 art. 2. See also Hugo Rahner, "Eutrapelia: A Forgotten Virtue," in *Holy Laughter: Essays on Religion in the Comic Perspective*, ed. M. Conrad Hyers, 188, 194 (New York: The Seabury Press, 1969); David L. Miller, *Gods and Games: Toward a Theology of Play* (New York: Harper Colophon Books, 1973), 110–11; and Daniel Ménager, *Le Renaissance et le rire* (Paris: PUF, 1995), 87–89.

4. For a discussion of the position of the Catholic church regarding games and entertainment

in the sixteenth century, see Michel Roulos, "Jeux interdits et réglementés" in *Les Jeux à la Renaissance*, ed. Philippe Ariès and Jean-Claude Margolin, 637–43 (Paris: Librairie Philosophique J. Vrin, 1982).

5. Francisco de Alcocer, *Tratado del juego* (Salamanca: Andrea de Portonariis, 1559), 7.

6. Juan de Palafox, *Luz a los vivos y escarmiento en los muertos* (Madrid: María de Quiñónez, 1661), 118. Similarly, Renaissance gambling scholar Gerolamo Cardano was convinced that "a confirmed gambler is a perjurer and a blasphemer," an opinion apparently shared by many at the time. See, Gerolamo Cardano, *Liber de Ludo Aleae*, trans. Sydney Henry Gould, notes by Oysten Ore, in Oysten Ore, *Cardano: The Gambling Scholar* (New Jersey: Princeton, 1953), 195.

7. Francisco Luque Fajardo, *Fiel desengaño contra la ociosidad y los juegos* (Madrid: Miguel Serrano de Vargas, 1603), 142v; Francisco de Alcocer, *Tratado del juego*, 8; Pedro de Covarrubias, *Remedio de jugadores* (Salamanca: Juan de Junta, 1543), 51v; Antonio de Ezcaray, *Vozes del dolor*, 343–45. This satanic image was first advanced by Bernardino de Siena in 1423 in his *Sermo LXII: De alearum ludo*, chap. 2 (Venecia: Giunta, 1596), quoted in Jean-Pierrre Étienvre, *Márgenes literarios del juego*, 314.

8. *Commentary on Matthew*, Homily 6.6, cited in Hugo Rahner, *Man at Play*, trans. B. Battershaw and E. Quinn, 98 (New York: Harper and Row, 1968); Bernardin of Siena, *Opera omnia* (Florence: Quaracchi, 1950), vol. II, 20–34, cited in Robert Sauzet, "La Réforme, le magistrat et le jeu à Strasbourg au xviè siècle," in *Les jeux à la Renaissance*, ed. Philippe Ariès and Jean-Claude Margolin, 651.

9. Francisco Luque Fajardo, *Fiel desengaño*, 147.

10. See Nicolás de Avila, *Suma de los mandamientos, y maremagnum del segundo* (Alcalá: Juan Gracián, 1610), 458.

11. Francisco de Alcocer, *Tratado*, 8–9.

12. F. Luque Fajardo, *Fiel desengaño*, t. II, 142–43; see also Jean-Pierre Etienvre, "Le symbolisme de la carte à jouer dans l'Espagne des XVIe et XVIIe siècles," in *Les jeux à la renaissance*, 435–36; and Joan Corominas, *Breve diccionario etimológico de la lengua castellana*, 3rd rev. ed.

(Madrid: Gredos, 1996 [1961]), 84. Jean-Pierre Etienvre further discusses the metaphor of the deck of cards as a book in *Márgenes literarios*, 100–104, 322–26.

13. Étienvre, "Le symbolisme," 433–34. The idea of a satanic origin of cards was widely extended in early modern Europe. See Pietro Aretino, *Le carte parlanti* (Palermo: Sellerio, 1992 [1543]), 39. In seventeenth-century Tuscany a Father Giovanni Dragoni was convinced that card games were inventions of the devil; see Carlo M. Cipolla, *Faith, Reason, and the Plague in Seventeenth-Century Tuscany*, trans. Muriel Kittel, 17 (New York: Norton, 1979). Similarly, cards were referred to as "the devil's picture book" in Protestant countries. See David Parlett, *The Oxford Guide to Card Games* (Oxford and New York: Oxford University Press, 1990), 11.

14. Blasphemy could indeed assume a carnivalized form of prayer at the games. See for instance the case of Gaspar de Zalaya (Mexico City), who was denounced to the Holy Office in 1573 for uttering "blessed is God's prick (*carajo*) for I won the game!" Archive of the Archbishopric of Mexico, box 1, exp. 8, unfoliated. Maureen Flynn raises a similar point in her "Blasphemy and the Play of Anger in Sixteenth-Century Spain," *Past and Present* 149 (1995): 29–56.

15. Pedro de Covarrubias, *Remedio de jugadores*, xxxvi–xxxvii.

16. See "Gobernación espiritual y temporal de las Indias," numbers 22 to 26, in *Colección de Documentos Inéditos de Ultramar* (Madrid: Imprenta de Archivos, 1928), vol. XXI, 105; see also *Recopilación de leyes de los reynos de las Indias*, 4 vols. Facsimile of 1681 original edition, (Madrid, 1979), book VIII, title ii, laws 1. Among the games listed as unlawful in the pragmática of 1771 were those called banca, faraón, baceta, quince, carteta, banca fallida, sacanete, parar, treinta y cuarenta, flor, and many others. See Angel López Cantos, *Juegos, fiestas y diversiones en la América española* (Madrid: MAPFRE, 1992), 272–73.

17. Archivo General de Indias, Indiferente, 415, book 2, f. 3; Luis Weckman, *The Medieval Heritage of Mexico*, trans. Frances M. López-Morillas, 128–29 (New York: Fordham University Press, 1992); Arthur Scott Aiton, *Antonio de Mendoza. First Viceroy of New*

Spain (Durham, NC: Duke University Press, 1927), 100. In ordering the closure of the gambling houses as a preventive measure, Mendoza probably followed the precedent established by King Alphonse X when he decided to put an end to the "immorality" accompanying the games by closing the *tafurerías*, or gambling houses in 1314. See *Los códigos españoles concordados y anotados*, vol. VI (Madrid: Imprenta de la Publicidad, 1849), 236.

18. See *Documentos cortesianos I*, ed. José Luis Martínez, 49 (México: UNAM/FCE, 1990).

19. Manuel Orozco y Berra, *Historia antigua de la conquista de México*, 4 vols. (México, DF: FCE, 1978), vol. 4, 296.

20. See *Documentos cortesianos II*, ed. José Luis Martínez, 37, 116, 174 (México, DF: UNAM/FCE, 1991). See also Angel López Cantos, *Juegos, fiestas y diversiones en la América española*, 292.

21. John L. Phelan, *The Kingdom of Quito in the Seventeenth Century: Bureaucratic Politics in the Spanish Empire* (Madison: University of Wisconsin Press, 1967), 163.

22. R. Douglas Cope, *The Limits of Racial Domination: Plebeian Society in Colonial Mexico City, 1660–1720* (Madison: University of Wisconsin Press, 1994), 41.

23. Jerónimo Castillo de Bobadilla, *Política para corregidores y señores de vassallos* (Amberes: 1704 [1597]), vol. I, 377, quoted in Jean-Pierre Étienvre, *Márgenes literarios del juego*, 43.

24. Antonio de Ezcaray, *Vozes del dolor*, 346–48.

25. See *Recopilación*, book II, title xvi, laws 74 and 75; book vii, title ii, laws 1–3; Félix Zubillaga, *Historia de la iglesia en la América Española* (Madrid: Editorial Católica, 1965), vol. I, 383; Francisco Antonio de Lorenzana, *Concilios provinciales primero, y segundo, celebrados, en la muy noble, y muy leal ciudad de México* (México, 1769), 117–18. As late as 1703, the chief ecclesiastical judge or *provisor* of Mexico City issued a new edict forbidding clerics to assist gambling houses or cockfights on pain of excommunication. See Antonio de Robles, *Diario de sucesos notables (1665–1703)* (México: Porrúa, 1946), vol. III, 256.

26. *Colección de Documentos Inéditos relativos al descubrimiento, conquista y organización de las antiguas posesiones de ultramar*,

25 vols. (Madrid: Sucesores de Rivadeneyra, 1885–1932), vol. 10, 396.

27. María Angeles Cuello Martinell, *La renta de los naipes en Nueva España* (Sevilla: Escuela de estudios hispano-americanos, 1966), 9, 15, 18, 26; Bartolomé Benassar, *The Spanish Character*, trans. Benjamin Keen, 165–66 (Berkeley and Los Angeles: University of California Press, 1979); María Antonia Colomar, "El juego de naipes en Hispanoamérica. Las pruebas y muestra de naipes conservados en el Archivo General de Indias," *Buenavista de Indias*, no. 7: 55–87 (Madrid: Ediciones Aldoba, 1992).

28. Luis Weckman, *The Medieval*, 129; López Cantos, *Juegos, fiestas*, 312. A good example of the discriminatory attitude against female players was offered by bishop Palafox who stated that, in playing at cards, women could lose not only precious time and money, but also their own *honra*. See his *Luz a los vivos*, 28. As late as 1625, Thomas Gage wrote that in México City women were passionate gamblers. See his *Nuevo reconocimiento de las islas occidentales* (México: SEP-FCE, 1982), 179–80. In eighteenth-century Chihuahua, authorities were convinced that "loose" women were responsible for men's transgressions and thus prevented women from mixing with men at gambling establishments not only because "women might be corrupted by such entertainment but because their presence might lead to disorder." See Cheryl E. Martin, *Governance and Society in Colonial Mexico: Chihuahua in the Eighteenth Century* (Stanford, CA: Stanford University Press, 1996), 151–52.

29. William A. Christian Jr., *Local Religion in Sixteenth-Century Spain* (Princeton, NJ: Princeton University Press, 1981), 47. Keith Thomas, *Religion and the Decline of Magic* (New York: Charles Scribner's Sons, 1971), 120–22.

30. See for instance Leviticus 16:8; Numbers 26:52–56; 1 Sam. 10:17; Neh. 11:1; and 1 Chron. 24:5. For similar examples in the New Testament, see Luke 1:9 and Acts 1:26.

31. Pedro Ciruelo, *Tratado de las supersticiones*, facsimile edition, 1628 (México: Universidad Autónoma de Puebla, 1986), 50–51. Ciruelos's distinction between the different kinds of *suertes* is based on Aquinas. See *The Summa Theologica*, trans. the Fathers of the English

Dominican Province (1920), II–II, q. 95, art. 8; Keith Thomas, *Religion and the Decline of Magic*, 121; see also Jean Céard, "Jeu et divination à la Renaissance," in *Les Jeux à la Renaissance*, 408–9. This providentialism was also widespread among Protestant countries; see Alexandra Walsham, *Providence in Early Modern England* (New York: Oxford University Press, 1999), 21–22.

32. AGN Inq., 14.10, f. 98–101.

33. AGN Inq., 1.10f, f. 82.

34. AGN Inq., 14.3, f. 65–69.

35. AGN Inq., 14.2bis, f. 60–74.

36. AGN Inq., 514.18, f. 105–50.

37. For Juan Baeza, see AGN Inq., 14.46, unfoliated; the denunciation against Diego Moreno is included in the trial that followed against Hernando Botello in the mines of Huachinango, see AGN Inq., 21.5, f. 302–37v.

38. AGN Inq., 3.5a, unfoliated. In an interesting inversion of these relations of reciprocity, moralists also referred to blasphemy as the *barato del diablo*, thus intimating that gamesters blasphemed in order to secure satan's help to win the games. See Lucas de Santo Thomas, *Excelencias del nombre de Jesús y su cofradía contra juradores, blasfemos y maldicientes* (Madrid: Diego Martínez Abad, 1696), 30. On the practice of giving *el barato* as a talisman in the games, see Andrés López Cantos, *Juegos, fiestas, y diversiones*, 274–76.

39. A popular card game in which players bet that their chosen card will be drawn from the deck before that of their opponent.

40. AGN Inq., 560.6, f. 146–191v.

41. Catherine Bates, *Play in a Godless World* (London: Open Gate Press, 1999), 7. See also Brian Sutton-Smith, *The Ambiguity of Play* (Cambridge, MA: Harvard University Press, 1997), 54–55, who reminds us that Erik Erikson was the first to advance a theory of play as "an illusion of mastery over life's circumstances."

42. AGN Inq., 45.9, f. 149–96.

43. Bancroft Library, MSS 72/57m, Box 1, File 7, unfoliated.

44. Like Yrregui, many other gamblers expressed a feeling of betrayal and deep injustice after losing in the games. For instance, an angered Pedro Correa asked in 1666 in the mines of Sombrerete, Zacatecas, after losing an albur, "Does God ignore perchance that I deserve this money [*hacienda*] much more than these cuckolds to whom He has just given it?" Huntington Library HM35131, vol. 37, Part II, unfoliated.

45. Pedro Covarrubias, *Remedio*, xlix. The notion that games are a privileged occasion in which the real self of the player is disclosed was also advanced by Aquinas in his *Commentary to Aristotle's Ethic IV*, 16, 4. See L. Jean Lauand, "Ludus in the Fundamentals of Aquinas's World-View," trans. Alfredo H. Alves, *International Studies on Laws and Education* 2 (Sao Paulo, Brazil, 1999).

46. On gestures as "expression" of the soul's movements, see Jean-Claude Schmitt, *La raison des gestes* (Paris: Gallimard, 1990), 25–26, and Keith Thomas, "Introduction," in *A Cultural History of Gestures*, ed. Jan Bremmer and Herman Roodenburg, 8–9 (Ithaca, NY: Cornell University Press, 1991). On Spanish gravity as the European ideal of bodily control during the Counter Reformation, see Peter Burke, "The Language of Gesture in Early Modern Italy," in his *Varieties of Cultural History* (Ithaca, NY: Cornell University Press, 1997), 72–73; see also Anthony Cascardis, "The Subject of Control," in *Culture and Control in Counter-Reformation Spain*, ed. Anne J. Cruz and Mary Elizabeth Perry, 231–54 (Minneapolis: University of Minnesota Press, 1992). For the Roman roots of the idea of gravity (gravitas) as masculine exceptional self-control, see Carlin Barton, "All Things Beseem the Victor; Paradoxes of Masculinity in Early Imperial Rome," in *Gender Rhetorics: Postures of Dominance and Submission in History*, ed. Richard C. Trexler, 86–87 (New York: State University of New York at Binghampton, 1994). For Pedro de Covarrubias's remark, see his *Remedio de jugadores*, li verso.

47. See Sonya Lipsett-Rivera, chapter 4 of this volume.

48. See for example Betty J. Bäuml and Franz H. Bäuml, *A Dictionary of Gestures* (Metuchen, NJ: The Scarecrow Press, 1975).

49. See Jean-Claude Schmitt, ed., "Gestures," *History and Anthropology* 1, no. 1 (1984): 1–2; Jacques Le Goff, "Los gestos del purgatorio," in *Lo maravilloso y lo cotidiano en el occidente*

medieval, trans. Alberto L. Bixio, 50 (Barcelona: Gedisa, 1986); see also, Jacques Le Goff, "Los gestos de San Luis. Enfoque de un modelo y de una personalidad," in *Lo maravilloso*, 52. For a fine discussion of the religious and political implications of the antinomy high/low at the time, see Carlo Ginzburg, "High and Low: The Theme of Forbidden Knowledge in the Sixteenth and Seventeenth Centuries," *Past and Present* 73 (1976): 28–42. The religious significance of right and left is discussed in the classical essay by Robert Hertz, "La prééminence de la main droite. Etude sur la polarité religieuse," in *Sociologie religieuse et folklore* (Paris: PUF, 1970), 84–109.

50. Nicolás de Avila, *Suma de los mandamientos*, 489–90. A good example of the indexical character of looking at the sky was offered in 1536 by gamester Alonso Carrión, who used to utter "all kinds of blasphemies" at the games, and also added raising his eyes to the ceiling "I know very well Who I am talking to" (AGN Inq., 14.3, f. 67).

51. Melchor Cano mentions the fig as a gesture of anger in his "Tratado de la victoria de sí mismo," *Biblioteca de Autores Españoles* (BAE), vol. LXV (Madrid: Imprenta de los sucesores de Hernando), 310. Origins and extended use of the fig among Spaniards are discussed in Rodrigo Caro, *Días geniales o lúdicos*, ed. Jean-Pierre Etienvre, vol. II, 104, 233–34 (Madrid: Espasa-Calpe, 1978), and Francisco del Rosal, *La razón de algunos refranes*, introduction and ed. B. Russell Thomson, 136 (London: Tamesis Books, 1975); Pedro Covarrubias registers the use of this gesture against Godhead in his *Remedio*, lv verso.

52. See the case of Gaspar de los Reyes in Mexico City (1572) in AGN Inq., 52.1, f. 36v–37r. Biting one's thumb and giving a fig were gestures usually attributed to Jews in canvases and retables dealing with Christ's passion; see plates IX and X, in Jean-Claude Schmitt, *La raison*, 42–43.

53. *Las Siete Partidas del Rey Don Alfonso el Sabio*, partida ii, título 4, ley 4, quoted in Sebastián de Horozco, *El libro de los proverbios glosados*, 2 vols, ed. Jack Weiner, vol. I, 257 (Kasel: Reicherberger, 1994).

54. AGN Inq., 5.12, f. 292–95v.

55. AGN Inq., 18.8, f. 45–72.

56. Juan de Vargas threw an agnus dei after losing the huge amount of 2,000 gold pesos on October 3, 1607. See AGN Inq., 467.59, f. 272–73.

57. AGN Inq., 15.3, f. 8–18.

58. For a rich analysis of the discourse of possession as "a language without a subject," see the interesting remarks of Michel de Certeau in his *La possession de Loudun* (Paris: Gallimard/Juillard, 1980), chapter three, esp. 63–69. The relation between "automatism" and blasphemy in medieval culture is discussed in Carla Casagrande and Silvana Vecchio, *Les péchés de la langue*, preface by Jacques Le Goff, trans. Phillippe Baillet, 177–78 (Paris: CERF, 1991). Jean-Claude Schmitt analyzes demonic possession as an extreme case of complete loss of mastery over bodily gestures in the Middle Ages; see *La raison*, 127–28. For an excellent recent discussion of the ambivalence of reception of gestures of possession in Medieval Europe when it came to discerning the nature (divine or demonic) of the invading spirit, see Nancy Caciola, "Mystics, Demoniacs, and the Physiology of Spirit Possession in Medieval Europe," *Comparative Studies of Society and History* 42, no. 3 (July 2000): 268–306.

59. Fernando Cervantes, *The Devil in New Spain* (New Haven and London: Yale University Press, 1994), 123.

60. AGN Inq., 520.25, f. 402–14v.

61. Juan Luis Vives, "Diálogo XX: El juego de naipes" (1538), and "Diálogo XXI: Las leyes del juego," in his *Obras completas*, trans. Lorenzo Riber, vol. II, 952–53 and 957–61, respectively (Madrid: Aguilar, 1948); Gerolamo Cardano, *Liber de Ludo Aleae*, in Oysten Ore, *Cardano*, 187.

62. For a case in which conversation gambits were controlled by asking a gamester to deal with issues "que fuesen de los tejados para abajo," a phrase that restricted their conversation to the sublunar world, see AGN Inq., 18.8, f. 97–104; for an example of fines established by the players themselves, see AGN Inq., 14.5, f. 75–81.

63. AGN Inq., 14.5, f. 75–81.

64. AGN Inq., 14.2bis, f. 60–74.

65. AGN Inq., 14.5, f. 75–81; AGN Inq., 14.4, f. 70–74; AGN Inq., 14.3, f. 65–69; AGN Inq., 14.10, f. 98–101.

ON DIVINE PERSECUTION

66. On welshing, see T. Slater, "Betting," in *The Catholic Encyclopedia*, vol. VI (New York: Robert Appleton Co., 1909). Catherine Bates offers interesting insights on "paying up" gambling debts in her *Play in a Godless World*, 2–3; for a discussion of gambling and self-fashioning among Renaissance courtesans, see Thomas M. Kavanagh, *Enlightenment and the Shadows of Chance* (Baltimore, MD: John Hopkins University Press, 1993), 42.

67. AGN Inq., 17.12, f. 258.

68. AGN Inq., 45.18, f. 233–314; AGN Inq., 45.19, f. 233–314.

69. The Holy Office ordered those who were penanced to abjure of their crimes in two forms: *de levi*, for minor offenses, and *de vehementi*, for serious ones.

70. AGN Inq., 591.4, f. 437–95v.

71. Juan Martínez de la Parra, *Luz de verdades catholicas, segunda parte* (Madrid: Diego Fernández de León, 1692), 159, 170. Following his advice, the crown banned cockfights. See Juan Pedro Viqueira Albán, *Propriety and Permissiveness in Bourbon Mexico*, trans. Sonya Lipsett-Rivera and Sergio Rivera Ayala, 6 (Wilmington, DE: Scholarly Resources, 1999).

72. For a thorough analysis of this famous riot, see Douglas R. Cope, *The Limits of Racial Domination: Plebeian Society in Colonial Mexico City, 1660–1720* (Madison: University of Wisconsin Press, 1994), 125–60.

73. Juan Pedro Viqueira Albán, *Propriety*, 9.

74. María Angeles Cuello Martinell, *La renta*, 57–58, 63, 68.

75. Brian Sutton-Smith, *The Ambiguity of Play* (Cambridge, MA: Harvard University Press, 1997), 67. The ancient relationship between play and religion (or play and the sacred) was pointed out long ago by Johan Huizinga, who in his *Homo Ludens: A Study of the Play-Element in Culture* (Boston: Beacon Press, 1950) traced the origins of play to the idea of the sacred in primitive religions, see 18–24. Unfortunately, since he was profoundly convinced that playing for money was a corruption of play—which Huizinga defined as an activity deprived of economic interest—the Dutch historian did not explore the relationship between gambling and the sacred.

76. See for example the classic study by Edmund Bergler, *The Psychology of Gambling* (New York: Hill and Wang, 1957), who was convinced that gamblers were regressed neurotics who engaged in the games with the purpose of losing and thus obtaining a masochist gratification. See 30–31. For a recent update in the same vein, see also Bettina L. Knapp, *Gambling, Game, and Psyche* (Albany: State University of New York Press, 2000), 9.

77. Roger Caillois, *Man, Play, and Games*, trans. Meyer Barash, 46 (New York: The Free Press of Glencoe, 1961).

78. Clifford Geertz, "Deep Play: Notes on the Balinese Cockfight," in his *The Interpretation of Cultures* (New York: Basic Books, 1973), 433–35.

79. This important shift in Christian religion has been described by Keith Thomas, *The Decline*, 120.

PART SIX

MUSIC AND MARTYRDOM
ON THE NORTHERN FRONTIER

They [the Franciscan friars] made for them in their own Anahuac language metrical versions of the commandments, the articles of faith, and the sacraments, also set to music. The Indians sing them even today in many parts of New Spain.

—fray Toribio Motolinia, d. 1568

The priests have gone to great efforts to introduce ecclesiastical music. Accordingly, in the pueblos on these first rivers there are church choirs that can compete with those in the great and civilized pueblos in and around Mexico City.... Today these schools where singing is taught serve purposes other than training singers. They are also where the students are instilled with the most important civilized and proper customs.

—Andrés Pérez de Ribas, 1645

We traveled through much land and we found all of it deserted, because the inhabitants of it went fleeing through the sierras without daring to keep houses or work the land for fear of the Christians. It was a thing that gave us great sorrow, seeing the land very fertile and very beautiful and very full of waterways and rivers, and seeing the places deserted and burned and the people so emaciated and sick, all of them having fled and in hiding.

—Alvar Núñez Cabeza de Vaca, 1542

But the peoples we are discussing here are truly fierce, and although they are human beings, some nevertheless murdered other human beings for no other reason than to feed on their flesh and to hold dances and barbarous celebrations.

—Andrés Pérez de Ribas, 1645

There should be no doubt that our missionaries, who have the good fortune of dying at the hands of barbarians while preaching the word of God, die out of obedience to the Supreme Pontiff and to God in him.

—Andrés Pérez de Ribas, 1645

Mexico City was the heart of New Spain and thus the center of all political, economic, social, and religious activity. For this reason, most clergy lived in the metropolis. However, Mexico City was also a launching point for people moving out beyond its borders and into new territories. The discovery of silver in Zacatecas in the 1540s was additional incentive for pressing north, though the region lacked the large settled populations of native peoples to furnish the requisite labor. The silver mines prompted the settling of towns, which then had streams of people moving in or passing through in search of new mines or a way of making a living.

Although the north was generally sparsely inhabited, the terrain was well known to the peoples who lived there. Wary and hostile after suffering the ravages and enslavement of Nuño de Guzmán and waves of epidemic diseases in the 1530s, these peoples saw their territory invaded by a force of Spaniards and thousands of native allies led by New Spain's Viceroy don Antonio de Mendoza to quell all other resistance. Nahuatl-speaking Indians from the central valley soon began to move into the frontier and set up model colonies, intending by their good example to draw the rebellious natives into or at least near their communities.

Franciscan and Jesuit religious were often in the vanguard of the move north, making overtures of peace and Christianity to the heathen and setting up mission outposts. They traversed the countryside, spreading the Gospel as they went. In the early years of the mission enterprises, the religious had learned the natives' languages, or brought guides and interpreters along to facilitate their preaching. The Jesuits, in particular, were exemplars in their linguistic erudition. The crown, for better or for worse, also provided for presidios to be established in the same regions, reportedly to protect the missions and wagon trains against marauding Indians.

The Franciscans took up the charge of evangelizing the native peoples in the central region and as far north as Santa Fe, New Mexico. The Jesuits worked with the natives of the northwest. Once established, the priests enlisted their charges to build churches and outfit them with the necessary ornaments. They also began to inculcate local peoples with Catholic practices—the meaning of the liturgical calendar, the sacraments, holy images, prayer, processions, and the like. Church music had great appeal, for the natives already enjoyed ceremonial singing, dancing, and instrumental performance. They had their own percussion and wind instruments which were adapted to ecclesiastical scores. The Indians subsequently learned to make and play a great variety of string and brass instruments and singing and organ playing became their specialties. Numerous other aspects of native religious pageantry were suited to Catholic ritual ceremony; thus it was not uncommon for any number of neophytes to attend church functions on a regular basis.

Kristin Dutcher Mann, in "*Opus Dei—*'The Work of God': Franciscan and Jesuit Music," writes of the good deeds of religious on the northern frontier. But her interest is in music and how missionaries used it in its many forms to evangelize and maintain social control. Mann finds that, although music was already very much a part of the indigenous world and European church music was widely and readily accepted by native peoples, music could also be the basis for the construction of individual and communal religious identity.

In spite of the missionaries' best intentions, though, indigenous traditional culture was increasingly compromised and the priests and newcomer Spaniards were in constant need of labor. When the loss outweighed the gain, the Indians rebelled and frequently raged against the missions, killing the priests. Maureen Ahern, in "Martyrs and Idols: Performing Ritual Warfare on Early Missionary Frontiers in the Northwest," focuses on the Jesuits and their experiences. Tentative, yet determined, the Jesuits had reformed communities and built churches as they moved north. Expecting compliance, even gratitude from the converts, they did not perceive the irreparable harm that was being done to the natives' way of life. As a result, the priests were mocked and, worse, killed, and churches and sacred images were desecrated. Ahern relates how, extraordinarily, both the religious and the natives came to use martyrdom to suit their own purposes.

NOTES

Epigraph citations, in order of appearance, are as follows: fray Toribio Motolinia, *History of the Indians of New Spain*, trans. Elizabeth Andros Foster (Westport, CT: Greenwood Press, 1977), 190; Andrés Pérez de Ribas, *History of the Triumphs of Our Holy Faith Amongst the Most Barbarous and Fierce Peoples of the New World (1645)*, ed. and trans. Daniel T. Reff, Maureen Ahern, and Richard K. Danforth, 440–41 (Tucson: University of Arizona Press, 1999); Alvar Núñez Cabeza de Vaca, *His Account, His Life, and the Expedition of Pánfilo Narváez*, vol. 1, ed. and trans. Rolena Adorno and Patrick Charles Pautz, 239 (Lincoln: University of Nebraska Press, 1999); Pérez de Ribas, *History of the Triumphs of our Holy Faith*, 193.

CHAPTER THIRTEEN

Opus Dei—"The Work of God"

Franciscan and Jesuit Music

KRISTIN DUTCHER MANN

As trumpets blared and drums rolled, banners bearing the sign of the king and the cross rippled in the breeze. Hernando Cortés announced to the gathered assembly that he would undertake a voyage to the newly discovered lands to conquer and settle them in the name of his Majesty.[1] Weeks later, the volunteers gathered before their vessels, chanted mass, and sailed for the land that would be called New Spain. Music, then, was linked to colonialism before the conquest of the indigenous peoples of Mexico was even underway. Before boarding ships or beginning a march, the entire company heard and participated in mass.[2] Territory was claimed by the Spaniards through a combination of military victories and ritual acts such as processions, chanting mass, and erecting altars or crosses. Bernal Díaz del Castillo reports that on Easter Sunday,

1519, fray Bartolomé de Olmedo, "who was a fine singer, chanted mass with the assistance of Padre Juan Díaz, while the two governors and the other caciques who were with them looked on."[3] The meal and a ritual gift exchange were further rites of possession practiced by the Spaniards in their conquest of new territory.[4]

Although mass was said or sung by a member of the regular clergy, the soldiers also participated in the liturgy, including vespers, in their encampments. Díaz perhaps overstates the piety of the soldiers when he writes, "It was the hour of Ave Maria, and at the sound of the camp bell we all fell on our knees, in front of a cross which we had erected on a sand hill, to say our prayers,"[5] but the rituals of Catholicism were embedded in the Spanish culture of conquest. Later, as the Spanish conquistadors moved north into the deserts and mountains and south into the highlands, music continued to be a part of the ritual actions of conquest and colonization.

As the early expeditions gave way to congregations of indigenous groups in pueblos and missions, music continued to be present in the daily routines of the missionaries. Indian children were taught to read, write, and sing, and the catechism was more easily learned when set to music. Schools were established by the missionary orders to educate indigenous children and aid in the conversion process among the larger population. Music was an important component of this education from the first efforts of Franciscan fray Pedro de Gante and its use was endorsed by royal officials. In 1573, a decree directed authorities in New Spain to use singers, instruments, and music to soothe, pacify, and influence indigenous peoples who otherwise would not peacefully accept Catholicism and Spanish authority.[6] Conquest was undertaken not only by the sword, but also through ritual speech, such as the *Requerimiento*, and through the ritual actions of the liturgy.

Music, then, was an integral, royally sanctioned part of the spiritual and cultural conquests of the native population of Mexico. But what type of musical training equipped the missionaries, what music did they employ, and in what contexts was it used? This chapter is part of a larger project in which I examine sacred music in the missions of northern New Spain as not only an evangelization tool, but as an instrument of colonialism embedded in power relations between the conquerors and conquered.[7] The Jesuits and Franciscans who worked in the northern frontier employed music as a teaching tool, but it also served to establish and preserve order and social relations. Music was a way that indigenous communities could continue to shape their cultural and religious practices, and it played a role in ethnogenesis—the continual recreation of group identity. Both missionaries and Indians came to mission communities with sacred musical traditions from their cultural backgrounds. The cultural confrontations of these encounters produced new forms of sacred music and dance.

The Place of Music in the Construction of Religious Identity

For Franciscan and Jesuit missionaries of the sixteenth and seventeenth centuries, Catholicism and membership in religious orders involved not only sets of beliefs and practices, but also social and cultural processes that restructured their daily lives. Music was a catalyst in the formation of religious identity, not only in the public sphere of evangelization and teaching, but also in the private sphere of daily devotions and prayer.

Sixteenth- and seventeenth-century Catholic religious identity was constructed within the context of the Counter Reformation. The Protestant Reformation and the Catholic Counter Reformation brought about changes in response to a dramatic expansion in the body of sacred music in the late Renaissance period. Martin Luther's complaints against liturgical music were that the liturgy was too vast and complicated and that it was sung in Latin, an elite language that was not meaningful to a majority of the population. He promoted the use of chorales and hymns in the vernacular

OPUS DEI—"THE WORK OF GOD"

instead of the sung mass and canonical hours. The Catholic church responded with the reforms of the Council of Trent. Both Franciscans and Jesuits were affected by the Tridentine musical legislation. These decrees stated that clergy must be trained in ecclesiastical song. The Gregorian chant melodies were preferred, as were the simple polyphonic works of composers like Giovanni di Palestrina. Musical excesses, such as inserted organ compositions, tropes containing excess words not found in the mass, and elaborate polyphony, were prohibited. These ornamentations were seen as detrimental to a congregation's ability to understand the meaning of the mass. In all, the Counter Reformation signaled a return to simplicity and religious conformity in the liturgy. These themes became part of the foundation upon which Catholic identity was constructed in the sixteenth century.

The Society of Jesus was founded against the backdrop of the Counter Reformation. Jesuits differed from other monastic and mendicant orders because of their apostolic focus, a fervent concern with saving souls. When writing the constitution of the Society of Jesus, Ignatius of Loyola struggled with the place of music in the new order:

> If I were to follow my taste and inclination, I would put choir and singing in the Society; but I do not do it because God our Lord has given me to understand that it is not his will—nor does he wish to be served by us in choir, but in other matters of his service.[8]

Thus the original ministries of the Society of Jesus did not include communal singing of the office or mass. Although music was not an official part of Jesuit practice, it was tied closely to the spirituality of many of the early Jesuits, who continued to chant and sing hymns as part of their daily routines. Jesuit superiors throughout Europe encouraged Ignatius to reconsider his restrictions on music. They feared the effectiveness of the Jesuit evangelization efforts would deteriorate because of Jesuit policy on the issue of music in worship.[9] In practice, despite the restrictions of the constitutions, music formed an important part of Jesuit devotions, particularly on special occasions, when vespers and the litany of Mary were commonly sung. Religious processions involved music, and Marian congregations sang hymns and produced religious dramas to honor the Virgin. Music was also an important part of the general curriculum of Jesuit colleges in Europe and in the missionary field.

The Franciscans, on the other hand, were governed by rules that stressed *Opus Dei*, the work of God, or the praying of the divine office, as one of their ministries, along with preaching and missionary work. St. Francis was not liturgically minded like other religious of his time, and the order at first did not have a rule that required choral duties.[10] After St. Francis's death, the friars became more attached to a monastic lifestyle at his shrine in Assisi.[11] At this time, they began to recite the divine office together, although they continued to travel extensively and perform missionary work within their home communities. The Franciscan breviary came into use as the Franciscan order spread throughout Europe. This style of liturgy could be

KRISTIN DUTCHER MANN

adapted for use in choir or by traveling friars, but it was different from that used by the monastic orders, stripped of excess, and better suited for missionaries with other important work besides Opus Dei.[12]

Franciscans in New Spain also recited or sang mass and the divine office at their *conventos* while they evangelized. Occasionally music was more elaborate and additional singers were enlisted. In the 1530s, for example, six unpaid Indians served as *cantores*, singers who assisted with the daily office and masses, at the Franciscan convento in San Luis Obispo.[13] As Franciscans experienced the power of music as an evangelization tool, musical accompaniment became much more elaborate, involving both singers and instrumentalists. The convento at Veracruz was praised for its musicians and instruments by Comisario General fray Juan Fogueras. He was impressed by the choir that sang the divine offices as well as the organ used to accompany hymns.[14]

Music, Education, and Evangelization

Franciscans were involved with education from the first century of their founding. Each provincial chapter ran a school for boys, and many provided an advanced school for promising students to continue their education and progress to the university level. While education had previously been offered only to children of the upper classes, Franciscan schools began to emphasize basic education for a larger population.[15] An emphasis on the popular spread of religion can be also seen in the composition of *laude spirituali*, for which the Franciscans were known. Used throughout Europe and in worldwide missionary efforts, the laude

were simple religious songs in the vernacular that gained enormous popularity and were sung by confraternities of lay people in towns. These songs were based on the "worldly and amorous" songs commonly sung in the villages.[16] The practice of Christianizing popular secular songs became common in the church throughout Europe, as *chansons* (French secular polyphonic songs) were used as the bases for simple polyphony during the late Renaissance period. When Franciscans established schools in their foreign missions, they also used this technique. It was a way of blending acceptable elements of culture with new Christian teachings to help in conversion efforts.

Early Work in Mexico

Fray Pedro de Gante was among three Franciscans who arrived in Mexico in 1523 charged with the task of converting the native population to Catholicism. He was a native of Ghent, an area known for its production of illustrious musicians. Pedro de Gante founded a school at Tetzcoco before moving to Mexico City and establishing the school at the convento de San Francisco, where he taught music along with Franciscans Arnaldo de Bassacio and Juan Caro. He learned the Nahuatl language and used music in his teaching. At the school, students studied reading, writing, and singing in the mornings and Christian doctrine in the afternoons. They participated in religious celebrations and chanted the office daily.[17] Soon fray Pedro's students became renowned for their proficiency in music and Christian devotion. He wrote to King Charles V in 1532 to praise his indigenous students:

There are already Indians here who are very capable of writing, and teaching, or preaching . . . I can attest that there are now trained singers among them who could sing in Your Majesty's Chapel so well that you might have to see them actually singing in order to believe it possible.[18]

Fray Pedro de Gante also encouraged the spread of Catholic rituals among the Indians by drawing on their talents in painting and dance. Like many missionaries who followed him, he encouraged dancing and singing of Christian hymns on special occasions, such as Holy Week, saints' feast days, Christmas, and Corpus Christi.[19] These special festivities involved a larger population than those boys educated at Franciscan schools, and fray Pedro believed their impact to be even more widespread. He wrote to his Flemish Franciscan brothers that after one Christmas dance festival, "the churches and their courtyards have continued [to be filled] with more people than they can hold, paying honors to our Savior Jesus Christ that formerly had been paid the devils."[20] Although his account of the power of music and dance and the sincerity of the new religious devotions may be inflated, many missionaries reported the remarkable effects of music as an evangelization tool.

Others used fray Pedro's methods with success. Fray Martín de Valencia reported that "we devote much time to them, teaching them how to read, write, and sing both plainsong and polyphonic music. We teach them how to sing the canonical hours and how to assist at mass; and we try to encourage the highest standards of living and conduct."[21] Pedro de Gante's educational techniques were praised by Motolinia in *Historia de los Indios*,[22] and were even used by Franciscans in Peru and Quito.[23] Fray Juan Caro, a contemporary of fray Pedro, organized a *schola cantorum*, or singing school, in the chapel of San José to enhance the celebration of the mass.[24] Franciscans established schools throughout New Spain in an effort to convert indigenous children, who were viewed as more receptive to the new religious and cultural traditions.

Jesuits also used music in their educational efforts. In Europe, the Jesuits had focused their efforts on a strong missionary movement to combat the advances of Protestantism. An equal emphasis was placed on education in Catholic countries with the goal of promoting instruction of youth and ignorant persons in the Catholic faith.[25] This emphasis on education was carried to New Spain, where children of indigenous elites were brought to study at the Jesuit Colegio de San Gregorio. Musical education was part of the required curriculum in the college and reports from teachers and observers attest to its popularity. Teaching the catechism was an important component of missionary work both in the secondary schools and in the mission field. Father Gerónimo Ripalda prepared a version of the catechism developed by the Council of Trent for Jesuit educational use. Missionaries further translated this catechism into indigenous languages, and some set the words to music to aid in memorization and to interest the Indians.

The importance of music and musical education in the religious communities of

KRISTIN DUTCHER MANN

New Spain is indicated by the large numbers of religious texts and scores printed in Mexico City. Choir books and musical treatises were among the items printed for the use of clerics. Juan de Tovar, one of the first creoles to join the Society, wrote a musical treatise printed in the sixteenth century. Franciscan friar Bernadino de Sahagún's book, *Psalmodia Christiana*, was one of the most influential books of any type printed in Mexico City. It was a response to the legislation of the First Provincial Council of the church in New Spain and attempted to replace the words of Nahuatl songs and dances with texts that taught the catechism and praised God.[26] This book provided materials that the local missionary could use in preaching, teaching, and adapting native music and dances to make them appropriate for performance in churches. The book's hymns and canticles, written in Spanish, Latin, and Nahuatl, were approved by New Spain's ecclesiastical authorities; in 1585 the Third Provincial Council recommended it for use in converting the Indians.

Although liturgical legislation from the Council of Trent, the Mexican provincial councils, and the individual religious clerical organizations was important in defining rough boundaries of music use, these boundaries were often tested when in the mission field. The ways missionaries used music are most reflective of their personal instrumental and vocal backgrounds and attitudes about music. To illustrate the place of music in conversion, it is useful to consider two examples: Franciscan fray Antonio Margil de Jesús and Jesuit Padre Juan María Salvatierra, men who rose to positions of prominence within their orders

and served as role models for younger men who followed them.

Fray Antonio Margil de Jesús

Antonio Margil was born in 1657 in Valencia, Spain, and joined the Franciscans in 1673. After studying theology in Spain, he was ordained a priest in 1682, and he joined twenty-two other Franciscans in a journey from Cádiz to Veracruz the following year. Their mission was to open the first *Colegio de Propaganda Fide* in the Americas at Querétaro in New Spain. The members of the Colegio de Santa Cruz had the dual purpose of preaching parish missions in Spanish towns and establishing teaching missions among unconverted indigenous groups. Fray Antonio worked in the southern edges of New Spain for thirteen years, establishing missions and *hospicios* (temporary way stations for missionaries) throughout the territory, and he served as Father Guardian of the Colegio de Santa Cruz from 1697–1700 before returning to the mission field. He helped found the Colegio de Cristo Crucificado in Guatemala in 1701, and another college at Guadalupe near Zacatecas in 1705. From 1711–1726, he established missions among the Indians of the north. He died in the Franciscan convento of San Francisco el Grande in 1726.

Although there are no specific references to Margil's musical training while in Spain, he was certainly familiar with the music of the liturgy. By the sixteenth century, daily corporate recitation of the canonical hours among Franciscans was expected. Elaborate musical celebration was generally limited to feast days, Sunday mass, and evening vespers. In Spain, where

Margil studied, instruction in the basics of singing and playing of some musical instruments was included in seminary education. The divine office was chanted in choir in the morning, at noon, late in the afternoon, and again in the evening.[27] Some of these students, upon hearing of the effectiveness of music as a conversion aid from early overseas missionaries, copied music from their home provinces for use in the mission field.[28] This resulted in a vast dispersion of European liturgical music throughout the colonies of Spain and Portugal in the sixteenth and seventeenth centuries. The copying of European liturgical music may also explain the similarity between the *alabados* (hymns of praise), used in many mission communities, and the *saetas* (sacred songs) in the vernacular, such as those sung by confraternities in Spain.[29]

Music was a part of fray Antonio's missionary work from his first days in New Spain. Upon arrival in a new town, the liturgy of the mass often furnished a way for Spaniards to provide closure for a journey and give thanks for a safe passage. Masses were chanted by clerics who traveled with invading Spanish forces as well as by missionaries entering new territory. Margil seems to have routinely ended his journeys in this manner: "We arrived at this town of Our Lady of El Viejo on the 16th of this month; and here we sang a mass in honor of Our Lady with great solemnity for the success of our mission."[30]

Similarly, Franciscans from the convento of San Francisco el Grande who were assigned to the Coahuila missions sang an *alabanza* (praise song) with newly converted Indians who traveled with them to aid in evangelization efforts.[31] On the way to the pueblo of Analco, the friars and their indigenous companions sang the *Te Deum Laudamus* (Glory Be to God) in strong voices.[32]

Fray Antonio, like later Franciscans such as Junípero Serra, also sang the alabado as he walked from his college through villages and towns where he was preaching missions.[33] While singing may have simply been a way to pass time during a long walk, it also reminded indigenous peoples of his presence and intent. For both Franciscan and Jesuit missionaries, singing the Te Deum or hymns of praise was part of the *entrada* (entrance) into a new area—a musical conquest of the space for God.

When founding new missions among the Talamancas Indians, Margil and his companion occupied a house in hostile territory before meeting with indigenous leaders. Margil wrote to the Father Guardian, "We stayed all day and night in that house, beating at times the drum that was there and singing many songs of devotion."[34] In this instance, Margil appropriated a native instrument to accompany his songs of Christian devotion. Singing strengthened their faith, announced their presence, and claimed the territory as holy space. In any event, it was not successful in convincing the Talamancas, nor were the other rituals they performed the next day; as a result, Margil and his companion were forced to leave.

Once their presence was initially accepted in the frontier territories, missionaries tried many techniques to interest indigenous peoples in the Catholic faith while establishing mission infrastructure. Routine duties included building and upkeep of the mission church, baptisms, instruction of children, and the praying of the liturgy of the mass and the Office. Although they often had some success baptizing and indoctrinating children, they met obstacles in trying to convert adults. Margil wrote to the viceroy that his missionaries from the college of Zacatecas in Texas were "always trying to find ways and means of attracting the adults."[35] Margil was known for his techniques involving the use of music. He taught the doctrine by setting it to music and used saetas to teach parents their biblical duties in raising their children.[36] He modeled piety by singing the alabado at the conclusion of masses, at mealtimes, and before sleeping.[37]

Another evangelization technique was to invite neighboring Indians to participate in celebrations surrounding a feast day. Indians were attracted by the food, singing, processions, and dancing allowed at these gatherings. Margil describes the activities associated with Corpus Christi in 1695 during his time evangelizing the Lacandons in Guatemala:

> We had four altars and arches, the usual procession, the foot soldiers on each side, discharging their guns effectively both during the mass and the procession . . . Some of the Lacandons carried the cross and candles, and served as sacristans and acolytes . . . With all the reverence we could show we raised the cross and planted it in the same place, and on our knees we sang the *Adoro Te, Santa Cruz*.[38] Some of the natives responded, especially the ones called don Pedro Ytzquin and Nicolás.[39]

This fiesta was held in conjunction with the burning of indigenous icons and punishment of the offending individuals. The music of the mass and the melody of the canticle were linked with the show of force associated with the gunshots and the bonfire. This celebration provided an alternative to the indigenous music of the Lacandons who were painted black and playing the cane flutes of the community as part of their spiritual rituals.[40]

For Margil, chanting and the liturgy were part of a daily routine connected to being a pious individual. In a letter to the Carmelite nuns in Guadalajara, he expressed his passion for Jesus Christ and revealed his Opus Dei.

> Jesus and Jesus only will live in us sacramentally, and really by grace; and . . . he will be the one who prays during prayer, the one who chants in the choir, and he will be in us entirely. . . . So let us die always for Jesus, so that Jesus may always live in us and we only in Jesus and for Jesus alone.[41]

Fray Simón del Hierro recognized that Margil's piety was reflected in his daily devotions. According to Hierro's *Testimonio*, he never failed to say mass and hear confessions each day. He participated with fervor at communal spiritual devotions, and sang and prayed as he walked from the college at Guadalupe to his mission work. Father Margil died in the Franciscan convento of San Francisco el Grande on August 6, 1726. It is not surprising that one who sang often during his ministry reportedly said before he died, "My heart is steadfast, O God,

OPUS DEI—"THE WORK OF GOD"

my heart is steadfast; I will sing and chant praise. I shall praise you and sing in the company of the angels in glory."[42]

Father Juan María de Salvatierra

Juan María de Salvatierra was born in Milan in 1658. He was educated at the Jesuit college in Parma, where he studied philosophy, music, Latin, and French. In 1675, entering the Society of Jesus in Genoa, he sailed for Mexico. He continued his studies in New Spain and taught rhetoric, serving as rector of the Guadalajara colegio from 1693–1696, and as the *maestro de novicios* (master of novitiates) at Tepotzotlan the following year. In 1680 he set out for the northern frontier, where he worked among indigenous peoples of Chínipas for ten years. He was appointed Father Visitor of the Jesuit missions in northwestern New Spain in 1690. With Father Eusebio Kino, he undertook the exploration and evangelization of Baja California in 1697. Apart from his duties as padre visitador from 1704–1707, he worked for the remainder of his life in the missions that he helped to found. Salvatierra died in Guadalajara in 1717.

Unlike Margil, Salvatierra is known to have had formal music training in Europe. His family was wealthy, and he learned to play the lute as a child. When the Spanish infanta doña Margarita passed through Milan on her way to marry Emperor Leopold, young Juan was chosen to perform at the ceremonies.[43] Jesuit colleges in Europe were renowned for their rigorous curriculum, which included music as well as languages, rhetoric, and philosophy. Many of the men who served the church in New Spain as chapel masters, while not Jesuits themselves, were educated at Jesuit colleges in Europe.[44]

During his studies at the Jesuit College in Parma, Salvatierra reportedly excelled in music. Jesuit novitiates throughout Europe completed the spiritual exercises of St. Ignatius, studied the lives of the saints, and participated in music at daily communal worship. At their Roman College, seminarians participated in the choir for liturgical functions, took singing lessons, and learned liturgical melodies for an hour each day. All students had to learn both Gregorian plainchant melodies as well as figured chant.[45]

After completing his novitiate, Salvatierra wrote Jesuit General Juan Paolo de Oliva asking permission to be sent to the mission field in the Americas. He listed his proficiency on the lute as among the many characteristics that made him suitable for the task of evangelization.[46] In 1675 he received his orders to travel to New Spain. After arriving, Salvatierra served in teaching and administrative capacities. As in his later work in the missions of northwestern New Spain, he found time to give special attention to the devotion of Our Lady of Loreto. In Guadalajara, while functioning as superior of the colegio, Salvatierra oversaw the founding of a holy house and chapel dedicated to Loreto. It was dedicated on November 25, 1695, in a ceremony that involved a solemn procession and sung vespers with "excellent" music. Miguel Venegas wrote that townspeople gathered at the chapel on Saturdays to hear a choir sing the rosary and the litany to the Virgin, followed by a sermon from Salvatierra.[47]

Like Margil, Salvatierra found music to be a useful way of teaching Christian

KRISTIN DUTCHER MANN

doctrine. He set the doctrine to music and played a flute to attract the children. Salvatierra "would sing about these mysteries, and following him, like a choir of angels, came the devout band of children who had already been baptized and who also sang the same thing in the settlements to their parents. Carried along by the same harmonious melody of this music, the parents came to learn about these same mysteries, and were moved to ask to be admitted within the portals of the Holy Church."[48] On special occasions, such as Corpus Christi and Holy Week, special masses were sung in conjunction with ceremonies including feasting, dancing, and processions. These rituals were essential elements in drawing Indians to the missions throughout Latin America, and Salvatierra considered them the most efficient way of achieving conversion, since "it was through the eyes [and ears and mouth] that devotion and charity entered the heart."[49]

In his role as a Jesuit administrator in Baja California, Salvatierra was concerned about the morale of his missionaries. Each year the padres were required to go to Loreto to perform the spiritual exercises of Ignatius of Loyola. While there, Salvatierra invited them to stay for chocolate, conversation, singing with the guitar, and dancing.[50] In this instance, music and dancing were used as ways to combat depression and homesickness. The exchange of folk songs and dances must have also fostered a sense of collegiality among the missionaries, who hailed from different parts of Europe and worked in Baja California in lonely settings.

Salvatierra also recognized the importance of dance among the indigenous peoples of Baja California. He described the dances of the Indians with great admiration, and even joined in the dance called the *Nimbe*, pulling Padre Pedro de Ugarte with him.[51] This reportedly earned him the admiration and affections of the *californios*. On one occasion Salvatierra gave permission for the californios to dance as a way of distracting them from the horrors of an epidemic that was sweeping through their community. He wrote to Padre Provincial Antonio Xardón of this decision:

> Before going to sleep, I said to Ambrosio that these people were very saddened by the deaths of their people from the epidemic of measles, and that they could have permission to dance that evening. And he told them that they could dance, and they were very happy; and then they began at midnight with a dance so sorrowful and hideous that had I not been prepared for it, I would have been fearful of treachery. And it lasted until the dawn.[52]

Perhaps Salvatierra recognized that both the Jesuits and their indigenous counterparts used music and dancing as a way of preserving group identity in the face of social upheaval, either in the form of loneliness and separation, or in the measles epidemic that decimated a native community. Despite official decrees that limited dancing to religious dances on special occasions, it was practiced by the missionaries and allowed among indigenous groups as a form of recreation and renewal.

As it was with fray Antonio, music was reportedly part of Salvatierra's final hours. En route to Mexico City to meet with the viceroy, Father Salvatierra fell ill and was forced to stop in Guadalajara. According to Venegas's biography, Juan María de Salvatierra died on July 18, 1717, while chanting the hymn *Ave Maria Stella* to Our Lady of Loreto.[53]

Conclusions

As the careers of Margil and Salvatierra illustrate, music was a routine part of missionary work in New Spain, whether it was the chanting of the liturgy, a doctrina set to music for teaching purposes, or a celebration for a special occasion. It was intertwined with piety in practices of the regular clergy in colonial Mexico. Missionaries brought their European-style liturgical music and their ideas about piety to their evangelization efforts. In the missions, distinct cultures encountered and contested one another within the context of unequal power relationships. The inner meanings of the outward signs of piety displayed by Indians in conventos or missions as they participated in mass or celebrations are unclear; these liturgical performances may have been infused with meanings the missionaries would have considered purely heathen.

It is interesting that missionary accounts and hagiographies consistently grant importance to the role of music in the conquest and conversion of New Spain's native inhabitants. Biographies of missionaries such as Margil and Salvatierra emphasize the ways they used music to convert Indians and illustrate their holiness and piety with tales of their singing. Music, then, was an essential element in the construction of Catholic identity, and thus music was glorified in the epic accounts of the missionaries.

Jesuit Eusebio Francisco Kino wrote in his biography of Francisco Javier Saeta, "the greatness of new missions will shine not only in the eternity of heaven, but also in the most desolate and remote regions of the world. It will live on in the splendid construction of temples, churches, buildings, and houses. It will reflect in the solemnities of the saints, in gay fiestas, and in the treats of religious banquets; it will be heard in music and the choirs of singers."[54] Even today, this is the legacy of the Franciscan and Jesuit missionaries who worked in New Spain. Music was an important component of colonial piety for the missionaries; it also became an important component of piety in the syncretic religious culture that developed in Mexico during the colonial period. As this culture has continued to be refashioned, music and dance have remained important components of Catholic identity.

NOTES

1. Bernal Díaz, *The Conquest of New Spain*, trans. J. M. Cohen (London: Penguin Books, 1963), 47.

2. Ibid., 49, 57, 74, 326, 333.

3. Ibid., 89.

4. For more on the Spanish ceremonies of possession, see Patricia Seed, *Ceremonies of Possession in Europe's Conquest of the New World, 1492–1640* (Cambridge: Cambridge University Press, 1995).

5. Díaz, *The Conquest of New Spain*, 96.

6. *Recopilación de leyes de los reynos de las Indias* (Madrid, 1681), lib. I, tit. I, ley iiii; Kristin Dutcher Mann, "The Power of Song in the

Missions of Northern New Spain" (PhD diss., Northern Arizona University, 2002).

7. For music in the missions, see Robert Stevenson, *Music in Mexico: A Historical Survey* (New York: Robert Y. Crowell Company, 1952) and *Music in Aztec and Inca Territory* (Berkeley: University of California Press, 1968); Alfred Lemmon, "Jesuits and Music in Mexico," *Archivum Historicum Societatis Iesu* 46 (1977): 191–98, and "Preliminary Investigation: Music in the Jesuit Missions of Baja California," *Journal of San Diego History* 25 (1979): 287–97, and William Summers, "The Spanish Origins of California Mission Music," *Miscellanea Musicologica* 12 (1987): 109–26.

8. Thomas D. Culley and Clement J. McNaspy, "The Place of Art in the Old Society," *Archivum Historicum Societatis Iesu* 40 (1971): 218.

9. T. Frank Kennedy, "Jesuits and Music: Reconsidering the Early Years," *Studi Musicali* 17 (1988): 77–79.

10. Stephen J. Van Dijk, "The Liturgical Legislation of the Franciscan Rules," *Franciscan Studies* 12 (1952): 185.

11. John R. H. Moorman, *A History of the Franciscan Order from its Origins to the Year 1517* (Oxford: Clarendon Press, 1968), 14–15.

12. John Harper, *The Forms and Orders of Western Liturgy from the Tenth to the Eighteenth Century* (Oxford: Clarendon Press, 1991), 18.

13. Carlos González Salas, *Las misiones franciscanas en la Colonia del Nuevo Santander* (Ciudad Victoria: Universidad Autonoma de Tamaulipas, 1975), 10.

14. Fray Juan Fogueras to the governor, 5/10/1747, Archivo General de las Indias (hereafter cited as AGI) Guadalajara, 205.

15. Pius J. Barth, *Franciscan Education and the Social Order in Spanish North America* (Chicago, 1950), 7.

16. Mary Berry, "Franciscan Friars," *New Grove Dictionary of Music and Musicians*, vol. 6 (London: Macmillan, 1980), 776–77.

17. Joaquín García Icazbalceta, "Fray Pedro de Gante," *Artes de México* 19, no. 150 (1972): 100.

18. Pedro de Gante to the king, 1532, transcribed in *Cartas de Indias* (Madrid: Imprenta de M. G. Hernández, 1877), 52.

19. Charles Verlinden, "Fray Pedro de Gante y su época," *Revista de Historia de América* 101 (Jan.–June 1986): 117, includes excerpts describing the use of music and dance at a Christmas celebration at the chapel of San José.

20. Arthur J. O. Anderson, "Introduction," to Bernardino de Sahagún's *Psalmodia Christiana* (Salt Lake City: University of Utah Press, 1993), xix.

21. Martín de Valencia to Charles V, 1532, transcribed in *Cartas de Indias* (Madrid: Imprenta de M. G. Hernández, 1877), 56.

22. E. A. Foster, *Motolinía's History of the Indians of New Spain* (Berkeley: The Cortés Society, 1950), 8, 52.

23. Agustín Moreno Proaño, "El influjo de Pedro de Gante en la cultura de Sudamérica," *Artes de México* 19, no. 150 (1972): 113–14.

24. Barth, *Franciscan Education*, 208.

25. See Karl Braunschweig, "Gradus ad Parnassum: A Jesuit Music Treatise," *In Theory Only* 12, no. 7–8 (November 1994): 40.

26. Anderson, "Introduction," x.

27. Regina Maria Gormley, "The Liturgical Music of the California Missions, 1769–1833" (DMA diss., Catholic University of America, 1992), 27.

28. Owen DaSilva, *Mission Music of California* (Los Angeles: Warren F. Lewis, 1941), 19.

29. Richard B. Stark, "Notes on a Search for Antecedents of New Mexican Alabado Music," in *Hispanic Arts and Ethnohistory in the Southwest*, ed. Marta Weigle (Santa Fe: Ancient City Press, 1983).

30. Margil de Jesus to Fr. Tomas de San Diego Arrivillaga, February 17, 1703, Archivo de la Recolección Guatemala, no. XXIX, in *Nothingness Itself: Selected Writings of Ven. Fr. Antonio Margil*, comp. and trans. Benedict Leutenegger and ed. Marion A. Habig, 93 (Chicago: Franciscan Herald Press, 1976). See also descriptions of Margil's travel in Fr. Simón del Hierro's "Testimonio," reprinted in the above book, 325, 328.

31. Alabanza refers to a song of praise, whereas alabado refers more specifically to one beginning with the word "alabado."

32. "Informe de los autos que se hicieron para la misión de la Provincia de Coahuila," 1673,

f. 10, Archivo San Francisco el Grande, Biblioteca Nacional, copy in Eugene C. Barker Texas History Collection, Center for American History, University of Texas at Austin.

33. *Testimonio* of Fr. Simón del Hierro in *Nothingness Itself*, 325, 328. See Owen DaSilva, *Mission Music of California*, 8, for Father Serra's singing of the alabado.

34. Margil to Fr. Sebastián de las Salas, February 10, 1691, in *Nothingness Itself*, 21. This trip is also recounted by Eduardo Enrique Ríos, *Life of Fray Antonio Margil* (Washington, DC: Academy of American Franciscan History, 1959), 35.

35. Margil to Viceroy Marqués de Valero, June 23, 1722, Querétaro reel 18, Old Spanish Missions Historical Research Collection, Our Lady of the Lake University Special Collections, San Antonio, Texas. See also fray Isidro Félix Espinosa, *El peregrino septentrional atlante: delineado en la exemplarissima vida del venerable padre F. Antonio Margil de Jesus*, Mexico, por Joseph Fernando de Hogal, 1737, f. 27.

36. One of these saetas is translated and reprinted in *Nothingness Itself*, 315–16.

37. There were many different versions of the alabado used in New Spain, but all seem to share the first three stanzas. Father Margil's version contained seven verses and was commonly sung in Texas. Marion A. Habig Collection, Our Lady of the Lake University Special Collections, San Antonio, Texas.

38. A liturgical song proclaiming adoration for the cross.

39. AGI Guatemala 153, f. 9v–14v, as transcribed in *Nothingness Itself*, 63.

40. *Nothingness Itself*, 64.

41. Ibid., 152, from Margil to the Carmelite convent, June 9, 1710.

42. This is a paraphrase of verses from psalms 36 and 37, *Nothingness Itself*, x.

43. Miguel Venegas, *Juan Maria de Salvatierra of the Company of Jesus; Missionary in the Province of New Spain, and Apostolic Conqueror of the Californias*, trans. Marguerite Eyer Wilbur (Cleveland: The Arthur H. Clark Company, 1929), 66–67. Venegas says that Salvatierra had been chosen, however, the ceremony never took place.

44. For example, Ignacio de Jerusalem, *maestro de capilla* (chapel master) of the Mexico City Cathedral from 1750–1769, and an illustrious composer, attended the Jesuit college in Leece, Italy. See Robert Murrell Stevenson, "Ignacio Jerusalem, 1707–1769," *Inter-American Music Review* 16, no. 1 (Summer–Fall 1997): 59.

45. Ricardo García Villoslada, "Algunos documentos sobre la música en el antigua seminario romano," *Archivum Historicum Societatis Iesu* 31 (1962): 116.

46. Salvatierra to Gian Paolo Oliva, June 8, 1671, cited in Ernest Burrus, ed., *Juan María Salvatierra: Selected Letters about Lower California* (Los Angeles: Dawson's Book Shop, 1971), 19.

47. Venegas, *Juan María de Salvatierra of the Company of Jesus*, 149.

48. Ibid., 187–88.

49. Ibid., 188.

50. Miguel Venegas, *El apostol Mariano representado en la vida del V. P. Juan María de Salvatierra.* (México, 1734), 132, 250–51.

51. Ibid., 188–89.

52. Salvatierra to Padre Provincial Antonio Xardón, April 3, 1710, AGN Historia 308, f. 398v., transcribed by Luis González Rodríguez in "Juan María de Salvatierra y los seris, 1709–1710," *Estudios de historia novohispana* 17 (1997): 254.

53. Venegas, *Juan María de Salvatierra of the Company of Jesus*, 224.

54. Ernest Burrus, ed., *Kino's Biography of Francisco Javier Saeta, S.J.*, trans. Charles Polzer (Rome: Jesuit Historical Institute, 1971), 215.

KRISTIN DUTCHER MANN

CHAPTER FOURTEEN

Martyrs and Idols

Performing Ritual Warfare on
Early Missionary Frontiers in the Northwest

MAUREEN AHERN

Donald Weinstein and Rudolph M. Bell's dictum that "wherever Christianity encountered a frontier, it had need of martyrs,"[1] reverberates throughout the narrative histories of the Franciscan and Jesuit enterprises in the northern borderlands. Yet these same accounts contain extensive testimony of the fierce resistance that indigenous peoples mounted in defense of their own spiritual practices and ethnic identities in response to militant evangelization and invasion. In Jalisco, in late spring of 1541, at the outbreak of the great rebellion known as the Mixton War, Caxcan warriors drove back a troop of Spanish soldiers from their mountain fortress. Defiantly they performed a victory mass at which they raised a large white tortilla in simulation of the Host. Soon after, when the Franciscan friar Juan Calero went to talk to them of peace, they riddled his body with arrows and constructed an idol out of his habit, adding a new cult to their annual cycle of ritual practices. Sixty years later, on the western flank of the Sierra Madre, an Acaxee shaman declared that he was God the Holy Spirit, come from heaven as their bishop to preach a new doctrine that would overcome the false one the Jesuit missionaries had brought. He baptized the young, married and unmarried the adults, said mass, and appointed two disciples, Santiago and San Pedro, to help him spread a new gospel of warfare that would "not leave a single Spaniard alive in the land."[2] At the height of the Tepehuan Revolt in 1616, on the eastern flank of the Sierra Madre north of Durango, rebel forces at Santiago Papasquiaro vented the brunt of their fury on the Jesuit martyr Diego de Orozco in a gruesome parody of the Latin mass as they dismembered his body in a visual replica of the cross.

The foregoing are some of the many stunning examples of how Christian ritual and liturgical signs generated performative meanings that mocked and repelled the authority from which they emanated, raising complex cultural issues about the construction of the northern frontier as transformative cultural and discursive spaces.[3] This chapter proposes a study that asks new questions about the multivalent nature of frontier martyrdom and the counter responses of indigenous resistance, as narrated in the missionary literature, judicial records, and iconography of their time. What do the constructions of symbolic arsenals among both indigenous and Spanish factions reveal about the early northwest frontier as a site of radical spiritual transformations? What can they inform us about the uses to which hagiography from an "old" frontier is put in the construction of "new" affirmations of native identity and survival? How do martyr narratives function as volatile sites of destabilization, decentering, and negotiation that question the triumphalist authority from which they emanate as well as traditional views of the frontier mission and literature they created? What is the relationship of these discourses to the pictorial narratives they generated, in indigenous as well as European iconography?

The discourses of this ritual warfare are embedded in the martyr narratives that abound in the histories of the Franciscan and Jesuit enterprises in northwest New Spain—so full of miracles and glorious deaths imbued with Tridentine zeal.[4] To pursue these issues I propose a postcolonial, against the grain, reading of three major missionary histories: the *Historia* *eclesiástica indiana* completed in 1596 by the apocalyptic Franciscan thinker and leader of the pro-Indian Franciscan faction, fray Gerónimo de Mendieta,[5] the *Crónica miscelánea de la sancta provincia de Xalisco* by the Franciscan historian, fray Antonio Tello (ca. 1656),[6] and the *Historia de los Triumphos de nuestra Santa Fee*, published in 1645 by Father Andrés Pérez de Ribas, provincial of the Society of Jesus in New Spain who had labored on the Sinaloa frontier among the Ahome and the Yaqui for seventeen years.[7] While indigenous accounts are known to us largely through missionary perspectives of a single true Christian God and his Holy Faith versus the idols and demons of the heathen, what "bleeds through"[8] can offer significant insights about the ways Christian ritual objects and symbols, once released by the missionaries, took on transformative powers of their own, beyond the control of the friars, to became focal points of rebellion and negotiation by indigenous peoples on the northern frontier in the sixteenth and early seventeenth centuries. I also read beyond these clerical authors, into the same prime sources the friars used to compile their histories, the letters (*cartas annuas*) sent by individual missionaries from their frontier posts, as well as testimony from indigenous and military witnesses who participated in the combat.

These narratives contain extensive chapters about the lives and deaths of their brothers who were killed by native peoples, ostensibly martyr stories that presented models of missionary victories. Yet tucked away in the baroque folds of their discourses or *pli*, as Gilles Deleuze would call them, we find embedded stories, often inserted or retold from oral or written witness testimony, where the slippage of narrated events and language buckles into other levels of meaning that reveal alternative accounts of indigenous reception and reaction to the missionary thrust.[9] Among these pages that have traditionally been read as official histories of heroic evangelism, these deeper pleats or twists reveal the battles of another war that Serge Gruzinski has called "*la guerra de las imágenes*" (images at war).[10] In this study I want to examine how these martyr stories can be cracked open to reveal performative forms of resistance: that is, how indigenous peoples of northern Mexico reacted to Christian images by appropriating them, manipulating, and resemanticizing them to affirm their own social and religious agency.[11] How, in Gruzinski's words, "the spaces of the idol and the saint continually intersect and overlap."[12]

Martyr Narratives as Warfare

In his study of the fourth-century Spanish poet and hagiographer, Prudentius, and the cult of the martyrs, Michael Roberts has pointed out that martyr narratives are really war stories, for the life and death of martyrs was a model of spiritual combat and celestial reward.[13] As Franciscan and Jesuit martyr narratives moved easily between the apostolic past, the apocalyptic present, and a utopian future, between history, earth, and heaven, their multiple semantic levels drew in other kinds of combat that were waging on the colonial periphery. Martyr experiences are also stories of reversals because they essentially narrate how the protagonists experience physical death in life as they seek to find spiritual life in death.[14] Writing about

this essential irony opens up other contradictions that are occurring in the same temporal and geographical contexts—for these narratives also tell how evangelization campaigns occurred on symbolic as well as historic levels.[15] The polysemic discourses they generated bend in ways that reveal the outer folds or pli of Franciscan and Jesuit action and the inner creases of indigenous reaction, producing alternative levels of meaning through syncretic signs imbued with new values. As hagiographic narratives, the blood of the new Franciscan and Jesuit martyrs consecrated powerful foundational models; yet at another level—albeit through a heavily mediatized lens—the testimonials to the indigenous appropriation of Christian symbology reveal potent new semantics that transform and transmit ritual objects and performances into formidable offensives against the invaders of their territories.

The Mixton War: Prophecy and Parody

Spanish attempts to establish missions in Nueva Galicia provoked a widespread rebellion that came close to annihilating their presence in central New Spain. It began in 1540, almost as soon as the Franciscans founded the first convent in Jalisco and sent their zealous missionaries into the field imbued with the conviction that the eleventh hour of Christianity was near, as John Phelan and Pauline Moffitt Watts have affirmed.[16] There Franciscan first contact took the form of mass baptisms, public destruction of idols, prohibition of traditional polygamy, indoctrination of the young, and resettlement of *serrano* or mountain groups in towns accessible to *encomiendas* (grants of indigenous labor and tribute), mines, and monasteries. Evidence from a variety of primary sources confirms that the ferocious response of the Caxcan was as much resistance to this aggressive missionary thrust to incorporate them into Christian life and practice as a response to the material and social pillage of a decade of rape and enslavement of large segments of the population by Nuño de Guzmán and his troops, the abuses and dispossession of ancestral lands by his *encomenderos* (possessors of encomiendas), and the heavy burdens imposed by requirements for provisions for the Coronado expedition that departed in 1539.[17] "It can be affirmed that in terms of its scope and force, [the Mixton War] seemed to be an organized attempt at reconquest on the part of the Indians. Tired of being the object of demands and abuses, and impelled by a deep religious motivation to return to their ancestral beliefs and practices, its objective was to expulse those they called 'the bearded Christians' from their country forever."[18] Their war cry in Nahuatl: *Axcan quema, tehuatl, nehautl*! (Ahora sí, tú o yo!)[19] proclaimed total war to the death against all invaders. Indigenous testimony inserted in Tello's *Crónica miscelánea* and also recorded in the *descargos* or judicial defense provided by Viceroy don Antonio de Mendoza during the legal inquisition into the causes of the Mixton War[20] pinpoint its outbreak in three ritual performances.[21] In the mountains of Guayanota when the performance of a traditional gourd dance was disrupted by a strong wind that snatched the gourd up into the air, the elder *hechiceras*, or female shamans, proclaimed that just as the wind had swept up the gourd, so would all the Spaniards be swept from the land if they went to battle against them, and not a single one would be left alive.

[At] a dance in a town named Tlaxicoringa, where they danced around a gourd. . . , a strong wind blew the gourd up into the air. Some old women shamans said they should rebel, because just as the wind had blown away the gourd, with the same force they would expel the Spaniards from [their] lands, and they should not doubt because it would come true. They should go to battle against the Spaniards because when they did, a wind would blow up a great dust storm and not a single Spaniard would remain alive, and they would celebrate it with grand dances and drinking.[22]

The insurrection spread like wildfire throughout the sierra, from Nayarit and southern Sinaloa into Jalisco and Zacatecas. However, Viceroy Mendoza testified a few years later that the "real" instigation of the rebellion was *"el habla del diablo que se llama tlatol"* (the messianic messages brought by shamans) from the "highlands of Tepeque and Zacatecas" through which their deity Tecoroli promised eternal youth, good health, abundant food, and weapons to those who rejected the teachings of God and the friars. Fields would flourish without labor or rain and followers could have as many women as they wanted instead of only one as the friars commanded. All the Spaniards would be driven from their lands and killed. The messages brought an immediate response in Zacatecas, Suchipila, and "throughout the land."[23]

MAUREEN AHERN

The Caxcan and their allies fortified themselves in a chain of *peñoles* or mountain strongholds at Suchipila, Teptiztaque, Nochistlan, and Mixton, from which they ambushed and drove back all the Spanish commanders and troops who went against them. At Teptiztaque the Caxcan reply to an official reading of the *Requerimiento* by Captain Miguel Ibarra and two Franciscans was a burlesque mass performed in full view of the Spaniards.

> Said Indians continued in rebellion at the fortress where they committed many offenses against Our Lord, celebrating a mass where they raised high a tortilla as the Host that reviled the Most Holy Sacrament . . . and these are the true and real causes of the rebellion by the Indians of the province of Jalisco and not those stated in this charge, as so declare the eye witnesses and was public and notorious as was demonstrated to Your Grace by the information that I ordered taken about this case *ad perpetuam rei memoriam* which the prosecutor cites.[24]

In July 1541, the arrogant Adelantado Pedro de Alvarado, or "Tonatiuh," the Sun, as he was called by the Nahua peoples, perished during the chaotic rout of Spanish forces at the fortress of Nochistlan.[25] The inhabitants of Apozol and el Teul burned the monastery, churches, and chapels the Franciscans had erected, disfigured the cross, "and incited the others to do the same, and they joined together and fortified themselves at El Mixton."[26]

This, then, is the ritualized stage upon which Mendieta's account of the first Franciscan martyrs plays out in a combat inspired in indigenous forms of prophecy and *tlatol*, or sacred speech, that preached its own message of victory and utopian rewards here on earth. The inserted accounts from indigenous testimony that foreground the messianic elements emit a very "Indian" view of the rebellion and its causes rarely found in other representations. The Caxcan are persuaded to begin war by a prophecy foretold by an unusual disturbance of a ritual object at a ceremonial dance, and by the *tlatolli* or sacred pronouncements of a shaman.[27] When Mendoza and a huge army of Indian allies were finally able to quell the rebellion in late autumn of 1541, large numbers of rebels threw themselves over steep precipices rather than surrender, while others slipped away to the north to the canyons of Nayarit and Tepic, where they joined the Cora and the Huichol and remained in perpetual rebellion.[28]

From Habit to Idol in Mendieta's *Historia eclesiástica indiana*

It is in this context of intensely sacralized performance that the first Franciscan martyrdoms occur, as friars walk into the war zones to attempt to convince the groups they have baptized in Nueva Galicia not to abandon the new religion. "The first Franciscans were dominated by an aspiration to the absolute that burned within them, more so in the peripheral zones where it was easy to approach martyrdom."[29]

In Book 5 of fray Gerónimo de Mendieta's *Historia eclesiástica indiana*, the Franciscan lay brother Juan Calero met his martyrdom on June 10, 1541, when

MARTYRS AND IDOLS

he walked into the mountains to entreat the Caxcan to abandon their idolatry and return to Christian settlements. After preaching to one group, apparently in their own language (according to Mendieta and Mendoza), a second group of latecomers who had not heard him shot him full of arrows, struck blows to his head with *macanas* (maces); then, according to an indigenous witness who had escaped, beat upon his mouth and his teeth, saying: "Now you won't preach any more about heaven or hell nor do we need your instruction."[30] Thus, Mendieta writes, Calero, who is the first Franciscan martyr in New Spain, suffered the same physical torture as four ancient martyrs: saints Stephen, Sebastian, Apolonia, and Thomas, Archbishop of Canterbury. When Calero's body was finally recovered after five days, it was found to be, "fresh, without any decomposition whatsoever and the blood as fresh as though they had just killed him," while the corpses of the three Christian Indian companions who were killed with him had been eaten by wild birds and animals. "It was a miracle," Mendieta adds.[31] But Calero's body was naked, the author notes, because his killers had taken his habit. When his companion friar dressed the body for burial in his own habit, the Spaniards who were attending the funeral ripped that habit off the cadaver and tore it into shreds, fighting for a piece of it when they perceived the fragrant aroma the corpse emitted.

Mendieta cast the circumstances of Calero's death and burial in the register of Christian hagiography or life stories of early saints. His analogy to the same physical tortures that were endured by the apostolic martyrs enlarges the ferocity of the Caxcan, evoking those earlier sufferings over the present one to create a montage of old and new imagery. But it is the representation of the mauling of Calero's speech organs that alerts us to a turn in the discourse that unfolds in the direction of the indigenous reaction. In missionary as well as in indigenous culture, speech, especially preaching, not text, was the primary vehicle for transmission of symbolic codes. The mauling of the lips and teeth reveals that, for the Caxcan warriors, the speech organs of the body *are* the presence of missionary power. It is a concept similar to the one that Gruzinski identified as the Nahua idea of *ixiptla*, that is, the receptacle or presence of forces imbued in a material object or body—the presence of the power of its material.[32] In other words, the lips and teeth that utter the preaching and instruction were the receptacles or site of Calero's power as they were the site of hated language that must be physically destroyed. Even this mediatized account effects a reversal of the Christian symbology of speech and the tongue as the traditional site and sign of the Holy Spirit. On the frontiers of Nueva Galicia the objective of war was to exterminate the sources of each other's words.

Several chapters later, in another martyr narrative contained in the *Historia eclesiástica indiana*, fray Francisco Lorenzo learns from the rebellious Tecoxquines that the warriors who killed Calero had taken his habit and made it into an idol—one that had already inspired its own cult. Each year on the anniversary of the day they had killed fray Juan, the indigenous community held a celebration in memory of that victory, when, they said, they had killed a destroyer of idols. Yet, after listening to a sermon from fray Francisco, the rebels returned Calero's habit to him.[33]

Thus we see that as the habit moves from Franciscan space to native space it is decontextualized, then resemantized and invested with a new identity of power as a parallel cult. The ironic reversals of this story are striking indeed. The first and founding image of Franciscan martyrdom in New Spain among the new Indian church of a new City of God—the very image of valiant martyrdom in the manner of renowned martyrs of the early church—becomes yet another idol among the many the Franciscans sought so zealously to destroy in the early stages of their enterprise. The very vestment that identified Calero as a Christian priest becomes a deity that generates a cult commemorating Calero's defeat as an indigenous victory. The Mixton War had begun with the tlatolli or words of shamans. When Calero is killed it is his mouth and tongue the Caxcan attempt to exterminate. There is a sharp sense of the word as the essential element that constitutes religious power, whether as prophecy or preaching, idol or relic: as they crisscross, ritual objects strive to exterminate each other.

In Mendieta's telling there are actually two endings or "deaths" to Juan Calero's martyrdom. First, his Christian death, which required that the body be reclothed or reinvested with the Christian covering of a friar's habit for burial, but which was then ripped to shreds by his own countrymen when they perceived the traditional "aroma of sanctity." Thus the Spaniards also perceived the material habit as a receptacle of power. The second ending, displaced and enfolded into the later account of fray Francisco's martyrdom, relates the conversion of Calero's habit into an idol that inspired a new annual feast day in the local religion and its own celebration as the sign of victory over an idol smasher. Thus, in the Calero hagiography, two different episodes converge in the object of the habit and then diverge again in their receptions. The dual sites that depicted the habit as power, whether as a referent or as an ixiptla, constructed a startling foundational figure in Mendieta's pantheon of frontier martyrs, as Calero's body and his dress inspired powerful new cults in both Christian and Indian factions. The inversion of valences resemanticized regional sacred practices through the investment of opposing values generated by a single ritual object. The lines between spiritual frontiers intersect to generate new cults. The power of the visual image and the early mendicant goal of the annihilation of images of the enemy, waging war on idols—was countered by a native understanding of the corresponding power of the images of colonial authority and how mimicry and inversion could become weapons against the colonizing forces from which they emanated.[34]

The Caxcan affirmed their rejection of Christianity through prophecy, parody, and appropriation. Some of these same elements or counter-ritual performances reappear in later rebellions among the Acaxee in 1601–1602 and along the mining frontiers of the Tepehuan from 1616 to 1618.[35]

A Visual Narrative

A visual depiction of the performances we have just discussed is the engraving that opens Book 5 of Mendieta's *Historia eclesiástica indiana* that narrates the lives and death of the Franciscan martyrs in sixteenth-century New Spain (see Figure 14.1). We can see that there are eight native warriors to only four Franciscans. The figures of the natives are smaller but their spaces are actually larger, while the Franciscans figures are fewer but larger. Framed by European scrolls, that at times look like plumes, the background of open spaces with some grass corresponds more to a stylized European landscape than to the rocky, cactus-studded deserts of northern Mexico. The drawings in Mendieta's *Historia* were done by an anonymous illustrator who copied four of the five plates in the volume from other engravings done by fray Diego Valadés, a sixteenth-century mestizo Franciscan writer and engraver and author of the *Rhetórica christiana*, who had worked on the northern frontier among the Chichimecas for several years. However, this last illustration was apparently carved by Valadés specifically for this last section of Mendieta's Book 5 on martyrs.[36]

This depiction of frontier martyrdom is not one of well-ordered civic spaces and citizens such as those that characterized European religious engravings of the time.[37] On the contrary, here the Chichimecas seem to be overpowering the space of evangelization. I suggest the drawing can also be thought of as a kind of visual fold—yet another alternative reading among the many pleated into Gerónimo de Mendieta's martyr narratives, for it could seem to depict a contradiction to the Franciscan achievements that he is narrating—perhaps yet another point of resistance, where the

elements work to sabotage themselves, as in Foucault's concept of discourse. Actually it may be closer to what Phelan pointed to as Mendieta's "apocalyptic gloom" at a time of severe demographic and economic crisis in New Spain at the end of the sixteenth century and his doubts regarding the authenticity of the indigenous reception of Christianity. On the other hand, in the code of martyrdom, it does depict "winning" when the martyr achieves the victory of everlasting life through earthly death. Thus it also presents "model martyrs," with the fingers of three friars pointing to heaven, in a gesture that identifies the position of the raised forefinger as the Christian gesture of blessing, which in medieval narrative functioned as a "speaking gesture."[38]

The spatial syntax of this engraving also allows for more than one decoding. It could be seen as what both Bernadette Boucher and Edwin Panofsky call "the rotative image," which reproduces on a single plate, in sequence and by contiguity, the temporal order of events as they occurred.[39] That interpretation would view Calero as the figure at top and center preaching; then Calero kneeling with crucifix in hand, enclosed by archers with drawn bows, and in the lower left hand space, two warriors with club and spear bend over the inert body of the friar. In other words, a vertical and temporal depiction of the stages of a single martyr's preaching and death, if read from top to bottom. But, when viewed from bottom to top, it might be seen as the course of ascension into heaven from the battered body to the friar looking toward the reward of heaven. However, if one takes into account the semantic content of Book 5 that explicitly

MAUREEN AHERN

Figure 14.1: Woodcut that introduces Book V, Part II, of *Historia eclesiástica indiana* by fray Gerónimo de Mendieta (ca. 1596), "De los Frailes Menores que han sido muertos por la predicación del Santo Evangelio en esta Nueva España." Illustration on folio 304. The anonymous engraver probably was fray Diego de Valadés. From the original manuscript with permission of the Benson Latin American Collection, The University of Texas at Austin.

MARTYRS AND IDOLS

records the lives and deaths of Franciscan martyrs in New Spain, and which this plate introduces, more probably it depicts the martyrdom of the four Franciscans, Calero among them, who meet their deaths within the same year in the same region and were buried at the monastery in Ezatlan. One of them is described in the text as dying with his crucifix raised in his hand, while the others are reported to have died preaching, as their hand gestures would indicate.

A Shaman Performing as a Bishop

The mission field of the Sierra de los Acaxee was located in the northwestern sector of the modern state of Durango in the high canyons and mountains of the Sierra Madre Occidental. The Jesuit Hernando de Santarén established a mission at Topia in 1598 followed by Alonso de Ruiz in San Andrés in 1600.[40] Acaxee religion centered on stone and wooden idols and fetishes with altars that were both personal and communal deities strongly connected to agriculture and war. Their custodians were the shamans who had special supernatural powers. In Acaxee ceremonial life the bones and skulls of enemies killed previously were also important elements connected with war and planting.[41] A letter written in 1602 by Francisco Báez, Jesuit Provincial of New Spain, and probably compiled from the annual letters sent to him by Santarén and Ruiz, documents the aggressive campaign that these two missionaries immediately undertook. In huge public bonfires they set fire to all the idols, skulls, and bones they could collect while they preached "the abomination of their idols and superstitions" and attempted to resettle the

mountain groups into accessible villages.[42] The Acaxee immediately rebelled against this disruption of their spiritual and physical lifeways. Santarén, however, extolled the potential harvest of Acaxee souls as comparable to the glorious Jesuit enterprises in the East, the seedbed of martyrs: "As far as I am concerned, here is Japan, here is China, and here is New Mexico."[43] His jubilation places the Acaxee within the global frame of Jesuit enterprise.

When Santarén recognizes the power of the cult of the slain enemy's bones ("which they believe endow one with bravery") the missionary mounts a dramatic Jesuit performance. He puts the idols on trial and sentences them to burn in an *auto de fe* that is held on the occasion of a mass baptism.

All the idols that were discovered were publicly burned, and a sermon was preached to those who had congregated for the auto [de fe] and the sentence of execution that was carried out against them. A great number of people were baptized and recognized the vanity of their superstitions and idols. Nor did any die [as a result of baptism] as their deceitful old men had predicted.[44]

But the priests reported that "because the idols had been destroyed the devil was restless," and that even though people handed over their idols voluntarily, "some [native] Christians pledged to support a conspiracy, whose goal was to return once and for all to the life of their ancestors and shamans."[45] The Acaxee killed all the Spaniards and mulattoes they encountered in the outlying areas, initiating a ferocious cycle of rebellions that inspired the revolt of their neighbors, the Xixime within the same decade, and a more extensive one by the Tepehuan a few years later.[46] Although their grievances were in part against the disruption that the influx of mining camps had caused their communities, they aimed their attacks directly at the churches and the persons of the missionaries.

Andrés Pérez de Ribas's mammoth *Historia de los Triumphos de nuestra Santa Fee*, the history of Jesuit evangelization in northwest Mexico, published in Madrid in 1645, cast his accounts of the Acaxee, Xixime, and Tepehuan rebellions in terms of the Jesuits who were martyred in those uprisings.[47] It was his discussion of the Acaxee Revolt in the region of Durango in 1601–1603 that first called my attention to the ritual reversals effected by the great shaman who led that rebellion by casting himself as their "bishop." Pérez de Ribas based his chapters on the Acaxee on the letters of the saintly Father Hernando de Santarén, whose mission deep into the sierra in 1598 had so violently conflicted with the Acaxees' animistic worship of stone idols, trees, and bones. However, reading beyond Pérez de Ribas into the thick description of the judicial sources, other witnesses offer even more explicit accounts of the Acaxee invention of a mission campaign of their own to combat the one that had taken their followers. The testimony of Captain Francisco Romero de Arellano, a resident of the mining camp of Topia, who served with Governor Francisco de Urdiñola's brutal campaign against the Acaxee, spells out the compelling appropriation of Catholic liturgy, a statement well worth considering in full.[48]

For this purpose they again conspired under the leadership of an Indian of the pueblo of Chacala, called Perico, a vicious inventor of great evils. He went among the rebels and others of the Acaxee and Sobaibo nations and told them and convinced them that he was God the Holy Spirit who had come down from heaven, that he was a bishop and had come to teach them how to be saved. He said that the teachings of the religious of the Society of Jesus were false and that he would teach them another and better doctrine. The Indians believed this, and many received baptism from him. He married and unmarried and remarried many of them and changed their names. He said mass and taught them prayers other than the Catholic ones. In order to have assistants who would go to the places where he could not and teach this false doctrine, he sent one named Santiago and another San Pedro. He had the whole country so stirred up that much mischief was to be expected at great cost to the royal treasury. In the meetings he held his purpose was none other than to persuade everyone to join in the conspiracy of the Indians of the aforementioned pueblos of Alayá and others and not leave a single Spaniard alive either on the roads or in their settlements. He promised to help them with heavenly power and to blind the Spaniards and change them into cows, sheep, and horses so they could more easily be killed.[49]

Perico led his followers in ferocious attacks against the mining camps at Topia,

San Andrés, and Las Vírgenes, burning the grinding mills and killing Spanish settlers and religious alike. Book 8, Chapter 8 of Pérez de Ribas's *Historia* completes the rest of the story. At the height of the rebellion, the bishop of Guadalajara, don Alonso de la Mota, traveled to the region to sue for peace. He sent on ahead of him his white miter on a standard to the Acaxee as a sign that he would intercede on their behalf with the governor, if they would settle down in pueblos and continue to receive instruction from the Jesuits: "He sent a message to them that he was their true Bishop and not the false one who was deceiving them." Eventually these groups returned peacefully to their pueblos and the miter was placed "as a peace trophy" to the side of the main altar in the church in Culiacán. Later, after the shaman-bishop was captured and executed, one of his accomplices "publicly confessed that he had pretended to be Santiago, or Saint James, because he had heard the Spaniards say that this saint was their patron and captain."[50]

The Acaxee enactment of parallel liturgy perceived that great power resided in the sacramental performances of baptism and marriage by a bishop and in the saints as well. They appropriated the title and the liturgy; re-performing them in a new Acaxee mission campaign of their own. Their parallel performances by a native officiator conferred new agency and therein new power to retain their followers. This episode, woven into military as well as Jesuit telling, reveals the inner workings of the fierce warfare between the shaman and the priests for spiritual control over the native population that lay at the core of early frontier conflicts. Religious figures, titles, liturgy,

saints, and vestments of the Spaniards were as vulnerable to raids as were their mines and churches. The Acaxee appropriated not the role of a priest but rather that of a bishop to enhance their own religious and military prowess among their followers, as they infused this traditional role of European episcopal power with native valences to affirm their own spirituality and deflect their power back against the usurpers.[51] In another twist of dueling signs, the battle is decided by sending the liturgical sign of Christian ritual authority, the white miter, against the proselytizing of the shaman bishop. Clearly, the archbishop who travels into the high sierra to offer his miter views the native cult in rivalry with Catholicism and himself as rival of the shaman.

Also worth noting is this very early indigenous transculturation of Santiago, the Iberian saint of military conquests, a phenomenon that will continue to grow in Mexican folk lore and art as Santiago also becomes an "Indian" saint.[52] The Acaxee bishop, in an effort to infuse his own mission with the power of the Christian saints, renames his deputies with the names of two apostles that signify dual domains of power: Santiago, who brings the military might of the Reconquest, and Saint Peter, who stands for the power of Rome. In his reinvention in the ecclesiastical figure of a bishop, the Acaxee shaman reversed the direction of power and legitimized his actions to the point where they had to be met by a corresponding level of authority from the Christian side: the bishop of Guadalajara. This masterful appropriation transformed Christian symbols into a formidable affirmation of Acaxee spiritual power and

MAUREEN AHERN

identity by turning the tables on the Jesuits in "ways that could win them back disciples in many of the same ways that priests had first lured them away."[53]

The Tepehuan and Diego de Orozco: Death in the Form of the Cross

In the first surge of the Tepehuan Revolt in 1616, large areas of the eastern flanks of the Sierra Madre and the mining settlements that had flourished there reverted to the control of the Tepehuan. They mounted a carefully coordinated rebellion that targeted the Jesuit missionaries, killing eight of them, including Hernando Santarén who had managed to survive both the Acaxee and the Xixime revolts.[54] The last books of Pérez de Ribas's *Historia* reconstruct those Jesuit martyrdoms in vivid detail.[55] One example is especially cogent for our discussion of ritual reversal: the death at Santiago Papasquiaro of Father Diego de Orozco whose body the Tepehuan chopped into a visual replica of the cross. Pérez de Ribas narrates it as a terrifying parody of the Latin mass at which Orozco had officiated for them:

> Before they killed him eight Indians raised him in the air, mocking him with the words they had heard in mass: *Dominus vobiscum* while others answered, *Et cum spiritu tuo*. As they carried him in this way, from a distance they shot an arrow that passed through one side of his torso to the other. Then— so that his death would be crueler— three of them grabbed him and two of them held him by his arms in the form of the Cross, so that he would die like

His Lord and Our Redeemer, Jesus Christ. The third Indian split open his body from top to bottom with an ax. Before he expired the blessed priest said, "Do with me what you will, my sons, for I die for my God," and with this he gave his soul to God in sweetest holocaust.[56]

By all measures the image of the "sweetest holocaust" (*suavíssimo holocausto*) is striking, as are the Indian parody of the mass and the havoc wreaked upon the image of Our Lady that prefigure the execution of Orozco. Drawing on the explicit equivalence of this martyr for Christ, Pérez de Ribas notes that the entire body of the priest is cloven through.[57] In Pérez de Ribas's construction the body of the martyr visually configures the cross—becoming literally and figuratively what the author calls "the blood altar of the cross." It is at once site and symbol of the central sacrifice or Passion of Christ, the "validating basis of Christian salvation and Catholic sacramentalism."[58] From another perspective, the parody of the mass told with the oral force of the Latin phrase of the greeting of the priest and the response of the faithful underscores the Tepehuan's clear understanding of the power of parody to desacralize and humiliate. Their dispatch of Orozco's body in the visual form of the emblem by which he lived fires a terrifying image back against the miners and settlers. The Tepehuan flout their defiance by imbuing the most sacred Christian emblem of victory with the valence of defeat as this sacrificial body is made to celebrate a Tepehuan covenant of rebellion.

The narratives of the first missions to the Acaxee and Tepehuan illustrate several important points. First, they demonstrate how at different moments and in different places Christian ritual had to some extent been incorporated or acculturated into the native conceptual system. They also reveal how porous the frontier zone had become in terms of ritual penetration.[59] On the one hand, the Acaxee and Tepehuan were willing to move onto Christian ground to fashion a symbolic arsenal to defend their traditional spiritual and cultural practices. The Jesuit countermoves of burning the idols at a formal auto de fe and the journey of the Christian bishop to display his miter in the battle zone show how much church authorities were willing to move onto indigenous grounds in order to combat indigenous cults. Historian Cynthia Radding has pointed to the dualities of defiance and accommodation as modes of spiritual defense and survival in her discussion of the Tarahumar and other late seventeenth- and eighteenth-century frontier rebellions, but our examination of the Acaxee and Tepehuan cases demonstrates that these processes were already operating much earlier in the first decade of the seventeenth century in almost immediate reaction to the arrival of the Jesuits to their communities.

Conclusions

The indigenous appropriation of ritual signs in Nueva Galicia and Nueva Vizcaya became the weapons of war. Meanings inverted as often as did the sites, bodies, speeches, and actors who performed them. At the intersection of frontier martyrs and idols, their iconography performed the "mimicry and mockery of authority . . . that characterize the classical colonial situation" as Homi Bhabha has discussed. The accounts of the tortilla that mimicked the host; a Franciscan habit transformed into an idol; the shaman who cast himself as a bishop; the accomplice who called himself Santiago; a Jesuit body split into a cross, all reveal the remarkable quality of how performance transforms the direction of power through reversal and parody. An examination of the contradictions inherent in the textual operations of official Franciscan and Jesuit histories uncovers the symbolic spaces and practices of colonial religious culture at moments of extreme crisis. In the postcolonial process of dismantling them, we can perceive how the indigenous objects of evangelization reinvent their symbolic arsenals to capture social agency and mount a counteroffensive through transformative reversals of semiotic meanings. The martyr stories become the flash points of textual and cultural instability that disrupt the patriarchal "We" and "I" of Franciscan and Jesuit subjectivity and their paradigms of hagiographic *vitae*.

The transculturation of Christian symbols into native performances became a way of affirming their lifeways and spiritualities—in sum, the survival of their own cultures.[60] The martyr heroes of the Franciscans and Jesuit texts were consumed in spectacles of parody and inversion that signified victories for the insurgents. This fundamental reversal contained a lesson that continued to be played out in the recurring rebellions that followed on into the eighteenth and nineteenth centuries. It is the essential one that the Yaqui so brilliantly employ to this day in their Pascua celebrations, as Richard Schechner has revealed in

MAUREEN AHERN

an illuminating analysis that links present performances with past ritual frontiers.[61]

Finally, the narration of the early missionary frontier in these discourses brings actors and tellers, spectators and readers, face to face with the perpetual questioning of power that language and images contain, as they constantly fulfill David Murray's haunting observation that "missionaries could not control the meanings of what they gave or introduced."[62] In the narratives and testimonies of early missionary contact on the northwestern frontiers of New Spain, ritual objects and liturgies that are the focal points of martyr deaths become the flashpoints of regional native resistance through transformative reversals and resemantization of semiotic meanings. The martyr stories in the missionary literature of colonial Mexico construct the northern frontier as a volatile stage of transformative ritual, whether textual, visual, or performative.

NOTES

For the research contained in this study, I wish to acknowledge the support of the College of Humanities and the Department of Spanish and Portuguese of the Ohio State University for a research quarter leave in spring 2001 that allowed me to reconceptualize the preliminary versions of this chapter.

1. Donald Weinstein and Rudolph M. Bell, *Saints and Society* (Chicago: University of Chicago Press, 1982), 160.

2. Testimony of Capt. Francisco Romero de Arellano at Topia, Nueva Vizcaya, December 31, 1603, "Investigation Made for Francisco de Urdiñola" (Original in Archivo General de Indias, Audiencia de México 1254), transcribed and translated in Thomas Naylor and Charles Polzer, *The Presidio and Militia on the Northern Frontier of New Spain 1570–1700. A Documental History* (Tucson: University of Arizona Press, 1986), 176–79.

3. Cynthia Radding and Susan Deeds have both analyzed symbolic exchanges in frontier rebellions in essays that deal largely with seventeenth- and eighteenth-century frontiers. Their discussions have provided significant insights for this essay. See Cynthia Radding, "Cultural Boundaries between Adaptation and Defiance: The Mission Communities of Northwestern New Spain," in Nicholas Griffiths and Fernando Cervantes, *Spiritual Encounters: Interactions between Christian and Native Religions in Colonial America* (Lincoln: University of Nebraska Press, 1999), 116–35; Susan Deeds, "First Generation Rebellions in Seventeenth-Century Nueva Vizcaya," in *Native Resistance and the Pax Colonial in New Spain*, ed. Susan Schroeder, 1–29 (Lincoln and London: University of Nebraska Press, 1998a), "Indigenous Rebellions on the Northern Mexican Mission Frontier," in *Contested Ground: Comparative Frontiers on the Northern and Southern Edges of the Spanish Empire*, ed. Donna J. Guy and Thomas E. Sheridan, 32–51 (Tucson: The University of Arizona Press, 1998); and "Indigenous Responses to Mission Settlement in Nueva Vizcaya" in *The New Latin American Mission History*, ed. Eric R. Langer and Robert H. Jackson, 77–108 (Lincoln and London: University of Nebraska Press, 1995).

4. See my discussions of the construction of Jesuit martyrdom and verbal and visual narrative of the period in two essays: Maureen Ahern, "Dichosas Muertes": Jesuit Martyrdom on the Northern Frontier of La Florida," *Romance Philology* 53, Special Issue, Part 1 (fall 1999): 1–21, and "Visual and Verbal Sites: The Construction of Jesuit Martyrdom in Northwest New Spain in Andrés Pérez de Ribas' *Historia de los Triumphos de nuestra Santa Fee* (1645)," *Colonial Latin American Review* 8, no. 1 (1999): 17–33.

5. Fray Gerónimo de Mendieta (ca. 1596), *Historia eclesiástica indiana*, 2nd ed. facsimilar y primera con reproducción de los dibujos originales

del códice (México, DF: Editorial Porrúa, S.A., 1971).

6. Fray Antonio Tello (ca. 1656), *Crónica miscelánea de la sancta provincia de Xalisco por Fray Antonio Tello*, 2 vols. (Guadalajara, Jalisco, México: Gobierno del Estado de Jalisco, Universidad de Guadalajara, Instituto Jalisciense de Antropología e Historia/Instituto Nacional de Antropología e Historia, Libro Segundo, vol. II, 1968).

7. Andrés Pérez de Ribas, S.J., *Historia de los Triumphos de nuestra Santa Fee entre Gentes las más bárbaras y fieras del nuevo Orbe* [*sic*] (Madrid: Por Alonso de Paredes, 1645), *History of the Triumphs of Our Holy Faith Amongst the Most Barbarous and Fierce People of the New World*, trans. by Daniel T. Reff, Maureen Ahern, and Richard Danford, intro. by Daniel T. Reff (Tucson: University of Arizona Press, 1999). All references are to this translation.

8. See Tuer's discussion of Spanish-Guaraní interaction in Ruiz de Montoya's account of the Jesuit enterprise in Paraguay in Dot Tuer, "Old Bones and Beautiful Words: The Spiritual Contestation between Shaman and Jesuit in the Guarani Missions," in *Colonial Saints: Discovering the Holy in the Americas, 1500–1800*, ed. Allan Greer and Jodi Bilinkoff, 77–97 (New York: Routledge, 2003).

9. Gilles Delueze, *The Fold: Leibniz and the Baroque*, trans. Tom Conley (Minneapolis and London: University of Minnesota Press, 1993).

10. Serge Gruzinski, *La guerra de las imágenes: De Cristóbal Colón a 'Blade Runner' (1492–2019)* (México, DF: Fondo de Cultura Económica, 1994). The English translation is *Images at War: Mexico from Columbus to Blade Runner (1492–2019)*, trans. Heather MacLean (Durham and London: Duke University Press, 2001).

11. My application of the concept of cracks or fissures in discourse is from Martin Heidegger, *The Question Concerning Technology and Other Essays*, trans. and intro. by William Lovitt (New York and London: Garland Publishing, 1977). As pointed out by David Spurr, in his *The Rhetoric of Empire* (Durham and London: Duke University Press, 1993), 184: "There are always cracks in the edifice; language is constantly sabotaging the very structures it supports." The concept of language as a point of resistance is from Michel Foucault, *The Order of Things: Archaeology of the Human Sciences* (New York: Pantheon Books, 1970) and *The History of Sexuality*, vol. 1, trans. Robert Hurley (New York: Vintage Books, 1980).

12. Gruzinski, *La guerra de las imágenes*, 179.

13. Michael Roberts, *Poetry and the Cult of the Martyrs: The Liber Peristephanon of Prudentius* (Ann Arbor: University of Michigan Press, 1993), 39–77.

14. Ibid., 75.

15. See David Sweet's discussion of "conversion" as a voluntary process and thus "not an accurate term for the real transformations that took place among Indians in the frontier missions. The missionary record makes it clear that Indians were frequently persuaded or even required, at least as a survival strategy, to accept the Catholic rite of baptism . . . Nothing about the mission enterprise is self-evident . . . nothing . . . about it should be taken for granted or at face value" in "The Ibero-American Frontier Mission in Native American History," in Langer and Jackson, *The New Latin American Mission History*, 44–45.

16. Thomas Calvo dates the founding of the first Franciscan convent in Jalisco at 1540. Thomas Calvo et al., *Xalisco, la voz de un pueblo en el siglo XVI* (México, DF: Centro de Investigaciones y Estudios Superiores en Antropología Social, Centro de Estudios Mexicanos y Centroamericanos, 1993), 17. Also see Pauline Moffitt Watts, "The New World and the End of the World: Evangelizing Sixteenth-Century Mexico," in *Imagining the New World: Columbian Iconography*, ed. Irma B. Jaffe et al., 29–39 (Rome and New York: Instituto della Encyclopedia Italiana, 1991), and John Leddy Phelan, *The Millennial Kingdom of the Franciscans in the New World*, 2nd. rev. ed. (Berkeley and Los Angeles: University of California Press, 1970), for the Franciscan ideals of founding a millennial and utopian kingdom in New Spain. Mendieta, in particular, was convinced they were founding the City of God, the New Jerusalem that would grow from the labors of the friars of evangelical poverty and the "angelic" Indians.

17. Miguel León-Portilla points out that the Caxcan and Zacatec were not nomadic or "primitive" Chichimecas but rather sedentary

groups whose related languages were part of the Nahua linguistic family in *La flecha en el blanco. Francisco Tenamaztle y Bartolomé de las Casas en la lucha por los derechos de los indígenas, 1541–1556* (México, DF: Editorial Diana 1995), 10–11.

18. León-Portilla, *Flecha en el blanco*, 23, my translation.

19. Cited in José López Portillo y José Weber, *La Rebelión de Nueva Galicia* (México, DF: Instituto Panamericano de Geografía e Historia, 1939), 403. León-Portilla, *Flecha en el blanco*, 23, adds that a mural at the entrance to the municipal building in Tlaltenango represents the rebellious Caxcan and Zacatec, with the transcription *axcan quema, tehuatl, nehuatl*! Robert Ricard pointed to "sharp resistance, although invisible" in early missionary efforts, in *The Spiritual Conquest of Mexico*, trans. by Lesley Byrd Simpson, 2nd. ed. (Berkeley and Los Angeles: University of California Press, 1982), 269. However, in the case of the Caxcan, it was dramatically visible.

20. "Los descargos del Virrey, don Antonio de Mendoza, números 35 al 43 inclusive, del interrogatorio de la Visita del licenciado Francisco Tello de Sandoval" (hereafter cited as Mendoza, "Descargos") (Original in Archivo General de Indias, Justicia 259, f. 1–78), reproduced in part in Ciriaco Pérez Bustamante, *Los orígenes del gobierno virreinal en las Indias españolas. Don Antonio de Mendoza, primer virrey de la Nueva España, 1535–1550* (Santiago de Compostela: Anales de la Universidad de Santiago, v. III, 1928), 152–68.

21. According to León-Portilla, *Flecha en el blanco*, 27, the testimony written in Nahuatl by don Francisco Pantecatl, Señor de Tzapotzinco, that narrated many of the events was later incorporated by Antonio Tello into his *Crónica miscelánea*, libro II, vol. I, 1973.

22. Tello, *Crónica miscelánea*, CIII 147, my translation.

23. In Article XXXV of his defense of the charges pressed by Tello de Sandoval, the viceroy inserted a detailed account of the cause of the Mixton War as due to the preaching of these shamans. Given such graphic detail in the testimony, it probably came from Indian informants (Mendoza, "Descargos," 1928, 154–53).

24. Mendoza, "Descargos," 1928, 157, my translation.

25. For an indigenous pictorial account of the siege of Nochistlan, the death of Alvarado and Franciscan evangelization at the height of the Mixton War in 1541, see f. 46r of Eloise Quiñones Keber's edition of the *Codex Telleriano-Remensis: Ritual, Divination, and History in a Pictorial Aztec Manuscript* (Austin: University of Texas Press), 1995.

26. Mendoza, "Descargos," 1928, 157, my translation.

27. León-Portilla, *Flecha en el blanco*, 53–54, comments that the viceroy seemed to be unaware of the meaning of tlatol, which would confirm that he was repeating what other witnesses who were aware of the significance of events had communicated to him. In this context the reference is to an abbreviated form of *tlahtolli*, a holy command to action for the Chichimecas.

28. León-Portilla, *Flecha en el blanco*, 135.

29. Calvo, *Xalisco*, 17.

30. Mendieta, *Historia eclesiástica indiana*, 738.

31. Ibid., 739.

32. Gruzinski, *La guerra de las imágenes*, 61.

33. Mendieta, *Historia eclesiástica indiana*, 756–57.

34. For a discussion of these tactics in terms of rhetoric and colonialism, see Spur, *Rhetoric*, 186, and also Homi Bhaba, "Signs Taken for Wonders: Questions of Ambivalence and Authority under a Tree Outside Delhi, May 1817," in *The Location of Culture* (London and New York: Routledge, 1994), 102–22.

35. Deeds, "First Generations" and "Indigenous Rebellions."

36. According to Francisco de la Maza in his *Fray Diego de Valadés, escritor y grabador franciscano del siglo XVI* (México, DF: Universidad Nacional Autónoma de México, 1945), this illustration is not a copy of any of the illustrations by Valadés contained in his *Rhetórica christiana* (Perugia, 1579), Intro. de Esteban J. Palomera, trad. Tarcicio Herrera Zapién (México, DF: Universidad Nacional Autónoma de México, Fondo de Cultura Económica, 1989). I hypothesize that it may well have been drawn by him specifically for fray Gerónimo

de Mendieta's *Historia eclesiástica indiana*. It is interesting to note that the Mexican scholar and collector, García Izcabalceta, did not include the prints in his first edition of the *Historia* published in 1870, because he found some of them to be too "*horrendos*"(horrible). Francisco Solano y Pérez-Lila, 1973, "Estudio Preliminar," fray Jerónimo de Mendieta, *Historia eclesiástica indiana. Biblioteca de Autores Españoles*, 2 vols. (Madrid: Ediciones Atlas, 1973), vol. 1, ix–cxi, lxxx.

37. As discussed by Edward E. Muir in a lecture, "The Eye of the Procession: Ritual Ways of Seeing in the Renaissance," April 15, 1999, at the Ohio State University. See also his *Ritual in Early Modern Europe* (Cambridge, UK: Cambridge University Press, 1997).

38. See Pauline Moffitt Watts, "Languages of Gesture in Sixteenth-Century Mexico: Some Antecedents and Permutations," in *Reframing the Renaissance: Visual Culture in Europe and Latin America 1450–1650*, ed. Claire Farago, 140–51 (New Haven: Yale University Press, 1995), and E. H. Gombrich, *The Image and the Eye* (Oxford, UK: Phaidon Press, 1982), 63–77.

39. Bernadette Boucher points out that "The grammar of graphic forms lets the graphic narrative develop autonomously; though supported by the written texts, the message it conveys is something other than the sum of the elements that compose it," in *Icon and Conquest* (Chicago and London: University of Chicago Press, 1981), 30. For the rotative image, see Edwin Panofsky, *Studies in Iconology: Humanistic Themes in the Art of the Renaissance* (New York: Harper Torch Books), 1962.

40. Naylor and Polzer, *The Presidio*, 154.

41. Ralph L. Beals, *The Acaxee: A Mountain Tribe of Durango and Sinaloa* (Berkeley: University of California Press, 1933), 22, 27, 31.

42. Francisco de Báez [1602], Annual Letter of April 1602, transcribed and translated in Naylor and Polzer, *The Presidio*, 154–71, from the Vatican, Archivum Romanum Societatis Iesu, México, 14, f. 289–94 (Original in Archivo General de Indias, México 1254) (hereafter cited as "Annual Letter"), 158–59.

43. Ibid., 156.

44. Ibid., 159, my translation.

45. Ibid., 160.

46. See Susan Deeds's lucid analysis of these two revolts in her essay, "First Generation Rebellions" in Schroeder, *Native Resistance*, 1–29.

47. See my essays in note 4, "Dichosas Muertes" and "Visual and Verbal Sites." For an historical perspective see Charlotte Grady, *The Tepehuan Revolt of 1616* (Salt Lake City: University of Utah Press, 2000).

48. Capt. Francisco Romero de Arellano, "Investigation Made for Francisco de Urdiñola," in Naylor and Polzer, *The Presidio*, 176–79. The Acaxee had already defeated two previous military expeditions against them. When the old frontier veteran Urdiñola was finally able to capture forty-eight of their war captains he ordered twelve to be hanged along the roads and the rest at the spot where they had robbed and killed Spaniards, finally subduing them in 1603. Naylor and Polzer transcribe a number of testimonies about the Acaxee and the Xixime rebellions dictated by members of the expedition as well as the testimony of Santarén himself.

49. Romero de Arellano, "Investigation," 177.

50. Pérez de Ribas, *History of the Triumphs*, book 8, chapter 8, 510.

51. Deeds mentions another case of an Indian shaman called Quautlatas, a "bishop" said to be from New Mexico, who had begun preaching among the Tepehuan around Durango in 1615. See "Indigenous Rebellions," 9.

52. See Marian Oettinger Jr.'s discussion of Santiago in his *Folk Art of Spain and the Americas* (San Antonio: San Antonio Museum of Art/Abbeville Press Publishers, 1997), and William B. Taylor's essay on the "growing ambivalence" of Santiago's meanings to Indians in Central Mexico in the late colonial period in "Santiago's Horse: Christianity and Colonial Indian Resistance in the Heartland of New Spain," in *Violence, Resistance and Survival in the Americas*, ed. William B. Taylor and Franklin Pease G. Y., 153–89 (Washington, DC and London: Smithsonian Institution Press, 1994).

53. Griffiths and Cervantes, *Spiritual Encounters*, 30.

54. Naylor and Polzer, *The Presidio*, 152, 245.

55. Ahern, "Dichosas Muertes" and "Visual and Verbal Sites."

56. Pérez de Ribas, *History of the Triumphs*, book 10, chapter 18, 602–3.

57. Stephan Gilman has pointed to the baroque compulsion to catch and hold the attention of the convert, reader, or audience through the effect of horror. See "An Introduction to the Ideology of the Baroque in Spain," *Symposium* (November 1946): 83–107, esp. 97 for quotation.

58. Thomas J. Steele, S.J., *Santos y Saints: The Religious Folk Art of Hispanic New Mexico*, rev. ed. (Santa Fe, NM: Ancient City Press, 1982), 51.

59. See the discussion of porous and fluid frontiers in Radding, "Cultural Boundaries," 116–18, and throughout Guy and Sheridan, *Contested Ground*.

60. Sweet points out that "Resistance of whatever sort, however manifested, was a reaffirmation of self or community that gave people a purpose and served to limit the effectiveness of the colonial mission as a system for the conversion, civilization, and exploitation of Indian society. . . . it was the mission as space, and as new context for organization that enabled the resistance itself to be attempted." See "The Ibero-American Frontier Mission," in Langer and Jackson, *The New Latin American Mission History*, 42–43.

61. Richard Schechner, "Waehma: Space, Time, Identity and Theatre at New Pascua, Arizona," in *The Future of Ritual: Writing on Culture and Performance* (London: Routledge, 1993), 94–130.

62. "What entered into circulation, whether a word, an idea, or a religious object, then took on a value given by its circulation within that particular material and discursive economy, and it could not from that point onward be restricted or authorized only by its Christian origins." See David Murray, "Spreading the Word: Missionaries, Conversion and Circulation in the Northeast," in Griffiths and Cervantes, *Spiritual Encounters*, 43.

PART SEVEN

TANGENTIAL CHRISTIANITY ON OTHER FRONTIERS

Business and Politics as Usual

I assign you to voluntary poverty. . . . Learn to be poor, to live without pretensions. . . . Be a canal, not a reservoir. . . . Strip yourself of all property and you will fly.

—Bishop Juan de Palafox
y Mendoza, 1664

From this calculation it can be determined that the metropolitan church of Mexico has a budget exceeding three hundred thousand pesos.

—Fray Iliarione da Bergamo, d. 1778

The Church is the congregation of the faithful who fight at their own expense to acquire the celestial inheritance, without any temporal matter the object of so holy a mother.

—Pedro Rodríguez Campomanes, 1769

It was principally through the secular and regular clergy that the Americans have been and are loyal to God and the king. . . . he who has the priests has the Indies.

—Archbishop Francisco Javier
de Lizana y Beaumont, 1809

Over the course of the colonial era, regions beyond Mexico City began to develop. Local resources and their demands determined which would prosper, but over time new cities with bishoprics, courts, and flourishing economies appeared in the north and south of New Spain. Populations, too, began to recover in the seventeenth century, and haciendas and plantations supplied the silver mines and the cities with food and livestock, and *obrajes* (factories) furnished locals with all sorts of consumable goods. These regions were often great distances from the capital and its trunk line connecting the silver mines to Veracruz on the Gulf of Mexico. Goods and people also came from the Philippines, traversed the isthmus, and went on to Spain along with the colony's precious metals and other commodities.

As the new districts developed, they became self-sufficient; they were involved in and benefited from investments in the local economy. In many ways, they became their own hubs, with a full complement of political and ecclesiastical officials and a society as complex and sophisticated as any other.

By the middle years of the colonial period, the church was heavily invested in the colony, whether through its clergy and their family connections or through its entrepreneurial activities, such as real estate loans, property rentals, or the revenues from large estates. Affluent families with sons and daughters as priests and nuns connected the church to the countryside, and money flowed between the two to finance festivals, purchase ornaments, sponsor a charitable project, or build a new chapel. Other family members might also be engaged in local politics, which inevitably benefited their estate and likely the church too.

James Riley, in "Priests and the Provincial Social Order in Tlaxcala, 1650–1792," treats career patterns of secular priests in the eastern province of Tlaxcala and the priests' relationships to family, business, and evolving politics. It is a comprehensive study that includes native-Spanish relations, concerns about mestizaje and entitlement, priestly activities and their diminishing place in Tlaxcala as other opportunities materialized, and the pervasiveness of corporatism in later Bourbon times. Business and politics also influenced eighteenth-century religious developments even in the southern reaches of Chiapas. Michael Polushin, in "Apostles of Reform: Local Elites and *Patronato Real* in Late Colonial Chiapas," gives us a fine example of how religious celebrations were manipulated for economic and political gain. In this instance the festival day of Our Lady of Merced was used to oust a royal official from his position. Probably harmless enough, but Polushin reveals that the Catholic church was often the means by which the machinations of elites brought great political and economic advantage to themselves, especially in faraway Chiapas in later Bourbon times, and had little to do with the spiritual needs of their community.

NOTES

Epigraph citations, in order of appearance, are as follows: William B. Taylor, *Magistrates of the Sacred: Priests and Parishioners in Eighteenth-Century Mexico* (Stanford: Stanford University Press, 1996), 144; Fray Ilarione da Bergamo, *Daily Life in Colonial Mexico: The Journey of Friar Ilarione da Bergamo, 1761–1768*, trans. William J. Orr, ed. Robert Ryal Miller and William J. Orr, 140 (Norman: University of Oklahoma Press, 2000); D. A. Brading, *The First America: The Spanish Monarchy, Creole Patriots, and the Liberal State, 1492–1867* (Cambridge: Cambridge University Press, 1993), 504; D. A. Brading, *Church and State in Bourbon Mexico: The Diocese of Michoacán, 1749–1810* (New York: Cambridge University Press, 1994), 129–30.

CHAPTER FIFTEEN

Priests and the Provincial Social Order
in Tlaxcala, 1650–1792

JAMES D. RILEY

A great deal of the recent work on colonial religion has focused on religious culture, particularly on indigenous understandings of Catholic belief systems and manipulation of Catholic structures to support their own social and ideological objectives.[1] That work offers many useful insights into how Catholicism functioned in a colonial environment. But the interest devoted to the study of cultural matters has not extended to another key element of colonial Catholicism, the diocesan priesthood. This lack of attention is somewhat puzzling since the secular parish priest was the lynchpin of the colonial religious system and the man most involved with the interpretation of European values for the indigenous communities.[2] While recent work mentions them in passing, it is usually analysis based on litigation and focuses on clergy as the source of controversy and conflict with the local community.[3] This approach gives us little insight into diocesan priests as individuals, or as representatives of the local notability from which they sprang. It is the purpose of this chapter to address this lacuna. What most interests me, specifically, is how local hispanicized elites used the priesthood to further their own social and ideological agendas.

In a recent book, Kathryn Burns showed that religious institutions could play a complex role in sustaining the values and identity of a local community. She argues, referring to Peru, that convents of women were central to the economic, social, and spiritual strategies pursued by local colonial elites, and were considered crucial to the identity of their communities.[4] Could the same have been true of the priesthood? Our understanding of why men became priests has usually emphasized individual motives: it was a bureaucratic career that offered a comfortable living and status, or it was a spiritual and intellectual vocation that led to personal growth.[5] But there are other possible motives that might be considered. Rik Hoekstra's work on the interpenetration of Hispanic and indigenous cultures in the region of Puebla-Tlaxcala, in particular, raises the possibility that communal objectives linked to economic necessity might explain why families of gente decente pushed sons to enter the clergy. His analysis of Spanish-indigenous relations from the middle of the sixteenth to the middle of the seventeenth century convinces him that controlling local indigenous resources required more than the brute application of power and the networking of Spanish landowners with other landowners and merchants. He argues that to penetrate eastern Nahua regions substantially controlled by the indigenous population after the conquest, Spanish landowners had to accommodate themselves to indigenous conceptions of authority. Such an accommodation, he concluded, was not as difficult as it might seem because the northern European concept of *herrschaft* (lordship) was very similar to the intimate link between political authority and religious authority characteristic of indigenous societies in Puebla and Tlaxcala. Herrschaft involved legitimating the authority of the ruler through a deeply personal relationship claimed by the lord over his followers on religious and moral grounds.[6] Hoekstra's most provocative conclusion is that Spanish landowners understood this basis for authority and adapted the concept to their relationship with the indigenous populations. They assumed the

mantle of indigenous lordship with all of its rights and responsibilities and used Nahua communal values to legitimate their claims to labor and land.[7]

The issues that Burns and Hoekstra address have importance for my own research. For a number of years I have been engaged in an effort to understand Hispanic society in the Mexican province of Tlaxcala. This has focused on the reconstruction of individual landholding families and their relationship to each other, as well as their involvement in the political life of their community and that of the larger society that surrounded them. During the sixteenth century, the province was the political bastion of the Tlaxcalan indigenous community, a community that had received a great deal of autonomy as a result of its support for the initial conquests and whose leadership had used that autonomy to control its economic development.[8] But toward the end of the sixteenth century, the dynamic growth of the Pueblan economy created economic opportunity for Hispanic settlers and a portion of the indigenous elite who decided to join the Hispanic commercial effort.[9] Ultimately, this development led to the indigenous political elite's loss of control over economic life, but it also resulted in the establishment of a very prosperous hispanicized landholding and commercial community that supplied food and raw materials for Pueblan development.[10]

One thing that stands out clearly in this process is that local hispanicized elites who dominated the province's economic life did not individually possess the money or status necessary to defend their interests and gain control over vital resources on a continuing basis. One way to overcome their weakness was to use networking. Even the most important of the local families married and exchanged godparents with other local landowners and local merchants in an effort to gain control of the local environment through collective action.[11]

But there were limits to the applicability of this tactic when it came to gaining access to resources controlled by the Indian community—particularly labor. Intermarriage with the indigenous governing elite, the *pipiltin*, did occur and at times created significant alliances, but by the middle of the seventeenth century it was not a favored strategy.[12] Adopting Hoekstra's model of herrschaft provided an alternative. That there was a moral economy linking landowners and indigenous communities is clear, particularly in labor relations. Labor systems in much of central Mexico depended on a set of patriarchal relationships that in 1687 gained the force of law and prevented indigenous residents of haciendas from moving.[13]

But if Hoekstra is correct about Spanish adoption of indigenous cultural conceptions of authority, we must see more than just a paternalistic moral economy in operation. Spanish landowners and merchants who claimed indigenous resources had to connect themselves to religious power as well, because spiritual and political power were linked in the same individual in the Nahua world. Given the obvious difference between this situation and the Catholic world where spiritual power was separated from the secular political authority, the person of the priests became quite important. In a personal way, they had to be identified with the local elites who were claiming herrschaft and using their moral power and control of access to the spiritual world to sustain the position of those elites.

Regrettably, testing whether this was the case cannot be done in a straightforward way. Priests never talked of their motives for entering the priesthood (in any records I have seen), and examples of priestly use of their authority to further family interests can only be found in court records that by their nature distort reality.[14] But I would suggest that it is possible to offer some confirmation of the thesis by examining the degree to which members of families belonging to the Tlaxcalan provincial elite entered the priesthood and obtained positions in areas where they could use their spiritual authority to support family activities.

The diocesan priesthood in Tlaxcala really began in 1641 when the bishop of Puebla, Juan de Palafox, secularized the Franciscan *doctrinas* (spiritual districts). Between that moment and 1732, I have identified 309 individuals who provided sacramental services to the Tlaxcalan community as more than short term visitors to the province. Since I have not examined all of the parishes fully (see the source note to Table 15.2), these figures are not absolute totals. There are, moreover, significant gaps in the careers of all but a relative few of the number. Nevertheless, even with the sources I have available, several conclusions about priests are very clear. First, there was a significant correlation between the amount of time individual priests spent in the province and their connection to local society. Second, there was also a correlation between the strength of Spanish landholding and Spanish commercial activity in a given parish and the degree to which men whose families had identifiable provincial interests dominated the priesthood.[15] Third, while local men infrequently obtained pastorates, they routinely served as assistants in the most attractive parishes. Moreover, in areas where haciendas were primary population centers, though not formally employed in significant numbers, they provided the sacramental services for the workers of their own, or their family, estates. Finally, both the total number of priests available for services and the number of local priests rose dramatically after 1660. The numbers reached a peak between 1710 and 1730 before declining just as dramatically thereafter. The surge corresponded almost exactly to the period of greatest economic and social strength of the local elites and suggests that there was a connection between the two phenomena.[16]

To explain these conclusions, I would like to examine the general conditions of the priesthood in Tlaxcala between 1641 and 1730 along with what can be ascertained regarding priestly visions of community during this period of efflorescence, and how the priesthood available for services changed in the latter colonial period.

Parish and Society in Colonial Tlaxcala

The parishes of San Luis Apizaco, Santa Ana Chiautempan, San Dionisio Yauhquemeca, San Agustín Tlaxco, San Luis Huamantla, and San José Tlaxcala were at the heart of the commercial development and growth of Spanish landholding but their indigenous and hispanicized populations pursued different economic activities and had different relationships. Apizaco and Santa Ana were the centers for *obrajes* (textile mills) and an indigenous system of household production (*telares sueltos*), which dominated textile production in the province until 1710. San Dionisio supported a ranching economy centered on the pasturing of sheep that produced wool for the nearby textile works, and its Indians provided workers for nearby projects. Haciendas producing pigs and wool for the markets of Puebla in the seventeenth century, and pigs and pulque in the eighteenth century, dominated San Agustín Tlaxco. Huamantla produced wheat and pork, likewise for Puebla, throughout the seventeenth and eighteenth centuries. The city of Tlaxcala was the administrative center and the residence of major merchants who moved Tlaxcalan goods northward to the Real del Monte and southward to Puebla, and acted as middlemen for Pueblan houses distributing imported wares to the eastern heartland. The indigenous communities that surrounded the city, however, were relatively independent with little connection to the Spanish economy.

The indigenous community constituted approximately 90 percent of total population in 1681 and 80 percent in 1792, a gradual downward trend that can be assumed to have fluctuated little during the intervening period.[17] Residential patterns and subordination to Spanish authority, however, varied. At a moment when the provincial Hispanic economy was at its height in 1675, approximately 50 percent of the tributary population in the province as a whole lived on Spanish estates.[18] But in the parish of Santa Ana, where the manufacture of cloth was the primary activity, the parish census of 1681 revealed relatively small landholdings with few Indian residents.[19] Indigenous communities under the social authority of the pipiltin dominated the center and center-south of the province in general and Spanish entrepreneurs had to share resources with these villages. Because of the critical role they played in this exchange, indigenous elites could not be ignored, and the leading families reflected the intermarriage of Spanish entrepreneurs and the pipiltin. Rather than landowners and *hacendados* (possessors of haciendas), the key authority figures were these Spanish and indigenous intermediaries between indigenous producers and the markets in Puebla and elsewhere.

Table 15.1. The Parishes of Tlaxcala in 1791 (date of erection)

San José Tlaxcala (1641)	Santa Ana Chiautempa (1641)	San Felipe Ixtacuintla (1641)*	San Agustín Tlaxco (1641)*
San Luis Huamantla (1641)	Santa María Nativitas (1641)*	San Ildefonso Hueyotlipa (1641)*	San Dionisio Yauquemecan (1641)
San Luis Apizaco (1641)*	San Francisco Topoyango (1643)*	Santa Inés Zacatelco (1646)	San Pablo del Monte (1670s?)
San Lorenzo Cuapiastla (1693)	Sanctuary of San Miguel el Milagro (1680s)	Santa Cruz Tlaxcala (1693)	San Martín Jaltocan (1693)
San Nicolás Panotla (1693)	San Juan Ixtenco (1709)	San Pablo Citlaltepec (1714)	San Juan Baptista Atlangatepec (1758)
San Luis Teolocholco (1766)	San Pablo Apetatitla (1767)	San Salvador Tzompantepec (1772)	Santa Isabel Tetlatlahuaca (1778)
Sanctuary of Nuestra Señora de Ocotlan (1780)			

Sources: Peter Gerhard, "Un censo de la diócesis de Puebla en 1681," *Historia Mexicana* 30, no. 4 (1981), 522, gives the parishes with curas beneficiados. William B. Taylor, *Magistrates of the Sacred: Priests and Parishioners in Eighteenth-Century Mexico* (Stanford: Stanford University Press, 1996), 79–82, describes the various types of assistants to the cura beneficiado. In 1791 there were twenty-three parishes and one visita plus two pilgrimage sites—the sanctuaries of San Miguel el Milagro and Nuestra Señora de Ocotlan—and one permanently staffed hacienda chapel with a private chaplain (AGN, ramo de padrones, vol. 22). Claude Morin, *Santa Inés Zacatelco (1645–1812): Contribución a la demografía histórica del Mexico Colonial* (México, DF: Instituto Nacional de Antropología e Historia, 1973), 11–12, and 92, n. 3, discusses Bourbon plans that led to these further changes.

* These parishes were established on the sites of Franciscan doctrinas when the Franciscans were removed. The doctrina of San Juan Atlangatepec was transferred to the Spanish settlement of San Agustín Tlaxco at this time, the church of the doctrina of Tescalac was abandoned and the parish established in the already existing church in the Spanish settlement of Santiago Tetla. In the late seventeenth century, this became known as the parish of San Luis Apizaco. There were three Franciscan convents remaining in 1791: in Tlaxcala, Huamantla, and San Francisco Topoyango.

Huamantla and the parish of San Agustín Tlaxco were at the other extreme. In 1681, the parish of Huamantla served one town, four barrios, forty-five haciendas, and four ranchos. While the census gave no breakdown of population by residence, in 1717 a crown inspection of labor conditions among resident workers (*gañanes*) revealed that possibly three-quarters of the indigenous households in Huamantla were found on Spanish estates.[20] Residence on an estate in this period required a submission to the patriarchal authority of the Spanish landlord, and his acceptance of the responsibilities involved, which Hoekstra used the model of herrschaft to describe.[21] But did religious authority in the person of the priest also supplement the social and economic basis for *gañanía* in these districts where it was strongest, as Hoekstra's model suggests it should?

Until 1641, local elites could not contemplate the use of priestly authority to support a patriarchal social order because Franciscans who established the system of doctrinas and convents that controlled provincial religious life had little link to provincial society.[22] In January of that year, however, bishop Juan de Palafox of Puebla swept into the provincial capital in the middle of the night (according to the Indian chronicler) and dispossessed the Franciscans, replacing them with diocesan priests.[23] In short order, all of the Franciscans were returned to their convents and their eight doctrinas were transformed into the first provincial parishes (see Table 15.1).

The number of parishes continued to grow due to population increase. By 1681, there were twelve, along with six *visitas*

(small churches without a resident priest) keeping separate sacramental registers and possibly served by permanent *vicarios de pie fijo* (permanent resident assistant pastors), three in the parish of San José Tlaxcala and three in Huamantla. By 1730, each of these six had become a parish in its own right with a *cura beneficiado* (permanent pastor). The priests who served these eighteen parishes in 1730 controlled the religious ritual life of the indigenous population and had the greatest opportunity to provide spiritual reinforcement to the economic and social regimes. As I will show, priests with connections to local families took advantage of the opportunities offered.

Priests and Parish Life, 1641–1730

Few of the first secular priests to serve in Tlaxcala after 1641 can be identified with local interests. Of the seven men we can securely identify as the initial pastors only one, Licenciado Diego de Nava y de la Mota, pastor of San Felipe, had a provincial attachment (though probably distant). He, however, was the only man in this group who did not pursue a salaried career. Although a relatively young man, he served as a pastor for only a few years and then established a residence in the town of San Francisco Tepeyanco where he remained into the 1670s occasionally assisting in the local parish.[24]

The same lack of local connections also characterized the initial assistants. The early registers are quite jumbled and fragmentary, but of the thirty-eight men identified as delivering the sacraments for at least a year before 1655, only eight can be securely identified as having local connections. At that point, however, the number of local priests began to increase significantly. Including these early men, Table 15.2 shows that over the entire period between 1641 and 1730 approximately 30 percent of the pastors and 54 percent of the assisting priests were men with local connections. When broken down by length of service, moreover, we find that the contribution of local priests to total numbers in both categories rises significantly the longer the time spent in the province. While 41 percent of the assisting priests and 14 percent of the pastors who worked for less than ten years were local, sixty-four of the eighty-two assisting priests (78 percent), and eighteen of the thirty-seven pastors (49 percent) who served more than ten years can be shown to have had local interests.

Most of the priests and pastors found in the province for less than ten years, whether local or non-local, were clearly using their

Table 15.2. Length of Service of Priests in Tlaxcala, 1641–1730*

Pastors			Other Priests	
Service recorded	Total number	Number connected to local families or interests	Total number	Number connected to local families or interests
less than 5 years	26	3	124	49
5–9 years	16	3	24	11
10–19 years	25	14	41	27
20+ years	12	4	41	37
Totals	79	24	230	124

Sources: I have explored the records of fourteen of the eighteen parishes extant in 1730 (including those visitas that became parishes during the period). Only scattered information from the parishes of San Nicolás Panotla, Santa Inés Zacatelco, San Pablo del Monte, and San Ildefonso Hueyotlipa are included in the above calculations. Following are the relevant roll numbers from the Genealogical Society of Utah collections:

San Agustín Tlaxco: *Baptisms,* 645860–61, 646519; *Marriages,* 645893–97; *Burials,* 645500
San Dionisio Yauhquemecan: *Baptisms,* 641278–80; *Marriages,* 641288; *Burials,* 641825
San Felipe Ixtacuixtla: *Baptisms,* 305324–25; *Marriages,* 305354–57
San Francisco Tepeyanco: *Baptisms,* 698804
San José Tlaxcala: Baptisms, 240968; *Marriages,* 241008–11, 241027–28; *Burials,* 241107–08
San Juan Ixtenco: *Baptisms,* 641387–89; *Marriages,* 641423–24
San Lorenzo Cuapiastla: *Baptisms,* 642403; *Marriages,* 642415–18; *Burials,* 642481

San Luis Apizaco: *Baptisms,* 698801–04, 698831; *Marriages,* 697449, 698820–21; *Burials,* 698831
San Luis Huamantla: *Baptisms,* 305144–47, 305149–51; *Marriages,* 305194–203, 305210; *Burials,* 305310–12
San Martín Jaltocan: *Baptisms,* 713110; *Marriages,* 704966
San Pablo Citlaltepec: *Baptisms,* 641434; *Marriages,* 641439, 641446
Santa Ana Chiautempan: *Baptisms,* 248329–31; *Marriages,* 304791, 304815–16; *Burials,* 304926
Santa Cruz: *Baptisms,* 641472; *Burials,* 641478, 641483
Santa María Nativitas: *Marriages,* 305087–88; *Burials,* 305106

Note: *The category of **Pastors** refers only to *curas beneficiados* (permanent pastors). The category of **Other Priests** includes all others who served in salaried positions as well as those who regularly performed sacramental services but held no salaried position. The category of **Connected to local** identifies priests who were members of extended families with interests in the province, or possessed haciendas or other property in the province.

PRIESTS AND PROVINCIAL SOCIAL ORDER IN TLAXCALA, 1650–1792

posts as steppingstones to other assignments. Licenciado Lorenzo de Sempertegui, pastor of San José Tlaxcala from 1716 to 1721, was probably typical. His name only appears in provincial records at the moment he became pastor, he seems to have established no provincial ties while a resident, and quickly moved on when he received his doctorate in theology in 1720.

The fact that a considerable number of local men (34 percent of the locals stayed less than five years) had equally brief employment cannot be ignored. It indicates that motivations were complex, and that these men probably were not using their ordination simply to maintain family control of the local environment. It is more likely that, to use the expression offered by one of William Taylor's sources, they were "desirous of rising in the profession."[25] There is no way of determining their career path because they left the provincial records I have examined. The cases of a few individuals who do resurface, however, suggest the possibility that important local landowners and merchants were capable of making the connections that gave their sons education and entree into the levels of episcopal bureaucracy where personnel decisions were made. At least two individuals belonging to important landholding families who began their careers in the province went on to major pastorates outside of Tlaxcala. The first man was Bachiller Bernardo Durán de Huerta who began his service in 1709 as an assistant to the pastor in the parish of San Agustín Tlaxco where his family had considerable landholdings. In 1717, he disappeared from the registers but resurfaced

as the pastor of Santa María Coronango in the district of Cholula in 1741.[26] The second man, Doctor Nicolás Rojano Mudarra, began as a *teniente* (deputy) in the parish of Santa Ana in 1722. He left the post in 1728 but was identified in 1743 as pastor of the parish of Huejotzingo where he stayed until 1771.[27]

The motives of the local men whose length of service totaled between ten and twenty years are almost equally as indiscernible. It seems, though, from at least some examples that a goodly number of those working in salaried positions were probably returning to the province at the end of their careers. We know little about their career paths from the evidence available, though one pastor whose roots lay outside the province, Bachiller Pedro Camacho del Campo of Santa María Nativitas (1677–1694) gives us some insight into the paths these men typically followed. He created a memorial to himself at the beginning of a new baptismal register in 1679 in which he declared that he had been pastor of two other parishes, Nopaluca and Tlatlauhquitepec (in Tepeaca), and for fifteen years was a professor of Latin, philosophy, and moral theology in the colleges of San Pedro and San Juan in Puebla.[28] We do not know what happened to Camacho but the fact that he served seventeen years in Santa María, well beyond the normal tenure, suggests that this was the end of his working life.

We can assume the same thing with those fourteen pastors who were locally connected. Although we can be absolutely certain they ended their careers in the post in only two cases where they died in office,

JAMES D. RILEY

there is a strong suspicion in at least six other cases that their post in Tlaxcala ended their active professional life. Judging purely from the decline of their signatures, these six men were seriously infirm when they disappeared from the registers.[29]

The motives for their appearance in the province later in their careers are never given but some evidence suggests the importance of family considerations. Take, for example, the case of Doctor Ignacio Diez de Urdanivia, who served as pastor of San Agustín Tlaxco from 1717 until his death in 1728. Doctor Ignacio's father and mother had owned the hacienda of Santa María Jalostoc in Tlaxco that they had inherited from the pastor's grandfather. Although Jalostoc passed out of family hands around 1715, individuals who were either his brothers and sisters, or nieces and nephews, were still property owners in the district while he was pastor.[30] It can be surmised that with his doctorate, he probably could have served in an urban area if he had chosen to do so. This suggests that what pulled him back were family connections, not individual interest.

We can even see the strong possibility of family economic interests operating in the case of outsiders. Licenciado Antonio López de Oropesa was pastor of Santa Ana between 1707 and 1718. His family was of Pueblan origin and intertwined in the Pueblan commercial elite.[31] But although focused in Puebla, this family was also involved in the commerce of Tlaxcala and, very likely, in the cloth trade of Santa Ana. In 1713 and 1717, the pastor baptized children of a family member, don Miguel López de Oropesa. In López's baptism, members of a family of obrajeros in the town served as godparents.[32] This along with other possible links suggests that the licenciado chose to end his career in a town that was useful to his family interests, and possibly used his ministry to support those activities.

It is the final group of local priests—four pastors and thirty-seven men who served in assisting roles for more than twenty years—that are the most important for our analysis. It is in their activities that we see the most significant evidence for the use of religious authority to sustain the local social order. Some of these men definitely spent their entire careers in Tlaxcala and all of them spent a very substantial portion of them there. Bachiller Pedro de Arriaga held the record for longevity in a single salaried position among the local men. He is identified without break as a salaried assistant in the parish of Santa Ana between 1729 and 1768. Another local man, Bachiller Diego de Nava y Loaysa, was a *teniente de cura* (associate pastor) in San José Tlaxcala for thirty-three years (1657–1690). He also owned a hacienda within the parish that had probably belonged to his father.

No individual held a single pastorate for that length of time, but one man born in Huamantla, Bachiller Martín Cid de Olivares, served for fourteen years (1688–1702) as a teniente de cura in that parish before being assigned as pastor to the newly separated parish of San Juan Ixtenco where he remained from 1702 until his death in 1728. His total service of forty years constitutes the longest tenure in a single parish by any individual, although a number of individuals combined employment in multiple parishes to rival or surpass

PRIESTS AND PROVINCIAL SOCIAL ORDER IN TLAXCALA, 1650–1792

him. Bachiller Antonio Benítes, for example, alternated in the parishes of San José Tlaxcala and Santa Ana between 1670 and 1720. There are significant gaps in his career so that only twenty-eight of the total of fifty years can be accounted for, but it seems clear that this son of a prominent merchant of the town focused his activity on Tlaxcalan districts where his father had had considerable commercial interests.[33]

These four men all pursued salaried careers in the church and might have been influenced by motives of personal advancement as well as familial interests. But most of the local priests who can be identified in the parish records for more than twenty years appear most frequently in the registers with the notation "by license of the pastor," meaning that they did not have a formal position. An important element links many of these men: landholding. We can identify twenty-six of the forty-one individuals positively as either members of a family that owned land while they were active, or who owned land in their own right.[34] Of these twenty-six men, only seven had a career in the salaried clergy, five worked as salaried assistants in local parishes irregularly but consistently, and the remaining fourteen appear infrequently in any salaried category. We can also make the same connection to landowning for eighteen of the fifty-five locally connected priests (including four pastors) who served from five to nineteen years. Of that group of eighteen, ten were pursuing salaried careers, two were employed only occasionally, and six infrequently.

The total group of twenty-seven men with a connection to land but no permanent position in the clerical bureaucracy played a major role in delivering the sacraments in Tlaxcalan parishes. Table 15.3 identifies priests who worked selected parishes of Tlaxcala during three separate three-year periods between 1679 and 1732. Locally-connected priests who could not be identified with land (*), and those who could ($), are marked.

Table 15.3 Priests of Tlaxcala

1679–1682			
Parish	Pastors	Assistants	Other Priests
San José Tlaxcala	Licenciado Juan Merino de Pineda Licenciado Antonio González Laso Licenciado Diego Martínez Valdes	Diego de Nava $ Francisco de la Soledad Joseph de Gracia Juan Vásquez de Quiroz Alonso Benítes *	Licenciado Gabriel del Rio * Miguel de Cepeda Diego Ruiz de Olivares * Juan Cortés de Brito Andrés López Almazán Joseph de Cepeda $ Juan Merino de Manzano Juan de Escobar *

Parish	Pastors	Assistants	Other Priests
San Agustín Tlaxco	Antonio de Bonilla Godinez	Joseph Beltrán Dávila Francisco de Anaya	Blas Yáñez $ Juan de Urdaneta $ Juan González Miguel López Antonio de Huerta $ Bernardo Cortés $
Santa Ana Chiautempa	Licenciado Mateo de Rivera	Nicolás Calderón Velarde *	Juan de Escobar * Antonio Benítes * Alonso Benítes
San Felipe	Licenciado Antonio de los Rios *	Marcos de la Peña Gaspar Domínguez	None
San Luis Apizaco	Doctor Miguel de Sierra Vargas * Joseph Martínez Mazanón	Joseph Cortés de Soría $ Diego de Sierra Vargas * Luis Rodríguez Lascari * Antonio Rodríguez Lascari * Cristóbal López de Cabrera *	Antonio Cortés de Calva Gálvez $ Antonio de Villela
San Dionisio Yauhquemeca	Fernando de Arellano * Diego de Gárate y Vargas *	Gregorio Romano $ Lorenzo Rodríguez de Molina *	Miguel de Villegas Miguel de Medina $ Antonio Rodríguez Lascari * Joseph Cortés de Soría ($) Francisco Gárate y Vargas * Miguel de Cepeda $ Jacinto Sánchez de la Vega $
San Luis Huamantla	Miguel Guzmán José Cid *	Sebastián de Villar Juan González * Francisco de Escobar Francisco López Quiroz $ Blas de Mayorga Juan Guerra	Pedro Hernández de Huerta $ Juan de Morón Diego de Olivares $ Antonio de Huerta $ Joseph Donis Montaño Joseph de Olivares y de la Vara $ Miguel de Medina
San Lorenzo Cuapiastla	Vicario of Huamantla	Miguel Rendón de Soria *	None

Parish	Pastors	Assistants	Other Priests
San José Tlaxcala	Doctor Mateo de Munabe y Vargas	Joseph de Gracia Antonio de Mora Miguel de Soria	Joseph Bernal $ Miguel Alvarez de Luna * Juan de Alarcón Joseph de Santiago *
San Agustín Tlaxco	Joseph del Castillo y Altia * Licenciado Diego Perdomo, cura interino Doctor Juan Fernández de Priego, cura interino Juan Ortiz de Espinal Montalvo	Marcos Ximénez de Bonilla $ Miguel Joseph del Castillo Altia * Nicolás del Castillo Altia Velásquez * Ildefonso de la Torre y Girón	Juan Ximénez de Vera $ Bernardo de Huerta $ Antonio de Huerta $ Joseph Bernal $
Santa Ana Chiautempa	Licenciado Antonio López de Oropesa *	Luis de Santiago * Antonio Benities * Miguel López Diego Calderón * Luis Valadés Joseph Gómez Cataño Doctor Diego Escalona Matamoros * Diego de Salamanca Manuel Cárdenas	Bernabé Pacheco Manuel Castelarios Carlos de Ocaña Francisco Fernández de Silva $ Juan Isusorbe * Jacinto Sánchez de la Vega $
San Felipe	Juan de la Cea Joseph Antonio de Villela (interino) Antonio Linares *	none	none
San Luis Apizaco	Joseph Pérez de Salazar	Juan Alonso Matamoros $ Bernardo de Huerta $ Juan García de Nájera $ Joseph Ruiz	Licenciado Jacinto Sánchez de la Vega $ Joseph García de Cepeda $ Joseph Martín de Sosa Joseph Muñoz Joseph Bernal $
San Dionisio Yauhquemeca	Francisco Felix Mendrice Br Joseph Sebastián Pimentel (interim) Nicolás Gómez de la Corte $	Antonio Calcanio de Timey $ Miguel López de Fuentes * Juan Baptista de Isusorbe * Bernabé Pacheco	Marcos Ximénez de Bonilla $ Sebastián Vásquez Gastelu $

1709–1712 *continued*			
Parish	Pastors	Assistants	Other Priests
San Luis Huamantla	Pedro Vargas	Licenciado Miguel Báez Santiso $ Joseph Berriel $ Antonio de Olivares $ Luis de Ortega Valdés Juan de Rojas * Manuel de Barrios y Salcedo Blas de Mayorga Felipe Patiño Valenzuela * Antonio de Olivera Tomás de Malpica Dn Joseph Bello y Vargas	Francisco Durán de Huerta $ Licenciado Francisco Díaz de Huerta $ Licenciado Francisco Franco $ Licenciado Ignacio Durán de Huerta $ Licenciado Joseph Blásquez de Velasco $ Juan Moreno Pena * Joseph de Olivares $ Francisco Hernández $ Agustín de Abrego $ Pedro Cortés $ Antonio de Huerta $ Joseph de la Caxica Oropesa $ Luis de Tovar * Ignacio de Tovar $ Luis Hernández $ Diego Díaz de Huerta $ Juan García
San Lorenzo Cuapiastla	Manuel de los Santos y Salazar * Nicolás Simeón de Salazar y Flores *	Luis de Santiago Salazar y Tapia *	Pedro de la Vega

1729–1732			
Parish	Pastors	Assistants	Other Priests
San José Tlaxcala	Licenciado Toribio de la Puente	Antonio de Mora Juan García de la Carrera * Francisco Malpica Miguel Rescalvo	Miguel de Fuente * Sebastián Ramírez de Cepeda Juan Xavier Colín * Cristóbal Montiel Miguel Alvarez de Luna * Joseph del Aguilar Rafael Corona Antonio Ortiz Antonio García Cayetano López Nicolás de Isusorbe * Juan Farfán * Francisco de Ortega *

PRIESTS AND PROVINCIAL SOCIAL ORDER IN TLAXCALA, 1650–1792

Parish	Pastors	Assistants	Other Priests
San Agustín Tlaxco	Antonio Riva de Neira *	Joseph Cortés de Soria $ Felipe Gordillo * Fernando Calderón $	Nicolás de Nava y de la Mota $ Antonio de Cueva y Zúñiga Antonio Miguel Robledo Francisco Ramos de Hinojosa * Francisco Miguel Merino * Miguel Alvarez de Luna * Francisco de Vera $
Santa Ana Chiautempa	Juan de Escalona Matamoros *	Pedro de Arriaga * Antonio Rosete Farfán * Manuel de Aguilar Nicolás de Escalona Matamoros * Miguel de Torres Francsico Pedraza * Felipe de Bonilla * Cristóbal de Matamoros * Joaquín de Medina y Romano	Juan Antonio Fernández Joaquín Fernández de Oropesa * Francisco Gálvez Juan Astacio Lucas Pérez de Oropesa $ Francisco Xavier de Ortega $ Francisco López de Fuentes * Matias del Razo * Doctor Nicolás de Ugalde
San Felipe	Juan Medrano Avendaño Doctor Juan Joseph de Ochoa (interino)	Manuel de Alcocer $ Antonio de Matamoros * Joseph de Villa Nicolás Fernández de Silva $	Juan Francisco Losada Bartolomé Ortiz Licenciado Fulgencio Miguel de Alcocer $
San Luis Apizaco	Licenciado Domingo Martín de Fonseca Bachiller Miguel Pantaleón Díaz de Acosta	Bachiller Diego Amesqueta Bachiller Antonio Ventura Marquez * Bachiller Sebastián Pérez de Oropesa $ Juan Merino Velarde * Doctor Miguel de Sierra Valle Rioseco Bachiller Jacinto Sánchez de la Vega $ Bachiller Pedro de Herrera	Bachiller Joseph Gutiérrez Bachiller Antonio Rosete Farfán de los Godos * Bachiller Francisco Martínez Lobatón Bachiller Sebastián Vásquez Gastelu $ Manuel Mellado y Estrada Bachiller Francisco Xavier de Ortega $

1729–1732 *continued*			
Parish	Pastors	Assistants	Other Priests
San Dionisio Yauhquemeca	Ildefonso de la Torre	Juan Antonio de los Santos y Aguila	Felipe Gordillo * Antonio de Mora Juan Farfán de los Godos * Cayetano López
San Luis Huamantla	Gerónimo Pérez de Gálvez	Ignacio de Tovar $ Licenciado Miguel Báez Santiso $ Joseph Blásquez de Velasco $ Manuel Grajales Pedro Cortés $ Francisco de Huerta $ Luis de Tovar * Joseph Berriel $	Licenciado Cayetano Franco de Olivares $ Licenciado Joseph Franco de Olivares $ Diego Báez Santiso * Antonio López Moreno de Huerta $ Juan García Francisco Estebán de Torreblanca Joseph Sardo Ignacio de Huerta $ Joseph de la Caxica Oropesa $
San Lorenzo Cuapiastla	Nicolás Simeón de Salazar y Flores *	Miguel Hernández Madueño Tadeo Hernández Calmecahua * Juan Buenaventura Báez	Estanislao del Puerto y Vergara

Source: See Table 15.2.
* Locally connected priests who could not be identified with land.
$ Locally connected priests who could be identified with land holdings.

The information depicted on these charts suggests that priests associated with land played a major role in areas such as Huamantla and San Agustín Tlaxco whose economies were geared to hacienda production, but were less represented in areas where other economic activities predominated. The commercial economies of San Luis Apizaco and Santa Ana, for example, were geared to cloth manufacture, not agricultural production, so landowners were not the most important social group. The important authority figures in these areas were priests whose families were involved in the cloth trade. In San Luis Apizaco and the neighboring parish of San Dionisio Yauhquemeca, for example, between 1679 and 1682 we find two sons of an obrajero family, the Rodríguez Lascari brothers, and Bachiller Gregorio Romano de Nájera y Becerra, a member of the most important family in the district active, as assisting priests.[35]

Equally as important in these parishes were the clergy, Bachiller Miguel de Cepeda, Bachiller Miguel de Medina, Bachiller

Jacinto Sánchez de la Vega, and Bachiller Joseph Cortés de Soría, who owned haciendas producing wool for the obrajes within the boundaries of the parishes in which they ministered. Cortés de Soría was a frequent salaried assistant (and one of the twenty-year career men) with family connections to the district that went back to the beginning of the seventeenth century.[36]

In later years, as the cloth economy declined in Apizaco, the mix changed. But the parish of Santa Ana where the industry remained vibrant continued to attract local priests from commercial backgrounds. In all three periods in Santa Ana, it was the sons of merchants and individuals with connections to the weaving complexes and their supply that predominated. Both pastors of the eighteenth century on the list, Licenciado Antonio López de Oropesa and Bachiller Juan de Escalona y Matamoros were of this type. As in Apizaco earlier, the landowning clergy identified on this list were in the main individuals whose families raised sheep for their wool and whose livelihood was connected to the town.

On the other hand, landowners who supplied grain and livestock for the markets of Puebla totally dominated the list of the parish of Huamantla. Many of these priest-landowners were identified in the parish registers for more than twenty years and even though not salaried, performed multiple sacramental services during any given year. Bachiller Diego de Olivares, for example, worked in Huamantla for more than fifty years (1641–1693) without ever being identified as a paid assistant to the pastor. Yet, up until 1691 he is present in the books of San Lorenzo Cuapiastla giving last rites

and performing burials for Indians on his estate. In the 1710s, sixteen priests owned property in the parish of Huamantla and performed sacramental services that are recorded in the books I have examined.

The same presence of landlord priests is recorded in the parish of San Agustín Tlaxco, the other major center of dispersed indigenous population. Unlike the situation in Huamantla, however, in San Agustín, the farthest estates were perhaps twenty kilometers away from the parish center. As a result, throughout the 1680s members of the indigenous communities resident on the estates of the Yáñez and Muñoz de Cote families received sacramental services from family clergy. The parish books linked to these haciendas record an occasional visit by the pastor, but the day-to-day religious life of the workers was under the control of the patriarchs. Similarly, the Bernal Bejarano family that owned the haciendas of Santa Clara and San Juan Atlangatepec controlled services in the town of San Juan Atlangatepec. Bachiller Joseph Bernal Bejarano appeared often enough in the records of the first decades of the eighteenth century to make it seem that the visita of that town was his personal chapel.

Priest and Community

The data on which this study is based offer numerous examples of locally connected priests establishing strong links to parish life in areas where their family interests could be served. But did they view their role in this fashion? Since we have no extant sermons from these priests and we have no idea what they told their indigenous communicants about the proper social order and their role in it, there are no supportable conclusions that we can make. There is one parish, however, in which it seems that a clear connection can be made between the social values of the priests who served it and a broader sense of community. This was the small parish of San Lorenzo Cuapiastla that was separated from San Luis Huamantla in 1693. The distinctiveness of its relationship to its priests does not lie in the fact that, from the beginning of its books in 1681 until the mid-1730s, it was totally controlled by priests with local connections, but in the fact that from its inception as a parish, these priests were from the same family of indigenous caciques, the Salazars, and that we know more about its first pastor and his social philosophy than we do about any other priest in Tlaxcala.

Bachiller Manuel de los Santos y Salazar was very proud of being a member of one of the oldest pureblooded families of the pipiltin in the province. Both his father, who was the leader of the traditional faction on the cabildo, and his mother traced their lineages untainted by Spanish blood back to the conquest. Moreover, unlike many of the Tlaxcalan indigenous elite, including the great chroniclers of the Tlaxcalan nation, the Muñoz Camargos, they had resisted assimilation into the Spanish social and economic sphere. Their power derived from their *cacicazgo* (patrimonial estate), not from Spanish friends and relatives. Because of his education and his loyalty to the traditional sector, Bachiller Manuel inherited the task of maintaining the yearly chronicle of the cabildo of Tlaxcala from Juan Buenaventura Zapata y Mendoza in 1689.[37] Bachiller Manuel said his first mass in 1685 and was employed as a vicario de pie fijo in the parish of San Salvador el Seco in Tepeaca. He became the first pastor of San Lorenzo Cuapiastla in 1693 where he remained until 1710 when he took up the leadership of another Indian parish, Santa Cruz, nearer Tlaxcala. There he died in 1715.[38]

If there was a project in which Bachiller Manuel participated, it was a project to reassert the prerogatives and the authority of the full-blooded indigenous elite. The crónica was one method of achieving this end through propaganda. Others among his relatives attempted to do the same politically.[39] Bachiller Manuel also gave a religious dimension to this assertion of loyalty and authority. While at San Lorenzo, he employed his brother, Bachiller Nicolás Simeón de Salazar y Flores, as his assistant and another relative, Bachiller Joseph Luis de Santiago y Salazar, from time to time. Bachiller Nicolás inherited the pastorate of San Lorenzo when Bachiller Manuel moved on and remained pastor until he died in 1733. Like his brother, he also employed only priests with roots in the indigenous elite. These included Bachiller Bernardo de Lima y Mendoza, Bachiller Augustín Flores Corona, and another relative, Bachiller Antonio Marcial de Salazar. In the final stage of his life, Bachiller Nicolás chose as an administrator Bachiller Tadeo Hernández Calmecahua, who would go on to become the first pastor of San Nicolás Terrenate in 1735.[40]

The intellectual component to this assertion of indigenous authority over religious life is to be found in Santos y Salazar's depiction of the consequences of mestizaje for Tlaxcala. The entries for the late sixteenth century attacked Diego Muñoz Camargo, the mestizo chronicler of the history of Tlaxcala, for his role in permitting Spaniards to gain a hold in Tlaxcala. But his strongest language was reserved for his father's rival for the governorship of Tlaxcala, don Nicolás Méndez de Luna. He reasoned that the decline of Tlaxcala and of its pipiltin was the result of the loss of its traditions due to the successful claims to political authority of men like Méndez de Luna. Both Zapata and Salazar were convinced that these men were corrupted by money gained pandering to the Spanish and vilified them as *"mestizos del infierno"* (the damnable mestizos).[41] Salazar's ultimate judgment in 1703 on the alcalde, don Antonio Pérez de Lira, reflected his sense of what was wrong, *"no es bueno que los champurros gobiernen porque su mala sangre los precípita a hacer iniquidades"* (It is not good that half breeds be allowed to govern because their bad blood pushes them to do evil things).[42]

It is possible to see in the Salazars' sequential pastorates and their use of indigenous priests a desire to carve out a place where indigenous nobility could rule and where traditions that were the basis of communal harmony could be restored. But creole priests, as well, could lament a world in which money ruled and a proper deferential social order was being lost. Doctor Ignacio Diez de Urdanivia, the pastor of San Agustín Tlaxco between 1717 and 1728, became involved in a dispute in which he showed frustration over the decline of his family and the rise of moneyed mestizos.

During the second half of the seventeenth century, his grandfather, Francisco

Díaz Garci Díaz had been a dominant man in the district with numerous powerful friends and a confident sense of his social position and the rights it gave him.[43] But family fortunes shifted and in 1715 their ancestral hacienda, Santa María Jalostoc, was sold to Domingo de León after Doctor Ignacio's father's death. A local man, León's marriage sometime prior to 1720 to doña Getrudis de Nava y de la Mota marked him as one of the current leaders of the community in Tlaxco. That other landowners used the couple frequently as godparents was a sign of their position. In 1725, Domingo's status was further affirmed by his identification as one of the district representatives in the elections for provincial *diputados* (representatives of the business community) and the administrator of sales tax known as the *alcabala*.[44]

Doctor Ignacio baptized the couple's first two children in the parish church and nothing extraordinary occurred. But the baptism of their third child in 1724 showed that a social conflict had developed. In the text of the record, the pastor noted very ostentatiously that the child was a mestizo and in the margin, wrote in large letters *"entre renglones mestizo-española"* (between the categories of mestizo and española).

That the description was accurate was not the point. Earlier pastors recorded the children of Domingo's first marriage to María Xaimes in the 1690s as mestizos. But after she died in 1707, no one noted the fact of his background until Diez brought it up. The pastor's notation, then, was a calculated insult and expression of disdain for the man who had taken over his father and grandfather's position. He reinforced the point in the baptism of Domingo's fourth child in 1726. In this case, he did not permit his assistant, Bachiller Nicolás de Nava, Getrudis's brother, to record the baptism that Nicolás had performed on the hacienda of Santiago belonging to the Navas. Since it was the common practice in this register for Bachiller Nicolás to record the baptisms he himself performed, it can only mean that Diez de Urdanivia used his prerogative as pastor to record and sign the document himself because he knew that Bachiller Nicolás would not state that Domingo was a mestizo.[45]

The pastor would have understood the stand taken by Bachiller Manuel de los Santos y Salazar. The social insult he offered to this prominent landowner could have been motivated by snobbery, but the context suggests that it resulted from a deeply felt concern over the decline of proper social order similar to that expressed by Salazar. The next pastor, Bachiller Antonio Vásquez Riva de Neira, did not follow his lead. He labeled Domingo as "don" and made no reference to mestizaje in the marriage of his daughter in 1738.[46] Times were changing and more modern men accepted the new basis for the social order.

Provincial Priesthood in the Late Colonial Period

Just as Medieval values reflected in the Habsburg state were giving way in the mid-eighteenth century to law and the new Bourbon political order, so concepts of social order and economic relations were changing. At the local level, gañanía declined significantly in the middle of the eighteenth century because rural laborers rejected the patriarchal environment of the haciendas. As a result, Indian villages gained more autonomy and more population and local elites were forced to find new ways of acquiring the resources they needed from the indigenous populations.[47] Bourbon modifications also changed the religious order. The late colonial period saw the priest transformed from a father to a teacher, from a patriarchal leader concerned with all aspects of his parishioners' lives to a role model of sanctity and internal spiritual development.[48]

Tlaxcalan elites reflected these new realities in their decisions about entering the priesthood. By the time of the census of 1791 the number of priests active in the province had declined substantially. In the eight parishes included in Table 15.3 there were a total of sixty-nine individuals in 1680, ninety-three in 1710, and one hundred in 1730 performing sacramental services. In all twenty-three parishes in the province in 1791, including chaplains for two pilgrimage sites and one hacienda, there were only sixty-five total priests available for service. If we only consider the eight parishes in Table 15.3, even allowing for the divisions after 1730, there were only forty priests where there had previously been one hundred. This decline stands in stark contrast to the situation described by Taylor for the Archbishopric of Mexico and the bishopric of Guadalajara that during the late colonial period had large and growing numbers of clergy.[49]

Explanations for this 60 percent decline must be very tentative, and are beyond the scope of this paper, but one element stands out in these figures. Provincial elites were

PRIESTS AND PROVINCIAL SOCIAL ORDER IN TLAXCALA, 1650–1792

not present in the priesthood in 1791 as they had been previously. Of the fifty-four resident priests for whom birth places are given in the census, only seventeen were born in Tlaxcala. A connected and equally noticeable trend lies in the fact that while thirty priests in the 1710s, and twenty-three in the 1730s, can be identified with landowning in the eight parishes, in 1791 the census found a total of only three haciendas and ranchos in the hands of diocesan clergy resident in the province, and only six other priests who were connected to landholding families.[50]

In Huamantla, the leading landholding families of the period from 1710 to 1730—the Durán de Huertas, Díaz de Huertas, and the Blásquez de Velascos—are present only in the person of Domingo Durán de Huerta. The Durán de Huertas alone contributed nine priests to the province between 1680 and 1730. Likewise, in Tlaxco the Muñoz de Cote- and Yáñez de Vera-connected family provided seven priests in the period we have examined, but had no representatives in

1791. It is ironic, and indicative of the change of intellectual climate, that although four or more of the most important haciendas in the province were held by Yáñez family members, with the owners resident and enumerated, the only individual in the family in 1791 even possibly focusing on a clerical career was José Ignacio Yáñez y Isquierdo, a graduate in theology of the Colegio Carolina of Puebla, resident on the hacienda of San Blas Cuajomulco belonging to his mother doña María Getrudis Yáñez.[51]

So it was that the most important families stopped supplying priests to provincial life, and the lesser families did not take their place. With the expansion of political administration and the declining social utility of the priesthood, landowners and merchants dedicated their sons to different careers after the 1750s. The gentry of Tlaxcala found it expedient to fend off the Bourbon state and their own economic problems, not with herrschaft and priests, but with bureaucrats and lawyers.

NOTES

Archival Abbreviations appearing in notes:

AGN   Archivo General de la Nación, México

AGT   Microfilm copy of selected documents of the Archivo General del Estado de Tlaxcala in the Library of Congress, Washington DC

ANEP   Archivo de Notarias del Estado de Puebla

BNAF   Biblioteca Nacional de México, Archivo Franciscano

GSU   Genealogical Society of Utah

1. The literature has grown enormously in the past twenty years, but for examples see recent books by Kenneth Mills, *Idolatry*

and its Enemies: Colonial Andean Religion and Extirpation, 1640–1750 (Princeton: Princeton University Press, 1997); James Lockhart, *The Nahuas after the Conquest: A Social and Cultural History of the Indians of Central Mexico, Sixteenth through Eighteenth Centuries* (Stanford: Stanford University Press, 1992); Carolyn Dean, *Inka Bodies and the Body of Christ: Corpus Christi in Colonial Cuzco, Peru* (Durham: Duke University Press, 1999); Sabine MacCormick, *Religion in the Andes: Vision and Imagination in Early Colonial Peru* (Princeton: Princeton University Press, 1991); and Louise Burkhart, *The Slippery Earth: Nahua-Christian Moral Dialogue in Sixteenth-Century Mexico* (Tucson: University of Arizona

Press, 1989). There is also a good summation provided by John F. Schwaller's recent selection of articles, *The Church in Colonial Latin America* (Wilmington: Scholarly Resources Press, 2000).

2. William B. Taylor, *Magistrates of the Sacred: Priests and Parishioners in Eighteenth-Century Mexico* (Stanford: Stanford University Press, 1996), is the only recent scholar to deal with secular priests in detail. His work, however, only addresses the very late colonial period. See also John F. Schwaller, *The Church and Clergy in Sixteenth-Century Mexico* (Albuquerque: University of New Mexico Press, 1987); A. C. Van Oss, *Catholic Colonialism: A Parish History of Guatemala, 1524–1821* (Cambridge, UK: Cambridge University Press, 1986), 153–78; David A. Brading, *Church and State in Bourbon Mexico: The Diocese of Michoacán, 1749–1810* (Cambridge, UK: Cambridge University Press, 1994), 105–49; Antonine Tibesar, "The Lima Pastors, 1750–1820: Their Origins and Studies as Taken from Their Autobiographies," *The Americas* 28, no. 1 (1971): 39–51; and three doctoral dissertations from the Catholic University of America, José García Leduc, "La iglesia y el clero católico de Puerto Rico (1800–1873): su proyección económica y política" (1990), Raymond Harrington, "The Secular Clergy in the Diocese of Mérida de Yucatán, 1780–1850: Their Origins, Careers, Wealth and Activities" (1983), and Michael Fallon, "The Secular Clergy in the Diocese of Yucatán, 1750–1800" (1979).

3. See Mills, *Idolatry and its Enemies*, and Brading, *Church and State*, 120–30, 150–70. Even Taylor, *Magistrates of the Sacred*, is forced to base his analysis of the relationship on litigation (see 207–64 and Part 4). But he persistently seeks a middle ground in judging the reality of the portrait (see his comments, 180).

4. Kathryn Burns, *Colonial Habits: Convents and the Spiritual Economy of Cuzco, Peru* (Durham: Duke University Press, 1999), 2–4.

5. Taylor, *Magistrates of the Sacred*, 98.

6. Rik Hoekstra, *Two Worlds Merging: The Transformation of Society in the Valley of Puebla, 1570–1640* (Amsterdam: Centro de Estudios y Documentación Latinoamericanos, 1993), 40–45. See particularly his comments about the roots of authority on 43.

7. Ibid., 238.

8. See Charles Gibson, *Tlaxcala in the Sixteenth Century* (Stanford: Stanford University Press, 1952) for a description of the cabildo's fight against Spanish encroachments.

9. The best, although distinctly slanted, source for this process is provided by the chronicles of Juan Buenaventura Zapata y Mendoza (with emendations by Bachiller Manuel de Santos y Salazar), *Historia cronológica de la noble ciudad de Tlaxcala*, transcripción paleográfica, traducción, presentación y notas por Luís Reyes García y Andrea Martínez Baracs (Tlaxcala, Mexico: Universidad Autónoma de Tlaxcala, [1692] 1995). For the view of indigenous elites who joined with the Spanish, see Diego Muñoz Camargo, *Suma y epíloga de toda la descripción de Tlaxcala, 1589*, paleografía, presentación y notas de Andrea Martínez Baracs y Carlos Sempat Assadourian, prólogo de Wayne Ruwet (Tlaxcala, Mexico: University Autónoma de Tlaxcala, Secretaría de Extensión Universitaria y Difusión Cultural; México, DF: Centro de Investigaciones y Estudios Superiores en Antropología Social, 1994), 189. See also Hoekstra, *Two Worlds Merging*.

10. The best study on the rise of Puebla is María de las Mercedes Gantes Tréllez, "Aspectos socioeconómicos de Puebla de los Angeles (1624–1650)," *Anuario de Estudios Americanos* 60 (1983): 497–613. There are no good studies of the regional economy but for the general character of the cloth industry consult Richard Salvucci, *Textiles and Capitalism in Mexico: An Economic History of the Obrajes, 1539–1840* (Princeton: Princeton University Press, 1987), 9–31, 135–50. For Tlaxcala's role in the agricultural economy of the Puebla-Tlaxcala region, see Arístides Medina Rubio, *La iglesia y la producción agrícola en Puebla, 1540–1795* (México, DF: Centro de Estudios Históricos, El Colegio de México, 1984). While Tlaxcala benefited from Pueblan expansion, it also suffered when the Pueblan economy stagnated. The consequences for Tlaxcala's elites are considered in James Riley, "Landlords, Laborers and Royal Government: The Administration of Labor in Tlaxcala, 1680–1750," in *El trabajo y los trabajadores en la historia de México*, ed. Elsa Cecilia Frost et al., 221–41 (México, DF: el Colegio de México, 1979).

11. James Riley, "Petty Elites and the Social Order in Tlaxcala: The Family of the Durán de Huertas," paper delivered to the History Faculty Colloquium, The Catholic University of America, March 1997.

12. There are numerous examples of this racial mixing, but the most significant one is that of Captain Antonio de Nava y de la Mota, leader of a prominent family involved in the cloth trade in Santa Ana Chiautempan. He had one complete family with a *cacica* (noblewoman), doña Isabel Pérez, to whom he was not married. In 1656, after he began to marry off the sons and daughters of this relationship to Spaniards and Indian caciques, he married doña Teresa Guevara de Altamirano y Amarillas of Puebla and began a second entirely Spanish family. The local registers record the marriages of the children of this union to merchants and landowners in the 1670s. See GSU, roll 304815, and roll 248329.

13. James Riley, "Crown Law and Rural Labor in New Spain: The Status of Gañanes During the Eighteenth Century," *Hispanic American Historical Review* 64 (1984): 259–86.

14. I have found only two references in court records to abuse by a priest of his flock that could be construed as serving family interests. See AGN, ramo de Tierras, Legajo 393, exp. 1, cuaderno 2, f. 7, (1721), and AGT, #299 (1732). For one additional case see Claude Morin, *Santa Inés Zacatelco (1645–1812): Contribución a la demografía histórica del Mexico Colonial* (México, DF: Instituto Nacional de Antropología e Historia, 1973), 92, n. 2.

15. Linking specific priests to specific families is an aspect of my broader project to link families and landholding. Important cadastral sources for family reconstruction include Isabel González Sanchez, ed., *Haciendas y ranchos de Tlaxcala en 1712* (México, DF: Instituto Nacional de Antropología e Historia, 1969), and AGN, ramo de padrones, vol. 22, which offers fairly complete lists of landowning families in 1712 and 1791. The most important resources, however, are the Tlaxcalan parish registers of baptisms, marriages, and burials filmed by the Genealogical Society of Utah. These registers not only allowed the reconstruction of elite families, and identified the priests serving the churches of Tlaxcala, but

also allowed the significant expansion of our knowledge of ownership of particular pieces of property. Until 1730, the sacramental records routinely identified the owner of the estate on which the individuals involved resided. These almost yearly lists of landowners combined with family names derived from the sacramental events in which they were directly involved became my benchmarks. I then fleshed out family histories using court cases found in the Archivo General de la Nación in Mexico, particularly in the ramos of Civil, Tierras, and Indios, administrative records and litigation found in the Archivo General del Estado de Tlaxcala, and a sampling of notarial records found in the Archivo de Notarias del Estado de Puebla, also microfilmed by the Genealogical Society of Utah.

16. The economic cycles affecting Tlaxcala on which this conclusion is based are considered in Medina Rubio, *La Iglesia y Producción*; Salvucci, *Textiles and Capitalism*; Riley, "Crown Law," 270–73; and Riley, "Landlords, Laborers."

17. For 1681 see Peter Gerhard, "Un censo de la diócesis de Puebla en 1681," *Historia Mexicana* 30, no. 4 (1981). Gerhard's figures are incomplete, but adding numbers from other sources to fill the gaps does not change the percentages. The Indian population of approximately 59,000 for 1793 is given in AGN, ramo de Historia, vol. 523, exp. 1. The census of 1791, AGN, padrones, vol. 22, provides the figure for the Spanish population, approximately 14,000.

18. Riley, "Crown Law," 263, n. 10.

19. Peter Gerhard, "Un censo," 548.

20. AGT, #249. This total number does not include individuals making less than 3 pesos, or women workers. Since a wage of 3 pesos per month was the minimum wage paid an adult worker, it can be assumed that these figures reflect the number of heads of households. The parameters of the estimate are obtained by multiplying this number by a family size of 3–4 and assuming that the Indian population had not grown explosively between 1681 and 1717.

21. See Riley, "Crown Law," in particular, on these social issues.

22. Among other sources, see Hoekstra, *Two Worlds Merging*, chapters 2 and 5, for information regarding the Franciscan experience.

23. Zapata, *Historia cronológica*, 271.

24. AGT, #149. He is identified as a vecino of Tlaxcala and a resident of San Francisco who occasionally administered the parish. The registers of Tepeyanco confirm this statement.

25. Taylor, *Magistrates of the Sacred*, 98.

26. He was the child of Captain Nicolás Durán de Huerta and doña Josefa Muñoz de Vera. See AGN, ramo de Tierras, Legajo 186, exp. 4 for information on these properties and the family connection. He was brought as a witness in a lawsuit in 1741 over ornaments in the church of San Agustín Tlaxco that had been donated by his uncle. See AGN, ramo de Tierras, legajo 624.

27. We can follow the progress of his career because he owned land in San Felipe. See AGN, ramo de Tierras, legajo 691, exp. 6, and AGT, #299.

28. GSU, roll 305106, register beginning April 1679.

29. For one example of rising decrepitude, see the signatures of Bachiller Nicolás Simeón de Salazar, pastor of San Lorenzo Cuapiastla, GSU, roll 642481. Pastors could use notaries to record the body of the entry, but both pastors and assistants always signed entries in their own hand. Except in the two instances where a burial is recorded, no reference is made in these books to the fate of the last man.

30. His burial record is found in GSU, roll 646500, January 7, 1728. See the listing for the family estate in González Sánchez, *Haciendas y ranchos*, 143. There are numerous references in the Tlaxco registers to this family's ownership of this and other property. Doctor Diez de Urdanivia, himself, is identified in 1712 as the executor of his father's estate in that burial record.

31. For his family connections see the marriage records of the Sagrario of Puebla, GSU, roll 227704, 1/24/1697.

32. See baptisms of 11/9/1713 and 5/5/1717, GSU, roll 248329.

33. He is found in the books of San José Tlaxcala from 1687 to 1695, and 1716 to 1720, but appears in Santa Ana from 1670 to 1680, 1697, 1700–1701 and 1709–1712. A comparison of the signatures in these different registers makes me confident it was the same man.

34. We can also identify the family occupation of nine of the remaining fifteen priests. Of those nine (including three pastors), two came from families associated with the cloth trade, three were involved in essentially local commerce (one from a family that held the abasto de carne for Tlaxcala), and three were from families connected to the political activity of the Indian cabildo. One individual whose father was a shopkeeper in Tlaxcala city, Licenciado Juan Bautista de Isusorbe, served as an occasional assistant in various parishes and later became pastor of the parish of San Nicolás Panotla (1740), but his main occupation was as a lawyer (he drafted several lawsuits of which we have a record) and at the end of his career he was the *procurador de causas* (state attorney) of the court of the Spanish governor of Tlaxcala.

35. The Nájera y Becerra clan owned land but made their fortune as middlemen in the cloth trade. They formed a mayorazgo based on their Tlaxcalan holdings in the 1640s (Gantes Tréllez, "Aspectos socio-económicos de Puebla," 514). In the 1650s, they married into the Romano Altamirano family and sat on the Pueblan cabildo for the remainder of the colonial period. See González Sanchez, *Haciendas y ranchos*, 114, for the description of the mayorazgo holdings in 1711.

36. The parish records identify him as early as 1656 owning the hacienda of San Jacinto in the parish of San Dionisio but his family was active in Apizaco as early as 1604. See AGT, protocolos de notarias, 1604, f. 248, July 11, 1604.

37. Zapata, *Historia cronológica*. His contribution seems to have been the introduction of marginal notes, mostly comments about the events or individuals involved. This is the element that is most interesting in the purpose here. He continued his notes until at least 1703, although the text ends in 1692.

38. Ibid., 19–20, gives this brief biography.

39. One of Manuel's relatives, don Antonio Simón Rico de Salazar, probably a nephew, inherited the mantle of leadership of the traditionalists in the 1720s and embarked on one of the

most unusual projects in Tlaxcalan history. In 1723, he proposed to the viceroy that the Indian nobility of Tlaxcala be allowed to raise a militia regiment organized and armed in the European fashion to defend the realm. See AGT, #259, #278, #283, and #284 for this story. The offer was at first accepted but then the regiment was disbanded in 1729. Don Antonio, however, continued to be referred to as Colonel Antonio de Salazar until his death in the 1750s. Despite the failure of this scheme, it was in line with the Tlaxcalan nobility's assertion that their honor and prestige were based on their military service to the crown during the conquest and their support of the crown thereafter. It was a mark of their distinctiveness that they were trying to resurrect and publicize. Although the effort ultimately failed, it was indicative of what the traditional elites were trying to accomplish, how to remain Indian in an ever-expanding Hispanic world.

40. See the documents of erection September 1735 in GSU, roll 737437. The new parish was judged a failure in the 1760s and absorbed into the parish of San Salvador Tzompantepec, which was created in 1777.

41. Zapata, *Historia cronológica*, 511. Don Nicolás Méndez de Luna was an alcalde on the Tlaxcalan cabildo, becoming governor on multiple occasions during the 1660s and 1670s. His mother was a cacica and his father a European merchant. He is also mentioned in a legal case in 1722. In the course of a petition to the viceroy concerning laws preventing mestizos from serving, the cabildo of Tlaxcala alleged that Méndez had exploited the Indians by using his power as Indian governor to force them to work for free in obrajes he and his Spanish friends established (AGT, #254). It is of note that his brother (or half brother), Bachiller Andrés Méndez de Luna, was active as a teniente in Santa Ana Chiautempan between 1655 and 1664 at the moment when don Nicolás was manipulating the population as described in the lawsuit.

42. Zapata, *Historia cronológica*, 623.

43. Doctor Ignacio's parents were married in San José Tlaxcala April 8, 1668 before the most powerful men in the province. It is also interesting to note that through his mother he could trace his lineage to the *primeros pobladores* of Puebla and that a maternal uncle or grandparent, don Cristóbal de Linares Urdanivia, was a longtime notary of the Indian cabildo of Tlaxcala. See Gantes Tréllez, "Aspectos socioeconómicos," for information on the Pueblan family.

44. Domingo de León was one of seven electors from the district of Tlaxco (AGT, #273). See James Riley, "Public Works and Local Elites: The Politics of Taxation in Tlaxcala, 1780–1810," *The Americas* 58, no. 3 (2002): 361–62, for the use of the diputados and administrator, as well as their election.

45. GSU, roll 645861, 7/24/1724 and 10/17/1726.

46. GSU, roll 645896, 4/16/1738.

47. The process of change and the rise of the authority of law, as it was reflected in labor relations on haciendas, is described in Riley, "Crown Law and Rural Labor."

48. Taylor, *Magistrates of the Sacred*, 162–73.

49. Taylor, *Magistrates of the Sacred* (78–79), estimates that the number of parish priests grew 29 percent in the archdiocese of Mexico, and 27 percent in the diocese of Guadalajara between 1767 and the first decade of the nineteenth century. This growth occurred despite the fact that nearly one-half of the diocesan priests in Guadalajara were not employed in parish work in 1796, and two-thirds of all priests (diocesan and regular) in the viceroyalty of Mexico were not employed in 1810.

50. My in-depth research into landed families ends in the 1730s, so I am not as confident about these identifications as I am in the earlier analysis. Some cases are obvious. Bachiller Francisco Alcocer, vicar of San Felipe, lived on the hacienda of his father (hacienda of la Compañia). Licenciado Domingo Durán de Huerta, though retired in 1791, rented the hacienda of San Miguel Tlacotepec in 1759 and 1763, and operated the hacienda of Concepción, which belonged to his father, in 1763 and 1771 (see the rental agreement ANEP, GSU, roll 650792, April 1759, f. 284; AGT, #421 and #440). The identifications of the other men are based on a comparison of names in the census.

51. For the Yáñez holdings and fortunes, see AGN, ramo de Civil, tomo 41, exp. 4. For the Muñoz de Cote family see AGN, ramo de Tierras, legajo 1375, exp. 1.

CHAPTER SIXTEEN

Apostles of Reform

Local Elites and *Patronato Real* in Late Colonial Chiapas

MICHAEL A. POLUSHIN

As he sat below the image of King Ferdinand VII on September 21, 1809, with his staff of office in hand, José Mariano Valero must have been overwhelmed by the events that had transpired in Ciudad Real earlier that day. Midway through the fiesta devoted to the Virgin of Merced, a raucous civil disturbance instigated by local elites had broken out in the central plaza of the city. During the ensuing melee, Valero was placed under house arrest by leading members of the city's *ayuntamiento* (city or town council) and he was left to ponder his fate beneath the portrait of *El Deseado*. The actions undertaken by local elites during the feast day, he later stated, clearly were an affront to his authority as both assessor and acting intendant of Chiapas, and thus the Spanish king. Valero further characterized the seditious behavior of his adversaries as being akin to the blasphemy committed against the sacred image of the Virgin during the ceremonies held in her honor, which he, as the Spanish monarch's chief official in the region, had the primary responsibility to oversee.[1]

These indeed were serious times in the Spanish Empire. The invasion of the Iberian Peninsula by Napoleon Bonaparte prompted the emergence of municipal *juntas* (committees) who claimed to rule on behalf of Ferdinand VII, which also meant that they laid claim to complete control over ecclesiastical and royal finances.[2] The merging of the image of the Spanish monarch with that of the Virgin implicit within Valero's accusations serves as a metaphor for royal patronage of the church in the Spanish Americas (*patronato real*) during the era.[3] Regalist Bourbon policies, after all, were not restricted to the effort to gain control of ecclesiastical wealth and privilege, but to strict oversight of religious celebrations as well.[4] Yet the arrest of Valero cannot be reduced to a knee-jerk reaction to Bourbon reform that supposedly excluded *criollo* (American-born Spanish) elites from enjoying traditional sociopolitical perks and privileges associated with provincial administration.[5] To the contrary, from the 1780s onward local patricians were included in the process of reform and their socioeconomic power was enhanced through royal legislation, including those policies directed toward patronato real.

The appropriation of the Virgin Mary for sociopolitical purposes during the period would be hardly unique to Chiapas as exemplified by the importance given to the Virgin of Guadalupe during the *Grito de Dolores* in 1810.[6] Obviously, the disturbance in Ciudad Real needs to be distinguished in its scope. Participation in it was restricted to local elites and their clients. Within the context of local identity and the nascent nationalism sometimes associated with the appropriation of the Virgin for political purposes, the episode foreshadowed the decision of local elites from Ciudad Real to orchestrate the incorporation of Chiapas into the Mexican Republic in 1824.[7] At this juncture, however, the city's patricians could not foresee nor fathom the future political landscape. Instead, they were motivated to solidify the place of the city in the current horizon of regional affairs by legitimizing their control over the traditional hierarchies implicit in religious fiestas, especially those associated with local, non-Spanish society. The Virgin de la Merced was the *patrona* (protectress) of the capital city, a matter of no small consequence or symbolic political value.[8]

The Entangled Destinies of Church and State

The apparent festive bonding by local elites of the interests of church and state was a fitting denouement to the peninsular official's career that began quite noisily with his appointment as assessor for the Intendancy of Comayagua (Honduras) in 1794. There he became embroiled in a dispute with the local *tesorero* (treasurer) over the appropriation and disbursement of the tithe.[9] Within a year of his appointment as assessor of the Intendancy of Ciudad Real de Chiapa, a myriad of lawsuits instigated by local elites appeared before the *Audiencia* of Los Confines (high court of Guatemala), which accused the well-educated Valero of fraudulent practices involving royal levies and ecclesiastical finance.[10] The assessor's legal education, befitting an *abogado* (lawyer) of the Royal Councils, proved helpful contending with his local adversaries in Ciudad Real before the courts in matters relating to secular and ecclesiastical affairs in Chiapas.[11] On one occasion, he successfully sued the ayuntamiento for not including him in the ceremonies devoted to Santiago, held each year in the cathedral to celebrate the Spanish conquest of the Americas.[12] On another occasion, he became involved in yet an additional nasty territorial dispute with the *contador* (accountant) and the tesorero of the provincial treasury of Chiapas over the right of assessors to supervise the transactions of the *junta de diezmos* (tithe committee).[13]

Notions of political legitimacy as they pertained to the entangled destinies of church and state were not limited to Valero, as local elites from Ciudad Real made a

MICHAEL A. POLUSHIN

spirited defense of what they perceived as their legitimate interests in the context of royal policies. In their effort to discredit Valero before the courts they argued that there could be no separation between the interests of the state, religion, and the patria.[14] Disputes between Valero and local elites were exacerbated by the fact that the administration of intendants in Chiapas was distinguished by their disinterest, incompetence, or by their untimely deaths, and especially since 1,000 of the 1,500 peso salary of the assessor was drawn from the city's general fund and taxes (*propios* and *arbitrios*).[15] A few years after Valero's expulsion, the representative to the Cortes de Cádiz (Spanish parliament) for Chiapas, the canon Mariano Robles, published an account in 1813 that attributed local administration to what had gone wrong with the Spanish Empire.[16] Robles, a member of one of the most prominent elite families in Ciudad Real, argued that the activities of intendants and subdelegates in Chiapas were comparable to the hideous atrocities committed by the conquistador Enrique de Guzmán centuries earlier. Conversely, the actions of the noble ayuntamiento of Ciudad Real and local *curas* (parish priests) throughout the history of Chiapas were as pristine as the efforts of the sixteenth-century bishop of Chiapas, fray Bartolomé de las Casas. Acting in the tradition of the "Apostle of the Indies," both the ayuntamiento and local curas had an unbroken past in their denunciation of morally repugnant royal officials.[17] In this instance, the canon's historical memory was selective. The ayuntamiento of the capital city had only been revived in 1782 after more than a thirty-year suspension for revolting

twice against *alcaldes mayores* (provincial magistrates) sent to Chiapas specifically to contend with corrupt practices that had emerged in local administration.[18]

While it is hardly surprising that Robles celebrated the works of parish priests, the tenor of his argument regarding the ayuntamiento was consistent with that used by local elites in the lengthy litigation that followed Valero's arrest and eventual appearance before the *Tribunal de Infidencia* (a court established to weed out traitors or French sympathizers) in 1810.[19] Within the realm of finance, the *regidores* (councilmen) of the ayuntamiento suggested that, unlike Valero, they had always ensured that ecclesiastical rents and royal taxes were liquidated in a timely fashion.[20] As part of his credentials presented to the Cortes de Cádiz, Robles himself had noted how he assisted in the liquidation of outstanding accounts for the *Consolidación de Vales Reales* (amortization of ecclesiastical loans) in 1806.[21]

The union of church and state within the process of reform that contributed to the expansion of the sociopolitical power of local elites and their conditioned attitudes toward patronato real can be first understood through an examination of jurisdictional changes involving the creation of the intendancy of Chiapas after 1786.[22] There was no immediate administrative precedent for the intendancy, and the geographical jurisdiction of the diocese of Chiapa actually served as its template.[23] From the sixteenth century onward royal government within the diocese was divided into the *alcaldía* (administrative district) of Chiapa and the *gobernación* (provincial unit) of Soconusco, and the chief royal official in each district acted as the focal point for all political, military, and fiscal administration. By 1769, the alcaldía of Chiapa was divided into two, with one alcalde mayor residing in the town of Tuxtla and the other in Ciudad Real.[24] The three administrative regions were incorporated into the intendancy in 1789 as subdelegations.[25] Along with the introduction of a provincial treasury, the cluster of new officials in the capital Ciudad Real that included intendant, assessor, and treasury officials, now served as the epicenter for royal administration, much like the bishop of Chiapa had always provided a centrifugal focus for ecclesiastical affairs.[26] The apparent rationalization of the region via jurisdictional change should not be overstated. The jurisdictions of royal and parochial districts in the countryside zigzagged, intersected, and overlapped, while the three subdelegations were continually subdivided, extinguished, and reconstituted well into the first two decades of the nineteenth century.[27]

Corporate Interests, Clients, and Agency within Fiscal Reform

The process of reform did not necessarily mean the complete abandonment of other traditional forms of administrative practice. Despite the introduction of salaried officials, venality and tax farming continued to be prominent features in the administration of ecclesiastical levies.[28] As noted elsewhere, from the late 1780s until 1810, the venal, titled regidurías of Ciudad Real's ayuntamiento were given key roles within the administration and dominated all fiscal juntas introduced by the Bourbons, including those specifically geared toward church finance.[29] This provided the city's elites privileged access to capital and traditional perquisites of office, while expanding upon their own mercantile and landed interests. Within six years of purchasing his office for 350 pesos in 1800, for example, the alférez real (regidor and royal standard bearer) José María Robles acquired control over almost 17,000 pesos during his tenure as calpixqui (tribute receptor) and de facto tesorero of the cathedral chapter, an amount he retained control over for ten years.[30] The apparent contradiction between venality and enlightened fiscal reform was not unique to Chiapas. Peter Guardino notes the price of four municipal offices for the ayuntamiento of Antequera (Oaxaca) sold by the crown in 1798 ranged from 1,300 to 1,525 pesos.[31]

As the only Spanish república (here, chartered Spanish city or town) here in the region, Ciudad Real remained the sole sociopolitical outlet for local elites from throughout Chiapas until the first decade of the nineteenth century. Its ayuntamiento was a closed, oligarchical institution where age, rank, and family connections mattered most. Status of municipal office was a key variable for expanding upon wealth and power and, thus, a society of orders was the guiding principle behind the local Spanish social hierarchy.[32] Landed and mercantile elites from throughout the intendancy needed to ensure their interests were represented in the city's council or the cathedral chapter, and they either controlled or became clients of extensive familial networks to that end.[33] Elected offices of the ayuntamiento, such as alcalde ordinario (municipal magistrate) and procurador *síndico* (city attorney) were typically reserved for young elites. This not only confirmed their status in provincial society, but helped them acquire vocational training to contend with the socioeconomic intricacies of the region.[34] Before he assumed his posting for the *partido* (local district) of Huixtán, the notorious subdelegate Cayetano Robles began his journey through the provincial *ascenso* (professional hierarchy of promotion) as an alcalde ordinario in Ciudad Real.[35] The Esponda family, whose landed and mercantile activities dominated the area of Tuxtla, buttressed their interests in provincial affairs when Sebastián Esponda was elected alcalde ordinario of the ayuntamiento in 1805.[36]

The titled, venal regidurías of the noble ayuntamiento represented the apex of the local hacendado-merchant elite social pyramid, only matched by the dignitaries of the cathedral chapter (*cabildo eclesiástico*). Close economic links were maintained by the ayuntamiento with the church, and titled, venal regidores always acted as fiscal agents for the chapter until Independence in 1821.[37] In their effort to control internal markets and agricultural prices and to obtain liquid capital, regidores acted as *fiadores* (bondsmen) for tithe collectors and subdelegates, helping in the liquidation accounts through the sale of goods paid in kind.[38] Again, consistent with the local version of a society of orders, a regiduría (council seat) not only confirmed social status, but also provided the means to expand upon wealth. A commission for a fiscal portfolio meant that the municipal official was responsible for a debt to the provincial treasury, yet this requirement allowed

for complete control over a capital fund and amounts owed to royal coffers by officials could take years to liquidate. By 1806, the alférez real Robles had acquired five haciendas and four houses in Ciudad Real. As a tribute receptor for the cathedral chapter, he manipulated tithe revenues, mortgaged his property to the church, and acquired personal loans in the effort to access liquid capital to diffuse any personal loss resulting from the Consolidación de Vales Reales in 1806.[39] It is highly plausible to assume that his efforts in this regard were not hurt by the future canon Mariano Robles's involvement in the Consolidación's proceedings.

The control the venal officers exerted over church levies cannot be overstated. Their belief that they had the legitimate authority to do so, moreover, was not unfounded and related in part to the ambiguous nature of Bourbon reform as it was extended to the local level. There was considerable overlap between the institutional scope of each of the fiscal juntas introduced by the Bourbons, a facet of provincial administration that related in part to the way levies were assessed, collected, and liquidated. The junta de diezmos, included within intendancy reform, was expected to oversee the fiscal administration of cathedral chapters. It corresponded to the introduction of the *junta municipal*, a committee that included two titled regidores and an alcalde ordinario elected on a yearly basis.[40] Aside from the payment of the 1,000 pesos of the assessor's salary, one of the main functions of the junta municipal was to liquidate taxes and tribute paid in kind (*especie*) or via a wide array of *escrituras* (financial notes or bills) used

APOSTLES OF REFORM

by officials to liquidate their debts to both church and state.

Here, too, it is important to stress in specie-starved Chiapas mechanisms of credit dominated all levels of society. In 1796 alone, for example, the *mayordomo* (steward) of the junta municipal accepted a wide array of *libranzas* (bills of exchange) ranging in value from 60 to 300 pesos, which were intended to serve as a guarantee for the solubility of the city's central fund.[41] The notes used for remissions were considered open until they were completely liquidated. This meant that the regidor, as acting mayordomo, controlled the aggregate capital until the mercantile mechanisms of exchange were cleared. Nevertheless, venal offices of the ayuntamiento still had to contend with the fiscal burdens resulting from Bourbon expansion of provincial administration under the auspices of intendancy reform. In order to facilitate the liquidation of the assessor's salary, legislation was enacted in 1795 that expanded the junta municipal's jurisdiction over propios and arbitrios for all of the *cabeceras* (head towns of districts) of the intendancy.[42]

An examination of corresponding church levies, moreover, demonstrates why the economic power of the local elites was actually extended over ecclesiastical accounts following the creation of the intendancy in 1786. Members of the ayuntamiento of Ciudad Real were always anxious to use their privileged position to become fiscal agents of rural officials, a process that was often tempered by elite kinship networks. The regidor Antonio Gutiérrez de Arce acted on behalf of his brother Joaquín, a *hacendado* (owner of a landed estate) and

tithe collector from San Bartolomé de los Llanos in the liquidation of tax remissions owed the church throughout the first two decades of the nineteenth century.[43] From 1790 onward, regidores and the occasional alcalde ordinario from Ciudad Real frequently appear in treasury documentation as fiadores and as fiscal agents for tax farmers collecting the tithe directed toward first fruits (*primicias*) of private landowners.[44] This related to a large extent to the overall effort of the venal officials of the ayuntamiento to gain control over the provincial economy and to establish an artificial central market in the capital of the intendancy.[45] The imposition of these taxes, after all, had a direct effect on the price of goods for sale in the city and outlying municipal areas, particularly since the triennial contracts for primicias stipulated the value of livestock, maize, beans, and cotton.[46]

The ambiguity of reform as it pertained to ecclesiastical jurisdiction and the involvement of venal officials from the ayuntamiento in fiscal affairs can also be seen in the tribute remissions. From at least the 1750s onward, an additional tithe was buried within tribute accounts in order to offset the penury faced by the church and to ensure that parish priests could expect payment for their service from *sínodos* (salaries).[47] Tribute payments (*tercios*) were collected twice a year during June (*San Juan*) and December (*Navidad*). An examination of tribute assessments from the 1790s through 1810 reveals at least four types of subcategories of tribute for all *repúblicas de indios* (here, native communities) and an additional fifth (*pierna de manta*) that was applied to highland native communities.

MICHAEL A. POLUSHIN

During each round of collection, these subcategories were listed for the provincial treasury as "*tributos*," "*el mitad de communidades*," "*el mitad de laborias*," and, to ensure the sanctity of church wealth, "*el mitad del diezmo*."[48]

While the collection of tribute fell squarely on the shoulders of subdelegates, the distribution of payments following the liquidation of accounts was hardly expedited in a timely or rapid fashion. Even though regidores of the ayuntamiento often acted as fiadores for subdelegates, the process of liquidation of the official's debt to the royal treasury could take years and was complicated by the fact that rural communities paid tribute in kind, specie, or, if they were unable to meet the demands of tribute payments due to natural disaster, via a promissory note.[49] In their effort to gain access to both liquid capital and the produce of rural communities, regidores as fiadores for subdelegates placed a note in the provincial treasury that covered the assessed amount the official was required to collect each year.[50] Only after these notes were liquidated was the subdelegate paid for his services in specie from the royal treasury. This process extended to the payments made curas as well. In 1798, Estevan de Vargas y Rivera complained that he still had not been paid from his sinodo during his tenure as cura of Escuintla between 1783 and 1787. He was forced to wait another six years while accounts from the district were cleared through the elaborate hierarchy of fiscal administration that included the subdelegate and his fiadores, the junta municipal of Ciudad Real, the *junta of sínodos* of the cathedral chapter, and lastly, the *junta*

provincial (the committee directly responsible for the provincial treasury).[51]

Here, too, we need to consider how the relationship between church and state in the countryside was tempered by clientele networks emanating from the ayuntamiento of Ciudad Real following its revival in the 1780s. As the case of the assessor Valero demonstrates, a failure to heed provincial sociopolitical hierarchies could have serious consequences. The animosity directed toward subdelegates and intendants by the canon Mariano Robles before the Cortes de Cádiz, moreover, seems to have been related to a matter of insiders and outsiders. Within the complex web of credit and debt that characterized provincial administration in the intendancy, local curas sometimes acted as fiscal agents for subdelegates. The cura and native son Pedro Borrego, for example, arranged the *fianzas* (bonds) needed to confirm his brother Andrés's appointment as subdelegate.[52] There were several native sons in Chiapas who served as subdelegates, and Bourbon reform did not necessarily preclude vocational opportunities for local elites within the church.[53] Within the context of church and state, ties of kinship also affected the economic relationship between secular and ecclesiastical officials. Aside from the alférez real José María Robles's tenure as tribute receptor for the cathedral chapter, the interests of the Robles family within its courts lasted well after independence from Spain because of Mariano Robles's stellar rise through the local ecclesiastical ascenso. Following his days as a cura of Tonalá, he became canon during the first decade of the nineteenth century before he was selected to represent Chiapas as a *diputado* (deputy) for the Cortes de Cádiz.[54] In 1818, he secured the offices of *maestre de escuela* (one of the prebends), *vicario capitular y gobernador* (acting head of a vacant see) in 1821, and was elected dean by the chapter in 1831. As one of the *dignidades* (dignitaries) of the cathedral chapter, he continued to wield enormous influence in local ecclesiastical and political affairs since there was no prelate to guide the fortunes of the church for the decade following independence from Spain.[55]

Invariably, there were still instances where curas struggled with subdelegates for control over community resources. In his virulent denunciation of subdelegates and intendants, the canon Mariano Robles described the various transgressions of subdelegates within the context of his experiences as the cura of Tonalá.[56] As found elsewhere in the viceroyalty of New Spain, intendancy reform in Chiapas was not restricted to an assault on the community chests (*cajas de communidad*), but was extended to pious works (*obras pias*), and especially *cofradías* (confraternities). Traditionally, local cofradías were used by leaders of repúblicas de indios and curas to preserve the sanctity of community wealth and, ultimately, to buttress their power while serving as what the historian Murdo Macleod describes as "broker institutions" to the outside world.[57] In order to expand or maintain the principal funds of cofradías, native elites from rural communities gave out short-term loans. The profit derived from the loans helped defer the costs incurred by the priest's involvement in the fiesta. Thus, parish priests had a strong interest in ensuring that the economic sanctity of cofradía

funds was maintained.[58] It is hardly surprising that the local cura of the town of Tonalá was at the front of a long line in his denunciation directed toward the subdelegate Domingo Olaysala for the subdelegates's failure to pay back a 1,139-peso loan made to him by the cofradía. Olaysala defended his position by stating that no such loan existed, and that he had taken the funds as part of his responsibility for the implementation of the Consolidación de Vales Reales. Thus, he argued, the amount was part of the corpus of capital that he owed to the provincial treasury for the revenues he collected for both church and state.[59]

The example of the dispute between the cura and the subdelegate may have related to the broader pattern found in rural societies throughout history that pits insiders (in this instance the cura) against outsiders (the subdelegate).[60] What is key, however, is the way curas promoted the activities of cofradías during feast days for self-serving economic ends, despite the so-called heresy and paganism identified by regalist prelates that were associated with celebrations devoted to local saints. For their part, subdelegates and their lieutenants would denounce the excesses of the fiestas in order to justify their intrusions into community resources.[61] The *subdelegado teniente* Francisco Tallada complained in 1805 that the real reason for the outstanding tribute owed by the highland community Amatenango related entirely to the *desórdenes* (disturbances) and *decadencia* (here, moral decadence) of the fiesta devoted to the Lady of Rosario. Along with funds spent on alcohol, music, and candles, mayordomos of the local cofradía and the

MICHAEL A. POLUSHIN

community itself were left destitute after paying the parish priest for mass.[62]

Viewed from the perspective of elites associated with the ayuntamiento of Ciudad Real, there was little reason to interfere in the jurisdiction of ecclesiastical courts in matters of faith, unless it directly affected their idealized vision of the hierarchies that guided the provincial sociopolitical order. They were not about to jeopardize legitimacy of their privileged offices and institution, especially since such regally endorsed privilege gave them unprecedented access to ecclesiastical wealth. While overzealous prelates carried out episcopal campaigns against nagualism and other traditional native beliefs practiced during local fiestas throughout Chiapas, elites associated with ayuntamiento of Ciudad Real maintained a cautious silence, and neither applauded nor chided the efforts of bishops in such matters.[63] To be sure, their ambivalence was again guided by no shortage of self-interest, for they were not beyond appropriating the economic bridge between the sacred and the profane to intrude upon community resources. Shortly after the revival of the ayuntamiento in the 1780s, members of the city's political elite were only too willing to lend monetary and material support to all of the native cofradías falling within Ciudad Real's jurisdiction. In exchange for their debts, communities were expected to provide goods and labor services to facilitate the ayuntamiento's administration.[64] In this context, it is hardly surprising to find that the ayuntamiento tied the city's central fund to the support of twenty-three feast days by 1795.[65] With the assistance of select regidores, the cathedral chapter had gained

control and consolidated the principal funds of several cofradías within the capital city and its barrios. This meant that they exerted enormous influence over capital and expenditures for religious celebrations and, ultimately, control over the labor and goods used to pay off debts acquired by cofrades (members of a cofradía) during fiestas.

To this point our discussion has focused largely on how ambiguous administrative reform lent itself to the expansion of the socioeconomic power of the emergent oligarchy in Ciudad Real. A careful reading of the Ordinance of Intendants of 1786 reveals that local elites were taking advantage of what was prescribed by law, which, in turn, was linked to broader questions regarding political power and legitimate authority.[66] Furthermore, the enormous influence local elites wielded over church wealth and taxes was probably helped by the career ambitions, disinterest, incompetence, or the untimely deaths of successive intendants in Chiapas. Bishops for the period should be interpreted in the same regard. Since local elites were conditioned to the regally endorsed privileges of office and the perks resulting from their cozy relationship with both church and state, it should be of no surprise that the ongoing political struggle between the assessor Valero and the ayuntamiento was linked to the control over corporate funds and finance. Heated disagreements regarding payment and liquidation of accounts between Valero and the ayuntamiento had been going on for quite some time, beginning with his arrival to the intendancy in 1798. Careful examination of the lengthy litigation that corresponded to each dispute reveals that Valero's consistent effort to discredit his enemies in Ciudad Real before the courts was a thinly veiled attempt to gain control over capital funds associated with the various fiscal juntas in the effort to either secure or augment his own salary.[67]

Aside from not recognizing his place as an outsider who needed to learn his place in the scheme of the hierarchy of the provincial sociopolitical order, Valero continually exacerbated each disagreement involving his salary because of his innate sense of superiority and arrogance. In the midst of a salary dispute with the ayuntamiento in 1804, he had accused the alférez real José María Robles of fraud in the liquidation of tribute during the municipal official's tenure as a calpixqui for the cathedral chapter.[68] On this occasion, the assessor did not confine his accusations to Robles but included several other local elites as well, including the royal official's bitter adversary Sebastián Esponda. Valero argued that Esponda was behind the series of insults and the fairly large flaming gunpowder-filled sacks attached to sticks (as he stated, "coetones" comprised of "pólvora inglesa de contrabando") hurled through the windows of his home shortly afterward in 1805.[69] Again, a careful reading of these ongoing disputes between the much-maligned assessor and the ayuntamiento reveals that they originated in disagreements from the 1,000 pesos of the assessor's 1,500-peso salary that was drawn from the city's general account. Much to Valero's chagrin, the ayuntamiento consistently stalled in its payment, and he responded by bringing attention to their previously ignored personal affairs.[70] Following the legal resolution of the incident in 1805 in Valero's favor, it was hardly a coincidence in this context that José María Robles and Esponda found themselves before the Junta de Consolidación the following year. While his family had escaped any implementation of the 1804 legislation until then, Valero's arch enemy Esponda now had to stall and then to renegotiate the immediate repayment of more than 59,000 pesos owed by the estate of his recently deceased mother to a wide array of pious funds. Even though his efforts proved successful by early 1808 (the estate ended up paying only a couple of thousand pesos in interest and renegotiated all loans), the damage done to the Esponda's landed and mercantile interests in both the long- and short-term were enormous.

Hierarchy and Legitimacy within a Festive Expulsion

The political struggle between the hated assessor and local elites for control over the entangled destinies and resources of church and state had indeed reached their boiling point long before the overthrow of Valero during the fiesta devoted to the Virgin of Merced. From the perspective of local elites, the death of the Intendant Tomás de Mollineda in 1808 was an immediate cause of consternation because, by law, assessors assumed the responsibilities of interim intendants (as intendente accidental) until a new official was appointed.[71] Once news of the events of Bayonne reached Ciudad Real, early in January 1809, the ayuntamiento decided to suspend payment of the accidental intendant's salary and use the 1,000 pesos of the city's general fund for patriotic observances instead. The attitudes of local

MICHAEL A. POLUSHIN

elites toward the union between church and state were given political expression when King Ferdinand's image made a tour of the churches found throughout the city and its barrios during the following months.[72] Valero seemingly could not appreciate the cost of the masses and candles purchased to illuminate the king's splendor during the ceremonies held in each of the churches, especially since the patriotic celebrations were conducted at his own personal expense. A few months after suspending the patriotic celebrations, Valero responded to the ayuntamiento's affront to his authority by arresting Antonio Gutiérrez de Gallo, the procurador síndico of the city.[73]

Although disputes between Valero had reached their limits and church ceremonies devoted to the Bourbon monarchs were hardly new, it was no accident that local elites chose the fiesta for the Virgin de la Merced to topple the assessor. The narratives detailing the events that occurred during the fiesta are at times confusing, given the contrasting viewpoints presented by the local political officers and Valero to the courts following his arrest.[74] Nevertheless, they help explain the notions held by the ayuntamiento toward the inseparable union between church and state and the legitimacy of local sociopolitical hierarchy. Early in the morning, the conspirators from the ayuntamiento met under the pretext of a cabildo extraordinario (special executive meeting) to plot their actions later that day. After taking care of some mundane administrative matters, Valero continued his morning by making personal preparations for the procession for the Virgin de la Merced, which included the preparation of

a speech explaining his fealty to the Spanish king. The assessor clearly believed that his place as interim intendant was secure following the incarceration of the ayuntamiento's procurador síndico, as he watched the religious procession pass his residence. His delusions of power and authority were probably confirmed in his mind as all participants in the procession bowed down to the assessor to demonstrate their deference to his authority.[75]

The procession, as it had been from time immemorial, was witnessed by local vecinos (citizens) and inhabitants from the barrios of the city. In accordance with custom, the statue of the Virgin de la Merced was the most conspicuous feature of the procession. Valero observed how she was preceded by what he termed as different types of dancers and musicians, all of whom could be distinguished by their dress. The appearance of the Gran Turco (Captain of the Turks) and the elaborate decorations only helped instill a sense of order to all of the city's inhabitants who were in attendance. After he thanked the participants in the parade for their devotion, Valero reminded them that it was just as important to demonstrate such religious fervor in their loyalty to King Ferdinand. As the procession made its way to the central plaza of the city, he undoubtedly believed that his speech had ensured that all sense of order was maintained.[76] The confirmation of the union between religious and imperial affairs intrinsic to the assessor's description of the political hierarchy found in the parade was given further sanction when the bishop of Chiapas likely blessed the proceedings.

Any sense of stability and hierarchy,

however, was disrupted by a civil disturbance moments after the procession arrived at the central plaza, involving some of the principal citizens of Ciudad Real as well as the former and current members of the city council. According to Valero, the Virgin was temporarily left to her own devices in the central plaza as the apparent anarchy engulfed the celebration. The bishop apparently rushed to the assessor's residence to warn Valero of his impending political fate. Confused, Valero tried to take stock of the situation, and shortly afterward he heard the noise of pounding drums announcing the arrival of the local *commandante de armas* (chief of the militia) Tiburcio Farrera and his troops. Farrera informed the assessor that he was under arrest.[77]

Many of the subsequent events that transpired during that fateful day and the next fit well into the pattern of revolts against royal officials.[78] There was no shortage of violence during Valero's incarceration, and the wayward bayonets of Farrera's overzealous troops were the cause of several wounds inflicted upon the assessor. Later in the afternoon, amid the screams of Valero to be recognized as intendant, the *alférez real* José María Robles appeared to despoil the assessor of his *vara de justicia* (staff of office) and to once again pronounce a sentence of treason.[79] Consistent with the shame associated with the public spectacle found within *autos de fe*, the following day the assessor was placed in a chair and paraded through the streets on his way to the city jail.[80] By stripping Valero of his vara and subjecting him to public humiliation during a religious holiday, the local political officials asserted what they perceived to

be their right to rule on behalf of the king. The use of drums to announce the arrest of Valero during the fiesta, while consistent with public manifestations of punishment, was strangely reminiscent of the *rompimiento de música* (loud or "rough" music) used by local *cofradías* to begin fiestas and processions honoring their saints, a local practice consistently condemned by bishops in Chiapas during the late eighteenth and early nineteenth centuries.[81]

Despite Valero's exaggerated description of the stability and hierarchy of the procession, there were other local customs pertinent to the fiesta that explain why elites chose to act when they did. All of the elements found in Thomas Gage's seventeenth-century description of native ceremonies were present during the fiesta of the Virgin of Merced, including *mascaradas* (masked and/or costumed participants) and the symbolism inherent in mock battles.[82] The combative elements of the fiesta certainly intersected with what the Virgin de la Merced meant for local Spanish society. She was first associated with the triumph of the reconquista over the Moors and then the conquest of what became the kingdoms of New Spain and Guatemala.[83] Aside from becoming the *patrona* of Ciudad Real years later, she needs to be distinguished from the Virgin de Caridad, the city's protectress of the military who originated from the Chamula assistance in the defeat of insurgents during the Tzeltal rebellion in 1712.[84] The celebration for the Virgin de la Merced, however, had distinguished itself before regalist bishops in Chiapas for its carnivalesque character and the license of impunity it gave its participants. A few years after Valero's arrest, for example, bishop Salvador Samartín denounced the drunkenness and gambling that were associated with the fiesta and how during processions men appeared masked and dressed as women.[85] We now know enough about popular culture to conclude that the public anarchy the prelate witnessed had broader sociopolitical meaning that assured that the traditional parochial order would live to see another day.[86] Aside from native traditions present during fiestas (which included ritual drinking), the role reversal and social inversion implicit in the transvestism politically articulated the limits of Spanish imperial rule.[87]

Local elites were extremely cognizant of the audience who witnessed the arrest of Valero, which included natives, *castas* (people of mixed European, indigenous, and/or often African heritage), and vecinos from the city and its environs.[88] The symbolism embodied in the revolt was scripted in a manner which participants in the celebration could easily appreciate within the context of contested hierarchy and legitimacy. The civic anarchy that broke out in the central plaza, the appearance of the local militia, and the ceremonial stripping of the assessor's staff of office were not far removed from the mocking of Spanish society or the desórdenes and *excesos* (here, drinking to excess) associated with the fiesta. In this instance, local elites had appropriated the Virgin de la Merced to legitimize their vision of provincial sociopolitical hierarchies. Hence, the overthrow of Valero had little to do with the notions of liberty or nascent elite nationalism often associated with the Virgin of Guadalupe in New Spain.[89] In choosing this day of the fiesta elites also recognized the crucial role of local custom and traditions in the maintenance of stability. Moreover, the violent assault against the assessor during his arrest bears a striking similarity to the festive coetones used by elites to burn his residence in 1805.

Conclusion

While the problems with the assessor Valero were not resolved until several years later, the sociopolitical importance local elites associated with the ayuntamiento placed on the fiesta devoted to the Virgin de la Merced during his arrest was comparable to arguments they used against him before the courts. There could be no separation between interests of patria, religion, and state, and their appropriation of the fiesta for political purposes suggests that they sincerely did not believe otherwise.[90] Royal policies toward patronato real, after all, had provided them privileged access to ecclesiastical wealth and taxes, while regalist interference in religious celebrations had set a precedent that they were only too willing to use for their personal political gain. This would have vast repercussions for instability in the region during the 1830s and, thus, serves as a reminder that any interpretation of the processes integral to nation and state formation in Chiapas (or indeed elsewhere in Mexico and Central America) needs to consider the continued role of the church in socioeconomic and political affairs. The historian Ana Carolina Ibarra's study of the activities of the cathedral chapter of Antequera, for example, suggests an analogous situation underway in Oaxaca during the eighteenth and nineteenth century.[91] A careful examination of the actual mechanics of civil and ecclesiastical administration in El Salvador likely would reveal similar reasons behind church and state struggles before and after Independence. In Chiapas, at least, ambiguous Bourbon administrative reform did not quash the sociopolitical pretensions of local elites from Ciudad Real, but, ironically, created them.

NOTES

This chapter is an updated and expanded English version of "Por la Patria, El Estado, y la Religión: la expusión del intendente accidente de Ciudad Real, Chiapas (1809)" in *La independencia en el sur de México*, coord. Ana Carolina Ibarra, 291–317 (México, DF: Facultad de Filosofía y Letras, UNAM, 2004). I must thank Juan Pedro Viqueira for his careful critique and suggestions.

1. Archivo General de Centro América (hereinafter AGCA), B2.7, leg. 31, exp. 768; Mills Memorial Library, McMaster University, Hamilton Ontario, Central American Microfilm Collection (hereinafter MMC), rollo 49B, A1.206.1541.

2. Latin American Library, Tulane University, Chiapas Collection (hereinafter TChC), box 2, folder 18; Timothy E. Anna, *Spain and the Loss of America* (Lincoln: University of Nebraska Press, 1983), 27–63; Jaime E. Rodríguez O., *The Independence of Spanish America* (New York: Cambridge University Press, 1999), 51–74. For a different interpretation of the Napoleonic period in Chiapas than the one found below, see Robert M. Laughlin, *Beware the Great Horned Serpent! Chiapas Under the Threat of Napoleon* (Albany, NY: Institute for Mesoamerican Studies, University of Albany, 2003).

3. On patronato real see D. A. Brading, *Church and State in Bourbon Mexico: The Diocese of Michoacán* (Cambridge, UK: Cambridge University Press, 1994); Nancy M. Farriss, *Crown and Clergy in Colonial Mexico, 1759–1821: The Crisis of Ecclesiastical Privilege* (London: The Athlone Press, 1968); Robert C. Padden, "The Ordenanza del Patronazgo of 1574: An Interpretative Essay," *The Americas* 12 (1956): 333–54; John Frederick Schwaller, "Ordenanza del Patronazgo in New Spain,

1574–1600," *The Americas* 42, no. 3 (January 1986): 253–74; William Eugene Shiels, *King and Church: The Rise and Fall of Patronato Real* (Chicago: Loyola University Press, 1961); Adriaan C. Van Oss, *Catholic Colonialism: A Parish History of Guatemala, 1524–1821* (New York: Cambridge University Press, 1986), 2, 51–52, 57–58, 79, 82–83.

4. Linda Curcio-Nagy, "Native Icon to City Protectress to Royal Patroness: Ritual, Political Symbolism, and the Virgin of Remedies," *The Americas* 52, no. 3 (January 1996): 387–88; William B. Taylor, *Magistrates of the Sacred: Priests and Parishioners in Eighteenth-Century Mexico* (Stanford: Stanford University Press, 1996), 250–64; Juan Pedro Viqueira Albán, *Propriety and Permissiveness in Bourbon Mexico*, trans. Sonya Lipsett-Rivera and Sergio Rivera Ayala (Wilmington, DE: Scholarly Resources Press, 1999), 103–21.

5. On the Bourbon reforms in this context, see D. A. Brading, *Miners and Merchants in Bourbon Mexico, 1763–1810* (Cambridge, UK: Cambridge University Press, 1971); John Fisher, "The Intendant System and the Cabildos of Peru," *Hispanic American Historical Review* 49, no. 3 (August 1969): 430–53; Cheryl Martin, *Governance and Society in Colonial Mexico: Chihuahua in the Eighteenth Century* (Stanford: Stanford University Press, 1996); John Lynch, *Spanish Colonial Administration, 1782–1810: The Intendant System in the Viceroyalty of Río de la Plata* (London: Athlone Press, 1958); John Lynch, *The Spanish American Revolutions, 1808–1826*, 2nd ed. (New York: Norton, 1986); John Preston Moore, *The Cabildo in Peru under the Bourbons: A Study in the Decline and Resurgence of Local Government in the Audiencia of Lima* (Durham, NC: Duke University Press, 1966); Robert Patch, "The Bourbon Reforms, Town

Councils, and the Struggle for Power in the Yucatan, 1770–1796," in *Mexico in the Age of Democratic Revolutions, 1750–1850*, ed. Jaime Rodríguez O., 57–70 (Boulder and London: Lynne Rienner Publishers, 1994); Guy P. Thomson, *Puebla de los Angeles: Industry and Society in a Mexican City, 1700–1850* (Boulder and London: Westview Press, 1989); Miles Wortman, *Government and Society in Central America, 1680–1840* (New York: Columbia University Press, 1983).

6. Linda Curcio-Nagy, *The Great Festivals of Colonial Mexico City: Reforming Power and Identity* (Albuquerque: University of New Mexico Press, 2004), 74–78, 137–40; Stafford Poole, *Our Lady of Guadalupe* (Tucson: The University of Arizona Press, 1995); Taylor, *Magistrates of the Sacred*, 277–300; Eric Van Young, *The Other Rebellion: Popular Violence, Ideology, and the Mexican Struggle for Independence, 1810–1821* (Stanford: Stanford University Press, 2001), 315–20. For the importance of the Virgin in the context of rebellion in colonial Chiapas, see Kevin Gosner, *Soldiers of the Virgin: The Moral Economy of a Colonial Maya Rebellion* (Tuscon: University of Arizona Press, 1992); Juan Pedro Viqueira, *Indios rebeldes e idólatras: Dos ensayos históricos sobre la rebelión india de Cancuc, Chiapas, acaedidada en el año de 1712* (México, DF: CIESAS, 1997).

7. TChC, box 3, folder 7; TChC, box 3, folder 8; TChC, box 3, folder 10; TChC, box 4, folder 3; Thomas Benjamin, *A Rich Land, Poor People: Politics and Society in Modern Chiapas* (Albuquerque: University of New Mexico Press, 1989), 1–12; Prudencio Moscoso Patrana, *México y Chiapas: Independencia y federación de la provincia chiapaneca* (San Cristóbal de las Casas: Instituto Chiapaneco de Cultura, 1988); Manuel B. Trens, *Historia de Chiapas desde los tiempos más remotos hasta la caída del Segundo Imperio* (México, DF: n.p., 1957), 249–377.

8. Manuel García Vargas y Rivera, *Relaciones de los pueblos de la Obispado de Chiapa, 1772, 1774*, ed. Jorge Lujan Muñoz, 13 (San Cristóbal de Las Casas, Patronato fray Bartolomé de Las Casas, Programa Cultura de Fronteras, Instituto Chiapenco de Cultura, and Ayuntamiento Constitucional, 1988).

9. AGCA, A1.15, leg.4400, exp.36160.

10. AGCA, A1.20, leg.1483, exp.9963; "Atentado contra el Asesor Ordinario de la Intendencia de Chiapas, 1805," *Boletín del Archivo Histórico del Estado* 11 (enero–agosto 1961): 79–114.

11. On the office of assessor see Charles Cutter, *The Legal Culture of Northern New Spain, 1700–1810* (Albuquerque: University of New Mexico Press, 1995), 56–57; Lillian Estelle Fisher, *The Intendant System in Spanish America* (Berkeley: University of California Press, 1929), 39, 45, 63–64, 85, 88, 95, 111, 113, 150; John Lynch, *Spanish Colonial Administration, 1782–1810: The Intendant System in the Viceroyalty of Río de la Plata* (London: Athlone Press, 1958), 81–84, 226–27, 241, 288; John Preston Moore, *The Cabildo in Peru under the Bourbons: A Study in the Decline and Resurgence of Local Government in the Audiencia of Lima* (Durham, NC: Duke University Press, 1966), 33, 76–77, 148, 190.

12. AGCA, A1.55, leg.301, exp.2061.

13. Church of Jesus Christ of Latter Day Saints, Salt Lake City, UT, Genealogical and Family History Library, San Cristóbal de las Casas (hereinafter MorF), rollo 0732484.

14. MMC, rollo 49B, A1.206.1541. See also Alma Margarita Carvalho, *La ilustración del despotismo en Chiapas* (México, DF: Consejo Nacional para la Cultura y las Artes, 1994), 210–11.

15. Michael A. Polushin, "Bureaucratic Conquest, Bureaucratic Culture: Town and Office in Chiapas, 1780–1832" (PhD diss., Tulane University, 1999), 44–82. For salaries of royal officials in Chiapas, see Archivo General de Indias, Seville (hereinafter AGI), Guatemala 686, exp. "*Lista de los Empleados de Real Hacienda de aquel Reyno y sus dotaciones*"; AGI, Mexico 2121, exp. "*Real Tribunal y Audiencia de cuentas del Reino de Guatemala, año de 1804.*"

16. Mariano Robles Domínguez de Mazariegos, *Memoria histórica de la provincia de Chiapas, una de las de Guatemala* (Cádiz: Imprenta tormentaria, 1813). See also Nettie Lee Benson, *The Provincial Deputation in Mexico: Harbinger of Provincial Autonomy, Independence and Federalism* (Austin: University of Texas Press, 1992), 20; Carvalho, *La ilustración*, 127–28; Mario Rodríguez, *The Cádiz Experiment in Central America, 1808 to 1826* (Berkeley and

Los Angeles: University of California Press, 1978), 33–92.

17. Robles, *Memoria histórica de la provincia de Chiapas*, 6–20, 23–27, 30–32, 62.

18. Archivo Histórico Diocesano de San Cristóbal de Las Casas (hereinafter AHDSC), TXA. 10.6.2, "Año de 1782. Testimonio del Real Título de Regidor, librado a favor de Don Bartolomé Gutiérrez"; MMC, rollo 5B, A1.5.67; MMC, rollo 15B, A1.45.520; MMC, rollo 17B, A1.51.583; MMC, rollo 17B, A1.51.584; MMC, rollo 45B, A1.190.1467.

19. MMC, rollo 49B, A1.206.1541. On the tribunal see Hubert Howe Bancroft, *The Works of Hubert Howe Bancroft, Volume VIII: The History of Central America* (San Francisco: The History Company Publishers, 1887), 6; Timothy Hawkins, "José de Bustamante and the Preservation of Empire in Central America, 1811–1818," *Colonial Latin American Historical Review* 4, no. 4 (fall 1995): 442.

20. MMC, rollo 49B, A1.206.1541.

21. *Relaciónes de los méritos y exercicios literarios del bachiller en sagradas canones Don Mariano Nicolas Robles* (Cádiz: n.p., 1811). On the Consolidación de Vales Reales, see Brading, *Church and State*, 222–27; Brian R. Hamnett, "The Appropriation of Mexican Church Wealth by the Spanish Bourbon Government: The 'Consolidación de Vales Reales,' 1805–1809," *Journal of Latin American Studies* 1, no. 2 (November 1969): 85–113; Asunción Lavrin, "The Execution of the Laws of *Consolidación* in New Spain: Economic Gains and Results," *Hispanic American Historical Review* 53, no. 1 (February 1973): 27–49.

22. AGI, Guatemala 690 "Expediente sobre establecimiento de Intendencia de Chiapa, Tuxtla y Soconusco."

23. See Van Oss, *Catholic Colonialism*, 60–71.

24. Peter Gerhard, *The Southeast Frontier of New Spain* (Princeton: Princeton University Press, 1979), 153–54.

25. MMC, rollo 47B, A1.196.1489; MMC, rollo 47B, A1.199.1502.

26. AGI, Guatemala 686, exp. "Lista de Empleados de Real Hacienda de aquel Reyno y sus dotaciones."

27. Polushin, "Bureaucratic Conquest," 29–31, 173–79.

28. On venality, see J. H. Parry, *The Sale of Public Office in the Spanish Indies Under the Hapsburgs* (Berkeley and Los Angeles: University of California Press, 1953); Martin, *Governance and Society*, 87–91; Robert Patch, "Imperial Politics and Local Economy in Colonial Central America," *Past and Present* 143 (May 1994): 77–107. In comparative terms, see William Doyle, *Venality: The Sale of Offices in Eighteenth-Century France* (New York: Oxford University Press, 1996), 312–13.

29. Polushin, "Bureaucratic Conquest," 129–67.

30. MMC, rollo 18B, A1.55.615; MMC, rollo 162B, A3.236.2908.

31. Peter Guardino, *The Time of Liberty: Popular Political Culture in Oaxaca, 1750–1850* (Durham, NC: Duke University Press, 2005), 29. Unfortunately, he does not distinguish between types of office. This may explain why he seemingly missed how ayuntamientos governed on behalf of the king or the material rewards that would result from the purchase of a regimiento. He states, for example, "town council members did not have the power needed to reap direct profits" (Ibid.).

32. Polushin, "Bureaucratic Conquest," 145–46. On the difference between a society of orders and a society of classes, see William Beik, *Absolutism and Society in Seventeenth-century France: State Power and Provincial Aristocracy in Languedoc* (Cambridge, UK: Cambridge University Press, 1985), 6–9.

33. For significant creole representation on cathedral chapters elsewhere for the period see Brading, *Church and State*, 192–210; and Ana Carolina Ibarra, *El Cabildo de Antequera, Oaxaca y el Movimiento Insurgente* (México, DF: El Colegio de Michoacán, 2000).

34. Polushin, "Bureaucratic Conquest," 138–67.

35. AGI, 675, "Expediente de todas las causas pendientes contra D. José Joaquín Arriola subdelegado del Partido de Istacomitán"; AGCA, A1.30.11, leg.203, exp.1530; MMC, Rollo 50B, A1.214.1586.

36. "Atentado contra el Asesor Ordinario de la Intendencia de Chiapas," *Boletín del Archivo Histórico del Estado* 11 (enero–agosto 1961) 79–145.

37. AHDSC, VI.C.8, "Ixtacomitán Diezmos, 1809–1836"; AHDSC, VI.C.8, "Tuxtla Diezmos, 1773–1903"; AHDSC, VI.C.2, "San Cristóbal Dinero y Bienes 1786–1919"; MorF, rollo 0733637.

38. AHDSC, VI.C.8, "Ixtacomitán. Diezmos, 1776–1798"; MMC, rollo 50B, A1.214.1586; MMC, rollo 50B, A1.214.1583; MMC, rollo 50B, A1.213.1577.

39. MMC, Rollo 18B, A1.55.615. For a similar pattern in Mexico, see Lavrin, "The Execution of the Laws of *Consolidación*," 37–41.

40. AGCA, A1.2, leg.7, exp.108; Moore, *The Cabildo*, 144–45. On the liquidation of ecclesiastical levies, also see Farriss, *Crown and Clergy*, 154–55; Brading, *Church and State*, 192–227; Marcela Corvera Poiré, "De la bonanza al ocaso: las Colecturías de Taxco," in Ibarra, *La Independencia*, 103–64.

41. AGCA, A1.2, leg.7, exp.108.

42. Ibid.

43. AHDSC, VI.C.8, "San Bartolomé Diezmos, 1818–1899."

44. AHDSC, VI.C.8, "Ixtacomitán Diezmos, 1776–1798"; AHDSC, VI.C.8, "Ixtacomitán Diezmos, 1809–1836"; AHDSC, VI.C.8, "San Bartolomé Diezmos, 1818–1899."

45. Polushin, "Bureaucratic Conquest," 163–64.

46. AHDSC, VI.C.8, "Ixtacomitán Diezmos, 1809–1836"; AHDSC, VI.C.8, "San Bartolomé Diezmos, 1818–1899."

47. Van Oss, *Catholic Colonialism*, 81–85.

48. AHDSC, III.G, "Comitán Asuntos Indígenas, 1762–1837"; MMC, rollo 186B, A3.304.4099; MMC, rollo 186B, A3.306.4118.

49. AHDSC, "Comitán Asuntos Indígenas, 1762–1837"; AHDSC, VI.C.2, "San Cristóbal Dinero y Bienes, 1786–1919"; MMC, 187B, A3.306.4143; MorF, rollo 0733205.

50. MMC, rollo 77B, A3.2.11.

51. MMC, rollo 15B, A1.44.512; MorF, rollo 0733637.

52. MMC, rollo 50B, A1.214.1583.

53. Carvalho, *La ilustración*, 143–44.

54. Robles, *Memoria histórica*, 32; *Relaciones de los méritos*.

55. MorF, rollo 0734877; AHDSC, VI.C.8, "San Bartolomé Diezmos, 1818–1819"; "Imp. de la sociedad," *El Para-Rayo* 3 de octubre de 1827.

56. Robles, *Memoria histórica*, 32.

57. Murdo J. MacLeod, "Papel social y económico de las cofradías indígenas de la colonia en Chiapas," *Mesoamérica* año 4, cuaderno 5 (junio 1983): 64–86. See also Dolores Aramoni Calderón, *Los refugios de lo sagrado: Religiosidad, conflicto y resistencia entre los zoques de Chiapas* (México, DF: Consejo Nacional para la Cultura y las Artes, 1992), 383–400; Nancy M. Farriss, *Maya Society Under Colonial Rule: The Collective Enterprise of Survival* (Princeton: Princeton University Press, 1984), 320–51; Taylor, *Magistrates of the Sacred*, 250–64, 301–23; Juan Pedro Viqueira, "Unas páginas de los libros de cofradías de Chilón (1677–1720)," *Anuario* (1995): 207–32.

58. MacLeod, "Papel social," 64–86; Taylor, *Magistrates of the Sacred*, 252.

59. AGCA, A1.30, leg.42, exp.492.

60. Van Young, *The Other Rebellion*, 391–99.

61. Taylor, *Magistrates of the Sacred*, 263–64.

62. MMC, rollo 187B, A3.306.4138.

63. Aramoni Calderón, *Los refugios de lo sagrado*, 111–12, 117–20, 125–28, 219–42, 271–92.

64. MMC, rollo 5B, A1.5.70.

65. AGCA, A1.2, leg.7, exp.108.

66. Fisher, *The Intendant System*, 97–331.

67. AGCA, A1.30, leg.26, exp.376.

68. MMC, rollo 186B, A3.405.4115.

69. "Atentado contra el Asesor," 79–114; Carvalho, *La ilustración*, 212–14.

70. MMC, rollo 6B, A1.7.111.

71. AGCA, A1.30, leg.42, exp.489.

72. MMC, rollo 6B, A1.7.112; Laughlin, *Beware the Great Horned Serpent*, 92–93; Timothy Hawkins, *José de Bustamante and the Central American Independence: Colonial Administration in an Age of Imperial Crisis* (Tuscaloosa: University of Alabama Press, 2004), 50–52.

73. MMC, rollo 49B, A1.206.1541.

74. AGCA, B2.7, leg. 31, exp.767; AGCA, B2.7, leg.31, exp.768; AGCA, B2.7, leg.31, exp.769; AGCA, B2.7, leg.31, exp.772; AGCA, B2.7, leg.31, exp.776;

Hawkins, *José de Bustmante*, 51–52; Laughlin, *Beware the Great Horned Serpent*, 93.

75. AGCA, B2.7, leg. 31, exp.768.

76. Ibid.

77. Ibid.

78. Murdo J. MacLeod, "Motines y cambios en las formas de control económico y político: Los acontecimientos de Tuxtla, 1693" in *Chiapas: Los rumbos de otra historia*, ed. Juan Pedro Viqueira and Mario Ruz, 90–91 (México, DF: UNAM, 1995); William B. Taylor, *Drinking, Homicide, and Rebellion in Colonial Mexican Villages* (Stanford: Stanford University Press, 1979), 113–51.

79. AGCA, B2.7, leg.31, exp.768.

80. Maureen Flynn, "Mimesis of the Last Judgment: The Spanish *Auto de fe*," *Sixteenth Century Journal* 22, no. 2 (1991): 281–97.

81. AHDSC, II.B.3, "Asuntos Ecclesiasticos."

82. J. Eric S. Thompson, ed., *Thomas Gage's Travels in the New World* (Norman: University of Oklahoma Press, 1958), 146–47.

83. On the associated Mercederians, see Van Oss, *Catholic Colonialism*, 14, 34–35.

84. García Vargas, *Relaciones de los pueblos*, 13; Francisco Orozco y Jiménez, *Colección de documentos relativos á la milagrosa Imagen de la Santísima Virgen de la Presentación Llamada Caridad que venera en su templo de San Cristóbal* (San Cristóbal Las Casas: Tip. de la Sociedad Católica, 1903); TChC, Box 1, F01.1.

85. "El Obispo de Chiapas se propone abolir las orgies y derroche de dinero que los miembros de los Cofradías y Hermandades de Ciudad Real, practicaban por costumbre durante las ferias religiosas, año de 1819," *Boletín del Archivo Histórico del Estado* 10 (enero–junio 1960): 24–32.

86. William H. Beezley, *Judas at the Jockey Club and Other Episodes of Porfirian Mexico* (Lincoln: University of Nebraska Press, 1987); Natalie Zemon Davis, *Society and Culture in Early Modern France* (Stanford: Stanford University Press, 1975); Martin, *Governance and Society*, 100–120; Viqueira Albán, *Propriety and Permissiveness*, 103–21.

87. Viqueira Albán, *Propriety and Permissiveness*, 105–7. Also see Peter Sahlins, *Forest Rites: The War of Demoiselles in Nineteenth-century France* (Cambridge, MA: Harvard University Press, 1994).

88. AGCA, B2.7, leg.31, exp.768.

89. Taylor, *Magistrates of the Sacred*, 292–93. Curcio-Nagy finds a very different situation with the Virgin de Remedios and the Virgin Guadalupe in Mexico City shortly afterwards that presents intriguing possibilities for comparison. See Curcio-Nagy, *The Great Festivals*, 74–78, 137–40.

90. AGCA, B2.7, leg.31, exp.772; MMC, rollo 49B, A1.206.1541.

91. Ibarra, *El Cabildo*, 213–64; Ana Carolina Ibarra, "Reconocer la soberanía de la nación americana, conservar la independencia de América y restablecer en el trono a Fernando VII: la ciudad de Oaxaca durante la ocupación insurgente (1812–1814)," in Ibarra, *La Independencia*, 233–70.

MICHAEL A. POLUSHIN

LIST OF CONTRIBUTORS

Maureen Ahern is a professor of Spanish at the Ohio State University, Columbus, Ohio, where she teaches Latin American colonial literatures and cultures. She is co-translator of the critical edition of Andrés Pérez de Ribas, S.J., *History of the Triumphs of Our Holy Faith* (1645), and is currently working on "Martyr Narratives and Ritual Performance on Missionary Frontiers in New Spain (1530–1645)."

John Chuchiak IV is an assistant professor of colonial Latin American history and coordinator of the Latin American studies minor in the Department of History at Missouri State University. His research specialty is colonial Latin American history with a particular focus on the ecclesiastical history of New Spain, the Franciscan order in Yucatan, and Maya ethnohistory.

Mónica Díaz is an assistant professor at the University of Texas-Pan American, where she teaches colonial Latin American literature. She has published various articles on Mexican literature and is working on a book-length manuscript about the writings of indigenous nuns in colonial Mexico.

Martha Few is an associate professor of Latin American history at the University of Arizona. She is the author of *Women Who Live Evil Lives: Gender, Religion and the Politics of Power in Colonial Guatemala*, and is currently working on a history of colonial medicine and local healing cultures in southern New Spain.

Stanley M. Hordes is an adjunct research professor at the Latin American and Iberian Institute of the University of New Mexico and former New Mexico State Historian. His book, *To the End of the Earth: A History of the Crypto-Jews of New Mexico* is based on research conducted in the archives of New Mexico, Mexico, Spain, Portugal, and France.

Asunción Lavrin is a professor of history at Arizona State University and author of several books and numerous articles on feminism, female religious, and church history. She has a book on colonial Mexican nuns in press and has begun research on the topic of masculinity and the mendicant orders in colonial Mexico.

Sonya Lipsett-Rivera is a professor of history at Carleton University in Ontario, Canada. She is the author of *To Defend Our Water with the Blood of Our Veins: The Struggle for Resources in Colonial Puebla*, and the coeditor of *The Faces of Honor: Sex, Violence and Illegitimacy in Colonial Latin America*.

Kristin Dutcher Mann is an assistant professor of history and a social studies education coordinator at the University of Arkansas at Little Rock. She is the author of several articles on music in the Franciscan and Jesuit missions of northern New Spain.

María Elena Martínez received her doctorate in history from the University of Chicago in 2002. Currently she is an assistant professor of Latin American history at the University of Southern California and is completing her book manuscript, entitled "Genealogical Fictions: *Limpieza de Sangre*, Religion, and Gender in Colonial Mexico."

Jeanette Favrot Peterson is an associate professor in the Department of History of Art and Architecture at the University of

California, Santa Barbara, specializing in the precolumbian and colonial arts of the Americas. Among her interests are the intersection of indigenous and European visual culture, text, and image in the Florentine Codex, and the imaging of the Virgin of Guadalupe, from Black Madonna to Queen of the Americas, is her current book project.

Stafford Poole, C.M., is a Roman Catholic priest of the Congregation of the Mission of Saint Vincent de Paul (Vincentian Community) and a full-time research historian. His latest book is *The Guadalupan Controversies in Mexico*.

Michael A. Polushin received his doctorate from Tulane University under the direction of Richard E. Greenleaf and is currently an assistant professor of history at the University of Southern Mississippi. He has just completed a book manuscript devoted to church, state, and local society in eighteenth- and nineteenth-century Chiapas.

James D. Riley is an associate professor of history at the Catholic University of America. He has published work on the Jesuits, hacienda labor, and society in colonial Tlaxcala. His forthcoming book is entitled *Provincial Elites in Colonial Mexico: The Labradores of Tlaxcala, 1640–1792*.

Susan Schroeder is France Vinton Scholes Professor of colonial Latin American history at Tulane University and the author of numerous works relating to colonial Mesoamerican society and politics, religion, resistance, and women. She is general editor and coeditor and cotranslator of the two-volume *Codex Chimalpahin* and the Series Chimalpahin.

Lisa Sousa is an associate professor of Latin American history at Occidental College in Los Angeles. She has coedited and translated *The Story of Guadalupe* with James Lockhart and Stafford Poole, and is the author of several articles on indigenous culture and gender in colonial Mexico.

David Tavárez is an assistant professor of anthropology at Vassar College. His articles have appeared in *Historica Mexicana, Colonial Latin American Review, Journal of Early Modern History,* and *The Americas,* and he is coeditor and cotranslator of the forthcoming work *Chimalpahin and the Conquest of Mexico by Francisco López de Gómara.*

Kevin Terraciano is a professor of history and director of Latin American studies at the University of California, Los Angeles. He specializes in the history of colonial Latin America, especially the indigenous cultures and languages of Mesoamerica.

Javier Villa-Flores is an assistant professor at the University of Illinois at Chicago. He is the author of *Carlo Ginzburg: el historiador como teórico* (1995), several articles in journals and edited volumes, and has a forthcoming book, *Dangerous Speech: Blasphemy and Authority in New Spain, 1520–1700.*

INDEX